Basic Marketing Research Using Microsoft® Excel Data Analysis

Third Edition

ALVIN C. BURNS
Louisiana State University

RONALD F. BUSH
University of West Florida

Prentice Hall

Boston   Columbus   Indianapolis   New York   San Francisco   Upper Saddle River
Amsterdam   Cape Town   Dubai   London   Madrid   Milan   Munich   Paris   Montreal   Toronto
Delhi   Mexico City   São Paulo   Sydney   Hong Kong   Seoul   Singapore   Taipei   Tokyo

Editorial Director: Sally Yagan
Editor in Chief: Eric Svendsen
Acquisitions Editor: Melissa Sabella
Editorial Project Manager: Meeta Pendharkar
Editorial Assistant: Elisabeth Scarpa
Director of Marketing: Patrice Lumumba Jones
Senior Marketing Manager: Anne Fahlgren
Marketing Assistant: Melinda Jensen
Senior Managing Editor: Judy Leale
Project Manager: Becca Richter Groves
Senior Operations Supervisor: Arnold Vila
Creative Director: Cristy Mahon
Senior Art Director: Kenny Beck

Text and Cover Designer: Ray Cruz
Cover Art: Michael Clutson/SPL/Photo Researchers, Inc.
Manager, Rights and Permissions:
    Hessa Albader
Media Editor: Denise Vaughn
Media Project Manager, Production:
    Lisa Rinaldi
Full-Service Project Management:
    S4Carlisle Publishing Services
Composition: S4Carlisle Publishing Services
Printer/Binder: Banta dba RRD–Menasha
Cover Printer:
    Lehigh-Phoenix Color/Hagerstown
Text Font: Times

Library of Congress Cataloging-in-Publication Data

Burns, Alvin C.
    Basic marketing research : using Microsoft Excel data analysis / Alvin
C. Burns, Ronald F. Bush.—3rd ed.
        p. cm.
    Includes bibliographical references and index.
    ISBN 978-0-13-507822-8 (alk. paper)
    1. Marketing research.   2. Microsoft Excel (Computer file)   I. Bush,
Ronald F.   II. Title.
    HF5415.2.B7787 2012
    658.8'30285554—dc22

                                                                    2010030838

10 9 8 7 6 5 4 3 2 1

www.pearsonhighered.com

ISBN 10:   0-13-507822-9
ISBN 13: 978-0-13-507822-8

Brief Contents

Contents

Preface

What Makes Basic Marketing Research: Using Microsoft® Excel Data Analysis, 3rd Edition, Unique?

This book provides:

- a concise presentation of the fundamentals of marketing research
- an improved software package, XL Data Analyst™, which runs using Microsoft® Excel 2010 or earlier versions
- input from many professionals in the marketing research industry
- an integrated case complete with a data set that gives students an experiential learning exercise throughout the course

What's New in the 3rd Edition?

- Significantly more information about qualitative research with a new section in the chapter on research design covering qualitative vs. quantitative research and new material discussing several methods used in qualitative research.
- Secondary data analysis is now combined with standardized information into one chapter and we have extensive coverage of the new, annual census information available through the American Community Survey. The text features a complete illustration of how to use the ACS for a marketing research objective.
- New Chapter (Chapter 10) on data issues and inputting data into XL Data Analyst, describes data matrices and data coding plus data quality issues. We also describe the organization of data and variables in the XL Data Analyst.
- New flow charts on data analysis identify key considerations such as categorical or metric data and provide guides to the selection of proper analyses.
- *iReportWriting Assistant* is an online tool to help students with the report writing process. It contains PowerPoints, templates for various aspects of a marketing research report, grammar and citation help, and an example marketing research report to use as a model. The *iReportWriting Assistant* can be accessed through any chapter by clicking on the Companion Website at http://www.pearsonhighered .com/burns.
- Numerous tweaks and small improvements to make the presentation as understandable and useful as possible have been made after a careful examination of every section of the text.

Why Excel for Data Analysis?

Most students will not become marketing researchers and only a small percentage of them, in their future careers, will have access to powerful software programs designed specifically for data analysis. By having this book, they will continually have access to our Excel add-in program, XL Data Analyst™. In this course students will learn how to use this powerful software program, which they can access as long as they can access Excel. Instructors told us they want to teach students a software program they will have and use in the future. Once students learn to use XL Data Analyst™ they can use it with their Excel programs for years to come.

Microsoft Excel is a powerful computing tool that is widely used and understood by students. Developers commonly program applications, called add-ins, that simplify Excel spreadsheet operations. Our add-in, XL Data Analyst™, opens up Excel's computing capabilities for marketing research applications in an easy-to-use format. Many features of XL Data Analyst™ make it more desirable than some of the most widely used dedicated stat packages because it takes the mystery and confusion out of data analysis.

Who Should Use This Textbook?

This book is written for the introductory marketing research course at the undergraduate level. We assume students have not had a prior course in marketing research, and that they have had at least one elementary statistics course. We focus on teaching the process of marketing research so that students will be better users of marketing research. They should be able to evaluate the need for marketing research and also determine the adequacy of research proposals. At the same time, we give the students of this book the tools to conduct basic analysis techniques on their own.

A Concise Presentation

We wanted to provide a book with the basics of marketing research. Adopters have told us they want to teach the basics of marketing research in depth as opposed to covering a large amount of material superficially. Many professors desire to teach a course with less text material, allowing them to supplement the course with projects or to spend more time on the basics. *Basic Marketing Research: Using Microsoft® Excel Data Analysis* is shorter in length but covers the essential, basic components of marketing research. We made every effort to write a shorter book without sacrificing knowledge on what we consider the "basics."

Features of XL Data Analyst™

XL Data Analyst™ is unique in that it only requires Excel, to which many students have access, and it is written expressly for the purpose of conducting marketing research data analysis. When we wrote the first edition of this book we knew we didn't want to just write a shorter version of a marketing research book. We wanted a new approach to data analysis. Specifically, we wanted a program that would operate without statistical terms that are difficult for students to navigate. We wanted the program to operate in a user-friendly format that was intuitive. Secondly, with many years of teaching marketing research experience, we wanted our program to offer output in a way that allowed students to interpret the output correctly and more easily. Those who have studied statistics realize that many of the presentations of statistical output are based upon tradition. We offer users an alternative. The XL Data Analyst™ has both traditional and classical statistical format as well as output in our new easy-to-interpret format. However, the essence of our new software is output that students can immediately interpret without a need to consult the statistical values: our program generates polished tables with "plain English" presentations of the various findings. This allows students to have greater focus on using marketing research to make decisions; the purpose of marketing research. The XL Data Analyst has been tested and is fully compatible with Excel 2010. Students may download XL Data Analyst™ at http://www.xldataanalyst.com.

About the Text: Key Strengths

Aside from being the first marketing research text to fully integrate Excel for data analysis, this book offers several key strengths.

Time-Tested, 11-Step Approach

The framework of our best-selling SPSS® text is the same framework for our Excel version. Our logical 11-step process is a time-tested process used throughout this book.

New Examples

In every chapter we searched for new examples for opening vignettes that would wake the students' interest and understanding of marketing research. Several of these vignettes were supplied from our professional contacts in the marketing research industry. Several of them reflect current marketing research practice. In addition to these all-new chapter-opening vignettes, new examples, many from marketing research industry sources, are integrated throughout the text.

(New) Integrated Case with Data Set

As with our previous textbooks, we wanted an integrated case which relates to students' interests and which was realistic. Consequently, for the 3rd edition, we developed "Advanced Automotive Concepts," a fictitious case about a major automobile manufacturer attempting to develop fuel-efficient and environmentally friendly vehicles. The case addresses consumer concerns about rising gasoline prices, global warming, and their reactions to automobile concepts the company is capable of manufacturing. The case is integrated throughout the textbook. The case resonates with students' interests and, at the same time, is an excellent example of teaching the marketing research process. The cases and topics covered are:

- **Chapter 1, Case 1.2:** The Need to Conduct Marketing Research
- **Chapter 2, Case 2.2:** Searching for a Marketing Research Firm
- **Chapter 3, Case 3.2:** Putting It All Together Using the Integrated Case for This Textbook: Defining Problems and Research Objectives
- **Chapter 4, Case 4.2:** Understanding Research Design
- **Chapter 5, Case 5.2:** Using Secondary Data
- **Chapter 6, Case 6.2:** Advanced Automobile Concepts Data Collection
- **Chapter 7, Case 7.2:** Turning Measurement Principles into Survey Questions
- **Chapter 8, Case 8.2:** Questionnaire Design
- **Chapter 9, Case 9.2:** Balancing Sample Error with Sample Cost
- **Chapter 10, Case 10.2:** The Advanced Automobile Concepts Survey Data Quality
- **Chapter 11, Case 11.2:** Advanced Automobile Concepts Summarization Analysis
- **Chapter 12, Case 12.2:** The Advanced Automobile Concepts Survey Generalization Analysis
- **Chapter 13, Case 13.2:** The Advanced Automobile Concepts Survey Differences Analysis
- **Chapter 14, Case 14.2:** The Advanced Automobile Concepts Survey Relationships Analysis
- **Chapter 15, Case 15.1:** Advanced Automobile Concepts: Using *iReportWriting Assistant*
- **Chapter 15, Case 15.2:** Advanced Automobile Concepts: Making a PowerPoint® Presentation

Also, we use the Advanced Automobile Concepts case data set to illustrate all of our data analyses procedures discussed in our four data analyses chapters. Of course, we have an Advanced Automobile Concepts XL Data Analyst data set for students to use in applying the various types of data analysis covered in the textbook.

Our Approach to Teaching Data Analysis

When we introduced the first edition of this book we said "Finally there is an alternative!" After many years of teaching marketing research and talking with dozens of colleagues who do the same, the authors decided it was time to do some things a different way. Weary of students struggling with levels of measurement, we present measurement in terms of categorical or metric variables. Instead of having students baffled by data analysis, we present data analysis in an easy-to-learn process. In this edition, we have provided flow charts that instruct students on the key factors to consider when deciding what analysis to use. In addition, data analysis keystrokes are illustrated through colorful, annotated screen captures. Experience has shown us that the students, using XL Data Analyst™, quickly learn the tools of data analysis and complete their projects much faster than with traditional software programs. They focus more on getting the answers and writing their reports instead of staring at hard-to-interpret output.

Datasets

In addition to the Advanced Automobile Concepts dataset (AAConcepts.xlsm), we have a dataset on retail store target marketing, Case 14.1, "Friendly Market Versus Circle K" (Friendlymarket.xlsm). Chapter 10 describes how students can set up their own datasets, such as those obtained with a team marketing research project, in the XL Data Analyst.

Ethics, Global Marketing Research, and Practical Applications

In our Marketing Research Applications, when we touch on ethical issues or give examples of the global use of research, we use icons to alert readers to these special topics. When we illustrate a practical application we denote this with an icon as well.

Marginal Notes, Key Terms, Review Questions, Application Questions, and Case Studies

These proven pedagogical aids are included in *Basic Marketing Research: Using Microsoft*® *Excel Data Analysis*, 3rd Edition.

Teaching Aids

PowerPoint Presentations (0135078261)

A comprehensive set of PowerPoint slides that can be used by instructors for class presentations or by students for lecture preview or review.

Instructor's Manual (0135078245)

A complete instructor's manual, prepared by the authors, can be used to prepare lecture or class presentations, find answers to end-of-chapter questions and case studies, and even to design the course syllabus.

Test Item File (0135078253)

The test bank for the 3rd Edition contains over 50 questions for each chapter. Questions are provided in both multiple-choice and true/false format. Page numbers corresponding to answers to the questions are provided for each question.

   This Test Item File supports Association to Advance Collegiate Schools of Business (AACSB) International Accreditation. Each chapter of the Test Item File was prepared with the AACSB learning standards in mind. Where appropriate, the answer line of each question indicates a category within which the question falls.[1] This AACSB reference helps instructors identify those test questions that support that organization's learning goals.

---

[1]Please note that not all test questions will indicate an AACSB category.

What Is the AACSB?

AACSB is a not-for-profit corporation of educational institutions, corporations, and other organizations devoted to the promotion and improvement of higher education in business administration and accounting. A collegiate institution offering degrees in business administration or accounting may volunteer for AACSB accreditation review. The AACSB makes initial accreditation decisions and conducts periodic reviews to promote continuous quality improvement in management education. Pearson Education is a proud member of the AACSB and is pleased to provide advice to help you apply AACSB Learning Standards.

What Are AACSB Learning Standards?

One of the criteria for AACSB accreditation is the quality of the curricula. Although no specific courses are required, the AACSB expects a curriculum to include learning experiences in such areas as:

- Communication abilities
- Ethical understanding and reasoning abilities
- Analytical skills
- Use of information technology
- Dynamics of the global economy
- Multicultural and diversity understanding
- Reflective thinking skills

These seven categories are AACSB Learning Standards. Questions that test skills relevant to these standards are tagged with the appropriate standard. For example, a question testing the moral questions associated with externalities would receive the Ethical understanding and reasoning abilities tag.

How Can I Use These Tags?

Tagged questions help you measure whether students are grasping the course content that aligns with AACSB guidelines noted above. In addition, the tagged questions may help to identify potential applications of these skills. This, in turn, may suggest enrichment activities or other educational experiences to help students achieve these goals.

Instructor's Resource Center

All your teaching resources in one place. Electronic versions of the instructor's manual, test item file, TestGen test generating software, plus PowerPoints are available online at http://www.pearsonhighered.com/burns. (Select Instructor Resources.)

Companion Website for Students

At http://www.pearsonhighered.com/burns, students should go to the "Companion Website." Here, by clicking on a chapter, they can take the self study quiz. The self study quizzes are automatically graded. To get the most out of the self study quizzes, students should study the chapter *first*, and then take the sample test to assess how well they have learned chapter material.

Also, at the "Companion Website" students will have access to: a. *iReportWriting Assistant*, b. a link where they can download the XL Data Analyst™ software, and c. find information about careers in marketing research.

CourseSmart for Students

CourseSmart goes beyond traditional expectations providing instant, online access to the textbooks and course materials students need at lower cost. They can also search, highlight and take notes anywhere at anytime. See all the benefits to students at www.coursesmart.com/students.

Acknowledgments

It takes many people to create a book. First, we wish to acknowledge the expert assistance we have received from the professional staff at Pearson Prentice Hall. First, we thank our editor, Melissa Sabella. Meeta Pendharkar served as our Editorial Project Manager. Meeta, you could not have been more helpful, thank you! Also, thank you to Elisabeth Scarpa our Editorial Assistant and Becca Richter Groves, our Production Product Manager. We owe Becca a very special thank you for her capable assistance. We have been with Prentice Hall now for over a decade and we are forever grateful we found such a great partnership. The entire Prentice Hall staff is courteous and professional. Thank you all for being so good at what you do!

In the 3rd Edition we again benefited from the capable experience of Heather Donofrio, Ph.D. Heather has been involved in different aspects of helping with our textbook for several years. Her highly qualified editorial assistance is reflected throughout this book. We also wish to thank Ashley Roberts who cheerfully and professionally helped us with many tasks during the preparation of this book.

We both enjoy keeping up with industry trends and practice through our extensive contacts in the marketing research industry. The following professionals made contributions to the 3rd Edition:

Baltimore Research—Ted Donnelly
Burke, Inc.—Ron Tatham
Decision Analyst—Jerry W. Thomas
ESRI—Brent Roderick & Lisa Horn
Experian Simmons—John Fetto
Inside Research—Jack Honomichl & Laurence Gold
Intercampo—Luis Pamblanco
Ipsos Forward Research—Richard Homans
Ipsos Public Affairs—Paul Abbate
Moore Research Services—Colleen Moore-Mezler
MRA—Kristen Darby
NewProductWorks, GfK Strategic Innovation—Marilyn Raymond and Penny Wamback
Ozgrid Business Applications—Raina Hawley
QRCA—Shannon Pfarr Thompson
Qualtrics, Inc.—Scott M. Smith
SDR Consulting—William D. Neal
Socratic Technologies—William H. MacElroy
Sports & Leisure Research Group—Jon Last
Survey Sampling International—Kees de Jong, Ilene Siegalovsky
Talking Business—Holly M. O'Neill
TNS Global/Retail & Shopper Practice—Herb Sorensen
United States Census Bureau

We'd like to thank the professors who took part in our focus groups and shared their ideas for this text and XL Data Analyst:

Reviewers

Brian Buckler	Avila University
Aslihan Cakmak	Lehman College
Doug Grisaffe	University of Texas at Austin
Steven Moff	Pennsylvania College of Technology
Mike Petrochuk	Walsh University
Emanuel Stein	Queensborough Community College, CUNY
James Swartz	California State Polytechnic University-Pomona
Diane Whitney	University of Maryland-College Park

As always, we wish to thank our life partners who put up with our book writing exploits and, no matter what, always smile. Thank you, Jeanne and Libbo, for your steadfast support of our professional endeavors.

Al Burns
Louisiana State University
alburns@lsu.edu

Ron Bush
University of West Florida
rbush@uwf.edu

About the Authors

Alvin C. Burns is the Ourso Distinguished Chair of Marketing and Chairperson of Marketing in the E.J. Ourso College of Business at Louisiana State University. He received his doctorate in marketing from Indiana University and an MBA from the University of Tennessee. Professor Burns has taught undergraduate and master's level courses and doctoral seminars in marketing research for over 35 years. During this time period, he has supervised a great many marketing research projects conducted for business-to-consumer, business-to-business, and not-for-profit organizations. His articles have appeared in the *Journal of Marketing Research, Journal of Business Research, Journal of Advertising Research*, and others. He is a Fellow in the Association for Business Simulation and Experiential Learning. He resides in Baton Rouge, Louisiana, with his wife Jeanne and Yellow Labrador Retriever, Shadeaux (it's a Louisiana thing).

Ronald F. Bush is Distinguished University Professor of Marketing at the University of West Florida. He received his B.S. and M.A. from the University of Alabama and his Ph.D. from Arizona State University. With over 35 years of experience in marketing research, Professor Bush has worked on research projects with firms ranging from small businesses to the world's largest multinationals. He has served as an expert witness in trials involving research methods, often testifying on the appropriateness of research reports. His research has been published in leading journals including the *Journal of Marketing, Journal of Marketing Research, Journal of Advertising Research, Journal of Retailing, Journal of Business,* among others. In 1993 he was named a Fellow by the Society for Marketing Advances. He and his wife, Libbo, live on the Gulf of Mexico where they can often be found playing "throw the stick" with their Scottish Terrier, Maggie.

An Introduction to Marketing Research

Why and How We Conduct Marketing Research at the Sports & Leisure Research Group

SPORTS& LEISURE
RESEARCH GROUP

What do organizations like Callaway Golf, Unilever, Carnival Cruises, Time Inc., and the PGA of America have in common? They are all actively seeking to efficiently communicate with their target market, many of whom are heavily involved in sports or recreation activities. As these organizations seek to optimize their product offerings, and the ways in which they communicate the benefits of these offerings, they face numerous marketing decisions. At the Sports & Leisure Research Group (SLRG) we help our clients make these decisions and devise optimal marketing strategies, going "beyond the numbers" by using marketing research to better understand what customers want and how to position their products and services most effectively to meet those needs.

Marketing research is the tool that we use to bring information to our clients which allows them to make the best decisions. At SLRG we use a variety of marketing research: qualitative and quantitative techniques such as focus groups, one-on-one interviews, telephone interviews and online surveys, and purchase diaries. We custom design research studies so our clients receive the best value from our service. In this book you will learn about these and other marketing research techniques.

Jon Last has over twenty years in marketing research including experience with Conde Nast's Golf Digest Publications Division, PGA of America, and a major cruise ship line. He holds an MBA from the Wharton School of the University of Pennsylvania and graduated magna cum laude from Tufts University. Last has served as president of the Marketing Research Association and is a recipient of the MRA's Award of Excellence.

Visit Sports & Leisure Research Group at www.sportsandleisureresearch.com.

Source: Jon Last, Sports & Leisure Research Group.

Jon Last, Founder and President, Sports and Leisure Research Group

We wish to welcome you to the world of marketing research! Any time business managers need to make decisions and they lack adequate information, they are likely to need marketing research. In our opening vignette, Jon Last, CEO of Sports & Leisure Research, collects marketing research information that is needed by magazine executives, advertisers, manufacturers of sports equipment, and service providers such as the lodging and restaurant business to make better decisions. In this chapter we introduce you to marketing research by (a) examining how marketing research is a part of marketing, (b) exploring definitions, purposes, and uses of marketing research, (c) learning how to classify marketing research studies, and (d) providing you with an understanding of how marketing research fits into a firm's marketing information system.

You will find in this book a successful statistical analysis software program that is easy to use and interpret. The program runs off Microsoft's Excel® spreadsheet program, so as long as you have access to Excel® you will be able to use this. We have developed XL Data Analyst™ to allow you to easily tap the power of Excel for purposes of marketing research analysis.

Now, we will show you *why* you conduct marketing research analyses by introducing you to the field of marketing research.

Marketing Research: Part of Marketing?

Before we discuss marketing research, we need to first discuss marketing. The reason is, marketing research is part of marketing, and you cannot fully appreciate marketing research and the role it plays in the marketing process unless you know how it fits into the marketing process. What is **marketing?**

> Because marketing research is part of marketing, you cannot fully appreciate marketing research and the role it plays in the marketing process unless you know how it fits into the marketing process.

The American Marketing Association [AMA] has defined marketing as an organizational function and a set of processes for creating, communicating and delivering value to customers and for managing customer relationships in ways that benefit the organization and its stakeholders.[1]

This definition recognizes that marketing is an organizational function. The other basic functions of business include production, finance, and human resources. It also recognizes that marketing is a set of processes that creates something of value such as products and services, communicates or promotes the value, and delivers or distributes the value (which includes the notion of pricing) to consumers. This definition recognizes the domain of marketing, namely, the four Ps (product or service; promotion, distribution (also known as "place") and pricing). This definition also recognizes that marketers need to manage customer relationships. This means it is not wise for a marketer to think of a one-time transaction. "Making the sale" is not the end of marketing if marketers want repeat buying and positive word-of-mouth promotion of their products and services. In addition, the AMA definition points out that marketing is carried out for the benefit of the organization and its stakeholders. A for-profit organization, for example, must earn a respectable return on investment (*ROI*) in order to remain in business.

For many years marketing focused on providing the customer with value through a physical product that emerged at the end of the distribution channel. Marketing managers focused on creating a physical product and then making efficient promotion, distribution, and pricing decisions. Current thinking, proposed primarily by Vargo and Lusch,[2] calls for a framework that goes beyond a "manufacturing-tangible product" view of marketing (e.g., Ford creates value by building cars). Rather, Vargo and Lusch argue that we should adopt a service-centered view of marketing which (a) identifies core competencies, the fundamental knowledge and skills that may represent a potential competitive advantage; (b) identifies potential customers who can benefit from these core competencies; (c) cultivates relationships with these customers, allowing them to help create values that meet their specific needs; and (d) allows one to gauge feedback from the market, learn from the feedback, and improve the values offered to the public.

One implication of this new framework is that firms must be more than customer oriented (making and selling what firms think customers want and need). Rather, firms must *collaborate with* and *learn from* customers, adapting to their changing needs. A second implication is that products are not viewed as separate from services. Isn't Ford really marketing a service, a service that happens to include a by-product called a car?[3] This framework is referred to as the service-dominant logic for marketing.

We do not wish to provide a discourse on how marketing thought is evolving. After all, we are still trying to answer the question: Why do we need to know about marketing in order to better understand marketing research? The answer is, in order to practice marketing, marketing decision makers need information in order to make better decisions. And, in our opinion, current definitions and frameworks of marketing mean that information is *more* important, not less important, in today's world. For example, the service-dominant logic for marketing implies that decision makers need information to know what their real core competencies are; how to create meaningful relationships with customers; how to create, communicate, and deliver value to customers; how to gather feedback to gauge customer acceptance; and how to determine the appropriate responses to the feedback. Keeping these information needs in mind, think about the information needed by Ford, as the company prepared to produce the Fusion hybrid to compete with the Prius and other successful hybrids already on the market; or by the managers at Sony, as they decided to go head to head with Apple with an online service to compete with iTunes®; or at Apple as they prepared to launch the iPhone and the iPad. Think about all the decisions managers made at General Mills when they launched their successful organic food line, Small Planet Foods, or how the managers at CBS's highly watched television show, *60 Minutes,* have continued to make good decisions regarding their broadcasts year after year. The same applies to not-for-profits such as the American Red Cross, which earns donations and support by creating value in the sense that it provides donors with "piece of mind for helping others." In order to make the decisions necessary for

Why do we need to know about marketing in order to better understand marketing research? The answer is, in order to practice marketing, marketing decision makers need information in order to make better decisions.

Current definitions and frameworks of marketing mean that information is *more* important, not less important, in today's world.

such actions, the decision makers in these organizations needed information. As you will learn, marketing research provides information to decision makers.

The phrase "hearing the voice of the consumer" has been popularized to mean that companies have the information they need to effectively satisfy wants and needs in the marketplace. While we just cited some successful firms, we recognize that not all firms hear this voice. They do not conceive of products or services that meet the needs and wants of the market. They do not provide value, and their sales come from short-term exchanges, not enduring customer relationships. These companies produce the wrong products or services. They have the wrong price, poor advertising, or poor distribution. Then they become part of the many firms that experience product failure. The Irridium telephone needed 500,000 customers to break even yet attracted only 50,000 subscribers.[4] General Motors's first electric vehicle, the EV1, was a failure. McDonald's veggie burger, the MacLean, was taken off the market.

The GfK Strategic Innovation's NewProductWorks® studies product failure in order to help clients glean ideas for successful new innovations. For example, a firm introduced scrambled frozen eggs in a push-up tube. The eggs came with cheese, bacon, or sausage and the idea was to quickly heat it up and take it with you for a convenient, eat-on-the-go breakfast. You could have eggs and bacon while driving to work! Although this sounded great in the board room, IncrEdibles were taken off the market as buyers found the eggs often ended up in their lap as they tried to push up another bite. There was inadequate information on how real consumers would use the product. Out! International, Inc. came up with what sounded like a cute name for a new bug spray: "Hey! There's a Monster in My Room!" What information did the company fail to pick up on? The name alone scared kids when Mommy told them there was "a monster in the room!" The product failed. Marketing Research Application 1.1 illustrates other examples of product failures supplied to us from the marketing researchers at NewProductWorks®.

Of course, it is easy to play "Monday morning quarterback" and keep in mind that all these companies have many successful products to their credit. Peter Drucker wrote that successful companies are those that know and understand the customer so well that the product conceived, priced, promoted, and distributed by the company is ready to be bought as soon as it is available.[5] Drucker is on target with his statement, but how can a marketer know and understand how to deliver value to the customer so well? The answer, as you can now see by our examples, is by having information about consumers. So to practice marketing correctly, managers must have information, and this is the purpose of marketing research. This is why we say that marketing research is a part of marketing; it provides the necessary information to enable managers to market ideas, goods, and services *properly*. But how do you market ideas, goods, and services *properly*? You have probably already learned in your studies that you must begin by having the right philosophy, followed by proper marketing strategy. We call that philosophy the "marketing concept."

The Marketing Concept: The "Right" Philosophy

Often we find that students do not understand how important philosophies are to them. First, what is a philosophy? We can think of it as a system of values, or principles, by which to live. But, more importantly, why is one of your philosophies important to you? The answer may be a surprise. Your philosophy is important because it dictates the decisions you make and what you do every day. Think about your philosophy regarding the importance of higher education. Isn't this philosophy affecting your daily decisions?

You go to college classes daily, you listen to professors lecture daily, and you are reading this book, aren't you? Well, the same is true for business managers. A manager's philosophy will affect how he or she makes day-to-day decisions in running a firm. There are many different philosophies that managers may use to guide them in their decision making. "We are in the locomotive business; we make and run trains." Or, "To be successful, we must sell, sell, sell!" The managers who guided their companies by these philosophies guided them right out of business. A much better philosophy that grew in popularity in the mid-1950s we call the marketing concept.[6]

Not all firms "hear the voice of the consumer." They do not conceive of products or services that meet the needs and wants of the market.

How can a marketer know and understand how to deliver value to the customer so well? The answer is, by having information about consumers. So to practice marketing correctly, managers must have information, and this is the purpose of marketing research. This is why we say that marketing research is a part of marketing; it provides the necessary information to enable managers to market ideas, goods, and services *properly*.

Philosophies are principles, values by which to live. They are important because they dictate how we behave every day.

MARKETING RESEARCH APPLICATION 1.1

Practical Applications

Could Better Information Have Helped to Avoid These Failures?

Practical Application

Ice Breakers Pacs went into distribution in November 2007. Pacs were small, dissolvable pouches with a flavored-powder sweetener, in orange and cool mint flavors. By January 2008, The Hershey Company stopped the

Ice Breakers Pacs

production in response to criticism that the mints looked too much like the tiny heat-sealed bags used to sell powdered illegal street drugs (cocaine). Hershey stated the mints were not intended to resemble anything of the sort. CEO David West disclosed the decision to stop production: "We are sensitive to these viewpoints and thus have made the decision that we will no longer manufacture Ice Breaker Pacs." What seemed like a breakthrough, innovative way to deliver a mint form turned out to be the opposite when consumer behaviors toward safety (for self, community, world) made this product unacceptable to the marketplace. Would better information as to the market's reaction to the packaging been helpful?

Introduced in April 2006, Coca-Cola's Blak entered the U.S. marketplace as a carbonated fusion beverage, a taste blend of Classic Coke and coffee "essence." Coke spent two

years developing Blak in hopes of making inroads into consumers' growing taste for coffee and a booming premium beverage market, targeting over-thirty, savvy, sophisticate-achiever consumers. Weak product performance in the United States resulted in its being discontinued seventeen months after launch. Coke would have benefited by taking a look at more information on product history in this category. Blak was not the first of its kind; similar blends were released in the past and failed as well. In 1994, Pepsi began to test-market a soda called Pepsi Kona, which tasted more like coffee than soda. In 1995, Starbucks partnered with Pepsi and began to market a coffee product called Mazagran. It was a

Coca-Cola Blak

lightly carbonated iced coffee beverage. Customers were willing to try it once, based on the Starbucks name alone, but the drink failed to encourage repeat sales.

One question is whether it was the carbonation or the coffee that put consumers off. It is true that premium coffee sales have boomed and carbonated beverages are still a mainstay in the U.S.

Coca-Cola C2

marketplace, and Coke saw that in Japan the combination of coffee and carbonation was popular. Causes for failure may include (a) consumers in the United States were not ready to accept the taste; (b) there may have been some confusion as to when and how this type of blended beverage could meet the needs currently being provided by coffee and soda separately; and (c) perhaps consumers love their coffee and they love their colas, but they don't want a combination. Would better information, prior to the launch of Blak, have been helpful?

Coca-Cola spent an estimated $30 to $50 million to promote C2, a cola-flavored beverage introduced first in Japan, then later in the United States in June 2004, in response to the low-carbohydrate diet trend. This was Coca-Cola's biggest product launch since Diet Coke in 1982. Despite this support, C2 (as well as its competitor Pepsi Edge) failed to meet sales expectations and was pushed out a year later. This failure is due mostly to the decline of the low-carb fad, and partly to the success of Coca-Cola Zero, a zero-calorie version launched within the same

Wolfgang Puck's Self-Heating Latte

time frame. Zero-calorie beverages had already been established, and with the advancement in the taste of

MARKETING RESEARCH APPLICATION 1.1 *(continued)*

Practical Applications

Could Better Information Have Helped to Avoid These Failures?

sweeteners, the combined effect made reduced-carb beverages obsolete.

Sources reported the Wolfgang Puck self-heating coffee containers technology took ten years and $24 million to develop. The self-heating can technology is by OnTech and is based on a two-part container. The outer chamber holds the beverage and the inner chamber holds calcium oxide and a water puck, which when its seal is broken mixes with the calcium oxide and creates a heating effect. Launched in the spring of 2005, the product was quickly picked up for distribution by Kroger, Albertsons, and Sam's Club. Less than a year later, Puck's namesake company demanded brand-licensee BrandSource Inc. to pull the products

from stores nationwide after complaints of faulty technology, ranging from the product's failure to reach an appropriately hot temperature to it actually overheating, and spurting or leaking product from the can. While self-heating and self-chilling technology could help meet the needs of many on-the-go consumers, any future use of an improvement in the technology will have to face an even higher hurdle to regain consumers' trust.

Visit NewProductWorks® at www.gfkamerica.com.

Source: NewProductWorks®, the innovation resource center of GfK Strategic Innovation (formerly Arbor Strategy Group).

Kotler and Keller characterize the marketing concept as one that "senses and responds. The job is not to find the right customers for your products, but to find the right products for your customers."[7] They define the marketing concept as follows:

> The **marketing concept** is a business philosophy that holds that the key to achieving organizational goals consists of the company's being more effective than competitors in creating, delivering, and communicating customer value to its chosen target markets.[8]

For many years, business leaders have recognized that this is the "right" philosophy. Although the term *marketing concept* is often used interchangeably with other terms such as *customer oriented* or *market driven*, the key point is that this philosophy puts the customer first. Time has proven that such a philosophy is superior to one in which company management focuses on production, the product itself, or some promotional or sales gimmick. If you satisfy consumers, they will seek to do business with your company. Thus, we've learned that having the right philosophy is an important first step in being successful. Still, just appreciating the importance of satisfying consumer wants and needs isn't enough. Firms must put together the "right" strategy.

> Although the *marketing concept* is often used interchangeably with other terms such as *customer oriented* or *market driven*, the key point is that this philosophy puts the customer first.

The "Right" Marketing Strategy

The term *strategy* was borrowed from military jargon that stressed developing plans of attack that would minimize the enemy's ability to respond. In other words, using strategy involves a plan, and that plan should anticipate competitors' reactions. Firms may also have strategies in different areas, such as financial strategy, production strategy, and technology strategy. So, what exactly is marketing strategy?

A **marketing strategy** consists of selecting a segment of the market as the company's target market and designing the proper "mix" of product/service, price, promotion, and distribution system to meet the wants and needs of the consumers within the target market.

We have to develop the "right" strategy—the strategy that allows our firm to truly meet the wants and needs of the consumers within the market segment we have chosen. Think of the many questions we now must answer: What is the market? How do we segment the market? What are the wants and needs of each segment? How do we measure the size of each market segment? Who are our competitors, and how are they meeting the wants and needs of each segment? Which

> Managers must make many decisions in order to implement a strategy and they need good information in order to make the "right" decisions.

segment(s) should we target? Which model of a proposed product will best suit the target market? What is the best price? Which promotional method will be the most efficient? How should we distribute the product/service? In order to make the right decisions, managers must have objective, accurate, and timely information; and, because environments are forever changing, marketers constantly need updated information about them. A strategy that is successful today may need to be changed as the competitive, economic, social, political, legal, global, and technological environments change. Therefore, the bottom line of this discussion is that to make the right decisions, managers continuously need information. As we shall learn next, marketing research supplies much of this information.

> The bottom line of this discussion is that to make the right decisions, managers continuously need information.

How Do We Define Marketing Research?

At this point you understand something about marketing, the marketing concept, and marketing strategy. You also know that marketing managers need information to carry out marketing, to implement the marketing concept, and to design the "right" strategy. What, then, is marketing research? **Marketing research** is the process of designing, gathering, analyzing, and reporting information that may be used to solve a specific marketing problem.

> Marketing research is the process of designing, gathering, analyzing, and reporting information that may be used to solve a specific marketing problem.

This definition tells us that marketing research is a *process* that results in reporting information that can be used to solve a marketing problem (e.g., price determination or advertising). The focus is on a process that results in information that will be used to make decisions. (We introduce you to this eleven-step process in Chapter 3.) Notice also that our definition refers to information that may be used to solve a *specific* marketing problem. We explain the importance of this later on in this chapter when we discuss marketing information systems. Ours is not the only definition of marketing research. The American Marketing Association formed a committee several years ago to establish a definition of marketing research. The AMA definition is:

> Marketing research is the function that links the consumer, customer, and public to the marketer through information—information used to identify and define marketing opportunities and problems; generate, refine, and evaluate marketing actions; monitor marketing performance; and improve the understanding of marketing as a process.[9]

Each of these definitions is correct. Our definition is shorter and illustrates the process of marketing research. The AMA's definition is longer because it elaborates on the function (we call it the *purpose*) as well as the *uses* of marketing research. Note that market research, a part of marketing research, refers to applying marketing research to a specific market area. One definition of **market research** is the systematic gathering, recording, and analyzing of data with respect to a particular market, where *market* refers to a specific customer group in a specific geographic area.[10] The Marketing Research Association (MRA) defines market research as "the process used to define the size, location and/or makeup of the market for a good or service."[11] Notice the focus on a geographical market area. The MRA defines marketing and opinion research in a manner consistent with the way we have defined marketing research: "a process used by businesses to collect, analyze and interpret information used to make sound business decisions and successfully manage the business."[12] In the next two sections, we will talk more about the purpose and uses of marketing research.

> Market research refers to the systematic gathering, recording, and analyzing of data with respect to a particular market, where *market* refers to a specific customer group in a specific geographic area.

What Is the Purpose of Marketing Research?

The AMA definition of marketing research includes a reference to the consumer: The purpose of marketing research is to link the *consumer* to the marketer by providing information that can be used in making marketing decisions. The AMA definition expands our definition by telling us that the information provided by marketing research for decision making should represent the consumer. In fact, by mentioning the consumer, this implies that marketing research is consistent with the marketing concept because it "links the consumer . . . to the marketer." The AMA definition is normative. That is, it tells us how marketing research *should be* used to ensure the firm is consumer oriented. We certainly agree with this, but what *should be* done isn't always followed. Our examples of poor product decisions we discussed previously illustrate this point, and managers have been implored to use marketing research instead of their own intuition to make decisions. Even though the AMA definition makes the point that marketing research links the firm to the consumer, we want to point out that marketing research information is also collected on entities other than the consumer. Information is routinely gathered on members of distribution channels, employees, and competitors as well as the economic, social, technological, and other environments.[13]

One could argue that the point of all this research is to do a better job of satisfying consumers. To illustrate how marketing research helps link managers to consumers, imagine what is taking place in the golf industry during the economic slowdown we have experienced since 2008. Managers of firms that market golf clubs and equipment, clothing, and managers in related industries, such as the lodging and resort industry, want to know how the recession is affecting golfers' attitudes and buying practices. Marketing Research Application 1.2 shows how one marketing research firm is linking these managers to their consumers.

Sometimes marketing research studies lead to the wrong decisions. We should point out here that just because a manager uses marketing research doesn't mean that the decisions based on the research are infallible. In the examples of "failed" products we examined earlier, some marketing research was conducted but may have been inaccurate. There are plenty of examples in which marketing research showed a product would fail, yet it turned out to be a resounding success. Stella Artois beer appealed primarily to people in urban areas. The company's advertising agency developed an advertisement showing a peasant selling flowers in a rural setting, but the marketing research results showed the ad to be a failure, citing below-average brand awareness and the fact that the ad positioned the beer away from the group to which it primarily appealed. Management at Stella Artois, however, believed that the ad was good and the marketing research was flawed. The ad was so successful it is credited with helping to turn the company's product from a niche beer to one of the top-selling grocery-store beer brands in the United Kingdom.[14] Another example occurred when marketing research showed the pilot for the *Seinfeld* show, starring Jerry Seinfeld, was "bad." Later, however, a doubting executive resurrected the show, which became one of the most successful shows in television history.[15] Likewise, marketing research studies also predicted that hair-styling mousse and answering machines would fail if brought to market.[16]

As we've mentioned, there are plenty of failures where marketing research predicted success. Most of these failures are removed from the shelves with as little fanfare as possible. Another classic example of this was Beecham's cold-water wash product, Delicare. The new product failed even though marketing research predicted it would unseat the category leader, Woolite. Beecham sued the research company that had predicted success.[17] When Duncan Hines introduced its line of soft cookies, marketing research studies showed that 80% of customers who tried Soft Batch® cookies stated that they would buy them in the future, but didn't.[18] Sainsbury's, the U.K. grocery chain, had an ad prepared by their agency that tested favorably in marketing research testing. However, the company received negative reactions from customers and staff alike when the ad ran. Sainsbury's switched ad agencies.[19]

These examples do not imply that marketing research is not useful. Remember, most marketing research studies are trying to understand and predict consumer behavior—a difficult task, indeed. The fact that the marketing research industry has been around for many years means that it has passed the toughest of all tests to prove its worth—the test of the marketplace. If the industry did not provide value, it would cease to exist. For each one of these examples of "failure" there are tens of thousands of success stories supporting the use of marketing research.

MARKETING RESEARCH APPLICATION 1.2

Practical Applications

Using Marketing Research to Better Understand Customer Attitudes

Practical Application

Golf is a multibillion-dollar industry. Managers in both manufacturing and retailing of golf clubs and equipment, golf apparel, golf courses, resorts, lodging, and restaurants that serve golfers are greatly concerned about golfers' attitudes. The Sports & Leisure Research Group has conducted marketing research studies to help these managers better understand golfers. What if you were a manager in this industry today? How will golfers react to harder economic conditions? Are they likely to play less golf? Are they likely to buy less golf equipment, clothing, and other items? What will keep them interested in following the PGA tour?

The SLRG regularly provides answers to these questions. This research not only provides current golfer attitudes, but because of multiple studies, they also identify how attitudes among golfers are changing. For a regular series of studies, SLRG focuses on (1) golfers' expectations to play golf, and spending and retail channel preferences; (2) how clubs are purchased; and (3) attitudes for the year ahead and how these attitudes will affect the industry.

SLRG collected data during three time periods: January 2009, July 2009, and January 2010. The 2010 online survey included a sample of 1,050 golfers and a control sample of 900 nongolfing sports fans. Key findings of the research include:

- A large percentage (94%) of the golfers expect to play the game the same or more in 2010, which is up from the 2009 figure (77%).
- Golfers expect to pay more for irons, drivers, and wedges in 2010 than they did in 2009.
- More golfers are purchasing from sporting goods retailers; brand loyalty is not as important. Technology is a "trigger" for purchasing and the ability to demo the clubs, especially "on-course trial" is important.
- Golfers view magazines as trustworthy, television ads as entertaining and memorable, and the Internet as informative and unique.
- Golfers showed an improved outlook toward being better off in retirement years, an important segment for the golfing industry.

Source: Jon Last, Sports & Leisure Research Group.

What Are the Uses of Marketing Research?

Now that you understand the purpose of marketing research, let's take a closer look at its uses. In our short definition, we simply refer to the use of marketing research as providing information to solve a specific marketing problem, and the AMA definition spells out what some of these problems may be.

Identify Market Opportunities and Problems

For example, the *identification of market opportunities and problems* is certainly a use of marketing research. Today many managers are asking, "What opportunities are in the market?" When everyone saw the music industry facing a terrible decline due to pirating of songs on the Internet, Apple saw an opportunity for iTunes, which has been an overwhelming success. Some auto manufacturers are contemplating a future where auto buyers will greatly value emission-free automobiles. Even though there is no existing infrastructure to recharge totally electric cars, Nissan sees an opportunity for this and has designed the Leaf® to capitalize on it. There are all sorts of opportunities, but companies must be aware and determine if they can provide a good or a service to fill that opportunity while achieving company objectives such as ROI. Problems are typically defined as times when we fail to meet objectives. Companies experience problems when market share, sales, profits, customer satisfaction, among others, fall below expectations. In either case, when there are opportunities or problems, managers need information to help them make the right decisions.

Generate, Refine, and Evaluate Potential Marketing Actions

Marketing research can also be used to generate, refine, and evaluate a potential marketing action. When Apple created the iPhone, both Apple and AT&T had to evaluate the proposed strategy of offering the wireless service for the iPhone only through AT&T. This turned out to be a good strategy as the iPhone was a huge success and both companies benefited from the partnership. Sometimes research is needed to generate actions. For example, a series of focus groups generates information that many consumers want cookies flavored with "dark chocolate." Additional research could help the company refine a strategy of bringing out a line of "dark chocolate" cookies by testing a proposed appeal that the "cookie is heart-healthy."[20] Once several strategies are in consideration, research can be conducted to evaluate each.

> Marketing research is used to generate, refine, and evaluate a potential marketing action.

Monitor Marketing Performance

The AMA definition also states that marketing research may be used to *monitor marketing performance.* Many research dollars are spent by firms to simply "see where we are." They not only want to know how they are doing, but also they want information about their competitors. So, marketing research may be used to monitor marketing performance. After companies have implemented their marketing strategies, they want to monitor the effectiveness of their ads, sales force, in-store promotions, dealer effectiveness, competitors, and customer satisfaction. Companies may also wish to monitor sales and market shares. This monitoring is often done through what is called "tracking research." Tracking research is used to monitor how well products of companies such as Hershey's, Campbell's Soup, Kellogg's, and Heinz are performing in the supermarkets and other distribution outlets (e.g., in mass merchandisers like Wal-Mart, Target, and K-Mart or drugstores or convenience stores). These "consumer packaged goods" firms want to monitor the sales of their brands, and sales of their competitor's brands. Research firms Nielsen and IRI are two of several firms monitoring the performance of products in supermarkets and other retail outlets. They monitor how many units of these products are being sold, through which chains, at what retail price, and so forth.

> Marketing research is used to "see where we and our competitors are."

Improve Marketing as a Process

The AMA definition says that one use of marketing research is to improve marketing as a process. To improve our understanding of the marketing process means that some marketing research is conducted to expand our basic knowledge of marketing. Typical of such research would be

Though they represent a very small part of the total marketing research studies, another use of marketing research is for studies that are designed to improve our basic understanding of marketing as opposed to solving a particular problem facing a business.

attempts to define and classify marketing phenomena and to develop theories that describe, explain, and predict these phenomena. Such knowledge is often published in journals such as the *Journal of Marketing Research* or *Marketing Research*. Much of this research is conducted by marketing professors at colleges and universities and by other organizations, such as the Marketing Science Institute. The latter use could be described as the only part of marketing research that is basic research. **Basic research** is conducted to expand our knowledge rather than to solve a specific problem. Research conducted to solve specific problems is called **applied research,** which represents the vast majority of marketing research studies. We will revisit the idea that marketing research solves specific problems a little later in this chapter.

A Classification of Marketing Research Studies

You are making progress at learning about marketing research. Let us now examine a way of classifying the different types of marketing research studies being conducted in the industry. In Table 1.1 we organize the major types of studies under the usage categories from the AMA definition. Under each of these four categories we provide example studies.

TABLE 1.1

A Classification of Marketing Research Studies

A. Identifying Market Opportunities and Problems

As the title implies, the goal of these studies is to find opportunities or to identify problems with an existing strategy. Examples of such studies include the following:

Market-demand determination
Market segments identification
Marketing audits SWOT analysis
Product/service-use studies
Environmental analysis studies
Competitive analysis

B. Generating, Refining, and Evaluating Potential Marketing Actions

Marketing research studies may be used to generate, refine, and then evaluate potential marketing actions. Marketing actions could be as broad as a proposed marketing strategy or as narrow as a tactic (a specific action taken to carry out a strategy). Typically these studies deal with one or more of the marketing-mix variables (product, price, distribution, and promotion). Examples include the following:

Proposed marketing-mix evaluation testing
Concept tests of proposed new products or services
New-product prototype testing
Reformulating existing product testing
Pricing tests
Advertising pretesting
In-store promotion effectiveness studies
Distribution effectiveness studies

C. Monitoring Marketing Performance

These studies are control studies. They allow a firm that already has a marketing mix placed in the market to evaluate how well that mix is performing. Examples include the following:

Image analysis
Tracking studies
Customer-satisfaction studies

Employee-satisfaction studies
Distributor-satisfaction studies
Web site evaluations

D. Improving Marketing as a Process[a]

A small portion of marketing research is conducted to expand our knowledge of marketing as a process rather than to solve a specific problem facing a company. By having the knowledge generated from these studies, managers may be in a much better position to solve a specific problem within their firms. This type of research is often conducted by institutes, such as the Marketing Science Institute, or universities. Examples include the following:

How can we determine our ROI for marketing expenditures such as advertising or digital communications, especially in B-to-B markets?

How can we better understand consumers, organizational buyers, and channel members—their decision-making processes; how, in a digital world, does peer-to-peer influence them?

What new tools can be generated to help us better understand consumers/customers? Ethnography? Virtual/simulated shopping experiences?

What are new methods for innovation of new products and services?

What can we learn about new ways to develop marketing strategy? Are there new ways to segment the market, position products, or to create value? How can we develop better metrics to measure response to marketing efforts?

How can we use the "new media" such as social networking and blogs and what is the role of the "old media" such as radio, TV, print?

---

[a]These study topics were taken from the Marketing Science Institute's research priorities list and former award-winning research papers. See www.msi.org for additional studies designed to improve marketing as a process.

The Marketing Information System

In order to stay abreast of competitive markets, firms must attempt to have the right information at the right time in the right format in the hands of those who make decisions. We have learned that this is not an easy task. In fact, one author suggests that more than 25% of critical data within Fortune 1000 companies is inaccurate or incomplete.[21] To manage information properly, companies develop information systems. So far, we have presented marketing research as if it were the only source of information. This is not the case, as you will understand by reading this section on marketing information systems.

Marketing decision makers have variable sources of information available to them. We can understand these different information sources by examining the components of the **marketing information system (MIS).** The MIS is a structure consisting of people, equipment, and procedures to gather, sort, analyze, evaluate, and distribute needed, timely, and accurate information to marketing decision makers.[22] The role of the MIS is to determine decision makers' information needs, acquire the needed information, and distribute that information to the decision makers in a form and at a time when they can use it for decision making. However, this sounds very much like marketing research—providing information to aid in decision making. We can understand the distinction by understanding the components of the MIS.

Components of the MIS

As noted previously, the MIS is designed to assess managers' information needs, to gather this information, and to distribute the information to the marketing managers who make decisions. Information is gathered and analyzed by the four subsystems of the MIS: internal reports, marketing intelligence, marketing decision support, and marketing research. We discuss each of these subsystems next.

So far, we have presented marketing research as if it were the only source of information, but this is not the case.

The MIS is a structure consisting of people, equipment, and procedures to gather, sort, analyze, evaluate, and distribute needed, timely, and accurate information to marketing decision makers.

There are four subsystems of a marketing information system (MIS): internal reports, marketing intelligence, marketing decision support, and marketing research.

The internal reports system gathers information generated by internal reports, which includes orders, billing, receivables, inventory levels, stock-outs, and so on. In many cases, the internal reports system is called the "accounting information system."

INTERNAL REPORTS SYSTEM The **internal reports system** gathers information generated by internal reports, which includes orders, billing, receivables, inventory levels, stock-outs, among others. In many cases, the internal reports system is called the "accounting information system." Although this system produces financial statements (balance sheets, income statements, etc.) that generally contain insufficient detail for many marketing decisions, the internal reports system also contains details on both revenues and costs that can be invaluable in making decisions. Other information is also collected, such as inventory records, sales calls records, and orders. A good internal reports system can tell a manager a great deal of information about what has happened within the firm in the past. When information is needed from sources *outside* the firm, other MIS components must be utilized.

The marketing intelligence system is defined as a set of procedures and sources used by managers to obtain everyday information about pertinent developments in the environment.

MARKETING INTELLIGENCE SYSTEM A second component of the MIS is the **marketing intelligence system,** defined as a set of procedures and sources used by managers to obtain everyday information about pertinent developments in the environment. Such systems include both informal and formal information-gathering procedures. Informal information-gathering procedures involve activities such as scanning newspapers, magazines, and trade publications. Formal information-gathering activities may be conducted by staff members who are assigned the specific task of looking for anything that seems pertinent to the company or industry. They then edit and disseminate this information to the appropriate members or company departments. Formerly known as "clipping bureaus" (because they clipped relevant newspaper articles for clients), several online information service companies, such as Lexis-Nexis, provide marketing intelligence. To use its service, a firm would enter key terms into search forms provided online by Lexis-Nexis. Information containing the search terms appears on the subscriber's computer screen as often as several times a day. By clicking on an article title, subscribers can view a full-text version of the article. In this way, marketing intelligence goes on continuously and searches a broad range of information sources in order to bring pertinent information to decision makers.

A DSS is defined as collected data that may be accessed and analyzed using tools and techniques that assist managers in decision making.

MARKETING DECISION SUPPORT SYSTEM The third component of the MIS is the decision support system. A **marketing decision support system (DSS)** is defined as collected data that may be accessed and analyzed using tools and techniques that assist managers in decision making. Once companies collect large amounts of information, they store this information in huge databases that, when accessed with decision-making tools and techniques (such as break-even analysis, regression models, and linear programming), allow companies to ask what-if questions. Answers to these questions are then immediately available for decision making.

We have already defined marketing research but now we should ask: If marketing research and an MIS both are designed to provide information for decision makers, how are the two different?

MARKETING RESEARCH SYSTEM Marketing research, which we have already discussed and defined, is the fourth component of the MIS. Now that you understand the three other components of an MIS, we are ready to discuss the question we raised at the beginning of this section—that is, if marketing research and the MIS both are designed to provide information for decision makers, how are the two different? In answering this question we must see how marketing research differs from the other three MIS components.

First, the **marketing research system** gathers information not gathered by the other MIS component subsystems: Marketing research studies are conducted for a *specific* situation facing the company. It is unlikely that other components of the MIS have generated the particular information needed for the specific situation. General Motors is working on changes in the appearance of its new electric car, the Volt. From the several design options available, will GM be able to get information from the internal reports system to know what today's new car consumer will most prefer? No. Can GM get useful information from its intelligence system? No. Can GM get information from its DSS? You could argue that GM's DSS has design preference data stored from the past and that this information may be helpful. Yet, when you consider the change in the car-buying public due to a renewed enthusiasm for fuel efficiency, should GM rely on old data on design preferences? GM will have to use marketing research to help design the Volt for today's consumer.

When *People* magazine wants to know which of three cover stories it should use for this week's publication, can its managers obtain that information from internal reports? No. What about from the intelligence system or the DSS? No.

This, then, is how marketing research plays a unique role in the total information system of the firm. By providing information for a specific problem at hand, marketing research provides information not provided by other components of the MIS. This is why persons in the industry sometimes refer to marketing research studies as "ad hoc studies." *Ad hoc* is a Latin word, meaning "with respect to a specific purpose." (Recall that earlier in the chapter when we defined marketing research, we told you we would revisit the word *specific*. Now you see why we used that word in our definition.)

> By providing information for a specific problem at hand, marketing research provides information not provided by other components of the MIS.

There is another characteristic of marketing research that differentiates it from the other MIS components. Though this difference doesn't justify the existence of marketing research in the MIS, the difference is notable. Marketing research projects, unlike the previous components, are not continuous—they have a beginning and an end. This is why marketing research studies are sometimes referred to as "projects." The other components are available for use on an ongoing basis. However, marketing research projects are launched only when there is a justifiable need for information that is not available from internal reports, intelligence, or the DSS.

> Because marketing research studies are not continuous they are often referred to as "projects."

Before Reading Further . . .

Before moving on let's take a moment to help you better understand where you are headed. Chapter 1 was written to introduce you to marketing research. At this point you understand how marketing research is a part of the marketing process, and the role marketing research plays in providing managers with information to help them make more informed decisions. You also understand the unique role marketing research plays in a firm's marketing information system (MIS). You are ready to continue learning about marketing research. In the next chapter we introduce you to the marketing research industry. Here you will learn about the structure of the industry. How many firms are there? What are the different types of firms and what do they do? We will also look at significant issues facing the industry, and you will learn about the Marketing Research Association's certification program, called the Professional Researcher Certification (PRC). In Chapter 3 we will introduce you to the eleven-step marketing research process. Pay attention to these steps as they will serve as an outline for the remainder of the book. We will then cover the steps in the marketing research process in the remainder of the chapters.

Summary

Marketing research is part of marketing. The American Marketing Association has defined marketing as an organizational function and a set of processes for creating, communicating, and delivering value to customers and for managing customer relationships in ways that benefit the organization and its stakeholders. The new service-dominant logic for marketing means that marketers need *more* information. To practice the marketing concept and to develop sound marketing strategies, managers are required to make numerous decisions. The marketing concept is a philosophy that states that the key to business success lies in determining and fulfilling consumers' wants and needs. Marketers attempting to practice the marketing concept need information in order to determine wants and needs and to design marketing strategies that will satisfy customers in selected target markets. Environmental changes mean that marketers must constantly collect information to monitor customers, markets, and competition.

Marketing research is the process of designing, gathering, analyzing, and reporting information that may be used to solve a specific problem. The purpose of marketing research is to link the consumer to the marketer by providing information that can be used in making marketing decisions. Not all firms use marketing research and sometimes marketing research leads to the wrong decisions. But marketing research has been around for many years and is growing—it has passed the "test of the marketplace."

The uses of marketing research are to (1) identify and define marketing opportunities and problems; (2) generate, refine, and evaluate marketing actions; (3) monitor marketing performance; and (4) improve our understanding of marketing. We classified marketing research studies using these four types, and we identified specific marketing research studies that would be found within each type. Marketing research is one of four subsystems making up a marketing information system (MIS). Other subsystems include internal reports, marketing intelligence, and decision support systems. Marketing research gathers information not available through the other subsystems. Marketing research provides information for the specific problem at hand. It is conducted on a project basis as opposed to an ongoing basis.

Key Terms

Marketing (p. 3)
Marketing concept (p. 7)
Marketing strategy (p. 7)
Marketing research (p. 8)
Market research (p. 8)

Basic research (p. 12)
Applied research (p. 12)
Marketing information system (MIS) (p. 13)
Internal reports system (p. 14)

Marketing intelligence system (p. 14)
Marketing decision support system (DSS) (p. 14)
Marketing research system (p. 14)

Review Questions

1. Explain how marketing research can be used in the leisure and sports industry.
2. What is marketing? Explain the role of marketing research in the process of marketing management.
3. Give examples of products that have failed.
4. Why are philosophies important to decision makers? What is the marketing concept?
5. What is strategy, and why is marketing research important to strategy makers?
6. Define marketing research. Define market research.
7. What is the purpose of marketing research?
8. Name the uses of marketing research.
9. Which use of marketing research is considered basic research?
10. Give two examples of the types of studies in each of the four classes of marketing research studies provided in this chapter.
11. Distinguish among MIS (marketing information system), marketing research, and DSS (decision support system).

Application Questions

12. Go to your library, either in person or online, and look through several business periodicals such as *Advertising Age, Business Week, Fortune*, and *Forbes*. Find three examples of companies using marketing research.

13. Select a company in a field in which you have a career interest and look up information on this firm in your library or on the Internet. After gaining some knowledge of this company, its products and services, customers, and competitors, list five different types of decisions that you believe this company's management may have made within the last two years. For each decision, list the information the company's executives would have needed to make these decisions.

14. Think of the following situations. What component of the marketing information system would a manager use to find the necessary information?

a. A manager of an electric utilities firm hears a friend at lunch talk about a new breakthrough in solar panel technology she read about in a science publication.

b. A manager wants to know how many units of each of three of the company's products were sold during each month for the past three years.

c. A manager wants to estimate the contribution to company ROI (return on investment) earned by ten different products in the company product line.

d. A manager is considering producing a totally new type of health food. But first, he would like to know if consumers are likely to purchase the new food, at which meal they would most likely eat the food, and how they would prefer the food to be packaged.

Case 1.1 **Starlight Films**

Marketing research is used to help managers in the movie industry make better decisions. There are many factors that go into making a great movie: Good scripts, directors, producers, actors, and all the support staff are fundamental. For many years, movies have been improved upon by using marketing research to gather consumer reactions. Two of the earliest users of marketing research, though primitive, were Carl Laemmie and Adolph Zukor. In the early 1900s, small, neighborhood theaters called nickelodeons showed films of the day; admission was a nickel. Laemmie observed audience and sales data for Hale's Tours in Chicago. He made notes on what types of people saw the films and determined the most popular hours of the day. Zukor, a nickelodeon operator in New York City, watched audience faces to see their reactions to different parts of the films and claimed he learned to "feel" reactions of laughter, pleasure, and boredom. Both Laemmie and Zukor must have learned something. They created the two companies Universal and Zukor Paramount—both large motion picture giants even today.

Over the years marketing research has increasingly played a role in movie making. When marketing research, conducted by the Gallup Poll, predicted a huge market success for the movie *Gone With the Wind*, MGM decided to price the movie between $0.75 and $2.20, when the average movie ticket of the day was about $0.25. The result was huge profits, as the Gallup predictions turned out to be correct. Marketing research has continued to be used to determine if scripts are profitable, rate the market attractiveness of the actors and actresses, profile the movie-going market segments, determine the effectiveness of advertising, and determine which type of movie ending the audience most prefers. Today, marketing research is heavily used by Hollywood to help make movies.[23] By answering the questions that follow our case material, you will have a better understanding of the role of marketing research.

Daniel Lee Yarbrough is a director and producer with Starlight Films in San Francisco, California. As part of his normal duties as a director and producer, Daniel constantly seeks scripts that he can turn into successful movies. The movie business is strongly driven by profits. While a few firms exist to make films purely for their artistic value, the cost of movie making is so huge today that few firms can afford to make movies that do not earn a respectable ROI for their investors. Daniel knows he must make "good" decisions—those that result in a film that will attract sufficient audience numbers to earn a good return.

Daniel has recently received a manuscript by a successful author, Warren St. John, who wrote the highly successful book, *Rammer Jammer Yellow Hammer* (a book about football fans following their team in RVs). Recently St. John turned out another manuscript about a boy's soccer team that has Daniel's interest. As he reads through the manuscript, Daniel begins thinking about decisions he will need to make if he wants to turn the manuscript into a movie.

How much should he offer St. John for the manuscript rights? Daniel knows the manuscript is very good and he assumes other film companies are going to make offers. Although Daniel has paid for manuscripts in the past, it has been about three years since he was actively involved in bidding for an author's script. Though the amount paid the author will be a small part of the total cost of the movie, it could still be a significant amount of money.

Casting decisions must be made early because they could greatly influence costs. Who should play the lead roles? Supporting roles? As always, there is a plentiful stock of talented, yet unknown actors available. On the other hand, there are "hot" actors who are very popular and draw audiences through name recognition alone.

Daniel's filmmaking experience allows him to adequately predict many of his costs. He knows, for example,

what it takes to film on location versus in a studio. He also knows the costs of equipment and costs of various personnel such as camera crew, grips, and copy editors. However, of all the issues facing Daniel, the most important issue will be how many people will buy a ticket to see this movie? Emmy Awards are great, but to make the needed ROI, Daniel knows he needs people to walk into movie theaters to see his movies. Of course, while some can estimate this number, no one can assure Daniel of the exact number. But, he can get some good estimates as to whether samples of an audience like the script.

1. Do you think Daniel Yarbrough needs to conduct marketing research? Why or why not?
2. Based on the case material alone, list decisions that Daniel needs to make.
3. For each decision you list in question 2, provide a description of the information that you think Daniel needs in order to make the decision.

Case 1.2 **Your Integrated Case**

Advanced Automobile Concepts

Nick Thomas is CEO of Advanced Automobile Concepts (AAC), a new division of a large automobile manufacturer, ZEN Motors. ZEN is a multinational manufacturer headquartered in the United States. It has multiple divisions representing several auto and truck brands. ZEN's divisions have been slowly losing market share to other competitors. AAC was created to revive the aging ZEN automobile brands by either reengineering existing models or developing totally new models that are more in tune with today's changing automobile market.

Nick is very familiar with the automobile industry, as his entire adult life has been in the business. He follows trade publications carefully and believes ZEN's most significant losses are due to the growing popularity of several foreign brands, particularly brands from Japan and Korea. As CEO, Nick has been given the authority to do what he believes is needed to revive the company's brands and help return ZEN to prominence in automobile manufacturing.

Nick has retrieved company sales data for all ZEN models for the last decade from ZEN's internal reports system, part of ZEN's management information system (MIS). He has accessed the intelligence system to obtain trade industry articles written about the market, including evaluations of top competitors' models. He notices that several highly evaluated models are small and fuel efficient. He also has recognized that foreign competition has severely eroded ZEN's

market share of their only large, luxury car brand. ZEN's brand has been around for many years and now fails to compete with the newer luxury car models on the market.

ZEN has been reluctant to move into the very small and highly fuel-efficient market for a couple of reasons. First, historically, ZEN has earned higher profits on larger vehicles. Every ZEN division has a large and extra-large model SUV. Historically these SUV models, ZEN's large trucks, and their larger family cars have been very profitable. Secondly, as sales have eroded in recent years, ZEN has been reluctant to invest the funds needed to develop radically different designs from those models that have been their "bread and butter" cars for decades. However, in recent months ZEN's sales have plummeted as fuel prices have soared. ZEN management realizes they must innovate and that is why they created the AAC division.

Nick Thomas realizes that he must develop innovations in automobile design and engineering, but he is not certain in which direction he should guide his division. He realizes that, for now, oil prices are high and he understands the increases in sales of fuel-efficient gasoline, diesel, and electric hybrids. However, Nick has seen these environmental changes come and go. He tells his younger vice presidents, "When the crises are over, the car buying public wants big vehicles and we have earned our standing in the industry by giving the market what they want." Nick wonders to himself if this oil crisis is here to stay. He has also been concerned about the prospects of real global warming. He's read the reports on climate change and is confused—he doesn't know whether to believe Al Gore or Rush Limbaugh. Nick also isn't certain about the future of alternative fuels. Will the U.S. government really encourage the reduction of the country's dependence on foreign energy? He vividly recalls this being an issue in the 1970s and President Carter calling for a switch to alternative fuels. He also knows that the country didn't follow through on this at the time. Nick wonders if today's promises by politicians of reducing foreign dependence on energy will be forgotten just as it has in the past. Nick is not sure what will happen but he knows that continued high prices of fuel and increasing evidence of global warming will affect consumer behavior with regard to automobiles.

1. Should Nick Thomas use marketing research?
2. What components of ZEN's marketing information system will Nick Thomas need?

The Marketing Research Industry

How the Marketing Research Association Serves the Marketing Research Profession

Marketing Research Association

Visit the MRA website at www.mra-net.org.

In this chapter you will gain knowledge of the marketing research industry and learn about several associations that serve the profession. The Marketing Research Association (MRA) is devoted to improving the quality and ensuring the future of the profession. MRA creates and facilitates education and networking for the profession, in the attempt to create a well-informed and united marketplace. To this end, MRA creates forums for clients and research company CEOs to advance their professional development.

In 2005, the MRA became the certifying body in the United States for individuals involved in research. The Professional Researcher Certification (PRC) was quickly adopted by clients and research providers. In the first three years since inception, over 1,000 individuals have been awarded the PRC. The program is aimed at evaluating the competencies of individuals in different areas and levels of the profession. Applicants are vetted based upon experience, education, and ethics. Certificates are renewable every two years, and individuals must be revetted upon renewal.

In 2009, the MRA launched a review program to provide transparency and quality assurance to the research process. It is the only program to provide critical information from panel providers which researchers and panel purchasers can use to make smart purchasing decisions. The MRA also joined with other associations to promote best practices in online research. This collaboration has produced an online glossary of terms, creating a common language among survey research professionals. The need to provide assurances of individual and company competencies is critical to the advancement of the profession. The MRA through these initiatives and through its advancement of technology as a solution agent seeks to secure good decision making based on knowledge.

The MRA not only works hard to provide quality services, but also works to protect the opinion and survey research profession now and into the future through its leading state and federal legislation program. The MRA's government affairs team works on issues of consumer and data privacy, in defense of most every mode and method of research. The MRA also helps to educate members of the profession in compliance and best practices for state and federal laws that impact research, to assist members in responding to litigation, and to review and file amicus briefs with the courts.

Source: Kristen Darby.

Kristen Darby, COO, Marketing Research Association

E very major industry is served by one or more professional organizations. The Marketing Research Association assumed a major leadership role in the industry with the introduction in 2005 of the Professional Researcher Certification (PRC), a certification for marketing researchers as explained by MRA's Kristen Darby, COO, in our opening vignette. In this chapter we will introduce you to several facets of the industry itself, including a brief history, different types and sizes of firms, an evaluation of the industry, and methods the industry uses for self-improvement. We also will examine the ethical issues facing the industry. Some of you may have become interested in marketing research as a career. If you want to know more about a career in the industry, including seeking a master's degree in marketing research, we encourage you to visit our website, under "Careers."

Interested in a career in marketing research? Visit www .pearsonhighered.com/ burns.

The Marketing Research Industry

Evolution of the Industry

THE EARLY DAYS Robert Bartels, a marketing historian, wrote that the earliest questionnaire surveys began around 1824. In 1879, N. W. Ayers and Company conducted a study for a client, to look at grain production by individual states. However, Bartels believes the first continuous and organized research began in 1911 by **Charles Coolidge Parlin,** a schoolmaster from a small city in Wisconsin. Parlin was hired by the Curtis Publishing Company to gather information about customers and markets to help Curtis sell advertising space. Parlin was successful, and the information he gathered led to increased advertising in Curtis's *Saturday Evening Post* magazine.[1] Parlin is recognized today as the "father of marketing research," and the AMA provides an award each year at the annual marketing research conference in his name.[2]

GROWTH OF THE NEED While there are a few reported instances of the use of marketing research in the early days of the history of the United States, it was not until the 1930s that marketing research efforts became widespread. The reason for this was that prior to the Industrial Revolution, businesses were located close to consumers. In an economy based on artisans and craftsmen involved in barter exchange with their customers, there was little need to "study" consumers, because business owners saw them daily. The owners knew the consumers' needs and wants and their likes and dislikes. However, when the Industrial Revolution led to manufacturers producing goods for distant markets, the need for marketing research emerged. Manufacturers in Boston needed to know more about the consumers, and their needs, in "faraway" places such as Denver and Atlanta. A. C. Nielsen started his firm in 1922. In the 1930s, colleges began to teach courses in marketing research, and during the 1940s, Alfred Politz introduced statistical theory for sampling in marketing research.[3] Also during the 1940s, Robert Merton introduced focus groups, which today represent a large part of what is known as "qualitative marketing research." Computers revolutionized the industry in the 1950s.[4] By the 1960s, marketing research had not only gained acceptance in the organization but was also recognized as being a key to understanding distant and fast-changing markets. It was needed for survival.

A MATURING INDUSTRY According to Jack Honomichl,[5] president of the Marketing Aid Center and publisher of *Inside Research,* the industry in the 1950s was largely composed of small, privately owned firms that didn't report their revenues.[6] There was "no sense of industry."

However, according to Honomichl, the industry evolved and by the 1990s many of the smaller firms had consolidated. This trend continued into the 2000s, leading to a very different structure in the industry today.

The current industry has quite large "behemoths" that operate around the globe with revenues in excess of $1 billion. Many of these firms are publicly listed or operate as subsidiaries of publicly listed parent companies and their revenues are in the public domain, along with statements of profitability and executive remuneration. Honomichl prepares annual reports of the industry's revenues, which are provided to you in the following section. These reports, which track industry structure and revenues, the growth of the professional organizations serving the industry, globalization of the industry, and the introduction of certification in the industry through the PRC, are all earmarks of a maturing industry.

Honomichl Global Top 25

Each year, Honomichl publishes the **Honomichl Global Top 25,** a report of the top twenty-five marketing/advertising/public opinion research services firms ranked in terms of worldwide revenues received. The report is published in *Marketing News,* a publication of the American Marketing Association. You can view the Honomichl Global Top 25 by going to www.marketingpower.com, and search for "Honomichl Global Top 25."

As we noted earlier, marketing research firms serve the entire globe. The top twenty-five firms are located all over the world. Headquarters among the Global Top 25 include France, Germany, Brazil, the Netherlands, the United Kingdom, Japan, and the United States. Reflecting the true global nature of marketing research, over half of the total revenues generated by the

Global Top 25 firms in 2009 came from operations/subsidiaries outside the home country. The largest research firm in the world is The Nielsen Company, headquartered in New York City and a dominant firm in the industry.

Worldwide Spending on Marketing Research

Total global spending for the industry was about $32.5 billion in 2008 according to the European Society of Opinion and Marketing Research (ESOMAR). The 2009 estimates indicate that this figure will be lower due to the worldwide recession. From 2007 to 2008, when the recession began, only North America experienced a net decrease in spending. Latin America had the highest growth rate from 2007 to 2008 of net 5.6%.[7] It is safe to say that, as of 2010, the marketing research industry is about a $30 billion industry.

Honomichl Top 50

REVENUES OF U.S. FIRMS Honomichl also publishes the **Honomichl Top 50** each year which is reported in *Marketing News*.[8] This report is a ranking of the top fifty U.S.-based firms in terms of the revenues these firms earn from U.S. operations only (see Table 2.1). Honomichl reported that the top fifty earned total revenues in the United States of $7.8 billion in 2009. Due to the recession, this represents a decline from 2008 of 3.2%. To get a better estimate of the revenue of most marketing research firms in the United States, based upon earnings in this country, Honomichl reports revenues from firms that are too small to make the Top 50 who are members of the Council of American Survey Research Organizations (CASRO). This council has many member firms not large enough to make the Top 50, and when 153 CASRO firms are added, the total revenue of the 203 U.S.-based research firms rises to $8.6 billion for 2009, which represents a decrease of 3.7% from 2008. Actually, 2009 revenues are close to what they were in 2007.

What is significant is that for over twenty years we have seen a growth in revenues spent on marketing research in real dollars. However, the recession, beginning in 2008, has hit the industry hard. For 2008 and 2009, we have seen revenues go down. Two factors seem to account for firms with lower revenues. The smaller, CASRO-member firms had a larger decline than those in the Top 50. Secondly, of all firms, those fairing the best were the firms that offer syndicated data to client firms that sign long-term contracts. The nine large firms that specialize in this show no revenue change from 2008—a positive factor during a recession. According to Honomichl, the forty-one firms of the Top 50 who are basically survey and/or qualitative research firms had revenues decline by 7% in 2009.[9] Marketing research, like most industries, has experienced difficult times during this period of economic unrest in the United States and worldwide.

STRONGER COMPETITION THROUGH M&A AND STRATEGIC ALLIANCES Over the years the Top 50 firms have powered their growth largely by merger and acquisition (M&A). Larger firms often gobble up smaller firms that have developed a growing service or niche in the market. Recent examples include the following: National Research Corp. acquired MyInnerView Inc.,[10] Nielsen acquired IAG Research,[11] and the Kantor Group made several acquisitions including Foresight International Inc., Teenage Research Unlimited, Cheskin Inc., and Yankelovich Inc., among others.[12] Many of these resulted in the formation of **strategic alliances** which allow firms with strong expertise in one area to form partnerships with firms offering expertise in other areas. For example, a firm with a strength in client consultation may form an alliance with a firm specializing in data collection and another firm specializing in data analysis. The combination of these strengths means higher levels of competition in the industry. These alliances may be formed through acquisition, merger, or contractual agreements. For example, in 2008, GfK acquired the Arbor Strategy Group which gave them expertise in several selected areas (see our discussion of failed products in Chapter 1) in the United States.[13] When the Kantar Group acquired TNSplc they were already in acquisition of Sorenson Associates

Jack Honomichl is president of the Marketing Aid Center and founder of *Inside Research,* a trade publication serving the industry. He is a recognized authority on the marketing research industry. In 2002, he was inducted into the Market Research Council's Hall of Fame at the Yale Club in New York City. Other members of the MRC Hall of Fame include such notables as Arthur C. Nielsen Sr., George Gallup Sr., David Ogilvy, Marion Harper, Daniel Yankelovich, Daniel Starch, Ernest Dichter, Alfred Politz, and Elmo Roper.

Each year, Honomichl publishes the Honomichl Global Top 25, a report of the top twenty-five marketing/advertising/public opinion research services firms ranked in terms of worldwide revenues received.

The marketing research industry is about a $30 billion industry.

Visit ESOMAR at www.esomar.org.

TABLE 2.1

The Honomichl Top 50

The Honomichl Top 50 is a list of the top fifty U.S.-based marketing/advertising/public opinion research firms, ranked according to revenues earned.

Top 50 U.S. Market Research Organizations

U.S. Rank 2009	U.S. Rank 2008	Organization	Headquarters	Web Site: www.	U.S. Research Revenues** ($ in millions)	Percent Change from 2008***	WW Research Revenues** ($ in millions)	Non-U.S. Research Revenues** ($ in millions)	Percent Non-U.S. Revenues	U.S. Full-Time Employee	From Other MR Companies
1	1	The Nielsen Co.	New York	nielsen.com	$2,298.0	3.0%	$4,628.0	$2,330.0	50.3%	9,110	
2	2	Kantar*	London & Fairfild, Conn.	kantar.com	850.9	−10.4	2,823.2	1,972.3	69.9	3,940	
3	3	IMS Health Inc.	Norwalk, Conn.	imshealth.com	801.1	−5.9	2,189.7	1,388.6	63.4	1,595	
4	4	Westat Inc.	Rockville, Md.	westat.com	502.4	7.0	502.4			2,087	
5	5	SymphonyIRI Group	Chicago	symphonyiri.com	441.7	−0.7	706.3	264.6	37.5	1,172	
6	6	Arbitron Inc.	Columbia, Md.	arbitron.com	379.1	4.0	385.0	5.9	1.5	971	
7	8	Ipsos	New York	ipsos-na.com	288.8	−7.3	1,315.0	1,026.2	78.0	880	
8	7	GfK USA	Nuremberg, Germany	gfk.com	288.5	−11.7	1,622.0	1,334.5	82.3	936	
9	9	Synovate	London	synovate.com	214.5	−12.4	816.3	601.8	73.7	754	
10	11	J.D. Power and Associates*	Westlake Village, Calif.	jdpower.com	164.4	−13.7	244.6	80.2	32.8	512	11.6
11	12	The NPD Group Inc.	Port Washington, N.Y.	npd.com	164.1	−2.6	225.8	61.7	27.3	770	
12	10	Maritz Research	Fenton, Mo.	maritzresearch.com	132.1	−13.2	154.6	22.5	14.6	554	
13	15	comScore Inc.	Reston, Va.	comscore.com	108.0	2.1	127.7	19.7	15.4	466	
14	14	Harris Interactive Inc.	New York	harrisinteractive.com	100.1	−24.0	167.0	66.9	40.1	464	4.0
15	-	dunnhumbyUSA LLC	Cincinnati	dunnhumby.com/us/	87.4	33.0	133.4	46.0	34.5	146	
16	16	Market Strategies International	Livonia, Mich.	marketstrategies.com	66.8	−13.8	80.1	13.2	16.5	244	
17	13	Opinion Research Corp.	Princeton, N.J.	opinionresearch.com	63.3	−16.2	97.9	34.6	35.3	245	
18	17	Lieberman Research Worldwide	Los Angeles	lrwonline.com	58.8	−20.2	73.4	14.9	20.3	317	
19	20	Abt SRBI Inc.	Cambridge, Mass.	abtassociates.com	57.5	16.2	57.5			208	
20	18	OTX	Los Angeles	otxresearch.com	56.2	10.2	61.3	5.1	8.3	224	14.8
21	24	National Research Corp.	Lincoln, Neb.	nationalresearch.com	43.8	−1.8	48.6	4.8	9.9	248	
22	22	MVL Group Inc.	Jupiter, Fla.	mvlgroup.com	39.9	3.1	39.9			118	
23	19	Burke Inc.	Cincinnati	burke.com	38.9	−23.4	42.8	3.9	9.1	205	
24	26	International Communications Research	Media, Pa.	icrsurvey.com	36.3	13.1	37.4	1.1	2.9	206	18.2
25	21	Knowledge Networks Inc.	Menlo Park, Calif.	knowledgenetworks.com	35.4	−4.9	35.4			156	3.2
26	29	Communispace Corp.	Watertown, Mass.	communispace.com	34.7	18.0	36.7	2.0	5.4	245	
27	25	Directions Research Inc.	Cincinnati	directionsresearch.com	33.7	−7.9	33.7			116	
28	23	Phoenix Marketing International	Rhinebeck, N.Y.	phoenixmi.com	31.4	−16.5	36.2	4.8	13.3	115	

Rank '22	Rank '21	Organization	Headquarters	Website	U.S. Research Rev. ($)	% Change***	Worldwide Rev. ($)	Non-U.S. Rev. ($)	% Non-U.S.	Employees	
29	27	MarketCast	Los Angeles	marketcastonline.com	28.5	–3.7	30.6	2.1	6.9	48	
30	32	Service Management Group Inc.	Kansas City, Mo.	servicemanagement.com	28.4	6.0	29.3	0.9	3.1	155	
31	30	Radius Global Market Research	New York	radius-global.com	27.6	–7.0	28.9	1.3	4.5	89	0.1
32	28	Lieberman Research Group	Great Neck, N.Y.	liebermanresearch.com	25.1	–14.9	25.1			72	
33	35	Informa Research Services Inc.	Calabasas, Calif.	informars.com	23.4	–0.4	23.4			181	
34	33	National Analysts Worldwide	Philadelphia	nationalanalysts.com	23.2	–11.8	23.2			76	
35	36	C&R Research Services Inc.	Chicago	crresearch.com	22.8	–2.1	22.8			100	
36	34	Morpace Inc.	Farmington Hills, Mich.	morpace.com	22.2	–13.6	25.6	3.4	13.3	104	
37	37	MarketVision Research Inc.	Cincinnati	mv-research.com	21.7	1.4	21.7			95	
38	39	KS&R Inc.	Syracuse, N.Y.	ksrinc.com	19.7	5.9	24.7	5.0	20.2	135	
39	38	Market Probe Inc.	Milwaukee	marketprobe.com	18.5	–19.1	41.1	22.5	54.7	85	
40	42	Q Research Solutions Inc.	Old Bridge, N.J.	qresearchsolutions.com	15.8	1.3	16.3	0.5	3.1	85	0.9
41	43	The Link Group	Atlanta	tlg.com	15.8	4.6	17.4	1.6	9.2	44	
42	45	CMI	Atlanta	cmiresearch.com	15.0	6.4	15.0			41	
43	–	Rentrak Corp.	Portland, Ore.	rentrak.com	14.4	22.0	14.9	0.5	3.4	22	
44	48	Gongos Research Inc.	Auburn Hills, Mich.	gongos.com	13.2	8.2	13.2			72	
45	–	StrategyOne	New York	strategyone.net	12.8	4.9	14.5	1.7	11.7	71	
46	41	Bellomy Research Inc.	Winston-Salem, N.C.	bellomyresearch.com	12.4	–25.7	12.4			65	0.1
47	48	RTi Market Research & Brand Strategy	Stamford, Conn.	rtiresearch.com	12.2	NC	12.2			50	
48	44	RDA Group Inc.	Bloomfield Hills, Mich.	rdagroup.com	11.9	–18.5	14.2	2.3	16.2	86	0.1
49	31	Public Opinion Strategies	Alexandria, Va.	pos.org	11.7	–57.8	11.8	0.1	0.1	27	
50	46	Savitz Research Companies	Dallas	savitzresearch.com	11.5	–8.7	11.5			45	
		Total			$7,825.6	–3.2%	$17,171.7	$9,347.2	54.4%	28,752	
		All other (153 CASRO companies not included in the Top 50)****			$770.2	–8.5%	$899.1	$128.9	14.3%	3,380	
		Total (203 companies)			$8,595.8	–3.7%	$18,070.8	$9,476.1	52.4%	32,132	

* Estimated by Top 50
** U.S. and WW revenues may include non-research activities for some companies that are significantly higher, as well as revenues from other MR companies. See individual company profiles for details.
*** Rate of growth from year to year has been adjusted so as not to include revenue gains or losses from acquisitions or divestitures. See company profiles for explanation.
**** Total revenues of 153 survey research companies that provide financial information on a confidential basis to the Council of American Survey Research Organizations (CASRO).
Source: By permission, InsideResearch.com.

The Honomichl Top 50 report is a ranking of the top fifty U.S.-based firms in terms of the revenues these firms earn from U.S. operations alone. Honomichl reported that the top fifty earned total revenues in the United States of $7.8 billion in 2009.

You can view the Honomichl Top 50 report by going to the AMA website, at www .marketingpower.com/. Go to "Search" and type in "Honomichl Top 50."

Strategic alliances allow firms with strong expertise in one area to form partnerships with firms offering expertise in other areas.

We can classify all research suppliers as either internal or external suppliers.

An internal supplier is an entity within the firm that supplies marketing research.

which gives the Kantar Group expertise on doing in-store research (see the opening vignette to Chapter 4).[14]

Classifying Firms in the Marketing Research Industry

In the marketing research industry we refer to providers of marketing research information as **research suppliers.** There are several ways we can classify suppliers. We use a classification developed by Naresh Malholtra,[15] slightly modified for our purposes here. This classification system is shown in Figure 2.1. Note that suppliers may be classified as either internal or external.

Internal Suppliers

An **internal supplier** is an entity within the firm that supplies marketing research. It has been estimated that firms spend roughly 1% of sales on marketing research, whether it is supplied internally or externally.[16] Most large firms such as Kraft Foods, IBM, Kodak, General Mills, and Ford have research departments of their own.

How Do Internal Suppliers Organize the Research Function?

Internal suppliers of marketing research can elect several organizing methods to provide the research function. They may (1) have their own formal departments, (2) have no formal department but place at least a single individual or a committee in charge of marketing research, or (3) assign no one responsibility for conducting marketing research.

ORGANIZING THE FORMAL DEPARTMENT OF INTERNAL SUPPLIERS   Most large organizations have the resources to staff their own formal marketing research departments. Firms with higher sales volumes (over $500 million) tend to have their own formal marketing research departments, and many large advertising agencies have their own formal research departments.[17] Companies with their own research department must justify the large fixed costs of supporting the personnel and facilities. The advantage is that the staff is fully cognizant of the firm's operations and the changes in the industry, which may give them better insights into identifying opportunities and problems suitable for marketing research action.

Marketing research departments are usually organized according to one or a combination of the following functions: area of application, marketing function, or the research process. By "area of application," we mean that these companies organize the research function around the "areas" to which the research is being applied. For example, some firms serve both ultimate consumers

FIGURE 2.1

A Classification of Marketing Research Suppliers

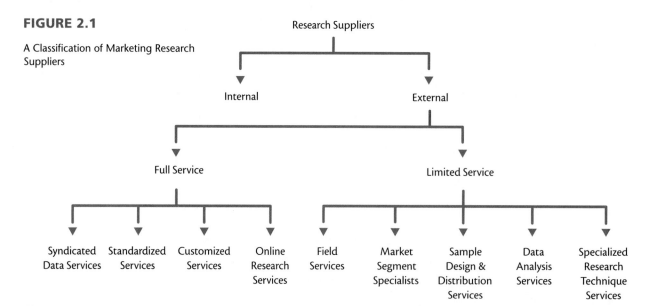

and industrial consumers. Therefore, the marketing research department may be organized into two divisions: consumer and industrial. Other areas of application may be brands or lines of products or services. Secondly, marketing research may be organized around functional areas (the four Ps) such as product research, ad research, pricing research, and place/channel of distribution research. Finally, the research function may be organized around the steps of the research process, such as data analysis or data collection.

ORGANIZING WHEN THERE IS NO FORMAL DEPARTMENT If internal supplier firms elect not to have a formal marketing research department, there are other organizational possibilities. When there is no formal department, *responsibility for research may be assigned to existing organizational units* such as departments or divisions. A problem with this method is that research activities are not coordinated; a division conducts its own research, and other units of the firm may be unaware of useful information. One way to remedy this is to organize by having a *committee or an individual assigned marketing research* to ensure that all units of the firm have input into and benefit from any research activity undertaken. In some cases, committees or individuals assigned to marketing research may actually conduct some limited research, but typically their primary role is that of helping other managers recognize the need for research and coordinating the purchase of research from external research suppliers. Obviously, the advantage here is limiting fixed costs incurred by maintaining the full-time staff required for an ongoing department. *No one may be assigned* to marketing research in some organizations. This is rare in large companies but not unusual in smaller firms. In very small firms, the owner/manager plays many roles, ranging from strategic planner to salesperson to security staff. This individual must also be responsible for marketing research, being certain to have the right information before making decisions.

External Suppliers

External suppliers are outside firms hired to fulfill a firm's marketing research needs. In most cases, internal suppliers of marketing research also purchase research from external suppliers. Both large and small firms, for-profit and not-for-profits, and government and educational institutions purchase research information from external suppliers.

Of course, there are many other research firms in the marketing research industry. These research firms range in size from one-person proprietorships to the large, international corporations you will find in the Honomichl Global Top 25. You can get an idea of the type, number, and specialities of these firms by looking at online directories of marketing research firms. For example, review the New York chapter of the American Marketing Association's website, and look through the *Greenbook*, a directory of marketing research firms, at www.greenbook.org. This website will provide you with a better understanding of how to classify external supplier firms. Also visit the different "directory" listings at www.quirks.com. The MRA publishes the *Blue Book*, which can be viewed at www.bluebook.org.

How Do External Suppliers Organize?

Like internal supplier firms, external supplier firms organize themselves in different ways. These firms may organize by function (data analysis, data collection, etc.), by type of research application (customer satisfaction, advertising effectiveness, new-product development, etc.), by geography (domestic versus international), by type of customer (health care, government, telecommunications, etc.), or another combination.

Classifying External Supplier Firms

As you may recall from Figure 2.1, we can classify all external supplier firms into two categories: full-service or limited-service firms. In the following paragraphs, we will define these two types of firms and give you examples of each.

FULL-SERVICE SUPPLIER FIRMS **Full-service supplier firms** have the ability to conduct the entire marketing research project for the buyer firms. Full-service firms will often define the problem, specify the research design, collect and analyze the data, and prepare the final written report. Typically, these are larger firms that have the expertise as well as the necessary facilities to conduct research studies in their entirety. Most of the research firms found in the Honomichl Global Top 25 and Honomichl Top 50 would qualify as full-service firms. Although many of these firms may specialize in, say, survey research or qualitative research, they are so large that they offer a full range of services and specializations.

SYNDICATED DATA SERVICE FIRMS **Syndicated data service firms** collect information that is made available to multiple subscribers. The information, or data, is provided in standardized form (the information may not be tailored to meet the needs of any one company) to a large number of companies, known as a syndicate. Therefore, these companies offer syndicated data to all subscribing members of the syndicate.

STANDARDIZED SERVICE FIRMS **Standardized service firms** provide syndicated marketing research services, as opposed to syndicated data, to clients. Each client gets different data, but the *process* used to collect the data is standardized so that it may be offered to many clients at a cost less than that of a custom-designed project. Burke's Customer Satisfaction Associates provides the service of measuring customer satisfaction. Maritz offers a service to help firms develop customer loyalty programs. Parties involved in litigation sometimes use "mock juries" to listen to different presentations by attorneys. This allows the litigant's attorneys to present testimony in a way that will have the greatest communication impact on jurors. Several marketing research firms, such as Baltimore Research, offer a service of "mock trials" to prospective clients. Baltimore Research has a proven process for conducting this service.

Baltimore Research, among other services, offers clients involved in litigation "mock trials."

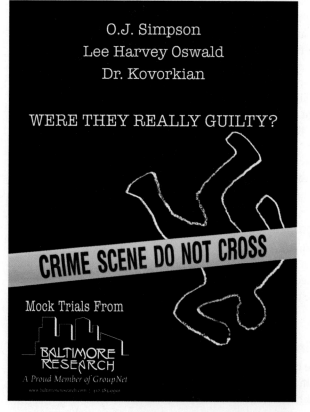

CUSTOMIZED SERVICE FIRMS **Customized service firms** offer a variety of research services tailored to meet the client's specific needs. Each client's problem is treated as a unique research project. Customized service firms spend considerable time with a client firm to determine the problem and then design a research project specifically to address the particular client's problem.

ONLINE RESEARCH SERVICES FIRMS **Online research services firms** specialize in providing services online. First, let's clear up some terms that are used loosely when dealing with "online" research. We define **online research** as the use of computer networks, including the Internet, to assist in any phase of the marketing research process, including development of the problem, research design, data gathering, analysis, and report distribution. Secondly, we need to distinguish between online research and Web-based research. **Web-based research** is conducted *on* Web applications. This type of research, sometimes confused with online research, may use traditional methods as well as online research methods in conducting research on Web-based applications.

Some Web-based applications would include research on the popularity of the Web pages themselves, such as "site hit counts," effectiveness studies of pop-up ads on websites, or research measuring consumers' reactions to various components of websites. Another term, online survey research, is often confused with online research. Online survey research has experienced rapid growth in the past several years, and many erroneously think that this is the same as online research. **Online survey research** refers to the collection of data using computer networks.

Virtually all research firms today use online research in the sense that they make use of online technology in at least one or more phases of the research process. These firms would be better categorized in one of the other types of firms shown in Figure 2.1. However, there are many firms that *specialize* in online services. Their "reason for being" is based on the provision of services online. Affinnova®, for example, exists because it has proprietary software that allows consumers to design preferred product attributes into new products online. InsightExpress® was formed by NFO Inc. in 1999, to allow clients to easily develop questionnaires and quickly conduct surveys online. The firm has grown rapidly and now offers many innovative services online. Knowledge Networks® came into being because its founders wanted to provide clients with access to probability samples online.

LIMITED-SERVICE SUPPLIER FIRMS **Limited-service supplier firms** specialize in one or, at most, a few marketing research activities. Firms can specialize in types of marketing research techniques such as eye-testing (tracking eye movements in response to different promotional stimuli), mystery shopping (using researchers to pose as shoppers to evaluate customer service), specific market segments such as senior citizens, or certain sports segments such as golf or tennis. The limited-service suppliers can be further classified on the basis of their specialization. These include field services, market segment specialists, sample design and distribution services, data analysis, and specialized research technique service suppliers. Many of these limited-service firms specialize in some form of online research.

Field service firms specialize in collecting data. These firms typically operate in a particular territory conducting telephone surveys, focus group interviews, mall-intercept surveys, or door-to-door surveys. Because it is expensive and difficult to maintain interviewers all over the country, firms will use the services of field service firms in order to quickly and efficiently gather data. There is specialization even within firms that specialize in field services. Some firms, for example, conduct only in-depth personal interviews; others conduct only mall-intercept surveys. Irwin, located in Jacksonville, Florida, specializes in collecting data and recruits participants for focus groups and collecting data door-to-door, at in-store locations, and a number of other data gathering techniques to suit the needs of clients. Some firms, such as Mktg. Inc., are known as **phone banks** because they specialize in telephone surveying.

Other limited-service firms, called **market segment specialists,** specialize in collecting data for special market segments such as African Americans, Hispanics, children, seniors, gays, industrial customers, or a specific geographic area within the United States or internationally. Strategy Research Corporation specializes in Latin American markets. JRH Marketing Services Inc. specializes in marketing to ethnic markets, especially to black markets. Other firms specialize in children, mature citizens, pet owners, airlines, beverages, celebrities, college students, religious groups, among other market segments. C&R Research has a division called Latino Eyes that specializes in U.S. Hispanic and Latin American markets. They have another division specializing in kids, tweens, and teens, called KidzEyes, and another division specializing in the fifty-year-and-over market called Sage Advice.[18] By specializing, these limited-service suppliers capitalize on their in-depth knowledge of each client's industry.

Survey Sampling Inc. and Scientific Telephone Samples (STS) are examples of limited-service firms that specialize in **sample design and distribution.** It is not uncommon, for example, for a company with an internal marketing research department to buy its sample from a firm

We define online research as the use of computer networks, including the Internet, to assist in any phase of the marketing research process, including development of the problem, research design, data gathering, analysis, and report distribution.

Web-based research is research that is conducted *on* Web applications and is sometimes confused with online research. Web-based applications would include research on the popularity of the Web pages themselves, such as "site hit counts," effectiveness studies of pop-up ads on websites, or research measuring consumers' reactions to various components of websites.

Online survey research refers to the collection of data using computer networks.

Read about Affinnova's IDDEA℠ service at www.affinnova.com.

specializing in sampling and then send the samples and a survey questionnaire to a phone bank for completion of the survey. This way, a firm may quickly and efficiently conduct telephone surveys using a probability sample plan in markets all over the country. Survey Sampling Inc. provides Internet samples, B2B samples, global samples, and low-incidence samples which are samples requiring persons with characteristics, i.e., incomes over $1million, that make them a small percentage of the total population. There are limited-service marketing research firms that offer **data analysis services.** Their contribution to the research process is to provide the technical assistance necessary to analyze and interpret data using the more sophisticated data analysis techniques such as conjoint analysis. SDR Consulting, SPSS, now an IBM Company, and Applied Decision Analysis LLC are examples of such firms.

Specialized research technique firms provide a service to their clients by expertly administering a special technique. Examples of such firms include Eye Tracking Inc., which specializes in eye movement research. Eye movements are used to determine effectiveness of ads, direct-mail pieces, and other forms of visual promotion. Other firms specialize in mystery shopping, taste tests, fragrance tests, creation of brand names, generating new ideas for products and services, and so on.

We should not leave this section without saying that our categorization of research suppliers does not fit every situation. Many full-service firms fit neatly into one of our categories, but some do not: The Kantar Group, for example, is a large, full-service firm, but it also offers very specialized data analysis services. In addition, there are other entities supplying research information that do not fit neatly into one of our categories. For example, universities and institutes supply research information. Universities sponsor a great deal of research that could be classified as marketing research.

Challenges Facing the Marketing Research Industry

Now that you've learned some of the basics about the industry and know some of the companies themselves, we pause here to address issues challenging the industry. The marketing research industry has been the subject of constructive criticism over the years.[19] These reviews are mixed. Earlier reviews would indicate that, although the marketing research industry is doing a reasonably good job, there is room for improvement.[20] More recent reviews, however, are not as complimentary.[21] We review some of the issues facing the industry, industry criticisms, and suggestions for remedies in the following section.

Issues with the Economy

If you were to ask a sample of marketing researchers today what their biggest concern is, it would no doubt be "the future economy." Late 2008 saw the introduction of startling problems arising in the world economy. By 2010, there are some reasons to be optimistic, yet forecasts are that a vibrant economy may still be several years away. We have already witnessed fallout and change in the marketing research industry. Surviving marketing research firms will have to demonstrate value-added by their services more than ever. Firms that can innovate and produce services that can help firms better deal with their own uncertainties, and firms that can be flexible in reducing costs during hard times, will survive. We will also likely see more consolidation in the industry, as firms having strong expertise in one or more areas but unable to weather economic downturns will be acquired by other firms. Mergers and acquisitions as well as other forms of strategic alliances will likely grow during the next few years.

The Lifeblood of the Industry—Consumer Cooperation

To compound a struggling economy, marketing research costs have been climbing as it takes more resources to obtain samples of respondents today than ever before. Response rates to requests for respondents to cooperate in research (mainly surveys) have been steadily declining for

> A struggling world economy will require marketing research firms to demonstrate value-added by their services in the years ahead.

> Marketing research firms will have to demonstrate value-added by their services more than ever in a down economy. Firms that can innovate and produce services that can help firms better deal with their own uncertainties, and firms that can be flexible in reducing costs during hard times, will survive.

several years. Marketing researchers have struggled with growing consumer resentment to their invasion of privacy. Marketing research, because it often seeks information from consumers, is "invasive." Weary from abuse from telemarketers and other direct marketers, potential respondents have grown resentful of any attempt by others to gather information from them. In the *2007 Confirmit* industry survey of firms in several countries in the world, Wilson and Macer reported that the number-one mentioned "challenge" facing the marketing research industry was "falling response rates."[22] As telephone survey response rates were lowered to new lows of about 7%, marketing researchers switched to online surveys. Soon after the online revolution, response rates for online surveys plummeted as well. B2B research has also experienced a similar decline in response rates.[23] Desperately needing respondents, research firms invested heavily in creating panels of consumers who agree to serve as research respondents.[24]

Making respondent cooperation more difficult has been the long battle between marketing researchers and telemarketers. The FTC's "do not call" registry has been very successful.[25] Fortunately, the marketing research industry is excluded from the ban placed on telemarketers in the "do not call" regulations. However, the industry is very concerned about this trend as research has shown that many consumers believe marketing research calls should be covered by the "do not call" ban.[26] In mid-2008, the FCC passed a new ruling which forbids companies, including research firms, from using an automatic telephone dialing system to call a cell phone without prior consent.[27]

Consumers have responded to their sense of loss of privacy by refusing to participate in research studies, so the industry must devote considerable time and effort to maintaining trusted relationships with consumer respondents. Respondents are the "lifeblood" of the marketing research industry. Ethical treatment of respondents is necessary if marketing research firms are to stop the growing resentment by consumers.

Marketing Research No Longer Represents "Voice of the Consumer"

Schultz, in 2005, claimed that marketing has lost its prominence in top management and partially blames marketing research for the decline. Schultz believes that supply-chain management, by stressing economies of scale and excellence in logistics, with the assumption that lower prices will attract consumers, means that marketing's former role of representing the consumer is lost. Marketing is now viewed as being an after-the-fact function that moves the goods, using promotional tools, at the end of the supply chain. Consumers are unimportant in the process. The assumption is that if we get the product to them at a low price, they will acquire it. Consequently, knowledge of consumers is less important. Schultz believes this is a short-sighted affair, and that marketing research must regain its role of providing top management with the "voice of the consumer."[28]

Marketing Research Is Parochial

Several critics of marketing research believe it is too parochial; it is isolated with a narrow focus. Mahajan and Wind[29] and Schultz complain that managers misapply research by not having research professionals involved in high-level, strategic decision making. Marketing research left to report to lower levels in the firm is not part of the strategic planning process. Their role is limited to routine reports and being involved in assessing promotion methods *after* the strategic decisions have been made. This occurs even when marketing research is outsourced to external suppliers. Too many executives view marketing research as providing a commodity to be outsourced to "research brokers," who are hired to conduct a component of the research process when they should be involved in the entire process. Schultz would agree with Mahajan and Wind that marketing research has become too comfortable in providing standard reports using simple measures. Honomichl has also levied this same criticism.[30] This information, although useful, does not allow marketing research to contribute to the important central issues of determining overall strategy. Young, Weiss, and Stewart have provided some suggestions for improving this issue in their book, *Marketing Champions*.[31]

Response rates to requests for respondents to cooperate in research (mainly surveys) have been steadily declining for several years.

A worldwide industry survey reported that the number-one mentioned "challenge" facing the marketing research industry was "falling response rates."

The "do not call" registry has been effective in the United States. Fortunately, the marketing research industry is excluded from the ban placed on telemarketers in such regulations.

The industry must devote considerable time and effort to maintaining trusted relationships with consumer respondents. Respondents are the "lifeblood" of the marketing research industry.

One critic believes marketing research must once again represent the "voice of the consumer" to top management.

Several critics of marketing research believe it is too parochial; it is isolated with a narrow focus. Too often marketing research left to report to lower levels of the firm is not part of the strategic planning process.

Marketing Research Operates in a "Silo"

Marketing researchers can add greater value if, instead of providing tactical reports, they provide information useful for determining and guiding the overall strategy of the firm.

The criticism that marketing research operates in a "silo" is closely related to marketing research being too parochial, albeit different. As we just learned, marketing research that is too parochial fails to address issues at the strategic planning level; it has been relegated to tactical issues within marketing. Schultz and Mahajan and Wind also believe that marketing research fails to communicate with other entities within the firm. Shultz states that because firms are organized in a functional structure (e.g., finance, operations, marketing departments), marketing (and marketing research) is viewed as just another function. The problem is that each function has its own knowledge and skills and operates in a "silo," with little interaction across functions. Each function reports up to top management. By being just another of several functions reporting to top management, marketing has become less important, as has its components, including marketing research. Consequently, marketing research has importance only within marketing. Marketers and marketing researchers have contributed to the demise of their own importance in the organization because, in recent years, they have come to view themselves not as managers but as staff members who supply management with information. Marketing research could add value to other departments as well, but it must break down the "silos."

Critics of marketing research believe that researchers do not adequately communicate with other entities within the firm.

Mahajan and Wind[32] believe that marketing researchers have created silos, which separate themselves from other information. For example, by separating research into qualitative and quantitative data, researchers tend to use one or the other when, in fact, more insights may be gained by integrating the two approaches. Other silos are created when decision support systems are not linked with marketing research. Firms should integrate experiments they conduct instead of conducting one-shot projects that investigate a single issue. Mahajan and Wind also suggest greater integration of marketing research with existing databases and other information sources such as customer complaints, other studies of product/service quality, and external databases. In other words, marketing researchers would improve their results by taking a closer look at all existing information instead of embarking on isolated research projects to solve a problem.

Marketing Research Is Tool Oriented

Marketing researchers have been criticized for developing tools, and instead of trying to diagnose the market and come up with creative solutions, they screen through issues until they find one on which they can apply one of their tools.

Critics of marketing research claim that marketing researchers develop tools, and instead of trying to diagnose the market and come up with creative solutions, they screen through issues until they find one on which they can apply one of their tools. The problem with this is that the "cart is leading the horse." Just because the tool fits the issue doesn't mean that the chosen issue is the one that deserves attention. Schultz[33] stated that external suppliers of marketing research, by focusing on their tools, have furthered this perception. Unfortunately, too often the research problem is defined in terms of being compatible with one of the existing tools (can use conjoint analysis to solve this problem). Researchers too readily apply a tool instead of focusing on the more complex strategic issues facing the firm. The end result is that marketing researchers are used to supplying "ingredients" instead of being involved in making strategic decisions.

Using IT to Speed Up Marketing Research

Online research has grown significantly because it can speed up the research process.

With globalization and firms outsourcing functions to "low bidders" worldwide, there has never been a more important time for marketing research to show value. One way to increase value is to provide the same information faster and at lower cost. Years ago, Roger D. Blackwell, a long-time marketing consultant, stated that the marketing research cycle must be stepped up because of fierce competition.[34] Blackwell's statement is even more applicable to today's business environment. It has long been recognized that there is a trade-off between quickly producing marketing research information and doing research in a thorough manner. Marketing researchers want time to conduct projects properly. However, Mahajan and Wind point out that researchers must remember that time is money. Real dollar losses result from introducing products and services to the marketplace too late. So much so, in fact, that many companies cut corners in the research they conduct or do no marketing research at all. This, of course, often leads to disastrous "death-wish" marketing.[35] The suggested prescription is for marketing researchers to utilize information technology (IT) for speed and economical efficiency. This is exactly why online research has become a significant factor of the research industry.[36]

Other Criticisms of Marketing Research

There have been several other investigations of the research industry over the years. Some of these reviews have been made by knowledgeable persons' critiques while others have asked buyers of marketing research studies whether the value of the research performed by the suppliers in the industry is worthwhile. Criticism has focused on the following areas of concern: There is a lack of creativity, the industry is too survey-oriented, the industry does not understand the real problems that need studying, market researchers show a lack of concern for respondents, the industry has a cavalier attitude regarding nonresponse error, the price of the research is high relative to its value, and academic marketing research should be more closely related to actual marketing management decisions.[37]

Critical reviews are good for the industry. John Stuart Mill once said that "custom is the enemy of progress."[38] One entire issue of *Marketing Research*, edited by Chuck Chakrapani, was devoted to a number of articles questioning customary practices in marketing research.[39] The debate these articles stirred is good for the industry. In summary, the basic conclusion of these evaluations is that the industry has performed well, but there is room for improvement. We discuss some of the suggestions for improvement in the following paragraphs.

Certification and Education: Means to Improving the Industry

We must point out that while the preceding discussion centered on criticism of the industry and we fully agree that constructive criticism is good, the marketing research industry has great reason to be proud. The industry has performed well by the toughest of all standards, the test of the marketplace. Clients obviously see value in the marketing research that is being generated. However, the industry is not complacent. Many suggest that the problems are created by a very small minority of firms, most of which simply are not qualified to deliver quality marketing research services. There is obviously a concern among buyers and suppliers with the lack of uniformity in the industry as well. In a study of buyers' and suppliers' perceptions of the research industry, Dawson, Bush, and Stern found that the key issue in the industry is a lack of uniform quality; there are good suppliers and there are poor suppliers.[40] Two areas in which the industry is seeking self-improvement are certification and education.

CERTIFICATION **Certification** is a designation that indicates the achievement of some minimal standard of performance. For many years, it has been argued that marketing research attracts practitioners who are not fully qualified to provide adequate service to buyer firms due in large part to the fact that there have been no formal requirements, no education level, no degrees, no certificates, no licenses, and no tests of any kind required to open a marketing research business. Certainly, the vast majority of research firms have staffs thoroughly trained in research methods and have years of excellent performance. However, industry observers have stated that it is those few firms with unqualified personnel and management that tarnish the industry's image.

The **Professional Researcher Certification (PRC)** program was started in 2005 after several years of planning by the Marketing Research Association. The certification program took the effort of many people, and the MRA coordinated the certification plan with several other organizations that serve the industry. The program,

Go to the PRC website at www.mra-net.org/prc.

Source: By permission, Marketing Research Association.

mentioned by COO Darby in our opening vignette, has been very successful and continues to adapt in order to make the certification program a viable service to the industry.

EDUCATION There are varied opportunities for members of the marketing research industry to learn more about their profession. For many years, the marketing research industry has offered a wide variety of educational opportunities for its members. Certification, by requiring CEUs (continuing education units) to maintain certification, will have a positive effect on educational programs in the industry. Several industry organizations offer programs designed to increase the knowledge and skills of those in the industry. The AMA, for example, sponsors several programs, including an annual marketing research conference. Second, the AMA sponsors the Advanced School of Marketing Research, a program conducted at Notre Dame University designed to benefit the analyst, project supervisor, or manager of marketing research. Yet another AMA program is an annual conference that focuses on advanced analytical techniques. In addition, the Marketing Research Association (MRA) started an introductory program on marketing research several years ago. Coordinated at the University of Georgia, this program is designed to develop the research skills of those being transferred into marketing research or those who want to enter the profession. In addition to the MRA, several other industry associations have excellent training classes and programs frequently scheduled to meet industry needs. These include the Council for the Association of Survey Research Organizations (CASRO, at CASRO University), the Qualitative Research Consultant's Association (QRCA), the Advertising Research Foundation (ARF), and the European Society of Opinion and Marketing Research (ESOMAR). Burke Institute (of Burke Inc.) has trained thousands of marketing research practitioners over the years and has an excellent, high-quality reputation. Several universities now offer a master's degree in marketing research. Well-regarded master's programs are available at Southern Illinois University–Edwardsville and the University of Texas–Arlington.

> There are varied educational opportunities for members of the marketing research industry to learn more about their profession.

> Certification, by requiring CEUs to maintain certification, will likely have a positive effect on educational programs in the industry.

> To see some of the types of classes taken by marketing research practitioners, visit the Burke Institute, at www.burkeinstitute.com/Seminars.

Ethics and Marketing Research

A few years ago we wrote, "Recent history has shown that ethical issues are rife in religion, government, politics and business." Unfortunately, that history has continued. The problems of Enron, WorldCom, and HealthSouth are now seemingly miniscule compared to the unethical practices of Wall Street and the financial industry during the last decade. These were not isolated incidents involving business managers who took advantage of others for personal gain. As in most areas of business activity, there exist many opportunities for unethical (and ethical) behavior in the marketing research industry.[41] Unfortunately, the marketing research industry is not immune to ethical problems.[42] Our purpose here is to introduce you to the areas in which unethical behaviors have existed in the past and hopefully to give you some framework for thinking about how you will conduct yourself in the future when confronted with these situations.

Ethics may be defined as a field of inquiry into determining what behaviors are deemed appropriate under certain circumstances as prescribed by codes of behavior that are set by society. Society determines what is ethical and what is not ethical. In some cases, this is formalized by our institutions. Some behavior, for example, is so wrongful that it is deemed illegal by statute.

Behavior that is illegal is unethical, by definition. However, other behaviors are considered by some to be unethical but are not illegal. When these types of behaviors are not spelled out by some societal institution (such as the justice system, legislature, Congress, or regulatory agencies such as the FTC), then the determination of whether the behaviors are ethical or unethical is open to debate.

> As in most areas of business activity, there exist many opportunities for unethical (and ethical) behavior in the marketing research industry.

> Unfortunately, the marketing research industry is not immune to ethical problems.

> Ethics may be defined as a field of inquiry into determining what behaviors are deemed appropriate.

Ethical Views Are Shaped by Philosophy: Deontology or Teleology

Numerous philosophies may be applied to explain one's determination of appropriate behavior given certain circumstances. In the following discussion we use the two philosophies of deontology and teleology to explain this behavior.[43] **Deontology** is concerned with the rights of the

> One's philosophy usually determines appropriate, ethical behavior.

individual. Is the behavior fair and just for each individual? If an individual's rights are violated, then the behavior is not ethical.[44] For example, consider the marketing research firm that has been hired to study how consumers are attracted to and react to a new form of in-store display. Researchers, hidden from view, record the behavior of unsuspecting shoppers as they walk through the supermarket. A deontologist considers this form of research activity unethical because it violates the individual shopper's right to privacy. The deontologist would likely agree to the research provided the shoppers were informed beforehand that their behavior would be recorded, giving them the option either to participate or not to participate.[45]

On the other hand, **teleology** analyzes a given behavior in terms of its benefits and costs to society. If there are individual costs but group benefits, then there are net gains, and the behavior is judged to be ethical.[46] In our example of the shopper being observed in the supermarket, the teleologist might conclude that, although there is a violation of the right to privacy among the shoppers observed (the cost), there is a benefit if the company learns how to market goods more efficiently, thus reducing long-term marketing costs. Because this benefit ultimately is shared by many more individuals than those whose privacy was invaded during the original study, the teleologist would likely declare this research practice to be ethical.

Thus, whether you view a behavior as being ethical or unethical depends on your philosophy. Are you a deontologist or a teleologist? It's difficult to answer that question until you are placed in an ethically sensitive situation. One thing is for certain: You will come across ethically sensitive situations during your career. Will you know it's an ethically sensitive situation? How will you respond? We hope you will at least know when you are in an ethically sensitive situation in marketing research. The rest of this section is devoted to teaching you this sensitivity.[47]

Ethical Behavior in Marketing Research Is a Worldwide Issue

As noted previously, there are many ways a society may prescribe wanted and unwanted behaviors. In business, if there are practices that are not illegal but are nevertheless thought to be wrong, trade associations or professional organizations will often prescribe a **code of ethical behavior.** This has been the case in marketing and, more specifically, in marketing research. The American Marketing Association (www.marketingpower.com), the Council of American Survey Research Organizations (www.casro.org), the Qualitative Research Consultants Association (www.qrca.org), the Marketing Research Association (www.mra-net.org), and the Canadian-based Professional Market Research Society (www.pmrs-aprm.com) all have codes of ethics. The European-based ESOMAR (www.esomar.org) also has a code of ethics referred to as "professional standards." ESOMAR was formed as the European Society for Opinion and Marketing Research. Most of these codes may be viewed online without a membership.

All over the world, marketing research organizations are striving to achieve ethical behavior among practitioners of marketing research. Marketing Research Application 2.1 illustrates how one firm follows the MRA Code of Ethics.

CODES OF ETHICS   As noted previously, the Marketing Research Association has a code of ethics. While we encourage you to look over the entire code, some of the issues covered are as follows:

- Prohibiting selling (sugging) or fund raising (frugging) under the guise of conducting research
- Maintaining research integrity by avoiding misrepresentation and omission of pertinent research data
- Treating outside clients and suppliers fairly

SUGGING AND FRUGGING   Marketing researchers are prohibited from selling or fund raising under the guise of conducting research. **Sugging** refers to "selling under the guise of a survey." Typically, sugging occurs when a "researcher" gains a respondent's cooperation to participate in a research study and then uses the opportunity to attempt to sell the respondent a good or service. Most consumers are quite willing to provide their attitudes and opinions of products and services

One philosophy is called deontology, which focuses on the rights of the individual. If an individual's rights are violated, then the behavior is not ethical.

Teleology is a philosophy that focuses on the trade-off between individual costs and group benefits. If benefits outweigh costs, the behavior is judged to be ethical.

To see the MRA's Code of Marketing Research Standards, visit www.mra-net.org, and go to "Resources" and then "Codes/Forms and Guidelines."

Sugging refers to "selling under the guise of a survey." Frugging refers to "fund raising under the guise of a survey."

MARKETING RESEARCH APPLICATION 2.1

Baltimore Research Follows MRA's Code of Ethics

Baltimore Research is a full-service marketing research firm. One of the many services we offer our clients is focus group research. There are ethical concerns with focus group facilities that "cut corners" in recruiting respondents. A given focus group will have strict specifications for the profile of qualified candidates. This can include household composition, demographics, brand and category usage, as well as a number of lifestyle and personality variables. Ideally, the focus group should be comprised of a cross section of consumers that meet the exact criteria needed by the client. For example, Frito-Lay may have a new, nutritious snack that they want to test with mothers of young children who purchase similar foods. While it takes time and effort to find the right individuals, we will only recruit the types of consumers our client expects to have in our focus groups. Baltimore Research utilizes a number of creative methodologies to target the harder to find segments. You will read more about this concept in this book when your authors discuss "incidence rates."

Clients expect us to recruit "typical" consumers into our focus groups. There are individuals who try to get into as many focus groups as possible to make a living from participation. This presents a number of concerns to researchers. For example, they may lie in the screening process and not really be the type of consumer sought. Consequently, their experiences may not be truly relevant. For a number of other reasons, these "professional respondents" may not be representative of the average consumer. We have implemented many procedures to safeguard against professional respondents, including software to track respondent participation by a number of variables, such as frequency and research topic. At Baltimore Research, we know that our enduring profitability and existence depend on providing quality information that will help our clients solve their research problems. If we give them the information that leads them to be more profitable, they will return to us when they have a future need for marketing research.

At Baltimore Research we "take the pledge" to avoid unethical shortcuts to ensure the long-term health of our industry. Many of our employees hold PRCs (Professional Researcher Certifications) from the MRA (Marketing Research Association). We are committed to continuing education for our employees and are proud custodians of the MRA's Code of Ethics.

Source: Ted Donnelly.

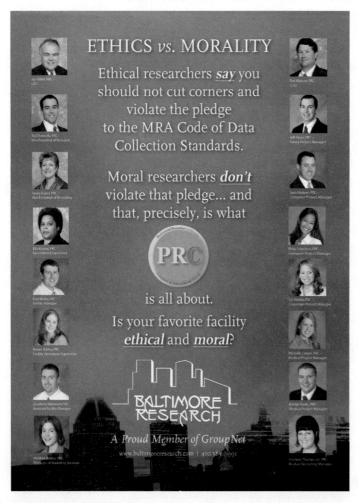

Ted Donnelly, Ph.D., PRC
Vice President
Baltimore Research

in response to a legitimate request for this information. Suggers (and fruggers), however, take advantage of that goodwill by deceiving unsuspecting consumers. Consumers soon learn that their cooperation in answering a few questions has led to their being subjected to a sales presentation. In sugging and frugging there is no good-faith effort to conduct a survey for the purpose of collecting and analyzing data for specific purposes. Rather, the intent of the "fake" survey is to sell or raise money. Of course, these practices have led to the demise of the pool of cooperative respondents. The Telemarketing and Consumer Fraud and Abuse Prevention Act of 1994 made sugging illegal. Under this act, telemarketers are not allowed to call someone and say they are conducting a survey, and then try to sell a product or service. Although telemarketers are not able to legally practice sugging, the act does not prohibit sugging via the mail.[48] **Frugging** is closely related to sugging and stands for "fund raising under the guise of a survey." Because frugging does not involve the sale of a product or service, it is not covered in the Telemarketing and Consumer Fraud and Abuse Prevention Act of 1994, but it is widely considered to be unethical. Actually, sugging and frugging are carried out by telemarketers or other direct marketers. It would be rare, indeed, to find a researcher practicing sugging or frugging. Telemarketers are the main offenders. However, we cover this topic because both sugging and frugging are unethical treatments of potential respondents in marketing research.

> Sugging is illegal.

> Frugging is unethical.

The marketing research industry recognizes that it must attempt to influence legislation in a way that will be favorable for the industry. For example, the industry fought hard to protect consumers from sugging and frugging. Also, when "do not call" bills were first introduced, the industry worked hard to educate lawmakers about the difference between telemarketers and researchers. Much of this work has been conducted by the Council for Marketing and Opinion Research (CMOR). CMOR was founded in 1992 by four industry associations and is now part of the Marketing Research Association.

RESEARCH INTEGRITY Sometimes research is not totally objective. Information is withheld, falsified, or altered to protect vested interests. Marketing research information is often used in making significant decisions. The outcome of the decision may have an impact on future company strategy, budgets, jobs, organization, and so forth. With so much at stake, the opportunity exists for a lack of total objectivity in the research process. The loss of **research integrity,** defined as performing research that adheres to accepted standards, may take the form of withholding information, falsifying data, altering research results, or misinterpreting the research findings in a way that makes them more consistent with predetermined points of view. As one researcher stated, "I refused to alter research results and as a result I was fired for failure to think strategically."[49] An example illustrates how research integrity is a serious issue. Forrester Research Inc. released a report concluding that developing and deploying Web-based portal applications is substantially less expensive using Microsoft technology than it is using a Linux/J2ee combination. When it was learned that the research was funded by Microsoft it brought about skepticism on the part of several CEOs, including one who stated, "I'm not a big fan of any of those marketing research firms. I don't believe them to be independent." Forrester CEO George Colony stated that the company was taking steps to "tighten" its internal processes and its integrity policy.[50] In examining reasons for product failure, Hodock addressed the issue of inflated sales forecasts that were unethically provided to upper management. Why? Because underlings knew that top management wanted a rosy picture for a new product innovation. Hodock notes that inflating sales forecasts is an ethical issue that goes on in the business world yet it is rarely noted in college classrooms.[51]

Another example of violating the integrity of the research has been noted in the automobile industry. As managers have learned that repeat sales and positive word of mouth (WOM) are strongly associated with customer satisfaction, many such programs have been implemented to track the level of customer satisfaction. Automobile firms have implemented many such systems among their dealer networks, often offering strong incentives for "high customer satisfaction scores." However, the scores themselves may not be an accurate reflection of true customer satisfaction. Half of the respondents to a 2007 TrueDelta Poll taken for the automotive industry

Some auto owners have reported being pressured into giving their dealer high customer satisfaction ratings.

reported that the dealership tried to influence their survey responses. Some manipulation techniques reported were asking or begging for perfect scores, commenting they would get a bonus for a perfect score, offering gifts for a perfect score, asking the customer to bring the survey to the dealership to fill it out, or even asking for the blank survey for the dealership to fill out on their own.[52]

A breach in research integrity may come from either the supplier or the buyer. If a research supplier knows that a buyer will want marketing research services in the future, the supplier may alter a study's results or withhold information, so that the study will support the buyer's wishes. Breaches of research integrity need not be isolated to those managing the research project. Interviewers have been known to make up interviews and to take shortcuts in completing surveys. In fact, there is some evidence that this is more of a problem than was once thought.[53] Maintaining research integrity is regarded as one of the most significant ethical issues in the research industry. In a study of 460 marketing researchers, Hunt, Chonko, and Wilcox found that maintenance of research integrity posed the most significant problem for one-third of those sampled.[54]

TREATING OTHERS FAIRLY   Several ethical issues may arise in the practice of marketing research that center around how others are treated. Buyers, suppliers, and the public may be treated unethically.

Sharing of "background knowledge" among firms raises ethical questions.

Buyers   In the Hunt, Chonko, and Wilcox study cited previously, the second most frequently stated ethical problem facing marketing researchers was fair treatment of buyer firms. Passing hidden charges to buyers, overlooking study requirements when subcontracting work out to other supplier firms, and selling unnecessary research are examples of unfair treatment of buyer firms. By overlooking study requirements, such as qualifying respondents on specified characteristics or verifying that respondents were interviewed, the supplier firm may lower its cost of using the services of a subcontracting field service firm. A supplier firm may oversell research services to naive buyers by convincing them to use a more expensive research design.

Marketing researchers try to avoid conflicts of interest by not working for two competitors.

Sharing confidential and proprietary information raises ethical questions. Virtually all work conducted by marketing research firms is confidential and proprietary. Researchers build up a storehouse of this information as they conduct research studies. Most ethical issues involving confidentiality revolve around how this storehouse of information, or "background knowledge," is treated. One researcher stated, "Where does 'background knowledge' stop and conflict exist [as a result of work with a previous client]?" [55] It is common practice among research supplier firms to check their existing list of buyer-clients to ensure that there is no conflict of interest before accepting work from a new buyer.

Suppliers. *Phony RFPs* Buyers also abuse suppliers of marketing research. A major problem exists, for example, when a firm with internal research capabilities issues a **request for proposals (RFP)** from external supplier firms. External firms then spend time and money developing research designs to solve the stated problem, estimating costs of the project, and so on. Now, having collected several detailed proposals outlining research designs and costs, the abusing firm decides to do the job internally. Issuing a call for proposals from external firms with no intention of doing the job outside is unethical behavior.

Failure to Honor Time and Money Agreements Often buyer firms have obligations such as agreeing to meetings or the provision of materials needed for the research project. Supplier firms must have these commitments from buyers in a timely fashion in order to keep to their time schedules. Buyer firms sometimes abuse their agreements to deliver personnel or these other resources in the time to which they have agreed. Also, buyers sometimes do not honor commitments to pay for services. Although this happens in many industries, research suppliers do not have the luxury of repossession, although there are, of course, legal recourses.

The Public Sometimes researchers are asked to do research on products thought to be dangerous to society. Ethical issues arise as researchers balance marketing requirements with social issues. This is particularly true in the areas of product development and advertising. For example, marketing researchers have expressed concern over conducting research on advertising to children. Some advertising has had the objective of increasing the total consumption of refined sugar among children via advertising scheduled during Saturday morning television programs. Other ethical concerns arise when conducting research on products researchers thought were dangerous to the public, such as certain chemicals, cigarettes, alcohol, and sugar.

Some marketing research firms take a proactive position on helping their clients implement strategy that considers ethical issues. For example, ABACO Marketing Research in São Paulo, Brazil, incorporates ethical considerations in its evaluations of clients' promotional materials. The company's AD-VISOR® service provides ethical scores and compares them with norms, thus allowing clients to understand consumers' ethical evaluations of proposed communication messages.

> Ethical concerns arise when marketing researchers are asked to conduct research on advertising to children or on products they feel are dangerous to the public, such as certain chemicals, cigarettes, alcohol, or sugar.

RESPONDENTS As we noted earlier in this chapter, respondents are the lifeblood of the marketing research industry. Respondent cooperation rates have been going down, and the industry is concerned with the ethical treatment of the existing respondent pool.[56] In 1982, some of the organizations that created CMOR began monitoring survey response cooperation. Response rates became such a problem that CMOR hired a director of respondent cooperation. Marketing researchers must honor promises made to respondents that the respondent's identity will remain confidential or anonymous if they expect respondents to cooperate with requests for information in the future. Some specific respondent abuses are discussed in the following paragraphs.

> Respondent cooperation rates have been going down, and the industry is concerned with the ethical treatment of the existing respondent pool.

Deception of Respondents Historically, respondents have been deceived during the research process in many fields, not just marketing research.[57] Kimmel and Smith point out that **deception** may occur during subject recruitment (they are told their participation will only take a "few minutes" when in fact it may take a quarter of an hour or much more; they are not told the true identity/sponsor or that of the research firm, etc.), during the research procedure itself (they are viewed without their knowledge, etc.), and during postresearch situations (there is a violation of the promise of anonymity). Also, these authors suggest that there are serious consequences to this deception.[58]

An example of where deception is used in marketing research is mystery shopping. **Mystery shopping** is the practice of gathering competitive intelligence by sending people posing as customers to gather price and sales data from unsuspecting employees. Shing and Spence argue

> Mystery shopping is the practice of gathering competitive intelligence by sending people posing as customers to gather price and sales data from unsuspecting employees.

Many of the research organizations to which we have referred in this chapter have specific codes of ethics dealing with mystery shopping.

Ethical issues arise when the respondents are promised confidentiality and anonymity and the researcher fails to honor this promise.

that though the information given out by the mystery shopper is not confidential, it is still given under false pretenses.[59] Mystery shopping is widely used in industry, and many would argue that it is not unethical. Few, however, would argue that it does not involve deception. Our purpose is to make certain you know when you are dealing with an issue that is ethically sensitive. Many of the research organizations to which we have referred in this chapter have specific codes of ethics dealing with mystery shopping.

Confidentiality and Anonymity   One way of gaining a potential respondent's trust is by promising confidentiality or anonymity. **Confidentiality** means that the researcher knows who the respondent is but does not identify the respondent with any information gathered from that respondent to a client. So the respondent's identity is confidential information known only by the researcher. A stronger appeal may be made under conditions of **anonymity,** where the respondent is, and remains, anonymous or unknown. The researcher is interested only in gathering information from the respondent and does not know the respondent's identity. Ethical issues arise when the respondents are promised confidentiality and anonymity and the researcher fails to honor this promise.

Invasions of Privacy   Marketing research, by its nature, is invasive. Any information acquired from a respondent has some degree of invasiveness. Ethical issues, some of them legal, abound in the area of invading others' privacy. The areas that are most responsible for consumer concern are unsolicited telephone calls and spam. Since marketing researchers rely heavily on telephone surveys and, more recently, online survey research, both areas are significant to the marketing research industry. Sending an email to someone without having either permission or some preexisting relationship with the person would be considered spam—and spam is illegal. An electronic message has been defined as **spam** if (1) the recipient's personal identity and context are irrelevant because the message is equally applicable to many other potential recipients; (2) the recipient has not verifiably granted deliberate, explicit, and still-revocable permission for it to be sent; and (3) the transmission and reception of the message appear to the recipient to give a disproportionate benefit to the sender.[60] The name *spam* comes from a Monty Python skit in which a restaurant customer is deluged with repeated requests to order canned Spam. Finally, the customer yells, "I don't want any Spam!"[61]

In conclusion, marketing research firms are working hard to protect the privacy of their respondents. The firms in the industry realize that they must rely on consumer cooperation for information requests. In order to achieve a cooperative pool of potential respondents, marketing researchers must attempt to separate themselves from unscrupulous direct marketers. The future is unclear in terms of how legal actions will affect research. Research firms have, for several years now, been moving in the direction of recruiting their own panels of willing respondents. Recruiting and maintaining a panel requires a considerable investment. **Panel equity,** the value of readily available access to willing respondents, may become increasingly important in the future. Marketing research firms, recognizing the value they have in panels, will make even greater effort to ensure fair and ethical treatment of their panel respondents. We discuss types of panels and how they are used in Chapter 4.

Summary

We describe several characteristics of the marketing research industry in this chapter. We begin by introducing you to one of the industry's premier professional associations, the Marketing Research Association. The chapter gives you a brief history of the evolution of the industry. Beginning with studies as early as the 1800s, marketing research was needed as the Industrial Revolution led to manufacturers being separated from their consumers by large distances. Companies had a growing need to know more about their customers, which led to the growth of marketing research firms that supplied information from distant markets. Charles Coolidge Parlin is credited for conducting the first continuous and organized research for the Curtis Publishing Company in 1911. Parlin is recognized as the "father of marketing research." Prior to the Industrial Revolution there was little need for formal marketing research. By the 1960s, the practice of marketing research gained wide approval as a method for keeping abreast of fast-changing, distant markets.

The research industry today is a multibillion-dollar industry, with firms operating worldwide. The Honomichl Global Top 25 is a listing of the top twenty-five firms, ranked in terms of revenue generated around the world. The Honomichl Top 50 is a list of U.S.-based firms ranked by revenues generated in the United States. Mergers and acquisitions and strategic alliances in the industry make it a highly competitive industry.

The research industry may be broadly classified as research buyers and suppliers. Suppliers may be internal (research is provided by an entity within the firm) or external. Internal suppliers organize by having their own formal departments, having a committee or individual responsible for research, or by not having anyone responsible. Formal departments of internal supplier firms typically organize by area of application (i.e., business to consumer, business to business, product a, product b), marketing function (product research, promotion research, etc.), or the research process (i.e., data collection, data analysis). External supplier firms may be classified as full-service or limited-service firms. Each of these types has several other classifications of firms. Full-service supplier firms have the ability to conduct the entire marketing research project for the buyer firms. Limited-service supplier firms specialize in one or, at most, a few marketing research activities. There are different types of both full-service and limited-service firms.

There are several challenges facing the marketing research industry. The industry must deal with the worldwide recession that began in 2008. Marketing research must deal with low response rates to requests of consumers to participate in research. The industry must take the steps necessary to safeguard consumer cooperation, the lifeblood of the industry. Marketing research has been accused of no longer representing the voice of the consumer, being too parochial (narrow view), operating in a "silo" without proper communication within the firm, being too tool oriented, not being fast enough, among other criticisms. The marketing research industry launched a certification program in 2005 to ensure a minimum standard of training and experience. The Professional Researcher Certification (PRC) program is coordinated by the Marketing Research Association. The industry offers varied educational programs from industry professional organizations such as CASRO, MRA, ARF, and the AMA. Also, there are private educational programs of excellent quality such as the Burke Institute. There are now several opportunities to earn a master's degree in marketing research.

All business students should be aware of the ethical issues in marketing research. Ethics is defined as a field of inquiry into determining what behaviors are deemed appropriate under certain circumstances, as prescribed by codes of behavior that are set by society. How you respond to ethically sensitive situations depends on your philosophy: deontology or teleology. Several organizations in the research industry have codes of ethical behavior for both buyers and suppliers of research. Sugging is illegal. Frugging is very unethical. Ethical issues include research integrity and treating others (buyers, suppliers, the public, and respondents) fairly. Respondent fairness issues include deception, confidentiality, and invasions of privacy.

Special standards are provided in codes of ethics and professional conduct of several industry organizations that apply to online survey marketing researchers in order to protect the privacy of online respondents. Research companies, faced with a declining pool of willing respondents in the general public, have come to rely more heavily on panels of respondents who have been recruited specifically to respond to research requests. The value, or "panel equity," of these panels has grown and we can expect to see even fairer treatment of panel respondents in the future.

Key Terms

Charles Coolidge Parlin (p. 22)
Honomichl Global Top 25 (p. 22)
Honomichl Top 50 (p. 23)
Strategic alliances (p. 23)
Research suppliers (p. 26)
Internal supplier (p. 26)
External suppliers (p. 27)
Full-service supplier firms (p. 28)
Syndicated data service
 firms (p. 28)

Standardized service firms (p. 28)
Customized service firms (p. 28)
Online research services
 firms (p. 28)
Online research (p. 28)
Web-based research (p. 29)
Online survey research (p. 29)
Limited-service supplier
 firms (p. 29)
Field service firms (p. 29)

Phone banks (p. 29)
Market segment specialists (p. 29)
Sample design and
 distribution (p. 29)
Data analysis services (p. 30)
Specialized research technique
 firms (p. 30)
Certification (p. 33)
Professional Researcher Certification
 (PRC) (p. 33)

Review Questions

1. Describe the PRC as discussed in the opening vignette by the COO of the Marketing Research Association.
2. Who is credited for conducting the first continuous and organized marketing research? (He is also known as the "father of marketing research.")
3. Explain why marketing research was not widespread prior to the Industrial Revolution.
4. Roughly, how much is the worldwide marketing research industry worth? How much is the U.S. marketing research industry worth?
5. What is the difference between the Honomichl Global Top 25 and the Honomichl Top 50 reports?
6. What is meant by a "strategic alliance"? Give an example of one.
7. We categorized firms as internal and external suppliers of marketing research information. Explain what is meant by each, and give an example of each type of firm.
8. Distinguish among full-service firms, limited-service firms, syndicated data services, standardized services, customized service, and online research services firms.
9. How would you categorize the following firms?
   a. One specializing in marketing to kids (ages six to twelve years)
   b. One specializing in a computerized scent generator for testing reactions to smells
   c. One that offers a method for conducting "mock trials"
   d. One that offers clients samples drawn according to the client's sample plan
   e. One that collects data over the Internet
10. What makes an online marketing research firm different from other marketing research firms?
11. What is the advantage in a firm having its own formal marketing research department? Explain three different ways such a department may be internally organized.
12. What are four challenges to the marketing research industry?
13. Explain how being "too tool oriented" may hurt the marketing research industry.
14. Explain how certification and education may improve the marketing research industry.
15. How would you define ethics?
16. What are the two fundamental philosophies that can be used as a basis for making ethical decisions?
17. List where you can find some codes of ethics applicable to the marketing research industry.
18. Name some of the ethical issues facing the marketing research industry.
19. Explain why sugging and frugging are bad for marketing researchers.

Application Questions

20. Go to the websites of either CASRO, MRA, or IMRO and look up their codes of ethics/professional standards. What do they have to say about doing online surveys?
21. Look up "marketing research" in your Yellow Pages directory. Given the information provided there, can you classify the research firms in your area according to the classification system of research firms we used in this chapter?
22. Comment on each practice in the following list. Is it ethical? Indicate your reasoning in each case.
   a. A research company conducts a telephone survey and gathers information that it uses later to send a salesperson to the home of potential buyers for the purpose of selling a product. It makes no attempt to sell the product over the telephone.
   b. Would your answer to (a) change if you found out that the information gathered during the telephone survey was used as part of a "legitimate" marketing research report?
   c. A door-to-door salesperson finds that by telling people that he is conducting a survey they are more likely to listen to his sales pitch.
   d. Greenpeace sends out a direct-mail piece described as a survey and asks for donations as the last question.
   e. In the appendix of the final report, the researcher lists the names of all respondents who took part in

the survey and places an asterisk beside the names of those who indicated a willingness to be contacted by the client's sales personnel.

f. A list of randomly generated telephone numbers is drawn in order to conduct a telephone survey.

g. A list of randomly generated e-mail addresses is generated using a "Spambot" (an electronic "robot" that searches the Internet looking for and retaining e-mail addresses) in order to conduct a random online research project.

h. Students conducting a marketing research project randomly select e-mail addresses of other students from the student directory in order to conduct their term project.

Case 2.1 **ABR Marketing Research**

The authors wish to thank Dr. Harriet Bettis-Outland, Assistant Professor of Marketing, University of West Florida, for revising this case.[62]

It was late Friday evening in December, and Barbara Jefferson, a senior research analyst for ABR Marketing Research, was working furiously to complete the media plan portion of the Precision Grooming Products report. PGP was considering introducing a men's hair gel, which required demographic characteristics and media habits of male hair gel users. In addition, attitudinal information about product attributes such as oiliness, stickiness, masculinity, and fragrance was needed.

The findings were to be presented Monday afternoon, and a long series of problems and delays had forced Barbara to stay late on Friday evening to complete the report. Complicating matters, Barbara felt that her boss, Michelle Barry, expected the statistical analysis to be consistent with ABR's initial recommendations to Precision. Barbara, Michelle, and David Miller, from Precision's advertising agency, were to meet Monday morning to finalize ABR's presentation to Precision.

Back in September, Barbara had recommended that 250 users of men's hair gel products be surveyed from each of fifteen metropolitan areas. Phillip Parker from Precision's marketing department had argued that conclusions about local usage in each city would not be accurate unless each city's sample size was proportional to its population. In other words, sample sizes for larger cities should be larger than for smaller cities. Furthermore, Phillip feared that males in metropolitan areas differed from males in rural areas with regard to usage or other important characteristics. Barbara finally convinced Phillip that sample sizes proportional to population would mean only twenty-five to fifty interviews in some smaller cities, which would be too few to draw statistically valid conclusions. Furthermore, expanding the survey to include rural users would have required committing more money to the project—money Precision didn't want to spend.

TABLE A.1
Proposed Budget

Phone survey (including pilot study)	$58,000
Focus group study	8,000
Advertising pretesting	25,000
Package pretesting	14,000
Miscellaneous expenses	5,000
Proposed total expenses	$110,000

In October, a Des Moines, Iowa, pretest revealed that the questionnaire's length was driving the cost per completed interview to about $18. Total expenses would be well over budget if that cost held for the fifteen metro areas. If the survey costs exceeded $65,000 (counting the pilot study), then precious little money would be left for the focus groups, advertising, and packaging pretesting in ABR's contract with Precision (see Table A.1).

Since Precision was a new account with big potential, a long-term relationship with them would be valuable. (Business at ABR had been slow this past year.) Feeling "under the gun," Barbara met with Michelle and Phillip, who agreed to reduce the sample to 200 men in only eleven metropolitan areas.

In early November, a new problem arose. After surveying eight metro areas, Barbara discovered that her assistant had accidentally deleted all questions on media habits from the questionnaire given to ABR's vendor for the phone interviews. When told of the missing questions problem, Michelle and Phillip became visibly angry at the vendor. After much discussion, they decided there was too little time to hire a new vendor and resample the eight areas. Therefore, they agreed to reinsert the media questions for the remaining three cities and just finish the survey.

Barbara's task now was to make the most of the data she had. Because responses from each of the three cities were reasonably similar, and each city was in a different region (East, West, and Midwest), Barbara felt confident

TABLE A.2

Comparison of Media Habits: Three-City Sample of Male Hair Gel Users Versus U.S. Adult Men

		Three-City Sample	All U.S. Men
Magazines: At least one subscription of . . .	News	28%	19%
	Entertainment	4%	3%
	Sports	39%	20%
	Other	9%	6%
Newspaper subscription (at least one daily)		35%	14%
Favorite radio format	Pop	41%	38%
	Country	21%	30%
	Jazz	15%	17%
	Easy listening	7%	6%
	News/talk	5%	4%
	Other	11%	5%
Hours watching television per week	Dramas	6.3	8.4
	Comedies	7.8	7.3
	News	1.1	3.9
	Other	2.3	3.9
	Total	17.5	23.5

that the three-city data were representative. Therefore, she decided to base the media plan on the large differences between her results and the national averages for adult men—making sports magazines and newspapers the primary vehicles for Precision's advertising (see Table A.2).

Barbara's confidence in the media plan was bolstered by a phone conversation with David Miller. Until a short time ago, his agency had handled the advertising for Village Toiletries, so he had valuable information about this competitor's possible responses to Precision's new product. David liked Barbara's recommendations, thought Phillip would also approve, and agreed to support the media plan in Monday's meeting. Indeed, Barbara thought, David had been a big help.

The Precision project had put a great deal of stress on Barbara, who hated spending evenings away from her family—especially near the holidays! If the presentation went well and more business was stirred up, then Barbara suspected that she would be spending even more evenings away from her family. But if the presentation went poorly or the data-collection errors became an issue, then Precision might look elsewhere for market research, thus jeopardizing Barbara's future with ABR. Either way, she was not feeling too comfortable.

1. After you have thoroughly read the case, list what you believe are the issues in the case.
2. For each issue in your list, rate its importance, from 7 (very important) to 1 (unimportant).

Case 2.2 **Your Integrated Case**

Advanced Automobile Concepts

In the last chapter we introduced you to Nick Thomas, CEO of Advanced Automobile Concepts (AAC), a new division of a large automobile manufacturer, ZEN Motors. If you have been assigned this case, you should briefly read over the information in Case 1.2 and in this case. You will recall that (1) AAC was created to revive the aging ZEN automobile brands by either reengineering existing models or

developing totally new models that are more in tune with today's changing automobile market, and (2) Nick Thomas has searched the company's MIS for information to help him make some major decisions. After reviewing these materials, Nick believes he must develop new models that will appeal to the market, but he is concerned that the recent interest in small, fuel-efficient cars will go away as it has done in the past when oil prices drop. He also wonders if consumers' interest in global warming is real enough that it will affect what they purchase. Nick knows he needs some help with additional information. ZEN Motors has its own marketing research department and Nick is considering using professionals in that department. Also, Nick has made several calls and learned that CMG Research has a good reputation; however, Nick is concerned about talking with a research firm outside ZEN Motors. Having never worked with a research firm before, Nick is afraid of sharing information that is so vital to AAC. He is concerned that such information may be given to competitors in the industry.

1. Why should Nick Thomas use the internal supplier, his own parent company's marketing research department? Why should he not use them?
2. Nick Thomas is concerned about using an external supplier of marketing research services, CMG Research. Go to the MRA's Code of Ethics and read what they have to say about researchers sharing confidential information (at www.mra-net.org, go to "Resources" and then "Codes, Forms and Guidelines"; then go to "(Expanded) Code of Marketing Research Standards, Section A").

3

The Marketing Research Process—Defining the Problem and the Research Objectives

A Practitioner Discusses the Marketing Research Process

Visit Moore Research at http://moore-research.com/.

In this chapter you will learn how to look at the marketing research process as a series of steps. Marketing research is fascinating yet complex. Here at Moore Research we deal with different types of problems, varying client industries, and changes in our clients' markets as their customers and competition adjust to seemingly constant environmental changes. To help us deal with this complexity, researchers have a stabilizing framework upon which we rely to help us sort out each client situation. We do not all share the same framework but many of us agree that there is great value in viewing marketing research as a series of steps making up the process. Some of us define the steps differently and some use fewer or more steps, but there is value in having this framework to help us conceptualize a path to obtaining the right information to solve a client's problem. For example, from having knowledge of this framework, I know we will spend several hours visiting with a client to ensure that we properly define that client's problem and the research objectives for the project. If we know the project entails collecting primary data, then we know the general steps necessary to follow; and this knowledge gives us a basis for planning the project. Without that general framework, coping with each client's situation would be much more difficult. This chapter provides an eleven-step process to help you develop a framework that will allow you to better understand marketing research. When you finish this chapter you will have a better understanding of marketing research. In addition, the eleven steps will serve you well as a framework for the remainder of the book.

Colleen Moore-Mezler, PRC and President, Moore Research Services Inc.

Colleen Moore-Mezler's comments in the opening vignette illustrate the importance of knowing the steps necessary to carry out a marketing research project. By having this framework of the marketing research process, Ms. Moore-Mezler is aided in her research planning by knowing the steps she will need to use in the proposed research project for her clients. Knowledge of these steps serves as a road map for planning a research project. Marketing researchers are familiar with the steps in the marketing research process. In this chapter we introduce you to these important steps, which will serve as a framework for the rest of this book. After we discuss the steps in the marketing research process we will focus on steps 2 and 3, defining the problem and establishing the research objectives.

The Marketing Research Process

The Process: Eleven Steps

In our effort to introduce you to marketing research in these first three chapters, recall that in Chapter 1 you learned what marketing research is and the role it plays in aiding managers in making marketing decisions; in Chapter 2, you learned specific aspects about the marketing research industry. Now, in this chapter, you are ready to learn the steps in the marketing research process. There is value in characterizing research projects in terms of successive steps. First, the steps give researchers and nonresearchers an overview of the entire research process. Second, they provide

FIGURE 3.1

Eleven Steps in the
Marketing Research
Process

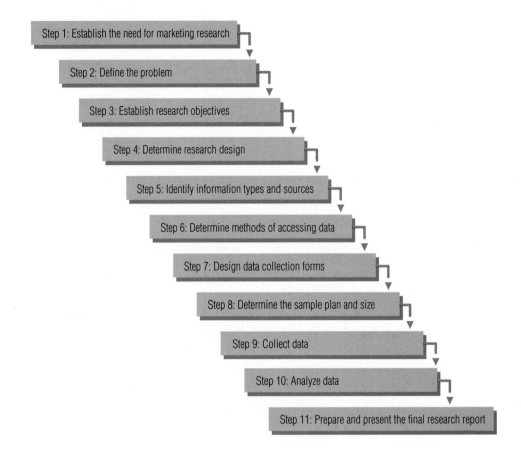

a procedure in the sense that a researcher, by referring to the steps, knows what tasks to consider and in what order. By introducing you to these steps we are also giving you a preview of what is in store as you read the remainder of this book. We identify the **eleven steps in the marketing research process** in Figure 3.1.[1]

The steps are (1) establish the need for marketing research, (2) define the problem, (3) establish research objectives, (4) determine research design, (5) identify information types and sources, (6) determine methods of accessing data, (7) design data-collection forms, (8) determine the sample plan and size, (9) collect data, (10) analyze data, and (11) prepare and present the final research report. We will discuss each of these steps in the following paragraphs, but first we discuss certain cautions associated with using a step-by-step approach to understanding the process of marketing research.

Step-by-Step Process: Words of Caution

WHY ELEVEN STEPS? We want to make certain that you understand some of the cautions you should exercise in learning the eleven-step process. First, while we conceptualize the research process as eleven steps, others may present the process in fewer or more steps. There is nothing sacred about eleven steps. We could present research as three steps: defining the problem, collecting and analyzing data, and presenting the results. We think this oversimplifies the research process. Or, we could present you with twenty-plus steps. In our opinion, this would provide more detail than is needed. We think that eleven steps are explicit without being overly detailed. Keep in mind, however, that everyone does not present the research process in the same way as we present it here.

NOT ALL STUDIES USE EVERY STEP A second caution is, not all studies follow all eleven steps. Sometimes, for example, a review of secondary research alone may allow the researcher to achieve the research objectives. Our eleven steps assume that the research process examines secondary data and continues on to collect primary data.

STEPS ARE NOT SEQUENTIAL Our third and final caution is, most research projects do not follow an orderly, sequential process. In fact, although it is difficult to understand at this point, the steps are interrelated. Sometimes, after beginning to gather data, it may be determined that the research objectives should be changed. Researchers do not move, robotlike, from one step to the next. Rather, as they move through the process, they make decisions as to how to proceed in the future, which may involve revisiting a previous step.

Introducing "Where We Are"

You have already learned that knowing the steps in the marketing research process provides you with a framework that will help you better understand marketing research. Colleen Moore-Mezler stated that her knowledge of these steps helps marketing researchers at Moore Research deal with the complex issues that arise in marketing research. Many of those same issues are presented as you go through this course and this textbook; therefore, we want to provide you with an aid to deal with the rest of the course material. From here on, we introduce a new section at the beginning of every chapter, called "Where We Are." As shown in the margin, this will feature a list of the eleven steps you will learn in this chapter and highlight the step being presented in that particular chapter. This way, even as you immerse yourself in the necessary details of marketing research, "Where We Are" will show you where the material at hand fits into the overall framework of marketing research. Now, let's take a look at our first step!

> **Where We Are:**
> 1. Establish the need for marketing research
> 2. Define the problem
> 3. Establish research objectives
> 4. Determine research design
> 5. Identify information types and sources
> 6. Determine methods of accessing data
> 7. Design data-collection forms
> 8. Determine the sample plan and size
> 9. Collect data
> 10. Analyze data
> 11. Prepare and present the final research report

Step 1: Establish the Need for Marketing Research

When managers try to make decisions with inadequate information, this signals the need for marketing research. Fortunately, not all decisions require marketing research. Because research takes time and costs money, managers must weigh the value that may possibly be derived from conducting marketing research and having the information at hand with the cost of obtaining that information. Fortunately, most situations do not require research. If they did, then managers would be mired down in the process instead of making timely decisions.

COMPANY POLICY REGARDING THE USE OF MARKETING RESEARCH The need for marketing research is affected by the company policy toward its use. Management must make a decision about the role marketing research will play in the organization. Some managers simply do not believe in investing time and money to conduct research. They have a *policy of not conducting marketing research*. However, good decision makers cannot make good decisions without the right information, and relying solely on intuition in today's complex and rapidly changing marketplace is risky business.

For firms that have a policy of using marketing research there are several choices to be made as to how much and how often marketing research will be used. For example, in some firms there is a *policy of conducting different types of studies on a continuous basis at specified intervals*. Some firms conduct customer satisfaction studies twice a year; some firms measure brand awareness quarterly. Conducting marketing research periodically allows management a method of monitoring company performance in order to spot problems early. Secondly, management may adopt a *policy regarding the use of certain types of studies being used whenever a particular situation occurs*. For example, when new products or services are considered, a concept test may be conducted very early in the company's new product development process; or brand awareness studies may be conducted prior to and following advertising campaigns.

> The need for marketing research arises when managers must make decisions without adequate information.

Other firms may elect to conduct marketing research on an *"as needed" basis*. Here, although marketing research is regarded as a useful tool, expenditures are made only when management feels the situation at hand justifies additional information. Company *policy regarding marketing research may also show a preference for the type of research* management prefers. Some managers use focus groups extensively; others rely on quantitative studies based upon large samples. Many packaged goods firms (primarily those products you see in supermarkets) make heavy use of tracking studies. They rely on data from these studies to estimate market shares and use these studies as feedback to tell them how well their strategies and tactics are working.

Regarding the *type* of research a company may require, William D. Neal of SDR Consulting has suggested that there are two broad uses of marketing research. Research information is gathered about markets and used primarily at the marketing department level to plan and assess marketing strategy. Large firms conducting tracking studies, for example, supply this type of information. Huge amounts of data are routinely collected showing sales per SKU in grocery stores, c-stores, and drug stores. Neal referred to this as market research as it reflected marketplace activity. However, Neal points out that marketing research is needed at a higher level in the firm to aid top management in strategic planning. These researchers should provide information that would help managers determine the company mission, objectives and goals, growth strategy, and the business portfolio plan by providing analyses focused on strategic issues such as market segmentation, strategic positioning, new-product development, market forecasting, and brand value analysis.[2] Both types of research are conducted and the company policy toward research will determine which is (or if both are) used.

Even in firms with a proactive policy regarding marketing research, it is sometimes determined inappropriate. The following section describes circumstances that indicate that research is not needed.

WHEN IS MARKETING RESEARCH NOT NEEDED?

The Information Is Already Available   Managers make a number of decisions, many of which are routine and require no additional information beyond a manager's own experience. When decisions require additional information, remember that there are other components of the MIS that the manager may use. Can the necessary information be obtained from the internal reports system, the marketing intelligence system, or the decision support system? All of these information systems are ongoing sources of information. Marketing managers can quickly and inexpensively (low variable cost) access this information. Coca-Cola®, for example, has an extensive database as part of its DSS. Large soft drink firms will have the data needed to forecast the effect on sales if they vary different levels of ingredients in their soft drink brand. When information is *not* available, the researcher should consider conducting marketing research. Marketing Research Application 3.1 provides examples of firms already having the information they need to make decisions.

The Timing Is Wrong   Often, by the time managers decide they need marketing research, time is critical. Consequently, time plays a critical role in making the decision to use marketing research. Even though online research speeds up the marketing research process considerably, other factors may indicate there is simply not enough time to conduct marketing research. As an example, let's assume that the new Nissan Leaf®, a total electric car, has runaway sales and slashes the market share of today's popular hybrids. Other auto firms do not need to do marketing research to "see" where the market preferences are!

Time may also be a factor for products that are nearing the end of their life cycle. When products have been around for many years and are reaching the decline stage of their life cycle, it may be too late for research to produce valuable results.

Knowledge of the steps involved in the marketing research process also helps a researcher determine how long a research project will take to complete. As we've just illustrated, time is

---

Company policy will dictate the use of marketing research in a firm. In some firms, marketing research is not used. In others, marketing research is used on an "as-needed" basis; and in other firms, marketing research studies are conducted periodically as well as a matter of routine for certain activities such as new-product development, advertising effectiveness, or dealer relationship management.

If the market reacts very strongly to a competitor's offering, then there simply isn't time to conduct a marketing research project.

MARKETING RESEARCH APPLICATION 3.1

Practical Applications

Do Not Conduct Research When Information Is Already Available

Marketing researchers John Goodman and David Beinhacker point out that many times companies execute surveys and collect data for information they already have.[3] They point out that clients can save money on research by not measuring variables that are known to be stable and exhibit high performance rates. Secondly, they state that firms should not conduct marketing research when internal metrics are already available.

In one financial services firm, management had commissioned research to measure customer satisfaction and quality. Over a period of time the company had developed and was administering eighty different surveys to cover every possible customer transaction in the firm. Upon examination, however, management determined that about thirty of the eighty transactions showed customer expectations were being met 98% to 99.5% of the time. Should the company be using marketing research to measure transactions for which they are consistently near perfect? The authors conclude that relying on a traditional complaint system would be a wiser method to monitor these transactions.

Goodman and Beinhacker tell the story of a major home repair services company that was spending large amounts to survey customers to find out if service personnel showed up on time. However, the company's call center already had data that tracked how many times customers were calling to complain about service personnel who were either late or failed to show. For a high involvement event such as having someone in your home, the researchers reported 90% of consumers will call when service personnel are late. So, the researchers ask, why conduct marketing research to collect data when you already have the information needed to make the decision?

A bank was surveying customers on their satisfaction with the readiness of automated teller machines (ATMs) because all ATMs must have some "downtime" for maintenance, repair, and daily reloading of cash. Management questioned the need to survey consumers about this when the bank already had internal metrics (data accurate to four decimal places) showing how often the ATMs were down.

The authors first recommend if you are executing eight of ten transactions with little or no error, do not conduct research on all ten transaction types. Focus on those that you do poorly. Neiman Marcus Direct has a good reputation for handling telephone customer service. However, management has identified two types of transactions that give them problems. Therefore, surveys of customers focus on these two transactions, enabling Neiman Marcus to continuously monitor and improve the trouble spots. Second, be certain the data does not already exist before you commission collecting more of the same. The researchers point out that they find many departments operate in silos; other departments in the same company already have internal metrics that will provide the information needed to make an informed decision.

Departments within a company often act as "silos" by not sharing information with other departments.

often critical. In the decision whether to conduct marketing research, knowledge of the steps necessary for any given project will help the researcher estimate the length of time the project will take. This time should be factored into the decision as to whether or not to conduct marketing research.

Funds Are Not Available Today's economic environment brings with it a new era of frugality.[4] In many cases, firms are minimizing marketing research expenditures. Small firms or those with cash-flow problems may not conduct marketing research simply because of the cost. Research, if conducted properly, can be expensive. A study to gather primary data for a representative sample can cost hundreds of thousands of dollars. Also, many times the total cost of research is not fully appreciated. Conducting the research is one cost but, to be useful, firms must also consider what it may cost to *implement* the research recommendations. The owner of a pizza restaurant saved money for a research project but was then unable to fund any of the recommendations (e.g., offer drive-through and delivery service). In this case, the research money was wasted.

> Small firms or firms with cash-flow problems may not conduct marketing research simply because of the cost.

Costs Outweigh the Value Managers should always consider the cost of research and the value they expect to receive from conducting it. Although costs are readily estimated, it is much more difficult to estimate the value that research is likely to add. As an example, consider a decision as to how best to package a new brand of toothpaste. The packaging required to send a few sample boxes to a new-products trade show would certainly not warrant research. The packaging needs only to ensure safe transit. If the packaging fails, little is lost and recovery is simple. However, what about the packaging of the toothpaste itself? The toothpaste must sit on a shelf among other brands, many of which have packaging that is easily recognized by brand-loyal customers. Chances are, a consumer quickly scanning the toothpaste section will see a favorite brand and make the purchase without even being aware of the existence of the new brand. If research can identify a package design that will draw greater attention and promote awareness of the brand on the shelf, sales will increase. This gives the research value, but how much value? Managers must try to estimate what impact there will be on sales if two of every ten shoppers are aware of the

Marketing research that can help a product get attention on supermarket shelves has value.

brand instead of one of every twenty shoppers. Though placing a dollar figure on value is difficult, value *can* be estimated and a more informed decision may be made justifying or not justifying marketing research. Some managers fail to compare research cost with its value, which is a mistake.[5] Recently, Hagins explained how to measure return on investment (ROI) from marketing research.[6]

A beneficial question to ask is, When will research more likely have greater value? Guidelines for answering this question include: Will the research help clarify problems or opportunities? Will research identify changes that are occurring in the marketplace among consumers and/or competitors? Will research clearly identify the best alternative to pursue among a set of proposed alternatives? Will the research help your brand establish a competitive advantage?[7] Once a decision is made that research is needed, managers (and researchers) must properly define the problem and the research objectives.

Step 2: Define the Problem

If a company decides to conduct marketing research, then the second step is to define the problem. This step is the most important, because if the problem is incorrectly defined, all else is wasted effort. As you will see in the latter section of this chapter, we prefer to view the "problem" as a statement of decision alternatives. If there are no alternatives, no decision is necessary. Researchers should only conduct marketing research when they have a decision to make but, as stated, lack the information available to make it.

> A decision consists of decision alternatives. If there are no alternatives, no decision is necessary.

We will devote a latter section of this chapter to issues that should be considered to properly define the problem.

Step 3: Establish Research Objectives

Research objectives, when achieved, provide the information necessary to choose between the decision alternatives identified in step 2. Research objectives tell the researcher exactly how to obtain the information necessary to allow the manager to choose between the decision alternatives. For example, if a manager must choose between two proposed ads, A or B, a research objective may look something like this:

> Research objectives tell the researcher exactly how to obtain the information necessary to allow the manager to choose between the decision alternatives.

> A sample of 300 members of our defined target market will be randomly split into two groups. Both groups will be exposed to a thirty-minute TV pilot program. For one group the pilot program will have ad A spliced into it, appearing as a regular TV ad; the other group will be exposed to ad B. After the pilot is run, respondents in both groups will be asked, "What can you recall about any ads you saw while viewing the pilot progam?" A "recall score" will be composed of the percentage of the audience in each group correctly recalling information about the ads, that is, the brand, product features/benefits presented in the ad, and so forth.

We will revisit research objectives in greater detail later in this chapter.

Step 4: Determine Research Design

Research design refers to the research approach undertaken to meet the research objectives. There are three widely recognized research designs: exploratory, descriptive, and causal designs. **Exploratory research,** as the name implies, is a form of casual, informal research that is undertaken to learn more about the research problem, learn terms and definitions, or identify research priorities. Going to a library to find background information on a topic is an example of exploratory research. **Descriptive research** describes the phenomena of interest. A marketing executive who wants to know what types of people buy the company's brand needs a study to *describe* the demographic profile of heavy users of the company brand. Many surveys are undertaken to describe factors: level of awareness of advertising, intentions to buy a new product, satisfaction level with service, and so on. The last type of research design is **causal research.** Causal studies attempt to uncover what factors *cause* some event. Will a change in the package size of our detergent cause a change in sales? Causal studies are achieved from a class of studies we call experiments. You will learn about these three research designs and when it is appropriate to use each in Chapter 4.

Step 5: Identify Information Types and Sources

Since research provides information to help solve problems, researchers must identify the type and sources of information they will use in step 5. There are two types of information: **Primary information** is collected specifically for the problem at hand; **secondary information** is already collected.

Secondary information should always be sought first, because it is cheaper and faster to access than primary information. Much secondary information is available in published sources and is either free or available for a small fee. Sometimes research companies collect information and make it available to all those wishing to pay a subscription to get the information. This type of information is referred to as syndicated data; Nielsen Media Research ratings, which report the number of persons who watch different television programs, are an example of syndicated data. Secondary information is discussed further in Chapter 5.

Secondary data are not always available, however, or the numbers are inadequate or outdated; then primary data must be collected. Beginning in Chapter 6, our discussion centers on how to gather, analyze, and report primary data.

Step 6: Determine Methods of Accessing Data

Data may be accessed through a variety of methods. While secondary data are relatively easy to glean, accessing primary data is much more complex. When the researcher must communicate with respondents, there are four main choices of accessing data: (1) Have a person ask questions (e.g., conduct an in-home or a telephone survey), (2) use computer-assisted or direct questioning (e.g., computer-assisted telephone interviewing [CATI] or online survey delivered to an e-mail address), (3) allow respondents to answer questions themselves without computer assistance (e.g., mail survey), or (4) use a combination of the first three modes.

> The most popular form of accessing data is through the Web. Furthermore, it seems as though more researchers believe their use of the Web to collect data will be increasing more than any other data collection method in the immediate future.

In the 2007 Confirmit Annual Market Research Survey, a study of 233 marketing researchers in 233 firms located in twenty-seven different countries, researchers Wilson and Macer measured the use of different methods for collecting data by looking at the percentage of total quantitative research revenues generated by each mode. The most popular method was Web-based data collection. The study also presented data that suggest Web, or online, surveys will increase the most in the immediate future. Both CATI and paper (and pencil) surveys are used extensively. In Asia-Pacific countries, paper surveys are used more often, as this area includes remote regions where technology is lacking. Computer-assisted personal interviewing (CAPI), using laptops or tablet PCs, generated 7% of total revenues and is used less in North America than other regions of the world. Hybrid, or mixed-mode, data collection represented just fewer than 6% of the revenues. It was reported that mixed-mode studies are mostly a combination of Web (online) and CATI (telephone) data collection.[8] We will discuss the methods of accessing data, along with their pros and cons, in Chapter 6.

Step 7: Design Data-Collection Forms

Step 7 involves designing the form used for gathering the data. If we communicate with respondents (ask them questions), the form is called a questionnaire. If we observe respondents, the form is called an observation form. In either case, great care must be given to designing the form properly. Care must be taken to ensure that the questions asked will generate answers that satisfy the research objectives and ultimately solve the "problem." The questions must be worded clearly and without bias. Care must also be taken to design the questionnaire so as to reduce refusals to answer questions in order to obtain as much information as desired from respondents. Software programs are available to researchers to assist in creating surveys. Most of these software programs allow users to post surveys on the Web, and data are automatically downloaded into software, such as Excel or Statistical Package for the Social Sciences (SPSS), when respondents complete answers to the survey questions. One such software program is Qualtrics®. You will learn about preparing an objective questionnaire in Chapter 8.

Step 8: Determine Sample Plan and Size

In many cases, marketing research studies are undertaken to learn about populations by taking a sample of that population. A **population** consists of the entire group that the researcher wishes to make inferences about based upon information provided by the sample data. A population could be "all department stores within the greater Portland, Oregon, area" or "college students enrolled in the College of Business at XYZ College." Populations should be defined by the research objectives. One firm, for example, defines its survey population as "between 17 and 70 years old and who make buying decisions for the household regarding technology products." A sample is a subset of the population. **Sample plans** describe how each sample element, or unit, is to be drawn from the total population. Objectives of the research as well as the nature of the sample frame (list of the population elements or units) determine which sample plan is to be used. The type of sample plan used determines whether the sample is representative of the population.

Qualtrics is an example of state-of-the-art online surveying software. Visit Qualtrics at www.qualtrics.com.

A second issue involves **sample size.** How many elements of the population should be used to make up the sample? The size of the sample determines how accurately your sample results reflect values in the population. In Chapter 9 you will learn about both sample plans and sample size. There are several marketing research firms that specialize in helping firms with the sampling process. One such firm is Survey Sampling International (SSI).

Visit Survey Sampling International at www.surveysampling.com.

Step 9: Collect Data

In Chapter 10 you will learn what issues to consider in collecting data. Errors in collecting data may be attributed to fieldworkers or to respondents, and they may be either intentional or unintentional. What is important is that the researcher knows the sources of these errors and implements controls to minimize them. For example, fieldworkers, those collecting the data, may cheat and make up data they report as having come from a respondent. Researchers minimize this from happening by undertaking a control referred to as "validation." Validation means that 10% (the industry standard) of all respondents in a marketing research study are randomly selected, recontacted, and asked if they indeed took part in a research study.

Step 10: Analyze Data

Marketing researchers transfer data from the data-collection forms to computer software programs that aid them in analyzing the data. In Chapter 10 you will learn how to enter data into a program and how to conduct data analysis using the XL Data Analyst™, the data analysis software program that comes with this book. You will learn **data analysis,** including basic descriptive analysis to summarize your data, in Chapter 11. In Chapter 12 you will learn how to generalize values you generate from your sample data to the population, and how to test hypotheses. In Chapter 13 you will learn how to test for differences between groups. For example, are there differences in intention to buy a new brand between different groups? Determining relationships among variables and using regression to predict are the topics covered in

Chapter 14. The objective of data analysis is to use the statistical tools that come with XL Data Analyst™ to present data in a form that satisfies the research objectives. If the research objective, for example, was to determine if there are differences in intention to purchase a new product between four levels of income groups, data analysis should be used to determine if there are any differences in intention to purchase between the income groups and to determine if these differences (based upon sample data) actually exist in the population.

Step 11: Prepare and Present the Final Research Report

The eleventh step in the research process is to prepare and present the marketing research report. The report is very important, because it is often the client's only record of the research project. In most cases, marketing research firms prepare a written research report and make an oral presentation to the client and staff. Marketing researchers follow a fairly standard report-writing format, which is illustrated for you in Chapter 15. Care must be taken to write clearly and to present data accurately using the most appropriate figures and tables. The most important criterion for the report is that it clearly communicates the research findings to the client.

We've just outlined and briefly discussed the steps in the marketing research process. If care is exercised by the researcher and the client, the research process will produce information that can be used to resolve the problem. Pay attention to "Where We Are" in these steps at the beginning of each chapter. This will help you appreciate the research process more as you learn about the details of each step in the marketing research process. We have already discussed step 1 in the marketing research process in the preceding section. Now, in the following sections of this chapter, we continue covering the steps in earnest by examining steps 2 and 3 in depth.

Defining the Problem

What Is the "Problem" and the "Research Objective"?

THE PROBLEM Before we go further, let's clear up what we mean by the concepts "problem" and "research objective." First, let's understand that the context of our discussion centers on a relationship between a researcher(s) and a client, or manager. When we refer to "problem," we are referring to the situation facing the manager or client. As we have discussed already in this chapter, managers must make decisions in order to manage. For our purposes here, we define **problems** as situations that call for managers to make choices among alternatives. When managers make decisions, they have a problem. Sometimes these decisions are so routine and easily made on past experience that they don't really cause much of a "problem" in the sense that they are difficult and they produce anxiety. Making a decision about ordering or not ordering diesel fuel to run a plant's machinery is a routine, straightforward process that is normally not thought of as a problem. Nevertheless, it is one, however minor. Choices must be made and the manager must make the decision. As an example of other problems, managers must choose among alternatives to select new products, choose among advertising copy alternatives, determine the price of the products or services, select dealers, and so on. Managers face a problem when they must decide what type of business they should be in! Notice how some of these problems can create a great amount of anxiety. As we will learn in this chapter, having the right information to make the decision reduces this anxiety. As an example, consider a situation once suggested by the marketing research director of Betty Crocker.[9] He stated: Our chefs bring us three new cookie recipes: A, B, and C. It is up to us to determine if any of these recipes are preferred over the other new recipes and, if so, is that

> Problems are situations calling for managers to make choices among alternatives.

most preferred recipe again preferred over any of our present cookie recipes for cookies now on the market? As we said earlier, a decision consists of decision alternatives, so in this case the decision alternatives are as follows (we assume that the marketing research director will pursue only one new recipe at a time):

Proceed with further consumer testing of the new cookie recipe (A or B or C).
Do not proceed with further consumer testing of new cookie recipe (A or B or C).

Notice it is because the manager has to choose between these decision alternatives and does not already have the information needed to make the choice that we need to conduct marketing research. So in defining the problem, managers must first determine what decisions they must make. Secondly, they must ask if they have adequate information already available to them to make the decision. Managers should not conduct marketing research just "to know something," because marketing research takes time and money to conduct. We will shortly revisit the issue of defining the problem in terms of decision alternatives, but for now you should have a good idea as to what is meant by the "problem." Now let's take a brief look at defining research objectives.

> In defining the problem, managers first determine decisions to be made and define those decisions in the form of alternatives. Second, managers ask if they have adequate information already available to them to make the decision.

THE RESEARCH OBJECTIVE What is a research objective? **Research objectives** are totally dependent on the problem but they are different in that they state what the researcher must do. Research objectives state specifically what information must be produced by the researcher so that the manager can choose the correct decision alternative to solve the problem. Research objectives are specific and tell the researcher exactly what information to collect in order to solve the problem by selecting a decision alternative. A research objective should be specific and should satisfy these four criteria: (1) Specify from *whom* information is to be gathered, (2) specify *what* information is needed, (3) specify the unit of measurement used to gather the information, and (4) word questions used to gather the information in the respondents' frame of reference. See how the example research objective below fulfills these four criteria to provide information for the Betty Crocker manager to determine which decision alternative to select.

> Research objectives are totally dependent on the problem but they are different in that, given the problem, research objectives state specifically what information must be produced by the researcher so that the manager can choose the correct decision alternative to solve the problem.

> Research objective: Conduct a taste test of 400 persons who have purchased cookies within the last month. Conduct a taste test of new cookie recipes A, B, C; and, following consumption of each, ask, "If given a choice, which brand (A, B, or C) would you most likely buy the next time you made a decision to buy cookies?" The latter is to be measured on a 7-point intensity continuum scale ranging from 1 = Very Unlikely to 7 = Very Likely.

Notice that our research objective specifies from *whom* we gather information (from those who have recently purchased cookies); *what* information (likelihood to purchase); the *unit of measurement* (a 7-point scale showing different degrees of likelihood); and the information is gathered using the *respondent's frame of reference* (most consumers will easily understand "most likely buy the next time you made a decision to buy cookies"). We will discuss the criteria for research objectives more thoroughly later in this chapter.

Now you should have a good idea as to the difference between the problem and the research objective. Later in this chapter we will discuss the process used to arrive at the proper problem definition and statement of research objectives.

> Research objectives should (1) specify from *whom* information is to be gathered, (2) specify *what* information is needed, (3) specify the *unit of measurement* used to gather the information, and (4) word questions used to gather the information in the *respondents' frame of reference.*

The Importance of Properly Defining the Problem

Most marketing research practitioners know the name Lawrence D. Gibson. Not only has Mr. Gibson had a long and notable career in marketing research, but he has also taught many seminars helping young practitioners focus on defining the problem correctly. Mr. Gibson states:

> "A problem well-defined is a problem half solved" says an old but still valid adage. How a problem is defined sets the direction for the entire project. A good definition is necessary if marketing

research is to contribute to the solution of the problem. A bad definition dooms the entire project from the start and guarantees that subsequent marketing and marketing research efforts will prove useless. Nothing we researchers can do has so much leverage on profit as helping marketing define the right problem.[10]

Clearly, properly defining the problem is extremely important. Other great problem solvers of our time have recognized the importance of the need to clearly define the problem. Albert Einstein said, "(T)he formulation of a problem is often more essential than its solution."[11] The statistician, Tukey, having discussed type I and type II errors in statistics, coined type III errors as those made solving the wrong problem![12] Tukey's type III error illustrates why problem definition is so important. Even though you defined a problem (incorrectly) there is nothing you can do in the research process to overcome this error. No matter if you use the proper sampling plan or a clear and unbiased questionnaire, achieve a very high response rate, use the proper data analysis techniques, and write a report that clearly and easily communicates to management, all is for naught if you solved the wrong problem.

In other words, properly defining the problem is *the* most important step in the marketing research process. Note that some may state that the first step, determining the need for marketing research, is more important. Their premise is, if we need marketing research and don't use it, this can have disastrous consequences. This may be true, but we're assuming you've made the decision to embark on a research project, so in this sense defining the problem is the most important of the steps.[13,14]

> When you define a problem incorrectly there is nothing you can do in the research process to overcome this error.

> Assuming we are going to conduct marketing research, defining the problem (and research objectives) is *the* most important step in the marketing research process.

A Process for Defining the Problem and the Research Objectives

There is no one universally agreed upon process for defining the problem and the research objectives. In fact, Gibson wrote, "Defining problems accurately is more an art than science."[15] In this next section we introduce you to an approach that practitioners have used successfully for many years in the marketing research industry. Figure 3.2 illustrates the components of this process. Remember, this process assumes management is already using marketing research. We will discuss each of these components in the following paragraphs.

Problem Sources

Failure to Meet an Objective

> There are two sources of problems: "failures to meet objectives" and "opportunities."

At the top of Figure 3.2, note the areas "Recognizing the Problem" and "Sources of Problems." Once we know the sources of problems, we will go back to the top of the figure and discuss what we use to recognize the problem sources. Figure 3.2 shows us two sources of problems, "failure to meet an objective" and "opportunities." First, we recognize that we have a problem when there is a gap existing between what was supposed to happen and what did happen.[16] We call this **"failure to meet an objective."** When, for example, our actual sales are below our sales objective, there is a gap between what was supposed to happen and what actually did happen. This situation is what we normally think of when we indicate a "problem." The manager must now determine what course of action to take in order to close the gap between the objective and actual performance.

Opportunity

> An opportunity occurs when there is a gap between what did happen and what could have happened. This is an opportunity because the situation represents a favorable circumstance or chance for progress or advancement.

The second source of a problem, however, is not often immediately recognized as the "problem." This second source, called an **opportunity,** occurs when there is a gap between what did happen and what could have happened. This is called an opportunity because the situation represents

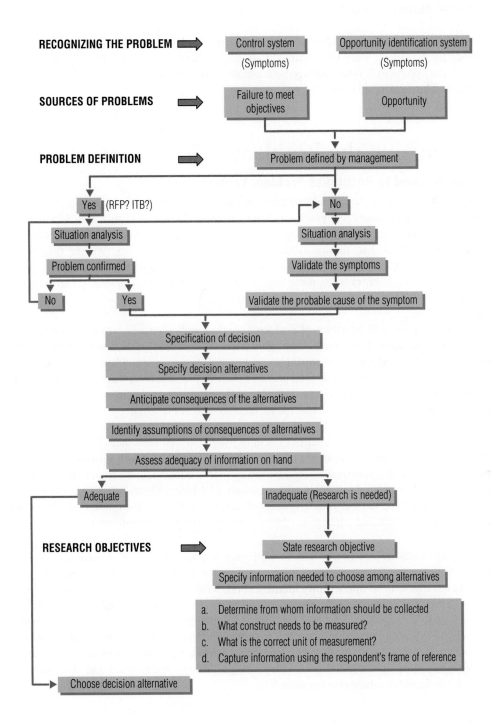

FIGURE 3.2

Defining the Problem and Determining the Research Objectives: Assuming the Use of Marketing Research

"a favorable circumstance or chance for progress or advancement."[17] In other words, a **marketing opportunity** has been defined as an area of buyer need or potential interest in which a company can perform profitably.[18] For example, our sales were $X but *could have been* $Y had we introduced a new, more competitive product. Volkswagen's decision to introduce a new CNG (compressed natural gas) car to the U.S. market represents an opportunity. Even though we refer to this as an opportunity, managers still have a problem in that they must determine whether and how to take advantage of it.

Both of these situations, "failure to meet an objective" and "opportunity," have the same consequence for managers: They must make decisions and, hence, we have what we have defined earlier as the "problem." What management can do to recognize either of these sources of the problem is discussed in the next section.

Recognizing the Problem

Systems Needed to Recognize Problem Sources

CONTROL SYSTEM   It has been said that the only thing worse than having a problem is to have a problem and not be aware that you have it! As we revisit the top of Figure 3.2, "Recognizing the Problem," note that there are different means for recognizing the problem depending on which source generated it: failure to meet an objective *or* opportunity. We see that for the source "failure to meet an objective," we use a control system to recognize this problem. To help them recognize failures to meet objectives, managers must have a control system. Secondly, to help them recognize opportunities, managers must have a system for identification of opportunities.

Good managers will be aware of problems, or they will soon cease to hold management positions. For managers to recognize a problem when the source is "failure to meet objectives," they must be knowledgeable of objectives and actual performance. They should be setting objectives and have a control system in place to monitor performance. This is just sound management practice. To "control" is one of the basic functions of management. Unless managers have a control system, they will not likely identify problems arising from failure to meet objectives.

Good managers will have a control system in place that will alert them to situations where performance is not achieving desired objectives. In fact, a good MIS will provide management with symptoms that this is occurring long before a predetermined date on which the objective is to be assessed. For example, a good sales manager will know which salespersons are ahead, behind, or on schedule to meet quarterly sales objectives early on in the quarter. This lead time allows the manager to make adjustments before the objective goes unrealized.

OPPORTUNITY IDENTIFICATION SYSTEM   Using Figure 3.2, how do managers recognize that they have an opportunity? Managers must have a system for monitoring opportunities, sometimes referred to as a process of **opportunity identification,** without which they will not likely identify these problems.[19] Kotler refers to this process as **market opportunity analysis (MOA).**[20] For example, research explains how we may use a combination of videography and personal introspection to identify opportunities.[21] We are not going to discuss MOA here, but we want to point out that if a company wishes to take advantage of opportunities then a system must be in place to help identify the opportunities when they emerge. Mintel International Ltd. is a firm that specializes in identifying new opportunities.[22]

The Role of Symptoms in Problem Recognition

Note again in Figure 3.2 that we have "symptoms" below both "Control System" and "Opportunity Identification System." What role do symptoms play in problem recognition? The classic statement "We have a problem—we are losing money" illustrates why researchers and managers, in properly defining problems, must be careful to avoid confusing symptoms with problems. The problem is not that "we are losing money." Rather, the problem may be found among all those factors that cause us to make (or lose) money; the manager, with help from the researcher, must identify all those possible causes in order to find the right problem(s).

To help them recognize failures to meet objectives, managers must have a control system. Secondly, to help them recognize opportunities, managers must have a system for identification of opportunities.

For managers to recognize a problem they must be knowledgeable of objectives and actual performance. They should be setting objectives and have a control system in place to monitor performance.

Managers must also be aware of opportunities; and unless they have a system for monitoring them, sometimes referred to as a process of opportunity identification, they will not likely identify these problems.

So managers must be aware that the symptoms are not the problem but the "signals" that alert us of the problem.

Symptoms are changes in the level of some key monitor that measures the achievement of an objective (e.g., our measure of customer satisfaction has fallen 10% in each of the past two months). In this case, the role of the symptom is to alert management to a problem; there is a gap between what should be happening and what is happening. A symptom may also be a perceived change in the behavior of some market factor that implies an emerging opportunity. A pharmaceutical company executive sees a demographic forecast that the number of teenagers will increase dramatically over the next ten years. This may be symptomatic of an opportunity to create new drugs designed for teenage problems such as acne or weight issues. One of the most successful publishing firms in college textbook history was started when Richard D. Irwin saw, while reading the *U.S. Statistical Abstract*, the rapid rise in college of business enrollments following World War II. Irwin recognized this "symptom" as an opportunity to specialize in the publication of textbooks targeted to college of business students. The key lesson, however, is that symptoms are not problems; their role is that they serve as the signals to be used to alert managers to recognize problems.

> Symptoms are not the problem but the "signals" that alert us of the problem.

> Symptoms are changes in the level of some key monitor that measures the achievement of an objective. A symptom may also be a perceived change in the behavior of some market factor that implies an emerging opportunity.

Problem Definition

Before we move on, let's state where we are and where we are headed. If we look back at the top of Figure 3.2, we assume we can "recognize the problem" because we have a system in place to identify either of the two sources of problems: "failures to meet objectives" or "opportunities." Regardless of the source, when managers recognize there is a problem, they must define the problem by identifying the decision alternatives. Sometimes management will define the problem on their own and realize they need additional information in order to make the choice among decision alternatives—thus seeking marketing research after they have defined the problem. If we look at Figure 3.2 we see this case depicted by following the "Yes" path under "Problem Defined by Management." Or, in some cases management is aware of the symptoms and they call upon the researcher to help define the problem. In Figure 3.2, we see this case depicted by following the "No" path under "Problem Defined by Management."

Whether management defines the problem independently and then calls upon marketing research, or management calls upon marketing research to help define the problem, in both cases, the researcher plays an important role. (Remember, we have already recognized that there are many problems that involve management defining the problem and selecting a decision alternative to solve the problem without marketing research. We assume in Figure 3.2 that management has decided to use marketing research.) In the next section we look at the role of the researcher when the problem has been defined by management and when it has not.

> Whether management defines the problem independently or calls upon marketing research to help define the problem, the marketing researcher plays an important role.

The Role of the Researcher in Problem Definition

WHEN MANAGEMENT DEFINES THE PROBLEM IN TERMS OF A DECISION TO BE MADE Our discussion here follows the "Yes" path under "Problem Defined by Management" in Figure 3.2. In some cases, managers have defined what they think the problem is and the decision that must be made to resolve the problem. In this case, the researcher has an obligation to help managers define the problem correctly, particularly when the researcher is called upon by the manager who already has the problem defined in specific terms. Researchers provide value at this junction in the process by bringing in a fresh view, unhindered by biases of recent events, trends, or influences which have dominated the manager's decision-making process. The manager who thinks the problem is choosing between two proposed advertising claims has

> When managers have already defined the problem prior to calling upon researchers, then researchers must resist the temptation to go along with the first definition suggested.

assumed that there are only two claims. Are there others that should be considered? Researchers are trained to think even broader and ask, Is it advertising that is really needed to address the problem? The manager who has defined the problem in terms of a decision to choose a better cookie recipe may be startled to learn that total cookie sales have been falling for the past five years. Perhaps the researcher should ask the question of the manager, "Are you sure you should be in the baked cookie business?" As a problem definition expert, Gibson wrote, "Researchers must resist the temptation to 'go along' with the first definition suggested. They should take the time to conduct their own investigation and to develop and consider alternative definitions."[23] Looking at Figure 3.2, under "Yes," management has already defined the problem for the marketing researchers to handle, so researchers should conduct an additional, preliminary investigation, which may take a different form of research sometimes called a situation analysis. A **situation analysis** is a form of exploratory research undertaken to gather background information and data pertinent to the problem area that may be helpful in properly defining the problem decision. A situation analysis may reveal, for example, that the problem lies not with promotion (so we shouldn't even be discussing the two proposed advertising claims) but with dealer motivation. The point is, researchers have a responsibility to ensure that they are going to address the right problem, even when the problem has been previously defined by management.

> A situation analysis is a form of exploratory research undertaken to gather background information and data pertinent to the problem area that may be helpful in properly defining the problem decision.

At this point we introduce you to a new concept, called invitation to bid (ITB), which resembles the request for proposal (RFP) discussed in Chapter 2. ITBs and RFPs are often used in the marketing research process. Both represent situations where the manager has predetermined the problem decision and is calling upon researchers to present a research proposal to be considered by management. (This is why we place them by the "Yes" in Figure 3.2.) We explain ITBs and RFPs in the following section.

THE ROLE OF ITBs AND RFPs Companies use an **invitation to bid (ITB).** Alternatively, some firms use RFPs, which stands for **"requests for proposals."** Companies use these documents to alert research firms that they would like to receive bids or proposals to conduct research. In either case, the role of the researcher and manager is changed in the problem definition process. As we noted above, when a company uses an ITB (or RFP) these people have already defined the problem and, in some cases, the research objectives; at the very least, management has already considered many of the issues revolving around defining the problem. This means that much of the dialogue that typically occurs between researchers and managers may be circumvented. For example, managers in a firm decide they need to assess customer satisfaction in a way that will allow them to prescribe remedial actions. The problem has been defined; they have specified the decision alternatives in the form of various methods they can use to improve customer satisfaction. They submit an ITB (or RFP) to several research firms who now bid on doing the necessary research. The significance of the ITB (RFP) is that researchers still have an obligation to ensure that the managers have defined the decision problem correctly even when responding to the ITB (RFP). A firm that sends out phony ITBs (RFPs) simply to get ideas for research is practicing highly unethical behavior.

> ITBs are "invitations to bid." Alternatively, some firms use RFPs, which stands for "requests for proposals."

Note in Figure 3.2 that when the problem has been defined by management and after the researcher conducts a situation analysis, the researcher makes a decision as to whether or not the problem is defined correctly. If, according to the researcher, the "Problem Is Confirmed," the decision to be made is stated and we are now ready to proceed to the "Specification of the Decision" which includes "Specify Decision Alternatives."

However, if the researcher cannot confirm the problem as stated by management, the researcher must discuss the situation with management, providing rationale as to why the decision specified by management is the one that should be pursued. If management agrees, the researcher proceeds as if management did not specify the problem decision. But, what if

> If, according to the researcher, the "Problem Is Confirmed," the decision to be made is stated and we are now ready to proceed to the "Specification of the Decision" which includes "Specify Decision Alternatives."

management does not agree? Certainly the researcher should listen carefully to arguments presented by the manager for his or her position and reevaluate the decision. However, if the researcher is still convinced the problem has been defined incorrectly, this creates an ethical situation for the marketing researcher.

WHEN MANAGEMENT DOES NOT DEFINE THE PROBLEM IN TERMS OF A DECISION TO BE MADE Sometimes managers call researchers when they sense that something is wrong and they need help in diagnosing the situation. They may be aware of symptoms but they are not sure what the problem is and hence they are not sure what decision they should make, if any. Here, the researcher's task is more involved. Again, referring to Figure 3.2, the researcher should also undertake a situation analysis.

Conduct a Situation Analysis

As mentioned, researchers should conduct a situation analysis regardless if management has defined the problem. This step may begin with the researcher learning about the industry, the competitors, key products or services, markets, market segments, among other things. The researcher should start with the industry in order to determine if any symptoms, to be identified later, are associated with the entire industry or only with the manager's firm. The researcher should then move to the company itself: the history of the company, its performance, products/services, unique competencies, marketing plans, customers, major competitors, and more. The primary method of conducting a situation analysis is to review both internal and external secondary data. Other methods of conducting a situation analysis include conducting experience surveys (discussions with knowledgeable persons both inside and outside the firm); case analysis (looking at examples of former but similar situations); pilot studies (conducting mini-studies that may reveal problem areas); and focus groups (having small groups discuss topics such as the company's product or service).

Validate Symptoms of the Problem

Next, the researcher should clarify or validate the symptoms. Are we certain we can place faith in the symptoms? After all, we are basing the fact that we have a problem on the symptoms themselves. Are we certain the symptoms are true indicators of what they supposedly represent?

To assess the veracity of the symptoms, the researcher needs to assess the control (or opportunity identification) system in place as well as the symptoms. Companies vary greatly in terms of defining objectives, monitoring results, and taking corrective action. Does the company have an adequate control system to identify symptoms? Are there other symptoms not identified? What are they? Are they accurate measures of performance? Are they reported in a timely fashion? Is there adequate screening of the environment to pick up on opportunities?

When assessing the symptoms, researchers ask specific questions: Are these symptoms true or are they artifacts of the control (or opportunity identification) systems in place? Can the symptoms be corroborated by other factors identified in the situation analysis? Are the symptoms aberrant? Are they likely to appear again? You are beginning to realize, no doubt, that the researcher acts much like a detective. It is the researcher's role to explore and to question, to properly define the problem. Upon validating the symptoms, the researcher is now ready to examine their causes.

Determine Probable Cause of the Symptom

At this point, the manager and researcher should be in agreement about which symptom or symptoms are in need of attention. Now it is time to determine what could possibly cause the symptom(s). To do this we must realize that symptoms do not just change—there is always some **cause** for change. Profits do not go down by themselves. Sales do not drop without customers doing something differently than in the past. Satisfaction scores do not drop without an underlying cause. First, it is important to determine *all* **possible causes.** If only a partial list of causes is made, it is possible that the real cause will be overlooked and we will specify the incorrect decision to be made. To help you visualize this process, let's look at an example of an apartment complex near your university. Let's assume the management has been alerted to symptoms that show the occupancy rate declining from 100% to 80% over the last three semesters. After discussion with the researcher, all possible causes may be categorized as follows: (1) competitors' actions, which had drawn prospective student residents away; (2) changes in the consumers (student target population); (3) something about the apartment complex itself; and (4) general environmental factors. The researcher should discuss these possible causes with management, knowing that there may be several possibilities within each of the four categories; for example, (1) competitors could be reducing rents or "lowering price" by providing free services such as free basic cable television, (2) the number of students at the university may be going down, (3) the apartment building itself may have not been adequately maintained and appears "aging," or (4) financial aid may have decreased on campus and students are less able to afford off-campus housing. The situation analysis should have identified these possible causes. After listing all possible causes under each of the above broad categories, the researcher and manager should narrow the possible causes to a small set of **probable causes,** defined as the most likely factors giving rise to the symptom. In our apartment example, we can assume that the manager and researcher have eliminated many causes for the symptom. For example, there has been no change in financial aid, student enrollment is up, and the apartment building's appearance is on par with, or even better than, competitive apartments. After evaluating all the other possible causes, assume the researcher and manager have reduced the probable cause to competitors offering students free cable television. Notice that something very important has now happened: Management now has a decision to make!

Specification of the Decision

The determination that the probable cause of the symptom in our previous example is "competitors offering free cable television" creates a decision for management. In terms of Figure 3.2, we are now ready to specify the decision to be made (see "Specification of Decision"). Management must now decide what to do to win back market share, and decisions consist of decision alternatives, which management must specify.

Specify Decision Alternatives to Alleviate the Symptom

Managers have at their disposal certain resources, and these resources may provide the decision alternatives they need to address the probable cause of the symptom. Essentially, possible **decision alternatives** include any marketing action that the marketing manager thinks may resolve the problem, such as price changes, product modification or improvement, promotion of any kind, or even adjustments in channels of distribution. It is during this phase that the researcher's marketing education and knowledge come into full play; often both the manager and the researcher brainstorm possible decision alternatives that may serve as solutions.

Once again, it is for the manager to specify *all* of the decision alternatives needed to address the probable cause of the symptom. In fact, one marketing research consultant has gone on record with the bold statement, "Unless the entire range of potential solutions is considered, chances of correctly defining the research problem are poor."[24]

Returning to our apartment complex example, assume the manager examines *all* types of television-delivery systems. One alternative is to offer what the other apartments are offering: free cable television. A second alternative is to try to gain a competitive advantage by offering free satellite television with premium channels. Now the decision alternatives become clear. If the apartment complex offers free satellite television with premium channels, will occupancy rates go back up high enough to offset the extra cost? Or, will occupancy rates rise if the apartment complex meets competition and offers free cable television? The other decision alternative, of course, is to do neither of these options. The latter could be chosen if the marketing research demonstrates that free television service does not affect students' likelihood of selecting an apartment.

Consequences of the Alternatives

Consequences are the results of marketing actions. What are the most likely consequences we can anticipate with each decision alternative? Note that we are *anticipating* a consequence. If we *know* the consequence, there is no need for marketing research. Assuming we don't know the consequence, then research on anticipated consequences, or most likely outcomes, of each alternative under consideration will help determine whether the alternative is correct.

Typically, the range of consequences of possible marketing decision alternatives is readily apparent. For example, if your advertising medium is changed from *People* magazine to *USA Today*, customers will either see less, more, or the same amount of advertising. If we go back to our apartment complex example, it would seem reasonable for the manager to speculate that if free satellite television with premium channels were made available for each apartment, the consequence of this alternative would be occupancy rates that are more than enough to offset the cost of providing the service. Likewise, the manager is making the same assumption for free basic cable television. But, we must ask, How certain is the manager that this will occur? Hasn't the manager made an *assumption* that providing satellite television with premium channels will create a greater demand for the apartment complex?

Identify the Manager's Assumptions About the Consequences of the Alternatives

Returning to Figure 3.2, after we have identified the consequences of the decision alternatives, we must address the assumptions we have made in stating these consequences. Decision makers make assumptions when they assign consequences to decision alternatives. **Assumptions** are assertions that certain conditions exist or that certain reactions will take place if the considered alternatives are implemented. Assumptions deserve researcher attention because they are the glue that holds the decision process together. Given a symptom, the manager *assumes* that certain causes are at fault; and further *assumes* that, by taking corrective actions (alternatives), the problem will be resolved and the symptoms will disappear. In our apartment complex example, the manager's assumption is that free satellite television with premium channels will be a strong enough incentive to cause current students to switch apartments for the next academic year and strong enough to attract new students to select the apartment over that of competitors who only offer free basic cable television. Another assumption is that this demand will be so much greater than the demand for apartments with free cable television that the increase in the demand will more than offset the additional cost of providing the satellite premium channels. As we can see from Figure 3.2, our next step is to determine if we have adequate information on hand to make these assumptions. If we do not feel that information is adequate to make these assumptions, then we will likely need new information. The new information will be gathered by conducting marketing research.

Assess the Adequacy of Information on Hand to Specify Research Objectives

We are almost ready to specify the research objectives, but before that, let's consider a key point: How strongly do we support our own assumptions? How adequate is the information we have upon which we made the assumption? If the manager is *completely certain* that the information is adequate to support the assumptions, then there is no need for research, and the decision may

What are the most likely consequences we can anticipate with each decision alternative? If we do not know these consequences, marketing research can help us by providing information that allows us to predict the consequences.

Decision makers make assumptions when they assign consequences to decision alternatives. Assumptions are assertions that certain conditions exist or that certain reactions will take place if the considered alternatives are implemented.

If we do not feel that information is adequate to make certain assumptions, then we will likely need new information. The new information will be gathered by conducting marketing research.

If the manager is *completely certain* that the information is adequate to support the assumptions, then there is no need for research and the decision may be made. The problem may now be resolved by simply choosing the correct decision alternative (see "Choose Decision Alternative" in Figure 3.2).

Perhaps a researcher questions a manager about his or her beliefs regarding the consequences of certain proposed alternatives. It may turn out that the manager is not really certain after all. It is imperative, therefore, that the manager's assumptions be analyzed for validity.

Information gaps are discrepancies between the current information level and the desired level of information at which the manager feels comfortable resolving the problem at hand. Ultimately, information gaps are the basis for establishing research objectives.

be made. The problem may now be resolved by simply choosing the correct decision alternative (see "Choose Decision Alternative" in the bottom left corner of Figure 3.2). In this case we do not need marketing research, do we? Perhaps a researcher questions a manager about his or her beliefs regarding the consequences of certain proposed alternatives. It may turn out that the manager is not really certain after all. It is imperative, therefore, that the manager's assumptions be analyzed for validity. To assess validity, the researcher assesses the existing **information state,** which is the quantity and quality of evidence a manager possesses for each assumption. During this assessment, the researcher should ask questions about the current information state and determine the desired information state. Conceptually, the researcher seeks to identify **information gaps,** which are discrepancies between the current information level and the desired level of information at which the manager feels comfortable resolving the problem at hand. Ultimately, information gaps are the basis for establishing research objectives. Now let's go back to the apartment complex situation and think about information gaps. Assume the manager felt quite confident about the accuracy of information that free cable television was offered by competitors because they had advertised this new feature as well as announced this new service with signs outside the apartment complexes. Plus, we can assume that the manager was confident that students were interested in having free basic cable television because of the knowledge that virtually all of the tenants had basic cable television in their apartments. However, when the researcher asked, "How do you know that students will desire the 'premium channels'?" the manager stated, "Because there are great movies on these channels. My wife and I watch a movie almost every night." Now, the researcher asked, "But, you don't have to study at night and you are not involved in campus activities and a fraternity or sorority, are you? How do you know that the college students will want the premium channels?" Now the manager admitted, "I really don't know. I haven't even asked any of my own tenants how many of them subscribe to premium channels." To this the researcher asked, "Would knowing that information help you make the decision? What if none of them subscribe to premium channels? Is it because they do not want premium channels or because they can't afford the premium channels?" Now the manager realized that his "certainty" had turned into high "*un*certainty." He has an information gap and he needs more information to close this gap in order to make the right decision. This situation is not unusual.

How confident are you with the assumption that free premium movie channels will be valued by college students?

We shouldn't be too hard on our apartment manager. We often make assumptions and are satisfied with those assumptions until we start asking ourselves hard questions. But, when the decision is important, it's wise to make the right decision alternative choice to solve that problem. In our example, the researcher has convinced the manager that he needs more information to make sure his assumptions are correct. Exactly what information is needed in order to close the information gap? This question leads us to the next step, creating research objectives.

Exactly what information is needed in order to close the information gap? Now, we are ready to create our research objectives!

Research Objectives

Defining Research Objectives

If the manager had the information to close the information gap we just identified, the decision alternative that will best solve the problem could be selected. Remember our discussion of research objectives earlier in this chapter? Recall that we said research objectives state specifically what information must be produced by the researcher so that the manager can choose the correct decision alternative to solve the problem. It is at this point that the researcher is ready to specify the research objectives. Since both the manager and the researcher agree as to the type of information that is needed to close the information gap, they can agree on the research objective. Sometimes hypotheses are stated which may be used to guide the development of the research objective. **Hypotheses** are statements that are taken for true for the purposes of argument or investigation. In making assumptions about the consequences of decision alternatives, managers are making hypotheses. For example, a successful restaurant owner uses a hypothesis that she must use X amount of food in an entrée in order to please customers. This restaurant owner bases her decisions on the validity of this hypothesis; she ensures that a certain quantity of food is served on every plate regardless of the menu choice. Businesspersons make decisions every day based on statements they believe to be true. Sometimes, those decisions are very important and the businessperson may lack confidence in making the correct hypothesis. This is very similar to what we have been discussing about assumptions, isn't it? Sometimes the manager makes a specific statement (an assumption) and wants to know if there is evidence to support the statement. In the instances in which a statement is made, we may use the term *hypothesis* to describe this "statement thought to be true for purposes of a marketing research investigation." Note that not all research is conducted through hypotheses. A research question is often used to guide research. In this case, the question, not being a statement, is not considered a hypothesis. You will learn how to test hypotheses using XL Data Analyst™ later in this book. However, for now, you should understand that when a manager makes a statement assumed to be true but is uncertain and wants the researcher to determine support for the statement, we call these statements hypotheses. Since hypotheses are essentially statements of the decision alternative's assumed consequences, they can be valuable in determining the research objective.

Hypotheses are statements that are taken for true for the purposes of argument or investigation. In making assumptions about the consequences of decision alternatives, managers are making hypotheses.

Stating the research objective is extremely important, for it defines what information will be collected from whom and in what format. The key assessment to be made of the research objective is, If this information, as stated in the research objective, is provided, can a decision alternative be selected? Before we discuss particulars of defining research objectives, let's look back at our apartment complex example. The researcher and the manager agree that they can make the choice in the decision alternatives if they know if students have a greater likelihood of signing a lease with an apartment with free satellite television with premium channels than an apartment with free basic cable service. Secondly, they agree that they will want this information to come from a sample of students who are presently enrolled at the university and will be returning next academic year and who also intend to rent an off-campus apartment.

Since hypotheses are essentially statements of the decision alternative's assumed consequences, they can be very helpful in determining the research objective.

An example of a research objective for our apartment complex example is as follows:

Research Objective: Conduct a survey based upon a representative sample of college students who have stated they intend to rent off-campus apartments during the next academic year to determine the likelihood (measured on a 5-point scale ranging from 1 = Very Unlikely to Rent to 5 = Very Likely to Rent) that, given all factors are equal, students will rent from an apartment providing "free basic cable TV" (with channels available clearly stated) or from an apartment complex providing "free satellite TV with premium channels" (with channels available clearly stated).

Is this a good research objective? Recall earlier in this chapter we listed criteria for writing research objectives. We said that a research objective should (1) specify from *whom* information be gathered, (2) specify *what* information (construct) is needed, (3) specify the *unit of measurement* used to gather the information, and (4) word questions used to gather the information in the *respondents' frame of reference*. Let's consider the criteria used in defining research objectives to answer our question just presented.

FROM WHOM ARE WE GATHERING INFORMATION? Research objectives should address *who* has the information we need. Political pollsters know they must seek information from registered voters. If we are studying factors consumers use in selecting an Internet service provider (ISP), then we should seek information from persons who have recently made this decision. We have already stated that for our apartment complex example we are seeking "students who intend to rent apartments off campus for the next academic year." The research objective should not only specify who is to provide the information sought, but also state *how* these persons are to be included in the sample.

Notice in our research objective above we stated that the students would be surveyed using a "representative sample." (You will learn which types of sampling plans give you a representative sample in Chapter 9.) Notice that other decisions are being made when we specify from whom we are gathering the information. We are assuming these persons we have specified will know the information and will provide it to us accurately. Since most students make their own decisions about where they live at college, the students should know the information we need. This is not always true. A researcher who asks "anyone in the household" about details of the families' financial plans will find that usually only one person in the household is familiar enough with these plans to answer specific questions. A researcher who asks high school seniors about their preferences for on-campus entertainment when they get to college is asking the wrong people. They do not know because they haven't experienced college campus life yet. Finally, not all respondents are willing to give us the information we seek. Will a respondent be willing to give you accurate information on such sensitive topics as speeding tickets, finances, or personal relationships? We must make sure we are asking for information that respondents are *willing* to provide.

WHAT CONSTRUCT DO WE WISH TO MEASURE? Exactly what information do we need to make our choice among the decision alternatives? Recall that earlier in this chapter we discussed a situation where a manager must choose between one of two proposed ads: A or B. Many would say we should choose the "better" of the two but this raises the question of what we mean by "better." It would be difficult to write a research objective without defining what is meant by "better." What information will tell us which ad is "better"? Is it the ad that is more memorable? More relevant? More believable? Least misinterpreted? Most likeable? Most likely to produce a favorable attitude? Most likely to produce an intention to buy the advertised product? Just what is "better"?[25] Each item in our list of different types of information we could collect is a separate **construct,** defined as an abstract idea inferred from specific instances that are thought to be related.[27] The following constructs have been mentioned: memory, relevance, believability, understandability, likeability, attitude, and intention to purchase. For example, marketers refer to the specific instances of someone buying the same brand nine out of ten times as a construct entitled "brand loyalty." Sometimes marketing researchers call the constructs they study variables. Variables are simply constructs that can be measured or quantified in some way. They are referred to as variables because they can take on different

---

Stating the research objective is extremely important, for it defines what information will be collected from whom and in what format. The key assessment to be made of the research objective is: "If this information, as stated in the research objective, is provided, can a decision alternative be selected?"

Memory, relevance, believability, under-standability, likeability, attitude, and intention to purchase are examples of constructs: abstract ideas inferred from specific instances that are thought to be related.[26]

values; that is, they can vary.[28] (Constants, however, do not vary.) A construct provides us with a mental concept that represents real-world phenomena. When a consumer sees an ad for a product and states, "I am going to buy that new product X," marketers would label this phenomenon with the construct called "intention to buy." Marketers use a number of constructs to refer to phenomena that occur in the marketplace. Marketing researchers are constantly thinking of constructs as they go through the problem definition process. Once they know the construct to be measured, they can determine the proper way to measure that construct, which we discuss in the next section.

Finally, it is important to measure the *right* construct. Can you state the construct we have suggested to measure in the research objective stated previously for our apartment complex research project? We could call it "likelihood to rent," which is similar to "intention to rent." To illustrate why the selection of the right construct is important, let's assume we asked a sample of students to tell us what television channels they presently "most *preferred*" to watch. Note that we would be measuring the construct "present preferences for TV channels." Can we make a decision based upon this factor? No, because students have only reported what they prefer to watch *from what is currently available* to them. Those who do not have premium television channels, such as those being considered in our decision, will not list them so we have no basis for making a decision as to how many students prefer them. Therefore, we cannot make a decision because we measured the wrong construct. What we really want to know is if the presence of free satellite television with premium channels will affect their *likelihood to rent* our apartment.

WHAT IS THE UNIT OF MEASUREMENT? Marketing researchers find constructs very helpful because, once it is determined that a specific construct is applicable to the problem, there are customary ways of *operationalizing*, or measuring, these constructs. The research objective should define how the construct being evaluated is actually measured. These definitions are referred to as operational definitions. An **operational definition** is a definition of a construct, such as intention to buy or satisfaction, which describes the operations to be carried out in order for the construct to be measured empirically.[29] For example, let's take the construct "intention to buy." (This is essentially the same as our "likelihood to rent" example.) This construct should represent a person's likelihood to purchase, or patronize, a particular good or service (or to rent an apartment). We know that since few people know with 100% certainty that they will, or will not, purchase something, we measure this construct using a scaled response format, that is, a scale ranging from either 1 to 5 or 1 to 7 or 1 to 10 points, say. (We are not concerned about the number of scale units here. We are simply illustrating that we should measure this construct using a scale of numbers, each representing a different likelihood.) This knowledge becomes very useful in properly formulating research objectives. Researchers can access sources of information that provide them with operational definitions needed to measure many constructs.[30]

What is critical in the formulation of research objectives is that the proper unit of measurement be measured for the construct. To answer what is "proper" we could ask, What unit of measurement will allow the manager to choose between decision alternatives? Let's suppose that the researcher and manager have agreed to make a decision based upon a statistically significant difference between the *mean* likelihood to rent apartments with (a) cable television versus (b) satellite television. By measuring likelihood to rent on a 1 to 5 scale for both apartments with free cable television and satellite television, we can calculate the mean score for each type of service. We can then calculate a significant difference between the two means. This should give us the basis for choosing between the two alternatives. What if we had decided to measure "likelihood to rent" by asking students, "If you had a choice between two similar apartments but one offered free satellite TV with premium channels (and provide list of channels) and the other offered free basic cable TV (and provide list of channels), which would you rent?" Certainly we could do this, but we now have "Yes" or "No" answers. We cannot calculate the means we said we needed in order to make our decision.

Whatever the unit of measurement, the researcher and manager must agree on it *before* defining the research objectives; this will ensure that the choice among alternatives can be made after the research project.

WORD THE INFORMATION REQUESTED IN THE RESPONDENTS' FRAME OF REFERENCE Often in our discussions we use jargon, which is terminology associated with a particular field. Researchers realize that, when formulating research objectives, the information requested of respondents must be *worded using the respondents' frame of reference*. A pharmaceutical manager who is about to initiate a marketing research project with physicians as respondents thinks of a particular drug in terms of dosage, form, differentiating characteristics from the nearest competitor, and so forth. On the other hand, physicians, from whom they must gather information, think first in terms of patient symptoms, disease severity, possible interaction with other drugs, willingness to comply with treatment, among others. The pharmaceutical manager must think of the information needed in terms of the respondent-physician's frame of reference, not his or her own.

If we apply this concept to our apartment complex example, we could say that cable and satellite television companies often speak of "basic," "advanced basic," and "premium" channels. Consumers do not think of television channels in these same terms. Consumers know channels by their names such as MSNBC, CBS, Golf, or HBO. This is why it is important in our example to provide consumers with the actual channels so that they can make an informed decision without having to guess as to what options "premium" channel service includes.

Completing the Process

Turn back and look over Figure 3.2. We started out several pages back by discussing the different sources of problems ("failure to meet objectives" and "opportunities") and the systems needed to recognize those problems. We then looked at problem definition and stated that problems must be couched in terms of decisions and decisions must be couched in the form of decision alternatives. We addressed two different routes for the researcher to take in defining the decision alternatives depending on whether the manager had already defined the problem. We then discussed how decision alternatives contain assumptions and how managers may be uncertain about these assumptions. Uncertainty of assumptions creates what we called information gaps, and those gaps are what research seeks to fill. The research objective specifies exactly what information the researcher must collect in order to fill the information gaps. Once this information is provided, the manager should be able to choose between the decision alternatives. But, exactly how will that decision choice be made? What must the information look like in order for a certain alternative to be selected and another not selected? This is the subject of the next section.

Action Standards

An action standard is the predesignation of some quantity of a measured attribute or characteristic that must be achieved for a research objective in order for a predetermined action to take place. The purpose of the action standard is to define what action will be taken given the results of the research findings.

We've seen how the problem definition and research objectives development process works (Figure 3.2) using our apartment complex example. However, there is another important element to be covered. We must specify action standards. An **action standard** is the predesignation of some quantity of a measured attribute or characteristic that must be achieved for a research objective in order for a predetermined action to take place. The purpose of the action standard is to define what action will be taken given the results of the research findings.[31] In other words, by specifying the action standard we will know, once we receive the information collected by the researcher, which decision alternative to select. In our apartment complex case, we have determined that one research objective should be to collect information that measures *the likelihood that students will rent an apartment which offers free satellite television service with premium channels (as well as the same for free basic cable television).* Recall that we stated in our research objective that we were going to measure the construct, likelihood to rent, measured on a 5-point scale ranging from 1 = Very Unlikely to Rent to 5 = Very Likely to Rent. When we get our research results, how do we know whether to select from our three decision alternatives: (1) Offer free satellite television with premium channels; (2) offer free basic cable television; or (3) do not offer either television service?

We know that we are going to get two means, one for "premium satellite" and one for "basic cable." Recall that we are asking respondents to choose an apartment, if all other factors are equal, based upon the provision of free "premium satellite" or "basic cable." Let's think about the two means and create a situation where it is easy to make the decision; the "premium satellite" mean is 4.8 (high likelihood) and the "basic cable" is 1.0 (very low likelihood) and these two means are statistically significant. Clearly, we should select the "premium satellite" decision alternative.

The manager and the researcher should try to determine, prior to collecting the data, at which point they will still make this decision. Let's assume they decide that if the "premium satellite" mean is above 3.5 and is statistically different from a lower mean for "basic cable," then they will stay with the decision alternative of "premium satellite." In other words, they believe that with any mean of 3.5 or above and with a mean for "basic cable" significantly (statistically) lower, the demand will be high enough to warrant the extra expense of providing the "premium satellite" service. A possible action standard that would warrant choosing neither would be two means that are both below 2. A possible action standard that would warrant installing "basic cable" would be a mean for "basic cable" that is above 3.5 and either is not statistically different from, or is statistically significant *above,* the mean for "premium satellite."

Action standards require you to make important decisions before you collect your information and serve as clear guidelines for action once the research is over. Ron Tatham, former CEO of Burke Inc., states the following:

> The action standard is an important component of the problem definition and research objective determination process because it requires the client to focus on predetermining what information he or she will need in order to take action. Using action standards helps the researcher determine the appropriate research objective because the specification of the action standards tells the researcher what information and in what format they must provide the client. Secondly, action standards allow clients to take action on research results. Without action standards, managers will often say "The results of the research are interesting. I learned a lot about the market but I am not sure what to do next."[32]

Impediments to Problem Definition

Now that you have an appreciation of the process that managers and researchers go through in order to properly define the problem and the research objectives, we can turn to examining why this process does not always go smoothly![33] Properly defining the problem is hampered by two factors: Managers fail to recognize the importance of communicating and interacting closely with researchers,[34] and the differences between researchers and managers may hamper communications.

Failure to Change Behavior for Problem Definition Situations

Sometimes, managers do not recognize that they need to change their normal behavior in order to properly define the problem. Managers are accustomed to dealing with outside suppliers efficiently. Suppliers are asked to present their products/services, they are evaluated against established purchasing criteria, and a decision is made. A minimum of interaction and involvement is required to make most purchasing decisions, and this is viewed as desirable; it leads to accomplishing business activities efficiently. Unfortunately, this behavior does not necessarily change when dealing with an external supplier of marketing research. Professor Sue Jones provides the following:

> It is an accepted wisdom that the stage within a marketing research project of defining the problem is critical; the solution to the research design problem is derived from a full understanding of the marketing problem. Still, it is not uncommon for initial discussions about a research project to involve relatively superficial dialog between clients and researchers; particularly if the latter are not members of the client organization.[35]

Chet Kane refers to this problem by saying that managers commission marketing research projects without direct involvement. He states that managers should be involved in designing the research and actually go out into the field and listen to some of the consumer responses firsthand. Kane says that had managers been more involved in the research they would have known that the positive findings of research for "clear" products (clear beer, clear mouthwash, and clear cola) were based on the novelty or "fad" of the clear products. Had the managers been more involved with the research process they would have understood this. Instead, the "clear" products were failures.[36]

Often, to be effective, this process is slow and tedious. Managers often are unaware of the required change in their behavior, and this causes difficulties in identifying the real problem. Veteran researchers are well aware of this situation and it is up to them to properly inform management of their expected role and the importance of this initial step in the research process.

Differences Between Managers and Researchers

Marketing managers and marketing researchers see the world differently because they have different jobs to perform and their professional backgrounds differ markedly. For example, managers possess line positions; researchers are in staff positions. Managers are responsible for generating profits; researchers are responsible for generating information. Managers are trained in general decision making, and researchers are trained in research techniques.[37] All of these differences hinder communications between two parties at a time when in-depth, continuous communications and trust are required. However, these differences have improved over the years and are growing smaller. The reason is that college students today, tomorrow's managers, are in a better position to learn and have greater appreciation for the technical side of marketing research. Many of the analyses you will learn using the XL Data Analyst™, for example, were once available only to computer specialists who could write the code required to run these analyses on mainframe computers. You will be far better equipped to communicate with marketing researchers than your predecessors.

Formulate the Marketing Research Proposal

Once a marketing researcher and client have agreed upon the problem decision alternatives and the research objectives, the marketing researcher prepares a **marketing research proposal,** the purpose of which is to convey to the manager, in written form, the problem and research objectives and the method that will be employed to collect and analyze the information needed to select the correct decision alternative. This formal document is prepared by the researcher; it serves several important functions: (1) It states the problem, (2) it specifies the research objectives, and (3) it details the research method proposed by the researcher to accomplish the research objectives; it also contains (4) a time table, and (5) a budget.

Summary

Although marketing research projects exhibit great variability, there are enough commonalities among these projects to enable us to characterize them in terms of "steps of the research process." Despite important caveats, the value in characterizing research projects in terms of successive steps are (1) the steps give researchers and nonresearchers an overview of the entire research process, and (2) they provide a procedure in the sense that a researcher, by referring to the steps, knows what tasks to consider and in what order. The eleven steps are (1) establish the need for marketing research, (2) define the problem, (3) establish research objectives, (4) determine research design, (5) identify information types and sources, (6) determine methods of accessing data, (7) design data-collection forms, (8) determine the sample plan and size, (9) collect data, (10) analyze data, and (11) prepare and present the final research report.

The first step is determining the need to conduct marketing research. Can the needed information be obtained from the internal reports system, the marketing intelligence system, or the decision support system? All of these information systems are ongoing sources of information. If these do not supply the information, then marketing research may be needed. Sometimes the need to respond quickly to competition means there isn't time to conduct marketing research. Though placing a dollar figure on value is difficult, value *can* be estimated and a more informed decision may be made justifying or not justifying marketing research.

Problems are situations calling for managers to make choices among alternatives. Research objectives state specifically what information must be produced by the researcher so that the manager can choose the correct alternative to solve the problem. Figure 3.2 depicts a process that may be used for defining the problem and determining the research objectives. There are two sources of problems. One arises when there is a gap between what was *supposed* to happen and what *did* happen. This type of problem is called "failure to meet an objective." The second type of problem arises when there is a gap between what *did* happen and what *could have* happened. We refer to this type of problem as an "opportunity." Managers recognize problems either through monitoring of control systems (in the case of "failure to meet an objective") or through opportunity identification systems (in the case of opportunities). Symptoms are changes in the level of some key monitor that measures the achievement of an objective. Symptoms alert managers to both types of problems. The researcher is responsible for ensuring that management has properly defined the problem even in cases when management has already defined the problem as in the case of ITBs or RFPs. In many cases, a situation analysis is required to help define the problem.

When defining the problem, researchers must validate the symptoms which alerted management to the problem so as to be certain that the symptoms are correctly reporting what they portend to report. Researchers should work with managers to determine *all possible causes* for the symptoms.

Researchers should work with managers to reduce all possible causes down to probable causes. The selection of a probable cause creates the decision. The decision itself must specify alternatives that may be used to stop the symptom. Researchers must work with managers to clearly state the decision alternatives and to determine the consequences of each alternative. Researchers should assess the assumptions managers have made in determining the consequences of each alternative. If the manager is completely certain in the assumptions made, a decision alternative may be selected without further research. However, in most cases, managers are not completely certain about their assumptions. Lack of sufficient information creates an information gap; and it is this information gap that serves as the basis for establishing research objectives. Sometimes hypotheses are stated, which help to guide the development of the research objective.

Research objectives should be specific and should address the following four criteria: (1) Specify from *whom* information is to be gathered, (2) specify *what* information (construct) is needed, (3) specify the *unit of measurement* used to gather the information, and (4) word questions used to gather the information in the *respondents' frame of reference*.

Action standards refer to the predesignation of some quantity of a measured attribute or characteristic that must be achieved for a research objective in order for a predetermined action to take place. Problem definition is sometimes impeded because (a) managers fail to change their normal behavior of dealing with outside suppliers in an efficient manner during problem-solving situations, and (b) managers are usually generalists and researchers tend to be technical. Marketing research proposals are formal documents prepared by the researcher to state the problem, specify research objectives, detail the research method, and specify a time table and budget.

Key Terms

Eleven steps in the marketing
   research process (p. 48)
Exploratory research (p. 53)
Descriptive research (p. 53)
Causal research (p. 53)
Primary information (p. 54)
Secondary information (p. 54)
Population (p. 55)
Sample plans (p. 55)
Sample size (p. 55)
Data analysis (p. 55)
Problems (p. 56)

Research objectives (p. 57)
Failure to meet an objective (p. 58)
Opportunity (p. 58)
Marketing opportunity (p. 59)
Opportunity identification (p. 60)
Market opportunity analysis
   (MOA) (p. 60)
Symptoms (p. 61)
Situation analysis (p. 62)
Invitation to bid (ITB) (p. 62)
Request for Proposals (RFPs) (p. 62)
Cause (p. 63)

Possible causes (p. 64)
Probable causes (p. 64)
Decision alternatives (p. 64)
Consequences (p. 65)
Assumptions (p. 65)
Information state (p. 66)
Information gaps (p. 66)
Hypotheses (p. 67)
Construct (p. 68)
Operational definition (p. 69)
Action standard (p. 70)
Marketing research proposal (p. 72)

Review Questions

1. What are the eleven steps in the marketing research process?
2. Use an example to illustrate that the steps in the marketing research process are not always taken in sequence.
3. Explain why firms may not have a need for marketing research.
4. Why is defining the problem the most important step in the marketing research process?
5. Explain why research objectives differ from the definition of the problem.
6. What are the three types of research that constitute research design?
7. Which part of the research process ensures that the sample is representative?
8. Which part of the research process ensures the accuracy of the results?
9. What is meant by the "problem"?
10. What is the research objective?
11. Briefly overview the process presented in the chapter for defining both the problem and the research objective.
12. What are the two sources of marketing problems?
13. Explain how managers should recognize they have a problem.
14. What is the role of symptoms in problem recognition?
15. What is the role of the researcher when management has already defined the problem?
16. What is a situation analysis and when would it likely be used when defining the problem?
17. How do ITBs and RFPs influence the problem definition process?

18. What is the role of the researcher when management has *not* already defined the problem?
19. What is meant by the researcher validating the symptoms?
20. What is the difference between (a) all possible causes and (b) probable causes?
21. Discuss why "defining the problem" is really stating the decision to be made along with the decision alternatives.
22. What is meant by "consequences" of the decision alternatives?
23. Explain how assumptions play a role in the problem definition process.
24. Use Figure 3.2 and explain what happens when the information on hand is adequate.
25. Explain the information state when there are information gaps.
26. What is needed to close information gaps?
27. What is the role of a hypothesis in defining the problem?
28. What are some factors considered to be important in determining research objectives?
29. What role do constructs play in the problem definition/research objectives process?
30. What is an operational definition and where would it likely be used?
31. What is an action standard?
32. Discuss impediments to problem definition.
33. What are the components of the marketing research proposal?

Application Questions

34. Go to the Internet and do a search for marketing research firms. Look through their Web pages. Can you identify examples of what they are presenting to you as relating to the eleven steps in the research process?

35. Go to your library's online databases or the Internet and look for examples of firms conducting a marketing research study. There are many examples reported in periodicals such as *Advertising Age, Marketing News, Business Week*, and *Forbes*. Typically, these articles will mention a few details of the research project itself. Identify as many of the steps in the marketing research process as possible that are referred to in the articles you find.

36. Observe any business in your community. Examine what it does, what products or services it provides, its pricing policy, its promotions, or any other aspect of its business. Try to determine whether you, as manager of the business, would have conducted research to determine the firm's products, their design, features, prices, promotion, and so on. If you decide that you would not have conducted marketing research on a given area, explain why.

37. Think of what you may imagine as being an opportunity in the marketplace. Explain how Figure 3.2 would help you in conducting or not conducting marketing research.

Case 3.1 **Golf Technologies Inc.**

Golf Technologies Inc. (GTI) relies on high-level scientific testing to design golf clubs that provide larger "sweet spots" resulting in fewer miss-hits and maximum yardage. In the last year, they discovered a technical breakthrough. Their newest designed clubs, for the same level of energy, hit the golf ball one-half club length longer than any existing clubs on the market. Harvey Pennick, CEO, is very excited about this new breakthrough and believes the new clubs will create a new level of excitement and enthusiasm among players. Pennick is well aware that many club manufacturers tout "new, scientific breakthroughs" with each year's new model clubs. He also knows that consumers have become fairly immune to these "breakthrough" claims made each year. He believes he must do something different to convince the potential buyers that the new line of GTI clubs actually does have a larger sweet spot and they actually do hit the ball farther. Armed with objective tests that prove these claims, Pennick and his marketing staff believe they need a highly credible golfer to be used in their promotional materials (television ads, magazine ads, infomercials, and special event promotions). The credibility of the message in GTI's promotions will be critical if golfers are to really believe this breakthrough in club design.

Pennick's staff present the two golfers whom they believe are the best known: Tiger Woods and Phil Mickelson. Both golfers are considered among the best golfers in the world and have very high name recognition. However, both these golfers have current exclusive contracts with other club manufacturers. Both contracts have buy-out clauses, so if GTI is to hire either one of them, it will be very expensive both to buy out the existing contract and to offer enough money to attract either of these world-class golfers. GTI will need only one of these golfers to be their new spokesperson.

1. Assuming Pennick agrees with his staff on the choice of Woods or Mickelson, what now is Pennick's decision in terms of decision alternatives?

2. Assuming that Pennick is not confident in his assumptions about the consequences of the outcomes associated with your decision alternative, what should Pennick consider doing?

3. Should Pennick decide to conduct marketing research, write the research objective.

Case 3.2 **Your Integrated Case**

Advanced Automobile Concepts

Recall in Case 1.2 that Nick Thomas is the new CEO of Advanced Automobile Concepts (AAC), a new division of a large automobile manufacturer, ZEN Motors. ZEN is a multinational manufacturer headquartered in the United States, and has multiple divisions representing several automobile and truck brands. ZEN's divisions have been slowly losing market share to other competitors. AAC was created to revive the aging ZEN automobile brands by either reengineering existing models or developing totally new models that are more competitive in today's new-car market.

Thomas is concerned about the strategic direction AAC should take. On the one hand, he knows the trend has been toward smaller, fuel-efficient automobiles; but on the other hand, he knows that this may be a passing trend, similar to what occurred in the 1970s when fuel costs soared. This previous spike led to greater demand for smaller cars and diesel engines for passenger cars. However, as soon as OPEC countries lowered their prices, Americans had a growing demand for larger cars for many years. This eventually led to the SUV craze of the 1990s through about 2006. Now, a few years after oil prices again spiked in 2008, he wonders if consumers really believe oil prices will remain high. If consumers believe this, they will probably prefer smaller, fuel-efficient vehicles. If they do not, he believes demand for these smaller vehicles will be a passing fad.

A second issue that concerns Thomas is the market's attitudes toward global warming. He is concerned because even though he realizes the scientific community is in reasonable agreement about global warming, there is enough controversy in the information environment to cause consumers to wonder if concern for global warming is real. Also, Thomas doesn't know how to deal with global warming in terms of the direction he should take with his automobiles. He knows consumers have varied thoughts about global warming. Some believe it is a hoax. These consumers enjoy citing record-low temperatures which appear from time to time. Other consumers believe there may be global warming but it is a natural phenomenon of the earth's temperature cycles. These consumers do not believe mankind contributes to global warming. If either of these arguments—either it doesn't exist or it exists but mankind does not affect it—becomes widely accepted, then global warming will have little effect on automobiles. On the other hand, if consumers believe their automobile exhaust affects global warming and it is a real potential threat to life on the planet Earth, there could be tremendous changes in the types of automobiles desired in the near future.

Not long after Thomas was hired as CEO, he hired Marilyn Douglass, former director of marketing research at Nord Motors, who has many years of experience working in the automotive industry. Nord Motors is a major competitor of ZEN. Thomas wanted Douglass on his team because he felt he needed someone to interpret consumers' future automotive needs. He asked Douglass to prepare a report summarizing what she felt were the major automobile alternatives for ZEN to consider. Her report, referred to in the company as the "Douglass Report," outlined the following major alternatives.

Regarding fuels, ZEN should consider only making hybrid autos in the near future. ZEN has another division of top researchers who are investigating new fuels and engines of the future. They have spent considerable time on developing a hydrogen cell but it will be several years before they have perfected a version that will be safe for public use. The rationale for Douglass's decision about hybrids is that some form of electric motor should be used. They are quiet, almost maintenance free, and the cost per mile is much cheaper than present internal combustion engines. But, the problem with all electric vehicles is their poor infrastructure to support the vehicle. For example, an all-electric car will not be useful except in very limited conditions due to restrictions on its range. For now, the range is not sufficient on the best of electric cars for use without the widespread availability of electrical plug-in receptacles needed to recharge the car. This is not something that will change overnight and even if there are plugs available, there must be meters with pay receptacles allowing users to pay for the electricity consumed. This may occur in limited situations but it will be many years before the driving public has such an infrastructure available.

Douglass believes that all electric cars will find a niche in the market but that the range limitation would cap sales. She believes that several manufacturers will enter this business and will develop different vehicles for different purposes. These vehicles will differ in terms of speeds, passenger space and storage payloads, range, and cost. She believes there will be many market entries, competition will be fierce, and no one will get an upper hand on the volume needed to earn respectable profits.

The Douglass Report suggests that ZEN's best opportunity will reside with hybrids that use both electric power and engine power, using either gasoline, diesel, biodiesel, or even CNG. The key to the future was thought to be hybrid cars with an electric motor charged by and alternating with an internal combustion engine. Her best choice for the engine fuel for now is biodiesel simply because diesel engines get higher miles per gallon (mpg) than gasoline and there is not likely to be a major change in the infrastructure needed to make biodiesel widely available. Some form of diesel will be necessary for the trucking industry, for example, for years to come. The Douglass Report recommends that this decision be confirmed by others at ZEN.

The report stated that ZEN's competitiveness will depend on selecting the car designs (models) that best meet market demand. The underlying premise is that all vehicles will need to have high mpg ratings and that demand will differ depending on the size of the vehicles. Generally speaking, the larger the vehicle the less the mpg; so the smallest vehicle will have "very high" mpg and the largest proposed model will have "good" mpg. Some broad choices include:

a. Very small, one-seat vehicle designed to get near maximum mpg
b. Small, two-seat vehicle designed to get high mpg

c. Larger, economy/compact size, four-seat vehicle designed to get good mpg
d. Large, standard size, five- to six-seat vehicle with conventional trunk space designed to get reasonably good mpg

How many of these models will ZEN want to create, manufacture, and market? The Douglass Report explains that there may very well be enough demand to justify several ZEN models. It will be critical to determine which models have the greatest demand. Secondly, Douglass warned that just because we have an energy and environmental crisis, the car-buying public will not be satisfied with one solution. Similar to the market today, there are varied segments and each may prefer a unique model to best satisfy their demands and to determine market segments.

Finally, the Douglass Report discusses the need to market vehicles in the future as efficiently as possible. Two factors are given for the additional efficiency requirements in the future. First, there will be increased competition. Start-up firms will be encouraged by new governmental policies to produce new, energy-saving vehicles. Second, profit margins will be lower on smaller vehicles of the future. As noted earlier, smaller cars traditionally have been priced competitively; they do not have the "higher" price points of some of the larger, luxury cars. Marketing efforts will need to clearly "reach" the market segments with promotional materials without wasting promotional dollars on market segments that are not interested in the vehicle being promoted. Media can be purchased that targets markets based upon knowledge of standard demographic data, such as gender, marital status, number of persons in a household, age, level of education, job category, income, dwelling type, number of vehicles owned/leased, and type of vehicle owned (economy, standard, luxury, SUV, pickup truck, van). Also, dealer locations can be selected based on other factors, such as size of the city.

Thomas read the Douglass Report carefully. He believed it was a good point to start the decision-making process, but he needed additional information.

1. How would you describe the "source" of the problem(s) facing Nick Thomas?
2. Focus just on one area identified in the Douglass Report: demand for the different basic models. How would you write this problem?
3. Given what you wrote in question 2, write the research objective.

Research Design Alternatives and Qualitative Research

4

Research Design Alternatives and Qualitative Research

LEARNING OBJECTIVES

- To understand what research design is and why it is significant

- To learn how exploratory research design helps the researcher gain a feel for the problem by providing background information, suggesting hypotheses, and prioritizing research objectives

- To know the fundamental questions addressed by descriptive research and the different types of descriptive research

- To explain what is meant by causal research and to describe types of experimental research designs

- To know the different types of test marketing and how to select test market cities

- To know the difference between qualitative and quantitative research and to know several approaches to conducting qualitative research

TNS Global Uses Experiments to Increase Client Sales in Convenience Stores

TM A salty snack brand manufacturer thought there was a potential for increased sales in the convenience store channel. In this case, two chains of stores, widely dispersed geographically, were selected to represent the channel, nationally. Obviously, there would be many variables across all the chains nationally, but understanding what drove sales in two chains could provide valuable insight for the channel. The basic experimental design here is referred to as a *controlled store test*, since two panels of matched stores were selected in each chain: Experimental A vs. Control A; Experimental B vs. Control B, where A and B are the chains. In this chapter you will learn about the importance of having equivalent experimental and control groups in an experiment.

The study began with tracking shopper behavior in stores, and interviewing them to learn more about their habits and practices in convenience stores *before* suggestions were made in terms of store design, layout, and merchandising.

The PathTracker® study of where shoppers went in a few stores, how long they spent there, and what categories they visited, as well as interviews at the exits, revealed that those who buy snacks on impulse are usually coming to the store to pay for gas. The primary path in a convenience store goes from the entrance to the checkout and/or to the cold vault. This is an example of doing preliminary exploratory research before the experiment.

Review of all the data from the exploratory research suggested that successful snack aisles will be located on the primary path to the

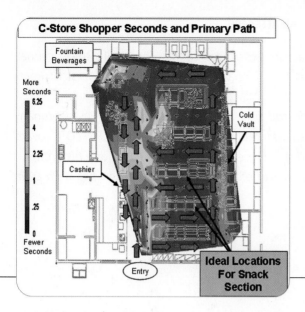

C-Store Shopper Seconds and Primary Path

Fountain Beverages

More Seconds
6.25
4
2.25
1
.25
0
Fewer Seconds

Cashier

Cold Vault

Entry

Ideal Locations For Snack Section

checkout and beverages and will vertically divide chips and other salty snacks (e.g., nuts). Salty snacks will be grouped by product type and within each type items will be brand blocked.

For the experiment, all of the experimental stores had the recommended new shelf location and merchandise configuration installed. These changes constituted manipulation of the independent variable. As you will also learn in this chapter, we kept the control stores in their pretest conditions. The dependent variable was sales, and sales were recorded for both experimental and control stores, on a week-by-week basis, for the entire prior year, plus the twelve weeks of the experiment, and four weeks of posttest. Not only did having pretest and posttest measures allow us to calculate the experimental effect (E), but we also obtained a good understanding of other variables such as seasonality, local neighborhood, and store-specific extraneous variables.

The net result of this project was that sales of chips and nuts/seeds increased with the new independent variable. Other salty snacks increased only slightly. Of great interest was that although the brand manufacturer's product sales increased significantly, from the retailer's point of view, more importantly, the sales of *all* of the category brands increased.

Herb Sorensen is a preeminent authority on observing and measuring shopping behavior and attitudes within the four walls of the store. He has worked with Fortune 100 retailers and consumer packaged goods manufacturers for more than thirty-five years, studying shopper behavior, motivations, and perceptions at the point of purchase. Sorensen's patented shopper tracking technology PathTracker® is helping to revolutionize retail marketing strategies from a traditional "product-centric" perspective to a new "shopper-centric" focus.

Herb Sorensen, Ph.D., Scientific Director, TNS Global/Retail & Shopper Practice

Sorensen has conducted studies in North America, Europe, Asia, Australia, and South America. His research has been published in AMA's Marketing Research, The Journal of Advertising Research, FMI Advantage Magazine, Progressive Grocer, *and* Chain Drug

Review, *and he has been utilized as an expert source for* The Wall Street Journal, Supermarket News, *and* BusinessWeek. *Additionally, he is currently a panelist of Retail Wire's "Brain Trust."*

Sorensen was named one of the top fifty innovators of 2004 by *Fast Company Magazine, and shared the American Marketing Association's 2007 EXPLOR Award for technological applications that advance research, with Peter Fader and his group at the Wharton School of Business, University of Pennsylvania. Sorensen has a Ph.D. in biochemistry.*

Source: Herb Sorensen, TNS Global.

Where We Are:

1. Establish the need for marketing research
2. Define the problem
3. Establish research objectives
4. **Determine research design**
5. Identify information types and sources
6. Determine methods of accessing data
7. Design data-collection forms
8. Determine the sample plan and size
9. Collect data
10. Analyze data
11. Prepare and present the final research report

We begin our journey into research design by looking at our opening vignette which is an example of one type of design, causal research. In this chapter we closely examine why some studies are called experiments, and why experiments alone can lead us to understand causality.[1] We will also learn that all studies are not experiments. In fact, relatively few studies are actually experiments. This takes us to other types of research designs: exploratory and descriptive research. In this chapter we will learn the circumstances that determine when to use a particular research design and lead you to a basic understanding of all three research designs: exploratory, descriptive, and causal. We will also look at test marketing and another way of classifying marketing research, qualitative and quantitative research.

Research Design

There are many different ways marketing research studies are carried out. Some projects are experiments of food tasting held in kitchenlike labs; others are focus groups, simulated test markets, or large, nationally representative sample surveys, among others. Some research objectives require only library research, whereas others may require thousands of personal interviews; other studies require observation of consumers in convenience stores, while another may involve two-hour-long, in-depth, personal interviews in respondents' homes.

Each type of study has certain advantages and disadvantages, and one method may be more appropriate for a given research problem than another. How do marketing researchers decide which method is the most appropriate? After thoroughly considering the problem and research objectives, researchers select a **research design,** which is a set of advance decisions that makes up the master plan specifying the methods and procedures for collecting and analyzing the needed information.

After thoroughly considering the problem and research objectives, researchers select a research design, which is a set of advance decisions that makes up the master plan specifying the methods and procedures for collecting and analyzing the needed information.

The Significance of Research Design

Marketing researcher David Singleton, of Zyman Marketing Group Inc., believes that good research design is the first rule of good research.[2] Every research problem is unique. In fact, one could argue that, given each problem's unique customer set, area of geographical application, and other situational variables, there are so few similarities among research projects that each study should be completely designed as a new and independent project. In a sense this is true; almost every research problem is unique in some way or another, and care must be taken to select the most appropriate set of approaches for the unique problem and research objectives at hand.

There are reasons to justify the significance placed on research design. First, as we just stated, even though every problem and research objective may seem unique, there are usually enough similarities among problems and objectives to allow us to make some decisions in advance about the best plan to use to resolve the problem. Second, there are basic marketing research designs that can be successfully matched to given problems and research objectives. In this way, they serve the researcher much like the blueprint serves the builder. Once the problem and the research objectives are known, the researcher selects a research design.

> Even though every problem and research objective may seem unique, there are usually enough similarities among problems and objectives to allow us to make some decisions in advance about the best plan to use to resolve the problem. There also are basic marketing research designs that can be successfully matched to given problems and research objectives.

Three Types of Research Designs

Research designs are classified into three traditional categories: exploratory, descriptive, and causal. The choice of the most appropriate design depends largely on the objectives of the research. It has been said that research has three objectives: to gain background information and to develop hypotheses, to measure the state of a variable of interest (e.g., level of brand loyalty), and to test hypotheses that specify the relationships between two or more variables (e.g., level of advertising and brand loyalty). Note also that the choice of research design is dependent on how much we already know about the problem and research objective. The less we know, the more likely it is that we should use exploratory research. Causal research, on the other hand, should only be used when we know a fair amount about the problem and we are looking for causal relationships among variables associated with the problem or the research objectives. We shall see how these basic research objectives are best handled by the various research designs.[3]

> Research designs are classified into three traditional categories: exploratory, descriptive, and causal. The choice of the most appropriate design depends largely on the objectives of the research.

Research Design: A Caution

Before discussing the three types of research design, we warn you about thinking of research design solely in a step-by-step fashion. Some may think that it is implied in this discussion that the order in which the designs are presented—that is, exploratory, descriptive, and causal—is the order in which these designs should be carried out. This mindset is incorrect. First, in some cases, it may be perfectly legitimate to begin with any one of the three designs and to use only that one design. Second, research is an "iterative" process; by conducting one research project, we learn that we may need additional research, and so on. This may mean that we need to utilize multiple research designs. We could very well find, for example, that after conducting descriptive research, we need to go back and conduct exploratory research. Third, if multiple designs are used in any particular order (if there is an order), it makes sense to first conduct exploratory research, then descriptive research, and finally causal research. The only reason for this order pattern is that each subsequent design requires greater knowledge about the problem and research objectives on the part of the researcher.

> It may be perfectly legitimate to begin with any one of the three designs and to use only that one design.

Exploratory Research

Exploratory research is most commonly unstructured, informal research that is undertaken to gain background information about the general nature of the research problem. By unstructured, we mean that exploratory research does not have a predetermined set of procedures. Rather, the nature of the research changes as the researcher gains information. It is informal in that there is no formal set of objectives, sample plan, or questionnaire. Other, more formal research designs are used to test hypotheses or measure the reaction of one variable to a change in another variable. Yet, exploratory research can be accomplished by simply reading a magazine or even observing a situation. Ray Kroc, the milkshake machine salesman who created McDonald's, observed that restaurants in San Bernardino, California, run by the McDonald brothers were so busy they burned up more milkshake machines than any of his

> Exploratory research is most commonly unstructured, informal research that is undertaken to gain background information about the general nature of the research problem.

You could say that Ray Kroc's idea to start McDonald's was based on exploratory research when he began to question why the McDonald brothers' restaurants used up so many milkshake machines.

other customers. Kroc took that exploratory observation and turned it into the world-famous fast-food chain. In another example, an eighteen-year-old college student sitting in line at a McDonald's drive-through awaiting a cheeseburger saw an old dilapidated truck, loaded with junk, with a sign "Mark's Hauling." This observation set in motion Brian Scudamore's ideas to launch a new type of junk service called "1-800-GOT-JUNK?" Soon he was making so much money he dropped out of college as the company grossed revenues near $100 million.[4] Exploratory research is very flexible in that it allows the researcher to investigate whatever sources he or she desires and to the extent necessary in order to gain a good feel for the problem at hand.

Exploratory research is usually conducted when the researcher knows little about the problem and needs additional information or desires new or more recent information. Often exploratory research is conducted at the outset of research projects.

USES OF EXPLORATORY RESEARCH Exploratory research is used in a number of situations: to gain background information, to define terms, to clarify problems and hypotheses, and to establish research priorities.

Exploratory research is usually conducted when the researcher knows little about the problem and needs additional information or desires new or more recent information.

Gain Background Information When very little is known about the problem or when the problem has not been clearly formulated, exploratory research may be used to gain much-needed background information. Even for experienced researchers it is rare that some exploratory research is not undertaken to gain current, relevant background information. There is far too much to be gained to ignore exploratory information.

Exploratory research is used in a number of situations: to gain background information, to define terms, to clarify problems and hypotheses, and to establish research priorities.

Define Terms Exploratory research helps to define terms and concepts. By conducting exploratory research to define a question, such as "What is satisfaction with service quality?" the researcher quickly learns that "satisfaction with service quality" is composed of several dimensions—tangibles, reliability, responsiveness, assurance, and empathy. Not only would exploratory research identify the dimensions of satisfaction with service quality but it could also demonstrate how these components may be measured.[5]

When very little is known about the problem or when the problem has not been clearly formulated, exploratory research may be used to gain much-needed background information.

Clarify Problems and Hypotheses Exploratory research allows the researcher to define the problem more precisely and to generate hypotheses for the upcoming study. For example, exploratory research on measuring bank image reveals the issue of different groups of bank customers. Banks have three types of customers: retail customers, commercial customers, and other banks for which services are performed for fees. This information is useful in clarifying the problem of the measurement of bank image because it raises the issue of which customer group bank image should be measured.

Exploratory research can also be beneficial in the formulation of hypotheses, which are statements describing the speculated relationships among two or more variables. Formally stating hypotheses prior to conducting a research study is very important to ensure that the proper variables are measured. Once a study has been completed, it may be too late to state which hypotheses are desirable to test.

Establish Research Priorities Exploratory research can help a firm prioritize research topics. A summary account of complaint letters by retail store may tell management where to devote valuable attention. One furniture store chain owner decided to conduct research on the feasibility of carrying office furniture after some exploratory interviews with salespeople revealed that their customers often asked for directions to stores carrying office furniture.

METHODS OF CONDUCTING EXPLORATORY RESEARCH A variety of methods are available to conduct exploratory research, and some of these we will cover in the section of this chapter that deals with qualitative research since the methods overlap. In this section we briefly discuss commonly used methods for conducting exploratory research: secondary data analysis, experience surveys, and case analysis. Other methods, common to both exploratory research and qualitative research, are discussed later in the chapter as part of our discussion of methods of conducting qualitative research.

Secondary Data Analysis By **secondary data analysis,** we refer to the process of searching for and interpreting existing information relevant to the research topic. Secondary data have been collected for another purpose and are almost always a part of a marketing research project. Secondary data, or information, are widespread and readily available. Thanks to the Internet and today's sophisticated search engines such as Google® you can conduct a search for secondary information on virtually any topic quickly and efficiently. Your library and the Internet give you access to large amounts of secondary data, which include information found in books, journals, magazines, special reports, bulletins, newsletters, and more. An analysis of secondary data is often the "core" of exploratory research.[6] A search of secondary data or information may come in many forms. Most executives subscribe to journals or trade publications for their particular industry. By reviewing these publications they are doing a form of exploratory research: looking for trends, new innovations, information about present or potential customers, competitors, the general economy, for example. We devote part of Chapter 5 to analyzing secondary data and sources.

Experience Surveys **Experience surveys** refer to gathering information from those thought to be knowledgeable on the issues relevant to the research problem. A manufacturer of a new building material that provides greater insulation at less cost may call a dozen contractors and describe the new material and ask them how likely it would be that they would consider using it on their next building. Volvo, believing that in the past autos had been designed by and for males, asked 100 women what they wanted in a car. They found major differences between what women want and what is available, and they used this information in designing vehicles.[7] Experience surveys differ from surveys conducted as part of descriptive research in that there is usually no formal attempt to ensure that the survey results are representative of any defined group of subjects. Nevertheless, useful information can be gathered by this method of exploratory research.

Case Analysis By **case analysis,** we mean a review of available information about a former situation(s) that has similarities to the present research problem. Usually, there are few research situations that do not have some similarities to past situations.[8] Even when the research problem deals with a radically new product, there are often similar past experiences that may be observed. For example, when Apple introduced the iPad® even though this was a product new to the market, Apple had plenty of experience with examining other new product introductions, such as Amazon's Kindle®. Though often useful, researchers must be cautious in using former case examples for current problems because situations change. For example, consumers are much savvier about buying electronic products than they were even a few years ago. Consumers today are also much more aware of the general economic situation than they were a few years ago.

Our concluding words about exploratory research are, first, some form of it should almost always be used to some extent, because this type of research, particularly secondary data analysis,

Our concluding word about exploratory research is that some form of it should almost always be used to some extent. Few researchers embark on a research project without doing some exploratory research.

is fast. You can conduct quite a bit of exploratory research online within a matter of minutes using online databases or a search engine to surf the net. Second, compared to collecting primary data, exploratory research is cheap. Third, sometimes exploratory research either provides information to meet the research objective or assists in gathering current information necessary to conduct either a descriptive or causal research design. Therefore, few researchers embark on a research project without doing some exploratory research.

Descriptive Research

Descriptive research is undertaken to describe answers to questions of who, what, where, when, and how.

Descriptive research is undertaken to describe answers to questions of who, what, where, when, and how. When we wish to know *who* our customers are, *what* brands they buy and in what quantities, *where* they buy the brands, *when* they shop, and *how* they found out about our products, we turn to descriptive research. Descriptive research is also desirable when we wish to project a study's findings to a larger population. If a descriptive study's sample is representative, the findings may be used to predict some variable of interest such as sales.

CLASSIFICATION OF DESCRIPTIVE RESEARCH STUDIES There are two basic descriptive research studies available to the marketing researcher: cross sectional and longitudinal. **Cross-sectional studies** measure units from a sample of the population at only one point in time.

A study measuring your attitude toward adding a required internship course in your degree program, for example, would be a cross-sectional study. Your attitude toward the topic is measured at one point in time. Cross-sectional studies are prevalent in marketing research, outnumbering longitudinal studies and causal studies. Because cross-sectional studies are one-time measurements, they are often described as "snapshots" of the population.

As an example, many magazines survey a sample of their subscribers and ask them questions about their age, occupation, income, educational level, and more. These sample data, taken at one point in time, are used to describe the readership of the magazine in terms of demographics. Cross-sectional studies normally utilize fairly large sample sizes, so many cross-sectional studies are referred to as sample surveys.

Sample surveys are cross-sectional studies whose samples are drawn in such a way as to be representative of a specific population. *ABC News* often conducts surveys on some topic of interest to report on the evening news. The surveys' samples are drawn such that ABC may report that the results are representative of the population of the United States and that the results have, for example, a "margin of error of + or −3%." So sample surveys may be designed in such a way that their results are representative and accurate, within some margin of error, of the true values in the population. (You will learn how to do this as you study this book.) Sample surveys require that their samples be drawn according to a prescribed plan and to a predetermined number. Later on, you will learn about these sampling plans and sample size techniques (see Chapter 9).

Longitudinal studies repeatedly measure the same sample units of a population over a period of time. Panels represent sample units who have agreed to answer questions at periodic intervals. Maintaining a representative panel of respondents is a major undertaking.

Longitudinal studies repeatedly measure the same sample units of a population over a period of time. Because longitudinal studies involve multiple measurements, they are often described as "movies" of the population. Longitudinal studies are employed by almost 50% of businesses using marketing research.[9] To ensure the success of the longitudinal study, researchers must have access to the same members of the sample, called a panel, so as to take repeated measurements. **Panels** represent sample units who have agreed to answer questions at periodic intervals. Maintaining a representative panel of respondents is a major undertaking.

Several commercial marketing research firms develop and maintain consumer panels for use in longitudinal studies. Typically, these firms attempt to select a sample that is representative of some population. Firms such as Knowledge Networks and Nielsen have maintained panels consisting of hundreds of thousands of households for many years. In many cases these companies will recruit panel members such that the demographic characteristics of the panel are proportionate to the demographic characteristics found in the total population according to Census Bureau statistics. Sometimes these panels will be balanced demographically not only to the United States in total but also within each of the various geographical regions. In this way, a client who wishes to get information from a panel of households in the Northwest can be assured that the panel is demographically matched to the total population in the states making up the northwestern region. Many companies maintain panels to target market segments such as "dog owners" or "kids" (ages six to fourteen years; see www.Kidzeyes.com). Note that panels are not limited to consumer households. They may consist of building contractors, supermarkets, physicians (Epocrates QuickRecruit® at www.epocrates.com/services/marketresearch/quickrecruit), lawyers, universities, or some other entity.

Online research created the opportunity for several new companies to emerge, offering panels recruited to respond to online queries. One such company is Lightspeed Research, which offers clients panels of consumer households. Greenfield Online is another firm that offers clients access to its online panel of consumers.

There are two types of panels: continuous panels and discontinuous panels. **Continuous panels** ask panel members the same questions on each panel measurement. **Discontinuous panels** vary questions from one panel measurement to the next.[10] Continuous panel examples include syndicated data panels that ask panel members to record their purchases using diaries or scanners. The essential point is that panel members are asked to record the *same* information (e.g., grocery store purchases) multiple times. Discontinuous panels are sometimes referred to as **omnibus panels**. (*Omnibus* means "including or covering many things or classes.") They may be used for a variety of purposes, and the information collected by a discontinuous panel varies from one panel measurement to the next. How longitudinal data are applied depends on the type of panel used to collect the data. Essentially, the discontinuous panel's primary usefulness is that it represents a large group—people, stores, or some other entity—and its members are agreeable to providing marketing research information. Discontinuous panels, like continuous panels, are also demographically matched to some larger entity, implying representativeness as well. Therefore, a marketer wanting to know how a large number of consumers, matched demographically to the total U.S. population, feel about two different product concepts may elect to utilize the services of an omnibus panel. The advantage of discontinuous (omnibus) panels is that they represent a group of persons who have made themselves available for research. In this way, then, discontinuous panels represent existing sources of information that may be quickly accessed for a wide variety of purposes. Ipsos Public Affairs Omnibus panel is a discontinuous panel.

The continuous panel is used quite differently. Usually, firms are interested in using data from continuous panels because they can gain insights into *changes* in consumer purchases, attitudes, and so on. For example, data from continuous panels can show how members of the panel switched brands from one time period to the next. Studies examining how many consumers switched brands are known as **brand-switching studies.** Such studies can be invaluable to brand managers because two cross-sectional studies may show changes in market shares between several brands but they can be misleading. If brands A and B increase, brands C and D remain the same, and brand E decreases, then a brand manager for E cannot determine to which brand or brands the customers are switching. However, with a brand-switching study conducted using a continuous panel, the brand manager may learn that former brand E customers are switching to brand B. This would enable the brand manager to focus on the marketing strategies being used by brand B.

Another use of longitudinal data is that of market tracking. **Market-tracking studies** measure some variable(s) of interest, that is, market share or unit sales over time.

Causal Research

Causal research determines causality. Causality may be thought of as understanding a phenomenon in terms of conditional statements of the form "If *x*, then *y*." These "if–then" statements become our way of manipulating variables of interest. For example, if the thermostat is lowered, then the air will get cooler. If I drive my automobile at lower speeds, then my gasoline mileage will increase. If I spend more on advertising, then sales will rise. Marketing managers are always trying to determine what

For an example of a panel company, visit www.greenfield-ciaosurveys.com.

Continuous panels ask members the same questions on each panel measurement. Discontinuous panels vary questions from one panel measurement to the next.

Causal relationships are determined by the use of experiments, which are special types of studies.

Ipsos' Omnibus Panel service can provide clients fast answers to their questions.

Source: By permission, Ipsos Public Affairs.

An experiment is defined as manipulating an independent variable to see how it affects a dependent variable, while also controlling the effects of additional extraneous variables.

will cause a change in consumer satisfaction, a gain in market share, or an increase in sales. In one experiment, marketing researchers investigated how color versus noncolor and different quality levels of graphics in Yellow Page ads caused changes in consumer attitudes toward the ad itself, the company doing the advertising, and perceptions of quality. The results showed that color and high-photographic graphics cause more favorable attitudes; but the findings differ depending on the class of product being advertised.[11] This illustrates how complex cause-and-effect relationships are in the real world. Understanding what causes consumers to behave as they do is extremely difficult. Nevertheless, there is a high "reward" in the marketplace for even partially understanding causal relationships. Causal relationships are determined by the use of experiments, which are special types of studies. Many companies conduct experiments online.[12]

Independent variables are those variables which the researcher has control over *and* wishes to manipulate. Some independent variables include level of advertising expenditure, type of advertising appeal (humor, prestige), display location, method of compensating salespersons, price, and type of product.

EXPERIMENTS An **experiment** is defined as manipulating an independent variable to see how it affects a dependent variable, while also controlling the effects of additional extraneous variables. **Independent variables** are those variables which the researcher has control over *and* wishes to manipulate. Some independent variables include level of advertising expenditure, type of advertising appeal (humor, prestige), display location, method of compensating salespersons, price, and type of product. **Dependent variables,** on the other hand, are those variables that we have little or no direct control over, yet we have a strong interest in. Typical dependent variables include sales, market share, customer satisfaction, sales force turnover, net profits, and ROI. Certainly, marketers are interested in changing these variables, but because they cannot change them directly, marketers attempt to change them through the manipulation of independent variables. To the extent that marketers can establish causal relationships between independent and dependent variables, they enjoy some success in influencing the dependent variables much like you know that to change your GPA (dependent variable) you must change certain independent variables such as amount of time devoted to study and class attendance.

Dependent variables, on the other hand, are those variables that we have little or no direct control over, yet we have a strong interest in.

Extraneous variables are those that may have some effect on a dependent variable but yet are not independent variables. To illustrate, let's say you and your friend wanted to know if the brand of gasoline (independent variable) affected gas mileage in automobiles (dependent variable). Your "experiment" consists of each of you filling up your two cars, one with brand A, the other with brand B. At the end of the week, you learn that brand A achieved 18.6 miles per gallon and brand B achieved 26.8 miles per gallon. Does brand B cause better gas mileage than brand A? Or could the difference in the dependent variable (gas mileage) be due to factors *other* than gasoline brand (independent variable)? Let's take a look at what these extraneous variables may be: (1) One car is an SUV and the other is a small compact. (2) One car was driven mainly on the highway and the other was driven in the city in heavy traffic. (3) One car has properly inflated tires, the other car does not. All these other, extraneous, variables could have caused the difference in the dependent variable.

> Extraneous variables are those that may have some effect on a dependent variable but yet are not independent variables.

Let's look at another example. Imagine that a restaurant chain conducts an experiment to determine the effect of supplying nutritional information on menu items (independent variable) on restaurant sales (dependent variable).[13] Management has a record of restaurant sales without menu-supplied nutritional information and then changes (manipulates the independent variable) the menu to include the nutritional information and measures sales once again. The experiment is conducted in one of the chain's restaurants. Assume sales increased. Does this mean that if the restaurant changes the menu information, then sales will increase in all the chain's restaurants? Could there be other extraneous variables that could have affected sales? Could the following two variables affect the restaurant's sales: (1) The restaurant selected for the experiment is located in a high-income area in California known for health spas and workout gyms; and (2) just prior to changing the menu, the FDA announced a study that caloric content for the same type of food had wide variation depending on the restaurant (coffee ranges in calories from 80 to 800 per cup; hamburgers range from 250 to over 1,000)? Yes, the clientele for the restaurant selected for the experiment could be unique and a new, highly publicized study about nutritional information from a respected source, the FDA, could certainly have had an effect on the acceptance of the new menu information. In fact, it could have helped create "buzz" or positive word-of-mouth influence. Both these possible influences are likely extraneous variables which have an effect on the dependent variable, yet themselves are not defined as independent variables. As this example illustrates, it would be difficult to isolate the effects of independent variables on dependent variables without controlling for the effects of the extraneous variables. Unfortunately, it is not easy to establish causal relationships, but it can be done. In the following section, we see how the design of an experiment allows us to assess causality.

EXPERIMENTAL DESIGN An **experimental design** is a procedure for devising an experimental setting such that a change in a dependent variable may be attributed solely to the change in an independent variable. In other words, experimental designs are procedures that allow experimenters to control for the effects on a dependent variable by an extraneous variable. In this way, the experimenter is assured that any change in the dependent variable was due only to the change in the independent variable.

> An experimental design is a procedure for devising an experimental setting such that a change in a dependent variable may be attributed solely to the change in an independent variable.

Let us look at how experimental designs work. First, we list the symbols of experimental design:

O = The measurement of a dependent variable
X = The manipulation, or change, of an independent variable
R = Random assignment of subjects (consumers, stores, and so on) to experimental and control groups
E = Experimental effect, that is, the change in the dependent variable due to the independent variable

When a measurement of the dependent variable is taken *prior to* changing the independent variable, the measurement is sometimes called a **pretest.** When a measurement of the dependent variable is taken *after* changing the independent variable, the measurement is sometimes called a **posttest.**

A **"true" experimental design** is one that truly isolates the effects of the independent variable on the dependent variable while controlling for effects of any extraneous variables.

A "true" experimental design is one that truly isolates the effects of the independent variable on the dependent variable while controlling for effects of any extraneous variables.

Designs that do not properly control for the effects of extraneous variables on our dependent variable are known as **quasi-experimental designs.** Control of extraneous variables is typically achieved by the use of a second group of subjects, known as a control group. By **control group,** we mean a group whose subjects have not been exposed to the change in the independent variable. The **experimental group,** on the other hand, is the group that has been exposed to a change in the independent variable. By having these two groups as part of our experimental design, we can overcome many of the problems associated with the quasi-experimental designs presented thus far. We shall use the following true experimental design to illustrate the importance of the control group.

Before-After with Control Group The **before-after with control group** design may be achieved by randomly dividing subjects of the experiment into two groups: the control group and the experimental group. If we assume that our restaurant chain has 100 restaurants around the country we could easily divide them randomly into two groups of 50 restaurants each. Management already has a pretest measurement of the dependent variable taken on both groups by virtue of knowing sales volume prior to changing the menus. Next, the independent variable, adding the nutritional information to the menus, is changed only in the experimental group (50 restaurants). Finally, after some time period, posttest measurements are taken of the dependent variable in both groups of restaurants. This design may be diagrammed as follows:

$$\text{Experimental group } (R) \; O_1 \times O_2$$
$$\text{Control group } (R) \; O_3 \quad O_4$$

Where:

$$E = (O_2 - O_1) - (O_4 - O_3).$$

By randomly dividing our 100 restaurants into two groups—50 in the experimental group and 50 in the control group—then the groups should be equivalent. That is, both groups should be as similar as possible, each group having an equal number of restaurants in high-income, middle-income, and low-income areas, and an equal number of restaurants in locales favoring exercising and nutrition concern. In fact, the average age of the restaurants should be equal, the average square footage should be equal, the average number of employees should be equal, and the average sales should be equal. In other words, randomization should yield two groups of restaurants that are equivalent in all respects. An experimenter should take whatever steps are necessary to meet this condition when using this design. There are other methods for gaining equivalency besides randomization. Matching on criteria thought to be important, for example, would aid in establishing equivalent groups. When randomization or matching on relevant criteria does not achieve equivalent groups, more complex experimental designs should be used.[14]

Looking back at our design, the R indicates that we have randomly divided our restaurants into two equal groups—one a control group, the other an experimental group. We also see that pretest measurements of our dependent variable, restaurant sales, were recorded for both groups of restaurants as noted by O_1 and O_3. Next, we see by the X symbol that only in the experimental group of restaurants were the menus changed to add the nutritional information for the menu items. Finally, posttest measurements of the dependent variable were taken at the same time in both groups of restaurants, as noted by O_2 and O_4.

Now, what information can we gather from this experiment? First, we know that $(O_2 - O_1)$ tells us how much change occurred in our dependent variable during the time of the experiment. But was this difference due solely to our independent variable, X? No, $(O_2 - O_1)$ tells us how many dollars in sales may be attributed to (1) the change in menu information, and (2) other extraneous variables, such as the FDA publicizing the wide variation in nutritional values obtained in restaurant meals or just that more people decided to eat in restaurants during this time interval. Now, let us look at what is measured by the differences in sales among our control restaurants $(O_4 - O_3)$.

Because it cannot account for changes in restaurant sales due to a change in menu information (the menus were not changed), then any differences in sales as measured by $(O_4 - O_3)$ must be due to the influence of all extraneous variables on restaurant sales. Therefore, the difference between the experimental group and the control group, $(O_2 - O_1) - (O_4 - O_3)$, results in a measure of E, the "experimental effect." We now know that if we change menu information, then restaurant sales will change by an amount equal to E. We have, through experimentation using a proper experimental design, made some progress at arriving at causality. However, we should point out here, though we have established causality, it did not come without cost and complexity. Notice our experiment went from changing menus in a single store to 50 stores, and our total experiment involved 100 stores!

As we noted earlier, there are many other experimental designs, and, of course, there are almost limitless applications of experimental designs to marketing problems. Although we have demonstrated how valuable experimentation can be in providing us with knowledge, we should not accept all experiments as being valid. How we assess the validity of experiments is the subject of our next section.

HOW VALID ARE EXPERIMENTS? How can we assess the validity of an experiment? An experiment is valid if (1) the observed change in the dependent variable is, in fact, due to the independent variable, and (2) the results of the experiment apply to the "real world" outside the experimental setting.[15] Two forms of validity are used to assess the validity of an experiment: internal and external.

Internal validity is concerned with the extent to which the change in the dependent variable was actually due to the independent variable. This is another way of asking if the proper experimental design was used and if it was implemented correctly. To illustrate an experiment that lacks internal validity, let us return to our change in menu information example. Recall that we took the effort to expand our restaurants to 100 and randomly divided them into two groups, to ensure that the experimental group and the control group were, in fact, equivalent. What would happen if the researcher did not ensure the equivalency of the groups? Our experimental effect, E, could be due to the differences in the two groups; that is, one group of restaurants was located in areas with clientele sensitive to nutrition. This difference in the groups, then, would represent an extraneous variable that had been left uncontrolled. Such an experiment would lack internal validity because it could not be said that the change in the dependent variable was due solely to the change in the independent variable. Experiments lacking internal validity have little value because they produce misleading results. Sometimes organizations will conduct studies and present them as "experiments" in order to intentionally mislead others.

External validity refers to the extent that the relationship observed between the independent and dependent variables during the experiment is generalizable to the "real world."[16] In other words, can the results of the experiment be applied to all the restaurants in the chain? There are several threats to external validity. How representative is the sample of test units? Is this sample really representative of the population? Additionally, there exist many examples of the incorrect selection of sample units for testing purposes. For example, some executives, headquartered in large cities in cold winter climates, have been known to conduct "experiments" in warmer, tropical climates during the winter. Although the experiments they conduct may be internally valid, it is doubtful that the results will be generalizable to the total population.

Another threat to external validity is the artificiality of the experimental setting itself. In order to control as many variables as possible, some experimental settings are far removed from real-world conditions.[17] If an experiment is so contrived that it produces behavior that would not likely be found in the real world, then the experiment lacks external validity.

TYPES OF EXPERIMENTS We can classify experiments into two broad classes: laboratory and field. **Laboratory experiments** are those in which the independent variable is manipulated and measures of the dependent variable are taken in a contrived, artificial setting for the purpose of controlling the many possible extraneous variables that may affect the dependent variable.

> Internal validity is concerned with the extent to which the change in the dependent variable was actually due to the independent variable.

> External validity refers to the extent that the relationship observed between the independent and dependent variables during the experiment is generalizable to the "real world."

> Laboratory experiments are those in which the independent variable is manipulated and measures of the dependent variable are taken in a contrived, artificial setting for the purpose of controlling the many possible extraneous variables that may affect the dependent variable.

To illustrate, let us consider a study whereby subjects are invited to a theater and shown test ads, copy A or copy B, spliced into a television "pilot" program. Why would a marketer want to use such an artificial, laboratory setting? Such a setting is used to control for variables that could affect the purchase of products other than those in the test ads. By bringing consumers into a contrived laboratory setting, the experimenter is able to control many extraneous variables. For example, you have learned why it is important to have equivalent groups (the same kind of people watching copy A as those watching copy B commercials) in an experiment. By inviting preselected consumers to the television pilot showing in a theater, the experimenter can match (on selected demographics) the consumers who view copy A with those who view copy B, thus ensuring that the two groups are equal. By having the consumers walk into an adjoining "store," the experimenter easily controls other factors such as the time between exposure to the ad copy and shopping, as well as consumer exposure to other advertising by competitive brands. As you have already learned, any one of these factors, left uncontrolled, could have an impact on the dependent variable. By controlling for these and other variables, the experimenter can be assured that any changes in the dependent variable were due solely to differences in the independent variable, ad copy A and copy B. Laboratory experiments, then, are desirable when the intent of the experiment is to achieve high levels of internal validity.

There are advantages to laboratory experiments. First, they allow the researcher to control for the effects of extraneous variables. Second, compared to field experiments, lab experiments may be conducted quickly and with less expense. Obviously, the disadvantage is the lack of a natural setting, and therefore, concern for the generalizability of the findings to the real world. **Field experiments** are those in which the independent variables are manipulated and the measurements of the dependent variable are made on test units in their natural setting. Many marketing experiments are conducted in natural settings, such as in supermarkets, malls, retail stores, and consumers' homes. Let us assume that a marketing manager conducts a *laboratory* experiment to test the differences between ad copy A, the company's existing ad copy, and a new ad copy, copy B. The results of the laboratory experiment indicate that copy B is far superior to the company's present ad copy A, but before spending the money to use the new copy, the manager wants to know if ad copy B will actually create increased sales in the real world. She elects to run the new ad copy in Erie, Pennsylvania, a city noted as being representative of the average characteristics of the U.S. population. By conducting this study in the field, the marketing manager will have greater confidence that the results of the study will hold up in other real-world settings. Note, however, that even if an experiment is conducted in a naturalistic field setting in order to enhance external validity, the experiment is invalid if it does not also have internal validity.

The primary advantage of the field experiment is that of conducting the study in a naturalistic setting, thus increasing the likelihood that the study's findings will also hold true in the real world. Field experiments, however, are expensive and time consuming. The experimenter must also be alert to the impact of extraneous variables, which are difficult to control in the natural settings of field experimentation.

The example we just cited of using Erie, Pennsylvania, for a field experiment would be called a "test market." Much of the experimentation in marketing, conducted as field experiments, is known as test marketing. For this reason, test marketing is discussed in the following section.

> Field experiments are those in which the independent variables are manipulated and the measurements of the dependent variable are made on test units in their natural setting.

Test Marketing

> Test marketing is the phrase commonly used to indicate an experiment, study, or test that is conducted in a field setting.

Test marketing is the phrase commonly used to indicate an experiment, study, or test that is conducted in a field setting. Companies may use one or several test market cities, which are selected geographical areas in which to conduct the test. There are two broad classes of use of test markets: (1) to test the sales potential for a new product or service, and (2) to test variations in the marketing mix for a product or service.[18]

Although test markets are expensive and time consuming, the costs of introducing a new product on a national or regional basis routinely amount to millions of dollars. The costs of the test market are then justified if the results of the test market can improve a product's chances of success. Sometimes the test market results will be sufficient to warrant further market introductions. Sometimes the test market identifies a failure early on and saves the company huge losses. The GlobalPC, a scaled-down computer targeted for novices, was tried in test markets. The parent company, MyTurn, concluded that the test market sales results would not lead to a profit, and the product was dropped before the company experienced further losses.[19] Test markets are conducted not only to measure sales potential for a new product but also to measure consumer and dealer reactions to other marketing-mix variables. A firm may use only department stores to distribute the product in one test market city and only specialty stores in another test market city in order to gain some information on the best way to distribute the product. Companies can also test media usage, pricing, sales promotions, and more, through test markets. Products and services in both the consumer (BtoC) and industrial (BtoB) markets may be test marketed.

Types of Test Markets

Test markets have been classified into four types: standard, controlled, electronic, and simulated.[20] The **standard test market** is one in which the firm tests the product or marketing-mix variables through the company's *normal* distribution channels. A negative of this type of test market is that competitors are immediately aware of the new product or service. However, standard test markets are good indicators as to how the product will actually perform because they are conducted in real settings.

Controlled test markets are conducted by outside research firms that guarantee distribution of the product through prespecified types and numbers of distributors. Companies specializing in providing this service provide dollar incentives for distributors to guarantee them shelf space. Controlled test markets offer an alternative to the company that wishes to gain fast access to a distribution system set up for test market purposes. The disadvantage is that this distribution network may or may not properly represent the firm's actual distribution system.

Electronic test markets are those in which a panel of consumers has agreed to carry identification cards that each consumer presents when buying goods and services. These tests are conducted only in a small number of cities in which local retailers have agreed to participate. The advantage of the card is that as consumers buy (or do not buy) the test product, demographic information on the consumers is automatically recorded. In some cases, firms offering electronic test markets may also have the ability to link media viewing habits to panel members as well. In this way, firms using the electronic test market also know how different elements of the promotional mix affect purchases of the new product. Obviously, the electronic test market offers speed, greater confidentiality, and less cost than standard or controlled test markets. However, the disadvantage is that the test market is one more step removed from the real market.[21]

Simulated test markets (STMs) are those in which a limited amount of data on consumer response to a new product is fed into a model containing certain assumptions regarding planned marketing programs, which generates likely product sales volume.[22]

There are many advantages to STMs. They are much faster and only cost 5% to 10% of the cost of a standard test market. STMs are confidential; competitors are less likely to know about the test. The primary disadvantage is that STMs are not as accurate as full-scale test markets because they are dependent on the assumptions built into the models.[23]

Selecting Test Market Cities

There are three criteria that are useful for selecting test market cities: **representativeness, degree of isolation,** and **ability to control distribution and promotion.** Because one of the major reasons for conducting a test market is to achieve external validity, the test market city should be representative of the marketing territory in which the product will ultimately be distributed. Consequently, a great deal of effort is expended to locate the "ideal" city in terms of comparability with characteristics of the total U.S. (or other country) population. The "ideal" city is, of

Test markets have been classified into four types: standard, controlled, electronic, and simulated.

Controlled test markets are conducted by outside research firms that guarantee distribution of the product through prespecified types and numbers of distributors.

Electronic test markets are those in which a panel of consumers has agreed to carry identification cards that each consumer presents when buying goods and services.

Simulated test markets (STMs) are those in which a limited amount of data on consumer response to a new product is fed into a model containing certain assumptions regarding planned marketing programs, which generates likely product sales volume.

The three criteria that are useful for selecting test market cities are representativeness, degree of isolation, and ability to control distribution and promotion.

course, the city whose demographic characteristics most closely match the desired total market. For instance, R. J. Reynolds chose Chattanooga, Tennessee, to test-market its Eclipse "smokeless" cigarette because Chattanooga has a higher proportion of smokers than most cities, and R. J. Reynolds needed to test Eclipse with smokers.[24]

When a firm test-markets a product, distribution of the product and promotion of the product are isolated to a limited geographical area, such as Tulsa, Oklahoma. If the firm advertises in the *Tulsa World* newspaper, the newspaper not only covers Tulsa but also has very little "spillover" into other sizable markets. Therefore, the company, along with its dealers, competitors, and so on, is not likely to get many calls from a nearby city wanting to know why it cannot buy the product. Distribution has been restricted to the test market, Tulsa. Some markets are not so isolated. If you were to run promotions for a product test in the *Los Angeles Times,* you would have very large spillover of newspaper readership outside the Los Angeles geographical area. Note that this would not necessarily be a problem as long as you wanted to run the test in the geographical area covered by the *Los Angeles Times* and you also had arranged for the new product to be distributed in this area.

The ability to control distribution and promotion depends on a number of factors. Are the distributors in the city being considered available and willing to cooperate? If not, is a controlled test market service company available for the city? Will the media in the city have the facilities to accommodate your test market needs? At what costs? All of these factors must be considered before selecting the test city. Fortunately, because city governments often consider it desirable to have test markets conducted in their city because it brings in additional revenues, they as well as the media typically provide a great deal of information about their city to prospective test marketers.

Pros and Cons of Test Marketing

The advantages of test marketing are straightforward. Testing product acceptability and marketing-mix variables in a field setting provides the best information possible to the decision maker prior to actually going into full-scale marketing of the product. Test marketing allows for the most accurate method of forecasting future sales, and it allows firms the opportunity to pretest marketing-mix variables. On the "con" side, first, test markets do not yield infallible results. Secondly, competitors intentionally try to sabotage test markets. Firms will often flood a test market with sales promotions if they know a competitor is test-marketing a product.[25] Another problem with test markets is their cost. Test markets involving several test cities and various forms of promotion can easily run costs into the millions. Third, test markets bring about exposure of the product to the competition. Competitors get the opportunity to examine product prototypes and to see the planned marketing strategy for the new product via the test market. Finally, test markets may create ethical problems. Companies routinely report test marketing results to the press, which allows them access to premarket publicity. But are negatives found in the test market always reported, or do we hear only the good news? Companies, eager to get good publicity, may select test market cities that they feel will return favorable results. Perhaps the company already has a strong brand and market power in the market. Is this method of getting publicity ethical? There have been efforts to make reporting of test markets more candid.[26]

This concludes our discussion of research design, per se. However, there is another way marketing researchers classify research studies: qualitative versus quantitative research. Since much of the rest of this textbook is devoted to quantitative research, we will look closely at qualitative research in the remainder of this chapter.

Qualitative Research

Marketing researchers often look at marketing research in terms of two broad approaches, qualitative research and quantitative research. Some firms specialize in only one type; others conduct both types of research. As we just noted, most of the material in the rest of this book is more applicable to quantitative research so we are taking this opportunity to give you information about qualitative research and its methods. We will begin by contrasting qualitative research with quantitative research. Quantitative research is the traditional mainstay of the research industry, and it is sometimes referred to as "survey research." For our purposes in this chapter, **quantitative research** is defined as research involving the use of structured questions in which the response options have been predetermined and numerous respondents are involved. When you think of quantitative research, you might envision a nationwide survey conducted with telephone interviews. That is, quantitative research often involves a sizable representative sample of the population and a formalized procedure for gathering data. The purpose of quantitative research is very specific, and this research is used when the manager and researcher have agreed that precise information is needed. Data format and sources are clear and well defined, and the compilation and formatting of the data gathered follows an orderly procedure that is largely numerical in nature. Much of the remainder of this text is written as if you are going to do quantitative research. For example, the software you will learn for data analysis, XLData Analyst®, was developed expressly to conduct quantitative research.

Qualitative research, in contrast, involves collecting, analyzing, and interpreting data by observing what people do and say. Observations and statements are in a qualitative or nonstandardized form. Because of this, qualitative data can be quantified, but only after a translation process has taken place. For example, if you ask five people to express their opinions on a topic such as a proposal for a national sales tax to replace income tax, you would probably get five different statements. But after studying each response, you could characterize each one as "positive," "negative," or "neutral." This translation step would not be necessary if you gave the respondents a description of the proposed tax and then instructed them to choose predetermined responses of "positive," "negative," or "neutral." Any study that is conducted using an observational technique or unstructured questioning can be classified as qualitative research, which is becoming increasingly popular in a number of research situations.[27] Marketing Research Application 4.1 illustrates how qualitative research was used to better understand the Latino market segment.

Qualitative research techniques afford rich insight into consumer behavior[28] and are sometimes conducted along with quantitative research. When both qualitative and quantitative research are used, this is referred to as **pluralistic research,** which is defined as the combination of qualitative and quantitative research methods in order to gain the advantages of both.

Methods of Conducting Qualitative Research

There are several methods commonly used in conducting qualitative research. First, many of these methods include observation, so we begin our discussion of methods by examining observation techniques. Other methods of qualitative research we will discuss are focus groups, depth interviews, protocol analysis, projective techniques, and ethnographic research.

Observation Techniques

Observation methods are those in which the researcher relies on his or her powers of observation rather than communicating with a person in order to obtain information. Observation requires something to observe, and because our memories are faulty, researchers depend on recording devices such as videotapes,[29] audiotapes, handwritten notes, or some other tangible record of what is observed. As we describe observation techniques, you will see that each is unique in how it obtains observations.

TYPES OF OBSERVATION At first glance, it may seem that observation studies can occur without structure; however, it is important to adhere to a plan so that the observations are consistent and comparisons or generalizations can be made without worrying about any conditions of the observation method that might confound the findings. There are four general ways of organizing observations: (1) direct versus indirect, (2) disguised versus undisguised, (3) structured versus unstructured, and (4) human versus mechanical.

Quantitative research involves the use of structured questions in which the response options have been predetermined and numerous respondents are involved.

Qualitative research involves collecting, analyzing, and interpreting data by observing what people do and say. Observations and statements are in a qualitative or non-standardized form.

Pluralistic research involves the combination of qualitative and quantitative research methods in order to gain the advantages of both.

One qualitative method is to observe others rather than communicate with them. Researchers observe behavior and record what they see.

There are four general ways of organizing observations: (1) direct versus indirect, (2) disguised versus undisguised, (3) structured versus unstructured, and (4) human versus mechanical.

MARKETING RESEARCH APPLICATION 4.1

Global

You Say Hispanic, They Say Latino: Using Qualitative Research Methods to Better Understand Latino Market Segments

Do *all* Latinos love baseball?

Many marketers refer to the "Hispanic market" not knowing that this is a term not used by Latino consumers. Rather, they prefer "Latino." Another misconception is that there is "*the* Hispanic" or "*the* Latino" market. Actually there is no one solution that can be used to reach the Latino market which is not a homogeneous group of people. Instead, the Latino market is a fragmented and complex tapestry of Latino backgrounds that includes more than 20 different countries of origin. Ricardo Lopez, president of Hispanic Research, Inc., states that "Latinos, like any other market segment, represent many levels of acculturation, education, income levels, and ethnic influences." To illustrate some of these differences, consider sports. Many Latinos who love baseball are primarily from the Caribbean islands of Puerto Rico, the Dominican Republic, and Cuba, as well as countries that border the Caribbean basin such as Venezuela, Colombia, Panama, and Nicaragua. But, other Latinos, primarily from the rest of Latin America including Mexico, prefer soccer, and baseball is not popular in those countries just as soccer is not popular in the countries that prefer baseball. Hispanic Research, Inc. used the qualitative technique of focus groups to help the magazine *Sports Illustrated* understand differences in its readers for their magazine, *SI Latino*. In markets consisting of many Mexicans, magazine covers showing soccer did not receive much interest. As a result of the research, *SI Latino* now prints with split covers: one to appeal to the baseball lovers and the other to appeal to the soccer fans.

Another example of using qualitative research to better understand the Latino market is provided by Rose Marie Garcia Fontana, president of Garcia Fontana Research in Half Moon Bay, California. Her company conducted 148 personal interviews with Latinos to determine perceptions, motivations, and barriers to using their non-profit client, the Monterey Bay Aquarium. For un-acculturated Latinos their greatest concerns were availability of public transportation to and from the aquarium and bilingual signage within the facility. Children were the most important motivation for going and research showed that it was the father who usually made the decision to go, particularly in Spanish-dominant households.

Whether using focus groups or any of a variety of qualitative research techniques, researchers understand that different markets require special attention. This is why the QRCA created the Latino Special Interest Group (SIG). This group of researchers shares best practices to help each other provide the greatest benefit to their clients. Some "best practices" already utilized by SIG members are: recruit focus group members that share the same acculturation levels; be wary of using results from one Latino market in another (Miami is different from Texas which is different from California); and using an interpreter who is able to focus on picking up nuances and emotions in participants' voices.

Source: Shannon Pfarr Thompson.

| Observing behavior as it occurs is called direct observation. | **DIRECT OBSERVATION** Observing behavior as it occurs is called **direct observation**.[30] For example, if we are interested in finding out how much shoppers squeeze tomatoes to assess their freshness, we can observe people actually picking up the tomatoes. Direct observation has been used by Kellogg to understand breakfast rituals, by a Swiss chocolate maker to study the behavior of "chocoholics," and by the U.S. Post Office's advertising agency to come up with the advertising slogan, "We Deliver."[31] |

INDIRECT OBSERVATION In order to observe types of hidden behavior, such as past behavior, we must rely on indirect observation. With **indirect observation,** the researcher observes the effects or results of the behavior rather than the behavior itself. Indirect observation could be based upon **archives,** secondary data representing historical records (e.g., files of salespersons' activity reports which could be used to determine how many sales calls it takes to lead to a sale), or **physical traces,** tangible evidence of some past event. A soft-drink company might do a litter audit in order to assess how much impact its aluminum cans have on the countryside. A fast-food company such as Wendy's might measure the amount of graffiti on buildings located adjacent to prospective location sites as a means of estimating the crime potential for each site.[32]

DISGUISED VERSUS UNDISGUISED With **disguised observation,** the subject is unaware of being observed. An example of this method might be a "mystery shopper" who is used by a retail store chain to record and report on sales clerks' assistance and courtesy. One-way mirrors and hidden cameras are other ways that are used to prevent subjects from becoming aware of being observed. This disguise is deemed important by those conducting the research because they believe if the subjects were aware of the observation, it is possible that they would change their behavior, resulting in observations of atypical behavior. Of course this raises an ethical issue for researchers. Should people be observed when they are unaware of the fact?

In **undisguised observation,** respondents are aware of being observed. Observing a sales representative's behavior on sales calls or observing how members of a focus group open packaging and eat food are examples of undisguised observation.

> With disguised observation, the subject is unaware of being observed.

> When the respondent is aware of being observed this is known as undisguised observation.

Focus Groups

A popular method of conducting exploratory research is through **focus groups,** which are small groups of people brought together and guided by a moderator through an unstructured, spontaneous discussion for the purpose of gaining information relevant to the research problem.[33] Although focus groups should encourage openness on the part of the participants, the moderator's task is to ensure that the discussion is "focused" on some general area of interest. This is a useful technique for gathering some information from a limited sample of respondents. The information can be used to generate ideas, to learn the respondents' "vocabulary" when relating to a certain type of product, or to gain insights into basic needs and attitudes.[34]

Focus groups have been popular for a number of years. They represent 85% to 90% of the total money spent on qualitative research.[35]

> Focus groups are small groups of people brought together and guided by a moderator through an unstructured, spontaneous discussion for the purpose of gaining information relevant to the research objectives.

HOW FOCUS GROUPS WORK Focus groups can be of several types. **Traditional focus groups** consist of six to twelve people who meet in a dedicated room, with a one-way mirror for client viewing, for about two hours. In recent years, **nontraditional focus groups** have emerged, which can differ from traditional focus groups in many ways: They may be online, with clients observing on computer monitors in distant locations, or they may have up to fifty respondents, allow client interaction with participants, last four or five hours, or take place in outside dedicated facilities such as a park.[36] A new innovation is to create panels using focus group members.[37] A marketing research firm offering traditional focus groups typically will have a **focus group facility,** which is a set of rooms especially designed for focus groups. The focus group is conducted in a room that seats about ten people (optimum size is thought to be somewhere between six and twelve participants) and a moderator.[38] One wall in the room is a large, one-way mirror. The one-way mirror allows clients in the adjoining room to watch the focus group without influencing what the focus group members say or do. Focus group members may be recruited randomly but are more often recruited from the focus group facility's database of potential respondents. Focus group companies exert great efforts to recruit potential participants. They often use clubs or church group lists from which to recruit. While payment varies, it is not uncommon for a participant to be paid $75 or more for participating in a one- to two-hour-long focus group.[39] Focus group participants are interviewed by **moderators,** often referred to as **qualitative research consultants (QRs or QRCs).**[40] QRCs have the responsibility of creating an atmosphere that is conducive to openness, yet they must make certain that participants do not stray too far from the central focus of the study. QRCs must also prepare a **focus group report,** which summarizes the information provided by the focus group participants relative to the research questions. Visit the professional organization of QRCs at www.qrca.org.

ADVANTAGES OF FOCUS GROUPS   The four major advantages of focus groups are (1) they generate fresh ideas; (2) they allow clients to observe their participants; (3) they may be directed at understanding a wide variety of issues such as reactions to a new food product, brand logo, or television ad; and (4) they allow fairly easy access to special respondent groups such as lawyers or doctors (it may otherwise be very difficult to find a representative sample of these groups).

DISADVANTAGES OF FOCUS GROUPS   Three major disadvantages to focus groups are (1) they do not constitute representative samples; therefore, caution must be exercised in generalizing their findings; (2) it is sometimes difficult to interpret the results of focus groups; the moderator's report of the results is based on a subjective evaluation of what was said during the focus group; and (3) the cost per participant is high, though the total spent on focus group research is generally a fraction of what may be spent on quantitative research.

WHEN SHOULD FOCUS GROUPS BE USED?   When the research objective is to describe, rather than predict, focus groups may be an alternative. Consider the following situations: A company wants to know, "How do we 'speak' to our market; what language and terms do the customers use?" "What are some new ideas for an ad campaign?" "Will a new service they are developing have appeal to customers and how can we improve it?" "How can we better package our product?"[41] In all these cases, focus groups can describe the terms customers use, their ideas for ads, why a service appeals to them, and so on.

WHEN SHOULD FOCUS GROUPS NOT BE USED?   Because focus groups are based on a small number of persons who are not representative of some larger population, care must be exercised in using focus groups. If the research objective is to predict, focus groups should not be used. For example, if we show twelve people in a focus group a new-product prototype and find that six people say they are going to buy it, can we predict that 50% of the population will buy our product? Hardly. Likewise, if our research is going to dictate a major, expensive decision for our company, we probably should not use focus groups. If the decision is that important, research that is representative of a population with a known margin of error (quantitative research) should be used.

Depth Interviews

A depth interview is a set of probing questions posed one-on-one to a subject by a trained interviewer so as to gain an idea of what the subject thinks about something or why the subject behaves in a certain way.

A **depth interview** is a set of probing questions posed one-on-one to a subject by a trained interviewer so as to gain an idea of what the subject thinks about something or why the subject behaves in a certain way. The interviews may be conducted almost anywhere including the respondent's home or possibly at a central interviewing location such as a mall-intercept facility. The objective is to obtain unrestricted comments or opinions and to ask questions that will help the marketing researcher better understand the various dimensions of these opinions as well as the reasons for them. Of primary importance is the compilation of the data into a summary report so as to identify common themes. New concepts, designs, advertising, and promotional messages can arise from this method.[42]

There are advantages and disadvantages to in-depth interviewing. Interviewers have the ability to probe, asking many additional questions, as a result of a respondent's response. This enables the research technique to generate rich, deep, in-depth responses. In-depth responses may be more revealing in some research situations than, say, responses to predetermined, yes–no questions typical of a structured survey. If used properly, depth interviews can offer great insight into consumer behavior.[43,44] However, this advantage also leads to the major disadvantage of in-depth interviewing which is the lack of structure in the process. Unless interviewers are well trained, the results may be too varied to give sufficient insight to the problem.

Depth interviews are especially useful when the researcher wants to understand decision making on the individual level, how products are used, or the emotional and sometimes private aspects of consumers' lives.[45,46] Obviously, the respondent in an in-depth interview is not influenced by others, as in a focus group.

In-depth interviews should be conducted by a trained fieldworker who is equipped with a list of topics or, perhaps, open-ended questions. This is necessary because the respondent is not provided a list of set responses and then instructed to select one from the list. Rather, the respondent is encouraged to respond in his or her own words, and the interviewer is trained in asking probing questions, such as "Why is that so?" "Can you elaborate on your point?" or "Would you give me some specific reasons?" These questions are not intended to tap subconscious motivations; rather, they simply ask about conscious reasons to help the researcher form a better picture of what is going on in the respondent's head. The interviewer may tape-record responses or may take detailed notes. Although it is typical to do face-to-face depth interviews, they can be done over the telephone when interviewees are widely dispersed.[47] Depth interviews are versatile, but they require careful planning, training, and preparation.[48]

Laddering is a technique used in in-depth interviews in an attempt to discover how product attributes are associated with desired consumer values. Essentially, values that are important to consumers are determined, such as "good health." Next, researchers determine which routes consumers take to achieve their values, such as exercise, eating certain foods, and stress reduction. Researchers also attempt to determine which specific product attributes are used as a means of achieving the end that is the desired value. Through in-depth interviews researchers may learn that low-sodium foods or "white meats" are instrumental in achieving "good health."[49] The term *laddering* comes from the notion that the researcher is trying to establish the linkages, or steps, leading from product attributes to values. We asked Professor Philip Trocchia to give additional insights on laddering (see Marketing Research Application 4.2).

Protocol Analysis

Protocol analysis involves placing a person in a decision-making situation and asking him or her to verbalize everything he or she considers when making a decision. It is a special-purpose qualitative research technique that has been developed to peek into the consumer's decision-making processes. Often a tape recorder is used to maintain a permanent record of the person's thinking. After several people have provided protocols, the researcher reviews them and looks for commonalities such as evaluative criteria used, number of brands considered, and types and sources of information used.

> Protocol analysis places a person in a decision-making situation and asks him or her to verbalize everything being considered.

Protocol studies are useful in two different purchase situations. First, they are helpful for purchases involving a long time frame in which several decision factors must be considered, such as when buying a house. By having people verbalize the steps they went through, a researcher can piece together the whole process. Second, when the decision process is very short, recall may be faulty, and protocol analysis can be used to slow the process. For example, most people do not give much thought to buying chewing gum, but if Dentyne wanted to find out why people buy spearmint gum, protocol analysis may provide important insights regarding this purchasing behavior.

Projective Techniques

Projective techniques involve situations in which participants are placed in (projected into) simulated activities in the hopes that they will divulge things about themselves that they might not reveal under direct questioning. Projective techniques are appropriate in situations in which the researcher is convinced that respondents will be hesitant to relate their true opinions. The situations may be sensitive such as behavior using public toilet facilities or the situation may require information about one's psyche that individuals do not freely provide such as the role of status in purchasing a Porsche SUV. Marketing Research Application 4.3 demonstrates how one marketing research firm uses projective techniques in focus groups to bypass the "rational controls" consumer use to cover up their bias, perceptions, and subconscious emotions.

> Projective techniques involve situations in which participants are placed in (projected into) simulated activities in the hopes that they will divulge things about themselves that they might not reveal under direct questioning.

In the following paragraphs we will discuss some common projective techniques used by marketers: the word association test, the sentence completion test, the cartoon or balloon test, and role-playing activity. A discussion of each follows.

WORD-ASSOCIATION TEST A **word-association test** involves reading words to a respondent, who then answers with the first word that comes to mind. These tests may contain over

> A word-association test involves reading words to a respondent, who then answers with the first word that comes to mind.

MARKETING RESEARCH APPLICATION 4.2

Practical Applications

The Laddering Interview

Professor Philip Trocchia

Professor Philip Trocchia is associate professor of marketing, at University of South Florida, St. Petersburg. He has employed qualitative research techniques for such organizations as The Poynter Institute, Computer Renaissance, and The Honda Grand Prix of St. Petersburg. He has also written an article on the laddering technique in the *Journal of Management Education.*

Laddering is a type of one-on-one depth interview technique that seeks to reveal how individuals relate the features of products they purchase to their personally held beliefs. In laddering interviews, consumers are asked to describe why they purchased a particular good or service. After uncovering relevant product attributes or features influencing their purchase decisions, the interviewer probes the consumer to reveal what benefits they associate with the product feature(s) identified earlier. The interviewer then attempts to uncover why those product benefits are of importance to the consumer subject. In this portion of the interview, the consumer's personal values are revealed.

The term *laddering* refers to the series of linkages described above: relevant features of the consumer's described product purchase are related to the perceived benefits of the product. Product benefits are then linked to the individual's personal set of values. For example, suppose a consumer regularly purchases a particular cereal. The interviewer would ask her why she buys that specific cereal. She might respond that it is high in fiber, a brand attribute. The consumer would then be asked why high fiber is important, and the respondent may express health reasons as a benefit of fiber. Finally, the interviewer would ask the consumer why good health is important to her, and the respondent might indicate that she associates good health with some personal value(s), such as happiness, freedom, or pleasure. The summary ladder for this consumer would be: high fiber (attribute or feature) → good health (benefit or consequence) → freedom (value). A typical report for the series of laddering interviews would contain a summary of the common attribute-benefit-value linkages among the respondents, along with demographic characteristics of the consumers who possess common linkage patterns. This information would help marketing managers make decisions such as: ensure our cereal has high fiber; promotional messages should be developed linking freedom derived from good health derived from high fiber diets. Demographic profiles of this target market could be used to buy media targeting this demographic group.

The summary report for the in-depth interview will look very similar to one written for a focus group study; that is, the analyst looks for common themes across several depth interview transcripts, and these are noted in the report. Verbatim responses are included in the report to support the analyst's conclusions, and any significant differences of opinion that are found in the respondents' comments are noted as well. Again, it is vital to use an analyst who is trained and experienced in interpreting the qualitative data gathered during depth interviews.

Source: Professor Philip Trocchia.

100 words and usually combine neutral words with words being tested in ads or words involving product names or services. The researcher then looks for hidden meanings or associations between responses and the words being tested on the original list. This approach is used to uncover people's real feelings about these products or services, brand names, or ad copy. The time taken to respond, called "response latency," and/or the respondents' physical reactions may be measured and used to make inferences. For example, if the response latency to the word "duo" is long, it may mean that people do not have an immediate association with the word.

With a sentence-completion test, respondents are given incomplete sentences and asked to complete them in their own words. The researcher then inspects these sentences to identify themes or concepts that exist.

SENTENCE-COMPLETION TEST With a **sentence-completion test,** respondents are given incomplete sentences and asked to complete them in their own words. The researcher then inspects these sentences to identify themes or concepts that exist. For example, suppose that General Motors is interested in today's perceptions about the company after its near insolvency. GM researchers may instruct a sample of potential auto buyers to complete the following sentences:

Someone who buys a GM car is _____.

The quality of GM cars today is _____.

The researcher would look at the written responses and attempt to identify central themes.

Using Projective Techniques to Discover New Insights

Holly M. O'Neill,
Founder and President,
Talking Business

Turbocharge Focus Groups with Projective and Interactive Exercises

Focus group moderators are charged with discovering actionable insights. Marketers understand that most purchase decisions are made subconsciously and steeped with emotional imagery—both positive and negative associations. So, how do moderators bypass the rational controls of consumers and strike up a meaningful dialogue that elicits emotions, perceptions, biases, and true buying motivations? Projective techniques and interactive exercises are the prescription here—tapping respondents' subconscious emotions and values that drive purchase behavior and shape brand relationships.

It is not enough to gather only rational thoughts in qualitative research. The challenge with pure questioning is that language is left brain–based, the part of the brain that also processes logic, analysis, science, and math. Yet, brand relationships live in the human right brain, the part of the brain responsible for intuition, creativity, imagination, art, and music. In *How Customers Think*, author Gerald Zaltman asserts that 95% of purchase decisions are made subconsciously.

In a focus group that relies solely on structured dialogue, respondents can become too analytical. Therefore, moderators can use projective techniques and interactive exercises to aid respondents' verbalizing of their subconscious motivations. Interactive exercises can also uncover issues and opinions that respondents may not otherwise be able to fully verbalize, or which they might be unaware. By increasing the variety of communication methods and modes, respondents can more easily express the whys behind their needs and feelings. As many of the techniques are tactile in nature, they promote insights from multiple senses, thus painting rich customer profiles.

According to *Qualitative Market Research* by Hy Miriampolski, projective techniques, which try to circumvent rational thinking, were adopted by the Freudians as another means of channeling into the unconscious mind. This book goes on to define projective techniques as a category of exercises that provoke imagination and imagery. Other practitioners more narrowly define projectives as unstructured techniques used to project emotions onto unrelated stimuli. However, in practice, both true projective techniques and the wider class of interactive exercises bring forth deep-rooted emotions and imagery associated with purchase decisions and provide marketers with exceptional, actionable insights.

Field research has proven that when respondents are more engaged in the focus group, they are more willing and more able to open up, speak honestly and express their inner thoughts, feelings, motivations, and biases. For the most part, respondents find these exercises described below to be fun, which further promotes their brains into stimulating new connections, and thus providing additional learning for marketers. Of course, each exercise should be customized, so that it is germane to the research at hand. Nonetheless, the more generic descriptions and instructions that follow are a great primer to introduce these exciting qualitative modalities.

Sort Me Up™

Sort Me Up is great for determining how target brands relate to their competition. This exercise uncovers similarities and differences across brands, product types, and product segments. It is valuable for segmentation studies, as it reveals frames of reference, thus allowing marketers to really understand what products the target brand most and least competes with. After several sorts (i.e., several focus groups), a purchase decision hierarchy emerges, which helps marketers understand not only consumer attitudes and usage patterns across different product segments, but also provides an understanding of how consumers shop and consume the category under study.

To begin, the moderator places about twenty-five actual products on the table and asks respondents to work together as a team to sort the products into groups that make sense to them. Respondents are encouraged to create as many product groupings as they see fit. They are also instructed to give each group of items they've placed together a descriptive title. Note that for product categories where the size/shape of individual products/services is not easily brought into the focus group room (e.g., large appliances, online banking sites), Sort Me Up can be executed with cards imprinted with brand names, logos, package graphics, etc. This exercise engages respondents in a tangible way. There is visual stimulation as well as physical activity (i.e., moving the products around the table). The ensuing lively, post-exercise discussion and probing provides marketers with key insights, largely unattainable through direct questioning.

Picture This, Picture That™

If a research goal is to learn about imagery and emotional associations for target brands, then Picture This, Picture That is a particularly insightful projective technique. In this exercise, pictures become metaphors for respondents to describe their perceptions. In brief, this technique allows respondents to

MARKETING RESEARCH APPLICATION 4.3 *(continued)*

Practical Applications

Using Projective Techniques to Discover New Insights

think more broadly, frame their ideas, and get over their inhibitions. The images trigger key perceptions and give consumers permission to divulge their inner-most thoughts (as they project their real attitudes onto the image).

This exercise begins with about fifty preselected images that represent a wide range of emotions. It's important that the images be rich, but they can be from almost any source—magazine ads, art books, furniture catalogs, etc. It's imperative that images that are related to the topic under discussion are not included (e.g., soup for a soup study, honeymoon vacation if researching online dating). The moderator places these images on the table and asks respondents to individually select a picture that depicts how they feel about brand/category/situation. Of course, the question should be crafted to be consistent with study goals. An easy variation is to ask each respondent to select two images, for example, one that depicts the best thing and one that depicts the worst thing about brand/category/situation or one that depicts how they feel about shopping at Store A and one for Store B.

The tangible aspects of implementing this exercise, combined with the intangible aspects of the deep-seated imagery, yield insightful stories for marketers. The discussion and active probing surrounding the emotional underpinnings of these images and how they relate to the target brand reveals fresh insights, which can greatly aid the advertising team's ability to create more engaging campaigns.

Dot, Dot, Dot™

This quali-quant technique helps marketers understand preferences among a set of brands, flavors, advertisements, etc. Dot, Dot, Dot yields weighted rankings, allowing marketers to iteratively narrow the range of ideas and concepts being researched. Most importantly, this exercise uncovers functional and emotional rationale behind consumer perceptions.

This easy-to-implement technique begins with the moderator presenting respondents with a short list of choices (e.g., brands,

flavors, advertisements) and ten small, round dot stickers (think purchase tokens). Respondents are instructed to allocate the dots according to their preferences, placing as many dots as they feel appropriate (or even zero dots) on each option. Of course, they should place a greater number of dots on their preferred option(s), but how many is up to them. While the results are not statistically significant, they can be considered directional. The ensuing discussion following Dot, Dot, Dot provides fresh insights about customer preferences. When "forced" to vote their preferences, it is often easier for respondents to later divulge their needs, emotions, and biases underlying these preferences.

About Talking Business

Talking Business delivers the truth behind brands and what motivates purchase behavior—vital insights decision makers need to drive competitive marketing solutions. Offering more than focus group moderating, we specialize in innovative marketing research and strategic brand development. Our category expertise includes consumer, financial, pharmaceuticals, technology, and hospitality with clients such as GlaxoSmith Kline, Princess Cruises, and Experian. Exceeding client expectations for fourteen years, Talking Business connects with target audiences to better understand brands, loud and clear.

You can visit Talking Business at www.TalkingBusiness.net.

Source: Holly O'Neill, Talking Business.

With a balloon test, a line drawing with an empty "balloon" above the head of one of the actors is provided to subjects who are instructed to write in the balloon what the actor is saying or thinking. The researcher then inspects these thoughts to find out how subjects feel about the situation described in the cartoon.

CARTOON OR BALLOON TEST With a **balloon test,** a line drawing with an empty "balloon" above the head of one of the actors is provided to subjects who are instructed to write in the balloon what the actor is saying or thinking. The researcher then inspects these thoughts to find out how subjects feel about the situation described in the cartoon. For example, when shown a line drawing of a situation in which one of the characters is making the statement, "What do think about your Apple iPhone®?" the participant is asked how the other character in the drawing would respond. Feelings and reactions of the subject are judged based on their answers.

ROLE-PLAYING ACTIVITY With **role playing,** participants are asked to pretend they are a "third person," such as a friend or neighbor, and to describe how they would act in a certain situation or to a specific statement. By reviewing their comments, the researcher can spot latent reactions, positive or negative, conjured up by the situation. It is believed that some of the respondents' true feelings and beliefs will be revealed by this method because they can pretend to be another individual.

As with depth interviews, all of these projective techniques require qualified professionals to interpret the results. This increases the cost per respondent compared with other survey methods. Because of this aspect, projective techniques are not used extensively in commercial marketing research, but each one has value in its special realm of application.[50]

Ethnographic Research

Ethnographic research is a term borrowed from anthropology; it is defined as a detailed, descriptive study of a group and its behavior, characteristics, culture, among others.[51] *Ethno* means "people" and *-graphy* means "to describe." Anthropologists have gained insights into human behavior by living with or among their subjects, called *immersion*, for prolonged periods to study their emotions, behaviors, and reactions to the demands of everyday events. Ethnography uses several different types of research, including immersion, participant observation, and informal and ongoing in-depth interviewing. Ethnographers pay close attention to words, metaphors, symbols, and stories people use to explain their lives and communicate with one another.[53] Marketers have increasingly used ethnographic research to study consumer behavior and many believe its use is increasing. However, unlike anthropologists, marketing researchers do not immerse themselves for months on end. Rather, ethnographic research involves direct observation, interviews, and audio and video recordings of consumers. Ethnographic research is not done at a point in time, as most other research is conducted. One researcher, Ann-Marie McDermott of Quaestor Research, stated that she worked on a new chicken burger project. Instead of doing the normal research, she decided to spend time with consumers. She went to their homes and watched them shop, cook in their homes, and eat.[54]

Ethnographic research is an area of ethical sensitivity. Researchers' immersing themselves in others' homes, schools, places of work, and play for purposes of recording behaviors, comments, reactions, and emotions of people naïve to the research is unethical. As the technique grows in marketing research, researchers must be adept in skills necessary to be "present and known" without interfering with normal behavior. Fortunately, most behaviors marketers are interested in are public behaviors—shopping, cooking, and eating, for example. Such public behaviors are easily observed.[55]

With role playing, participants are asked to pretend they are a "third person," such as a friend or neighbor, and to describe how they would act in a certain situation or to a specific statement. By reviewing their comments, the researcher can spot latent reactions, positive or negative, conjured up by the situation.

Ethnographic research is a term borrowed from anthropology; it is defined as a detailed, descriptive study of a group and its behavior, characteristics, culture, among others.[52] *Ethno* means "people" and *-graphy* means "to describe."

Ethnographers pay close attention to words, metaphors, symbols, and stories people use to explain their lives and communicate with one another. Marketers have increasingly used ethnographic research to study consumer behavior.

Summary

Research design refers to a set of advance decisions made to develop the master plan to be used in the conduct of the research project. There are three general research designs: exploratory, descriptive, and causal. Each one of these designs has its own inherent approaches. The significance of studying research design is that, by matching the research objective with the appropriate research design, a host of research decisions may be predetermined. Therefore, a research design serves as a "blueprint" for researchers. Selecting the appropriate research design depends, to a large extent, on the research objectives and how much

information is already known about the problem. If very little is known, exploratory research is appropriate. Exploratory research is unstructured, informal research that is undertaken to gain background information; it is helpful for more clearly defining the research problem. Exploratory research is used in a number of situations: to gain background information, to define terms, to clarify problems and hypotheses, and to establish research priorities. Reviewing existing literature, surveying individuals knowledgeable in the area to be investigated, relying on former similar case situations, as well as several methods used in qualitative research such as conducting focus groups and using projective techniques are methods of conducting exploratory research. Exploratory research should almost always be used because it is fast, inexpensive, and sometimes resolves the research objective or is helpful in carrying out descriptive or causal research.

If concepts, terms, and so on, are already known and the research objective is to describe and measure phenomena, then descriptive research is appropriate. Descriptive research measures marketing phenomena and answers the questions of who, what, where, when, and how. Descriptive studies may be conducted at one point in time (cross sectional), or several measurements may be made on the same sample at different points in time (longitudinal). Longitudinal studies are often conducted using panels. Panels represent sample units who have agreed to answer questions at periodic intervals. Continuous panels are longitudinal studies in which sample units are asked the same questions repeatedly. Brand-switching tables may be prepared based on data from continuous panels. Market-tracking studies may be conducted using data from continuous panels.

The second type of panel used in longitudinal research is the discontinuous panel. Discontinuous panels, sometimes called omnibus panels, are those in which the sample units are asked different questions. The main advantage of the discontinuous panel is that research firms have a large sample of persons who are willing to answer whatever questions they are asked.

Causal relationships provide such relationships as "If x, then y." Causal relationships may be discovered only through special studies called experiments. Experiments allow us to determine the effects of a variable, known as an independent variable, on another variable, known as a dependent variable. Experimental designs are necessary to ensure that the effect we observe in our dependent variable is due, in fact, to our independent variable and not to other variables known as extraneous variables. The validity of experiments may be assessed by internal validity and external validity.

Laboratory experiments are particularly useful for achieving internal validity, whereas field experiments are better suited for achieving external validity. Test marketing is a form of field experimentation. Test market cities are selected on the basis of their representativeness, isolation, and the degree to which market variables such as distribution and promotion may be controlled. Various types of test markets exist (standard, controlled, electronic, simulated, consumer, industrial, and lead country) and, although test markets garner much useful information, they are expensive and not infallible.

Qualitative research, unlike quantitative research, involves collecting, analyzing, and interpreting data by observing what people do and say. Using both qualitative and quantitative research is referred to pluralistic research. Observation techniques are often used in qualitative research. The four types of observation research are direct versus indirect, disguised versus undisguised, structured versus unstructured, and human versus mechanical observation. Focus groups are conducted by having a small group of people guided by a moderator through a spontaneous, unstructured conversation that focuses on a research problem. Focus group research is a type of qualitative research. Other forms of qualitative research include in-depth interviews, protocol analysis, projective techniques, and ethnographic research. Focus groups should be used when there is something that needs to be described. When something needs to be predicted, focus groups should not be used. Depth interviews are also used in qualitative research and "laddering" is a technique used in depth interviews to discover how product attributes are associated with desired values. Protocol analysis involves placing people individually in a decision-making situation and asking them to verbalize everything they consider when making a decision. Projective techniques include word-association tests, sentence-completion tests, cartoon or balloon tests, and role playing. Finally, ethnographic research, defined as a detailed, descriptive study of a group and its behavior, characteristics, culture, and more, is used in qualitative research.

Key Terms

Research design (p. 80)
Exploratory research (p. 81)
Secondary data analysis (p. 83)
Experience surveys (p. 83)
Case analysis (p. 83)
Descriptive research (p. 84)
Cross-sectional studies (p. 84)
Sample surveys (p. 84)

Longitudinal studies (p. 84)
Panels (p. 84)
Continuous panels (p. 85)
Discontinuous panels (p. 85)
Omnibus panels (p. 85)
Brand-switching studies (p. 85)
Market-tracking studies (p. 85)
Causal Research (p. 85)

Experiment (p. 86)
Independent variables (p. 86)
Dependent variables (p. 86)
Extraneous variables (p. 86)
Experimental design (p. 87)
Pretest (p. 87)
Posttest (p. 87)
"True" experimental design (p. 87)

Review Questions

1. What are the independent, dependent, and possible extraneous variables in our chapter opening vignette written by Herb Sorensen?
2. Give some examples illustrating the uses of exploratory research.
3. What type of research design answers the questions of who, what, where, when, and how?
4. What are the differences between longitudinal studies and cross-sectional studies?
5. In what situation would a continuous panel be more suitable than a discontinuous panel? In what situation would a discontinuous panel be more suitable than a continuous panel?
6. What type of panel is an omnibus panel?
7. Explain why studies of the "if–then" variety are considered to be causal studies.
8. Define each of the following types of variables and give an example of each in an experiment designed to determine the effects of an advertising campaign: independent, dependent, extraneous, control group, experimental group.
9. Explain the two types of validity in experimentation and also explain why different types of experiments are better suited for addressing one type of validity versus another.
10. Distinguish among the various types of test marketing.
11. How does qualitative research differ from quantitative research?
12. What is meant by pluralistic research?
13. What are the different methods of observation?
14. Why are focus groups called "focus" groups?
15. What is the difference between traditional and nontraditional focus groups?
16. What is the role of a focus group moderator and what is meant by QRC?
17. When should focus groups be used? When should focus groups not be used?
18. Discuss the advantages and disadvantages of in-depth interviewing.
19. Explain how "laddering" works.
20. What is meant by "protocol analysis"?
21. Explain the rationale behind using projective techniques.
22. Why do you think ethnographic research could be ethically sensitive?

Application Questions

23. Think of a past job that you have held. List three areas in which you, or some other person in the organization, could have benefited from having information generated by research. What would be the most appropriate research design for each of the three areas of research you have listed?
24. You are no doubt familiar with Internet search engine companies that find online sources pertaining to words, phrases, or questions that users enter. Can you identifiy research problems likely to be addressed by a search engine company such as Google™? What type of research design would you recommend for these problems?

25. Design an experiment. Select an independent variable and a dependent variable. What are some possible extraneous variables that may cause problems? Explain how you would control for the effects these variables may have on your dependent variable. Is your experiment a valid one?

26. The Maximum Company has invented an extra-strength, instant coffee brand to be called "Max-Gaff," positioned to be stronger tasting than any competing brands. Design a taste-test experiment that compares Max-Gaff to the two leading instant coffee brands to determine which brand consumers consider to taste the strongest. Identify and diagram your experiment. Indicate how the experiment is to be conducted, and assess the internal and external validity of your experiment.

27. Coca-Cola markets PowerAde as a sports drink that competes with Gatorade. Competition for sports drinks is fierce where they are sold in the coolers of convenience stores. Coca-Cola is thinking about using a special holder that fits in a standard convenience-store cooler but moves PowerAde to eye level and makes it more conspicuous than Gatorade. Design an experiment that determines whether the special holder increases the sales of PowerAde in convenience stores. Identify and diagram your experiment. Indicate how the experiment is to be conducted and assess the internal and external validity of your experiment.

28. SplitScreen is a marketing research company that tests television advertisements. SplitScreen has an agreement with a cable television company in a medium-size city in Iowa. The cable company can send up to four different television ads simultaneously to different households. SplitScreen also has agreements with the three largest grocery store chains, which will provide scanner data to SplitScreen. About 25% of the residents have SplitScreen scan cards that are scanned when items are bought at the grocery store and that allow SplitScreen to identify who bought which grocery products. For allowing SplitScreen access to their television hookups and their grocery-purchase information, residents receive bonus points that can be used to buy products in a special points catalog. Identify and diagram the true experimental design possible using the SplitScreen system. Assess the internal and external validity of SplitScreen's system.

29. A tire store chain is concerned that women have concerns about bringing their car to tire stores which are typically dominated by men—employees and customers. What type of research would you conduct to determine if this concern is prevalent among female drivers and what techniques the chain may adopt that would alleviate some of these concerns?

Case 4.1 **Memo from a Researcher**[56]

John Daniel, a researcher at Georgia Metro Research, made the following notes about several of his clients to you, a newly hired trainee who had just graduated from college.

Client A is a consumer packaged goods manufacturer with a well-established brand name. The client has focused on manufacturing and distribution for years while the marketing program has been set on "auto pilot." All had worked fine though there was a hint of emerging problems when, in the preceding year, market share had fallen slightly. Now, our client has just reviewed the current market share report and notices that over the previous twelve months their share has gradually eroded 15%. When market share falls, clients are eager to learn why and to take corrective action. In these situations we know immediately the problem is that we don't know what the problem is: There are many possible causes for this slippage. We need to determine the research design needed.

Secondly, Client B is a manufacturer of several baked goods products sold in grocery stores throughout the country. Marketing is divided up into five regional divisions in the United States. The five divisions have had total autonomy over their advertising though all of them have used television advertising almost exclusively. Each division has tried several different television ad campaigns and some were thought to be successful and others not as successful but no one had ever formally evaluated the ad expenditures. A new marketing VP now wants to evaluate the advertising. She's interested in knowing not only the sales of the client's products sold during the different campaigns but also what happened to sales of competitors' brands. In this case, the client needs us to *describe* sales by SKU in the client's product category for each television market and for each time period associated with each ad campaign. What research design do you recommend?

Finally, Client C is in a very competitive category with equal market share of the top three brands. Our client is convinced that they have changed every marketing-mix variable possible except for package design. Since the three competitive brands are typically displayed side-by-side, they want us to determine what factors of package design (i.e., size, shape, color, texture, and so on) cause an increase in awareness, preference for, and intention to buy the brand. What do you recommend for the appropriate research design?

1. Describe what research design you would recommend for each client.
2. For each research design you selected for the three clients, discuss *why* you believe your choice of design is the correct choice.

Case 4.2 **Your Integrated Case**

Advanced Automobile Concepts

Nick Thomas has been considering some of the issues identified in the Douglass Report (see Case 3.2). He is considering different directions to take. First, he is a little concerned that most of the information he and AAC have based their decisions on thus far are either industry reports or opinions of persons in the company. Granted, these persons are quite knowledgeable of the automobile industry. But, Thomas is concerned that he doesn't have input from some consumers. What do consumers think about global warming, future fuel costs, hybrids versus all electric cars? He knows the media has introduced a vast amount of information on these topics to consumers but he wonders if consumers are even aware of these issues. How important are these issues to consumers? What appears to be the most important: global warming, fuel costs, or giving up their SUVs? He begins to realize he doesn't know very much about what consumers think about these important issues. He doesn't know how much they talk about these issues with their neighbors or even what terms they use to speak of these issues.

Secondly, Thomas dwells on consumer attitudes and car purchasing intentions. That is, will a strong belief in global warming caused by mankind be highly associated with buying certain types of cars? Will this vary around the country? Will these relationships exist within definable market segments?

Finally, Thomas knows that AAC can retrofit some ZEN models that will improve fuel economy without drastic requirements of new technology or retooling or added costs. He wonders: "How much of an improvement in mpg would consumers require to buy the present ZEN models? What percentage increase in fuel economy (mpg) in current ZEN models will be required before ZEN becomes equally preferred with some of the better selling foreign autos?"

Thomas wonders how he could find answers to these questions. He is considering talking with a marketing researcher. Imagine you are the researcher hired by Thomas to address these questions.

1. To deal with the first set of issues—determining how consumers feel about certain issues, how important these issues are to them, and what terms they use to discuss these issues—what research design would you suggest? Why?
2. Consider the second paragraph in the case. What research design would you suggest to determine all of the following: Which attitudes are strongly associated with purchase intentions of different auto models? Will these relationships vary around the country and will they exist for definable market segments? Why?
3. Nick Thomas's last question deals with determining how much of an increase in mpg will be needed for consumers to have equal preference for ZEN models as those outselling ZEN today. What research design would you suggest?

5

Information Types and Sources: Secondary Data and Standardized Information

Marketing Researchers Use Secondary Data

Here at Decision Analyst we make certain we are fully aware of all existing information about an industry, a product category, and a company before we decide on the research objectives and methods for a research project. Even when we are dealing with a client in an industry in which we have conducted dozens of marketing research projects, a review of current secondary data can alert us to any recent developments. Any good marketing researcher should be adept at searching for and analyzing secondary data. As you will learn in this chapter, secondary data analysis is fast and inexpensive compared to collecting primary data. Sometimes, secondary data is all we need in order to provide the necessary information to solve our client's problem. Also, when we need to collect primary data for our clients, we provide current, relevant secondary data to help them better understand the implications of the primary data. We strive to add value for our clients and secondary data helps us accomplish that goal.

The Internet has been a catalyst for allowing faster searches and giving us access to more information than we thought possible just a few years ago. You have much of this information available to you through your university's databases. However, we are cautious in accepting any secondary data. Sometimes information is disseminated to serve special interests. At Decision Analyst we use secondary data from known and trusted sources. Go to our website at www.decisionanalyst .com, and click on SecondaryData.com. Here you will find a list of sources of secondary data. You will learn about some of these sources in this chapter as well as important ways to evaluate them.

Jerry W. Thomas
President/CEO
Decision Analyst®

The comments of marketing researcher Jerry W. Thomas demonstrate the importance of secondary data and online databases to marketing researchers. As he points out, even when the project involves collecting primary data, marketing researchers also consult secondary data. He also points out how online information databases have made this task much easier for the researcher. In this chapter, you will learn ways in which secondary data are used,[1] how we classify different types, its advantages and disadvantages, and some significant sources of secondary data for marketing researchers. In the next part of the chapter we will look at another type of information we call standardized information. We will examine its applications in marketing research and provide examples.

Visit Decision Analyst at www.decisionanalyst .com.

Secondary Data

Primary Versus Secondary Data

Data needed for marketing management decisions can be grouped into two types: primary and secondary. **Primary data** refers to information that is developed or gathered by the researcher specifically for the research project at hand.

Primary data refers to information that is developed or gathered by the researcher specifically for the research project at hand.

Visit Decision Analyst's secondary data site at www.secondarydata.com.

In this chapter we focus on secondary data, and one form specifically, standardized information. After this chapter, much of the remainder of this text focuses on how to collect and analyze primary data.

Secondary data have previously been gathered by someone other than the researcher and/or for some other purpose than the research project at hand. As commercial firms, government agencies, or community service organizations record transactions and business activities, they are creating a written record of these activities in the form of secondary data. When consumers fill out warranty cards or register their boats, automobiles, or software programs, this information is stored in the form of secondary data. It is available for someone else's *secondary* use. The Internet provides an incredible stock of free secondary data, the access of which, we believe, will continue to grow and become increasingly more important.

> Secondary data have previously been gathered by someone other than the researcher and/or for some other purpose than the research project at hand.

Uses of Secondary Data

There are so many uses of secondary data that it is rare for a marketing research project to be conducted without including some secondary data. Some projects may be totally based upon secondary data. The applications of secondary data range from predicting broad changes in a culture's "way of life" to specific applications such as selecting a street address location for a new car wash. Decision Analyst Inc., a marketing research firm, has a website entirely devoted to secondary data. Suggested applications include economic trend forecasting, corporate intelligence, international data, public opinion, and historical data, among others.

> The applications of secondary data range from predicting broad changes in a culture's "way of life" to specific applications such as selecting a street address location for a new car wash.

Marketers are very interested in knowing secondary data in terms of demographics, to help them forecast the size of the market in a newly proposed market territory. A researcher may use secondary data to determine the population and growth rate in almost any geographical area. Government agencies are interested in knowing secondary data to help them make public policy decisions. The Department of Education needs to know how many five-year-olds will enter the public school system next year. Health care planners need to know how many senior citizens will be eligible for Medicare during the next decade.

> Researchers Tootelian and Varshney have published secondary data on the size and market potential of the "grandparent" market.

Sometimes secondary data can be used to evaluate market performance. For example, since gasoline and fuel taxes collected per gallon are available in public records, petroleum marketers can easily determine the volume of fuels consumed in a county, thus making market share calculations both easy and reliable. Articles are written on virtually every topic and this storehouse of secondary data is available to marketers who want to understand a topic more thoroughly even though they themselves may not have firsthand experience. A wealth of secondary data is available concerning the lifestyles, including purchasing habits, of demographic groups. Because these demographic groups tend to make similar purchases and have similar attitudes, they have been scrutinized by marketers. The most significant of these demographic groups for decades has been the "baby boomer" population, defined as those born between 1946 and 1964.[2] As the baby boomers enter middle- and senior-age status, other demographic groups, such as the Gen Xers (born between about 1965 and 1979) and Gen Yers (born between about 1977 and 1994), are also studied by marketers.[3] Recently, Tootelian and Varshney provided research on "grandparents." This demographic group represents one-fourth of the U.S. population and spends about $55 billion a year on their grandchildren.[4] Is this a growing market as more and more of the baby boomers become grandparents?

Classification of Secondary Data

INTERNAL SECONDARY DATA Secondary data may be broadly classified as either internal or external. **Internal secondary data** have been collected *within* the firm. Such data include sales records, purchase requisitions, and invoices. Obviously, a good marketing researcher determines what internal information is already available. You may recall from Chapter 1 that we referred to internal data analysis as being part of the internal reports system of a firm's marketing information system (MIS). Today a major source of internal data is databases that contain information on customers, sales, suppliers, and any other facet of business a firm may wish to track. Kotler and Keller define **database marketing** as the process of building, maintaining, and using customer and other (*internal*) databases (products, suppliers, resellers) to contact, transact, and build customer relationships.[5]

Before we discuss internal and external databases, we should understand that a **database** refers to a collection of data and information describing items of interest.[6] Each unit of information in a database is called a **record.** A record could represent a customer, supplier, competitive firm, product, individual inventory item, among others. Records are composed of subcomponents of information called **fields.** As an example, a company having a database of customers would have *records* representing each customer. Typical *fields* in a customer database would include name, address, telephone number, e-mail address, products purchased, dates of purchases, locations where purchased, warranty information, and any other information the company thought was important.

Internal databases consist of information gathered by a company, typically during the normal course of business transactions. Marketing managers normally develop internal databases about customers, but databases may be kept on any topic of interest, such as products, members of the sales force, inventory, maintenance, and supplier firms. Companies gather information about customers when they inquire about a product or service, make a purchase, or have a product serviced. Companies use their internal databases for purposes of direct marketing and to strengthen relationships with customers, a process called **customer relationship management (CRM).**[7]

Internal databases can be quite large, and dealing with the vast quantities of data they contain can be a problem. **Data mining** is a type of software available to help managers make sense out of seemingly senseless masses of information contained in databases.[8] However, even simple databases in small businesses can be invaluable. Kotler and Keller describe five ways that companies use their databases: (1) to *identify prospects,* such as sorting through replies to company ads to identify customers who can be targeted with more information; (2) to decide *which customers should receive a particular offer,* such as sending a cross-selling suggestion two weeks after a sale; (3) to *deepen customer loyalty,* by remembering customer preferences and sending appropriately customized materials reflecting those preferences; (4) to *reactivate customer purchases,* such as automatically sending out a birthday card; and (5) to *avoid serious customer mistakes,* such as charging a fee to one of the firm's best customers.[9] Databases can tell managers which products are selling, report inventory levels, and profile customers by SKU. Coupled with geodemographic information systems (GIS), databases can provide maps indicating zip codes in which the most profitable and least profitable customers reside. Internal databases, built with information collected during the normal course of business, can provide invaluable insights for managers. We shall discuss GIS more completely later in this chapter.

What companies do with information collected for their internal databases can present ethical problems. Should your credit card company share the information on what types of goods and services you buy with anyone who wants to buy it? Should your Internet service provider be able to store information on which Internet sites you visit? As consumers become aware of these privacy issues, you see more companies adopt privacy policies.[10]

> Internal secondary data have been collected *within* the firm.

> Database marketing is the process of building, maintaining, and using customer (*internal*) and other (*internal*) databases (products, suppliers, resellers) to contact, transact, and build customer relationships.

> Internal databases consist of information gathered by a company, typically during the normal course of business transactions.

> Companies use their internal databases for purposes of direct marketing and to strengthen relationships with customers, a process called customer relationship management (CRM).

> Data mining is a type of software available to help managers make sense out of seemingly senseless masses of information contained in databases.

EXTERNAL SECONDARY DATA

Published Sources **External secondary data** are obtained from *outside* the firm. We classify external data into three sources: (1) published, (2) syndicated services data, and (3) external databases. **Published sources** of information are prepared for public distribution and are normally found in libraries or through a variety of other entities such as trade associations, professional organizations, or companies. Many published sources are now being made available via the Internet. Published sources of secondary information come from governments, not-for-profit organizations such as chambers of commerce, colleges and universities, trade and professional associations, and for-profits (e.g., *Sales & Marketing Management* magazine, Pearson Prentice Hall Inc., McGraw-Hill, and research firms). Many research firms publish secondary information in the form of books, newsletters, white papers, special reports, magazines, or journals. Many marketing research firms have white papers on varied topics on their website; for example, visit www.burke.com and click "Literature Library."

The sheer volume of published sources makes searching this type of secondary data difficult. However, understanding the function of the different types of publications can be of great help to you in successfully searching published secondary information sources. Table 5.1 depicts the different types of publications, their functions, and an example, to help make you a better user of secondary data.

Syndicated Services Data **Syndicated services data** are provided by firms that collect data in a standard format and make them available to subscribing firms. Such data are typically highly specialized and not available in libraries for the general public. We devote more attention to syndicated data services firms in a later section of this chapter.

External Databases **External databases** are supplied by organizations outside the firm. They may be used as sources for secondary data. **Online information databases** are sources of secondary data searchable by search engines online. Some online databases are available free of charge and are supplied as a service by a host organization. However, many online information databases are available from commercial sources that provide subscribers password (or IP address identification) access for a fee. Different databases are often packaged together by vendors that produce the software that retrieves the information. Sometimes called "aggregators" or "databanks," these services or vendors may offer a wide variety of indexes, directories, and statistical and full-text files all searched by the same search logic. Such services include Ibis World, Factiva, Gale Group, ProQuest, First Search, Lexis-Nexis, and Dialog, among others. Business databases comprise a significant proportion of these data banks.

Advantages of Secondary Data

The advantages of secondary data are, for the most part, readily apparent. There are five main advantages of using secondary data. First, data can be obtained quickly. Second, compared to collecting primary data, secondary data collection is inexpensive. Third, for almost any application, some secondary data are readily available. Fourth, secondary data may enhance primary data by providing a current look at issues, trends, yardsticks of performance, and so on, that may affect what primary data should be collected. Fifth, secondary data may be all that is needed to achieve the research objective. For example, a supermarket chain marketing manager wants to allocate television advertising dollars to the twelve television markets in which the chain owns supermarkets. A quick review of secondary data will show that retail sales on food is available by television market area. Allocating the television budget based on the percentage of food sales in a given market would be an excellent way to solve the manager's problem and satisfy the research objective.

TABLE 5.1

Understanding the Functions of Different Types of Publications

---

1. **Reference Guides**
   Function: Refer to *types* of other reference sources and recommended specific titles. Guides tell you where to look to find different types of information.

   Example: *Encyclopedia of Business Information Sources*. Detroit: Gale Group, 1970–present

2. **Indexes and Abstracts**
   Function: List periodical articles by subject, author, title, keyword, and more. Abstracts also provide summaries of the articles. Indexes allow you to search for periodicals by the topic of your research.

   Example: *ABI/Inform*. Ann Arbor, MI: Proquest, 1971–present

3. **Bibliographies**
   Function: List varied sources, such as books and journals, on a particular topic. Tells you what is available, from several sources, on a topic.

   Example: *Recreation and Entertainment Industries, an Information Source Book*. Jefferson, NC: Macfarland, 2000

4. **Almanacs, Manuals, and Handbooks**
   Function: As "deskbooks," provide a wide variety of data in a single, handy publication.

   Example: *Wall Street Journal Almanac*. New York: Ballantine Books, annual

5. **Dictionaries**
   Function: Define terms and are sometimes available for special subject areas.

   Example: *Concise Dictionary of Business Management* (2nd ed.). Abingdon, Oxon: Taylor & Francis Ltd., 2007

6. **Encyclopedias**
   Function: Provide essays, usually in alphabetical order, by topic.

   Example: *Encyclopedia of Busine$$ and Finance*. New York: Macmillan, 2001

7. **Directories**
   Function: List companies, people, products, organizations, among others, usually providing brief information about each entry.

   Example: *Career Guide: Dun's Employment Opportunities Directory*. Parsippany, NJ: Dun's Marketing Services, annual

8. **Statistical Sources**
   Function: Provide numeric data, often in tables, pie charts, and bar charts.

   Example: *Handbook of U.S. Labor Statistics*. Lanham, MD: Bernan Press, annual

9. **Biographical Sources**
   Function: Provide information about people. Useful for information on CEOs, and others.

   Example: *D&B Reference Book of Corporate Management*. Bethlehem, PA: Dun & Bradstreet, annual

10. **Legal Sources**
    Function: Provide information about legislation, regulations, and case law.

    Example: *United States Code*. Washington, DC: Government Printing Office

---

Disadvantages of Secondary Data

Although the advantages of secondary data almost always justify a search of this information, there are caveats associated with secondary data. Five of the problems associated with secondary data include incompatible reporting units, mismatch of the units of measurement, differing definitions used to classify the data, timeliness of the secondary data, and lack of information needed to evaluate the credibility of the data reported. These problems exist because secondary data have not been collected specifically to address the problem at hand but have been collected for some other purpose.

INCOMPATIBLE REPORTING UNITS Secondary data are provided in reporting units such as county, city, metro area, state, region, zip code, or core-based statistical areas. **Core-based statistical areas (CBSAs)** are geographic reporting units used by the Census Bureau. CBSAs consist of two smaller units, metropolitan and micropolitan statistical areas (SAs). **Metropolitan SAs** are defined by the Office of Management and Budget (OMB) as having at least one urbanized area of 50,000 or more population, plus adjacent territory that has a high degree of social and economic integration with the core as measured by commuting ties. **Micropolitan SAs** are a new set of statistical areas that have at least one urban cluster of at least 10,000 but less than 50,000 population, plus adjacent territory that has a high degree of social and economic integration with the core MSA as measured by commuting ties. A researcher's use of secondary data often depends on whether the reporting unit matches the researcher's need. For example, a researcher wishing to evaluate market areas when considering an expansion may be pleased with data reported at the county level. A great deal of secondary data is available at the county level. But, what if another marketer wishes to evaluate a two-mile area around a street address that is proposed as a site location for a retail store? County data would hardly be adequate. Another marketer wishes to know the demographic makeup of each zip code in a major city in order to determine which zip codes to target for a direct-mail campaign. Again, county data would be inappropriate. While inappropriate reporting units are often problems in using secondary data, more and more data are available today in multiple reporting units. Data at the zip +4 level are becoming more widely available. **Geodemographics** is the term used to describe the classification of arbitrary, usually small, geographic areas in terms of the characteristics of their inhabitants. Aided with GIS (geodemographic information systems), geodemographers can access huge databases and construct profiles of consumers residing in geographic areas determined by the geodemographer. Instead of being confined to fixed geographic reporting units such as a city, county, or state, geodemographers can produce this information for geographic areas thought to be relevant for a given marketing application (such as in our two-mile radius example). Geodemography is often at the core of many standardized services we discuss in the latter part of this chapter.

MEASUREMENT UNITS DO NOT MATCH Sometimes secondary data are reported in measurement units that do not match the measurement unit needed by the researcher. Available studies of income may measure income in several ways: total income, income after taxes, household income, and per capita income. Consider a research project that needs to categorize businesses by size in terms of square footage. Secondary data sources, however, classify businesses in terms of size according to sales volume, number of employees, profit level, and other ways.

CLASS DEFINITIONS ARE NOT USABLE The class definitions of the reported data may not be usable to a researcher. Secondary data are often reported by breaking a variable into different classes and reporting the frequency of occurrence in each class. For example, suppose a source of secondary data reports the variable household income in three classes. The first class reports the percentage of households having between $20,000 and $34,999, and the final class reports the percentage of households having incomes of $50,000 and over. For most studies, these classifications are applicable. However, imagine you are a manufacturer of high-end plumbing fixtures and you are

---

The five advantages of secondary data are data can be obtained quickly and inexpensively, are usually available, enhance primary data collection, and can sometimes achieve the research objective.

Five of the problems associated with secondary data include incompatible reporting units, mismatch of the units of measurement, differing definitions used to classify the data, the timeliness of the secondary data, and the lack of information needed to assess the credibility of the data reported.

These problems exist because secondary data have not been collected specifically to address the problem at hand but have been collected for some other purpose.

Secondary data are provided in reporting units such as county, city, metro area, state, region, zip code, or CBSAs.

Geodemographics is the term used to describe the classification of arbitrary, usually small, geographic areas in terms of the characteristics of their inhabitants.

looking to expand the number of distributorships. You have learned that your dealers are most successful in geographical areas with average household incomes above $80,000. You need another source of information since your source of secondary data only reports household incomes of $50,000 and over. What would a researcher do in this situation? Typically, if you keep looking you can find what you need, for example, in other sources of secondary data in other categories.

DATA ARE OUTDATED Sometimes a marketing researcher will find information reported with the desired unit of measurement and the proper classifications, however, the data are outdated. The reason is, some secondary data are published only once; and for secondary data that is published at regular intervals, the time that passed since the last publication can be a problem when applying the data to a current situation. The researcher must make the decision as to whether or not to use the data.

Evaluating Secondary Data

Hopefully, in the course of your studies, you have learned that not everything you read is true. In order to properly use secondary data, you must evaluate the information before you use it as a basis for making decisions. A reader must be most cautious when using an Internet source because few quality standards are applied to most sites. To determine the reliability of secondary information, marketing researchers must evaluate it. In the following paragraphs we look at five questions to evaluate secondary data.

WHAT WAS THE PURPOSE OF THE STUDY? Studies are conducted for a purpose, but readers may not know the true purpose. Some studies are conducted in order to "prove" a position or to advance the special interests of those conducting the study. In the 1980s, environmentalists became concerned over the growing mountains of disposable, plastic diapers that had all but replaced cloth diapers. More than a dozen state legislatures were considering various bans, taxes, and even warning labels on disposable diapers. Then "research studies" were produced whose "purpose" was to evaluate the environmental effects of disposable versus cloth diapers. It seemed that the "new" research proved that cloth diapers, by adding detergent by-products to the water table, were more harmful to the environment than the ever-lasting plastic disposables.

Soon after several of these studies were made available to legislators, the movement against disposables was dead. But, what was the real purpose of the studies? Procter & Gamble, owning the lion's share of the market for disposable diapers, commissioned the consulting firm of Arthur D. Little Inc. to conduct one of the studies. Another favorable study for the disposables was conducted by Franklin Associates, whose research showed disposables were not any more harmful than cloth diapers. But who sponsored this study? The American Paper Institute, an organization with major interests in disposable diapers. But wait, before you become too critical of the disposable diaper folks, let's consider another so-called scientific study in 1988, that showed disposable diapers as being "garbage" and contributing to massive buildups of waste that was all but impervious to deterioration. Who sponsored this study? The cloth diaper industry, of course.

The diaper industries are not the only ones playing the game: A more recent "study" appeared in news media citing the terrible condition of roads and bridges in the United States. Who sponsored the study? An organization representing road and bridge construction companies. It may well be that the study was objective and accurate. Users of secondary information, however, should be well aware of the *true purpose* of the study and evaluate the information accordingly.

WHO COLLECTED THE INFORMATION? Even when you are convinced that there is no bias in the purpose of the study, be sure to question the competence of the organization that collected the information, because organizations differ in terms of the resources they command and

Sometimes measurement units reported in secondary data sources do not match the researcher's needs. Household income is reported but the researcher needs per capita income.

There is a problem when the researcher needs to know the percent of households having incomes over $80,000 and the secondary data source provides the highest category at $50,000 and over.

To determine the reliability of secondary information, marketing researchers must evaluate it.

Users of secondary data should try to understand the true purpose of a study they are using as secondary data.

Research studies are often published and become a part of secondary data. However, not all research studies are conducted in a totally objective manner. You must ask who conducted the study.

their quality control. But how do you determine the competency of the organization that collected the data? First, ask others who have more experience in a given industry. Typically, credible organizations are well known in those industries for which they conduct studies. Second, examine the report itself. Competent firms will almost always provide carefully written and detailed explanations of the procedures and methods used in collecting the information contained in the report. Third, contact previous clients of the firm. Have they been satisfied with the quality of the work performed by the organization? Be wary of using information just because it is available on the Internet. While the Internet is a wonderful source of information, there are few restrictions as to who may place, or what information may be placed, on this information highway. Always check for the original source of the information if it is available.

It may be very important to know exactly what was measured in a report before using the results.

WHAT INFORMATION WAS COLLECTED? There are many studies available on topics such as economic impact, market potential, feasibility, and the like. But what exactly was measured in these studies that constitute impact, potential, or feasibility? There are many examples of studies that claim to provide information on a specific subject but, in fact, measure something quite different. In one study it was important to determine the number of businesses that existed in each county, to set a basis for projecting sales for a B2B service; but how was "number of businesses" actually measured? In one report, each existing business location counted as a business. This resulted in a high count as one business may have had a dozen distribution outlets. In another report, only the business, not its outlets, was counted. This resulted in a low count. Is this distinction important? Perhaps, depending on how the study's user intends to utilize the information. One would have to assess if the B2B service could be sold to each individual distribution outlet or only to the parent company. The important point here is that the user should discover exactly what information was collected.

Evaluate the method used to collect the primary data now available to you as secondary data. You will be much better at doing this when you finish this course.

HOW WAS THE INFORMATION OBTAINED? You should be aware of the methods used to obtain information reported in secondary sources. What was the sample? How large was the sample? What was the response rate? Was the information validated? As you will learn throughout this book, there are many alternative ways of collecting primary data, and each may have an impact on the information collected. Remember, even though you are evaluating secondary data, this information was gathered as primary data by some organization. Therefore, the alternative ways of gathering the data had an impact on the nature and quality of the data. It is not always easy to find out how the secondary data were gathered; however, as noted earlier, most reputable organizations that provide secondary data also provide information on their data-collection methods.

If two or more sources of secondary data differ you should investigate why they differ. Did they measure the same entity? Did they use different methods to collect their data?

HOW CONSISTENT IS THE INFORMATION AMONG SOURCES? In some cases, the same secondary data are reported by multiple, independent organizations, which provides an excellent way to evaluate secondary data sources. Ideally, if two or more independent organizations report the same data, you can have greater confidence in the validity and reliability of the data. Demographic data, for example, for metropolitan areas (CBSAs), counties, and most municipalities are widely available from more than one source. If you are evaluating a survey that is supposedly representative of a given geographic area, you may want to compare the characteristics of the sample of the survey with the demographic data available on the population. If you know, based on U.S. census data, that there are 45% males and 55% females in a city and a survey, which is supposed to be representative of that city, reports a sample of 46% males and 54% females, then you can be more confident in the survey data. It is indeed rare, however, that two organizations will report exactly the same results. Here you must look at the magnitude of the differences to determine validity. If all independent sources report very large differences of the same variable, then you may not have much confidence in any of the data. You should look carefully at what information was collected, how it was collected, and so on, for each reporting source.

Key Sources of Secondary Data for Marketers

We hope you understand by now that there are thousands of sources of secondary data that may be relevant to business decisions. In Table 5.2, we provide you with some of these major sources that are useful in marketing research. In the next section we will take an in-depth look at what will likely be a significant source of secondary data for marketing research for many years, the American Community Survey.

TABLE 5.2
Secondary Information Sources on Marketing

---

1. Reference Guides

Encyclopedia of Business Information Sources (Detroit: GaleGroup, annual)

For the researcher, this lists marketing associations, advertising agencies, research centers, agencies, and sources relating to various business topics. It is particularly useful for identifying information about specific industries.

2. Indexes

ABI/INFORM Global (Ann Arbor, MI: ProQuest, 1971–present)

Available online, this database indexes and abstracts major journals relating to a broad range of business topics. Electronic access to many full-text articles is also available. ABI/INFORM Global may be complemented by ABI/INFORM Archive; ABI/INFORM Dateline; ABI/INFORM Trade & Industry; and may be searched alone or in tandem with any or all of these databases at subscribing libraries.

Business File ASAP (Detroit: Gale Group, 1980–present)

Available online. This index covers primarily business and popular journals and includes some full-text articles.

Wilson Business Full Text (New York: H. W. Wilson, 1986)

Available online. The print version is *Business Periodicals Index* (1958–present). This basic index is useful for indexing the major business journals further back in time than other indexes.

3. Dictionaries and Encyclopedias

Dictionary of Marketing Terms, Fourth Edition (Hauppauge, NY: Barron's, 2008)

Prepared by Jane Imber and Betsy Ann Toffler, this dictionary includes brief definitions of popular terms in marketing.

Encyclopedia of Consumer Brands (Detroit: St. James Press, 2005)

For consumable products, personal products, and durable goods, this source provides detailed descriptions of the history and major developments of major brand names.

4. Directories

Bradford's Directory of Marketing Research Agencies and Management Consultants in the United States and the World (Middleberg, VA: Bradford's, biennial)

Indexed by type of service, this source gives scope of activity for each agency and lists names of officers.

Broadcasting and Cable Yearbook (New Providence, NJ: R. R. Bowker, annual)

A directory of U.S. and Canadian television and radio stations, advertising agencies, and other useful information.

Directories in Print (Detroit: Gale Research, annual)

Provides detailed information on business and industrial directories, professional and scientific rosters, online directory of databases, and other lists. This source is particularly useful for identifying directories associated with specific industries or products.

Gale Directory of Publications and Broadcast Media (Detroit: Gale Research, annual)

A geographic listing of U.S. and Canadian newspapers, magazines, and trade publications, as well as broadcasting stations. Includes address, edition, frequency, circulation, and subscription and advertising rates.

(continued)

TABLE 5.2 (continued)

Secondary Information Sources on Marketing

---

5. Statistical Sources

Datapedia of the United States, 1790–2005 (Lanham, MD: Bernan Press, 2001)

Based on the *Historical Statistics of the United States from Colonial Times* and other statistical sources, this volume presents hundreds of tables reflecting historical and, in some cases, forecasting data on numerous demographic variables relating to the United States.

Survey of Buying Power

Now available only through the website, at www.surveyofbuyingpower.com/. Formerly published in print in an annual copy of *Sales & Marketing Management* magazine. Includes statistics on population, income, retail sales, effective buying income, and more, for CBSAs and media markets.

Editor and Publisher Market Guide (New York: Editor and Publisher, annual)

Provides market data for more than 1,500 U.S. and Canadian newspaper cities covering facts and figures about location, transaction, population, households, banks, autos, and more.

Market Share Reporter (Detroit: Gale Research, annual)

Provides market share data on products and service industries in the United States.

Standard Rate and Data Service (Des Plaines, IL: SRDS, monthly)

In the SRDS monthly publications (those for consumer magazine and agrimedia, newspapers, spot radio, spot television) marketing statistics are included at the beginning of each state section.

Census 2010 and American Community Survey

The taking of a census of the U.S. population began in 1790. Prior to 1940, everyone had to answer all the questions that the census used. In 1940, the long form—a longer questionnaire distributed to only a sample of respondents—was introduced as a way to collect more data, more rapidly, and without increasing respondent burden. In Census 2000, the long form went to one in six housing units. As a result, much of the census data are based on statistical sampling.[11] **Census 2010** is different in that only the short form is used to collect data. The Census Bureau is more interested in an accurate count which they believe is more attainable with the short form that only takes a few minutes to complete. The short form asks only for name, sex, age, date of birth, race, ethnicity, relationship, and housing tenure. Data from the long form is still needed but will be collected through the American Community Survey. For many years the census has been the backbone of secondary data in the United States. Marketers use the information in many ways and marketing research firms have developed products to aid in the use of census data. You may learn more about Census 2010 by visiting the official website, at http://2010.census.gov.

Census 2010 is different in that only the short form is used to collect data.

You may learn more about Census 2010 by visiting the official website, at http://2010 .census.gov.

AMERICAN COMMUNITY SURVEY The **American Community Survey** may represent the most significant change in the availability of secondary data to be used for marketing research purposes in several decades. The U.S. Census Bureau created the American Community Survey (ACS) in 1996 to collect economic, social, demographic, and housing information as part of the Decennial Census Program. The survey is designed to help update Decennial Census data by collecting information on a small percentage of the population in all counties, American Indian areas, Alaska Native areas, and Hawaiian homelands on a rotating basis using a sample. The primary advantage is that the ACS will provide data annually instead of once every ten years. Since these data will have the U.S. Census Bureau's "high marks" for reliable data *and* will be current, the ACS is likely to become a major secondary data resource for marketing researchers.

The American Community Survey provides current data about communities every year, rather than once every ten years. Visit the American Community Survey at www.census.gov/acs/ www/.

As we just noted, the ACS will provide updated, annual estimates to help alleviate one of the major problems with the Decennial Census which, of course, is updated every ten years. The ACS will provide information each year and will provide a measure of accuracy of the yearly estimates. To do this, the ACS relies on a sampling plan that involves surveying

In 2007, the number of U.S. residents who identified themselves as Asian alone or in combination with one or more races was 15.2 million.

approximately 3 million Americans every year. Because a sample is used, data are reported with a margin of error, which is an estimate of the accuracy of the data. (You will learn more about this in Chapters 9 and 12.)

The ACS was first completed in 2005. Since then, the ACS has been offering yearly estimates for geographic areas with a population of 65,000 or more. Geographic areas with populations of 20,000 or more can access three-year estimates, and areas with populations less than 20,000 can access five-year estimates beginning in 2010. Whereas the one-year estimates are more current, they lack the sample size of the three- and five-year estimates. However, the three-year estimates have more sample size than the one-year estimates; and the five-year estimates have more sample size than the three-year estimates. Larger sample sizes mean more accurate (smaller margin of error) data. Figure 5.1 provides essential information needed to understand the basics of the ACS, and Marketing Research Application 5.1 provides you with an illustration of its use for a marketing research objective.

What Is Standardized Information?

We are now ready to turn to a special form of secondary data, standardized information. **Standardized information** is a type of secondary data in which the data collected and/or the process of collecting the data are standardized for all users. There are two broad classes of standardized information: syndicated data and standardized services.

Syndicated data are collected in a standard format and made available to all subscribers. Marketing Evaluations Inc. offers several Q Scores® services. For example, they measure the familiarity and appeal of performers in a number of categories such as actors, actresses, authors, athletes, and sportscasters. This information is used by companies to help them choose the most appropriate spokesperson for their company or help a movie producer select a performer for an upcoming movie. **Performer Q** is the service for ratings of approximately 1,700 performers.

Standardized information is a type of secondary data in which the data collected and/or the process of collecting the data are standardized for all users. Two broad classes of standardized information are syndicated data and standardized services.

How to Find
American Community Survey Data in American Factfinder (AFF)

Issued July 2009

American FactFinder,the U.S. Census Bureau's primary online data access tool, is the source for population, housing, economic, and geography data produced by the Census Bureau. Look inside for ways to use AFF to access American Community Survey data products, such as data tables, detailed profiles, thematic maps, and Public Use Microdata Sample (PUMS) files.

The American Community Survey in AFF

Subjects Found in American Community Survey

Housing	Population
☒ Vehicles Available	☒ Age
☒ Year Structure Built	☒ Sex
☒ Units in Structure	☒ Hispanic Origin
☒ Year Moved Into Unit	☒ Race
☒ Rooms	☒ Relationship to Householder (e.g., Spouse)
☒ Bedrooms	☒ Income
☒ Kitchen Facilities	☒ Food Stamps Benefit
☒ Plumbing Facilities	☒ Labor Force Status
☒ House Heating Fuel	☒ Industry, Occupation, and Class of Worker
☒ Telephone Service Available	☒ Place of Work and Journey to Work
☒ Farm Residence	☒ Work Status Last Year
☒ Tenure (Owner/Renter)	☒ Marital Status
☒ Housing Value	☒ Marital History
☒ Rent	☒ Fertility
☒ Selected Monthly Owner Costs	☒ Grandparents as Caregivers
	☒ Ancestry
	☒ Place of Birth
	☒ Citizenship
	☒ Year of Naturalization
	☒ Educational Attainment
	☒ Residence One Year Ago
	☒ Veteran Status
	☒ Period of Military Service
	☒ Disability
	☒ Undergraduate Field of Degree
	☒ And Other Subjects!

The American Community Survey (ACS) is the largest household survey in the United States and provides the most up-to-date social, economic, housing and demographic data for communities in the U.S.

The area to the left displays the many subjects produced from the ACS data collection. Data for the subjects are shown in a variety of ways and inside you will find descriptions of the ACS data products available through AFF.

Similar information is also available for Puerto Rico through the Puerto Rico Community Survey (PRCS).

<www.factfinder.census.gov>

USCENSUSBUREAU
Helping You Make Informed Decisions

United States®
Census
2010

FIGURE 5.1

Source: www.census.gov.

Advanced Automotive Concepts' Decision to Build a Total Electric Car

AAC is considering adding a car model to their product mix that will be *totally* electric. Buyers will never have to buy gasoline. The cost to operate this vehicle will be about $.02 per mile versus about $.12 per mile for a gasoline vehicle. AAC believes it can have a competitive advantage over other all electric vehicles by building a car whose body surface is made of solar panels. So, unlike other competitive vehicles that charge only when plugged into an electrical outlet, a car with a solar panel "skin" can absorb additional energy as long as the sun is out. This is significant for another reason and that is if an electric car owner charges their vehicle with electricity from a coal powered electric plant (which powers the dominant percentage of power plants in the U.S.) the greenhouse gas emissions are still .8 lbs per mile driven. While this is better than the 1 lb per mile for gasoline powered emissions, it means the vehicles are far from "emission free." Lange, K.E. (2009, November). The big idea: Electric cars. *National Geographic*, p. 24. A solar panel "skin" will help reduce the gas emissions and the AAC car would not only have greater range but come closer to a truly emission free vehicle. However, the range of electric cars is still a major concern even with the ability of a constant charge using the solar panels. While the solar panels will help, they cannot keep up with the energy needed to propel the car even on a very sunny day. It is estimated that the range of this new car will be 125 miles, an improvement over other cars whose range is between 60 to 100 miles. Before going further, AAC wants to know if this car will suffice for the bulk of commuter travel to and from work each day and still have sufficient range to run errands. AAC believes that *if the majority of workers commute under 30 minutes each way to work*, then the new car would have adequate range to get owners to and from work and run a few errands. Before going further with the concept of the new vehicle, secondary data may be assessed to answer the question: "What is the mean travel time, one way, for Americans to travel to work?" Let's examine how we could find the answer to this research objective.

First, go to www.census.gov and click on *American Factfinder*, which should give you access to another link–*American Community Survey*. Find *Get Data*. Now you will have a choice as to whether you want your results/estimates to be based on 1, 3, or 5 year reports. Select *5 year estimates*. (You can also use 3 year estimates if you wish). *Go to Subject Tables* and select *Geographic Type*–it should default to Nation so you can leave this in and click Next. (Take a look at other geographic types you may choose, i.e. counties, MSA's, etc.) Scroll down through the subjects, i.e. age and sex, aging, children . . . down to transportation. Click on *Commuting Characteristics by Sex* and scroll down to *Travel Time to Work*. Look for *Mean Travel Time to Work (minutes)*. Should AAC continue with development plans for the new car?

Lange, K.E. (2009, November). The big idea: Electric cars. *National Geographic*, p. 24.

Tom Hanks and Bill Cosby, for example, are performers that have high Q Scores. Data for all 1,700 performers studied is the same—standardized—regardless of who uses the data. Data are collected two times a year for all performers based on a sample of nearly 2,000 persons. Data are made available to all who subscribe to the data, and subscribers include advertisers, television and movie production companies, licensing companies, talent and public relations companies, among others. Another example is Nielsen Media Research's Nielsen Television Index (NTI). The NTI provides subscribers with data on television viewing. The resulting data are standardized in the sense that the same data are made available to anyone wishing to purchase the data. On the other hand, **standardized services** refers to a standardized marketing research *process* that is used to generate information for a particular user. **Esri's Tapestry™ Segmentation** is a standardized service that uses a *process* to profile residential neighborhoods. This information is purchased by clients desiring to better understand who their customers are, where they are located, how to find them, and how to reach them. We discuss both of these types of information next.

Syndicated data are a form of external, secondary data that are supplied from a common database to subscribers for a service fee. Recall from our discussion of the types of firms in the marketing research industry in Chapter 2 that we call firms providing such data "syndicated data service firms." Such information is typically detailed information that is valuable to firms in a given industry and is not available in libraries. Firms supplying syndicated data follow standard research formats that enable them to collect the same standardized data over time. These firms

> Syndicated data are collected in a standard format and made available to all subscribers.

> Go to www.qscores.com and visit the Market Evaluations Inc. site. Learn about the different Q Score studies that are available.

> Standardized services refer to a standardized marketing research *process* that is used to generate information for a particular user.

provide specialized, routine information needed by a given industry in the form of ready-to-use, standardized marketing data to subscribing firms. We mentioned the NTI ratings earlier. As another example, Arbitron supplies syndicated data on the number and types of listeners to the various radio stations in each radio market. This standardized information helps advertising firms reach their target markets; it also helps radio stations define audience characteristics by providing an objective, independent measure of the size and characteristics of their audiences. With syndicated data, the process of collecting and analyzing the data, as well as the data, is standardized; that is, neither is varied for the client.[12] On the other hand, standardized services rarely provide clients with standardized data. Rather, it is the *process* they are marketing. The application of that standardized process will result in different data for each client. For example, a standardized service may be a measure of customer satisfaction. Instead of a user developing a process for measuring customer satisfaction, the user may elect to employ a standardized service for measuring customer satisfaction. This is also true for several other marketing research services, such as test marketing, naming new brands, pricing a new product, or using mystery shoppers.

Advantages and Disadvantages of Standardized Information

SYNDICATED DATA One key advantage of syndicated data is *shared costs*. Many client firms may subscribe to the information; thus, the cost of the service is greatly reduced to any one subscriber firm. Secondly, because syndicated data firms specialize in the collection of standard data and because their viability, in the long run, depends on the validity of the data, the *quality of the data collected is typically very high*. Finally, another advantage of syndicated data is that the *data are normally disseminated very quickly* to subscribers and the more current the data, the greater their usefulness.

Although there are several advantages to syndicated data, certain disadvantages remain, as well. First, *buyers have little control over what information is collected.* Are the units of measurement correct? Are the geographical reporting units appropriate? A second disadvantage is that buyer firms often must commit to *long-term contracts* when buying standardized data. Third, there is *no strategic information advantage* in purchasing syndicated data because all competitors have access to the same information. However, in many industries, firms would suffer a serious strategic disadvantage by not purchasing the information.

STANDARDIZED SERVICES The key advantage of using a standardized service is *taking advantage of the experience of the research firm offering the service*. Imagine a firm setting out to conduct a test market for the very first time. It would take the firm several months to gain the confidence needed to conduct the test market properly. Taking advantage of others' experiences with the process is a good way to minimize potential mistakes in carrying out the research process. A second advantage is the *reduced cost* of the research. Because the supplier firm conducts the service for many clients on a regular basis, the procedure is efficient and far less costly than if the buyer firm tried to conduct the service itself. A third advantage is the *speed of the research service*. The efficiency gained by conducting the service over and over translates into reduced turnaround time from start to finish of a research project.

There are disadvantages of using standardized services as well. "Standardized" means "not customized." The *ability to customize some projects is lost* when using a standardized service. Second, the *company providing the standardized service may not know the idiosyncrasies of a particular industry,* resulting in greater burden on the client to ensure that the standardized service fits the intended situation. Client firms need to be very familiar with the service provided, including what data are collected on which population, how the data are collected, and how the data are reported before they purchase the service.

APPLICATIONS OF STANDARDIZED INFORMATION Standardized information may be applied to many marketing research decisions such as measuring consumer attitudes and opinions, defining market segments, conducting market tracking studies, and monitoring media usage and

---

Esri's Tapestry™ Segmentation is a standardized service that uses a *process* to profile residential neighborhoods. This information is purchased by clients desiring to better understand who their customers are, where they are located, how to find them, and how to reach them.

With syndicated data, the data and the process used to generate the data are standardized across all users. With standardized services, the process of collecting data is standardized across all users.

Advantages of syndicated data are shared costs, high quality of the data, and speed with which data are collected and made available for decision making.

Disadvantages of syndicated data include little control over what data are collected, buyers must commit to long-term contracts, and competitors have access to the same information.

Advantages of standardized services are using the experience of the firm offering the service, reduced cost, and increased speed of conducting the service.

promotion effectiveness. In the following section we illustrate a few of these applications with examples of firms that provide the service.

Market Segmentation Several marketing research firms offer a standardized service of providing client firms with sophisticated methods of identifying members of their target market, locating these members, and providing information that will help develop promotional materials to efficiently reach them. At the base of many of these services is geodemographics, as discussed earlier in this chapter. Esri's offers clients a geodemographic market segmentation system called Tapestry™ Segmentation. Tapestry Segmentation divides U.S. residential neighborhoods into sixty-five distinctive segments based upon selected demographic and socioeconomic characteristics. Some of these segments are as follows:[13]

Top Rung Tapestry's wealthiest consumer segment represents less than 1% of all U.S. households. The median household income of $182,041 is 3.5 times higher than that of the U.S. median; the median net worth of $1,120,886 is more than 5 times higher than the national figure. The median home value is approximately $864,923. The median age is 44.2 years. These residents are married couples with and without children, highly educated, and in

> Disadvantages of standardized services are the inability to customize services and the service firm not being knowledgeable about the client's industry.

> Tapestry Segmentation divides U.S. residential neighborhoods into sixty-five distinctive segments based upon selected demographic and socioeconomic characteristics.

their peak earning years of ages 45 to 64. Because they can afford anything, they travel in style both domestically and abroad. This is the top segment for owning or leasing a luxury car—new imported vehicles, especially convertibles equipped with a GPS. Exercise and community activities are part of their busy lifestyle. They'll read two or more daily newspapers and countless books.

Aspiring Young Families Young, married-couple families or single parents with children live in these large, growing metropolitan areas in the South and West, concentrated in California, Texas, and Florida. The median age is 30.9 years. Half of them live in owner-occupied single-family housing or townhouses; the other half rent, many in newer multiunit apartment buildings. They buy home furnishings, baby and children's products, and toys. They've recently bought electronics such as cameras and video game systems. They eat out; they go out dancing, to the movies, and to professional football games. They also fish, lift weights, play basketball, and visit chat rooms online. They would probably visit a theme park on vacation.

Practical Applications

MARKETING RESEARCH APPLICATION 5.2

Practical Application

Mavens are recognized by their peers as reliable information sources who give the facts and let people make their own decisions.

Tipping Point Segments

Growing use of viral campaigns, social media networking and other innovative new marketing strategies highlight the unchanged power of word-of-mouth advertising. By going to the source, Experian Simmons offers an industry-first solution so that you can identify the individuals most responsible for word-of-mouth advertising.[14]

- Created through partnership with Malcolm Gladwell, author of *The Tipping Point: How Little Things Can Make a Big Difference*
- Exponentially leverages your marketing spend by focusing on the small group of influential people, approximately 13% of the U.S. adult population, who take an idea, trend or behavior and help it spread like wildfire
- Tipping Point analysis allows you to precisely target the most influential consumers and tailor your messages for each of the different Tipping Point segments

Who Are These People?

Through Experian Simmons' ongoing National Consumer Survey, we are able to define the key characteristics of each Tipping Point segment. They are people with a powerful ability to spread information and trends who come from all walks of life. Describing them demographically is virtually impossible

but they do share attitudes and opinions that are typical of those who are "engaged in life."

- They are active socially, civically and politically
- They seek out information from a variety of sources
- They find activities that enhance relationships
- They engage in life by playing a key role in the lives of many people

Experian Simmons can help you identify which of your prospects and customers fall into the key Tipping Point segments:

1. *Connectors* Possessors of an extensive network of friends and acquaintances, these are the individuals who provide the links between people.
2. *Mavens* Recognized by their peers as reliable information sources who give the facts and let people make their own decisions.
3. *Salespeople* Persuaders who can motivate people to believe or try things through their energy and their enthusiastic personality and style.
4. *Innovators* People who are in at the birth of a new trend, they embrace whatever can set them apart from others, pioneer new products and categories, and respond to opportunities to provide positive change.

Source: Experian Simmons, by permission.

Given these descriptions, you can see how beneficial it would be to marketers to know which Tapestry Segmentation segments account for a dominant share of their target market. Knowing where these segments are located (even at the ZIP Code level), knowing their demographics, and knowing their media habits and purchasing preferences would give marketers keen insight into their target markets.

Monitoring Consumer-Generated Media Consumer-generated media (CGM) is content created by consumers on blogs, discussion boards, forums, user groups, and other social media platforms. Opinions, comments, and personal experiences are posted and made publicly available on a wide range of issues, including products and brands. CGM is also referred to as online consumer word of mouth or online consumer buzz—a fast growing form of media. Consumers, who value nonmarketer-controlled sources of information, often seek opinion, recommendations, and product reviews that are part of CGM. Companies desiring to track the "buzz" going on in CGM about their own brands and those of their competitors may purchase a service such as Experian Simmon's Tipping Point. Read more about Tipping Point in Marketing Research Application 5.2.

Both market segmentation and CGM are examples of standardized services; it is the process that these firms offer clients. A prevalent example of syndicated data services is Nielsen's Homescan® panel, which tracks the sales of products sold in grocery stores, warehouse clubs, and even on the Internet. Clients receive data for all SKUs in a category of products. In addition, Arbitron measures the number of persons listening to radio stations in a given market. These data are provided to all subscribers of Arbitron radio services.[15]

Summary

Data may be grouped into two categories: primary and secondary. Primary data are gathered specifically for the research project at hand. Secondary data have been previously gathered for some other purpose. There are many uses of secondary data in marketing research, and sometimes secondary data alone can achieve the research objectives. Secondary data may be internal, meaning they are data already gathered *within* the firm for some other purpose. Data collected and stored from sales receipts, such as types, quantities, and prices of goods or services purchased; customer names; delivery addresses; shipping dates; and salesperson identification, would be an example of internal secondary data. Storing internal data in electronic databases has become increasingly popular and may be used for database marketing. Databases are composed of records, which contain subcomponents of information called fields. Companies use information recorded in internal databases for purposes of direct marketing and to strengthen relationships with customers. The latter is a process known as customer relationship management (CRM). External secondary data are obtained from sources outside the firm. These data may be classified as (1) published, (2) syndicated services data, and (3) external databases. There are different types of published secondary data, such as reference guides, indexes and abstracts, bibliographies, almanacs, manuals, and handbooks. Different types of secondary data have different functions, and understanding these functions is useful in researching secondary data. Syndicated services data are provided by firms that collect data in a standard format and make them available to subscribing firms. Online information databases are sources of secondary data searchable by search engines online. Examples include Factiva, Ibis World, Lexis-Nexis, and ProQuest.

Secondary data have the advantages of being quickly gathered, readily available, and relatively inexpensive, adding helpful insights should primary data be needed, and sometimes being all that is necessary to achieve the research objective. Disadvantages are that the data are often reported in incompatible reporting units (county data are reported when zip code data are needed), measurement units do not match researchers' needs (household income is reported and per capita income is needed), class definitions are incompatible with the researchers' needs (income is reported in classes up to $50,000 but the researchers need to know what percent of the population earns $75,000 or more), and secondary data may be outdated. Evaluation of secondary data is important; researchers must ask certain questions in order to ensure the integrity of the information they use. The American Community Survey (ACS) may represent the most significant change in the availability of secondary data to be used for marketing research purposes in several decades. The ACS

will make data available on an annual basis instead of the ten-year interval required in the past to update census data.

Standardized information is a type of secondary data in which the data collected and/or the process of collecting the data are standardized for all users. There are two classes of standardized information. Syndicated data are collected in a standard format and made available to all subscribing users. An example is the Nielsen television ratings. Standardized services offer a standardized marketing research process that is used to generate information for a particular user. Tapestry™ Segmentation is a system of classifying residential neighborhoods into sixty-five different segments. That process is standardized; it is the same for all users. The information from the process is then applied to generate different data for each user. With syndicated data, the data are the same for each user and with standardized services the process of generating data for each user is the same.

Syndicated data have the advantages of sharing the costs of obtaining the data among all those subscribing to the service, high data quality, and the speed with which data are collected and distributed to subscribers. Disadvantages are that buyers cannot control what data are collected, buyers must commit to long-term contracts, and there is no strategic information advantage to buying syndicated data because the information is available to all competitors.

Standardized services have the advantage of using the supplier firm's expertise in the area, reduced costs, and speed with which supplier firms can conduct the service. The disadvantages of standardized services are the process cannot easily be customized, and the supplier firm may not know the idiosyncrasies of the industry in which the client firm operates.

Four major areas in which standardized information sources may be applied are measuring consumers' attitudes and opinions, defining market segments, conducting market tracking studies, and monitoring media usage and promotion effectiveness.

Key Terms

Primary data (p. 107)
Secondary data (p. 108)
Internal secondary data (p. 109)
Database marketing (p. 109)
Database (p. 109)

Record (p. 109)
Fields (p. 109)
Internal databases (p. 109)
Customer relationship management
  (CRM) (p. 109)

Data mining (p. 109)
External secondary data (p. 110)
Published sources (p. 110)
Syndicated services data
  (p. 110)

External databases (p. 110)
Online information databases
   (p. 110)
Core-based statistical area
   (CBSA) (p. 112)
Metropolitan SAs (p. 112)
Micropolitan SAs (p. 112)

Geodemographics (p. 112)
Census 2010 (p. 116)
American Community
   Survey (p. 116)
Standardized information
   (p. 117)
Syndicated data (p. 117)

Performer Q (p. 117)
Standardized services (p. 119)
ESRI's Tapestry
   Segmentation (p. 119)
Top Rung (p. 121)
Aspiring Young
   Families (p. 121)

Review Questions

1. What are secondary data, and how do they differ from primary data?
2. Describe some uses of secondary data.
3. How would you classify secondary data?
4. What is database marketing and what is CRM?
5. What are three types of external secondary data?
6. What are online information databases? Name three of them.
7. What are the five advantages of secondary data? Discuss the disadvantages of secondary data.
8. How would you go about evaluating secondary data? Why is evaluation important?
9. Describe the American Community Survey in terms of the advantage it will offer as well as how to find it to retrieve data.
10. What are the two types of standardized information?
11. Clearly distinguish between syndicated data and standardized services.
12. ESRI's market segmentation service, Tapestry™ Segmentation, would be classified as which type of standardized information? Why?
13. What are the advantages and disadvantages of syndicated data?
14. What are the advantages and disadvantages of standardized services?
15. Describe some areas in which standardized information may be applied.

Application Questions

16. Access your library's online databases. Describe how your library helps categorize the many databases such that you would know how to select databases appropriate for business.
17. Go online to your library's website. Can you locate a database that would be a good choice to find publications such as journal articles, trade publications, or newspapers? What are they?
18. Go online to your favorite search engine (e.g., Google, Yahoo) and enter "Demographics." Visit some of these sites and describe the kind of information you are receiving. Why would this information be considered secondary data?
19. Find your library's online databases and check if any of them have the ability to automatically put an article you retrieve in a format suitable for citing (e.g., MLA, APA).
20. Go to the website of Nielsen, at http://nielsen.com/. Select the region or country in which you live. Look at the services provided by Nielsen and read about them. Which ones would you classify as (a) syndicated data and (b) standardized services?
21. Go to www.maritz.com, and click on "Sales & Marketing Services" then "Marketing Research." Go to "Case Studies." Read any case in an industry in which you have an interest for future employment. Was the study conducted by Maritz using either syndicated data or a standardized service? If so, provide a description.

Case 5.1 **Secondary Data to Find Your Career Industry**

Soon you will be in the job market. Have you thought about which industry will provide you with a challenging and rewarding career? One thing you want to make certain is to pick a "growth" industry versus a "sunset" industry where sales are declining and layoffs will be inevitable. You can use secondary data to help you make this distinction.

As an example, Mark Eberhard is a retired marine officer and is well versed on firearms and has an intrinsic interest in marksmanship. He wondered if a chain of modern firing ranges would make a successful entrepreneurial investment. He asked himself these basic questions: Are firing ranges growing or declining in popularity? Since firing ranges are often used by hunters, is hunting, of all types, growing or declining? What is the general public's attitude toward firearms? Are American sentiments toward firearms favorable or will negative sentiment push Congress to pass legislation restricting the use of firearms?

These are basic questions potential entrepreneurs should ask about the industry they are planning to enter. Is this a viable industry? Is it growing or declining? Fortunately, for most of these types of questions secondary data are available.

It didn't take Eberhard long to find that the firing range industry had a trade association, the National Shooting Sports Foundation (NSSF). Trade associations often gather secondary data from various sources and make this information available to members or those who are thinking about entering the industry. NSSF, for example, gathers data from the U.S. Fish and Wildlife Service on the number of hunting licenses. These data are also available by state, which allows users to pinpoint the largest concentrations of hunters. Furthermore, the data are available for many years, which allow users to look at twenty-, ten-, and five-year trends. Since excise taxes are charged on the sale of firearms and ammunition, Eberhard was able to examine secondary data showing sales of weapons and ammunition over several years. The Bureau of Alcohol, Tobacco, Firearms, and Explosives (ATF) also publishes data on firearm licenses by state, as well as an annual report on how many firearms (pistols, rifles, shotguns, etc.) are manufactured each year, and the number of firearms imported and exported.

Eberhard also looked at other information, such as the declining number of firearm deaths published by the National Safety Council, and the low incidence of sports injuries due to hunting, paintball, trap and skeet shooting, and archery published by American Sports Data Inc. After studying this secondary data, Eberhard believed the outlook for the firing range industry was good to excellent. He continued to gather more secondary data, but eventually realized he needed data that was not available. He would have to collect primary data; data gathered for the first time for the purpose at hand. However, the secondary data he had studied would help him formulate the right questions for his primary data collection.

1. Go to your library and find publications that give you some assessment of industries. There are several sources that give you industry overviews. Your reference librarian may be able to help. Describe an industry in which you have a career interest in terms of its future outlook. Properly cite your source. (Hint: Some of the securities ratings services publish industry overviews.)

2. For your career industry, access some of the electronic databases available through your library. Find recent publications that describe issues currently facing your industry. Describe those issues and how your industry is trying to address them. Properly cite your sources.

Case 5.2 **Your Integrated Case**

Advanced Automobile Concepts

Nick Thomas is very concerned. He knows there are a number of issues that will impact consumers' decisions regarding automobiles they will demand in the future. What is likely to happen with gasoline prices in the future? Will alternative fuels such as compressed natural gas or electricity perform compared to gasoline in terms of miles per gallon, costs per gallon, and so forth? How many consumers believe in global warming? Of those who do believe in global warming, how many believe that it is a problem caused by mankind? How likely is it that consumer attitudes for the environment will manifest in terms of choices for automobiles?

If Zen Motors is really going to consider more fuel-efficient cars, Thomas knows he needs information on which fuel-efficient cars are selling well and which alternative fuels are the closest to being developed.

1. What types of secondary information should Nick Thomas seek?
2. Select one particular topic from those that concern Thomas. Go to your library's databases and find current articles on the topic. List the database and the search terms you used to find the articles.
3. Write a short summary of the contents of the articles you found relative to the issue selected in question 2.

6

Data Collection Methods

Intercampo

LEARNING OBJECTIVES

- To learn the four basic alternative modes for gathering survey data

- To understand the advantages and disadvantages of each of the alternative data gathering modes

- To become knowledgeable about the details of different types of survey data collection methods such as personal interviews, telephone interviews, and computer-assisted interviews, including online surveys

- To comprehend the factors researchers consider when choosing a particular survey method

Intercampo is a marketing research company based in Madrid, Spain, specializing in fieldwork, which is the topic of this chapter. Intercampo was founded in 1977 by Luis Pamblanco and Emma Cadarso, and since 1983, has undertaken more than 5,000 different projects for Spanish, British, French, Belgian, Dutch, German, and U.S. companies. Intercampo currently has twenty-one full-time employees with an average age of 34 and an average of eight years of service in the company.

Intercampo
nvestigación y Técnicas de Campo S.A.

Intercampo performs thousands of computer-assisted telephone interviews (CATIs) and face-to-face (personal) interviews every year. Both CATI and personal interviewing will be described in this chapter. In its monthly "omnibus" survey, Intercampo interviews a representative sample of 1,000 Spanish households. All CATI interviews are performed by interviewers working in Intercampo's central office in Madrid. These interviewers are carefully recruited, trained, and monitored. In addition, Intercampo has area agencies staffed with personal interviewers and local supervisors located in Spain's ten largest cities. All personal interviews are audio recorded and scrutinized by the local supervisors and Intercampo's Madrid office supervisors for quality control. Approximately 65% of Intercampo's fieldwork is personal interviews, and about one-third of these take place in a Spanish home. Apart from the impressive volume of fieldwork that Intercampo executes every year, it has built a reputation for strict quality control over the data collection process. In Pamblanco's words, "This has become our calling card, as our clients' fidelity proves." Intercampo is an example of a highly successful marketing research company that offers top-notch data collection and other marketing research services. For more information, visit Intercampo's website, at www .intercampo.es (the website offers both English and Spanish versions).

Source: Luis Pamblanco, Intercampo.

As you are learning in this course, there are many different ways of conducting marketing research studies. In Chapter 4 we discussed different forms of marketing research, such as focus groups, experiments, and survey research. A **survey** involves interviews with a large number of respondents using a predesigned questionnaire.[1] In this chapter, we focus on the various methods used to collect data for surveys, that is, how marketing researchers communicate with respondents taking surveys. Surely, you have personally experienced the wave of technological advances in communications. In the case of data collection where the marketing research industry is completely dependent on communications, profound shifts have taken place and continue to take place. These shifts are partly due to changes in the communication preferences of consumers. For example, wireless telephones with caller identification and conference calling capabilities are the communication standard of many consumers. At the same time, these changes are due to technological advances that make the data collection process faster, simpler, more secure, and less expensive. You will learn in this chapter that survey data collection methods range from traditional forms of communication to ones based on modern technology.

The four basic survey modes used are (1) person-administered surveys, (2) computer-administered surveys, (3) self-administered surveys, and (4) mixed-mode, sometimes called "hybrid," surveys. We describe each mode, enumerating its basic advantages and disadvantages. Then we discuss various alternative methods of collecting data within each basic data collection mode, for example, person-administered surveys may be conducted through mall intercepts or telephone. Finally, we identify four factors a market researcher should consider when deciding which data collection method to use.

Four Alternative Data Collection Modes

> Surveys involve interviews with a large number of respondents using a predesigned questionnaire. This chapter focuses upon data collection methods used for surveys.

There are four major modes of collecting survey information from respondents: (1) Use a person to ask the questions, either face-to-face or voice-to-voice, usually with some assistance from a computer; (2) use a computer to actively accomplish the questioning; (3) require respondents to fill out the questionnaire themselves, without computer assistance; or (4) use some combination of two or more of the above three modes. We will refer to these four alternatives as person-administered, computer-administered, self-administered, and mixed-mode surveys, respectively. Each one has special advantages and disadvantages that we describe in general before discussing the various types of surveys found within each category. Specific advantages and disadvantages of these various types are discussed later.

> The four basic survey modes used are (1) person-administered surveys, (2) computer-administered surveys, (3) self-administered surveys, and (4) mixed-mode or "hybrid."

Person-Administered Surveys

A **person-administered survey** is one in which an interviewer reads questions, either face-to-face or over the telephone, to the respondent and records the answers. Often the administration and recordkeeping is performed with a computer. Although less popular than some other methods, person-administered surveys are often used, and we describe the advantages and disadvantages associated with these surveys next.

> A person-administered survey is one in which an interviewer reads questions, either face-to-face or over the telephone, to the respondent and records the answers.

ADVANTAGES OF PERSON-ADMINISTERED SURVEYS Person-administered surveys have four unique advantages: They offer feedback, rapport, quality control, and adaptability.[2]

Feedback Interviewers often must respond to direct questions from respondents during an interview. Sometimes respondents do not understand the instructions, or they may not listen to the questions carefully. An interviewer may be allowed to adjust the questions according to verbal or nonverbal cues. When a respondent begins to fidget or look bored, the interviewer can say, "I have only a few more questions." Or if a respondent makes a comment, the interviewer may jot it down as a side note to the researcher.

Rapport Some people distrust surveys in general, or they may have doubts about the survey at hand. It is often helpful to have another person present to develop rapport with the respondent early on in the questioning process. Another person can create trust and understanding that nonpersonal forms of data collection cannot achieve.

> Personal interviewers can build rapport with respondents who are initially distrustful or suspicious.

Quality Control An interviewer sometimes must select certain types of respondents based on gender, age, or another distinguishing characteristic. Personal interviewers may be used to ensure respondents are selected correctly. Alternatively, some researchers believe that respondents are more likely to be truthful responding to a personal interviewer.

A good personal interviewer can build rapport and trust with respondents.

Adaptability Personal interviewers can adapt to respondent differences. It is not unusual, for instance, to find an elderly person or a very young person who needs step-by-step instruction during the answering process, to understand how to respond to questions. Personal interviewers are highly adaptable with respect to the context of the interview as it can take place in a respondent's living room, in a shopping mall, at a restaurant, over the telephone, or in a manager's office.

DISADVANTAGES OF PERSON-ADMINISTERED SURVEYS There are drawbacks to using human interviewers, including human error, slowness, cost, and interview evaluation.

> Personal interviewers can adapt to differences in respondents but they must be careful not to alter the meaning of a question.

Human Error Interviewers may ask questions out of sequence; they may inadvertently change the wording of a question, which may change its meaning altogether. People can make mistakes recording the information provided by the respondent.

Slowness Collecting data using human interviewers, particularly face-to-face interviewing, is slower than other modes. Although pictures, videos, and graphics can be handled by personal interviewers, they cannot accommodate them as quickly as, say, computers. Often personal interviewers simply record respondents' answers using pencil and paper, which necessitates a separate data-input step to build a computer data file. Increasing numbers of data collection companies have shifted to the use of portable computers that speed up personal interviews.

Cost Naturally, the use of a face-to-face interviewer is more expensive than, say, mailing the questionnaire to respondents. Ideally, personal interviewers are highly trained and skilled, and their use overcomes the expense factor. A less expensive person-administered survey is a telephone interview.

> The disadvantages of person-administered surveys are that humans can make errors, the method may be slower than other methods, it can be costly, and it can produce interview evaluation among certain respondents.

Interview Evaluation Another disadvantage of person-administered surveys is that the presence of another person may create apprehension, called interview evaluation, among certain respondents. We discuss this concept more fully in the following section.

Computer-Administered Surveys

A **computer-administered survey** is one in which computer technology plays an essential role in the interview work, often, but not always, completely eliminating the need for a personal interviewer. Computer-administered survey methods have grown so rapidly that they now surpass all other survey modes, the reason being that computer technology is highly adaptable. For instance, a computer may house questions asked by a telephone interviewer, a questionnaire may be posted on the Internet, or computer voice questioning may be used. In all cases, the computer actively administers the interview even if a human interviewer is its "voice." As with person-administered surveys, computer-administered surveys have their advantages and disadvantages.

> A computer-administered survey is one in which computer technology plays an essential role in the interview work. Here, either the computer assists an interview or it interacts directly with the respondent.

ADVANTAGES OF COMPUTER-ADMINISTERED SURVEYS As you can imagine, there are variations of computer-administered surveys. As one example, the respondent answers the questions on a

Computer-administered surveys are fast, error-free, capable of using pictures or graphics, able to capture data in real time, and less threatening for some respondents.

personal computer, often online, and the questions are tailored to the respondent's answers to previous questions, so there are no human interviewers. Another example is computer programs in which a telephone or personal interviewer is prompted by the computer as to what questions to ask and in what sequence. Regardless of which variation is considered, at least five advantages of computer-administered surveys are evident: speed; error-free interviews; use of pictures, videos, and graphics; real-time capture of data; and reduction of anxieties caused by interview evaluation (respondents' concern that they are not answering "correctly").

Speed The computer-administered approach is much faster than the human interview approach. Computers can quickly jump to questions based on specific responses, they can rapidly dial random telephone numbers, and they can easily check on answers to previous questions to modify or otherwise custom-tailor the interview to each respondent's circumstances. The speed factor translates into cost savings, and there is a claim that Internet surveys are about one-half the cost of mail or phone surveys.[3]

Error-Free Interviews Properly programmed, the computer-administered approach guarantees zero interviewer errors such as inadvertently skipping questions, asking inappropriate questions based on previous responses, misunderstanding how to pose questions, and recording the wrong answer. Also, the computer neither becomes fatigued nor cheats.

Pictures, Videos, and Graphics Visual presentations can take place whenever a respondent interacts with a computer monitor. Photos of products and brands, advertising video snippets, computer graphics and simulations, recorded customer testimonials, and practically any other digitalized exhibit is possible in high resolution. At least one author claims that this feature is the primary advantage of Web-based surveys.[4]

The real-time capture of data by computer-administered surveys is an important advantage of this data collection method.

Real-Time Capture of Data Because respondents are interacting with the computer, the information is directly entered into a computer's data storage system and can be accessed for tabulation or other analyses at any time. Once the interviews are finished, final tabulations can be completed in a matter of hours. Because research project deadlines are always critical, this time savings is extremely advantageous.

Reduced Interview Evaluation Interview evaluation occurs when another person is involved in the interviewing process and some respondents are apprehensive that they are answering

Interview evaluation may occur because another person is conducting the interview, and his or her presence creates anxieties in respondents which may cause them to alter their normal response.

"correctly." These people become anxious about the possible reaction of the interviewer to their answers. That is, they may be concerned as to how the interviewer evaluates their responses. This may be especially present when the questions deal with personal topics such as hygiene, political opinions, financial matters, and even age. Some respondents, for example, may try to please the interviewer by saying what they think the interviewer wants to hear. In any case, some researchers have found that respondents will provide less socially desirable, but truthful answers to potentially sensitive topics when interacting with a computer.[5]

Computerized surveys offer many advantages.

The advantages of using computers have created a growing demand for the use of online survey research. This has led to the growth of firms specializing in assisting companies in planning and conducting online surveys. Common Knowledge provides clients with the option to design their own surveys or utilize their programming services. They can target a sample from their online panel of millions of households and businesses, including subgroups such as consumers, B2B, health care, technology professionals, and teens. Common Knowledge has over 500 sample targets available and offers clients different ways to remind panelists to respond. Reminders are particularly important for low incidence targets. If necessary, Common Knowledge can use mixed-mode methods and call on partner panels to gain the needed responses.

DISADVANTAGES OF COMPUTER-ADMINISTERED SURVEYS The primary disadvantages of computer-assisted surveys are that they require some level of technical skill and costs may be significant.

Technical Skills Required There is a wide range of computer-assisted methods available to marketing researchers. However, even the simplest options require some technical skills, and some of them require considerable programming skills to ensure the systems are operational and free of errors. It is notable that the newest generation of online questionnaire development options have sought to reduce the technical skills requirement to be a very low barrier to their use.

High Setup Costs There are sometimes high setup costs associated with getting the computerized systems in place and operational. Programming and debugging costs must be incurred with each survey. One software evaluator implied that two days of setup time by an experienced programmer was fairly efficient.[6] Depending on what type of computer-administered survey is under consideration, these costs, including the time factor associated with them, can render computer-administered delivery systems for surveys less attractive relative to other data collection options. However, as noted, there are a number of moderate- to low-cost computer-administered options such Web-based questionnaires with user-friendly development interfaces that are very easy to learn.

> The disadvantages to computer-assisted data collection are the requirement of technical skills and high setup costs.

Self-Administered Surveys

A **self-administered survey** is one in which the respondent completes the survey completely on his or her own. It is different from other survey methods in that there is no agent—human or computer—administering the interview.[7] Instead, the respondent reads the questions and responds directly on the questionnaire, referred to as the prototypical "pencil-and-paper" survey. Normally, the respondent goes at his or her own pace, and in most instances selects the place and time to complete the interview. The respondent also may decide when the questionnaire will be returned. As with other survey methods, those that are self-administered have their advantages and disadvantages.

> A self-administered survey is one in which the respondent completes the survey on his or her own. It is different from other survey methods in that there is no agent—human or computer—administering the interview.

ADVANTAGES OF SELF-ADMINISTERED SURVEYS Self-administered surveys have three important advantages: reduced cost, respondent control, and no interview-evaluation apprehension.

Reduced Cost Eliminating the need for an interviewer or an interviewing device, such as a computer program, during a self-administered survey can lead to significant cost savings.

Respondent Control Respondents can control the pace at which they respond, so they may not feel rushed. Ideally, a respondent should be relaxed while completing the survey, and a self-administered survey may effect this state.

> Self-administered surveys have three important advantages: reduced cost, respondent control, and no interview-evaluation apprehension.

No Interview-Evaluation Apprehension As we just noted, some respondents feel apprehensive when answering questions, or the topic may be sensitive, such as gambling,[8] smoking, or dental work. The self-administered approach takes the administrator, whether human or computer, out of the picture, so the respondents may feel more at ease. Self-administered questionnaires have been found to elicit more insightful information than face-to-face interviews.[9]

There is potential for respondent error with self-administered surveys.

DISADVANTAGES OF SELF-ADMINISTERED SURVEYS The disadvantages of self-administered surveys are respondent errors, lack of supervision, and high questionnaire requirements.

Respondent Errors As we just mentioned, self-administration places control of the survey in the hands of the prospective respondent. Hence, this type of survey is subject to the possibility that respondents will answer questions incorrectly, will not respond in a timely manner, will fail to answer some questions, or will refuse to return the survey at all.

The disadvantages of self-administered surveys are respondent control, lack of monitoring, and high questionnaire requirements.

Lack of Supervision With self-administered surveys there is no opportunity to monitor or interact with the respondent during the course of the interview. Respondents who do not understand the meaning of a word or who are confused about how to answer a question cannot ask about these. There is no interviewer who can offer explanations and encourage the respondent to continue.

Stand-Alone Questionnaire Due to the absence of the interviewer or an internal computer check system, the burden of respondent understanding falls on the questionnaire itself. Not only must it have perfectly clear instructions, examples, and reminders throughout, but the questionnaire must also entice the respondents to participate and encourage them to continue answering until all questions are complete. With self-administered surveys in particular, the questionnaire must be thoroughly checked for clarity and accuracy before data collection begins. We will learn more about designing questionnaires in Chapter 9.

Mixed-Mode Surveys

Mixed-mode surveys, sometimes referred to as "hybrid" surveys, use multiple data collection methods.

Mixed-mode surveys, sometimes referred to as "hybrid" surveys, use multiple data collection methods. It has become increasingly popular to use mixed-mode surveys in recent years due to efficiencies of computer-administered methods and the communication preferences of respondents. Not everyone prefers to do online surveys; some people are more comfortable with face-to-face or telephone interviews. A mixed-mode survey seeks to increase the number of respondents in the survey by tapping into these communication proclivities. Like other forms of surveys, mixed-mode surveys have both advantages and disadvantages.

The advantage of mixed-mode surveys is that researchers are able to use the advantages of each of the various modes to achieve their data collection goals.

ADVANTAGE OF MIXED-MODE SURVEYS The advantage of mixed-mode surveys is that researchers are able to use the advantages of each of the various modes to achieve a better data collection result. For example, the European Social Survey was originally conducted in thirty countries using face-to-face or in-home interviews, each lasting about one hour. Declining response rates and rising costs have forced reconsideration of the use of this expensive data collection method. With extensive study, the survey is about to be conducted with a mixture of online data collection, telephone interviews, and face-to-face interviews. The mixed-mode approach will result in higher response rates, lower costs, and better representation of respondents for the thirty countries.[10] Another example is the American Cancer Society, which has determined that a mixed-mode approach using online and mail survey modes is optimal for its annual Volunteer Satisfaction Survey.[11]

Using mixed modes of data collection adds to the complexities of data collection, such as differences in instructions and integration of data from different sources.

DISADVANTAGE OF MIXED-MODE SURVEYS The one important disadvantage of using mixed-mode, or hybrid, data collection methods is that complexity will increase. In other words, using mixed modes adds to the complexities of data collection. For example, if you are conducting a survey online and by telephone, the wording of the instructions must be different to accommodate those reading instructions they themselves are to follow (for online respondents) versus someone else reading the instructions to the respondent (for telephone respondents). Further, data from the two sources will need to be integrated and care must be taken to ensure data are compatible. Responses must be coded in exactly the same way.

Descriptions of Data Collection Modes

Now that you have an understanding of the pros and cons of the four data collection methods (person-administered, computer-administered, self-administered, and mixed-mode surveys), we can describe the various interviewing techniques used in each method. There are ten different data collection methods used by marketing researchers, listed here and described in Table 6.1.

Person-administered surveys
1. In-home interview
2. Mall-intercept interview
3. In-office interview
4. Central location telephone interview

Computer-administered surveys
5. Computer-assisted telephone interview (CATI)
6. Fully computerized interview
7. Online surveys

TABLE 6.1

Ten Methods for Data Collection

Data Collection Method	Description
In-home Interview	The interviewer conducts the interview in the respondent's home. Appointments may be made ahead by telephone.
Mall-intercept Interview	Shoppers in a mall take part in the survey. Questions may be asked in the mall or in the mall-intercept company's facilities located in the mall.
In-office Interview	The interviewer conducts interviews with business executives or managers at the respondent's place of work.
Central Location Telephone Interview	Telephone interviewers work in a data collection company's office using individual cubicles or work areas. Often the supervisor has the ability to "listen in" on interviews and to check that they are being conducted correctly.
Computer-assisted Telephone Interview	The questions are programmed for a computer screen and the telephone interviewer then reads them sequentially. Responses are entered directly into the computer program by the interviewer.
Fully Computerized Interview	A computer is programmed to administer the questions. Respondents interact with the computer and enter in their own answers by using a keyboard, by touching the screen, or by using some other means.
Online Survey	Respondents fill out a questionnaire that is programmed to be administered on the Internet.
Mail Survey	Questionnaires are mailed to prospective respondents who fill them out and return them by mail.
Group-administered Survey	Respondents take the survey in a group context. Each respondent works individually, but they meet as a group and this allows the researcher to economize.
Drop-off Survey	Self-administered questionnaires are left with the respondent to fill out. The administrator may return at a later time to pick up the completed questionnaire, or it may be mailed in.

Self-administered surveys
8. Mail survey
9. Group-administered survey
10. Drop-off survey

Person-Administered Surveys

There are at least four variations of person-administered interviews commonly used by marketing researchers, and their differences are largely based on the location of the interview. These variations include the in-home interview, the mall-intercept interview, the in-office interview, and the central location telephone interview.

IN-HOME INTERVIEWS   Just as the name implies, an **in-home interview** is conducted in the home of the respondent. It takes time to recruit participants for in-home interviews, and trained interviewers must travel to and from respondents' homes. Therefore, the cost per interview is very high, but two important factors can justify the cost. First, the marketing researcher must believe that personal contact is essential to the success of the interview. Second, the researcher must be convinced that the in-home environment is conducive to the questioning process. In-home interviews are useful when the research objective requires respondents' physical presence to either see, read, touch, use, or interact with the research object (such as a product prototype) *and* the researcher believes that the security and comfort of respondents' homes is an important element affecting the quality of the data collected.

> In-home interviews are useful when the research objective requires respondents' physical presence to either see, read, touch, use, or interact with the research object *and* the researcher believes that the security and comfort of respondents' homes is an important element affecting the quality of the data collected.

Some research objectives require the respondents' physical presence in order to interact with the research object. For example, a company develops a new countertop grill that is designed to remain perfectly clean. However, in order to get the benefit of clean cooking, the grill must be configured differently for various cooking applications such as fish versus beef, and the throw-away "grease-catch foil" must be placed in just the right position to work properly. Will consumers be able to follow the instructions? This is an example of a study that would require researchers to conduct surveys in the home kitchens of the respondents. Researchers would observe respondents open the box, unwrap and assemble the grill, read the directions, and cook some item with it. All of this may take an hour or more. Again, respondents may not be willing to travel somewhere and spend an hour on a research project, but they would be more likely to do this in their own home.

MALL-INTERCEPT INTERVIEWS   Although the in-home interview has important advantages such as privacy and respondent interaction, it has the significant disadvantage of cost due to interviewer travel, even for local surveys. Patterned after "man-on-the-street" interviews pioneered by opinion-polling companies and other "high-traffic" surveys conducted in settings where crowds of pedestrians pass by, the **mall-intercept interview** is one in which the respondent is encountered and questioned while he or she is visiting a shopping mall. A mall-intercept company generally has its offices located within a large regional shopping mall. Typically, the interview company negotiates exclusive rights to do interviews in the mall and, thus, forces all marketing research companies that wish to do mall intercepts in that area to use that interview company's services. In any case, the interviewer travel costs are eliminated because the respondents travel to the mall. Mall-intercept interviewing has acquired a major role as a survey method due to its ease of implementation,[12] and it is available in many countries.[13] Shoppers are intercepted in the pedestrian traffic areas of shopping malls and either interviewed on the spot or asked to move to a permanent interviewing facility located in the mall office. Although some malls do not allow marketing research interviewing because they view it as a nuisance to shoppers, many permit them, and may rely on these data themselves to fine-tune their own marketing programs. Mall-intercept companies are adopting high-tech approaches such as electronic pads, and they are experimenting with kiosks to attract respondents.[14]

> Mall-intercept interviews are conducted in large shopping malls, and they are less expensive per interview than are in-home interviews.

In addition to low cost, mall interviews have many of the benefits associated with in-home interviewing. Perhaps the most important advantage is the presence of an interviewer who can interact with the respondent.[15] However, a few drawbacks are specifically associated with mall

> The representativeness of mall interview samples is always an issue.

MARKETING RESEARCH APPLICATION 6.1

Practical Applications

Has the Mall Intercept Become a Dinosaur?

A recent panel of data collection professionals concluded that mall data collection companies are falling in status and use.[18] Three trends have converged to greatly diminish the importance of mall intercepts. First, malls themselves have become less desirable shopping venues because of travel costs and online shopping, which has soared in popularity, plus the fact that shoppers now desire to have a "shopping experience." Second, the marketing research industry has come to realize the significant cost and other advantages of online surveys. Third, mall intercepts have become victimized by the fact that marketing researchers have increasingly used them for "difficult" surveys that were longer, more stringent in their qualifications for participants, and subject to faster turnaround requirements. As a consequence, the status of mall-intercept interviews has fallen dramatically.

So, are mall intercepts now dinosaurs? The panel members did not believe this to be the case. They did agree, however, that mall intercepts have an "image" problem, but offered strategies that mall-intercept companies can adopt to render this data collection method more attractive to the marketing research industry. These strategies include:

1. Adopt and keep pace with mobile data collection technology such as laptops, tablets, electronic pads, and handheld devices.
2. Establish kiosk locations in malls where they are more visible and more in tune with the "shopping experience" atmosphere desired by mall shoppers.
3. Work with marketing research buyers to make incentives more substantial and attractive to mall shoppers, thus recruiting higher quality respondents.
4. Work with marketing research buyers to reduce interview lengths and/or create an understanding of the amount of time necessary to obtain high-quality mall-intercept interviews.
5. Partner with full-service marketing research companies and thus become the preferred providers for their mall-intercept interviews.
6. Tighten quality assurance systems for interviewers, interview quality, time management, and close communications with marketing research buyers.
7. Publicize the fact that respondents typically experience more enjoyment and involvement with face-to-face interviews as compared to self-administered ones.

interviewing. First, sample representativeness is an issue, for most malls draw from a relatively small area in close proximity to their location. If researchers are looking for a representative sample of some larger area, such as a large geographic region, they should be wary of using the mall intercept. Some people shop at malls more frequently than others and, therefore, have a greater chance of being interviewed.[16] Recent growth of non-mall retailing concepts such as catalogs and stand-alone discounters such as Wal-Mart mean that more mall visitors are recreational shoppers than convenience-oriented shoppers, resulting in the need to scrutinize mall-intercept samples as to what consumer groups they actually represent.[17] Also, many shoppers refuse to take part in mall interviews for various reasons. Nevertheless, special selection procedures called quotas, described in Chapter 10, may be used to counter the problem of nonrepresentativeness.

A second shortcoming of mall-intercept interviewing is that a shopping mall does not have a comfortable home environment that is conducive to rapport and close attention to details. The respondents may feel uncomfortable because passersby stare at them; they may be pressed for time or otherwise preoccupied by various distractions outside the researcher's control. These factors may adversely affect the quality of the interview. As we indicated earlier, some interview companies attempt to counter this problem by taking respondents to special interview rooms located in the interview company's mall offices. This procedure minimizes distractions and encourages respondents to be more relaxed. A recent panel of mall-intercept company owners and managers convened with the Marketing Research Association to discuss trends in mall data collection. The essence of this panel's findings is summarized in Marketing Research Application 6.1.

> Mall-intercept companies use rooms in their small headquarters to conduct private interviews in a relaxed setting.

IN-OFFICE INTERVIEWS Although the in-home and mall-intercept interview methods are appropriate for a wide variety of consumer goods, marketing research conducted in the business-to-business or organizational market typically requires interviews with business executives, purchasing agents, engineers, or other managers. Normally, **in-office interviews** take place in person, in the respondent's office or another designated area. Interviewing businesspeople face-to-face has essentially the same advantages and drawbacks as in-home consumer interviewing. For example, if Knoll Inc. wanted information regarding user preferences for different adjustment features that might be offered in an ergonomic office chair designed for business executives, it would make sense to interview prospective users or purchasers of these chairs. It would also be logical that these people would be interviewed at their place of business.

> In-office interviews are conducted at the workplace because it is the most suitable location.

As you might imagine, in-office personal interviews are relatively expensive. Those executives qualified to give opinions on a specific topic or individuals who would be involved in product purchase decisions must first be located. Sometimes names can be obtained from sources such as industry directories or trade association membership lists. More frequently, screening must be conducted over the telephone by calling a particular company that is believed to have executives of the type needed. However, locating those people within a large organization may be time consuming. Once a qualified person is located, the next step is to persuade that person to agree to an interview and then set up a time for the interview. This may require a sizable incentive. Finally, an interviewer must go to the particular place at the appointed time. Even with appointments, long waits or cancellations are common because a businessperson's schedule can shift unexpectedly. Added to these cost factors is the fact that interviewers who perform businessperson interviews are more costly in general because of their specialized knowledge and abilities. They have to navigate around gatekeepers such as secretaries, learn technical jargon, and be conversant on product features when the respondent asks pointed questions or even criticizes questions as they are posed.

> In-office personal interviews incur costs due to difficulties in accessing qualified respondents.

CENTRAL LOCATION TELEPHONE INTERVIEWS Our next two data collection methods are similar in that they both utilize telephone communication, but they also are quite different as one is person-administered and the other is computer-administered. We will describe the pros and cons of telephone surveys in general and then describe the person-administered method in this section.

If the interviewer's physical presence is not necessary, telephone interviewing is an attractive option. The advantages of telephone interviewing are many.[19] First, the telephone is a relatively inexpensive way to collect survey data. Long-distance telephone charges are much lower than the cost of a face-to-face interview. Second, the telephone interview has the potential to yield a very-high-quality sample. If the researcher employs random-dialing procedures and proper call-back measures, the telephone approach may produce a better sample than any other survey procedure. Third, and very important, telephone surveys have very quick turnaround times. Most telephone interviews are of short duration anyway, but a good interviewer may complete several interviews per hour. Conceivably, a study could have the data collection phase executed in a few days with telephone interviews. In fact, in the political polling industry, in which real-time information on voter opinions is essential, it is not unusual to have national telephone polls completed in a single night.

> Advantages of telephone interviews are cost, quality, and speed.

Unfortunately, a telephone survey has several inherent shortcomings. First, the respondent cannot be shown anything or physically interact with the research object. This shortcoming ordinarily eliminates the telephone survey as an alternative in situations requiring that the respondent view product prototypes, advertisements, packages, or the like. Second, the telephone interview does not permit the interviewer to make various judgments and evaluations that can be made by a face-to-face interviewer. For example, judgments regarding respondent income based on the home they live in and outward signs of economic status cannot be made. Similarly, the telephone does not allow for the observation of body language and facial expressions, nor does it permit eye contact. A third disadvantage of the telephone interview is that the marketing researcher is more limited in the quantity and types of information that he or she can obtain. Very long interviews are inappropriate for the telephone, as are questions with lengthy lists of response

> The telephone is a poor choice for conducting a survey with many open-ended questions.

Central location telephone interviewers are professional and well-trained.

options that respondents will have difficulty remembering when they are read over the telephone. Respondents short on patience may hang up during interviews, or they may utter short and convenient responses just to speed up the interview. Obviously, the telephone is a poor choice for conducting an interview with many open-ended questions where respondents make comments or give statements as the interviewer will have great difficulty recording these remarks.

A last, and most significant, problem with telephone survey is the growing threat to its existence by the increased noncooperation by the public. This situation is compounded by use of answering machines, caller recognition, and call-blocking devices being adopted by consumers.[20] The research industry is concerned about these gatekeeping methods, and it is studying ways around them.[21] Another difficulty is that legitimate telephone interviewers must contend with the negative impression people have of telemarketers.[22] Despite their shortcomings and declining response rates, telephone surveys remain popular. In fact, when monetary incentives, assurance that it is not a sales call, and a short survey are involved, response rates are quite good according to one study conducted in New Zealand.[23] Furthermore, widespread adoption of mobile phones has excited researchers who believe that a wireless phone revolution is on the horizon.[24]

Telephone interviewers must contend with the negative impression people have of telemarketers.

The research industry's current standard telephone interview method is referred to as **central location telephone interviewing,** where a field data collection company installs several telephone lines at a central location, and the interviewers make calls from that spot. Usually, interviewers have separate enclosed work spaces and lightweight headsets that free both hands so they can record responses. Everything is done from this central location. Obviously, there are many advantages to operating from a central location. For example, resources are pooled, and interviewers can handle multiple surveys, such as calling plant managers in the afternoon and households during the evening hours. The reasons accounting for the prominence of the central location phone interview are efficiency and control. Efficiency is gained when everything is performed at a single location and further acquired by the benefit that multiple telephone surveys can be conducted simultaneously.

Central location interviewing is the current telephone survey standard.

Apart from cost savings, central location telephone interviewing provides excellent quality control. To begin, recruitment and training are performed uniformly at this location. Interviewers can be oriented to the equipment, they can study the questionnaire and its instructions, and they can practice the interview among themselves over their phone lines. Also, the actual interviewing process can be monitored. Most telephone interviewing facilities have monitoring equipment that permits a supervisor to listen in on interviewing as it is being conducted. Interviewers who are not doing the interview properly can be spotted and the necessary corrective action taken. Ordinarily, each interviewer will be monitored at least once per shift,[25] but the supervisor may focus attention on newly hired interviewers to ensure they are doing their work correctly. The fact that each interviewer never knows when the supervisor will listen in guarantees more overall diligence than would be seen otherwise. Also, completed questionnaires are checked on the spot as additional quality control. Interviewers can be immediately informed of any deficiencies in filling out the questionnaire. Finally, there is control over interviewers' schedules. That is, interviewers report in and out and work regular hours, even if they are evening hours, and make calls during the time periods stipulated by the researcher as appropriate interviewing times.

Computer-Administered Surveys

Computer technology has impacted data collection significantly to the point that completely computer-administered surveys are commonplace. There are variations of computer-administered interview systems. For example, a person asks the computer's questions over the telephone, a synthesized computer voice may be used, or the survey may be administered online.

COMPUTER-ASSISTED TELEPHONE INTERVIEWS The most advanced companies have computerized the central location telephone interviewing process; such systems are called **computer-assisted telephone interviews (CATIs).** Although each system is unique, we can describe a typical situation. Here each interviewer is equipped with a hands-free headset and is seated in front of a computer screen that is driven by the company's computer system. Often the computer dials the prospective respondent's telephone automatically, and the computer screen provides the interviewer with the introductory comments. As the interview progresses, the interviewer moves through the questions by pressing a key or a series of keys on the keyboard. Some systems use light pens or pressure-sensitive screens. The questions and possible responses appear on the screen one at a time. The interviewer reads the question to the respondent, enters the response code, and the computer moves on to the next appropriate question. For example, an interviewer might ask if the respondent owns a dog. If the answer is "yes," there could appear a series of questions regarding what type of dog food the dog owner buys. If the answer is "no," these questions would be inappropriate. Instead, the computer program skips to the next appropriate question, which might be, "Do you own a cat?" In other words, the computer eliminates the human error potential that would exist if this survey were done in non-CATI interviewing. The human interviewer is just the "voice" of the computer, but because telephone communication is used, the respondent usually does not realize that a computer is involved.

The computer can even be used to customize questions. For example, in the early part of a long interview, you might ask a respondent the years, makes, and models of all cars he or she owns. Later in the interview, you might ask questions about each specific car owned. The question might come up on the interviewer's screen as follows: "You said you own a Lexus. Who in your family drives this car most often?" Other questions about this car and others owned would appear in similar fashion. Questions like this can, of course, be dealt with in a central location manual interview, but they are handled much more efficiently in the computerized version because the interviewer does not need to physically flip questionnaire pages back and forth or remember previous responses.

The CATI approach also eliminates the need for checking for errors in completed questionnaires because there is no physical questionnaire. More to the point, in most computerized interview systems it is not permitted to enter an "impossible" answer. For example, if a question has three possible answers, with codes "A," "B," and "C," and the interviewer enters a "D" by mistake, the computer will ask for the answer to be reentered until an acceptable code is entered. If a combination or pattern of answers is impossible, the computer will not accept an answer, or it may alert the interviewer to the inconsistency and move to a series of questions that will resolve the discrepancy. Moreover, data are entered directly into a computer file as the interviewing is completed. Consequently, tabulations may be run at any point in the study, and such instantaneous results available with computerized telephone interviewing provide some real advantages. Based on preliminary tabulations, certain questions may be dropped, saving time and money in subsequent interviewing. If, for example, over 90% of those interviewed answered a particular question in the same manner, there may be no need to continue asking the question.

Tabulations may also suggest the addition of questions to the survey. If an unexpected pattern of product use is uncovered in the early interviewing stages, questions can be added to further delve into this behavior. So the computer-administered telephone survey affords an element of flexibility unavailable in the traditional paper-and-pencil survey methods. Finally, managers may find the early reporting of survey results useful in preliminary planning and strategy development. Sometimes survey project deadlines run very close to managers' presentation deadlines, and advance indications of the survey's findings permit managers to organize their presentations in advance rather than all in a rush the night before. In sum, computer-administered telephone interviewing options are very attractive to marketing researchers because of the advantages of cost savings, quality control, and time savings over the paper-and-pencil method.[26]

> CATI systems permit tabulation in midsurvey.

FULLY COMPUTERIZED INTERVIEWS (NOT ONLINE) Some companies have developed **fully computerized interviews,** in which the survey is administered completely by a computer, but not online. With one such system, a computer dials a phone number and a recording is used to introduce the survey. The respondent then uses the push buttons on the telephone to make responses, thereby interacting directly with the computer. In the research industry, this approach is known as a **completely automated telephone survey (CATS).** CATS has been successfully employed for customer satisfaction studies, service quality monitoring, election day polls, product/warranty registration, and even in-home product tests with consumers who have been given a prototype of a new product.[27]

> Completely automated telephone surveys (CATS) are administered only by a computer.

In another system, the respondent sits or stands in front of the computer and reads the instructions off the screen. Each question and its various response options appear on the screen, and the respondent answers by pressing a key or touching the screen. For example, the question may ask the respondent to rate the level of satisfaction, on a scale of 1 to 10 (where 1 is very unsatisfied and 10 is very satisfied), the last time he or she used a travel agency to plan a family vacation. The respondent is instructed to press the key with the number appropriate to the degree of satisfaction. So, the respondent might press a "2" or a "7," depending on the experience and expectations. If, however, a "0" or some other ineligible key were pressed, the computer could be programmed to beep, indicating that the response was inappropriate, and instruct the respondent to make another entry.

All of the advantages of computer-driven interviewing are found in this approach, plus the interviewer expense or extra cost of human voice communication capability for the computer is eliminated. Because respondents' answers are saved in a file during the interview itself, tabulation can take place on a daily basis. Even if the interviews are conducted in remote locations across the United States, it is a simple matter to download the files to the central facility for daily tabulations. Some researchers believe that the research industry should move to replace pen-and-paper questionnaires with computer-based ones.[28]

ONLINE INTERVIEWS The **Internet-based questionnaire,** in which the respondent answers questions online, has become the industry standard for surveys in virtually all high Internet penetration countries. Internet-based online surveys are fast, easy, and inexpensive.[29] These questionnaires accommodate all of the standard question formats; they can be easily programmed for "skips" so respondents will only see questions they should answer, and they are very flexible,

> Online surveys have significant advantages over traditional surveys, including fast speed, ease of use, and low cost.

MARKETING RESEARCH APPLICATION 6.2

Why Online Surveys Are Not Self-Administered

The chances are good that you have been a respondent to an online survey. If so, you can recall answering the questions at your own pace, and in fact, you may even have stopped responding and resumed your participation at a later time. Because you had control of the timing and pace of your responses, it surely must seem like an online survey is completely self-administered. However, there are at least three behind-the-scenes aspects of online questionnaires that create this illusion.

1. You must answer questions. Online questionnaires can be programmed such that all or specific, critical questions must be answered before the respondent is allowed to continue to the next page.
2. You never see the skips. Online questionnaires have "skip logic," which means that they can be programmed to skip over questions that are not appropriate given a respondent's answer to a previous question. For

example, if you say you have no children, it will not ask you their ages, but it will ask the ages of those who say they have children. Some respondents never see large numbers of questions because their answers activate the skip logic to not display the inappropriate questions.
3. You cannot make an error. Online questionnaires can be programmed to accept only certain ranges of answers, so respondents cannot go beyond the boundaries. For instance, when a respondent keys in "222" for his age by mistake, the program will alert him to this error and indicate that a correction is necessary.

As you can imagine, the hidden controls possible in online surveys are tremendously advantageous for researchers because they eliminate the need of human interviewers who implement the controls in person-administered surveys and they eliminate some of the errors that respondents commit with self-administered surveys.

including the ability to present pictures, diagrams, or videos to respondents. In fact, the graphics capability is a major reason why researchers tracking advertising effects prefer online surveys to telephone surveys, which have been a standard data collection method for advertising tracking for many years.[30] The researcher can check the website for current tabulations at any time, and respondents can access the online survey at any time of the day or night.

> Online surveys afford more control to the researcher than respondents realize.

Online data collection has profoundly changed the marketing research landscape,[31] particularly in the case of online panels.[32] For instance, in the case of customer satisfaction instead of "episodic" research in which a company does a large study one time per year, it allows for "continuous market intelligence" in which the survey is posted permanently on the Web and modified as the company's strategies are implemented. Company managers can retrieve tabulated customer reactions on a daily basis.[33] Some researchers refer to this advantage of online surveys as "real-time research."[34] The speed, convenience, and flexibility of online surveys make them very attractive.[35] Online surveys are generally believed to effect response quality equal to telephone or mail surveys; although, research of this belief is only now becoming evident.[36] One serendipitous aspect of online surveys is that because the researcher can monitor the progress of the online survey on a continual basis, it is possible to spot problems with the survey and to make adjustments to correct these problems. Finally, online questionnaires afford a great deal of control to marketing researchers, normally with respondents fully believing that the survey is self-administered when, in reality, it is not. We explain this advantage in Marketing Research Application 6.2.

Self-Administered Surveys

> With a self-administered survey, each respondent works at his or her own pace.

Self-administered survey methods are, for the most part, situations in which the respondent fills out a printed questionnaire copy normally at a leisurely pace. Probably the most popular type of self-administered survey is the mail survey, although researchers consider other variations, including the group-administered survey and the drop-off survey.

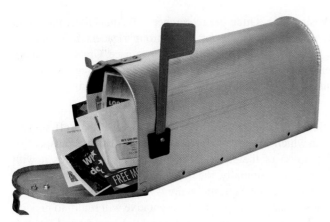

Mail surveys tend to have very low response rates.

MAIL SURVEYS A **mail survey** is one in which the questions are mailed to prospective respondents who are asked to fill them out and return them to the researcher by mail.[37] Part of its attractiveness stems from its self-administered aspect, meaning there are no interviewers to recruit, train, monitor, and compensate. Similarly, mailing lists are readily available from companies that specialize in this business, and it is possible to access very specific groups of target respondents. For example, it is possible to obtain a list of physicians specializing in family practice who operate clinics in cities larger than 500,000 people. Also, one may opt to purchase computer files, printed labels, or even labeled envelopes from these companies. In fact, some list companies will even provide insertion and mailing services. There are a number of companies that sell mailing lists, and most, if not all, have online purchase options. On a per-mailed respondent basis, mail surveys are very inexpensive. But mail surveys incur all of the problems associated with not having an interviewer present, which we discussed earlier in this chapter.

> Mail surveys suffer from nonresponse and self-selection bias.

The mail survey is plagued by two major problems. The first is **nonresponse,** which refers to questionnaires that are not returned.[38] The second is **self-selection bias,** which means that those who do respond are probably different from those who do not fill out the questionnaire and return it. In such cases, the sample gained through this method is nonrepresentative of the general population. Research shows that self-selected respondents can be more interested and involved in the study topic.[39] To be sure, the mail survey is not the only survey method that suffers from nonresponse and self-selection bias.[40] Failures to respond are found in all types of surveys, and marketing researchers must be constantly alert to the possibilities that their final samples are somehow different from the original set of potential respondents because of some systematic tendency or latent pattern of response. Whatever the survey mode used, those who respond may be more involved with the product, they may have more education, they might be more or less dissatisfied, or they may even be more opinionated in general than the target population of concern.[41]

> Self-selection bias means respondents who return surveys by mail may differ from the original sample.

Researchers have tried various tactics to increase the response rate, such as using registered mail, color, money, personalization, and reminder postcards.[42] Even with these incentives, response rates are low for mail surveys.[43] Despite this situation, mail surveys are viable in countries with high literacy rates and dependable postal systems.[44] Remember, however, that consumers and business respondents are constantly changing, and the inducement that works today may not necessarily work the same way in the future.

GROUP-ADMINISTERED SURVEYS A **group-administered survey** entails administering a questionnaire to respondents in groups, rather than individually, for convenience and to gain economies of scale. For example, twenty to thirty people might be recruited to view a television program sprinkled with test commercials. All respondents would be seated in a viewing room facility, and a video would run on a large television projection screen. Then they would be given a questionnaire to fill out regarding their recall of test ads, their reactions to the ads, and additional thoughts. As you would suspect, it is handled in a group context primarily to reduce costs and to provide the ability to interview a large number of people in a short time.

> Group-administered surveys economize in time and money because a group of respondents participates at the same time.

Variations for group-administered surveys are limitless. Students can be administered surveys in their classes; church groups can be administered surveys during meetings; social clubs and organizations, company employees, movie theatre patrons, and any other group can be administered surveys during meetings, work, or leisure time. Often the researcher will compensate the group with a monetary payment as a means of recruiting the support of the group's leaders. In all of these cases, each respondent works through the questionnaire at his or her own pace. Granted, a survey administrator may be present, so there is some opportunity for interaction concerning instructions or how to respond, but the group context often discourages the respondents from asking all but the most pressing questions.

> Drop-off surveys must be self-explanatory.

DROP-OFF SURVEYS   Another variation of the self-administered survey is the **drop-off survey,** sometimes called "drop and collect," in which the survey representative approaches a prospective respondent, introduces the general purpose of the survey to the prospect, and leaves it with the respondent to fill out on his or her own. Essentially, the objective is to gain the prospective respondent's cooperation. The respondent is told the questionnaire is self-explanatory, and it will be left and filled out at the respondent's leisure. Perhaps the representative will return to pick up the questionnaire at a certain time, or the respondent may be instructed to complete and return it by prepaid mail. Normally, the representative will return on the same day or the next day to pick up the completed questionnaire. In this way, a representative can cover a number of residential areas or business locations in a single day with an initial drop-off pass and a later pick-up pass. Drop-off surveys are especially appropriate for local market research undertakings in which travel is necessary but limited. They have been reported to have quick turnaround, high response rates, minimal interviewer influence on answers, and good control over how respondents are selected; plus, they are inexpensive.[45] Studies have shown the drop-off survey improves response rates with business or organizational respondents.[46]

> Several variations of drop-off surveys exist.

Variations of the drop-off method include handing out the surveys to people at their places of work and asking them to fill them out at home and then to return them the next day. Some hotel chains have questionnaires in their rooms with an invitation to fill them out and turn them in at the desk on checkout. Stores sometimes have short surveys on customer demographics, media habits, purchase intentions, or other information that customers are asked to fill out at home and return on their next shopping trip. A gift certificate drawing may even be used as an incentive to participate. As you can see, the term *drop-off* can be stretched to cover any situation in which the prospective respondent encounters the survey as though it were "dropped off" by a research representative.

Deciding Which Survey Method to Use

How does a marketing researcher decide which survey method to use? Because you have read our descriptions, you know that each data collection method has unique advantages, disadvantages, and special features. As a quick reference we have summarized these methods in Table 6.2. As you can see from the table, there is no "perfect" data collection method. The marketing researcher is faced with the problem of selecting the one survey system that is most suitable in a given situation.

How does a researcher decide which is the best survey method for a particular research project? When answering this question, the researcher should always have the overall quality of the data collected as a foremost concern. Even the most sophisticated techniques of analysis cannot make up for poor data. So, the researcher must strive to choose a survey method that achieves the highest quality of data allowable with the time, cost, and other special considerations[47] involved with the research project at hand.

We wish we could provide you with a set of questions about these considerations that, when answered, would point to the single most appropriate data collection method. However, this is not possible, because situations are unique and researchers have to apply judgment to narrow the many possible data collection methods to one that best fits the circumstances. In some cases, these judgments are obvious, but in others, they require careful thought. Also, as we have indicated in our descriptions, new data collection methods have emerged[48] and improvements in old ones have come about, so the researcher must constantly update information regarding these data collection methods.

TABLE 6.2

Key Advantages and Disadvantages of Alternative Data Collection Methods

Method	Major Advantages	Major Disadvantages	Comment
In-home Interview	Conducted in privacy of the home, which facilitates interviewer–respondent rapport	Cost per interview can be high; interviewers must travel to respondent's home	Often much information per interview is gathered
Mall-intercept Interview	Fast and convenient data collection method	Only mall patrons are interviewed; respondents may feel uncomfortable answering questions in the mall	Mall-intercept company often has exclusive interview rights for that mall
In-office Interview	Useful for interviewing busy executives or managers	Relatively high cost per interview; gaining access is sometimes difficult	Useful when respondents must examine prototypes or samples
Central Location Telephone Interview	Fast turnaround; good quality control; reasonable cost	Restricted to telephone communication	Long-distance calling is not a problem
CATI	Computer eliminates human interviewer error; simultaneous data input to computer file; good quality control	Setup costs can be high	Losing ground to online surveys and panels
Fully Computerized Interview	Respondent responds at own pace; computer data file results	Respondent must have access to a computer and be computer literate	Many variations and an emerging data collection method
Online Survey	Ease of creating and posting; fast turnaround; computer data file results	Respondent must have access to the Internet	Fastest growing data collection method; very flexible
Mail Survey	Low cost	Slow response and self-selection bias	Once very popular but now rarely used
Group-Administered Survey	Cost of interviewer eliminated; economical for assembled groups of respondents	Must find groups and secure permission to conduct the survey	Good for pretests or pilot tests
Drop-off Survey	Cost of interviewer eliminated; appropriate for local market surveys	Generally not appropriate for large-scale national surveys	Many variations exist

When deciding on a data collection method, most marketing researchers will ponder four questions: (1) How much time do I have for data collection? (2) How much money do I have for data collection? (3) What type of respondent interaction is required? (4) Are there special considerations to take into account? Each of these questions will be discussed in turn.

How Much Time Do I Have for Data Collection?

Sometimes data must be collected within a very tight deadline. There are many reasons for deadlines: A national campaign is set to kick off in four weeks and one component needs testing; an upcoming trademark infringement trial needs a survey of the awareness of the company's trademark and the

A tight deadline may dictate which data collection method to use.

trial starts in four weeks; an application deadline for a radio license with the FCC is in six weeks and a listenership study of other stations in the area must be conducted. Traditionally, if the short time horizon is the overwhelming consideration, telephone surveys were often selected due to their speed. Today, online surveys are exceptionally fast and can accommodate all but physical handling of research objects. Magazine ads, logos, and other marketing stimuli may be evaluated in online surveys. Naturally, in-home, personal interviews, and mail surveys are poor choices when time is critical.

As we just noted, when time is a factor in doing research, online surveys are fast. As online surveying has matured, marketing researchers soon learned that better quality data could be achieved by collecting data from established panels consisting of respondents who had previously agreed to provide information. Panels have been widely used in the research industry to ensure high response rates. However, recruiting panel members is costly and time consuming. e-Rewards® Market Research is an example of a firm that provides online panel access to clients, with over 3 million panel members. The e-Rewards panel members are recruited into the panel by invitation only and are offered valuable rewards for their time spent taking and responding to survey requests.

How Much Money Do I Have for Data Collection?

Costs vary greatly depending on the survey mode. Costs have been greatly reduced by some online survey companies.

With a generous budget, any appropriate data collection method can be considered, but with a tight budget, the more costly data collection methods must be eliminated from consideration. With technology costs dropping and Internet access becoming commonplace, online survey research options have become attractive when the data collection budget is austere. For example, certain online survey companies allow the client to design the questionnaire and select the target sample type and number from their panels. Here, surveys can be completed for a few hundred or a few thousand dollars which, most researchers would agree, is a small data collection budget. Of course, the researcher must be convinced that the panel members are desirable to survey. Other data collection methods that are relatively inexpensive include central location telephone surveys, mail surveys, and other self-administered methods.

What Type of Respondent Interaction Is Required?

The type of interaction with the respondent affects the data collection method decision. If respondents need only verbal communication, telephone interviewing will work.

Most certainly, the data collection method selection is swayed by any special requirements that are a vital part of the survey. That is, there might be a requirement that the respondent inspect an advertisement, package design, or logo. Or, the researcher may want respondents to handle a prototype product, taste formulations, or watch a video. Typically, when there are requirements such as these built into the survey, the researcher has discussed data collection issues early on with the client, and they have agreed that time and money will not be paramount or that the data collection mode will accommodate these requirements.

For example, if the respondent needs to view photos of a logo or magazine ad, mail surveys or online surveys may be considered. If the respondent needs to observe a short video or moving graphic, online surveys may be considered. If the respondent needs to watch a twenty-minute infomercial, then mall intercepts or special online systems can be considered. If the respondent is required to handle, touch, feel, or taste a product, the mall-intercept company services are reasonable. If a respondent is required to actually use a product in a realistic setting, in-home interviews may be the only data collection method that will work.

Are There Special Considerations to Take into Account?

The incidence rate—the percentage of the population that possesses some characteristic necessary to be included in the survey—affects the data collection mode decision.

A troublesome special consideration is the **incidence rate** which is the percentage of the population that possesses some characteristic necessary to be included in the survey. Rarely are research projects targeted to "everyone." In most cases, there are qualifiers for being included in a study. Examples are registered voters, persons owning and driving their own automobile, and persons over age eighteen. Sometimes the incidence rate is very low. A drug company may want to interview only men above age fifty with medicated cholesterol above the 250 level. A cosmetics firm may only want to interview women who were planning facial cosmetic surgery within the next six months. In low incidence situations such as these, certain precautions must be taken in selecting the data collection method. For example, in either of the above examples, it would be foolishly time consuming and expensive to send out interviewers door-to-door looking for members who have the qualifications to participate in the study. A data collection method that can easily and inexpensively screen respondents is desirable with a low incidence rate situation because a great many potential respondents must be contacted, but a large percentage of these would not qualify to take the survey. Of course, the marketing research industry has worked with low incidence populations for a long time, and online panels that are maintained by research providers are often touted as affordable ways for researchers to access the low incidence panel members who are preidentified.[49]

In addition, data collection method choice is sometimes influenced by cultural norms and/or communication or other systems that are in place. These considerations have become more of an issue as marketing research companies operate worldwide. For example, in Scandinavia, residents are uncomfortable allowing strangers in their homes. Therefore, telephone and online surveying is more popular than door-to-door interviewing. On the other hand, in India less than 10% of the residents have a telephone, and online access is very low; therefore, door-to-door interviewing is used often.[50] In Canada, where incentives are typically not offered to prospective respondents, there is heavy use of telephone surveys, but online research continues to grow.[51] It would be very important for a firm, conducting a study in a culture about which they are unfamiliar, to consult the services of local research firms before making the data collection method decision. Another example is a global marketing research study conducted across 100 counties with online and mail surveys to compensate for differences in Internet access and to obtain a representative sample.[52] In China, face-to-face interviews embody respect and are preferred; however, telephone and Internet surveys are now common as this country has become more dependent on these communication modes, as well.[53]

It is important that the manager allow the marketing researcher to decide on the survey mode because this person has a unique understanding of how question characteristics, respondent characteristics, and survey resources and objectives come into play. Choice of survey method can be made by answering the question, "What data collection method will generate the most complete and generalizable information within the time horizon and without exceeding the allowable expenditure for data collection?"

> A survey method can be chosen by answering the question, "What data collection method will generate the most complete and generalizable information within the time horizon and without exceeding the allowable expenditure for data collection?"

Summary

Marketing researchers must communicate with respondents in order to gather primary data. Marketing researchers refer to the process of communicating with study respondents as surveys. The four basic survey modes used are (1) person-administered surveys, (2) computer-assisted surveys, (3) self-administered surveys, and (4) mixed-mode, sometimes called "hybrid," surveys.

Person-administered survey modes are advantageous because they allow feedback, permit rapport building, facilitate certain quality controls, and capitalize on the adaptability of a human interviewer. However, they are prone to human error, slow, costly, and sometimes produce respondent apprehension known as interview evaluation.

Computer-administered interviews, on the other hand, are faster, are error-free, may have pictures or graphics capabilities, allow for real-time capture of data, and may make respondents feel more at ease because another person is not listening to the answers. Disadvantages are that technical skills are required and there may be high setup costs.

Self-administered survey modes have the advantages of reduced cost, respondent control, and no interview-evaluation apprehension. The disadvantages of self-administered surveys are respondent control in that they may not complete the task or make errors, lack of a monitor to help guide respondents, and the need to have a perfect questionnaire.

Mixed-mode surveys, sometimes referred to as "hybrid" surveys, use multiple data collection methods. The advantage of mixed-mode surveys is that researchers are able to take the advantages of each of the various modes to achieve their data collection goals. Disadvantages are that different modes may produce different responses to the same research question, and researchers must evaluate this. Secondly, mixed-mode methods result in greater complexities as researchers must design different question-naires and be certain that data from different sources all come together in a common database for analysis.

We described ten different survey data collection methods: (1) in-home interviews, which are conducted in respondents' homes; (2) mall-intercept interviews, conducted by approaching shoppers in a mall; (3) in-office interviews, conducted with executives or managers in their places of work; (4) telephone interviews conducted from a central location in a telephone-interview company's facili-ties; (5) computer-assisted telephone interviews, in which the interviewer reads questions off a computer screen and enters responses directly into the program; (6) fully computerized interviews, in which the respondent interacts directly with a computer; (7) online and other Internet-based surveys; (8) mail surveys, in which questionnaires are mailed to prospective respondents, who are requested to fill them out and mail them back; (9) group-administered surveys, in which the questionnaire is handed out to a group for individual responses; and (10) drop-off surveys, in which the questionnaire is left with the respondent to be completed and picked up or returned at a later time. The specific advantages and disadvantages of each data collec-tion method were discussed.

So, how do researchers choose the survey data collec-tion method? Researchers must take into account several considerations when deciding on a survey data collection mode. The major concerns are (1) the survey time horizon, (2) the survey data collection budget, (3) the type of respondent interaction required, and (4) special considera-tions such as the incidence rate or percent of those asked to take part in the survey who actually qualify to partici-pate. Ultimately, the researcher should select the data collection mode that will result in the highest quality and quantity of information without exceeding time or budget constraints.

Key Terms

Survey (p. 129)
Person-administered survey (p. 130)
Computer-administered
   survey (p. 131)
Interview evaluation (p. 132)
Self-administered survey (p. 133)
Mixed-mode surveys (p. 134)
In-home interview (p. 136)
Mall-intercept interview (p. 136)
In-office interviews (p. 138)

Central location telephone
   interviewing (p. 139)
Computer-assisted telephone
   interviews (CATIs) (p. 140)
Fully computerized
   interviews (p. 141)
Completely automated telephone
   survey (CATS) (p. 141)
Internet-based questionnaire (p. 141)
Mail survey (p. 143)

Nonresponse (p. 143)
Self-selection bias (p. 143)
Group-administered survey (p. 143)
Drop-off survey (p. 144)
Incidence rate (p. 146)

Review Questions

1. What is a survey?
2. What factors are affecting how marketing researchers conduct surveys?
3. What are the four basic survey modes?
4. What are the advantages of person-administered surveys over computer-administered ones?
5. What is interview evaluation, and which survey mode is most likely to produce it?
6. Discuss the advantages and disadvantages of self-administered surveys.
7. Discuss why a researcher would or would not use a mixed-mode survey. Give an example to illustrate your points.
8. Indicate the differences among (a) in-home interviews, (b) mall-intercept interviews, and (c) in-office inter-views. What do they share in common?
9. Why are telephone surveys popular?
10. What controls are possible with central location telephone interviewing?
11. What does CATI stand for? What does CATS stand for?
12. What advantages do online surveys have?
13. What are the major disadvantages of a mail survey?
14. How does a drop-off survey differ from a mail survey?
15. What are the major factors to be considered in the choice of the survey method?
16. What is the "best" data collection method?

Application Questions

17. Is a telephone interview inappropriate for a survey that has as one of its objectives a complete listing of all possible advertising media a person was exposed to in the last week? Why or why not?

18. NAPA Car Parts is a retail chain that specializes in stocking and selling automobile parts. It is interested in learning about its customers, so 100 questionnaires are sent to each of the 2,000 store managers with instructions that they are to give them to "the next" 100 customers. The customer is instructed to answer the questions and to place the completed questionnaire in the mail in a self-addressed envelope. There is a $500 NAPA coupon random drawing for a lucky respondent who returns the completed survey. What data collection method is being used, and what are its pros and cons in this situation?

19. Discuss the feasibility of each of the types of survey modes for each of the following cases:
    a. Fabergé Inc. wants to test a new fragrance called "Lime Brut."
    b. Kelly Services needs to determine how many businesses expect to hire temporary secretaries to replace secretaries who go on vacation during the summer months.
    c. The *Encyclopedia Britannica* requires information on the degree to which mothers of elementary-school-aged children see encyclopedia DVDs as worthwhile purchases for their children.
    d. AT&T Wireless is considering a television screen wireless phone application and wants to know people's reaction to it.

20. With a telephone survey, when a potential respondent refuses to take part or is found to have changed his or her telephone number or moved away, it is customary to simply try another prospect until a completion is secured. It is not standard practice to report the number of refusals or noncontacts. What are the implications of this policy for the reporting of nonresponse?

21. Compu-Ask Corporation has developed a stand-alone computerized interview system that can be adapted to almost any type of survey. It can fit on a palm-sized computer, and the respondent directly answers questions using a stylus once the interviewer has started up the program. Indicate the appropriateness of this interviewing system in each of the following cases:
    a. A survey of plant managers concerning a new type of hazardous-waste disposal system
    b. A survey of high school teachers to see if they are interested in a company's DVDs of educational public broadcast television programs
    c. A survey of consumers to determine their reactions to a nonrefrigerated variety of yogurt

22. A researcher is pondering what survey mode to use for a client who markets a home security system for apartment dwellers. The system comprises sensors that are pressed onto all of the windows and magnetic strips that are glued to each door. Once plugged into an electric socket and activated with a switch box, the system emits a loud alarm and simulates a barking guard dog when an intruder trips one of the sensors. The client wants to know how many apartment dwellers in the United States are aware of the system, what they think of it, and how likely they are to buy it in the coming year. Which consideration factors are positive and which ones are negative for each of the following survey modes: (a) in-home interview, (b) mall-intercept survey, (c) online survey, (d) drop-off survey, and (e) CATI survey?

Case 6.1 **Steward Research Inc.**

Joe Steward is president of Steward Research Inc. The firm specializes in customized research for clients in a variety of industries. The firm has a centralized location telephoning facility, and they have a division, "Steward Online," which specializes in online surveys. However, Joe often calls on the services of other research firms in order to provide his client with the most appropriate data collection method. In a meeting with four project directors, Joe discusses each client's special situation.

Client 1: A small tools manufacturer has created a new device for sharpening high-precision drill bits.

High-precision drill bits are used to drill near-perfect holes in devices such as engine blocks. Such applications have demanding specifications, and drill bits may be used only a few times before being discarded. However, the new sharpening device takes the bits back to original specifications, and the bits can be resharpened and used in as many as a dozen applications. After testing the device and conducting several focus groups in order to get modification suggestions, the client is now ready for more information on presentation methods. The project director and the client have developed several different presentation formats. The client wishes to have some market evaluation of these presentations before launching a nationwide training program of the company's 125-person salesforce.

Client 2:   A regional bakery markets several brands of cookies and crackers to supermarkets throughout California, Nevada, Arizona, and New Mexico. The product category is very competitive and competitors use a great deal of newspaper and television advertising. The bakery's vice president of marketing desires more analytics in making the promotional decisions for the firm. She has lamented that though she spends several million dollars a year on promotions in the four states, she has no analytic upon which to evaluate the effectiveness of the expenditures. Steward's project director has recommended a study that will establish baseline measures of top-of-mind brand awareness (called TOMA, this measure of awareness is achieved by asking respondents to name the first three brands that come to mind when thinking of a product or service category, such as "cookies"), attitudes, and preferences.

Client 3:   An inventor has developed a new device that sanitizes a toothbrush each time the brush is used and replaced in the device. The device uses steam to sanitize the brush, and lab tests have shown the mechanism to be very effective at killing virtually all germs and viruses. The inventor has approached a large manufacturer who is interested in buying the rights to the device but would like some information first. The manufacturer wants to know if people have any concerns with toothbrush sanitization and whether or not they would be willing to purchase a countertop, plug-in device to keep their toothbrush sterile. The project director states that the manufacturer is not interested in a sample that represents the United States. They only want to know what a few hundred people think about these issues. The inventor is anxious to supply this information very quickly before the manufacturer loses interest in the idea.

1. For each of the three clients, suggest one or more data collection methods that would be appropriate.
2. For each data collection method you select in question 1, discuss the rationale for your choice.
3. What disadvantages are inherent in the data collection methods you have recommended?

Case 6.2 **Your Integrated Case**

Advanced Automobile Concepts

Cory Rogers presented his interpretations of the focus groups he had subcontracted for Nick Thomas of Advanced Automobile Concepts to get a feel for what American consumers wanted in global warming initiatives, gasoline prices, alternative fuels, hybrid automobiles, and other aspects of the AAC division's mission. Thomas was impressed with the amount of information that had been collected from just a few focus groups. "Of course," noted Rogers, "we have to take all of this information as tentative because we talked with so few folks, and there is a good chance that they are just a part of your target market. But we do have some good exploratory research that will guide us in the survey." Thomas agreed with Rogers's assessment, and asked, "What's next?" Rogers replied, "I need to think about how we will gather the survey data. That is, in order to make an informed decision as to the type(s) of new automobiles to manufacture and market, it is important to understand the worries, beliefs, preconceptions, and preferences of potential automobile buyers. In other words, there must be a survey of prospective automobile purchasers, and it is time to start thinking about the method of data collection."

While specifics are still being hammered out, it is agreed upon by everyone involved that there should be a survey that reaches a large number of American households, perhaps 1,000 to 2,000 households. Again, with the details to come, the survey will include between forty and seventy-five questions on a variety of topics including demographics of the household, inventory of currently owned automobiles, beliefs about global warming, gasoline usage, reactions to various "new technology" automobiles, and all of the other constructs and questions identified in the research project objectives. The survey will be directed to either the male or female head of the household using a 50/50 split so both are equally represented. Other than this factor, the overriding objective of the survey method decision is to choose a method that will ultimately yield a respondent profile that reflects the demographic and automobile ownership profile of the American public. It is possible to purchase lists of American households in just about any quantity desired—hundreds, thousands, or even tens of thousands. These lists can be in the form of mailing addresses, email addresses, telephone numbers, or any combination. Following are questions that Rogers must answer.

1. If a mail survey was used, what would be the pros, cons, and special considerations associated with achieving the overriding objective of the survey?

2. There are many telephone data collection companies that offer national coverage. Some have centralized telephone interview facilities and some offer CATI services. If a telephone survey was used employing one of these companies, what would be the pros, cons, and special considerations associated with achieving the overriding objective of the survey?

3. The following data collection methods are not likely to achieve the overriding objective. For each one, indicate why not.
   a. Drop-off survey
   b. Group-administered survey
   c. Mall-intercept survey

4. Compare the use of an in-home method to the use of an online method for Advanced Automobile Concepts survey. What are the relevant pros and cons of each one? Indicate which one you would recommend and why.

7

Measurement Scales

Why Is Measurement Important?

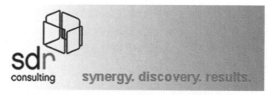

Visit SDR Consulting at www.sdr-consulting.com.

In most cases, we must actually measure higher-order constructs that we are studying as we conduct marketing research. How we measure "loyalty," "satisfaction," "sales potential," "demand," "brand value," and "brand equity," for example, is very important and seldom involves just a single question, but multiple measures. The way the researcher decides how to measure these constructs impacts what he or she can or cannot say about them and their impact on the development of successful marketing strategy and tactics. For instance, *brand loyalty* can be defined as the brand purchased most often, or it can be defined as the person's most preferred brand. The measure of "brand purchased most often" is behavioral and may be highly influenced by costs, convenience, and availability. The "brand most preferred" is attitudinal and may be highly influenced by perceptions of brand quality and esteem. "Most preferred" may not reflect what is actually bought.

A second consideration in determining how to measure constructs is the "level of measurement." In this chapter you will learn about open-ended, categorical, and metric "levels of measurement." The "level of measurement" is determined by the researcher and it is extremely important because it determines what statistical analyses may be performed. If the research objective, for example, calls for determining the "mean number of units forecast," a level of measurement necessary for calculating a mean must be selected by the researcher. You will learn about "levels of measurement" and how they are determined, and what statistical analyses are appropriate for each in this chapter.

Source: By permission, Bill Neal, SDR Consulting.

William D. Neal,
Senior Partner SDR
Consulting

This chapter is the first of two devoted to the questionnaire design phase of the marketing research process. Its primary goal is to develop the foundation for understanding measurement in marketing research. According to William Neal's comments in the opening vignette, measurement includes a definition of the concept you are studying and application of certain principles that you will learn in this chapter. Our chapter first describes six question–response formats, then defines basic concepts in measurement, and finally explains the various scale formats common in marketing research.

Question–Response Format Options

While it takes skill and experience to become a proficient questionnaire designer, there are some basic building blocks that you can learn quickly. One basic building block to understand is question–response formats. There are six response format options commonly found in questionnaires, diagrammed in Figure 7.1.

As can be seen in Figure 7.1, there are three basic question–response formats, and each one has two variations. Each of the six format options will be described in the following sections.

Where We Are:

1. Establish the need for marketing research
2. Define the problem
3. Establish research objectives
4. Determine research design
5. Identify information types and sources
6. Determine methods of accessing data
7. Design data-collection forms
8. Determine the sample plan and size
9. Collect data
10. Analyze data
11. Prepare and present the final research report

FIGURE 7.1

A Diagram of the Six
Question-Response
Format Options

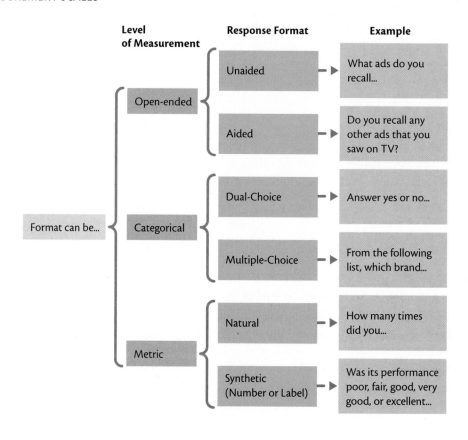

Level of Measurement	Response Format	Example
Open-ended	Unaided	What ads do you recall...
	Aided	Do you recall any other ads that you saw on TV?
Categorical	Dual-Choice	Answer yes or no...
	Multiple-Choice	From the following list, which brand...
Metric	Natural	How many times did you...
	Synthetic (Number or Label)	Was its performance poor, fair, good, very good, or excellent...

Format can be...

There are six response format options commonly found in questionnaires, diagrammed in Figure 7.1.

The open-ended response format is useful when the researcher wants the respondent to describe something in his or her own words.

Open-Ended Response Format Questions

With an **open-ended response format** question, the respondent is instructed to respond in his or her own words. That is, the response format is open-ended. This format is useful when the researcher wants the respondent to describe something in his or her own words.

For example, in exploratory research situations, it is often useful to let respondents say what is on their minds about the topic. Even in descriptive research studies, it is sometimes valuable to gather respondents' unfettered comments or answers. Sometimes the researcher wants a comment or statement from the respondent, or perhaps the researcher simply wants the respondent to indicate the name of a brand or a store. An **unaided open-ended format** does not prompt or probe the respondent beyond the initial question. When the researcher uses an **aided open-ended format,** there is a **response probe** in the form of a follow-up question instructing the interviewer to ask for additional information, saying, for instance, "Can you think of anything else you felt was important when you purchased your last automobile?" The intent here is to encourage the respondent to provide information beyond the initial and possibly superficial first comments.[1]

Categorical Response Format Questions

The **categorical response format** question provides response options on the questionnaire. Categorical response formats are used when the researcher already knows the possible response to a question. By listing the response options, the researcher ensures that the respondent can answer quickly and easily.[2] A **dual-choice question** is an instance where the respondent must select one answer from only two possible alternatives, such as "yes" or "no." This is like a true–false question that you might see on a test. With a **multiple-choice category question** format, there could be several options, such as a list of several cola brands, and the respondent indicates the one that answers the question posed. So, this format is like a multiple-choice question that you might see on your next marketing research test.

Both the dual-choice and multiple-choice categorical question formats are very common on questionnaires due to the fact that they allow respondents to answer effortlessly, because the response categories are predetermined and standardized.

Before we leave this section, we need to discuss the special case of the **"Check all that apply" question.** Here is an instance where what appears to be a multiple-choice category question is really a dual-choice question. Consider the following question that could appear on a questionnaire:

When you purchased your most recent automobile, what features do you take into consideration? (Check all that apply.)

_____ Style (e.g., sedan, coupe, wagon, SUV)

_____ Price

_____ Quiet ride

_____ Trunk space

_____ EPA mileage rating

This question looks like a multiple-choice category question because it has several categories listed as possible responses. However, it is a dual-choice category question because the respondent is actually answering the five separate "yes" or "no" questions that follow. So, a "check all that apply" question is actually a series of "yes/no" dual-choice questions, but the "yes" and "no" response options are not listed on the questionnaire. The researcher knows that when a respondent checks an item, it is a "yes," and if the item is not checked, it is a "no" answer. The "check all that apply" instruction is readily understood by respondents, and this format makes the questionnaire appear less cluttered.

Metric Response Format Questions

The **metric response question** calls for a number to be provided by the respondent or utilizes a scale developed by the researcher. "Metric" means that the answer is a number that expresses some quantity of the property being measured. With a **natural metric response format,** the respondent is asked to give a number that is the appropriate response to the property being measured, such as age, number of visits, or number of dollars.

The **synthetic metric format** uses an artificial number to measure the property. For instance, when respondents are asked to indicate their levels of satisfaction using a scale of 1 to 10, these numbers are assigned artificially by the researcher as a convenient way for respondents to express themselves. Alternatively, synthetic metric formats may include scale descriptors such as "poor," "fair," "good," "very good," and "excellent." As you will learn shortly, these labels, or scale descriptors, are assigned artificial numbers (1, 2, 3, and so on) to represent the different gradations of the property being measured.

Basic Measurement Concepts

Now that you have been introduced to the six major question–response formats, we describe the basic elements of measurement. Questionnaires are designed to collect information that is represented via **measurement,** defined as determining the description or amount of some element of interest to the researcher.

For instance, a marketing manager may wish to know how a person feels about a certain product, or how much of the product a person can use in a certain period. This information, once compiled, can help answer specific questions such as brand usage.

Both the dual-choice and multiple-choice categorical question formats are very common on questionnaires due to the fact that they allow respondents to answer effortlessly, because the response categories are predetermined and standardized.

With a natural metric response format, the respondent is asked to give a number that is the appropriate response to the property being measured, such as age, number of visits, or number of dollars.

The synthetic metric format uses an artificial number to measure the property.

Measurement is defined as determining the description or amount of some element of interest to the researcher.

Properties are the specific features or characteristics of an object that can be used to distinguish it from another object.

When a researcher specifies the procedure to measure a property of an object, the procedure is referred to as an operational definition. For example, assume we are doing a survey for Canon digital cameras. In Table 7.1 you can see that we have identified six different properties— gender, age, income level, preferred brand of digital camera, eval- uation of our (Canon) brand, and intention to buy our (Canon) brand. Table 7.1 illustrates the operational definition for each property, and it shows the measure- ment results for three different consumers who are our objects. That is, once the object's desig- nation on a property has been determined, we say that the object has been measured on that property.

Because every respon- dent uses his or her own words in the responses, open-ended measures are not standardized. It is therefore the most difficult level of mea- surement to analyze.

A categorical measure is one where the possible responses are cate- gories, meaning that the possible alternatives are labels that represent con- crete and very different types of answers.

But what are we really measuring? We are measuring properties—sometimes called attrib- utes or qualities—of objects. Objects include consumers, brands, stores, advertisements, or other construct of interest to the researcher working with a particular manager. **Properties** are the spe- cific features or characteristics of an object that can be used to distinguish it from another object.

Of course, research objectives specify which properties are to be measured in any particular research project. When a researcher specifies the procedure to measure a property of an object, the procedure is referred to as an **operational definition.**

Measurement underlies marketing research to a very great extent because researchers are keenly interested in describing marketing phenomena, and measurement is essential to this end. For instance, researchers are often given the task of finding relevant differences in the profiles of various customer types.

When a researcher specifies an operational definition for the measurement of a property of a con- struct, he or she explicitly identifies the response scale's **level of measurement,** meaning that the researcher has decided whether the scale is to be open-ended, categorical, or metric. If you refer back to Figure 7.1, you will notice that we have included the headings of "Level of Measurement," "Response Format," and "Example." It is now time to describe the level of measurement in more detail.

Open-Ended Measurement

As we indicated in our brief description of open-ended questions, researchers refrain from using these unless there are special reasons, such as conducting exploratory research. Because every respondent uses his or her own words in the responses, open-ended measures are not standard- ized. It is therefore the most difficult level of measurement to analyze.

In fact, it generally takes interpretation skills or even special computer programs to analyze open-ended responses, and for these reasons we will not dwell on open-ended measurement more than to mention it here.

Categorical Measurement

A **categorical measure** is one where the possible responses are categories, meaning that the possible alternatives are labels that represent concrete and very different types of answers.

TABLE 7.1

How Operational Definitions Lead to Measuring the Properties of Objects

Properties	Operational Definition	Measurement of Three Different Objects		
		Object: Mr. Able	Object: Ms. Baker	Object: Mrs. Carr
Gender	Male or female?	Male	Female	Female
Age	Number of years	35 years old	26 years old	40 years old
Income Level	From $0 to over $150,000, in $10,000 ranges	$30,000– $40,000	$40,000– $50,000	$80,000– $90,000
Preferred Brand	Brand person bought last	Panasonic	Sony	Panasonic
Evaluation of Our Brand	Rating of "poor," "fair," "good," "very good," or "excellent"	"Good"	"Very good"	"Fair"
Intention to Buy Our Brand	How likely to purchase, using scale of "not likely" to "very likely"	"Somewhat likely"	"Very likely"	"Unlikely"

By answering a categorical measure, a respondent is indicating to which group (or category) he or she belongs. For example, when you say "no" or "yes," you are expressing completely opposite expressions of your state of mind, so you are either in the affirmative group or the negative group. If you indicate you are a "male" or a "female," you have flatly stated what your gender group is. When you say you bought a "Domino's Pizza" the last time you ordered pizza, you belong to the Domino's Pizza buyers group, just as if you had said "Papa John's," you would belong to the Papa John's group. So, categorical measures are ones where the response options are very different from each other and the options are best envisioned as group or category labels. Also, there is practically no judgment involved for the respondent to answer a categorical measure question: The respondent simply indicates the category label that best describes him or her.

Metric Measurement

A **metric measure,** on the other hand, requires the respondent to think in terms of amounts or levels of the property being measured.

We might ask how many times a person shops in a supermarket per month, or how many soft drinks a person consumes in a week, or even how one feels about global warming. Metric measures have (1) *order*, meaning that each number that can be given is larger or smaller than other numbers that can be given, and (2) *distance*, meaning that the numbers can be compared to see how many units separate them. For example, a metric measure for how many times people shopped in a supermarket in a month may have one respondent answering with a "4," while another respondent with an "8." The number 8 is greater than the number 4 (*order*), and they are four units apart (*distance*).

Metric scales can be either natural or synthetic. Natural metric scales direct respondents to give a number that is appropriate or natural to the property being measured, such as the number of times, the number of dollars, or the number of years. So, natural metric scales measure properties that are inherently quantitative, such as frequency (times), value (dollars), or time (years).

A synthetic metric measure, you should recall, is one that utilizes *artificial* descriptors or numbers to indicate the amount of a property possessed by an object.

A metric measure, on the other hand, requires the respondent to think in terms of amounts or levels of the property being measured.

A synthetic metric measure is one that utilizes *artificial* descriptors or numbers to indicate the amount of a property possessed by an object.

How many times do you shop at a grocery store in a month? is an example of a natural metric measurement.

For example, if we were doing research for a travel agency, we could ask respondents to use a scale of 1 to 5, where 1 means "very dissatisfied" and 5 means "very satisfied," as to how satisfied they are with the travel agency's website. A respondent would give a number between 1 and 5 to indicate the amount of satisfaction with the website. The scale is metric because it uses artificial numbers selected by the researcher that reflect relative amounts of satisfaction. The numbers 1 to 5 are artificial because they are arbitrarily selected by the researcher to represent levels of satisfaction: The researcher can select for any $1–n$ number range, such as 1–10 or even 1–100.

> Researchers often use a number range, such as 1–5, 1–7, 1–10, when constructing a synthetic *number* metric scale. A synthetic number has meaning only in the context of the scale from which it originates.

Researchers often use a number range, such as 1–5, 1–7, 1–10, when constructing a **synthetic number metric scale.** A synthetic number has meaning only in the context of the scale from which it originates. In other words, you must know the range of the scale and the property the scale is measuring in order to understand the meaning of any number in the scale. For instance, if someone told you that he rates a new movie as a "5" for its action, you would not know if it was a low or a high rating until he told you his scale's range. If it was a 1–5 scale, the 5 rating would indicate high action, but if it was a 1–10 scale, the 5 rating would denote much less action.

> We might use a synthetic *label* metric scale such as a rating scale of "poor," "fair," "good," "very good," or "excellent." Here, we are using words to indicate different gradations or levels of the respondent's opinion of an object.

By the same token, we might use a **synthetic label metric scale** such as a rating scale of "poor," "fair," "good," "very good," or "excellent." Here, we are using words to indicate different gradations or levels of the respondent's opinion of the travel agency's website, for example. Again, a synthetic label has meaning only in the context of the scale from which it comes. As before, this means that if someone rates the action in a new movie as "very good," you would not know whether this was the highest rating until you were told that the labels ranged from "poor" to "very good." If the labels were "poor" to "excellent," you would realize that "very good" was not the highest rating possible. The reason these labels are called metric is they represent successive degrees, and it is customary for researchers to code them as "1," "2," "3," "4," and "5," respectively, when preparing responses for data analysis.[3] There will be more examples of synthetic label metric scales provided to you later in this chapter.

Although researchers know categorical and metric scale types very well, and they can identify the types effortlessly, these labels are no doubt confusing to someone learning about them for the first time. To help you keep these four types of scales separated in your mind, we have prepared Table 7.2, which illustrates some questions that might appear in a survey. We have identified each question as dual-choice categorical, multiple-choice categorical, natural metric, or synthetic metric. Take a few minutes to examine each type of question to help in your understanding of the four types.

Why the Level of a Scale Is Important

The choice of the level of measurement for a scale affects which analyses should or should not be performed. The analysis, in turn, greatly affects what may or may not be said about the property being measured.

> The choice of the level of measurement for a scale affects which analyses should or should not be performed. The analysis, in turn, greatly affects what may or may not be said about the property being measured.

When researchers wrestle with operational definitions of their scales, they are simultaneously taking into account the data analysis as well as the presentation layout they will be using in the final report. To illustrate why the level of a scale is important, answer this question: If you asked each of 1,000 respondents about how many dollars they spend on groceries each week, how would you summarize the findings? Would you count up how many respondents gave the answer of $50, then count up how many gave $51, and so on until you had accounted for every possible dollar amount? You could do this, but it would take a great deal of effort, and even when you were done you would have a very long list of dollar amounts with how many respondents gave each amount. So, doing frequency counts for natural metric scales is an inefficient way to summarize these numbers. The appropriate way is to calculate the average and say something like, "The average amount spent on groceries each week is $87.65." We were able to calculate the average *because* we used a metric scale where the numbers pertained to quantities of dollars.

TABLE 7.2

Examples of Questions with Categorical Scales and Metric Scales

---

A. Dual-Choice Categorical Scale Questions (Respondent selects one of two possible categories)

1. What is your gender?

   _____ Male _____ Female

2. Are you planning on purchasing a new automobile anytime during the next six months?

   _____ Yes _____ No

3. What is your marital status?

   _____ Unmarried _____ Married

B. Multiple-Choice Categorical Scale Questions (Respondent selects one of more than two possible categories)

1. Check the one automobile brand you would probably buy next.

   _____ Ford

   _____ Volvo

   _____ ZEN

   _____ Chevrolet

2. What is your age category?

   _____ Less than 18 _____ 18 to 24 _____ 25 to 34 _____ 35 to 49

   _____ 50 to 64 _____ 65 and older

C. Natural Metric Scale Questions (Respondent indicates an amount or quantity in a common denomination such as years, times, dollars)

1. Please indicate the number of persons in your household. _____

2. What is the probability (0% to 100%) that the next automobile you purchase will be a small, two-seat hybrid? _____ (enter a probability ranging from 0% to 100%)

D. Synthetic Metric Scale Questions (Respondent selects a location on a graduated scale developed by the researcher)

1. Now that we have described the Super Cycle, this very small, one-seat hybrid that gets over 120 mpg, how desirable is this vehicle to you? (Circle one)

Very Undesirable	Undesirable	Somewhat Desirable	Neutral	Somewhat Desirable	Desirable	Very Desirable
1	2	3	4	5	6	7

2. How well does this statement describe you: "Innovator – early adopter, less risk taker than novelist, but into new technology; likes new products, but not 'show offs.'"

1	2	3	4	5	6	7	8	9	10
"Does Not Describe Me at All"							"Describes Me Perfectly"		

For categorical measures, the researcher should use a percentage distribution, which can be depicted as a pie chart or a bar chart. With a metric measure, the most appropriate analysis is to compute the average.

Now, let's take the marital status question that these 1,000 respondents also answered. Recall that this is a categorical scale (Table 7.2). Would you calculate the average and say something like, "The average marital status is 1.6"? No, this would be meaningless. Instead, you would say something like, "48.7% of the respondents are unmarried and 51.3% are married." That is, the appropriate summarization analysis for a categorical scale is a percentage distribution (sometimes called a frequency distribution).

For categorical measures, the researcher should use a percentage distribution, which can be depicted as a pie chart or a bar chart. With a metric measure, the most appropriate analysis is to compute the average.

Commonly Used Synthetic Metric Scales

Scale development requires the marketing researcher to develop response formats that are very clear and that are used identically by the various respondents so that the respondents translate their mental constructs onto an intensity continuum.

The measurement of most properties is a simple task. It is simple as long as we are measuring **objective properties,** which are physically verifiable characteristics such as age, gender, number of bottles purchased, or store last visited. However, marketing researchers often desire to measure **subjective properties,** which cannot be directly observed because they are mental constructs such as a person's attitudes, opinions, or intentions. In this case, the marketing researcher must ask a respondent to translate his or her mental constructs onto an intensity continuum. To do this, the marketing researcher must develop response formats that are very clear and that are used identically by the various respondents. This process is known as **scale development.**

Scale development is primarily concerned with the creation or use of synthetic metric measures.[4] There are two goals of scale development: reliability and validity. A **reliable scale** is one in which a respondent responds in the same or in a very similar manner to an identical or nearly identical question.

A reliable scale is one in which a respondent responds in the same or in a very similar manner to an identical or nearly identical question.

Obviously if a question elicits wildly different answers from the same person and you know that the person is unchanged from administration to administration of the question, there is something very wrong with the question. A **valid scale,** on the other hand, is one that truly measures the construct under study.

A valid scale is one that truly measures the construct under study.

It is beyond the scope of this book to delve into reliability and validity of measures, so we will simply point out that the proper development of synthetic metric measures poses reliability and validity challenges.

The process of developing a synthetic metric scale can be long and difficult.[5] Marketing Research Application 7.1 shows how this may be an area of ethical concern. However, researchers are almost always under time and budget pressures, so they typically turn to scale formats that are most familiar. In this section, we will describe the basic scale formats that are most common in marketing research practice and that professional marketing researchers use quite frequently.

Symmetric Synthetic Scales

The neutral point is not considered zero or an origin; instead, it is considered a midpoint along the continuum.

Many scales are designed to measure psychological properties that exist on a continuum ranging from one extreme to another in the mind of the respondent. Table 7.3 serves as a useful visual aid in illustrating the intensity continuum that underlies the measurement of these types of constructs. Notice that we are illustrating an intensity continuum that ranges from extremely negative through neutral and to extremely positive. The **neutral point** is not considered zero or an origin; instead, it is considered a midpoint along the continuum, as you can see with the numbers we have *artificially* assigned to each label for each of the three examples in Table 7.3.

To relate to this visual aid, think about your own feelings about some brand. You may think it is a very good brand, so you have a strong positive rating. On the other hand, you may think it is a very bad brand, and you would have a strong negative rating. Finally, you may not have any opinion, in which case you would have a neutral rating. Of course, your strong feelings may not

MARKETING RESEARCH APPLICATION 7.1

Ethics

Why Marketing Researchers Face Ethical Issues in Scale Development

Researchers face an ethical dilemma in scale development. The proper way to develop a scale is lengthy and expensive because of the different criteria that should be used to assess the quality of a scale. To meet these criteria, it is expected that a scale will be developed over a series of administrations. Statistical tests are used after each one to refine the scale, and each subsequent administration tests the new version, which leads to further refinement. It is not unusual for scales that are published in academic journals to go through three or four administrations involving hundreds of respondents. (Many of these scales are published in books listed at the end of this application.) In other words, when a marketing researcher must develop a scale to measure a marketing construct, doing it properly may take several months or even years of work.

The few marketing research firms who have pursued scale development have developed proprietary instruments that are protected by copyright. That is, they have invested the time and money into the scale development so it will be one of their marketing research services, and they will enjoy a competitive advantage over other marketing research firms because of the legal protection afforded their work by a copyright.

As you would expect, the vast majority of marketing research practitioners do not have the time and their clients are unwilling to supply the monetary resources necessary to thoroughly develop scales. So, there is an ethical dilemma when a marketing researcher must measure some marketing phenomenon, but has neither the luxury of time nor the resources necessary to do so properly. Proper scale development simply cannot take place due to the fact that clients do not appreciate the time and cost factors. In fact, they may not even believe these procedures are warranted and will refuse to pay for them, meaning that if such tests are performed, they will reduce the marketing researcher's profits. Consequently, the vast majority of marketing researchers are forced to design their measures by relying on face validity alone, meaning that the researcher, and perhaps clients if they are inclined to take part, simply judges that the question developed to measure the marketing construct at hand "looks like" an adequate measure.

The unfortunate truth is that most marketing researcher practitioners cannot be concerned with rigorous scale development that relies on time-consuming reliability or validity measurements. The standard procedure is to use measures that are already well known to the researcher from either past experience or marketing research literature. On the other hand, it is unethical for a researcher to find reliability and/or validity problems and not strive to resolve them. A conscientious marketing researcher will devote as much time and energy as possible to ensure the reliability and validity of the research throughout the entire process.

The following resources focus on scale development:

Bearden, W. O., and Netemeyer, R. G. (1999). *Handbook of Marketing Scales: Multi-item Measures for Marketing and Consumer Behavior Research* (2nd ed.). Thousand Oaks, CA: Sage Publications.

Bruner, G. C., Hensel, P. J., and James, K. E. (2005). *Marketing Scales Handbook: A Compilation of Multi-item Measures for Consumer Behavior & Advertising* (vol. IV). Chicago: American Marketing Association, and South Melbourne, Victoria, Australia: Thomson/South-Western.

Marketing scales handbooks describe valid and reliable scales for many constructs.

be extreme, so your rating would not be at the endpoint of the scale; it would be somewhere between the neutral position and the extreme position.

We will briefly describe three symmetric synthetic metric scales that are commonly used by marketing researchers. Remember, with symmetric scales, we are measuring attitudes, feelings,

TABLE 7.3

The Intensity Continuum Underlying Commonly Used Symmetric Synthetic Scales

Extremely Negative			*Neutral*			*Extremely Positive*
	Strongly Disagree	**Somewhat Disagree**	**Neither Agree nor Disagree**	**Somewhat Agree**	**Strongly Agree**	
	1	2	3	4	5	
Slow Check Out	Very _____	Somewhat _____	No Opinion _____	Somewhat _____	Very _____	Fast Check Out
Extremely Unfavorable	Very Unfavorable	Somewhat Unfavorable	No Opinion	Somewhat Favorable	Very Favorable	Extremely Favorable
1	2	3	4	5	6	7

opinions, among others, where the response can be anywhere from a strong negative to a strong positive one.

The **Likert scale** format is commonly used by marketing researchers.[6] When using this scale, respondents are asked to indicate their degree of agreement or disagreement on a symmetric agree–disagree scale for each of a series of statements.

The value of the Likert scale should be apparent because respondents are asked how much they agree or disagree with the statement. That is, the scale captures the intensity of their feelings. The following example illustrates the use of a Likert scale in a telephone interview. Note the directions given by the interviewer to properly administer this scale.[7]

(INTERVIEWER: READ) I have a list of statements that I will read to you. As I read each one, please indicate whether you agree or disagree with it. Are the instructions clear? (IF NOT, REPEAT)
(INTERVIEWER: READ EACH STATEMENT, WITH EACH RESPONSE, ASK) Would you say that you (dis)agree VERY STRONGLY or (dis)agree STRONGLY or just (dis)agree?

Statement	Very Strongly Disagree	Strongly Disagree	Disagree	Neither Agree nor Disagree	Agree	Strongly Agree	Very Strongly Agree
Global Warming is a real threat	1	2	3	4	5	6	7
Americans use too much gasoline	1	2	3	4	5	6	7
We should be looking for gasoline substitutes	1	2	3	4	5	6	7
Gasoline prices will remain high in the future	1	2	3	4	5	6	7
Gasoline emissions contribute to global warming	1	2	3	4	5	6	7

To use the Likert response format, borrowed from a formal scale development approach developed by Rensis Likert,[8] a researcher generates a list of statements about the construct(s) under consideration. One such statement could be, "I find my bank's online bill-paying system easy to use," and another could be, "The charge for my bank's online bill-paying system is reasonable." Respondents read the statements and indicate the degree of agreement or disagreement to each one. Typically, statements should not have strong evaluative words in them, such as "very," "exceptionally," or "extremely," as the statement should make a simple claim, and the respondent is the one who indicates the direction and intensity of his or her reaction to the statement.

To demonstrate how much market researchers have come to rely on the Likert scale, we point out that consumer lifestyles are very often measured with the use of a lifestyle inventory composed of Likert scale questions. **Lifestyle** takes into account the values and personality traits of people as reflected in their unique activities, interests, and opinions (AIOs) toward their work, leisure time, and purchases. The underlying belief is that knowledge of consumers' lifestyles, as opposed to demographics alone, offers direction for marketing decisions.[9]

Many companies use consumer lifestyles as a market-targeting tool. Lifestyle can be used to distinguish among types of purchasers, such as heavy users versus light users of a product, store patrons versus nonpatrons, or media vehicle users versus nonusers. Likert scales can assess the degree to which a person is price conscious, fashion conscious, an opinion giver, a sports enthusiast, child oriented, home centered, or financially optimistic. Each respondent indicates his or her degree of agreement or disagreement by responding to the Likert-like categories.

The **semantic differential scale** is another symmetric scale that has sprung directly from the problem of translating a person's qualitative judgments into quantitative estimates.

The semantic differential scale contains a series of bipolar adjectives for the various properties of the object under study, and respondents indicate their impressions of each property by indicating locations along its continuum. The focus of the semantic differential is on the measurement of the meaning of an object, concept, or person. Because many marketing stimuli have

> Lifestyle takes into account the values and personality traits of people as reflected in their unique activities, interests, and opinions (AIOs) toward their work, leisure time, and purchases. The underlying belief is that knowledge of consumers' lifestyles, as opposed to demographics alone, offers direction for marketing decisions.

> The semantic differential scale is another symmetric scale that has sprung directly from the problem of translating a person's qualitative judgments into quantitative estimates.

Are American and Canadian lifestyles so different that marketers use different promotions for the same target markets?

meaning, mental associations, or connotations, this type of scale works very well when the marketing researcher is attempting to determine brand, store, or other images.

The construction of a semantic differential scale begins with the determination of a concept or object to be rated. The researcher then selects bipolar pairs of words or phrases that could be used to describe the object's salient properties. Depending on the object, some examples might be "friendly–unfriendly," "hot–cold," "convenient–inconvenient," "high quality–low quality," and "dependable–undependable." The opposites are positioned at the endpoints of a continuum of intensity, and it is customary, although not mandatory, to use seven line-segment separators between each point. The respondent then indicates his or her evaluation of the performance of the object, a brand for example, by checking the appropriate line. The closer the respondent checks to an endpoint on a line, the more intense is his or her evaluation of the object being measured.

Table 7.4 shows how this was done for a survey for Red Lobster. The respondents also rated Jake's Seafood Restaurant on the same survey. You can see that each respondent has been instructed to indicate his or her impression of various restaurants such as Red Lobster by checking the appropriate line between the several bipolar adjective phrases. As you look at the phrases, note that they have been randomly flipped to avoid having all of the "good" ones on one side. This flipping procedure is used to avoid the **halo effect,**[10] which is a general feeling about a store or brand that can bias a respondent's impressions on its specific properties.[11] For instance, if you

TABLE 7.4

The Semantic Differential Scale Is Useful When Measuring Store, Company, or Brand Images

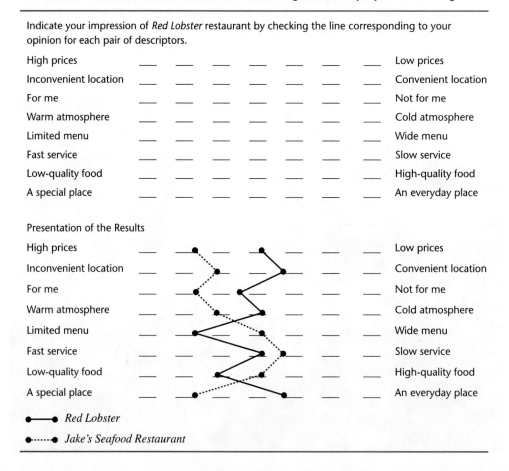

Indicate your impression of *Red Lobster* restaurant by checking the line corresponding to your opinion for each pair of descriptors.

High prices								Low prices
Inconvenient location								Convenient location
For me								Not for me
Warm atmosphere								Cold atmosphere
Limited menu								Wide menu
Fast service								Slow service
Low-quality food								High-quality food
A special place								An everyday place

Presentation of the Results

High prices								Low prices
Inconvenient location								Convenient location
For me								Not for me
Warm atmosphere								Cold atmosphere
Limited menu								Wide menu
Fast service								Slow service
Low-quality food								High-quality food
A special place								An everyday place

●——● *Red Lobster*

●·····● *Jake's Seafood Restaurant*

have a very positive image of Red Lobster, with all of the positive items on the right-hand side and all the negative ones on the left-hand side, you might be tempted to simply check all of the answers on the right-hand side without reading each characteristic carefully. It is entirely possible, however, that a specific aspect of this Red Lobster might not be as good as the others. Perhaps the restaurant is not located in a convenient area, or the menu is not as broad as you would like. Randomly flipping favorable and negative ends of the descriptors in a semantic differential scale minimizes the halo effect.[12] Also, there is some evidence that when respondents are ambivalent in the survey topic, it is best to use a balanced set of negatively and positively worded questions.[13]

Because it is a metric scale, one of the most appealing aspects of the semantic differential scale is the ability of the researcher to compute averages and then to plot a "profile" of the brand or company image. Each check line is assigned a number for coding. Usually, the bipolar properties are rearranged to be negative-to-positive, then numbers 1, 2, 3, and so on, beginning from the left side, are customary. Next, an average is computed for each bipolar pair. The averages are plotted as you see them, and the marketing researcher has a very nice graphical communication vehicle with which to report the findings to the client, as can be seen in the bottom half of Table 7.4. As you can see in our fictitious example, Red Lobster is viewed more favorably on some issues such as prices and convenient locations and Jake's Seafood Restaurant is viewed more favorably in terms of a wide menu and being more of a special place than an everyday place.

The **Stapel scale** is our last symmetric scale to be described. The basis of the Stapel scale format is numerical rather than verbal or visual; however, its purpose is the same as other symmetric synthetic scales—to obtain the degree of positive or negative feeling in the mind of the respondent concerning an attribute of some object.

A Stapel scale is easily recognized as it has numbers that range from a minus end to a corresponding plus end, and typically include "0" as the midpoint. The respondent circles the number that best corresponds to his or her feelings on the topic. For example, using a Staple scale, a respondent would be asked to rate his or her feelings toward Best Buy® on "competitive prices" on the following scale: +3 +2 +1 0 −1 −2 −3. See Table 7.5, appearing later in this chapter, for an example.

A Stapel scale is a good substitute for a semantic differential scale as it is easier to construct because the researcher does not need to think of bipolar adjectives for each attribute. It is also flexible to administer as respondents do not need to "see" the scale the way they do when responding to a semantic differential scale. However, in order to use a Stapel scale properly, respondents must feel comfortable with the use of negative numbers.

Before moving on to a variation of synthetic scales, we need to address a question that may have come to your mind as you examined our various examples. All of the examples in this section have a neutral or "no opinion" option in the middle of the scale. However, you may have wondered if the "no opinion" response option is really appropriate, and our answer is, "It depends."[14] If a respondent is not familiar with a brand, they are not forced to give an opinion. If you have reason to suspect that the respondents all have experience with the brand, then leaving out the "no opinion" option would make sense.[15] This may be the case if you had qualified respondents as being "familiar" through a screening question.

Nonsymmetric Synthetic Scales

A symmetric scale is sometimes called "balanced," as it has equal amounts of positive and negative positions.

The **one-way labeled scale** is one where the researcher is measuring some construct attribute with the use of labels that restrict the measure to the "positive" side. (See example on next page.)

The importance scale just described, which ran from "not important" to "extremely important," is a one-way labeled scale as it is primarily degrees of importance. Granted, there is a "not important" position on the scale, but this is the only instance of unimportance, and the rest of the positions on the scale are differing levels of importance. Ideally, respondents should respond to a one-way labeled scale as having equal intervals which gives you *distance* (described earlier).[17]

When using the semantic differential, be sure to control for the halo effect.

The basis of the Stapel scale format is numerical rather than verbal or visual; however, its purpose is the same as other symmetric synthetic scales—to obtain the degree of positive or negative feeling in the mind of the respondent concerning an attribute of some object.

A Stapel scale is easily recognized as it has numbers that range from a minus end to a corresponding plus end, and typically include "0" as the midpoint.

A symmetric scale is sometimes called "balanced," as it has equal amounts of positive and negative positions. But not all constructs that researchers deal with have counteropposing ends.[16] For example, suppose you were asked to indicate how important having jail bail bond protection was for you as a feature when you purchased automobile insurance. It is doubtful that you would differentiate between "extremely unimportant," "very unimportant," or "somewhat unimportant," but you could indicate how important it was to you with the response options of "not important" to "somewhat important," "very important," and "extremely important." That is, a nonsymmetric, or unbalanced, scale would be more appropriate because most people do not think in degrees of negative importance. We will describe two of these scales: the one-way labeled scale and the n-point scale.

The one-way labeled scale is one where the researcher is measuring some construct attribute with the use of labels that restrict the measure to the "positive" side.

The n-point scale, meaning a 5-point, 7-point, or 10-point scale format, is a popular choice for researchers measuring constructs on nonsymmetric attributes.

Example of a One-Way Labeled Scale

How important is each of the following to you when you are deciding on an automobile service center?

Factor	Not Important	Somewhat Important	Quite Important	Very Important	Extremely Important
Qualified mechanics	___	___	___	___	___
Convenient location	___	___	___	___	___
Will not try to do work I don't need	___	___	___	___	___
Provides me with transportation when my car is in the shop	___	___	___	___	___

The **n-point scale,** meaning a 5-point, 7-point, or 10-point scale format, is a popular choice for researchers measuring constructs on nonsymmetric attributes.

Here is an example: Indicate how you rate the friendliness of the wait staff at Olive Garden Restaurant, where 1 means "not friendly" and 5 means "extremely friendly." It is a one-way scale that uses synthetic numbers rather than verbal labels.[18] This is the **anchored n-point scale,** and there are two anchors used for this type of scale. The number "1" is anchored, and the highest number, "5" in our example, is also anchored. The anchors are important as they tell the respondent the context of the scale; that is, they indicate how to translate the range of the scale into a frame of reference to which the respondent can relate.

Recall that synthetic numbers have meaning only in the context of the scale in which they are used. Following is an example of an anchored 5-point scale. Note how crucial it is to have good instructions that communicate the anchors and the numbers in the scale.

Example of a 5-Point Anchored Scale

Rate the performance of your book bag from 1 to 5, where 1 means "poor" and 5 means "excellent."

Performance Factor	Your Rating				
	Poor				Excellent
Appearance	1	2	3	4	5
Roominess	1	2	3	4	5
Waterproofing	1	2	3	4	5
Easy to carry	1	2	3	4	5

Occasionally, a researcher will opt to not provide the anchors, in which case it will be an **unanchored n-point scale.** An example is, "On a scale of 1 to 5, how do you rate the friendliness of Olive Garden's wait staff?" As a general rule, anchors are desirable as they stipulate concrete ends of the scale to respondents, but anchors are not mandatory.

Whether to Use a Symmetric or a Nonsymmetric Scale

You are probably confused by all the scale options we have described in this chapter and particularly as to when to use a symmetric versus a nonsymmetric scale. In reality, this decision is a judgment call on the part of the researcher, and the judgment is based on the following logic. Ideally, when a synthetic scale is used in a survey, the researcher wants respondents to use all of the scale positions, meaning that for any one question, the responses should be spread across all of the scale positions. If the researcher believes there will be very few respondents who will make use of the negative side of a symmetric scale, the researcher should opt for a nonsymmetric scale. When in doubt, a researcher can pretest both the two-sided and the one-sided versions to see whether the negative side will be used by respondents. As a general rule, it is best to pretest a symmetric scale to make sure it is being used in its entirety.

Because individuals of different cultures, such as Hispanics, tend to use only one end of a scale,[19] pretests should be used to find a scale that will be completed appropriately. Marketing Research Application 7.2 describes how different cultures use extreme scale ends.

> The anchored *n*-point scale uses two anchors, to indicate both high and low ends. The anchors are important as they tell the respondent the context of the scale; that is, they indicate how to translate the range of the scale into a frame of reference to which the respondent can relate.

Choosing Which Scale to Use

It has been our experience that when students learn about each type of scale on an individual basis, then each one makes better sense. However, when faced with the actual decision as to which scale to recommend in a given situation, it is difficult for neophyte marketing researchers to sort these scales out. Since you now understand the basic concepts of measurement and have become acquainted with the basic scales used by marketing researchers, we have provided Table 7.5 as a quick reference to our recommended scales pertaining to the constructs most often measured by marketing researchers. Of course, this is not a complete list of marketing constructs, but the constructs in this table are often involved in marketing research undertakings. Also, as we indicated earlier, seasoned researchers may have preferences for other scales or variations of our recommended synthetic scales.[20]

> When in doubt, a researcher can pretest both the two-sided and the one-sided versions to see whether the negative side will be used by respondents. As a general rule, it is best to pretest a symmetric scale to make sure it is being used in its entirety.

TABLE 7.5
Recommended Synthetic Scales for Selected Constructs

The following scales are recommended to neophyte researchers who are seeking ways to measure the various constructs identified.

Construct	Recommended Scale(s)
Brand Image	**Recommend: Semantic Differential** scale using a set of bipolar adjectives
	Or **Recommend: Stapel Scale** (if researcher does not wish to develop bipolar adjectives)
	Example: Rate Folgers Decaffeinated Coffee on . . .

	+3		+3
	+2		+2
	+1		+1
Taste	0	Mild on stomach	0
	−1		−1
	−2		−2
	−3		−3

Frequency of Use	**Recommend: One-Way Labeled Scale**
	Example: How often do you buy take-out Chinese dinners?

_____ Never

_____ Infrequently

_____ Occasionally

_____ Often

_____ Quite Often

_____ Very Often

Construct *Importance*	**Recommended Scale(s)** **Recommend: One-Way Labeled Scale**

Example: How important is it to you that your dry-cleaning service has same-day service?

_____ Not Important

_____ Slightly Important

_____ Important

_____ Quite Important

_____ Very Important

Intention to
Purchase

Recommend: Symmetric Labeled Scale

Example: The next time you buy cookies, how likely are you to buy a fat-free brand?

_____ Very Unlikely

_____ Somewhat Unlikely

_____ Neither Unlikely nor Likely

_____ Somewhat Likely

_____ Very Likely

Lifestyle or
Opinion

Recommend: Likert Scale using a series of lifestyle or opinion statements

Example: Indicate how much you agree or disagree with each of the following statements.

Statement	Strongly Disagree	Disagree	Neither Disagree nor Agree	Agree	Strongly Agree
I have a busy schedule.					
I work a great deal.					

Performance

Recommend: Anchored 5-Point Scale

Example: Indicate with a number from 1 to 5, where 1 means "poor" and 5 means "excellent," as to how well you think Arby's performs on each of the following features.

	Poor				Excellent
a. Variety of items on the menu	1	2	3	4	5
b. Reasonable price	1	2	3	4	5
c. Location convenient to your home	1	2	3	4	5

(With respondents who are less comfortable with number ratings, **Recommend: One-Way Labeled Scale** of "poor," "fair," "good," "very good," and "excellent.")

Satisfaction

Recommend: Symmetric Labeled Scale

Example: Based on your experience with Federal Express, how satisfied have you been with its overnight delivery service?

_____ Extremely Satisfied

_____ Somewhat Satisfied

_____ Neither Satisfied nor Unsatisfied

_____ Somewhat Unsatisfied

_____ Extremely Unsatisfied

MARKETING RESEARCH APPLICATION 7.2

Global

How Cultural Differences Affect Respondents' Use of the Extreme Ends of Scales

Whenever a marketing researcher undertakes global studies, a host of considerations must be considered. Typically, language differences alone account for a great deal of concern, for often a literal translation of questions fails to include nuances, idioms, and subtleties that are built into the initial question's wording. Often two or three iterations of translations, interpretations, and pretests are necessary in order for the researcher to feel confident that the various language versions are equivalent.

However, even if the questions are equivalent, the possibility exists that cultural response styles will come into play. A cultural response style is a tendency among members of a cultural group to use the scale in a particular way. For instance, cultures where individualism and dogmatism are valued are perhaps more likely to use the extreme ends of scales than are cultures where collectivism and cooperation are valued. In the collective cultures, extremism is avoided, and one would expect that respondents in these cultures respond more in the "middle of the road" to the scales posed on a questionnaire.

This line of thinking was validated to some extent by the study. Note in Figure 7.2, respondents from Thailand and Taiwan (which are collective, communal cultures) exhibited a relatively strong "middle of the road" response tendency. That is, they tended not to use the extreme end response options such as "very strongly agree" or "very strongly disagree" in the test surveys. Chinese respondents, also representing a communal society, were found to have middle of the road response propensities as well. In contrast, Russian respondents displayed very pronounced extreme response tendencies, meaning that they used the "very strongly agree" and "very strongly disagree" end points of the scales in the study quite frequently and much more so than respondents in any other countries. Romanian and Argentinean respondents were also found with extreme response tendencies, although somewhat less pronounced.

The majority of countries in the study fell into a range of response moderation rather than response extremism as can be seen with many countries clustered closely to the "0" response. This extremism demarcation on the figure indicates that neither high numbers of extreme responses nor unusually large occasions of middle of the road responses are found.

If you choose a career in the marketing research business, you will realize that each marketing research company or marketing research department tends to rely on tried-and-true formats that they apply from one study to another. There are some very good reasons for this practice of adopting a preferred

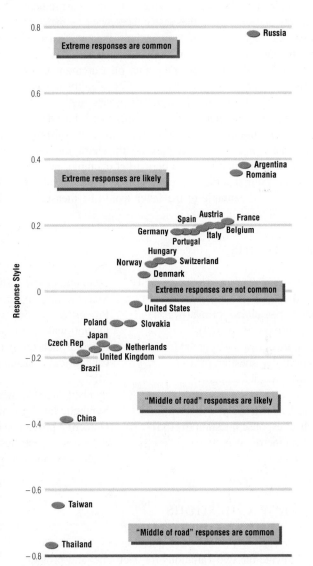

FIGURE 7.2

question format. First, it expedites the questionnaire design process. That is, by selecting a standardized scaled-response form that has been used in several studies, there is no need to be creative and to invent a new form. This saves both time and costs. Second, by testing a scaled-response format across several studies, there is the opportunity to assess its reliability as well as its validity.

Summary

This chapter discussed the concepts involved in measurement of the properties of objects of interest to marketing researchers. We began by reviewing the three basic question–response option formats of open-ended, categorical, and metric. We then introduced basic measurement concepts and explained that researchers want to measure properties (e.g., level of satisfaction, income, age) of objects (e.g., consumers), and they use operational definitions to describe precisely how this measurement takes place. There are two relevant levels of measurement: categorical, where the measure is based on groups such as male versus female; and metric, where the measure is based on a quantity or amount, such as how many times a consumer shops in a supermarket in the past month. Metric measures can be natural, such as our supermarket example, or synthetic, meaning that the researcher utilizes a rating scale of some sort. An example of the latter would be measuring your satisfaction with your bank on a 10-point scale ranging from "very unsatisfied" to "very satisfied." We explained that categorical measures are typically summarized using percents, while metric measures are summarized by using averages.

The chapter also describes synthetic metric scales commonly used by marketing researchers. We began this section by illustrating an underlying intensity-of-feeling continuum for symmetric synthetic metric scales, and we described and provided examples for three of these: the Likert scale, the semantic differential scale, and the Stapel scale. Next, we described two nonsymmetric synthetic scales where the rating scale is basically on the positive side of the intensity continuum: the one-way labeled scale and the *n*-point scale. Finally, we provided our recommended scales for a list of constructs that marketing researchers find themselves measuring over and over across surveys.

Key Terms

Open-ended response format (p. 154)
Unaided open-ended format (p. 154)
Aided open-ended format (p. 154)
Response probe (p. 154)
Categorical response format (p. 154)
Dual-choice question (p. 154)
Multiple-choice category
    question (p. 154)
"Check all that apply" question (p. 155)
Metric response question (p. 155)
Natural metric response
    format (p. 155)

Synthetic metric format (p. 155)
Measurement (p. 155)
Properties (p. 156)
Operational definition (p. 156)
Level of measurement (p. 156)
Categorical measure (p. 156)
Metric measure (p. 157)
Synthetic number metric scale (p. 158)
Synthetic label metric scale (p. 158)
Objective properties (p. 160)
Subjective properties (p. 160)
Scale development (p. 160)

Reliable scale (p. 160)
Valid scale (p. 160)
Neutral point (p. 160)
Likert scale (p. 162)
Lifestyle (p. 163)
Semantic differential scale (p. 163)
Halo effect (p. 164)
Stapel scale (p. 165)
One-way labeled scale (p. 165)
n-point scale (p. 166)
Anchored *n*-point scale (p. 166)
Unanchored *n*-point scale (p. 166)

Review Questions

1. List each of the three basic question–response formats. Indicate the two variations for each one, and provide an example for each.
2. What is measurement? In your answer, differentiate an object from its properties, both objective and subjective.
3. Discuss the meaning of an operational definition. How does a researcher use an operational definition? Provide an example of the operational definition for each of the following:
   a. Likelihood of buying car X
   b. Media habits such as reading the newspaper
   c. Attitude toward global warming
4. How does reliability differ from validity? In your answer, define each term.
5. What is meant by the "level of measurement"? Identify and define the two levels of measurement described in this chapter.
6. Distinguish a synthetic number scale from a synthetic label scale. What do these two types of scales have in common, and how do they differ?
7. Answer the following question: "Why is it important for a researcher to know the level of a scale that he or she uses to measure a property of a construct of interest?"

8. Distinguish a symmetric synthetic scale from a non-symmetric synthetic scale. Provide an example of each of these types of scales.
9. Explain what is meant by a continuum along which a subjective property of an object can be measured.
10. What are the arguments for and against the inclusion of a neutral response position in a symmetric scale?
11. Distinguish among a modified Likert scale, a semantic differential scale, and a Stapel scale.
12. What is the halo effect, and when and how does a researcher control for it?
13. What consideration should be foremost in a researcher's decision to use a symmetric synthetic rating scale versus a nonsymmetric one?
14. Distinguish among a one-way labeled scale and an *n*-point scale.
15. What is an "anchor" and how does an anchor give a context to an *n*-point scale?

Application Questions

16. Mike, the owner of Mike's Market, which is a convenience store, is concerned about low sales. He reads in a marketing textbook that the image of a store often has an impact on its ability to attract its target market. He contacts the All-Right Research Company and commissions you, a marketing researcher, to conduct a study that will shape his store's image. You are charged with the responsibility of developing the store-image part of the questionnaire.

    Design a semantic differential scale that will measure the relevant aspects of the market's image. In your work on this scale, you must do the following: (a) brainstorm ten convenience store properties to be measured, (b) determine the appropriate bipolar adjectives, (c) decide on the number of scale points, and (d) indicate how the scale controls for the halo effect.

17. Each of the following examples involves a marketing researcher's need to measure some construct. Devise an appropriate scale for each one. Defend the scale in terms of its level of measurement and use or nonuse of a "no opinion" or neutral response category.
    a. Mattel wants to know how preschool children react to a sing-along video game in which the child must sing along with an animated character and guess the next word in the song at various points in the video.
    b. TCBY is testing five new flavors of frozen yogurt and wants to know how its customers rate each one on sweetness, flavor strength, and richness of taste.
    c. A pharmaceutical company wants to find out how much a new federal law eliminating dispensing of free sample prescription drugs by doctors will affect their intentions to prescribe generic versus brand-name drugs for their patients.

18. Harley-Davidson is the largest American motorcycle manufacturer, and it has been in business for several decades. Harley-Davidson has expanded into "signature" products such as shirts that prominently display the Harley-Davidson logo. Some people have a negative image of Harley-Davidson because it was the motorcycle favored by the Hell's Angels and other motorcycle gangs. There are two research questions here. First, do consumers have a negative feeling toward Harley-Davidson, and, second, are they disinclined toward the purchase of Harley-Davidson signature products such as shirts, belts, boots, jackets, sweatshirts, lighters, and key chains? Design a Likert measurement scale that can be used in a nationwide telephone study to address these two issues.

19. Family Dollar store believes it has a niche market, and that its image in the minds of its customers is the following: *a self-service store with bargain prices and no sales hassles but with reasonably fast checkout and for household and clothing items that are functional.* Construct a Stapel scale approach that would measure Family Dollar's image to determine the extent to which customers have an opinion consistent with Family Dollar's belief.

20. Pick any fast-food chain (McDonald's, KFC, etc.) and construct a scale that measures the performance of that chain's units. Use a one-way labeled scale that measures the chain on at least five performance attributes that you think are relevant. Be sure to include any instructions for the respondents.

21. Check in your library's catalog for one of the handbooks mentioned in this chapter on marketing scales. Find a scale, and describe the construct the scale measures and show the scale items are used to measure the construct. Also describe any measures of the reliability and validity of the scale as reported in the handbook.

Case 7.1 **Extreme Exposure Rock Climbing Center Faces the Krag**

For the past five years, Extreme Exposure Rock Climbing Center has enjoyed a monopoly. Located in Sacramento, California, Extreme Exposure was the dream of Kyle Anderson, a former extreme sports enthusiast. Kyle's rock-climbing center has over 6,500 square feet of simulated rock walls to climb, with about 100 different routes up to a maximum of 50 vertical feet. Extreme Exposure's design permits the four major climbing types: top-roping, where the climber climbs up with a rope anchored at the top; lead-climbing, where the climber tows the rope that is affixed to clips in the wall while ascending; bouldering, where the climber has no rope but stays near the ground; and rappelling, where the person descends quickly by sliding down a rope. Climbers can buy day passes or monthly or yearly memberships. Shoes and harnesses can be rented cheaply, and helmets are available free of charge as all climbers must wear protective helmets. In addition to individual and group climbing classes, Extreme Exposure has several group programs, including birthday parties, a kids' summer camp, and corporate team-building classes.

Another rock-climbing center, called The Krag, will be built in Sacramento within the next six months. Kyle notes the following items about The Krag that are different from Extreme Exposure: (1) The Krag will have climbs up to a maximum of 60 vertical feet, (2) it will have a climber certification program, (3) there will be day trips to outdoor rock-climbing areas, (4) there will be group overnight and extended-stay rock-climbing trips to the Canadian Rockies, and (5) The Krag's annual membership fee will be about 20% lower than the one for Extreme Exposure.

Kyle chats with Dianne, one of his Extreme Exposure members who is in marketing, during a break in one of her climbing visits, and Dianne summarizes what she believes Kyle needs to find out about his current members. Dianne's list follows.

Objective 1: What is the demographic and rock-climbing profile of Extreme Exposure's members?

Objective 2: How satisfied are the members with Extreme Exposure's climbing facilities?

Objective 3: How interested are its members in (a) day trips to outdoor rock-climbing areas, (b) group overnight and/or extended-stay rock-climbing trips to the Canadian Rockies, and (c) a rock climber certification program?

Objective 4: What are members' opinions of the annual membership fee charged by Extreme Exposure?

Objective 5: Will members consider leaving Extreme Exposure to join a new rock-climbing center with climbs that are 10 feet higher than the maximum climb at Extreme Exposure?

Objective 6: Will members consider leaving Extreme Exposure to join a new rock-climbing center with climbs that are 10 feet higher than the maximum climb at Extreme Exposure and whose annual membership fee is 20% lower than Extreme Exposure's?

For each of Dianne's questions, identify the relevant construct and indicate how it should be measured.

Case 7.2 **Your Integrated Case**

Advanced Automobile Concepts

Cory Rogers of CMG Research talks on the phone with Nick Thomas, CEO of Advanced Automobile Concepts in Zen Motors, and, while they have not completely decided on the survey data collection method to be used in the AAC survey, they both agree that an online survey seems most attractive. There are a few issues to be decided, such as the specific online questionnaire system and the sample, but Thomas gives Rogers the go-ahead to begin the questionnaire design process. Being a good marketing researcher, Rogers knows that the first step in the questionnaire design process is to develop operational definitions, meaning the appropriate measurement scale, for the constructs in the survey.

There are several constructs involved with the research desired by Advanced Automobile Concepts. Each one is briefly described here. In each case, provide the operational definition. That is, identify what you think is the most appropriate scale format for Rogers to use. You are not being asked to develop the precise questions, but to recommend a response scale. In deliberating your recommendations, keep the following facts in mind: (1) There will be a very wide variety of individuals who will be responding, (2) the questionnaire will undoubtedly be quite long, meaning that the best response scale types will be those that are intuitive and easy for respondents to relate to, and (3) insofar as possible, it is desirable to use metric scales.

1. Current vehicle ownership (size and type of vehicle)
2. Beliefs about global warming and the effects of the use of gasoline on global warming
3. Beliefs about gasoline price levels and trends
4. Opinions as to the impact of alternative fuel automobiles (hybrids, synthetic fuels, electric, etc.) on global warming
5. Intentions to buy an alternative fuel automobile
6. Preferences for various sizes of alternative fuel automobiles (mini, economy two-door, economy four-door, standard)
7. Preferred: television show type (e.g., drama, mini-series, sports), magazine type (e.g., business and finance, family living, travel), radio music genre (e.g., rock, jazz, easy listening), and newspaper section (e.g., local news, sports, editorial)

8

Designing Data Collection Forms

What's Wrong with This Questionnaire?

Nick Thomas has decided he needs to collect primary information. He asks a newly hired intern, Jane Akin, to begin preparing a questionnaire form. Jane is a sophomore at the local university. She is majoring in marketing but has not yet taken the course in marketing research. Below are the notes and questions that Jane has written to present to her boss, Nick Thomas.

Memorandum

To: Mr. Nick Thomas, AAC Division President

From: Jane Akin, Marketing Intern

RE: Proposed Questions for Data Collection

I assume we will be gathering information from a randomly selected sample of adult consumers. First, we need an introduction and I suggest the following: *"Hello. I am Jane Akin with AAConcepts and I would like to ask you a few questions, OK?"* Since the Douglass Report strongly suggests we should move in the direction of hybrids I suggest the following as the first question: Question 1. *"Since most consumers want a car with excellent fuel economy, wouldn't you agree your next car will be a hybrid? Yes _____ No _____."* Secondly, if we want to efficiently target promotional messages to those consumers who are likely to be our customers, we should ask: Question 2. *"Where do you see most ads for automobiles?"* Third, from what I understand we need to determine which type of car model we want to design and manufacture. I suggest the following question: Question 3. *"Will your next car be one that is a good value in terms of fuel efficiency? Yes_____ No_____."* Fourth, I understand from what you have told me that you are concerned that only a small number of people are really worried about the future and gasoline

Jane Akin, AAConcepts marketing intern, prepares her first questionnaire.

prices. I propose the following question: Question 4. *"Since our nation's security depends on lessening our dependence on foreign petroleum supplies and since this means that we will have to drill for more expensive oil in our nation, much of it in deep water off our shores which are environmentally sensitive, are you going to be willing to pay for higher priced gasoline at the expense of being more secure? Yes _____ No _____."*

When you finish reading this chapter, you should be able to provide Jane Akin with some constructive criticism.

In this chapter we take a close look at the step 7, Designing data collection forms. We begin by noting the differences between survey questionnaires and observation forms. Then we take a look at the functions of a questionnaire and the process you may go through in designing questionnaires. Next, we look at what issues to consider as you develop specific questions including guidelines on the do's and don'ts of how to word questions.[1] We also teach you the components

Where We Are:

1. Establish the need for marketing research
2. Define the problem
3. Establish research objectives
4. Determine research design
5. Identify information types and sources
6. Determine methods of accessing data
7. Design data-collection forms
8. Determine the sample plan and size
9. Collect data
10. Analyze data
11. Prepare and present the final research report

you should address in the introduction to the questionnaire—an important and often overlooked component of a good questionnaire. We also will look at different concepts dealing with the flow of questions and we introduce you to computer-assisted questionnaire design. Finally, we take a look at coding and pretesting your questionnaire.[2]

Types of Data Collection Forms

Survey Questionnaires and Observation Forms

Once a decision has been made to conduct quantitative research using a descriptive research design, researchers may want to communicate with respondents through surveys or observe respondents' behavior through observation.[3] In Chapter 4 we discussed conducting observation studies. Observation studies have the advantage of recording what actually happens. A person may tell you that they snack on fresh squeezed juices, nuts, and whole grains but a researcher in an ethnographic study may observe boxes of Twinkies in the person's kitchen pantry! A researcher may be interested in seeing how shoppers behave when exposed to a promotional display in a supermarket rather than knowing what they think about the display. In this case, the researcher would want to observe the behavior of the shoppers.[4] Whether the researcher wishes to communicate through surveys or observe behavior, a form must be prepared upon which to record the information to be gathered. When we conduct surveys, the form is referred to as a "questionnaire" since the purpose is to ask questions of respondents. In observation studies, the form is referred to as an "observation form." Observation forms are thought to be easier than questionnaires as they do not need to address the psychological impact of questions. In determining what information needs to be recorded, observational forms "should specify the who, what, when, where, why, and way of behavior to be observed."[5] However, we do *not* mean to imply that preparing an observation form is easy. Consider a study one of your authors conducted. It was a study of factors related to shoe buying and it was decided that one of the variables that would be recorded was "type of shoe tried and type purchased." How would you record "type" of shoes? There are thousands of different types of shoes, not to mention colors and sizes! In the remainder of the chapter, we will examine the more onerous task of designing survey questionnaires.

> When we conduct surveys, the form is referred to as a "questionnaire" since the purpose is to ask questions of respondents. In observation studies, the form is referred to as an "observation form."

The Functions of a Questionnaire

> A questionnaire presents the survey questions to respondents.

A **questionnaire** is the vehicle used to present the questions that the researcher desires respondents to answer. Surely, you realize that questionnaires are important elements in surveys, but it might surprise you to learn that a questionnaire serves six key functions. (1) It translates the research objectives into specific questions that are asked of the respondents. (2) It standardizes those questions and the response categories so every participant responds to identical stimuli. (3) By its wording, question flow, and appearance, it fosters cooperation and keeps respondents motivated throughout the interview. (4) Questionnaires serve as enduring records of the research. (5) Depending on the type used, a questionnaire can speed up the process of data analysis. Online questionnaires, for example, can be transmitted to thousands of potential respondents in seconds, and respondents' submitted responses are available for analysis almost instantaneously. (6) Finally, questionnaires contain the information on which reliability assessments may be made, and they are used in follow-up validation of respondents' participation in the survey. In other words, questionnaires are used by researchers for quality control.

Given that it serves all of these functions, the questionnaire is indeed a very important ingredient in the research process. In fact, studies have shown that the design of a questionnaire directly affects the quality of the data collected. Even experienced interviewers cannot compensate for questionnaire defects.[6] The time and effort invested in developing a good questionnaire are well spent.[7] As you will soon learn, designing a questionnaire is a systematic process in which the researcher contemplates various question formats, considers a number of factors characterizing the survey at hand, and ultimately words the various questions carefully. It is a process that requires the researcher to go through a series of interrelated steps.

The Questionnaire Design Process

As you will soon learn, **questionnaire design** is a systematic process in which the researcher contemplates various question formats, considers a number of factors characterizing the survey at hand, ultimately words the various questions carefully, and organizes the layout of the questionnaire.

Figure 8.1 offers a flowchart of the various phases in a typical questionnaire design process. The first thing you should note is that the process begins with the research objectives. Remember how we stressed the importance of being very specific in wording each research objective in Chapter 3? The research objectives should specify who you wish to survey and what construct is to be measured and how. Questionnaire design begins with a well-thought-out research objective. Next, as you can see, a significant part of questionnaire design involves the development of individual questions in the survey, identified as "Question Development" in Figure 8.1. We have expanded and highlighted the "questionnaire design" steps so you can see that there are some specific activities the researcher must execute before any question is acceptable. As you can see in the figure, a question will ordinarily go through a series of drafts before it is in acceptable final form. In fact, even before the question is constructed, the researcher mentally reviews alternative question response scale formats to decide which ones are best suited to the survey's respondents and circumstances.

> Questionnaire design is a systematic process that requires the researcher to go through a series of considerations.

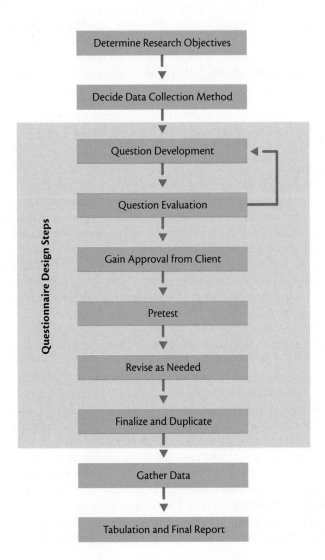

FIGURE 8.1

Steps in the Questionnaire Development Process

As the question begins to take shape, the researcher continually evaluates the question and its response options. Changes are made, and the question's wording is reevaluated to make sure that it is asking what the researcher intends. Also, the researcher strives to minimize **question bias,** defined as the ability of a question's wording or format to influence respondents' answers.[8] It is important to point out that question development takes place for every question pertaining to each research objective. We elaborate on question development and the minimization of question bias very soon.

With regard to questionnaire design, it is important only that you realize that with a custom-designed research study,[9] the questions on the questionnaire, along with its instructions, introduction, and general layout, are systematically evaluated for potential error and revised accordingly. Generally, this evaluation takes place at the researcher's end, and the client will not be involved until after the questionnaire has undergone considerable development and evaluation by the researcher. The client is given the opportunity to comment on the questionnaire during the client approval step, in which the client reviews the questionnaire and agrees that it covers all of the appropriate issues. This step is essential, and some research companies require the client to sign or initial a copy of the questionnaire as verification of approval. Granted, the client may not appreciate all of the technical aspects of questionnaire design, but the key issue the client must evaluate is, Will this questionnaire give the information needed to choose from among the decision alternatives? Prior to *finalizing* client approval, the questionnaire normally undergoes a pretest, which is an actual field test using a very limited sample to reveal any difficulties that might still lurk in wording, instructions, administration, and other areas. However, some researchers do pretests after *initial* client approval or in concert with client approval as pretests normally result in fine-tuning of the questionnaire. Before finalizing and duplicating the questionnaire, researchers should obtain *final* approval from the client. We describe pretesting more fully later in this chapter.[10] Response codes, to be described later in this chapter as well, are decided, and the questionnaire is finalized.

> Question bias occurs when the question's wording or format influences the respondent's answer.

> The key issue the client must evaluate is, Will this questionnaire give the information needed to choose from among the decision alternatives?

Developing Questions

Question development is the practice of selecting appropriate response formats and wording questions that are understandable, unambiguous, and unbiased. Marketing researchers are very concerned with developing research questions because they measure attitudes, beliefs, behaviors, and demographics,[11] and they desire reliable and valid answers to their questions. So, question development is a tall order, so to speak, but it is absolutely vital to the success of the survey.[12]

Developing a question's precise wording is not easy. A single word can make a difference in how study participants respond to a question, and there is considerable research to illustrate this fact. For example, in one study, researchers let subjects view a picture of an automobile for a few seconds. Then, they asked the participants a single question, but they changed one word. They asked, "Did you see *the* broken headlight?" to one group of participants; and asked, "Did you see *a* broken headlight?" to another group. Only the "a" and the "the" were different, yet the question containing the "the" produced more "don't know" and "Yes" answers than did the "a" question.[13] Our point is that as little as one word in a question can result in question bias that will distort the findings of the survey. Unfortunately, words that we use commonly in speaking to one another sometimes encourage biased answers when they appear on a questionnaire. Table 8.1 lists ten words to avoid in question development.[14] Again, the point to remember is that while we use these words in everyday language, they can introduce an element of bias into a questionnaire when they are used and respondents are using a literal interpretation in their efforts to answer the questions.

> Question development is the practice of selecting appropriate response formats and wording questions that are understandable, unambiguous, and unbiased.

As you can see from Table 8.1, it is important that questions do not contain subtle cues, signals, or interpretations that lead respondents to give inaccurate answers. Granted, not all respondents will be influenced by a question's wording, but if a significant minority is affected, this bias can cause the findings to be distorted or mixed as you saw in our broken headlight study example. Note the "better wording" questions in Table 8.1. These do not place respondents in the awkward position of answering to extreme absolutes. Rather, they give participants latitude to respond in

> Some words, when taken literally, introduce question bias.

TABLE 8.1

Ten Words to Avoid in Question Development: Example in a Survey
Performed with Home Theater System Purchasers

Word*	Poor Wording	Why Is the Wording Poor?	Better Wording
All	Did you consider **all** the options before you decided to purchase your home theater system?	There may be a huge number of options or too many for a consumer to even know about, let alone consider one by one.	What options did you consider when you decided to purchase your home theater system?
Always	Do you **always** buy audio products from Bose?	"Always" means every purchase, every time, with no exceptions.	How often do you buy audio products from Bose?
Any	Did you have **any** concerns about the price?	Even the smallest concern qualifies as "any," and small concerns are usually insignificant.	To what extent was the price a concern for you?
Anybody	Did you talk to **anybody** about home theater systems before you made your decision?	This includes family, friend, co-workers, sales personnel, neighbors, parents, teachers, and anybody else on the planet.	Which of the following people did you talk with about home theater systems before you made your decision? (Likely parties such as spouse or co-workers are listed.)
Best	What is the **best** feature on your new home theater system?	"Best" implies that there is a single feature that stands out, but it is possible that features were tied or combinations of features are important.	Please rate the following features of our new home theater system on their performance for you using "poor," "fair," "good," or "excellent."
Ever	Have you **ever** seen a home theater system?	"Ever" means on any occasion in one's past lifetime.	Have you seen a home theater system in the past thirty days?
Every	Do you do consult Consumer Reports **every** time you purchase a major item?	"Every" means without fail, or otherwise no way without doing this.	How often do you consult Consumer Reports when you purchase a major item?
Most	What was the **most** important factor that convinced you it was time to make this purchase?	There may not be a single most important factor; there may be ties or there may be combinations of factors that are relevant.	Please rate the following factors on their importance in convincing you it was time to purchase a home theater system using "unimportant," "slightly important," or "very important."
Never	Would you say that you **never** think about an extended warranty when making a major electronics purchase?	"Never" means not ever, without fail.	How often do you consider an extended warranty when making a major electronics purchase?
Worst	Is the high price the **worst** aspect of purchasing a home theater system?	There may not be a single worst aspect; there may be ties for last place or combinations that make for negative aspects.	To what extent did the high price concern you when you were considering your purchase of your home theater system?

*Why avoid these words? The words are **extreme absolutes,** meaning that they place respondents in a situation where they must either completely agree or completely disagree with the extreme position in the question.

degrees (such as how often or how important) that are more consistent with their actual deliberations or actions than are the extreme absolute–worded versions.

Four "Do's" of Question Wording

Question evaluation amounts to scrutinizing the wording of a question to ensure that question bias is minimized and that the question is worded such that respondents understand it and can respond to it with relative ease. As we noted earlier, question bias occurs when the phrasing of a question influences a respondent to answer wrongly or with other than perfect accuracy. Ideally, every question

> The researcher uses question evaluation to scrutinize a possible question for its bias and ease of understanding.

should be examined and tested according to a number of crucial factors known to be related to question bias. While question evaluation is a judgment process, we can offer four simple guidelines or "do's" for question wording. We strongly advise that you do ensure that the question is (1) focused, (2) brief, (3) simple, and (4) crystal clear. A discussion of these four guidelines follows.

THE QUESTION SHOULD FOCUS ON ONE TOPIC To the greatest extent possible, the researcher must stay focused on the specific issue or topic.[15] For example, consider the question, "What type of hotel do you usually stay in when on a trip?" The focus of this question is hazy because it does not narrow the type of trip or when the hotel is being used. For example, is it a business or a pleasure trip? Is the hotel at a place en route or at the final destination? A more focused version is, "When you are on a family vacation and stay in a hotel at your destination, what type of hotel do you typically use?" As a second example, consider how "unfocused" the following question is: "When do you typically go to work?" Does this mean when do you leave home for work or when do you actually begin work once at your workplace? A better question would be, "At what time do you ordinarily leave home for work?"

> A question should be focused.

THE QUESTION SHOULD BE BRIEF Unnecessary and redundant words should always be eliminated. This requirement is especially important when designing questions that will be administered verbally, such as over the telephone. Brevity will help the respondent to comprehend the central question and reduce the distraction of wordiness. Here is a question that suffers from a lack of brevity: "What are the considerations that would come to your mind when you are confronted with the decision to have some type of repair done on the automatic icemaker in your refrigerator assuming that you noticed it was not making ice cubes as well as it did when you first bought it?" A better, brief form would be, "If your icemaker was not working right, how would you correct the problem?" One source recommends that in order to be brief, a question be no more than twenty words in length.[16]

> A question should be brief.

THE QUESTION SHOULD BE A GRAMMATICALLY SIMPLE SENTENCE IF POSSIBLE A simple sentence is preferred because it has only a single subject and predicate, whereas compound and complex sentences are busy with multiple subjects, predicates, objects, and complements. The more complex the sentence, the greater the potential for respondent error. With more conditions to remember, there is more information to consider simultaneously, so the respondent's attention may wane or focus on only one part of the question. To avoid these problems, the researcher should strive to use only simple sentence structure[17]—even if two separate sentences are necessary to communicate the essence of the question. Take the question, "If you were looking for an automobile that would be used by the head of your household who is primarily responsible for driving your children to and from school, music lessons, and friends' houses, how much would you and your spouse discuss the safety features of one of the cars you took for a test drive?" A simple approach is, "Would you and your spouse discuss the safety features of a new family car?" followed by (if yes), "Would you discuss safety 'very little,' 'some,' 'a good deal,' or 'to a great extent'?"

> A question should be grammatically simple.

THE QUESTION SHOULD BE CRYSTAL CLEAR All respondents should "see" the question identically.[18,19] For example, the question, "How many children do you have?" is unclear because it can be interpreted in various ways. One respondent might think of only those children living at home, whereas another might include children from a previous marriage. A better question is, "How many children under the age of 18 live with you in your home?" One tactic for clarity is to develop questions that use words that are in respondents' core vocabularies. It is best to avoid words that are vague or open to misinterpretations. To develop a crystal clear question, the researcher may be forced to slightly abuse the previous guideline of simplicity, but with a bit of effort, question clarity can be obtained with an economical number of words.[20] One author has nicely summarized this guideline: "The question should be simple, intelligible, and clear."[21]

> A question should be crystal clear.

Question wording is difficult when the researcher is conducting a survey in a foreign country. That is, many countries have unique cultures with completely different languages, and creating a questionnaire in the country's language is an exceptionally difficult undertaking.[22] There are, however, ways to address the wording and translation issues confronting researchers who find themselves engaged in global research projects. You will find these guidelines in Marketing Research Application 8.1.

MARKETING RESEARCH APPLICATION 8.1

New Guidelines for Developing a Questionnaire in a Foreign Language

What about question wording in global marketing research situations where the researcher must create questionnaires that are in diverse languages? How can a manager avoid question bias when he or she does not speak the language of the respondents? For example, a researcher working with Burger King might need to design a survey that has respondents who speak only one of the following languages: English, Chinese, Spanish, Italian, Tamil, German, or Russian. One solution that might be put forth is to design the questionnaire in some "common" language and then only survey bilingual respondents.[23] However, this approach is generally unsatisfactory because there are many opportunities for miscomprehension. Instead, global marketing researchers use the following "back translation approach"[24] when attempting to do across-the-globe research.

- Create the questionnaire in the researcher's native language (e.g., English).[25]
- Translate the questionnaire into the other language (e.g., German).
- Have independent translators translate it back into the native language (e.g., from German to English) to check that the first translation was accurate.
- Revise the questionnaire based on the "back translation" (into a better German version).
- If an online survey is involved, make sure that the letters and characters (such as Chinese, Japanese, or Arabic) are faithful to the language being used.
- Carefully pretest the revised questionnaire using individuals whose native tongue is the other language (e.g., natives of Germany).

Even with these precautions, there may be translation errors where idioms or concepts do not relate well from one culture to the other.

The back translation approach has been found to be lacking when comparing equivalent words in one language to those of another language. For instance, "doing laundry" is very different for respondents who must use the local river (Thailand) versus those with washer and dryer units in their basements (United States); and "having wine for dinner" is not equivalent in a country where wine is consumed with every dinner (France) compared to another one where wine is only consumed on special occasions (China). To address this problem, it is advocated to use a systematic process and a committee that collaborates in the questionnaire translation effort. The following diagram shows how this process should work.

Ideally, the committee is comprised of multilingual individuals with expertise in translations and questionnaire design. The first task of the committee is to address the equivalences of words, behaviors, idioms, and other nuances between the languages. The committee translates the questionnaire various ways and decides on the best version. Then it is pretested with a small sample of native-speaking respondents who are debriefed as to difficulties, plus, if possible, statistical comparisons are made as to equivalence. The pretest results are reviewed by the committee which makes subsequent revisions and may require additional pretesting of the revisions until the questionnaire is ready for administration.

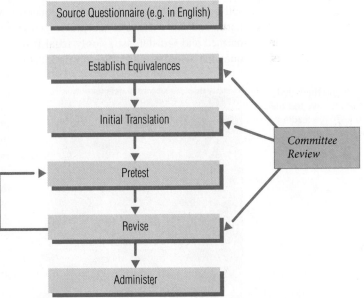

Recommended process for foreign language questionnaire development.

Four "Don'ts" of Question Wording

There are four situations in which question bias is practically assured, and it is important that you learn about these so you can avoid them or spot them when you are reviewing a questionnaire draft. Specifically, the question should not be (1) leading, (2) loaded, (3) double-barreled, or (4) overstated.

> Do not use leading questions that have strong cues on how to answer.

DO NOT "LEAD" THE RESPONDENT TO A PARTICULAR ANSWER A **leading question** gives the respondent a strong cue or expectation as to how to answer.[26] Therefore, it biases responses. Consider this question: "Don't you see problems with using your credit card for an online purchase?" The respondent is being led here because the question wording stresses one side (in this case, the negative side) of the issue. Therefore, the question "leads" respondents to the conclusion that there must be some problems, so they will likely agree with the question, particularly respondents who have no opinion. Rephrasing the question as, "Do you see any problems with using your credit card for an online purchase?" is a much more objective request of the respondent. Here the respondent is free—that is, not led—to respond "yes" or "no."

While you may think that leading questions are very easy to identify, and that they do not trick an intelligent person into a biased answer, we have just scratched the surface of this form of bias. Marketing Research Application 8.2 provides various examples of leading questions.

> Do not use loaded questions that have emotional overtones.

DO NOT HAVE "LOADED" WORDING OR PHRASING Leading questions are biased questions. **Loaded questions** are also biased but they differ from a leading question in that they contain wording elements that make reference to universal beliefs or rules of behavior. It may even apply emotionalism or touch on a person's inner fears. Some researchers refer to a loaded question simply as a "biased question."[27] Identifying this type of bias in a question requires more judgment. For example, a company that is marketing the product mace for personal use may use the question, "Should people be allowed to protect themselves from harm by using a taser as self-defense?" Obviously, most respondents will agree with the need to protect oneself from harm, and self-defense is acceptable, but these are loaded concepts because no one wants to be harmed and self-defense is only legal if one is attacked. Eliminating the loaded aspect of this question would result in the question, "Do you think carrying a taser is acceptable for someone

> "Don't you think that fast foods have too many calories?" is a leading question.

who believes it is needed?" A more obvious loaded question would be, "Since our Founding Fathers gave us the right to own guns, are you in favor of proposed laws restricting gun ownership?" Here there is an obvious reference to a universal belief in the term "Founding Fathers." As you can see, the phrasing of each question should be examined thoroughly to guard against the various sources of question bias error, for with the new wording we do not load the question with mention of harm or self-defense.

DO NOT USE A "DOUBLE-BARRELED" QUESTION A **double-barreled question** is really two different questions posed in one question.[28] With two questions posed together, it is difficult for a respondent to answer either one directly.[29] Consider a question asked of patrons at a restaurant: "Were you satisfied with the restaurant's food and service?" How do respondents answer? If they say "yes," does it mean they were satisfied with the food? The service? A combination? The question would be much improved by asking about a single

MARKETING RESEARCH APPLICATION 8.2

Ethics

The Many Ways That a Question Can Be Leading

Marketing and public opinion research associations hold deceptive practices such as leading questions to be unethical. Our definition of a leading question is rather simple, but consider the following, more complete definition to start.

A leading question is an interrogatory making use of a biasing mechanism. This mechanism may come in any one of, or any combination of, three forms: question structure; question content; question delivery.

This more formal definition of a leading question reveals that there are three different ways that a question can lead or strongly influence the respondent to give a particular answer. It can lead with form, facts, or phonics. Each is described in the following table. With each type, we have provided an example of a leading question dealing with fast food and overweight consumers.

As can be seen in the expanded definition of a leading question and these examples, there are both obvious and subtle ways that a question may lead a respondent to answer in a particular way. In order to be ethical, it is vital that marketing researchers examine their questions carefully and remove any question bias elements such as these.

Leading by form (*Question Structure*)

Common ways to make the form of the question leading include crafting a question that:

1. *Includes the answer in the question*

2. *Uses logic or apparent logic to steer the respondent to an answer (parallel examples)*

3. *Presumes the truth of an answer, or the truth of something logically leading to an answer*

Examples

1. *Don't you think that fast foods have too many calories?*

2. *Since most fast foods are fried, shouldn't these companies put warnings on their labels?*

3. *Since McDonald's is the largest fast-food company, shouldn't it set the example for more nutritious meals?*

Leading with facts (*Question Content*)

Common ways to use facts to make a question leading would be to include:

1. *Unsupported assertions presented as facts*

2. *Supported facts (or points presented as supported) presented in an unbalanced fashion*

3. *Loaded words/broadly held beliefs that generate an emotional/cognitive impetus toward an answer*

Examples

1. *Since everyone buys fast foods, shouldn't everyone be concerned about nutrition?*

2. *As studies have shown that overweight children buy fast foods, shouldn't "kids' meals" be healthier?*

3. *Do you think that Kentucky Fried Chicken should have warnings for obese people suffering from deadly diseases such as diabetes?*

Leading with phonics (*Question Delivery*)

Common ways to use phonics (or context) to make a question leading include:

1. *Make respondents aware of the desired outcome of, or "purpose" for, the survey*

2. *Make respondents aware of the sponsor*

3. *Use preceding questions to set up assumptions in the mind of the respondent*

Examples

1. *Will you take part in our survey that will alert consumers to the dangers of fast food?*

2. *Our survey is sponsored by the Vegetarian Council.*

3. *Since you have agreed that fast-food consumption contributes to eating disorders, shouldn't fast-food companies take responsibility for correcting them?*

Do not use double-barreled questions that ask two questions at the same time.

item: one question for food and another question for service. Sometimes double-barreled questions are not as obvious. Look at the following question designed to ask for occupational status:

_____ Full-time employment

_____ Full-time student

_____ Part-time student

_____ Unemployed

_____ Retired

How does one who is retired and a full-time student answer the question? An improvement could be made by asking one question about occupational status and another about student status.[30]

Do not use overstated questions that use words that overemphasize the case.

DO NOT USE WORDS TO OVERSTATE THE CONDITION An **overstated question** is one that places undue emphasis on some aspect of the topic. It uses what might be considered "dramatics" to describe the topic. Avoid using words that overstate conditions. It is better to present the question in a neutral tone rather than in a strong positive or negative tone. Here is an example that might be found in a survey conducted for Ray-Ban sunglasses. An overstated question is, "How much do you think you would pay for a pair of sunglasses that will protect your eyes from the sun's harmful ultraviolet rays, which are known to cause blindness?" As you can see, the overstatement concerns the effects of ultraviolet rays, and because of this overstatement, respondents will be compelled to think about how much they would pay for something that can prevent their blindness and not about how much they would really pay for the sunglasses. A more toned-down and acceptable wording of the question is, "How much would you pay for sunglasses that will protect your eyes from the sun's glare?"

To be sure, there are other question wording pitfalls.[31] For example, it is nonsensical to ask respondents about details they don't recall (How many and what brands of aspirin did you see the last time you bought aspirin?); questions that invite guesses (What is the price per gallon of premium gasoline at the Exxon station on the corner?); or to predict their actions in circumstances they cannot fathom (How often would you go out to eat at this new, upscale restaurant that will be built 10 miles from your home?). Our advice for you is to use common sense in developing questions for your questionnaire; you will probably avoid most other sources of question wording bias.

Table 8.2 is a convenient summary of the do's and don'ts of question wording. These questions may be developed for a survey on automobile global positioning systems (GPS). This table contains examples of bad questions that violate the associated question wording recommendation, and good examples that abide by the recommendation. Use Table 8.2 as a handy study guide or to keep our question wording recommendations foremost in your mind when you are involved in question development.

Seasoned researchers develop a sixth sense about the do's and don'ts we have just described; however, because the researcher can become caught up in the research process, slips do occur. This danger explains why many researchers use "experts" to review drafts of their questionnaires. For example, it is common for the questionnaire to be designed by one employee of the research company and then given to another employee who understands questionnaire design for a thorough inspection for question bias as well as **face validity,** that is, if the questions "look right."

Questionnaire Organization

Questionnaire organization pertains to the introduction and the actual flow of questions on the questionnaire.

Now that you have learned about question development, and specifically the guidelines and things to avoid when wording questions, we can turn to the organization of the questionnaire. Normally, the researcher creates questions by taking the research objectives in turn and developing the questions that relate to each objective. In other words, the questions are developed but not arranged on the questionnaire. **Questionnaire organization** is the sequence of statements and

TABLE 8.2

Examples of Do's and Don'ts for Question Wording

Do or Do Not Guideline	Bad Question	Good Question
Do: Be Focused	How do you feel about your automobile's GPS?	Please rate your automobile's GPS in each of the following features. (Features are listed.)
Do: Be Brief	When traffic conditions are bad, do you or do you not rely on your automobile's GPS to find the fastest way to work?	Does your automobile GPS help you arrive at work on time?
Do: Be Simple Structured	If you needed to find your child's best friend's house that was over 10 miles from your house for your child to attend a birthday party, would you rely on your automobile GPS to get you there?	To what extent would you rely on your automobile GPS to find a friend's house?
Do: Be Crystal Clear	Is your automobile GPS useful?	How useful is your automobile GPS for each of the following occasions? (Occasions are listed.)
Do Not: Lead	Shouldn't everyone have a GPS in their automobile?	In your opinion, how helpful is an automobile GPS?
Do Not: Load	If a GPS were shown to help us decrease our depletion of world oil reserves, would you purchase one?	How much do you think an automobile GPS might save you on gasoline?
Do Not: Double-Barrel	Would you consider purchasing an automobile GPS if it saved you time, money, and worry?	Would you consider buying an automobile GPS if you believed it would reduce your commuting time by 10%? (Separate questions for money and worry savings.)
Do Not: Overstate	Do you think that an automobile GPS can help you avoid traffic jams that may last for hours?	To what extent do you believe that an automobile GPS will help you avoid traffic congestion?

questions that make up a questionnaire. Questionnaire organization is an important concern, because the questionnaire's arrangement and the ease with which respondents complete the questions have potential to affect the quality of the information that is gathered. Well-organized questionnaires motivate respondents to be conscientious and complete, while poorly organized ones discourage and frustrate respondents and may even cause them to stop answering questions in the middle of the survey. We will describe two critical aspects of questionnaire organization: the introduction and the actual flow of questions in the questionnaire body.

The Introduction

The introduction is very important in questionnaire design.[32] If the introduction is written to accompany a mail survey or online survey, it is normally referred to as a **cover letter.** If the introduction is to be verbally presented to a potential respondent, as in the case of a personal interview, it may be referred to as the "opening comments." Of course, each survey and its target respondent group are unique, so a researcher cannot use a standardized introduction. In this section, we discuss the five functions to be provided by the introduction. Table 8.3 lists these five functions, and provides an example of the sentences that you might find in a survey on personal money management software. As you read our descriptions of each function, refer back to the example in Table 8.3 and the brief explanation.

TABLE 8.3

Functions of the Questionnaire Introduction

Function	Example	Explanation
Identifies the surveyor/ sponsor.	"Hello, my name is , and I am a telephone interviewer working with Nationwide Opinion Research Company here in Milwaukee. I am not selling anything."	The sponsor of the survey is divulged, plus the prospective respondent is made aware that this is a bona fide survey and not a sales pitch.
Indicates the purpose of the survey.	"We are conducting a survey on Internet browsers, sometimes called 'Web browsers.'"	Informs prospective respondent of the topic and the reason for the call.
Explains how the respondent was selected.	"Your telephone number was generated randomly by a computer."	Notifies prospective respondent how he/she was chosen to be in the survey.
Requests for/provides incentive for participation.	"This is an anonymous survey, and I would now like to ask you a few questions about your experiences with your Web browser program. Is now a good time?"	Asks for prospective respondent's agreement to take part in the survey at this time. (Also, here, notes anonymity to gain cooperation.)
Qualifies (or disqualifies) individual to be a respondent in the survey.	"Do you use Internet Explorer, Firefox, or Opera?"	Determines if prospective respondent is qualified to take part in the survey. Those who do not use one of these programs will be screened out.

First, as the interviewer, it is common courtesy to introduce oneself at the beginning of a survey. Note in Table 8.3 that the interviewer has done so, and the prospective respondent has been made aware that this is a bona fide survey and not a sales pitch. Additionally, the sponsor of the survey should be identified. There are two options with respect to sponsor identity. With an **undisguised survey,** the sponsoring company is identified; but with a **disguised survey,** the sponsor's name is not divulged to respondents. The choice of which approach to take rests with the survey's objectives or with the researcher and client who agree whether disclosure of the sponsor's name or true intent can in some way influence respondents' answers. Another reason for disguise is to prevent alerting competitors to the survey.

Second, the general purpose of the survey should be described clearly and simply. In a cover letter, the purpose may be expressed in one or two sentences. Typically, respondents are not informed of the several specific purposes of the survey as it would be boring and perhaps intimidating to list all the research objectives. Consider a bank having a survey conducted by a marketing research firm. The actual purpose of the survey is to determine the bank's image relative to that of its competitors. However, the research firm needs only say, "We are conducting a survey on customers' perceptions of financial institutions in this area." This satisfies the respondent's curiosity and does not divulge the name of the bank.

Third, prospective respondents must be made aware of how and why they were selected. Just a short sentence to answer the respondent's mental question of "Why me?" will suffice. Telling respondents that they were "selected at random" usually is sufficient. Of course, you should be ethical and tell them the actual method that was used. If their selection wasn't random, you should inform them as to which method was used but in a nontechnical manner.

Fourth, you must ask prospective respondents for their participation in the survey. With a mail survey, the cover letter might end with an invitation such as, "Will you please take ten minutes to complete the attached questionnaire and mail it back to us in the postage-paid, preaddressed envelope provided?" If you are conducting a personal interview or a telephone

The decision to use a disguised survey depends on the survey's objectives, possible undue influence with knowledge of the client, or desire to not alert competitors of the survey.

The introduction should indicate to the respondent the method of selection.

interview, you might say, "I would now like to ask you a few questions about your experiences with automotive repair shops. Would this be okay?" You should be as brief as possible yet let the respondent know that you are getting ready for him or her to participate by answering questions. This is also the appropriate time to offer an incentive to participate. **Incentives** are offers to do something for the respondent in order to increase the probability that the respondent will participate in the survey. There are various incentives that may be used by the researcher to encourage participation. As consumers have become more resistant to telemarketers and marketing researchers' pleas for information, researchers are reporting they must offer increased incentives. Offering a monetary incentive, a sample of a product, or a copy of study results are examples. Other incentives encourage respondents' participation by letting them know the importance of their participation: "You are one of a select few, randomly chosen, to express your views on a new type of automobile tire." Or the topic itself can be highlighted for importance: "It is important that consumers let companies know whether or not they are satisfied."

Other forms of incentives address respondent anxieties concerning privacy. Here again, there are methods that tend to reduce these anxieties and, therefore, increase participation. As you can see in Table 8.3, one is **anonymity,** in which respondents are assured that neither their name nor any identifying designation will be associated with their responses. The second method is **confidentiality,**[33] which means that the respondent's name is known by the researcher, but it is not divulged to a third party, namely, the client. Anonymous surveys are most appropriate in data collection modes where the respondent responds directly on the questionnaire.

> Anonymity means the respondent is never identified with the data collected, while confidentiality means that the respondent is not to be divulged to a client or any other third party.

> The introduction is important because it may determine whether the respondent cooperates or not!

Any self-administered survey qualifies for anonymity as long as the respondent does not indicate his or her identity and provided the questionnaire does not have any covert identification tracing mechanism. However, when an interviewer is used, appointments and/or callbacks are usually necessary, so there typically is an explicit designation of the respondent's name, address, telephone number, and so forth, on the questionnaire. In this case, confidentiality may be required. Often questionnaires have a callback notation area for the interviewer to make notes indicating, for instance, whether the phone is busy, the respondent is not at home, or a time at which to call back when the respondent will be available. Here the respondent will ordinarily be assured of confidentiality, and it is vital that the researcher guard against the loss of that confidentiality.

A fifth function of the introduction is to qualify prospective respondents. Respondents are screened for their appropriateness to take part in the survey. **Screening questions** are used to ferret out respondents who do not meet qualifications necessary to take part in the research study.[34] Whether you screen respondents depends on the research objectives. If the survey's objective is to determine the factors used by consumers to select an automobile dealer for the purpose of purchasing a new car, you may want to screen out those who have never purchased a new car or those who have not purchased a new car within the last, say, two years: "Have you purchased a new car within the last two years?" For all those who answer "no," the survey is terminated with a polite "Thank you for your time." Some would argue that you should put the screening question early on so as to not waste the time of the researcher or the respondent. This should be considered with each survey. We place screening questions as last in the introduction because we have found it awkward to begin a conversation with a prospective respondent without first taking care of the first four items we just discussed.

The creation of the introduction should entail just as much care and effort as the development of the questions on the questionnaire. The first words heard or read by the prospective respondent will largely determine whether he or she will take part in the survey. It makes sense, therefore, for the researcher to labor over a cover letter or opening until it has a maximum chance of eliciting the respondent's cooperation to take part in the survey. If the researcher is unsuccessful in persuading prospective respondents to take part in the survey, all of his or her work on the questionnaire itself will have been in vain.[35]

> Screening questions are used to screen out respondents who do not meet qualifications necessary to take part in the research study.

Question Flow

> Attention should be given to placing the questions developed into a logical sequence to ease respondent participation.

Question flow pertains to the sequencing of questions or blocks of questions, including any instructions, on the questionnaire. Each research objective gives rise to a question or a set of questions. As a result, as indicated in Figure 8.1, questions are usually developed on an objective-by-objective basis. However, to facilitate respondents' ease in answering questions, the organization of these sets of questions should follow some understandable logic in so far as possible. A commonly seen sequence of questions found in questionnaires is presented in Table 8.4 and, as the table title notes, there should be a logical or commonsense order to questions on a questionnaire.[36] Of course, it should be obvious that an objective is to keep the questionnaire as short as possible, because long questionnaires have a negative effect on the response rate.[37] The table points out that the first few questions are normally screening questions, which will determine whether the potential respondent qualifies to participate in the survey, based on certain selection criteria that the researcher has deemed essential. Of course, not all surveys have screening questions. A survey of the charge account customers for a department store, for example, may not require screening questions. This is true because, in a sense, all potential respondents have already been qualified by virtue of having a charge account with the store.

> Warm-up questions are used near the beginning of the survey to get the respondent's interest and demonstrate the ease of responding to the research request.

Once the individual is qualified by the screening questions, the next questions may serve a "warm-up" function. **Warm-up questions** are simple and easy-to-answer questions that are used to get the respondents' interest[38] and to demonstrate the ease of responding to the research request.

> Transitions are statements made to let the respondent know that changes in question topic or format are forthcoming.

Transitions are statements or questions used to let the respondent know that changes in question topic or format are about to happen. A statement such as, "Now, I would like to ask you a few questions about your family's television viewing habits" is an example of a transition statement. Such statements aid in making certain that the respondent understands the line of questioning.

TABLE 8.4

The Location of Questions on a Questionnaire Is Logical

Question Type	Location	Examples	Rationale
Screens	First questions asked	"Have you shopped at Old Navy in the past month?" "Is this your first visit to this store?"	Used to select the respondent types desired by the researcher to be in the survey
Warm-ups	Immediately after any screens	"How often do you go shopping for casual clothes?" "On what days of the week do you usually shop for casual clothes?"	Easy to answer; shows respondent that survey is easy to complete; generates interest
Transitions (statements and questions)	Prior to major sections of questions or changes in question format	"Now, for the next few questions, I want to ask about your family's television viewing habits." "Next, I am going to read several statements and, after each, I want you to tell me if you agree or disagree with this statement."	Notifies respondent that the subject or format of the following questions will change
Complicated and difficult-to-answer questions	Middle of the questionnaire; close to the end	"Rate each of the following ten stores on the friendliness of their sales-people on a scale of 1 to 7." "How likely are you to purchase each of the following items in the next three months?"	Respondent is committed to completing the questionnaire; can see (or is told) that there are not many questions left
Classification and demographic questions	Last section	"What is the highest level of education you have attained?"	Questions that are "personal" and possibly offensive are placed at the end of the questionnaire

Transitions include "skip" questions. A **skip question** is one whose answer affects which question will be asked next. For example, a skip question is, "When you buy groceries, do you usually use coupons?" If the person responds no, then questions asking the details of coupon usage are not appropriate, and the questionnaire will instruct the respondent (or the interviewer, if one is being used) to skip over or to bypass those questions. If the researcher has a great number of transition and skip questions, it may be a good idea to create a flow chart of the questions to ensure that there are no errors in the instructions.[39] Online questionnaires typically have a skip logic function that handles these transitions automatically.

As Table 8.4 reveals, complicated and difficult-to-answer questions should be placed deep in the questionnaire. Scaled-response questions, such as semantic differential scales, Likert-type response scales, or other questions that require some degree of mental activity, such as evaluation, voicing opinions, recalling past experiences, indicating intentions, or responding to what-if questions are found here. There are at least two good reasons for this placement. First, by the time respondents have arrived at these questions, they have answered several relatively easy questions and are now caught up in a responding mode in which they feel some sort of commitment. Thus, even though the questions in this section require more mental effort, the respondent will feel more compelled to complete the questionnaire than to break it off. Second, if the questionnaire is self-administered or online, the respondent will see that only a few sections of questions remain to be answered; the end is in sight, so to speak. If the survey is being administered by an interviewer, the questionnaire will typically have prompts included for the interviewer to notify the respondent that the interview is in its last stages. Also, experienced interviewers can sense when respondents' interest levels sag, and they may voice their own prompts, if permitted, to keep them on task.

> The more complicated and difficult-to-answer questions are placed deep in the questionnaire.

The last section of a questionnaire is traditionally reserved for classification questions. **Classification questions,** which almost always include demographic questions, are used to classify respondents into various groups for purposes of analysis. For instance, the researcher may want to classify respondents into categories based on age, gender, and income level. The placement of classification questions such as these at the end of the questionnaire is useful because some respondents will consider certain demographic questions "personal," and they may refuse to give answers to questions about the highest level of education they attained, their age, their income level, or marital status.[40] In these cases, if the respondent refuses to answer, the refusal comes at the very end of the questioning process. If it occurred at the very beginning, the interview would begin with a negative tone, perhaps causing the person to think that the survey will be asking any number of personal questions, and the respondent may very well object to taking part in the survey at that point.[41]

While most researchers agree in principal to these question flow recommendations, some prefer to think about questionnaire organization somewhat differently. That is, they tend to envision the questionnaire as comprised of areas, blocks, or elements that can be arranged efficiently and logically while still preserving the basic question flow suggestions just presented.

Computer-Assisted Questionnaire Design

Computer-assisted questionnaire design refers to software programs that allow users to use computer technology to develop and disseminate questionnaires and, in most cases, to retrieve and analyze data gathered by the questionnaire. Several companies have developed computer software that bridges the gap between composing questions on a word processor and generating the final, polished version complete with check boxes, radio circles, coded questions, graphics, and a variety of specialized features. These software programs allow users to publish their questionnaires on the Internet and enable respondents to enter data on the Internet. The data are then downloaded and made available for analysis, and practically all of these special-purpose personal computer programs generate data files that can be exported in a standard format.

The following paragraphs illustrate how these computer-assisted questionnaire design programs work. First, however, let us point out that there are at least four distinct advantages of computer-assisted questionnaire design software packages: They are easier, faster, friendlier, and provide significant functionality beyond that available with a traditional word processor.[42] Given this, here are descriptions of the basic functions of a computer-assisted questionnaire design program.

Questionnaire Creation

The typical questionnaire design program will query the user on, for example, type of question, number of response categories, whether multiple responses are permitted, if skips are to be used, and how response options will appear on the questionnaire. Usually, the program offers a selection list of question types such as closed-ended, open-ended, numeric, or scaled-response questions. The program may even have a question library[43] feature that provides "standard" questions on constructs that researchers often measure such as demographics, importance, satisfaction, performance, or usage.

Data Collection and Creation of Data Files

Computer-assisted questionnaire design programs create online survey questionnaires. Once online, the survey is ready for respondents who are alerted to the online survey with whatever communication methods the researcher wishes to use. Normally, a data file is built as respondents take part, that is, in real time. To elaborate, each respondent accesses the online questionnaire, registers responses to the questions, and, typically, clicks on a "Submit" button at the end of the questionnaire. The submit signal prompts the program to write the respondent's answers into a data file, so the data file grows in direct proportion to and at the same rate as respondents submit their surveys. Features, such as requesting an email address, are often available to block multiple submissions by the same respondent. The data file can be downloaded at the researcher's discretion, and, usually, several different formats, including Excel-readable ones, are available.

Data Analysis and Graphs

Many of the software programs for questionnaire design have provisions for data analysis, graphic presentation, and report formats of results. Some packages offer only simplified graphing capabilities, whereas others offer different statistical analysis options. In fact, it is very useful to researchers to monitor the survey's progress with these features.

Coding the Questionnaire

A final task in questionnaire design is **coding** questions, which is the use of numbers associated with question response options to facilitate data analysis after the survey has been conducted. The logic of coding is simple once you know the ground rules, and we have incorporated the basic rules of questionnaire coding in Table 8.5. The primary objective of coding is to represent each possible response with a unique number because numbers are easier and faster to use in computer tabulation programs.

TABLE 8.5

Examples of Codes on the Final Questionnaire

---

1. Have you purchased a Papa John's pizza in the last month?

    _____ Yes (1) _____ No (2) _____ Unsure (3)

2. The last time you bought a Papa John's pizza, did you (check only one):

    _____ Have it delivered to your house?   (1)
    _____ Have it delivered to your place of work?   (2)
    _____ Pick it up yourself?   (3)
    _____ Eat it at the pizza parlor?   (4)
    _____ Purchase it some other way?   (5)

3. In your opinion, the taste of a Papa John's pizza is (check only one):

    _____ Poor   (1)
    _____ Fair   (2)
    _____ Good   (3)
    _____ Very Good   (4)
    _____ Excellent   (5)

4. Which of the following toppings do you typically have on your pizza? (Check all that apply.)

    _____ Green pepper (0;1)   *(Note: the 0;1 indicates the coding system*
    _____ Onion (0;1)   *that will be used. Typically, no precode such*
    _____ Mushroom (0;1)   *as this is placed on the questionnaire. Each*
    _____ Sausage (0;1)   *response category must be defined as a*
    _____ Pepperoni (0;1)   *separate question. Also, you will want to*
    _____ Hot peppers (0;1)   *treat each topping as a separate question.)*
    _____ Black olives (0;1)
    _____ Anchovies (0;1)

5. How do you rate the speediness of Papa John's delivery service once you have ordered? (Circle the appropriate number.)

    Very   Very
    Slow   1   2   3   4   5   6   7   Fast

6. Please indicate your age: _____ Years (Note: No precode is used as the respondent will write in a number.)

7. Please indicate your gender.

    _____ Male (1) _____ Female (2)

The basic rules for questionnaire coding are as follows:

- Every closed-ended question should have a code number associated with every possible response.
- Use single-digit code numbers, beginning with "1," incrementing them by one and using the logical direction of the response scale.
- Use the same coding system for questions with identical response options regardless of where these questions are positioned in the questionnaire.
- Remember that a "check all that apply" question is simply a special case of a "yes" or "no" question, so use a "1" (= "yes") and "0" (= "no") coding system. You will want to consider each concept being tested as a *separate* question.
- When possible, set up the coding system before the questionnaire is finalized.

Codes are numbers associated with question responses to facilitate data entry and analysis.

Table 8.5 illustrates code designations for selected questions that exemplify our code system guidelines. For a hard-copy questionnaire, codes are normally placed in parentheses as you see in Table 8.5 (except for the "all that apply" question). In an online questionnaire, the codes are set up internally and not displayed. As you can see, when words such as "yes" and "no" are used as literal response categories, codes are normally placed alongside each response and in parentheses. For labeled scales, we recommend that the numbers match the direction of the scale. For example, notice in question 3 in Table 8.5 that the codes are 1–5, which match the Poor–Excellent direction of the scale. If we happened to have a 5-point Likert scale with a Strongly Disagree to Strongly Agree response option in our questionnaire, the codes would be 1–5. With scaled-response questions in which numbers are used as the response categories, the numbers are already on the questionnaire, so there is no need to use codes for these questions.

The codes for an "all that apply" question are set up as though each possible response was answered with "yes" or "no."

As you examine Table 8.5 please note the instance where coding becomes slightly complicated—the "all that apply" request in question 4. Again, once you learn the basic rules, the coding is fairly easy to understand. The researcher uses the **"all that apply" question** to ask the respondent to select more than one item from a list of possible responses.[44] With "all that apply" questions, the standard approach is to have each response category option coded with a 0 or a 1. The designation "0" will be used if the category is not checked by a respondent; a "1" is used if it is checked. It is as though the researcher asks about each item in the list, and a yes–no response (e.g., "Do you usually order green peppers as topping?" _____ No [0] _____ Yes [1]), but by listing them and asking "all that apply," the questionnaire is less cluttered and more efficient.

Performing the Pretest of the Questionnaire

A pretest is a dry run of a questionnaire to find and repair difficulties that respondents encounter while taking the survey.

Refer back to Figure 8.1, and you will find that as part of the questionnaire design process a pretest should be made of the entire questionnaire.[45] A **pretest** involves conducting a dry run of the survey on a small, representative set of respondents in order to reveal questionnaire errors before the survey is launched.[46] It is very important that pretest participants are in fact representative; that is, selected from the target population under study. Before the questions are administered, participants are informed of the pretest, and their cooperation is requested in spotting words, phrases, instructions, question flow, or other aspects of the questionnaire that appear confusing, difficult to understand, or otherwise problematic. Normally, five to ten respondents are involved in a pretest, and the researcher looks for common problem themes across this group.[47] For example, if only one pretest respondent indicates concern about a question, the researcher probably would not attempt modification of its wording, but if three mention the same concern, the researcher would be alerted to the need for a revision. Ideally, when making revisions, researchers should place themselves in the respondent's shoes and ask the following questions: "Is the meaning of the question clear?" "Are the instructions understandable?" "Are the terms precise?" and "Are there any loaded or charged words?"[48] However, because researchers can never completely replicate the respondent's perspective, a pretest is extremely valuable.[49]

Summary

This chapter described questionnaire design and some of the activities that are involved in the questionnaire design process. Forms that ask respondents questions are called questionnaires. Forms used to record observed behavior are called observation forms. Questionnaires serve several functions. The steps in the questionnaire development process begin by reviewing the research objectives and considering question development, including question evaluation, client approval, and a pretest of the questionnaire to ensure that the questions and instructions are clear to respondents. Certain words should be avoided in question wording, and we provided our "top ten" words to avoid, because these words are absolute extremes that force respondents to totally agree or totally disagree with the question. The objective of question development is to create questions that minimize question bias, and the four do's in question development stress that the ideal question is focused, simple, brief, and crystal clear. Question bias is most likely to occur when question wording is leading, loaded, double-barreled, or overstated.

The organization of questions on the questionnaire is important. The introduction should identify the sponsor of the survey, relate its purpose, explain how the respondent was selected, solicit the individual's cooperation to take part, and, if appropriate, qualify the respondent for taking part in the survey. We next provided general guidelines on the flow of questions on the questionnaire and pointed out the location and roles of screens, warm-ups, transitions, "difficult" questions, and classification questions. The chapter also introduced you to computer-assisted questionnaire design software, precoding the questionnaire, and pretesting the questionnaire. Pretesting should only be performed using a subsample of representative respondents to discover errors before the survey is launched.

Key Terms

Questionnaire (p. 176)
Questionnaire design (p. 177)
Question bias (p. 178)
Question development (p. 178)
Question evaluation (p. 179)
Leading question (p. 182)
Loaded question (p. 182)
Double-barreled question (p. 182)
Overstated question (p. 184)
Face validity (p. 184)

Questionnaire organization (p. 184)
Cover letter (p. 185)
Undisguised survey (p. 186)
Disguised survey (p. 186)
Incentives (p. 187)
Anonymity (p. 187)
Confidentiality (p. 187)
Screening questions (p. 188)
Question flow (p. 188)

Warm-up questions (p. 188)
Transitions (p. 188)
Skip question (p. 189)
Classification questions (p. 190)
Computer-assisted questionnaire design (p. 190)
Coding (p. 191)
"All that apply" question (p. 192)
Pretest (p. 192)

Review Questions

1. What is a questionnaire and what are the functions of a questionnaire?
2. Distinguish between questionnaires and observation forms.
3. What is meant by the statement that questionnaire design is a systematic process?
4. What is meant by question bias? Write two biased questions using some of the words to avoid described in Table 8.1. Rewrite each question without using the problem word.
5. What are the four guidelines or "do's" for question wording?
6. What are the four "don'ts" for question wording? Describe each.
7. What is the purpose of a questionnaire introduction, and what things should it accomplish?
8. Distinguish anonymity from confidentiality.
9. Indicate the functions of (a) screening questions, (b) warm-ups, (c) transitions, (d) skip questions, and (e) classification questions.
10. List at least three features of computer-assisted questionnaire design programs that are more advantageous to a questionnaire designer than the use of a word processor program.
11. What is coding and why is it used? Relate the special coding needed with "all that apply" questions.
12. What is the purpose of a pretest of the questionnaire and how does a researcher go about conducting a pretest?

Application Questions

13. The Marketing Club at your university is thinking about undertaking a moneymaking project. All coeds will be invited to compete, and twelve will be selected to be in the "Girls of (insert your school) University" calendar. All photographs will be taken by a professional photographer and tastefully done. Some club members are concerned about the reactions of other students who might think that the calendar will degrade women. Taking each of the "don'ts" of question wording, write a question that would tend to bias answers such that the responses would tend to support the view that the calendar is degrading. Indicate how the question is in error, and provide a version that is in better form.

14. Using the Internet, find a downloadable trial version of a computer-assisted questionnaire design program and familiarize yourself with it. With each of the following possible features of computer-assisted questionnaire design programs, briefly relate the specifics on how the program you have chosen provides the feature.

a. Question type options
b. Question library
c. Font and appearance
d. Web uploading (sometimes called "publishing")
e. Analysis, including graphics
f. Download file format options

15. Panther Martin invents and markets various types of fishing lures. In an effort to survey the reactions of potential buyers, the company hires a research firm to intercept fishermen at boat launches, secure their cooperation to use a Panther Martin lure under development sometime during their fishing trip that day, meet them when they return, and verbally administer questions to them. As an incentive, each respondent will receive three lures to try that day, and five more will be given to each fisherman who answers the questions at the end of the fishing trip.

What opening comments should be verbalized when approaching fishermen who are launching their boats? Draft a script to be used when asking these fishermen to take part in the survey.

Case 8.1 The SteakStop Restaurant: What Is Wrong with These Questions?

Professor Tulay Girard.

This case was contributed by Tulay Girard, PhD, Assistant Professor of Marketing, Pennsylvania State University-Altoona.

The SteakStop is a (fictitious) chain restaurant located in the southeastern United States. Working for its headquarters, the marketing manager, Brenda Bauer, hired you as a marketing intern to work on a customer satisfaction survey. On average, the twenty chain restaurants will receive about 150 phone surveys per store per month. Brenda would like to receive weekly, monthly, and quarterly reports generated from the customer feedback received. She drafted an automated telephone survey to collect information on customer satisfaction with the menu items and service in the restaurant. Below are the script and the questions that Brenda wants you to improve.

While looking at the survey questions, you notice violations of the basic questionnaire design rules based on what you learned from your marketing research course. Among such violations are double-barreled, loaded, leading or biasing, overstated, and vague questions, and questions with bad scales.

The SteakStop Restaurant Phone Survey Script

"Welcome to our customer feedback system. Please enter your access code followed by the pound sign. It is located on your purchase receipt next to the toll-free phone number you've just dialed."

Introduction Script

"Thank you for participating in SteakStop's customer satisfaction survey. By participating in this survey you will have a chance to win a $50 gift certificate. Winners will be notified by telephone. You must complete the entire survey to have a chance to win the gift certificate."

"If at any time during this survey you wish to repeat a question, just press the star key. Your feedback is important to us. Now, we will ask you questions regarding your latest dining experience at SteakStop."

Main Survey

1. *"What meal did you choose?* If steak, press 1. If seafood, press 2. If chicken, press 3. If sandwich, press 4."
2. *"Did you order one of our fantastic appetizers that everyone is raving about?* If yes, press 1. If no, press 2."
   (If the answer is yes, continue with 2a; if no, skip to 3.)

2a. *"How would you rate the quality of our appetizers?* If good, press 1. If very good, press 2. If excellent, press 3. If exceptional, press 4."

3. *"Were you pleased with the exceptional taste of your meal?* If yes, press 1. If no, press 2."

4. *"Please rate your hot and tasty meal based on your satisfaction.* If good, press 1. If very good, press 2. If excellent, press 3. If exceptional, press 4."

5. *"All of our health-conscious customers consider the portion size of our meals to be ideal. Do you?* If yes, press 1. If no, press 2."

6. *"Was your server attentive and responsive to your needs?* If yes, press 1. If no, press 2."

7. *"What does our competitor, Beef-O-Rama, charge for a complete meal?* If under $15, press 1. If between $15 and $20, press 2. If over $20, press 3."

Source: Tulay Girard.

8. "Now that you've completed the survey, please enter your ten-digit phone number followed by the pound key so we can notify you if you are a winner of the $50 gift certificate. If you prefer not to enter the drawing, press the pound key to skip this step."

Closing Statement

"Thank you for participating in our survey! We look forward to hearing from you each time you eat at SteakStop. Remember, 'When it's time to stop for a steak, stop at SteakStop!'"

Case Question

Carefully go over each question and identify what type of error was made. Then, correct the error using the "do's" and "don'ts" of question wording.

Case 8.2 **Your Integrated Case**

Advanced Automobile Concepts

(Note: This case requires that you have read and answered Case 7.2, Advanced Automotive Concepts.)

Cory Rogers now felt he had a good grasp of the research objectives needed in order to conduct the research study for Nick Thomas of Advanced Automobile Concepts. Furthermore, he had taken some time to write operational definitions of the constructs, so he had done most of the preliminary work on the questionnaire. Rogers began work on the questionnaire that he would need. Both Rogers and Thomas have decided that the most reasonable approach to the survey is to use an online panel. This alternative, although somewhat expensive, will guarantee that the final sample is representative of the market. That is, companies that operate such panels assure buyers of their services that the sample will represent any general target market that a buyer may desire to have represented. In the case of Advanced Automobile Concepts, the market of interest is "all automobile owners," meaning that practically all adults qualify.

Consequently, it is time to design a questionnaire suitable for administration to an online panel of adult consumers. The survey objectives have been agreed upon, and the ones relevant to questionnaire design for this phase of the research project are as follows:

1. What are (prospective) automobile buyers' attitudes toward:
   a. Global warming (do consumers believe it is real and this will affect their choice of car power source)?
   b. Fuel prices (do they believe they will remain high for several years)?
   c. Very small autos (one seat) with very high mpg ratings?
   d. Small autos (two seat) with high mpg ratings?
   e. Hybrid compact-size autos with moderately high mpg ratings?

2. Do attitudes (in question 1) vary by market segment? Market segments are defined by:
   a. Demographics
      i. Age ii. Income
      iii. Education iv. Gender
   b. Lifestyle

3. What are consumer preferences and intentions for various types and combinations of fuel-efficient automobiles?
   a. Very small (one seat), no trunk space, and very high mpg
   b. Small (two seat), very limited trunk space, and high mpg
   c. Hybrid models (compact and moderately high mpg)
      i. Synthetic fuel hybrids ii. Electric hybrids
   d. Alternative fuels models

4. What are media habits of those who prefer the new automobile types?
   a. Reading newspaper (local, state, national)
   b. Watching local news on television (6 A.M, 8 A.M, 6 P.M, 10 P.M.)
   c. Listening to FM radio (talk, easy listening, country, top 40, oldies)
   d. Reading magazine types (general interest, business, science, sports)

Go over the needed integrated case facts and information imparted to you in previous chapters, and design a survey questionnaire for Advanced Automobile Concepts. Naturally, you are responsible for proper construct measurement, clear question wording, appropriate question flow, and all other principles of good questionnaire design.

9

Determining Sample Size and the Sample Plan

LEARNING OBJECTIVES

- To become familiar with the basic concepts involved in sampling

- To learn how to calculate the minimum sample size needed to achieve a predetermined level of accuracy

- To understand the difference between "probability" and "nonprobability" sampling plans

- To become acquainted with the specifics of four probability and four nonprobability sampling plans

Survey Sampling International

Survey Sampling International (SSI) is the leading provider of sampling solutions for survey research all over the world. Founded in 1977, SSI has 17 offices in 15 countries, and reaches research respondents in 72 countries through a full range of online and offline sampling modes. SSI has an array of services to ensure market researchers access their target respondents and reach balanced and representative samples. With its broad coverage of modes, geographies and audiences, including both consumer and B2B, it can build sampling plans specific to each project's research objectives.

Not too many years ago, the marketing research industry heavily relied on a large percentage of households having landline telephone service. This was the main form of communication and it made sampling relatively easy compared to today. SSI provides us with the following information to illustrate how we have changed the way we communicate:

- Since 2000, Internet use worldwide has grown a staggering 380.3%. Every region has seen an explosion in Internet growth, including 134% in North America . . . 52% in Europe . . . and 545% in Asia. (*Internet World*)
- *Facebook* now has 350 million users—and not just teens! Baby boomers dominate—and "women, over 55" is one of the fastest growing segments.
- Email use has exploded! There are now 1.4 billion users world-wide. Over the last year, 90 trillion emails were sent—with 81% of them spam. (*Source: Radicati Group*)

- Google averages 299 million searches a day. C-level execs are among the most active searchers, conducting 6 or more searches a day. (*Google, Forbes*)
- 52% of consumers now blog about their brand experiences. (*Razorfish*)
- People who spend 10 hours a week on the Web cut use of traditional media by 65%. (*Stanford University*)
- Worldwide mobile phone penetration is now 61% and expanding. (*emarketer*)
- Nearly 25% of U.S. households are cell phone only and another 26% consider their cell phone their primary telephone. (*National Center for Health Statistics*)

What all this means is that consumers today communicate using methods other than traditional landline phones and this trend is increasing. Random Digit Dialed (RDD) telephone samples are still considered to be the "gold standard" as they provide accurate, representative samples. If, working with their sampling firm, researchers decide the research objectives require that the RDD/landline sample should be augmented, SSI has solutions created by adding samples drawn from other sources such as online consumers, cellphone users and/or creating sample by mailing sample to households without landline numbers. Or, if the research objectives call for it, SSI can use any *one* of these sources to create the sample. Regardless of the research objectives for a particular project, working with a professional sampling firm can ensure a representative sample.

One exciting new SSI service is SSI Dynamix.™ SSI Dynamix has the ability to draw sample from a full range of online sources—including SSI's own global online panels, web sites, social media, affiliate partnerships, online publishers, etc.—to create a balanced, dynamic access stream. This allows SSI to access people from anywhere they are on the Internet so researchers have every opportunity to drive target respondents to their surveys. Even people who would never join a panel may now be reached. Additionally, SSI Dynamix dynamically records and tracks their participation, just as if they were on a panel. Each time they take a survey, SSI matches them back to a stored profile. As a result, SSI Dynamix provides both tight quality and sampling control and broad reach. In addition, SSI Dynamix, delivers an improved respondent experience, reducing screen out and drop out rates . . . integrates advanced tools and process to optimize quality . . . and customized incentives to increase respondent engagement.

You can read more about these new methods at www.surveysampling.com.

Source: Ilene Siegalovski, Survey Sampling International.

Where We Are:

1. Establish the need for marketing research
2. Define the problem
3. Establish research objectives
4. Determine research design
5. Identify information types and sources
6. Determine methods of accessing data
7. Design data-collection forms
8. **Determine the sample plan and size**
9. Collect data
10. Analyze data
11. Prepare and present the final research report

Marketing researchers, when collecting primary data, typically rely on a sample because taking a census of everyone in a market is time consuming, very costly, and often leads to measurement errors. This chapter describes how researchers go about deciding sample size and taking samples. We begin with definitions of basic concepts such as population, sample, and census. Though sample size determination can be complicated,[1] we describe a simple way to calculate the desired size of a sample and illustrate how the XL Data Analyst can be used to do these calculations for you. We describe sample plans and describe in some detail four types of probability sampling plans and four types of nonprobability sampling plans.

Basic Concepts in Samples and Sampling

The **population** is the entire group under study as specified by the research project. For example, a researcher may specify a population as "persons in the household who are the primary decision makers for family finances residing in those counties defining the trading area for the Bank of Topeka." A **sample** is a subset of the population that should represent that entire group. How large a sample and the appropriate plan used to select the sample are the major topics of this chapter. A **census** is defined as an accounting of *everyone* in the population. As we stated earlier, a sample is used because a census is normally completely unobtainable due to time, cost, and because, as you will learn in this chapter, samples result in very accurate estimates of population values.

Since samples are used to estimate population values, we should be concerned with the accuracy of sample estimates. First, we must understand that because a sample is used, there will always be some error due to the unique properties of the sample. If the real[2] average height in your classroom of forty-five persons is 5'7" and we took a sample of say, ten persons, and found their height to be 5'9" then we have a 2" error simply due to the uniqueness of the height of the ten persons we happened to select for our sample. This difference between the real value in the population and the sample estimate is called sampling error. If we sampled another ten persons, we may have an error of 1.5." The point is, we would expect almost every sample to have what is known as sampling error. **Sampling error** is any error in a survey that occurs because a sample is used. Sampling error is caused by two factors: (1) the method of sample selection and (2) the size of the sample. You will learn in this chapter that larger samples represent less sampling error than smaller samples, and that some sampling plans allow for us to predict and control for sampling error while other plans do not.

In order to select a sample, you will need a **sample frame,** which is a master list of all the members of the population. For instance, if a researcher had defined a population to be all supermarkets in Greene County, then the master list would include these stores as a frame from which to sample. A physical list of supermarkets is readily attainable from research companies that provide such lists. However, sometimes a "frame" is not a physical list but a theoretical list. For instance, a researcher has defined the population as "female shoppers, age sixteen and older, who are shopping at City Mall." The "list" is a theoretical list of all the females, age sixteen and over, who happen to be walking in the mall on the day data is collected. As we all know, lists are not perfect representations of populations, because new members are added, old ones drop off, and there may be clerical errors in the list. So, researchers understand that **sample frame error,** be it

---

The population is the entire group under study as specified by the research project. A sample is a subset of the population that should represent that entire group. A census is defined as an accounting of *everyone* in the population.

This difference between the real value in the population and the sample estimate is called sampling error. Sampling error is any error in a survey that occurs because a sample is used.

MARKETING RESEARCH APPLICATION 9.1

Practical Applications

Sample Frame Error and How to Overcome It

The *Literary Digest*, an influential general interest magazine started in 1890, correctly predicted several presidential campaigns by using surveys. The world was becoming accustomed to viewing surveys as accurate predictors of future events. But the prediction the magazine made in the 1936 election was so bad that it is given credit for not only causing the collapse of the magazine (it was purchased by *Time* in 1938) but for stirring interest in refining surveying sampling techniques. Alf Landon, the Republican candidate and Governor of Kansas was running against Democratic President Franklin D. Roosevelt. The *Literary Digest* used three lists as its sample frame for polling American voters: its two million subscribers, a list of telephone owners and, third, a list of registered automobile owners.

The *Digest's* survey predicted Landon would win overwhelmingly but Roosevelt won in a landslide, taking

46 of 48 states! What went wrong? The *Literary Digest* had used an unusually large sample, yet the results were terribly wrong. The answer: the sampling frame was not a list of the potential voters from both parties. 1936 was the depth of the Great Depression. Those who could afford a magazine subscription, telephone, or automobile were much more likely to be Republican than Democrat. So the *Digest* was surveying, in very large numbers, voters who were mostly Republican. This illustrates the importance of having a sound sample plan which includes a sample frame with minimal error. Even a very large sample size will not help . . . you are just surveying more of the wrong people![3]

Every marketing research project must consider the extent of sample frame error in the sample frame to be used. Limiting sample frame error, as we illustrated in our opening vignette, can lead to samples that are more representative of some larger population.

---

great or small, exists for sample frames in the forms of misrepresentation, overrepresentation, or underrepresentation of the true population in a sample frame. Whenever a sample is drawn, the amount of potential sample frame error should be judged by the researcher.[4] Sometimes the only available sample frame contains much potential sample frame error, but it is used due to the lack of any other sample frame. It is a researcher's responsibility to seek out a sample frame with the least amount of error at a reasonable cost. The researcher should also apprise the client of the degree of sample frame error involved. Marketing Research Application 9.1 explains a classic mistake made by sample frame error.

> Sample frame error, be it great or small, exists for sample frames in the forms of misrepresentation, overrepresentation, or underrepresentation of the true population in a sample frame.

Determining Size of a Sample

The Accuracy of a Sample

A convenient way[5] to describe the amount of sample error due to the size of the sample, or the **accuracy of a sample,** is to treat it as a plus-or-minus percentage value.[6] That is, we can say that a sample is accurate to $\pm x\%$, such as $\pm 5\%$ or $\pm 10\%$. The interpretation of sample accuracy uses the following logic: If you use a sample size with an accuracy level of $\pm 5\%$, when you analyze your survey's findings, they will be about $\pm 5\%$ of what you would find if you performed a census. Let us give an example of this interpretation, as it is important that you understand how sample accuracy operates. We will take a sample that is representative of the population of people who bought birthday gifts in the past year, and let's say that we find that 50% of our respondents say "Yes" to the question, "The last time you bought a birthday gift, did you pay more than $25?" With a sample accuracy of $\pm 5\%$, we can say that if we took a census of the population of our birthday gift givers, the percent that will say "Yes" is between 45% and 55% (or 50% $\pm 5\%$). Think, for a minute, about the incredible power of a sample: We can interview a subset of the entire population, and we can extrapolate or generalize the sample's findings to

FIGURE 9.1

Relationship Between
Sample Size and Sample
Accuracy

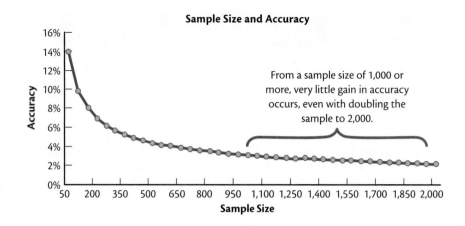

the population with a ±x% approximation of what we would find if we took all the time, energy, and expense to interview every single member of the population.

The relationship between sample size and sample accuracy is presented graphically in Figure 9.1. Here, sample error (accuracy) is listed on the vertical axis and sample size is noted on the horizontal axis. The graph shows the accuracy levels of samples ranging in size from 50 to 2,000. The shape of the graph shows that as the sample size increases, sample error decreases. However, you should immediately notice that the graph is not a straight line. In other words, doubling sample size does not result in halving the sample error. The relationship is a curved one. It looks a bit like a ski jump lying on its back.

There is another important property of the sample accuracy graph. As you look at the graph, note that at a sample size of around 500, the accuracy level drops below ± 5% (it is actually ± 4.4%), and it continues to decrease at a very slow rate with larger sample sizes. In other words, once a sample is greater than, say, 500, large gains in accuracy are not realized with large increases in the size of the sample. In fact, if it is already ± 4.4% in accuracy, there is not much more accuracy possible.

> With small increases in sample size, we can gain large increases in sample accuracy *up to a point* (about 500). Beyond that point, there are diminishing returns in accuracy as we increase sample size.

With the lower end of the sample size axis, however, large gains in accuracy can be made with a relatively small sample size increase. For example, with a sample size of 50, the accuracy level is ± 13.9%, whereas with a sample size of 250, it is ± 6.2%, meaning the accuracy of the 250 sample is roughly double that of the 50 sample. But as was just described, such huge gains in accuracy are not the case at the other end of the sample size scale because of the nature of the curved relationship. In summary, we learn from Figure 9.1 that with small increases in sample size, we can gain large increases in sample accuracy *up to a point* (about 500). Beyond that point, there are diminishing returns in accuracy as we increase sample size.

Formula to Determine Sample Accuracy

The amount of sample accuracy (error) can be calculated with a simple formula. Accuracy is expressed as a ± x% number. The **sample error formula** is:

Sample error formula

$$\pm \, Sample \, Error \, \% = 1.96 \, times \, \sqrt{\frac{p*q}{n}}$$

In this formula, *n* is the sample size that was used in the study. Let's assume we used a sample size of 400. (We will discuss the 1.96, which is a measure of our desired "level of confidence," and the "p and q" later in this chapter.) For now, to illustrate how the formula works, let us assume we have a 95% level of confidence (then we will always use a 1.96) and we will assume that $p = 50\%$ (i.e., 50% said "yes" they bought a birthday gift in the last year) and therefore $q = 50\%$ (i.e., 50% did not buy a birthday gift). What is the amount of error? If you enter these values in the formula, the result is $\pm$ 4.9%. As you will learn in this chapter, this means if you were to do the study one hundred times, then ninety-five of one hundred times your sample finding from these studies would fall between $\pm$ 4.9% of the sample finding you found in your study. In this chapter you are going to learn how to set your sample size so that you can *predetermine* the amount of sample accuracy—an important skill, indeed.

How to Calculate Sample Size When Estimating a Percentage

Since we never want to go to the effort and cost of doing a research project that results in inaccurate results, we want the minimum sample size that will afford us with some predetermined level of accuracy. Imagine this! We are saying that prior to conducting the study, we can predetermine the accuracy of the results by adjusting the size of the sample. If this is what you want, then there is only one proper way to calculate sample size—the **confidence interval formula for sample size.** When we are calculating the sample size needed to estimate a percentage value in the population, the formula is:

Sample size formula

$$n = \frac{z^2(p*q)}{e^2}$$

Where:

n = the calculated sample size
z = standard error associated with the chosen level of confidence (typically, 1.96)
p = estimated percentage in the population
$q = (100\% - p)$
e = acceptable error (desired accuracy level)

The confidence interval formula for sample size is based on three elements: variability, confidence level, and desired accuracy. We will describe each in turn.

VARIABILITY: p times q This formula is used if we are focusing on some categorically scaled question in the survey. For instance, let's assume we are doing a survey for our integrated case, Advanced Automobile Concepts. Since we are interested in knowing how to efficiently market to a target audience (those we identify who have a high preference for AAC's proposed models), we would want to know their media habits. Specifically, we may want to know how to reach them via television ads, so we would want to ask, "What is your favorite television show type? Comedy? Drama?" (For now let's assume there are only two types of televsion show types. Also, note this is a categorically scaled question.) Our primary interest will be to determine the percentage of the sample that answers each television show type. So this percentage will be the sample finding which is an estimate of the true population value. If our survey respondents have very little **variability,** then most will select one category (say, 90%) and few will select the other. In other words, there is much agreement (90%). Then this "low variability" will be reflected in the sample size formula as 90% times 10%, or 900. However, if there is great variability, meaning that no two respondents agree and we have a 50%–50% split, p times q becomes 50% times 50%, or 2,500, which is the largest possible p times q number possible. You should observe that since the p, q values are in the numerator of our formula, the more variability, given all else equal, the higher the sample size, n. Alternatively, the lower the variability, the lower the sample size. (There is a different formula for when you are trying to estimate an average. We will cover this later in the chapter.)

You should observe that since the p, q values are in the numerator of our formula, the more variability, given all else equal, the higher the sample size, n. Alternatively, the lower the variability, the lower the sample size.

The use of $p = 50\%$, $q = 50\%$ is a research industry standard of sorts. As you can see, it is the most conservative p-q combination because the sample results (which will show the actual variability) will never have variability exceeding 50%, 50%. While this will always generate a larger sample size, we will always achieve our minimum desired accuracy, which is why we call it a "conservative" choice. There are other ways of estimating p, q. If we have a former study on the same population, we could use past data reported in this study to estimate today's variance. Or, a third method would be to conduct a small pilot study to determine the approximate amount of variability.[7] So, in summary, there are three ways to estimate p, q: (1) Unless we have other information we can assume the most conservative case and use the maximum amount of variance we would expect in the population ($p = 50\%$, $q = 50\%$); (2) use data from a previous study conducted on the same population; and (3) conduct a small pilot study to estimate variance.

> There are three ways to estimate p, q: (1) Unless we have other information we can assume the most conservative case and use the maximum amount of variance we would expect in the population ($p = 50\%$, $q = 50\%$); (2) use data from a previous study conducted on the same population; and (3) conduct a small pilot study to estimate variance.

LEVEL OF CONFIDENCE: z We need to decide on a **level of confidence,** and it is customary among marketing researchers to use the 95% level of confidence, in which the z is 1.96. If a researcher prefers to use the 99% level of confidence, the corresponding z is 2.58. We use the phrase "level of confidence" because it refers to how confident we are that the sample finding will repeat itself if we conducted a different survey tomorrow or again the next day. Imagine that we learn that 55% of the respondents answered "comedy" to our question about favorite television show types. If we take this finding as an estimate of the real value in the population, then we should want to know that, if we redid the study tomorrow, we would get another estimate very close to the 55%. We know it would not likely be exactly 55% because we have already learned that sample error exists in every sample. As we will explain, by setting $z = 1.96$, it means that if we were to conduct our survey over a hundred times, ninety-five of these times we would get a sample finding that would fall within our predetermined level of accuracy. This gives us some confidence in the reliability of our sample finding.

> By setting $z = 1.96$, it means that if we were to conduct our survey over a hundred times, ninety-five of these times we would get a sample finding that would fall within our predetermined level of accuracy. This gives us some confidence in the reliability of our sample estimate.

DESIRED ACCURACY: e Lastly, the formula requires that we specify an acceptable level of sample error, meaning the predetermined ±% accuracy we have already introduced in the chapter. That is, the term e is the amount of sample error (**desired accuracy**) that will be associated with the survey. It is used to indicate how close your sample finding, in this case a percentage, will be to the true population percentage if the study were repeated many times.

EXPLAINING THE LOGIC OF OUR SAMPLE SIZE FORMULA Figure 9.2 illustrates how the level of confidence figures into sample size accuracy. First, we assume that $p = 50\%$ and $q = 50\%$. There is a theoretical notion (central limits theorem) that if the survey were repeated a great many

FIGURE 9.2

How Sample Error and the 95% Level of Confidence Theoretically Operate

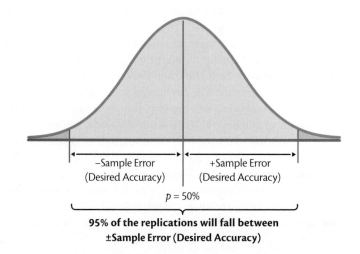

–Sample Error (Desired Accuracy) +Sample Error (Desired Accuracy)

$p = 50\%$

95% of the replications will fall between ±Sample Error (Desired Accuracy)

times—several thousands of times—and if you plotted the frequency distribution of each p for every one of these repeated samples, the pattern would appear as a bell curve, as you see in Figure 9.2. By setting $z = 1.96$ you are setting the interval in which 95% of the ps would fall, because $\pm 1.96z$ defines 95% of the area under the normal curve. Secondly, by setting e, you define the range within which these theoretical findings would fall. Observe that the smaller the e, the greater accuracy and the smaller this range will be. Also notice that e is in the denominator in our formula so, if we want to be more accurate, e will be a smaller number in the denominator resulting in a larger n, sample size. Note that 95% of the replications would fall between the population p (50%) in our example in Figure 9.2 and $\pm e$.

Here is an example of a sample size calculation that you can follow to make certain that you understand the logic of the sample size formula. Let us assume there is great expected variability (50%) and we want $\pm 5\%$ accuracy at the 95% level of confidence.

Sample size computed with $p = 50\%$, $q = 50\%$, and $e = 5\%$

$$
\begin{aligned}
n &= \frac{1.96^2(50 \times 50)}{5^2} \\
&= \frac{3.84(2,500)}{25} \\
&= \frac{9,600}{25} \\
&= 384
\end{aligned}
$$

Now, one final check to make sure you understand our logic. What does the $n = 384$ mean? It means that if you wish to conduct a survey to determine the percentage of respondents who prefer "comedy" television shows and you estimate variance to be 50% (prefer comedy) and 50% (prefer other than comedy), and you want your sample finding to fall within a range of $\pm 5\%$ if you were to do the study over and over, ninety-five of a hundred times, then you will need a sample size of 384! In this way, *as long as our variance estimate is accurate*, we will correctly *predetermine* the amount of accuracy we will have in our survey results. Just think how powerful this statement is. By being able to predetermine how accurate your result will be, you can confidently conduct surveys to estimate values of interest and be assured as to the accuracy of the sample findings.

How to Calculate Sample Size When Estimating a Mean

Thus far, we have presented the standard sample size formula in this chapter assuming the researcher is trying to estimate a percentage (p and q). However, there are instances when the researcher is more concerned with estimating the mean of a variable. In this case, a different formula is needed which expresses variability with the use of the standard deviation. That is, when determining the sample size needed to determine a mean, the situation calls for the use of the standard deviation, instead of pq, to indicate the amount of variation. In this case, the sample size formula changes slightly to be the following:

> A different sample size formula should be used when we are trying to estimate a mean.

Sample size formula for a mean

$$
n = \frac{s^2 z^2}{e^2}
$$

Where:

n = the sample size
z = standard error associated with the chosen level of confidence (typically, 1.96)
s = variability indicated by an estimated standard deviation
e = the amount of precision or allowable error in the sample estimate of the population

The formula and its application differ in two key ways from our percentages formula we have used thus far. First, as we just noted above, instead of using p, q to express variability, we use the standard deviation(s). Second, allowable error (e) is expressed in terms of the units being estimated instead of a percentage. For example, if we are estimating likelihood to purchase a car on a 7-point scale, we would express e in terms of scale units such as 0.25 or 0.5 scale units. Or, if we are estimating the mean number of miles driven by commuters in a city, e would be expressed in terms of miles. Finally, z is determined exactly the same way as it was in our percentages formula and will be either 1.96 or 2.58 depending on the desired level of confidence (95% or 99%). So, e and z are to be determined by the marketing manager working with the researcher.

There are three ways we can estimate variability, s, in the population. First, do you have a previous study on the same population from which we can calculate s? Second, do you have a pilot study to calculate s? Finally, when the first two choices are not available we estimate the range of values that may be derived from the question and divide this range by 6. Why 6? We are trying to estimate one standard deviation, and $\pm$ 3 standard deviations account for 99.9% of the area under the normal curve, so 6 standard deviations are synonymous with the range. By dividing the range by 6 we can estimate 1 s. For instance, the researcher might have a 7-point likelihood to purchase scale so $s = 7/6 = 1.17$. Or, for our commuter problem, we could assume that a few people drive zero miles to work and some may drive as many as 80 miles to work. So the range is 80 and $s = 80/6 = 13.3$.[8]

> There are three ways we can estimate variability, s, in the population: a previous study, a pilot study, or estimate the range and divide by 6.

THE EFFECTS OF INCIDENCE RATE AND NONRESPONSE ON SAMPLE SIZE   Whenever you calculate the sample size, you are computing the number of respondents you should have *complete* your survey. But invariably, surveys run into difficulties that require an upward adjustment in terms of the size of the sample you should begin with, or order from a sampling firm. We asked Kees de Jong of Survey Sampling International to explain how this works, in Marketing Research Application 9.2.

> Download XL Data Analyst at www.pearsonhighered.com/burns.

USING THE XL DATA ANALYST TO CALCULATE SAMPLE SIZE

It is time for you to be introduced to the XL Data Analyst Excel macro software that accompanies this textbook. A more formal introduction follows in Chapter 10, but there is a computational aid included in the XL Data Analyst that pertains to sample size. For now, simply open any Excel file that accompanies this textbook. Because the XL Data Analyst is an Excel macro, you will need to set the Excel 2010 Macro Settings via "Excel Options—Trust Center—Trust Center Settings—Macro Settings" to "Disable all macros with notification." Then, enable the macro content via the Security Warning feature after the file is loaded. If you have a problem, go to either www.xldataanalyst.com or www.pearsonhighered.com/burns, and read "Documentation."

After the file is loaded, you will see a "Data" worksheet and a "Define Variables" worksheet, but you can ignore whatever you see on these worksheets. Instead, use the XL Data Analyst to access the "Calculate" function available in its main menu. If you are using Excel 2010 or 2007, you will need to click on "Add-Ins" after you have clicked on "Enable this Content" in your Security Warning. Then click on XL Data Analyst and you will see the menu.) The XL Data Analyst will calculate sample size using the confidence sample size formula we have described in this chapter. As you can see in Figure 9.3, we have "pinned" the XL Data Analyst menu item on the Excel 2010 Quick Access tool bar, and the menu sequence is Calculate—Sample Size, which opens up the selection window where you can specify the allow able error (desired sample accuracy) and the estimated percent, p, value. In our example, we have set the accuracy level at 4% and the estimated p at 50%.

MARKETING RESEARCH APPLICATION 9.2

Practical Applications

Conducting a Telephone Survey? How Many Phone Numbers Will You Need?

Kees de Jong, CEO, Survey Sampling International

*I*n this chapter you are learning how to determine how many completed interviews you need to achieve as well as how many telephone numbers you need to dial to reach your desired number of completes, n. To answer this question, we asked an expert, Kees de Jong, CEO of Survey Sampling International, to tell you how it's done at the leading sample provider in the world.

You are going to learn how to calculate the size of a sample in this chapter. But, for a given sample size, n, how many telephone numbers are you going to need to dial? This may seem like a difficult task, but by following a few basic rules, it can become quite simple. To start,

Visit SSI at www.ssi.com.

two pieces of information are required. The first is an estimate of the incidence of qualified individuals in the particular geographic frame you've selected. The second is an idea of how many qualified individuals *contacted* will actually complete the interview. We call these two pieces of information the "incidence rate" and the "completion rate." It's useful to be somewhat conservative in projecting these rates, since these figures are rarely known as facts until the survey has been completed.

Next, you must know the number of completed interviews required, or the n. Then, it's necessary to have information on what we call the "working phones rate (WPR)." The Working Phone Rate is the percentage of telephone numbers in a sample that are working or assigned residential numbers (as opposed to non-working/disconnected numbers, businesses, etc.). The WPR varies by type of sample being used.

The equation we use to calculate the number of phone numbers needed for a project starts with the number of completed interviews required, n, divided by the working phones rate. That result is then divided by the incidence rate. Then, that quotient is divided by the contact and co-operation rates

to determine the total number of numbers you will need for your project.

SSI's Formula for Determining the Number of Telephone Numbers Needed

$$\text{Number of Telephone Numbers} = \frac{\text{Completed Interviews}}{\text{Working Phone Rate} \times \text{Incidence} \times \text{Completion Rate Needed}}$$

Where:

Completed Interviews = Number of interviews required for a survey (n)

Completion Rate = Percent of qualified respondents who complete the interview (taking into account circumstances such as refusals, answering machines, no answers, and busy signals).

Working Phone Rate = Percent of working residential telephone numbers for the entire sample. Rate varies by country and also depends on the selection methodology. Typically, in the U.S., Working Phone Rate ranges from 40% to 75%.

Incidence = The percent of a group which qualifies to be selected into a sample (to participate in a survey). Qualification may be based on one or many criteria, such as age, income, product use, or where the respondent lives. The incidence varies depending on three factors specified by the client.

Incidence = Product Incidence × Geographic Incidence × Demographic Incidence

Product Incidence = Percentage of respondents that qualify for a survey based on screening for things like product use, ailments, or a particular behavior.

Geographic Incidence = Likelihood of a respondent actually living in the targeted geographic area, expressed as a percentage.

Demographic Incidence = Percentage of respondents that qualify for a survey based on demographic criteria. The most common targets include age, income, and race.

For example, if 800 completed interviews are needed, the working phone rate is 60%, the incidence is 70%, and the completion rate is estimated to be 25%, 7,619 numbers should be ordered [800 / 0.60 / 0.70 / 0.25].

Source: Ilene Siegalovsky, Survey Sampling International.

FIGURE 9.3

XL Data Analyst Setup
for Sample Size
Calculation

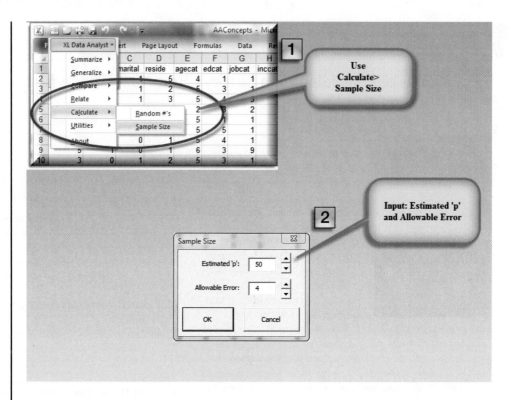

Figure 9.4 reveals that the XL Data Analyst has computed the sample size for the 95% level of confidence to be 600, while for the 99% confidence level, the calculated sample size is 1,040. There are two tables following the sample size table that a researcher can use to inspect the sensitivity of the sample size to slight variations of *e* (with estimated *p* constant), ranging in our example from 3% to 5% by 0.5% increments, or variations in the estimated *p* (with *e* constant), ranging from 40% to 60% by 5% increments. (Note: This part of the table is not shown in Figure 9.4.) The sensitivity analysis tables are provided so a researcher who is wrestling with a sample size decision can quickly compare the impact of small differences in his or her assumptions about variability in the population (*p*) as well as slightly loosening or tightening the sample accuracy requirements, or allowable error.

Marketing managers and other clients of marketing researchers do not have a thorough understanding of sample size. In fact, they tend to have a belief in a false "law of large sample size." That is, they often confuse the size of the sample with the representativeness of the sample. As you will soon learn in reading about sample selection procedures, the way the sample is selected, not its size, determines its representativeness. Also, as you have just learned, the accuracy benefits of excessively large samples are typically not justified by their increased costs.

It is an ethical marketing researcher's responsibility to try to educate a client on the wastefulness of excessively large samples. Unethical researchers may recommend very large samples as a way to increase their profits, which may be set at a percentage of the total cost of the survey. They may even have ownership in the data collection company slated to gather the data at a set cost per respondent. It is important, therefore, that marketing managers know the motivations underlying the sample size recommendations of the researchers they hire.

> It is an ethical responsibility of the marketing researcher to try to educate a client on the wastefulness of excessively large samples.

FIGURE 9.4

XL Data Analyst Sample
Size Calculation Output

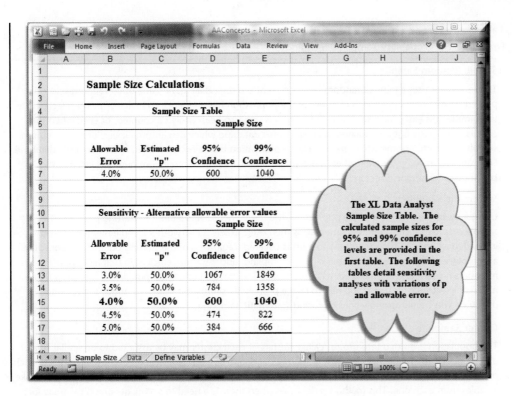

How to Select a Representative Sample

You now know that surprisingly few individuals can be chosen in a sample that represents a population with a small amount of sample error. What we wish to point out now is that the two sample size formulas you have learned in the preceding pages are only applicable when we have a representative sample. How we draw a sample, the sample plan, determines whether the sample is representative or not. There are two major types of sampling plans: probability and nonprobability sampling plans.

> The two sample size formulas you have learned in the preceding pages are only applicable when we have a representative sample. How we draw a sample, the sample plan, determines whether the sample is representative or not.

Probability Sampling Methods

A **random sample** is one in which *every* member of the population has an equal chance, or probability, of being selected into that sample. Sample methods that embody random sampling are often termed **probability sampling methods,** because the chance of selection can be expressed as a probability. Only probability sampling plans result in representative samples. Why? Think about it, if a certain subgroup of the population does not have a chance of being included in a sample, how could that sample possibly represent the subgroup? With probability sampling, all members of the population have a chance of being included in the sample and it is this characteristic that makes probability samples representative. We will describe four probability sampling methods: simple random sampling, systematic sampling, cluster sampling, and stratified sampling. You can use Table 9.1 as a handy reference, for it summarizes the basics of each of these sampling techniques.

TABLE 9.1

Four Different Probability Sampling Techniques

Simple Random Sampling

The researcher uses a table of random numbers, random digit dialing, or some other random selection procedure that guarantees each member of the population has an identical chance of being selected into the sample. It is easily used when the population is small and can easily be counted, or even when the population is large but is contained in an electronic database which can automatically "draw" a random sample. It is cumbersome when there is a large population that is not contained in an electronic database. For example, imagine the difficulties in drawing a simple random sample from numbers listed in the Los Angeles telephone directory!

Systematic Sampling

Using a list of the members of the population, the researcher selects a random starting point for the first sample member. A constant "skip interval" is then used to select every other sample member. A skip interval must be used such that the entire list is covered, regardless of the starting point. This procedure accomplishes the same end as simple random sampling, and it is more efficient in that all population members need not be enumerated. It is useful when you have a large list of population members that is not in an electronic format. If you had to take a probability sample from the Los Angeles telephone directory, you should strongly consider using systematic sampling.

Cluster Sampling

The population is divided into groups called clusters. If each cluster may be assumed to be similar to all other clusters, the researcher can then randomly select one or a few clusters and perform a census of each one. Alternatively, if the clusters are not similar, the researcher can randomly select more clusters and take samples from each one. This method is desirable when there is a need to survey geographical areas such as a city, as the resulting sample is selected from areas that are within clusters and are not spread out geographically. This lowers data collection costs.

Stratified Sampling

If the population is believed to have a skewed distribution for one or more of its distinguishing factors (e.g., size of firm, income, or product ownership), the researcher identifies subpopulations called strata. A random sample is then taken of each stratum. Weighting procedures may be applied to estimate population values such as the mean. This approach is better suited than other probability sampling plans when we believe that answers to significant research questions will vary between strata. If we believe there are significant differences on our research questions between strata, stratified sampling will give you more precise estimates, given the same sample size, from each subgroup and also ensure that each subpopulation of interest will be properly represented.

Simple Random Sampling

With **simple random sampling,** the probability of being selected into the sample is "known" and equal for all members of the population. This sampling technique is expressed by the following formula:

Formula for sample selection probability

$$\text{Probability of selection} = \text{Sample size/Population size}$$

So, with simple random sampling, if the researcher was surveying a population of 100,000 recent DVD player buyers with a sample size of 1,000 respondents, the probability of selection on any single population member into this sample would be 1,000 divided by 100,000, or 1 out of 100, calculated to be 1%. There are some variations of simple random sampling, but a table of random numbers technique best exemplifies simple random sampling.

The **random numbers technique** is an application of simple random sampling that uses the concept of a **table of random numbers,** which is a listing of numbers whose nonsystematic (or random) order is assured. Before computer-generated random numbers were widespread, researchers used physical tables that had numbers with no discernible relationship to each other.

If you looked at a table of random numbers, you would not be able to see any systematic sequence of the numbers regardless of where on the table you began and whether you went up, down, left, right, or diagonally across the entries.

USING THE XL DATA ANALYST TO GENERATE RANDOM NUMBERS

You can use the XL Data Analyst to generate your own table of random numbers. Figure 9.5 shows the menu command sequence and setup window to accomplish this end. Note that the menu sequence is Calculate—Random #'s, and the selection window allows you to specify how many random integer numbers you want (up to 9,999), and you can also specify the largest possible value (up to 999,999,999). In our example, we have specified 100 random numbers with a maximum value of 1,000.

Figure 9.6 displays our random numbers. Notice that they are arranged in five columns. You can experiment with the random-number-table-generator function of the XL Data Analyst, and you should discover that there is no systematic pattern relating these numbers to one another.

With the random numbers technique, you must have unique number values assigned to each of the members of your population. You might use social security numbers because these are unique to each person, or you may have the computer, such as in a database program, assign unique numbers to them, and do the matching work to determine what individuals are selected into the sample. Again, the use of random numbers assures the researcher that every population member who is present in the master list or file will have an equal chance of being selected into the sample.

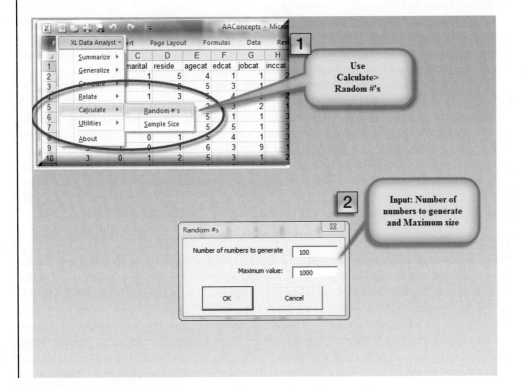

FIGURE 9.5

XL Data Analyst Setup for Random Numbers

FIGURE 9.6

XL Data Analyst Output
for Random Numbers

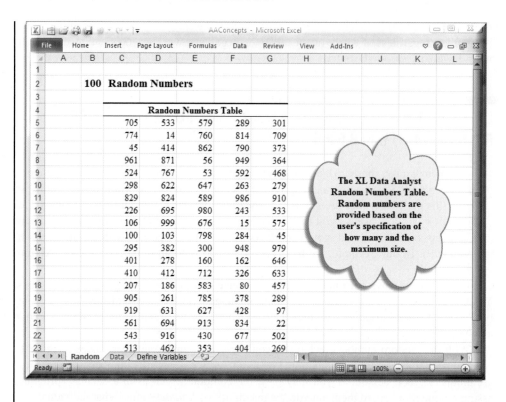

Random digit dialing
(RDD) is a method of
randomly generating
numbers to represent
telephone numbers. This
approach is used in
telephone surveys to
overcome the problems
of unlisted and new
telephone numbers.

Random digit dialing (RDD), a method of randomly generating numbers to represent telephone numbers. This approach is used in telephone surveys to overcome the problems of unlisted and new telephone numbers.[9] In random digit dialing, telephone numbers are generated randomly with the aid of a computer.

Simple random samples
are useful when you have
either a small population
or a large population
contained in an electronic
database such as a
spreadsheet program.

Simple random sampling is simple but the name should not imply that it is a weak sampling method. In fact, in the right circumstances it is desirable, because it is simple and it provides a sample representative of the population. This method is useful when you have either a small population or a large population contained in an electronic database such as a spreadsheet program. Imagine that a department store chain CEO wishes to sample the 823 persons (small population) who have sent in complaint letters to one of the chain's stores during the last year. It would be easy to take all the letters, number them, and then select a sample using a table of random numbers. Within a short time, the simple random sample could be drawn. Or, imagine the CEO wants to sample the chain's 127,000 credit card customers. Obviously, though this is a much larger population, an electronic list would be available. Downloading the list into a database management, spreadsheet, or statistical software program which has the ability to randomly select cases would result in a simple random sample within minutes.

Systematic Sampling

Before widespread use of computerized databases, researchers used hard-copy lists. In this situation, **systematic sampling** is a way to select a simple random sample from a directory or list that is much more efficient (uses less effort) than with simple random sampling, because with a physical list, the researcher must first enumerate (assign a unique identifier) each listing in order to select them using a random number.[10] To apply the systematic sampling technique in the special case of a physical listing of the population, such as a membership directory or a telephone book, systematic sampling can be applied with less difficulty and accomplished in a shorter time period than can simple random sampling. Furthermore, in many instances, systematic sampling has the potential to create a sample that is almost identical in quality to samples created from simple random sampling.

To use systematic sampling, it is necessary to obtain a hard-copy listing of the population, but it is not necessary to have a unique identification number assigned to each member on the list. (Think of the time this would save you if you had to go through a telephone book and number each listing!) The goal of systematic sampling is to literally "skip" through the list in a systematic way. To ensure that every member of the population has a chance of being included in the sample drawn, it is important to begin at a random starting point in the list. Then, in order to create this "systematic skip" through the list, the researcher calculates a **skip interval** using the following formula:

Formula for skip interval

Skip interval = Population list size/Sample size

For example, if the skip interval is calculated to be 100, the researcher will select every hundredth name in the list. This technique is much more efficient than searching for matches to random numbers. The use of this skip interval formula ensures that the entire list will be covered. The random sample requirement is implemented by the use of a **random starting point,** meaning that the researcher must use some random number technique to decide on the first name in the sample. Subsequent names are selected by using the skip interval.

Now, let's look at a brief example using a telephone directory of your city. First, to begin at a random starting point, select a page of the directory using a table of random numbers. Assume your directory has 280 pages, so you would select one number from among 280. Let's say you select number 26, so you begin on page 26. If there are five columns on each page, select a random number from 1 to 5. And, after taking a sample of a few columns, you conclude there are about fifty listings per column; so select a random number between 1 and 50. Assume you randomly draw listing 41 from column 2 on page 26. Every listing in the directory had a chance of being drawn and you now have a random starting point. Now, make a ruler that, on average is the length of the listings making your skip interval, 100 listings. Beginning at the starting point, record the number of the listing and then rule off the next 100 listings and select the next number and continue using the ruler to "skip" systematically through the directory. This will take a fraction of the time needed if you were to first have to enumerate every single listing as required in a simple random sample.

One problem with using a systematic sample to draw telephone numbers from a telephone directory is that you end up only drawing listed numbers. Therefore, you will have sample frame error by excluding the 20% or so of the population with unlisted numbers or persons new to your city whose listing was not included in the last printing of the telephone directory. For many years, researchers used a technique that would give them both listed and unlisted numbers. **Plus-one dialing** means that the number drawn from the directory has the last digit in the number replaced by a random number. In this way, the researcher is assured of drawing only numbers with central offices (the first three digits) that represent the city and blocks of the remaining four-digit numbers that have likely been assigned numbers by the telephone company.

Cluster Sampling

Another form of probability sampling is known as **cluster sampling,** in which the population is divided into subgroups, called "clusters," each of which may represent the entire population.[11] Note that the basic concept behind cluster sampling is very similar to the one described for systematic sampling,[12] but the implementation differs. The procedure identifies identical clusters. Any one cluster, therefore, could be a satisfactory representation of the population as long as the assumption is met that the clusters are identical. If they are not, as is often the case, multiple clusters should be drawn randomly using a simple random sample. Cluster sampling is advantageous when there is no electronic database of the population. It is easy to administer, and cluster sampling goes a step further in gaining economic efficiency over simple random sampling by

---

Systematic sampling is a way to select a simple random sample from a directory or list that is much more efficient (uses less effort) than with simple random sampling, because with a physical list, the researcher must first enumerate (assign a unique identifier) each listing in order to select them using a random number.

Plus-one dialing means that the number drawn from the directory has the last digit in the number replaced by a random number. This ensures that both listed and unlisted numbers are included in the sample.

In cluster sampling, the population is divided into subgroups, called "clusters," each of which may represent the entire population.

simplifying the sampling procedure used. We illustrate cluster sampling by describing a type of cluster sample that is sometimes referred to as "area sampling."

In **area sampling,** the researcher subdivides the population to be surveyed into geographic areas, such as census tracts, cities, neighborhoods, or any other convenient and identifiable geographic designation. As an example, think of a city map which typically divides the geographical area of a city by rows and columns in order to help you locate streets within the city. The resulting squares at the intersections of the rows and columns may be thought of as "clusters." Once the population has been divided into clusters, the researcher has two options: a one-step approach or a two-step approach. In the **one-step area sample** approach, the researcher may believe the various geographic areas to be sufficiently identical to permit him or her to center attention on just one area and then generalize the results to the full population. But the researcher would need to select that one area randomly and perform a census of its members. Alternatively, the researcher may employ a **two-step area sample** approach to the sampling process. That is, for the first step, the researcher could select a random sample of several areas (clusters), and then for the second step, could decide on a probability method to sample individuals within the chosen areas. The two-step area sample approach is preferable to the one-step approach because there is always the possibility that a single cluster may be less representative than the researcher believes. But the two-step method is more costly because more areas and time are involved.[13]

To illustrate why this is cost efficient, imagine that a researcher wishes to have a representative sample of a city and the research objectives require that respondents are to assemble and use a new kitchen appliance in their own kitchens. If you selected households using a simple random sample, you would have households that would be maximally distributed throughout the city. If a researcher showed up at a home at a prearranged time and the respondent was not home or, for some reason, was unavailable at that time, the researcher would have to drive to the next location. Using a cluster sample, the respondents in a particular cluster would be selected and a street in that cluster randomly selected. If one respondent were not available at a particular time, the researcher would simply walk next door. Sooner or later, all the respondents on that randomly selected street in the randomly selected cluster who had agreed to take part would be interviewed. The total costs would be much lower than the cost required for another sampling plan.

> In area sampling, the researcher subdivides the population to be surveyed into geographic areas, such as census tracts, cities, neighborhoods, or any other convenient and identifiable geographic designation.

Stratified Sampling

All of the sampling methods we have described thus far implicitly assume that the population has a normal or bell-shaped distribution for its key properties. That is, we assume that all the sample units are equivalent with respect to how they respond to our research question and any who are extreme in one way are perfectly counterbalanced by opposite extreme potential sample units. However, in marketing research it is common to work with populations that contain unique subgroupings, each responding to the research question differently. When we divide the population by these subgroupings we form different strata; each subgroup represents a stratum. The researcher should use some basis for dividing the population into strata that results in different responses to the key research question(s) across strata. There is no need to stratify if all strata respond alike.

To illustrate what we mean, let's assume a researcher is designing a marketing research project designed to determine the sales of a new photocopier that does not require ink and is jam-proof. The research objectives require that a sample of firms in the company territory be called to determine the likelihood that they will purchase the new machine and, if there is "high likelihood," the respondents are to be asked how many machines they will likely purchase. The sales territory is large and there are many small, medium, and very large firms within the territory. Would we think that all these firms would respond the same in terms of how many machines they may order? No, a firm with 10 employees may use only one machine but a firm with 10,000 employees may purchase several dozen machines. When we expect the responses to vary between strata, we should consider stratified sampling for two reasons. First, we want a sampling method that will ensure we

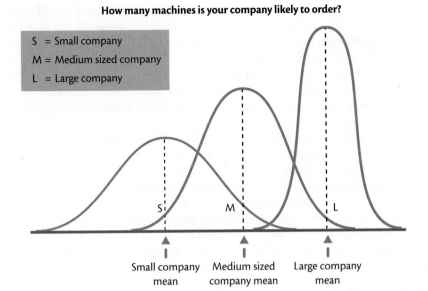

How many machines is your company likely to order?

S = Small company
M = Medium sized company
L = Large company

S   M   L

Small company
mean

Medium sized
company mean

Large company
mean

FIGURE 9.7

Research Question: How
Many Photocopy
Machines Do You Believe
Your Firm Will Purchase?
Illustration of Three
Strata in a Stratified
Sample of Business Firms

have representation of each stratum (small, medium, and large firms). Secondly, as we shall see, we can get more accurate estimates from each stratum by using stratified sampling without increasing the size of the total sample. **Stratified sampling** separates the population into different subgroups, or strata, and then samples all of these subgroups using a random sampling plan.

> Stratified sampling separates the population into different subgroups, or strata, and then samples all of these subgroups using a random sampling plan.

Why are stratified samples more accurate than simple random samples, given a sample size, n? To illustrate this, let's look at the distribution of possible responses to our photocopier research question described above. In Figure 9.7 we see three distributions of responses: one for each stratum—small, medium, and large firms. First, notice that the answers to the research question differ between the strata, as anticipated. Second, notice that the distributions vary in shape; the small firm has the flattest distribution, meaning there is more variance, and the most peaked distribution is for large firms, with the medium sized firms distribution fitting somewhere in between. We would expect there to be much variance among small firms as, depending on their business, some may not need copy machines at all and some need copy machines. Very large firms, because they have so many functions (e.g., HR, R&D) and so many employees, typically have photocopying needs regardless of the nature of their business. So we would expect there to be less variance on the number of machines needed.

Now, we should deal with the question, "How much sample size should we allocate to each stratum?" The answer to this question helps us understand one of the reasons to use a stratified question: They are more accurate than simple random samples given the same total sample size. What would happen if we used a simple random sample of equal size for each of our three strata? Because sample accuracy is determined by the variability in the population—regardless of whether you assess variability by using p times q for categorical questions or by using the standard deviation for metric scales—in our example, we would be least accurate in our estimate of machines to be purchased by small firms and most accurate with the large firms. To state this situation differently, we would be statistically overefficient with large firms and statistically underefficient with small firms, because we would be oversampling the large firms and under-sampling the small firms. To gain overall statistical efficiency, without increasing our total sample size, we should draw a larger sample of small firms and a smaller sample of large firms. (We can assume the medium sized firms sample size is about right for the level of accuracy we desire.) Having sample sizes for each stratum based upon the variances within each will result in a disproportionate sample size for each stratum. Intuitively, we would think that a proportionate sample size allocation would be preferred. A **proportionate sample size** would occur if we allocated sample size based upon each stratum's proportionate share of the total population; that is, if small firms represented 48% of the total population of business firms, then 48% of our total sample would be allocated to small businesses. A **disproportionate sample** is any other allocation that would occur if we based our sample size per stratum not on its proportionate share of the population but on its variance as per our sample size formula. So, going against our intuition, we should use a disproportionate sample size allocation in order to achieve the statistical efficiency possible by using a stratified sample plan.

> We should use a disproportionate sample size allocation with stratified sampling.

If we use a stratified sample, we would be estimating sample findings, that is, the mean number of photocopy machines desired per stratum. How would we calculate the overall mean for the entire population? There is a procedure that allows the estimation of the overall population mean by use of a **weighted average** for a stratified sample, whose formula takes into consideration the sizes of the strata relative to the total population size and applies those proportions to the strata's averages. The population average is calculated by multiplying each stratum by its proportion and summing the weighted stratum averages. This formula results in an estimate that is consistent with the true distribution of the population when the sample sizes used in the strata are not proportionate to their shares of the population. Here is the formula that is used for two strata:

Formula for weighted average

$$\text{Average}_{\text{population}} = (\text{average}_A)(\text{proportion}_A) + (\text{average}_B)(\text{proportion}_B)$$

Where:

A signifies stratum A, and B signifies stratum B.

Nonprobability Sampling Methods

The four sampling methods we have described thus far embody probability sampling assumptions. In each case, the probability of any unit being selected from the population into the sample is known, and it can be calculated precisely given the sample size, population size, and strata or cluster sizes, if they are used. With a **nonprobability sampling method,** all members of the population do not have a chance of being selected into the sample.[14] Because of this we cannot say that a sample drawn using a nonprobability sampling method is representative of some larger population. Also, the sample size formulas we learned at the beginning of this chapter may only be used with probability sampling plans. Yet, nonprobability samples are used often in marketing research. We explore why in the following paragraph.

> Since all members of the population do not have a chance of being included in a nonprobability sample, they are not representative of some larger population. Yet nonprobability sampling is used often.

Since nonprobability samples result in samples that are not representative of some larger population and when we use them, we cannot predetermine the accuracy of our findings because the sample size formulas are only used with representative samples, why are nonprobability samples used? There are several reasons, and these reasons explain their popularity. First, they are fast, simple to use, and less costly than probability sampling plans. As you will see when we describe the different plans, they may quickly and easily be administered at much less cost than the probability sample plans we have described above. The second reason, however, is also interesting. For many decisions, managers are perfectly happy to ask n number of persons a question to help them make a decision. A manager at Betty Crocker wants to know if a new cookie recipe is worth further development. By asking 100 people, the manager feels he or she will have enough information to make the decision. How can this be? If you just want enough information to tell you whether to continue development or drop the cookie and 95 of 100 people tell you that the cookie is the best tasting cookie they ever ate, wouldn't your decision be easy? Or, if 80 of 100 did not like the taste, you could also make a decision. Is the sample representative? Yes, but only of the 100 people you asked! Also, some managers will say,

> Nonprobability sampling is used because: (a.) they are faster and cheaper than probability sampling plans, and (b.) managers are willing to make decisions based upon the opinions of n number of respondents.

"So, what if I go to the time and effort to get a representative sample of residents of Des Moines? This won't tell me what people in Portland, Phoenix, or Atlanta think about the new cookie." So, our point here is that in some cases you want to make sure you use a representative sample and use the appropriate sample size formula to predetermine the accuracy of your results. This would be especially true for decisions that are deemed highly important or for decisions that require accurate estimates of population data (e.g., sales forecasts or research presented in litigation to establish damages).

There are four nonprobability sampling methods: convenience samples, judgment samples, referral samples, and quota samples. A discussion of each method follows, and you can refer to Table 9.2, which summarizes how each of these nonprobability sampling techniques operates.

Convenience Samples

A **convenience sample** is drawn at the convenience of the researcher or interviewer. Accordingly, the most convenient areas to a researcher in terms of time and effort turn out to be high-traffic areas such as shopping malls or busy pedestrian intersections. The selection of the place and, consequently, prospective respondents is subjective rather than objective. Certain members of the population are automatically eliminated from the sampling process.[15] For instance, there are those people who may be infrequent or even nonvisitors of the particular high-traffic area being used. On the other hand, in the absence of strict selection procedures, there are members of the population who may be omitted because of their physical appearance, general demeanor, or by the fact

> Convenience samples are drawn at the convenience of the researcher.

TABLE 9.2

Four Different Nonprobability Sampling Techniques

Convenience Sampling

The researcher selects respondents who are convenient. For example, the college professor surveys his or her class to learn about the attitudes of "college students." The television reporter interviews people at a busy intersection to learn how "people in the city" feel about an important upcoming event for the city. Sample selection error occurs in the form of the absence of members of the population who are not in the class or who are infrequent or nonusers of that location.

Judgment Sampling

The researcher uses his or her judgment or that of some other knowledgeable person to identify who will be in the sample. For example, the professor selects several different classes in different colleges to interview. The television reporter interviews some people who are shopping downtown and some people who are shopping at a suburban mall. Subjectivity enters in here, and perhaps the judgment includes more members of the population than a convenience sample, still certain members of the population will not have a probability of being selected into the sample.

Referral Sampling

Respondents are asked for the names or identities of others like themselves who might qualify to take part in the survey. Members of the population who are less well known, disliked, or whose opinions conflict with the respondent have a low probability of being selected into a referral sample.

Quota Sampling

The researcher identifies quota characteristics such as demographic or product-use factors and uses these to set up quotas for each class of respondent. The quota sizes are determined by the researcher's belief about the relative size of each class of respondent in the population. Often quota sampling is used as a means of ensuring that convenience samples will have the desired proportions of different respondent classes, thereby reducing the sample selection error but not eliminating it. Again, there will be members of the population who have no probability of ending up in the sample.

that they are in a group rather than alone. One author states, "Convenience samples . . . can be seriously misleading."[16]

Mall-intercept companies often use a convenience sampling method to recruit respondents. For example, shoppers are encountered at large shopping malls and quickly qualified with screening questions. For those satisfying the desired population characteristics, a questionnaire may be administered or a taste test performed. Alternatively, the respondent may be given a test product and asked if he or she would use it at home. A follow-up telephone call some days later solicits the respondent's reaction to product performance. In this case, the convenience extends beyond easy access of respondents into considerations of setup for taste tests, storage of products to be distributed, and control of the interviewer workforce. Additionally, large numbers of respondents can be recruited in a matter of days. The screening questions and geographic dispersion of malls may appear to reduce the subjectivity inherent in the sample design, but in fact the vast majority of the population was not there and could not be approached to take part. Yet, there are ways of controlling convenience sample selection error using a quota system, which we discuss shortly.

Judgment Samples

> Judgment samples require some educated guess, or judgement, about who should be included in the sample to represent the population.

A **judgment sample** is somewhat different from a convenience sample in concept because a judgment sample requires a judgment or an "educated guess" as to who should represent the population. Often the researcher or some individual helping the researcher who has considerable knowledge about the population will choose those individuals that he or she feels constitute the sample. It should be apparent that judgment samples are highly subjective and therefore prone to much error.

However, judgment samples do have special uses. For instance, in the preliminary stages of a research project, the researcher may use qualitative techniques such as depth interviews or focus groups as a means of gaining insight and understanding to the research problem. In this case, judgment sampling is a quick, inexpensive, and acceptable technique because the researcher is not seeking to generalize the findings of this sample to the population as a whole. Take, for example, a recent focus group concerning the need for a low-calorie, low-fat microwave oven cookbook. Twelve women were selected as representative of the present and prospective market. Six of these women had owned a microwave oven for ten or more years, three of the women had owned the oven for less than ten years, and three of the women were in the market for a microwave oven. In the judgment of the researcher, these twelve women represented the population adequately for the purposes of the focus group. It must be quickly pointed out, however, that the intent of this focus group was far different from the intent of a survey. Consequently, the use of a judgment sample was considered satisfactory for this particular phase in the research process for the cookbook. The focus group findings served as the foundation for a large-scale regional survey conducted two months later that relied on a probability sampling method.

Referral Samples

> Referral, or "snowball" samples require a respondent to provide the name of another respondent to be sampled. They are often used in B2B research.

A **referral sample** is sometimes called a "snowball sample," because it requires respondents to provide the names of additional respondents. Such lists begin when the researcher compiles a short list of potential respondents based on convenience or judgment. After each respondent is interviewed, he or she is queried about the names of other possible respondents. In this manner, additional respondents are referred by previous respondents. Or, as the other name implies, the sample grows just as a snowball grows when it is rolled downhill.

Referral samples are most appropriate when there is a limited sample frame and when respondents can provide the names of others who would qualify for the survey. For example, some foreign countries have low telephone penetration or slow mail systems that make these options unsuitable, whereas a referral approach adds an element of trust to the approach for each new potential respondent. The nonprobability aspects of referral sampling come from the selectivity used throughout. The initial list may also be special in some way, and the primary means of adding people to the sample is by tapping the memories of those on the original list.

Referral samples are often useful in B2B marketing research situations.[17] Because persons in various positions (e.g., sales managers, buyers, production managers) tend to know their counterparts in other businesses, by reaching one person, a researcher can often be referred to other respondents who have the necessary position to qualify them as a respondent.

Quota Samples

We have saved the most commonly used nonprobability sampling method for last. The **quota sample** establishes a specific quota for various types of individuals to be interviewed. The quotas are determined through application of the research objectives and are defined by key characteristics used to identify the population. In the application of quota sampling, a fieldworker is provided with screening criteria that will classify the potential respondent into a particular quota cell. For example, if the interviewer is assigned to obtain a sample quota of fifty each for black females, black males, white females, and white males, the qualifying characteristics would be race and gender. Assuming our fieldworkers were conducting mall intercepts, each would determine through visual inspection which category the prospective respondent fits into, and would work toward filling the quota in each of the four cells. So a quota system overcomes much of the danger of nonrepresentativeness that is inherent in convenience samples.[18]

> Quota samples establish quotas for various types of individuals to be interviewed, i.e. 50% males and 50% females.

The popularity of quota samples is attributable to the fact that they combine nonprobability sampling advantages with quota controls that ensure the final sample will approximate the population with respect to its key characteristics. Quota samples are often used by consumer goods companies that have a firm grasp on the features characterizing the individuals they wish to study in a particular marketing research project. These companies often use mall-intercept data collection companies that deliver fast service at a reasonable price, and the use of quota controls guarantees that the final sample will satisfactorily represent the population that the consumer goods company has targeted for the research project. Quota samples are also used in global marketing research where communication systems are problematic. For example, most companies performing research in Latin America use quota samples.[19] When done conscientiously and with a solid understanding of the quota characteristics, quota sampling can rival probability sampling in the minds of some researchers. The key assumption of quota sampling is that because the sample matches the population on certain quota characteristics, the sample will also match the population on the research questions of interest.

Online Sampling Techniques

Online or Internet surveys are popular because of their speed and low cost. Sampling for Internet surveys poses special challenges,[20] but most of these issues can be addressed in the context of our probability and nonprobability sampling concepts.[21] If you understand how a particular online sampling method works, you can probably interpret the sampling procedure correctly with respect to basic sampling concepts.[22] For purposes of illustration, we will describe three types of online sampling: (1) random online intercept sampling, (2) invitation online sampling, and (3) online panel sampling.

Random online intercept sampling relies on a random selection of website visitors. There are a number of Java-based or other html-embedded routines that will select website visitors on a random basis, such as time of day, or random selection from the stream of website visitors. If the population is defined as website visitors, then this is a simple random sample of these visitors within the time frame of the survey. If the sample selection program starts randomly and incorporates a skip interval system, it is a systematic sample;[23] and if the sample program treats the population of website visitors like strata, it uses stratified simple random sampling as long as random selection procedures are used faithfully. However, if the population is other than website visitors, and the website is used because there are many visitors, the sample is akin to a mall-intercept sample (convenience sample).

> Random online intercept sampling randomly selects website visitors to become part of the sample.

Invitation online sampling invites potential respondents to a survey website.	**Invitation online sampling** is when potential respondents are alerted that they may fill out a questionnaire that is hosted at a specific website.[24] For example, a retail store chain may have a notice that is handed to customers with their receipts notifying them that they may go online to fill out the questionnaire. However, to avoid spam, online researchers must have an established relationship with potential respondents who expect to receive an e-mail survey. If the retail store uses a random sampling approach such as systematic sampling, a probability sample will result. Similarly, if the e-mail list is a truly representative group of the population, and the procedures embody random selection, it will constitute a probability sample. However, if in either case there is some aspect of the selection procedure that eliminates population members or otherwise over-represents elements of the population, the result will be a nonprobability sample.
Online panel sampling relies on a preestablished panel of respondents to complete the survey request.	**Online panel sampling** refers to consumer or other respondent panels that are set up by marketing research companies for the explicit purpose of conducting online surveys with representative samples. There is a growing number of these companies, and online panels afford fast, convenient, and flexible access to preprofiled samples.[25] Typically, the panel company has several thousand individuals who are representative of a large geographic area, and the marketing researcher can specify sample parameters such as specific geographic representation, income, education, or family characteristics. The panel company then uses its database on its panel members to broadcast an e-mail notification to those panelists who qualify according to the sample parameters specified by the marketing researcher. Although most online panel samples are not probability samples, they are used extensively by the marketing research industry.[26] One firm, Knowledge Networks, specializes in offering an online panel which is a probability sample. In some instances, the online panel company creates the questionnaire; at other times, the researcher composes the questionnaire on the panel company's software, or some other means of questionnaire design might be used, depending on the services of the panel company. One of the greatest pluses of online panels is the high response rate, which ensures that the final sample closely represents the population targeted by the researcher. Other online sampling approaches are feasible and limited only by the creativity of the sample designers.

Summary

This chapter discusses both sample size determination and the sample plan choices. We began by defining basic terms such as *population*, *sample*, *census*, *sampling error*, *sample frame*, and *sample frame error*. Sample frame error is illustrated by the classic mistakes made in the survey used to predict the Landon/Roosevelt presidential election. Sample size accuracy is typically expressed as a $\pm x\%$ of what you would find if you conducted a census. Small increases in sample size give you great increases in accuracy up to a point, after which it takes large increases in sample size to achieve small increases in accuracy. There is a formula for calculating sample accuracy.

To calculate the required sample size to estimate a percentage, we use the confidence interval formula for sample size. The formula requires that variability in the form of p, q be estimated. Variability is measured by p, q in the formula. The higher the variability, the larger the sample size required, given all else equal. We can estimate p, q by assuming it to be the maximum (50%, 50%); or we can use a previous study on the same population; or we can conduct a pilot study to get an estimate of p, q. The formula also requires that we determine z, the level of confidence, and it is customary among marketing researchers to use the 95% level of confidence, or $z = 1.96$. If a researcher prefers to use the 99% level of confidence, then $z = 2.58$. We use the phrase "level of confidence" because it refers to how confident we are that the sample finding will repeat itself if we conducted a different survey tomorrow or again the next day.

Lastly, the formula requires that we specify an acceptable level of sample error, e. Here the formula allows us to predetermine the $\pm x \%$ accuracy. It is used to indicate how close your sample finding, in this case a percentage, will be to the true population percentage if the study were repeated many, many times. Many studies set e as 5%.

The sample size for calculating a mean is also presented. The formula and its application differs in two key ways from the percentages formula. First, instead of using p, q to express variability we use the standard deviation (s). Second, allowable error (e) is expressed in terms of the units being estimated instead of a percentage. Finally, z is determined exactly the same way as it was in our percentages formula. There are three ways we can estimate s. First, do you have a previous study on the same population from which we can calculate s? Second, do you have a pilot study to calculate s? Finally, when the first two choices are not available we estimate the range of values that may be derived from the question and divide this range by 6. We illustrate that the final sample size should be increased due to factors such as the working phone rate, incidence rate, and so on. You can automatically calculate the sample size required for a percentage using XL Data Analyst.

Sample plans are used to select units from the population into the sample. Sample size formulas are only applicable when you use a probability sampling plan. A random sample is one in which *every* member of the population has an equal chance, or probability, of being selected into that sample. Sample methods that embody random sampling are often termed probability sampling methods, because the chance of selection can be expressed as a probability. Only probability sampling plans result in representative samples. Sample size formulas are appropriate only when there is a probability sampling plan.

The chapter describes four probability sampling methods: (1) simple random sampling, (2) systematic sampling that utilizes a skip interval for a sample frame list, (3) cluster sampling, and (4) stratified sampling. Next, four nonprobability sample methods were described, and it was pointed out for each one how its application incurs some degree of sample selection error. With a nonprobability sampling method, all members of the population do not have a chance of being selected into the sample.[27] Because of this we cannot say that a sample drawn using a nonprobability sampling method is representative of some larger population. Yet, nonprobability samples are used often in marketing research because, first, they may quickly and easily be administered at much less cost than the probability sample plans. Secondly, for many decisions, managers are perfectly happy to ask n number of persons a question to help them make a decision. Nonprobability sampling techniques presented in the chapter are (1) convenience sampling, such as using customer traffic in a shopping mall as the sample frame; (2) judgment sampling, where someone arbitrarily specifies who will be in the sample; (3) referral sampling, in which case the respondents divulge the names of friends and acquaintances to the researcher; and (4) quota sampling, where the researcher attempts to minimize sample selection error by requiring that certain classes of individuals are in the sample in proportions that are believed to reflect their presence in the population. Finally, online sampling techniques are random online intercept sampling, invitation online sampling, and online panel sampling.

Key Terms

Population (p. 198)
Sample (p. 198)
Census (p. 198)
Sampling error (p. 198)
Sample frame (p. 198)
Sample frame error (p. 198)
Accuracy of a sample (p. 199)
Sample error formula (p. 200)
Confidence interval formula for sample size (p. 201)
Variability (p. 201)
Level of confidence (p. 202)
Desired accuracy (p. 202)
Completed interviews (p. 205)
Completion rate (p. 205)
Working phone rate (p. 205)
Incidence (p. 205)

Product incidence (p. 205)
Geographic incidence (p. 205)
Demographic incidence (p. 205)
Random sample (p. 207)
Probability sampling methods (p. 207)
Simple random sampling (p. 208)
Random numbers technique (p. 208)
Table of random numbers (p. 208)
Random digit dialing (RDD) (p. 210)
Systematic sampling (p. 210)
Skip interval (p. 211)
Random starting point (p. 211)
Plus-one dialing (p. 211)
Cluster sampling (p. 211)
Area sampling (p. 212)
One-step area sample (p. 212)

Two-step area sample (p. 212)
Stratified sampling (p. 213)
Proportionate sample size (p. 214)
Disproportionate sample (p. 214)
Weighted average (p. 214)
Nonprobability sampling method (p. 214)
Convenience sample (p. 215)
Judgment sample (p. 216)
Referral sample (p. 216)
Quota sample (p. 217)
Random online intercept sampling (p. 217)
Invitation online sampling (p. 218)
Online panel sampling (p. 218)

Review Questions

1. Define each of the following:
   a. Population
   b. Sample
   c. Census
   d. Sample frame
2. Indicate the sample frame error typically found in the households listing of a telephone book.
3. Explain why the *Literary Digest* survey of the Landon/Roosevelt election was so incorrect.
4. What is meant by accuracy of a sample and what is the formula to measure it?
5. What is the formula for estimating a percentage in the population? Explain what the variables *z, p, q,* and *e* represent.
6. What does *p, q* measure and what relationship does this have to the size of the sample, given all else is equal?
7. What do we mean by "level of confidence" and how is it expressed in the sample size formula?
8. What is the formula for estimating a mean in the population? Explain how its components are different/like the components in the formula for estimating a percentage.
9. What are three methods for estimating the variance in the population using the formula to calculate the sample size for estimating a mean?
10. Explain how you would use XL Data Analyst to calculate the desired sample size to estimate a percentage in the population.
11. How do probability samples differ from nonprobability samples and what is the significance of this difference?
12. What is simple random sampling and when would you use it?
13. What is systematic sampling and when would you use it?
14. What is cluster sampling and when would you use it?
15. What is stratified sampling and when would you use it?
16. How would you use XL Data Analyst to generate random numbers?
17. Explain how you would use the skip interval in a systematic sample if you had to draw a sample from your city telephone directory.
18. Would you use a proportionate or disproportionate stratified sample? Why?
19. Describe the four types of nonprobability samples.
20. What are the drawbacks of using a nonprobability sample and why are they used?
21. Briefly explain the three techniques presented in the chapter for online sampling.

Application Questions

22. Here are four populations and a potential sample frame for each one. With each pair, identify (1) members of the population who are not in the sample frame, and (2) sample frame items that are not part of the population. Also, for each one, would you judge the amount of sample frame error to be acceptable or unacceptable?

Population	Sample Frame
a. Buyers of Scope mouthwash	Mailing list of *Consumer Reports* subscribers
b. Listeners of a particular FM radio classical music station	Telephone directory in your city
c. Prospective buyers of a new day planner and prospective-client tracking kit	Members of Sales and Marketing Executives International (a national organization of sales managers)
d. Users of weatherproof decking materials (to build outdoor decks)	Individuals' names registered at a recent home and garden show

23. Here are some numbers that you can use to sharpen your computational skills for sample size determination. Crest toothpaste is reviewing plans for its annual survey of toothpaste purchasers. With each case that follows, calculate the sample size pertaining to the key variable under consideration. Where information is missing, provide reasonable assumptions. You can check your computations by using the sample size calculation feature of the XL Data Analyst.

Case	Key Variable	Variability	Acceptable Error	Confidence Level
1	Market share of Crest toothpaste last year	23% share	4%	95%
2	Percentage of people who brush their teeth per week	Unknown	5%	99%
3	How likely Crest buyers are to switch brands	30% switched last year	5%	95%
4	Percentage of people who want tartar-control features in their toothpaste	20% two years ago; 40% one year ago	3.5%	95%
5	Willingness of people to adopt the toothpaste	Unknown	6%	99%

24. A researcher has the task of estimating how many units of a new, revolutionary photocopy machine (it does not require ink cartridges and it is guaranteed not to jam) will be purchased among business firms in Cleveland for the coming annual sales forecast. She is going to ask the likelihood that they will purchase the new device and for those that are "very likely" to purchase, she wants the respondents at the companies to estimate how many machines their company will buy. She has data that will allow her to divide the companies into small, medium, and large firms based upon number of employees at the Cleveland office.

    What sampling plan should be used? Why?

25. Honda USA is interested in learning what its 550 U.S. dealers think about a new service program Honda USA provided the dealers at the beginning of last year. Honda USA wants to know if the dealers are using the program and, if so, their likes and dislikes about the program. Honda USA does not want to survey all 550 dealers but wants to ensure that the results are representative of all the dealers.

    What sampling plan should be used? Why?

26. Applebee's Restaurants has spent several thousand dollars advertising the restaurant during the last two years. They wish to have some input into what effect the advertising has made and they decide to measure top of mind awareness (TOMA). A TOMA "score" for such a restaurant is the ranking a firm has as a result of asking a representative sample of consumers in the service area to "Name a non-fast-food restaurant." The restaurant that is named by the most persons has the #1 TOMA score, and so on. It is important that Applebee's management conduct their TOMA survey on a representative sample in the metropolitan area.

    What sampling plan should be used? Why?

27. We have a 7-point scale to measure the construct: likelihood of buying a new car. We wish to estimate the mean score on the scale and we want to be 95% confident that our sample statistic (mean) is within $\pm$ 0.5 of a scale point from the true population parameter.
    a. Calculate the required sample size.
    b. After you calculate the sample size in 27a, you decide you want to halve the level of accuracy. What would the new sample size be?

28. A plan is set before all state universities to require classes to meet either three or four days a week in order to make better use of classroom facilities, because currently, classrooms sit empty Friday afternoons and evenings and on Saturdays. However, some schools that have a large percentage of commuter schools are concerned that this proposal will put a hardship on their commuter students because it will require more driving to/from the campus. University officials want to estimate the average number of miles driven, one way, to campus by its commuter students. It is estimated that some students drive as little as 0 mile to campus while at least one student reported driving one way as far as 60 miles. University officials want to be 95% confident that the sample mean is no more than $\pm$ 2 miles from the real average number of miles driven in the population.
    a. What is the required sample size?
    b. After the study is conducted we learn that the standard deviation in the sample data, which is now our best estimate of s, is actually 12.3. What impact does this new measure of variation have on the mean number of miles driven that we also derived from our sample?

Case 9.1 **Target: Deciding on the Number of Telephone Numbers**

Target is a major retail store chain specializing in good-quality merchandise and good values for its customers. Currently, Target operates about 1,700 stores, including over 200 Super Targets, in major metropolitan areas of forty-eight of the U.S. states. One of the core marketing strategies employed by Target is to ensure that the shopper has a special experience every time he or she shops at Target. This special shopping experience is enhanced by Target's department arrangements that are intuitive (e.g., toys are next to sporting goods). Another shopping experience feature is the "racetrack" or extra wide center aisle that helps shoppers navigate the store easily and quickly. A third feature is the aesthetic appearance of its shelves, product displays, and seasonal specials. Naturally, Target continuously monitors the opinions and satisfaction levels of its customers because competitors are constantly trying to outperform Target, and/or customers' preferences change.

Target management has committed to an annual survey of 1,000 of its customers to determine these very issues and to provide for a constant tracking and forecasting system of its customers' opinions. The survey will include customers of Target's competitors such as Wal-Mart, K-Mart, and Sears. In other words, the population under study is all consumers who shop in mass merchandise stores through Target's geographic markets. The marketing research project director has decided on the use of a telephone survey to be conducted by a national telephone survey data collection company, and he is currently working with Survey Sampling International (SSI) to purchase the telephone numbers of consumers residing in Target's metropolitan target markets. The SSI personnel have informed him of the basic formula they use to determine the number of telephone numbers needed.

The formula is as follows:

Telephone numbers needed = Completed interviews/(Working phone rate × Incidence × Completion rate)

Where:

Working phone rate = percent of telephone numbers that are "live"
Incidence = percentage of those reached that will take part in the survey

Completion rate = percentage of those willing to take part in the survey that actually complete the survey

As a matter of convenience, Target identifies four different regions that are roughly equal in sales volume: North, South, East, and West.

1. With a desired final sample size of 250 for each region, what is the lowest total number of telephone numbers that should be purchased for each region?
2. With a desired final sample size of 250 for each region, what is the highest total number of telephone numbers that should be purchased for each region?
3. What is the lowest and highest total number of telephone numbers to be purchased for the entire survey?

Region	North		South		East		West	
	Low	*High*	*Low*	*High*	*Low*	*High*	*Low*	*High*
Working rate	70%	75%	60%	65%	65%	75%	50%	60%
Incidence	65%	70%	70%	80%	65%	75%	40%	50%
Completion rate	50%	70%	50%	60%	80%	90%	60%	70%

Case 9.2 **Your Integrated Case**

Advanced Automobile Concepts

As you know, Nick Thomas, CEO of Advanced Automobile Concepts, has agreed with Cory Rogers of CMG Research to use an online method of survey. In particular, the decision has been made to purchase panel access, meaning that the online survey, developed with the use of Qualtrics, will be completed by individuals who have joined the ranks of the panel data company and agreed to periodically answer surveys online. Even though these individuals are compensated by their panel companies, the companies claim that their panel members are highly representative of the general population. Also, because the panel members have provided extensive information about themselves such as demographics, lifestyles, and product ownership that is stored in the panel company data banks, a client can purchase this data without the necessity of asking these questions on its survey.

Rogers's CMG Research team has done some investigation and they have concluded that there are several panel companies that can provide a representative sample of U.S. households. Rogers decides to purchase the sample from a company that can provide a probability sample of U.S. households. The company provides blended data, which is a combination of stored database information on the panel members and answers to online survey questions. The cost will be based on the number of respondents.

Rogers knows that his Advanced Automobile Concepts client is operating under two constraints. First, Zen Motors top management has agreed to a total cost for all of the research, and it is up to Thomas to spend this budget prudently. If a large portion of the budget is expended on a single activity, such as paying for an online panel sample, then there are less funds available for other research activities. Second, Rogers knows from his extensive experience with clients that both Thomas and Zen Motors top management will expect this project to have a large sample size. Of course, as a marketing researcher, Rogers realizes that large sample sizes are generally not required from a sample error standpoint, but he must be prepared to respond to any questions, reservations, or objections from Thomas or Zen Motors top management when the sample size is proposed. As preparation for the possible need to convince top management that Rogers's recommendation is the right decision for the sample size for the Advanced Automobile Concepts survey, he decides to make a table that specifies sample error and cost of the sample.

For each of the following possible sample sizes, calculate the associated expected cost of the panel sample and the sample error.

1. 20,000
2. 10,000
3. 5,000
4. 2,500
5. 1,000
6. 500

Data Issues and Inputting Data into XL Data Analyst

OzGrid Excels with Excel

Marketing researchers have turned to Microsoft Excel to manage data, and OzGrid Business Applications is a good example. They not only teach and tutor in Microsoft Excel, but they also use Microsoft Excel for marketing research on a daily basis. OzGrid has many clients who use the company's Excel add-ins to conduct marketing research. The company's expert knowledge of Excel, combined with industry experience, ensures clients that OzGrid knows exactly the type of problems that are encountered in business today and how to properly analyze data to solve those problems. According to Raina Hawley of OzGrid, "Microsoft Excel is used widely in business for analyzing data for market research projects." Ms. Hawley states, "Many businesses collect data to help them make better business decisions and the use of Microsoft Excel can make the data analysis tasks simple and can automate what once took many labor-intensive hours of research."[1]

Microsoft Excel is specifically designed for these sorts of tasks and has many useful and extremely powerful features that can aid businesses in their efforts to become successful in the marketplace. Microsoft Excel not only has useful built-in features that can make market research easy but also add-ins that have been or can be tailored to suit a company's needs. An add-in is a software product that adds extra functionality to an existing application, such as Microsoft Excel. The XL Data Analyst is an add-in that we developed to help

Raina Hawley oversees a staff member using Excel for a marketing research project at OzGrid.

make Microsoft Excel more useful to you for marketing research purposes. OzGrid Business Applications is far more extensive as it offers hundreds of Excel add-ins and business software designed for data analysis in all market areas through their website, at www.ozgrid .com. OzGrid Business Applications provides training and tutoring in all aspects of Excel and Visual Basic Applications Excel, enabling their clients to become proficient users of this Microsoft Office tool.

Source: Raina Hawley, OzGrid

This chapter begins by introducing you to the typical organization of the raw data gained from a survey. You will soon learn that the ideal configuration is a worksheet full of rows and columns of numbers. However, a variety of errors can take place during the data collection process, and we describe how these errors can occur with interviewers or administrators of surveys as well as in respondents themselves. It will become evident to you that the most troublesome data quality detractors are nonresponse errors, where respondents fail to answer questions. You will learn that a researcher necessarily scrutinizes his or her raw data in an effort to find only acceptable responses. Otherwise, subsequent analyses may be plagued by the low quality of the data being analyzed.

Next, the chapter introduces you to the XL Data Analyst which is the Excel add-in developed specifically for *Basic Marketing Research,* with the goal of making data analysis quick, easy, cheap, and understandable. You will learn how XL Data Analyst data are organized in Excel and how variable descriptions and value labels that ultimately appear in XL Data Analyst menus and ultimately on its output tables are handled. Finally, the chapter describes special aspects of the use of the XL Data Analyst such as inputting and setting up your own data set, working with subsets of data, and computing or adding variables to the data set.

Where We Are:

1. Establish the need for marketing research
2. Define the problem
3. Establish research objectives
4. Determine research design
5. Identify information types and sources
6. Determine methods of accessing data
7. Design data collection forms
8. Determine the sample plan and size
9. Collect data
10. Analyze data
11. Prepare and present the final research report

Data Matrix, Coding Data, and the Data Code Book

Prior to analysis, the data from a survey is arranged into a **data matrix,** which is an arrangement of rows and columns identical to a spreadsheet in Microsoft Excel. Some researchers refer to their data matrix as a "data set." Each row pertains to the answers provided by a single respondent to the questions on the questionnaire. Each column represents a question on the questionnaire. Of course, if a question has multiple parts to it, then it would take up multiple columns correspondingly. Because the answers vary from respondent to respondent, data pertaining to the questions or question parts are sometimes referred to as "variables."

Normally, the first row of a data matrix is where the researcher locates a label of some sort that identifies the question or question part associated with each column in the data matrix, and these designations are often called "variable labels" or "variable names." **Data entry** refers to the creation of a computer file that holds the raw data taken from all of the acceptable completed questionnaires. A number of data entry options exist, ranging from manual keyboard entry of each and every piece of data into the data matrix to systems that scan entire sets of questionnaires and convert them to a data file in a matter of minutes. The most common data entry situations are integrated questionnaire design and analysis software programs that capture each respondent's answers and convert them to computer files almost immediately.

> Data entry results in the creation of a data matrix that contains raw data from a survey.

Regardless of the method, data entry relies heavily on an operation called **data coding,** defined as the identification of code values that are associated with the possible responses for each question on the questionnaire. You learned about data coding in Chapter 8, where we described this same operation as "precoding." Typically, these codes are numerical because numbers are quick and easy to input, and computers work with numbers more efficiently than they do with letter or text codes. In large-scale projects, and especially in cases in which the data entry is performed by a subcontractor, researchers utilize a **data code book** which identifies (1) the questions on the questionnaire, (2) the variable name or label that is associated with each question or question part, and (3) the code numbers associated with each possible response to each question. With a code book that describes the data file, any analyst can work on the data set, regardless of whether that analyst was involved in the research project during its earlier stages.

> Data coding is the identification of code values that are associated with the possible responses for each question on the questionnaire.

Because precoded questionnaires have the response codes identified beside the various responses, it is a simple matter to create a code book. However, as we will soon point out, the researcher will no doubt encounter missing data where respondents have failed to answer a question. So what code is used when a missing item is encountered? The easiest and most acceptable code for a missing response is to use a blank, meaning that nothing is entered for that respondent on the question that was not answered. Practically all statistical analysis programs treat a blank as "missing," so a blank or empty cell is the universal default code to signify that there is missing data.

With online surveys the data file is built as respondents submit their completed online questionnaires. That is, with a Web-based survey, the codes are programmed into the html questionnaire document, but they do not appear on the questionnaire as code numbers such as those customarily placed on a paper-and-pencil questionnaire. Questions that are not answered are typically entered as a "blank" into the online survey's data set unless the researcher preprograms the software to insert a different code number. In the case of Web-based surveys, the code book is vital as it is the researcher's only map to decipher the numbers found in the data file and to match them to the answers to the questions on the questionnaire.

Errors Encountered During Data Collection

Regardless of the method of data collection, the data collection stage of a marketing research project can be the source of many **nonsampling errors,** which are errors in the research process pertaining to anything except the sample size. In this chapter, we describe nonsampling errors that directly affect the quality of the researcher's data. If the researcher uses **fieldworkers,** or individuals hired to administer the survey to respondents, there are dangers of **intentional fieldworker errors**[2] where the interviewer deliberately falsifies his or her work, such as cheating by submitting bogus completed questionnaires.[3] There are also dangers of **unintentional fieldworker errors,** where the interviewer makes mistakes such as those caused by fatigue or lack of understanding of how to administer the questions. The best way to minimize fieldworker errors is to hire a reputable data collection company that has excellent training, good supervision, and built-in validation techniques,[4] to ensure that fieldworkers will be very unlikely to commit fieldworker errors.[5]

There are also **respondent errors,** which are errors committed by respondents when answering the questions in a survey. **Intentional respondent errors** are those committed when the respondent knowingly provides false answers,[6] a global problem as is described in Marketing Research Application 10.1, or fails to give an answer.[7] Tactics such as incentives, assuring anonymity, providing confidentiality, or follow-up validation are utilized to reduce the level of intentional respondent error.[8] **Unintentional respondent errors,** on the other hand, occur when the respondent is confused, distracted, or otherwise inattentive. Here, the researcher uses tactics such as good questionnaire design, adequate pretesting of the questionnaire, "no opinion" or "unsure" response options, negatively worded items, or prompters such as "Do you have any other things that come to mind?" that minimize the amount of unintentional respondent error in a survey. No matter how diligently a researcher tries to control respondent errors, they will always be present, and the most troublesome data collection problems are nonresponse errors, which we will describe in detail.

Types of Nonresponse Errors

Nonresponse is defined as a failure on the part of a prospective respondent to take part in the survey or to answer specific questions on the questionnaire. Nonresponse is a respondent error, and it may be either intentional or unintentional. Although nonresponse was briefly described earlier in our discussion of mail surveys, we will now describe the nonresponse issue more fully and describe the various types of nonresponse that a researcher may encounter. Nonresponse has been labeled the marketing research industry's biggest problem,[10] it bedevils the polling industry,[11] and it is multinational in scope.[12] Some industry observers believe that the major problems leading to nonresponse are caused by fears of invasion of privacy, skepticism of consumers regarding the benefits of participating in research, and the use of research as a disguise for telemarketing.[13]

The identification, control, and adjustments necessary for nonresponse are critical to the success of a survey. There are three different types of potential nonresponse errors lurking in any survey: refusals to participate in the survey, breakoffs during the interview, and refusals to answer specific questions, or item omission. Table 10.1 is a quick reference that describes each type of nonresponse.

Global

MARKETING RESEARCH APPLICATION 10.1

Which Causes More Response Bias with Dutch Respondents: CAPI, CASI, or CATI?[9]

As in many other countries, Dutch marketing researchers have noticed dramatic declines in cooperation rates and sharp increases in interviewing costs. Advances in computer technology have enticed some marketing researchers to gravitate to "interviewer-less" surveys. In other words, there has been a movement toward self-administered online surveys and away from personal or telephone interviews that require the use of a trained interviewer. In a nutshell, there are three popular alternatives, and each one is briefly described here.

- **CATI,** computer-assisted telephone interviews, where the survey is programmed into a computer and the interviewer reads the questions to the respondent over the telephone
- **CASI,** computer-assisted self-interviews, where the respondent takes part in an online survey without any interviewer present
- **CAPI,** computer-assisted personal interview, where the interviewer conducts a face-to-face interview while using a laptop, handheld, or other computerized device to administer the survey

Among other questions, the Dutch researchers wondered whether or not and to what extent the presence (either face-to-face or over the telephone) of an interviewer caused response biases such as underreporting socially undesirable or overreporting socially desirable behaviors. An example of a socially undesirable behavior underreporting bias is not admitting to or not truthfully divulging how many traffic violations you committed in the past year. A socially acceptable behavior overreporting bias example is overstating one's income. As you would expect, the Dutch researchers hypothesized that face-to-face interviews would be associated with more bias, whereas self-administered surveys would be associated with less bias of both types.

The Dutch researchers used these three variations of the same survey with equivalent Dutch respondent samples. They found that CASI provided respondents with more privacy and anonymity, which translated into more "honest" or accurate reports of socially undesirable behaviors. Similarly, the CASI respondents gave more truthful responses when answering questions about socially desirable topics. Surprisingly there were minimal differences between CAPI and CATI. This finding strongly suggests that even a "remote" interviewer engenders some sort of "evaluation apprehension" in respondents, meaning that they may be worrying about how the interviewer regards their answers. So, the use an interviewer, regardless whether a face-to-face or a telephone interview is used, will most certainly sway some respondents to be untruthful in that they may understate their socially undesirable behaviors and overstate their socially desirable behaviors. Researchers working with such sensitive topics should take the interviewer out of the equation to the extent possible.

TABLE 10.1

Three Types of Nonresponse Encountered in a Survey

Type	Description
Refusal	A prospective respondent declines to participate in the survey.
Break-off	A respondent stops answering in the middle of the survey.
Item omission	A respondent does not answer a particular question, but continues to answer questions after that question.

Prospective respondents often refuse to take part in a survey.	**REFUSALS TO PARTICIPATE IN THE SURVEY** A **refusal** occurs when a potential respondent flatly rejects the offer to take part in the survey. Refusal rates for telephone surveys are estimated to be as high as 50%.[14] The reasons for refusals are many and varied.[15] The person may be busy or may have no interest in the survey, as is illustrated in Marketing Research Application 10.2, something about the interviewer's voice or approach may have turned the person off, the survey topic may be overly sensitive,[16] or the refusal may simply reflect how that person always responds to surveys. Some tactics that have been found to reduce the refusal rate include making an offer to call back at a more convenient time, identifying the name of the research company (and client if possible), making the interviews as short as possible, and emphasizing that the interviewer is not selling anything.[17]

MARKETING RESEARCH APPLICATION 10.2

Practical Applications

Do Respondents Participate in Surveys Due to Topic Interest?

There is a commonly held belief that survey respondents are more inclined to take part in a survey if the topic has some high level of interest to them. Three researchers[18] set out to test this belief. They employed five different surveys, each on a different topic and each with a different household population. The populations were teachers, new parents, senior citizens, political contributors, and a random sample. The topics were education and schools, child care and parenting, medicare and health issues, voting and elections, and issues facing the nation. Respondents were selected with random sampling methods, and all those selected were approached with a telephone survey. A total of 2,330 respondents participated in the surveys, with an overall response rate of 63%.

The results: People do cooperate more with surveys that have high topic interest to them. In fact, the researchers found that with a survey topic of high interest to the person, the chances of that person taking part are 40% higher than with a low interest topic. Clearly, if a marketing reseacher believes the survey topic will be interesting to potential respondents, it is vital to divulge the topic very early in the introduction. Alternatively, if the survey topic is not highly interesting to those who will be asked to particiapte in the survey, the researcher should give strong consideration to incentives and inducements for individuals who participate.

Prospective respondents often refuse to take part in a survey.

BREAK-OFFS DURING THE INTERVIEW A **break-off** occurs when a respondent reaches a certain point, and then decides not to answer any more questions for the survey. As you would expect, there are many reasons for break-offs. For example, the interview may take longer than the respondent initially believed; the topic and specific questions may prove to be distasteful or too personal; the instructions may be too confusing; a sudden interruption may occur; or the respondent may choose to take an incoming call on call-waiting and stop the interview. Sometimes with self-administered surveys, a researcher will find a questionnaire that the respondent has simply stopped filling out.

> Respondents sometimes break off or just stop responding to a survey.

REFUSALS TO ANSWER SPECIFIC QUESTIONS (ITEM OMISSION) Even if a refusal or break-off situation does not occur, a researcher will sometimes find that specific questions have lower response rates than others. In fact, if a marketing researcher suspects ahead of time that a particular question, such as the respondent's annual income for last year, will have some degree of refusals, it is appropriate to include the designation "refusal" on the questionnaire. Of course, it is not wise to put these designations on self-administered questionnaires, because respondents may use this option simply as a cop-out, when they might have provided accurate answers if the designation were not there. **Item omission** is the phrase sometimes used to identify the percentage of the sample that did not answer a particular question.[19] Research has shown that sensitive questions elicit more item omissions while questions that require more mental effort garner more "don't knows."[20] So it is useful for a researcher to offer the "don't know" option with the latter type of questions to reduce item omissions.

> Item omissions are occasions where respondents fail to answer some questions but continue on and answer other questions.

Preliminary Data Screening

As we have indicated, nonresponses appear in practically every survey. At the same time, there are respondents whose answers have a suspicious pattern to them. Both of these occurrences necessitate a separate phase of the data preparation stage in the marketing research process that involves the inspection of respondents' answers as they are being organized into a computer file for tabulation and analysis. Obviously, it is the researcher's goal to work with a set of data that has few data quality issues in it as is humanly possible to obtain. Consequently, the researcher must examine the responses for data quality problems prior to analysis.

> Raw questionnaire files should be screened for errors.

Researchers develop a sixth sense about the quality of responses, and they can often spot errors just by inspecting raw questionnaires or survey data files. Because of the role of computer technology in marketing research, is highly likely that the researcher will be scrutinizing the raw data in the form of an Excel or similar spreadsheet of numbers. After we describe what the researcher is looking for, we will develop this spreadsheet notion more formally for you.

What to Look for in Raw Data Inspection

> Raw data inspection determines the presence of "bad" respondents.

The purpose of raw data inspection is to determine the presence of "bad" respondents and, if deemed advisable, to throw out the ones with severe problems. Problem respondents are ones that fall into the following five categories: incomplete responses (break-offs), nonresponses to specific questions (item omissions), yea-saying patterns, nay-saying patterns, and middle-of-the-road patterns. We describe each problem in the text, and Table 10.2 illustrates an example of each one. In industry jargon, these are "exceptions," and they signal data quality errors to a researcher.

> Some questionnaires may be only partially completed.

INCOMPLETE RESPONSE An **incomplete response** is a break-off where the respondent stops answering in the middle of the questionnaire. For instance, the researcher might find that a respondent answered the first three pages of questions, and then, for some reason, the respondent stopped. As we noted earlier, perhaps the respondent became bored, or the questions might have been too complicated, or perhaps the respondent thought the topic was too personal. The reason that the questionnaire was not completed may never be known. In Table 10.2, the respondent stopped answering after question 3.

> When a respondent does not answer a particular question, it is referred to as an item omission.

NONRESPONSES TO SPECIFIC QUESTIONS (ITEM OMISSIONS) For whatever reasons, a respondent will sometimes leave a question blank. In a telephone interview, he or she may decline answering a question, and the interviewer might note this occurrence with the designation "ref" (refused) or some other code to indicate that the respondent failed to answer the question. In Table 10.2, the respondent did not answer questions 4 and 7.

> Yea-saying and nay-saying are seen as persistent tendencies on the parts of some respondents to agree or disagree, respectively, with most of the questions asked.

YEA-SAYING OR NAY-SAYING PATTERNS Even when questions are answered, there can be signs of problems. A **yea-saying** pattern may be evident on one respondent in the form of all "yes" or "strongly agree" answers,[21] identified as all "5" codes for questions 5 through 9 in Table 10.2. The yea-sayer has a persistent tendency to respond in the affirmative regardless of the question, and yea-saying implies that the responses are not valid. The negative counterpart to the yea-saying is

TABLE 10.2
Identification of Data Quality Errors Found in Raw Data Matrix Inspection

Error Type	Q1	Q2	Q3	Q4	Q5	Q6	Q7	Q8	Q9	Description of Error
Incomplete response (break-off)	1	2	3							Questionnaire is incompletely filled out. No answers after Q3.
Nonresponse to specific question(s) (item omission)	1	2	1		4	2		4	5	The respondent refused to answer particular question(s), but answered others before and after it. Q4 and Q7 are not answered.
Yea-saying	1	2	2	3	5	5	5	5	5	Respondent exhibits a persistent tendency to respond favorably (yea) regardless of the questions. Q5–Q9 are all 5, the code for "strongly agree."
Nay-saying	2	1	3	1	1	1	1	1	1	Respondent exhibits a persistent tendency to respond unfavorably (nay) regardless of the questions. Q5–Q9 are all 1, the code for "strongly disagree."
Middle-of-the-road	1	2	1	3	3	3	3	3	3	Respondent indicates "no opinion" to most questions. Q5–Q9 are all 3, the code for "neutral."
Acceptable questionnaire	1	2	3	2	5	3	4	1	2	No data quality issues are evident.

Data Matrix Column Labels

Code Book: Questions Q1–Q3 are 1 = Yes, 2 = No, 3 = No opinion; Questions Q5–Q9 are 1 = Strongly disagree, 2 = Disagree, 3 = Neutral, 4 = Agree, and 5 = Strongly agree

nay-saying, identifiable as persistent responses in the negative, or all "1" codes for questions 5 through 9 in Table 10.2. Repeating the same answer on grid-type questions is a variation called "straightlining," which also signals a response quality problem.[22]

MIDDLE-OF-THE-ROAD PATTERNS The **middle-of-the-road pattern** is seen as a preponderance of "no opinion" responses or "3" codes for questions 5 through 9 in Table 10.2. No opinion is in essence no response, and prevalent no opinions on a questionnaire may signal low interest, lack of attention, or even objections to being involved in the survey. True, a respondent may not have an opinion on a topic, but if one gives numerous "no opinion" answers, questions arise as to how useful that respondent is to the survey. It should be noted that our yea-saying, nay-saying, and middle-of-the-road examples in Table 10.2 are extreme cases, and sometimes these appear as tendencies such as almost all 4s and 5s for yea-saying, almost all 1s and 2s for nay-saying, and almost all "neutral" responses for middle-of-the-road errors.

Some respondents will hide their opinions by indicating "no opinion" throughout the survey.

Yea-saying and nay-saying are seen as persistent tendencies on the parts of some respondents to agree or disagree, respectively, with most of the questions asked.

OTHER DATA QUALITY PROBLEMS There are other bothersome problems sometimes encountered during questionnaire screening. For example, a respondent may have checked more than one response option when only one was supposed to be checked. Another respondent may have failed to look at the back of a questionnaire page and thus missed all of the questions there. A third respondent may have ignored a agree–disagree scale and simply written in personal comments. Usually, detecting these errors requires physically examining the questionnaires. With surveys that are done online, however, these problems can usually be blocked by selecting options or requirements in the online questionnaire program that prevent such errors from occurring.

HOW TO HANDLE DATA QUALITY ISSUES When a researcher encounters data quality issues such as those just described, there are three options. First, if there are several egregious errors, the researcher will most likely throw out the respondent's entire data row. Second, if the errors are minor and will not falsely sway the findings of the survey, the researcher will probably leave the respondent's entire row data in the data set. Last, if there are some obvious error-riden responses, while other responses by this respondent seem valid, the researcher may opt to set the bad data items to blanks or missing data and use only the good data items in subsequent analyses.

> The researcher must inspect and decide if a respondent is acceptable for data analysis.

WHAT IS AN "ACCEPTABLE RESPONDENT"? As we learned earlier, break-offs, item omissions, and problem respondents are common in the industry. At what point does an incomplete or problem respondent constitute an acceptable respondent that the researcher will allow into data analysis? A researcher must have a definition or otherwise specify the criteria for an "acceptable respondent." Almost all surveys have response quality issues. However, only in rare cases is it necessary that all respondents answer all of the questions satisfactorily. The researcher will usually adopt some decision rule that defines an acceptable respondent. For example, in most research studies there are critical questions directed at the primary purpose of the study, while other questions are of a lesser or secondary nature. An **acceptable respondent** may be defined as one who has answered all the primary questions satisfactorily. Of course, the best case is one where there are no data quality issues whatsover, as is the case in the example in Table 10.2.

Introduction to Your XL Data Analyst

XLDA

> The XL Data Analyst was created to make data analysis easier and simpler.

You have downloaded and used a few of the features (such as sample size determination) in the XL Data Analyst that was created to accompany this textbook. It is now time to give you a formal introduction to the XL Data Analyst. We created the XL Data Analyst so you can perform and interpret data analyses with ease. There are four reasons why we created the XL Data Analyst. First, practically everyone is acquainted with the Excel spreadsheet program that is included in Microsoft's Office Suite, so there is no need to learn a new software program. Second, commercial data analysis programs typically produce output with a great many statistical values and tables that are very confusing and, frankly, unnecessary for basic marketing research. We have programmed our XL Data Analyst so the findings of your analyses are not confusing. Granted, you will need to understand some basic statistical concepts, but you will not need to memorize formulas or deal with statistical procedures. (However, if you or your instructor wishes to look at the statistical output, you may do so.) Third, the XL Data Analyst produces tables that can be copied and pasted into word processor applications such as Microsoft Word without the need for extensive reformatting into professionally appearing tables. There are also graphs you can use or modify and copy, or you can make your own graphs in Excel. Finally, by creating a macro system for Excel, we have avoided the added cost (to you) of including a statistical program with this textbook.

TABLE 10.3

Your Data and Code Book in XL Data Analyst

Worksheet	Element	Description
Data	Variables	Each variable occupies a separate column.
	Variable labels	A unique descriptive word in row 1 of each variable column (e.g., Gender or Q1, Q2)
	Respondents	Rows of numbers in the various cells of each column, not including row 1
	Data set	The matrix of rows and columns
Define Variables	Variable labels	Variable labels that are in row 1 of the Data worksheet are *linked* to the Define Variables worksheet beginning at cell B1.
	Variable descriptions	You can type in or paste a long variable description for each variable in the cell beneath its variable label (e.g., "Gender of the Respondent").
	Value codes*	The related code values for each variable's possible answer (value label) are placed in row 3 with the codes separated by commas (e.g., 1, 2).
	Value labels*	The value labels for each set of variable's value codes are placed below them in row 4 with the value labels separated by commas and in the same order as your value codes (e.g., Male, Female).

*With metric variables that do not have value labels such as the case of a respondent giving his actual age in years or other open-ended questions, the Value Codes and Value Labels cells are left blank.

The Data Set and Data Code Book Are in the XL Data Analyst

Your XL Data Analyst is a Microsoft Excel program with customized features designed to perform data analyses. We will systematically introduce you to these data analyses in subsequent chapters of this textbook. We have set up the XL Data Analyst with a simulated data set pertaining to your integrated case, Advanced Automobile Concepts. As you will soon learn, the code book information for your Advanced Automobile Concepts case data set is contained in your XL Data Analyst. There are two named worksheets in an XL Data Analyst that are critical: the Data worksheet and the Define Variables worksheet. Both are described in Table 10.3.

Figure 10.1 is a dual screen capture of Excel with the XL Data Analyst installed and a dataset in the **Data worksheet.** We have pasted the **Define Variables worksheet** window so you can view both worksheets at the same time. As you can see in the Data worksheet, the columns include labels in the first row, meaning that each column pertains to a variable in the survey. Each row represents a respondent or a completed questionnaire. The way you set up your code book in XL Data Analyst is through the Define Variables worksheet. When a researcher sets up the data set for the first time in XL Data Analyst, each variable can be defined in three ways. First, there *must* be a **variable label,** or a unique, short, single-word description for that variable placed in the first row on the Data worksheet. This row is then linked (via Copy—Paste Special—Paste Link) into the Data Variables worksheet starting at cell B1.

The Define Variables worksheet accommodates the researcher's data code book as follows. There should be a **variable description,** which is a phrase or sentence that identifies the variable in more detail and refers to the question on the questionnaire. Then, depending on the nature of the variable, there can be **value codes** that are numerical values and **value labels,** which are responses that correspond to each data code number for that particular variable. You are not required to define your variables in XL Data Analyst; however, you will find that it will be much more convenient to use its menus and to read the various analyses results if you provide variable descriptions, and supply value codes and value labels where appropriate. Also, the data definition step is a one-time activity as XL Data Analyst will remember your data definitions as soon as you

> The Data worksheet contains data labels and rows and columns of raw data.

FIGURE 10.1

The XL Data Analyst Data and Define Variables Worksheets Showing Organization of Variable Labels, Data, Variable Descriptions, Value Codes, and Value Labels

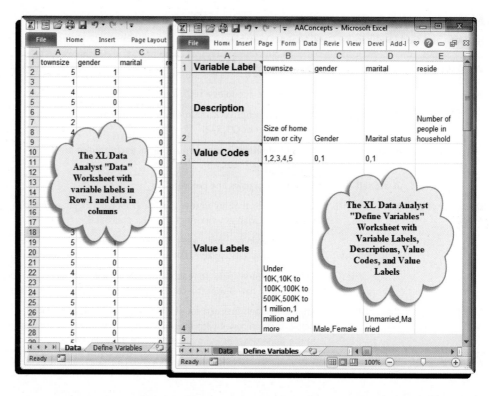

save your data set as an Excel file. You will see in Figure 10.1 that we have set up variable labels *townsize, gender, marital, reside,* and others with descriptions, value codes, and value labels.

> The Define Variables worksheet supplies variable descriptions, value codes, and value labels.

The Define Variables worksheet is the data code book because it identifies the column label, provides a long description of the variable, lists the answer value code numbers, and matches the answer value labels to these code numbers. It is also used by the XL Data Analyst to provide variable descriptions and answer labels in the tables and graphs it creates by its various analyses.

Case Data Sets and Building Your Own XL Data Analyst Data Set

There are three XL Data Analyst data sets that accompany your textbook: Advanced Automobile Concepts, Advanced Automobile Concepts Recoded and Friendly Market. You may download these from the XL Data Analyst website (www.xldataanalyst.com), or your instructor may make them available to you by some other means. Each of these Excel files has a Data worksheet and a linked Define Variables worksheet, and when you load the file and enable the XL Data Analyst macro, you will have full access to all XL Data Analyst operations.

However, you may wish to use a different survey data set such as a course team project or a data set provided to you by your instructor, so we will describe how to set up the XL Data Analyst with the code book information for any survey. However, we must warn you that only advanced users of XL Data Analyst should build their own data sets.

> Advanced users may build their own XL Data Analyst files either manually or by using the data import feature.

There are two options: (1) manually building the XL Data Analyst data set or (2) importing a comma separated variable (CSV) dataset. With the manual approach, you must replace the data in one of the case study XL Data Analyst files with your own data. The Data worksheet should have labels in row 1 and raw data in the associated columns. Next, clear all contents of rows 2 through 4 in the Define Variables worksheet. Copy the labels in row 1 of the Data worksheet and do Paste—Special—Paste Link with the cursor in cell B1 of the Define Variables worksheet. Type or paste in the variable descriptions, value codes, and value labels. The XL Data Analyst Utilities-Cleanup operation will catch errors, such as too few code numbers. Last, save the new XL Data Analyst dataset under a new macro-enabled Excel file name.

You can use the XL Data Analyst on your team marketing research data.

With the import option, you can use Utilities-Import Data. This operation will (1) completely replace the current XL Data Analyst data with the imported data, (2) link the data labels on the Data worksheet to the Define Variables worksheet, (3) place the data label in the Variable Description row (so you will know what data label is to be replaced with a long description), and (4) clear the value codes and value labels. Then, you must enter in the value codes and values associated with your imported data set. The Utilities-Cleanup operation will notify you of any errors that it catches. Last, you must save the data set under a unique, new XL Data Analyst Excel macro-enabled file name. If the CSV file data labels are not perfect, meaning punctuation or strange symbols in row 1 may cause problems, then the import operation may misalign the labels with the data column(s), so, again, this operation is recommended for advanced users of Excel and the XL Data Analyst.

Special Operations and Procedures with XL Data Analyst Data Sets

During the course of data analysis, researchers may encounter situations where they wish to modify the data to be analyzed. For example, the researcher may wish to analyze only certain respondents such as only males or only those who answered "yes" to a key question. Alternatively, a researcher may want to add or compute a new variable. Both cases are handled easily by the XL Data Analyst.

SELECTING SUBSETS OF THE DATA FOR ANALYSIS This data handling function is accomplished with the Utilities-Filter Data operation that will apply Excel's data filter feature and thus allow the researcher to select the code value(s) for any one or a number of variables. Once selected, only the data that qualifies according to the data selection criteria will be available for analysis. Any XL Data Analyst analysis can then be applied to the filtered data. To return the original data set, simply use the Utilities-Unfilter Data operation.

The Filter Data feature allows the user to select subsets within the XL Data Analyst.

COMPUTING OR ADDING VARIABLES Advanced users may wish to add a variable or to compute a variable by using Excel operations such as SUM, COUNT, a division operation, or some other data manipulation. Adding a variable in the middle of a data set means that a new column will be created in the Data worksheet, and the Data-Define Variable link will become misaligned, so any added variables should be done at the end of the data set (far righthand side). After the new variable(s) have been applied, the user can then copy the data labels in row 1 of the Data worksheet and Paste Special—Paste Link with the cursor in cell B1 on the

Define Variables worksheet. The added variable(s) will then be properly linked, and the user can enter in descriptions, value codes, and value labels in the appropriate cells on the Define Variables worksheet. Use of Utilities-Cleanup is advisable and necessary to eliminate any Excel function or data manipulation operations in the data set that may adversely affect subsequent analyses.

Summary

This chapter introduces you to some important issues about data quality, and it describes how to work with your XL Data Analyst. The chapter begins by defining a data matrix or data set, used by the researcher to analyze the responses to survey questions. A data matrix consists of rows (respondents) and columns (questions or question parts). The data matrix is created by a data coding or the assignment of code numbers to the various possible responses to the questions in the survey. Researchers keep track of this coding with use of a data codebook.

Unfortunately, there are many data errors in surveys. Apart from those attributed to fieldworkers, whether intentional or unintentional, there are respondent errors. With respect to data quality, there are three types of nonresponse: refusals to take part in the survey, break-offs where respondents stop responding, and item omissions where respondents fail to answer some questions but do complete the survey. During initial data screening, researchers must assess these errors and they must be vigilant for cases of yea-saying, nay-saying, or middle-of-the-road patterns in respondents' answers in order to judge for acceptable respondents. Occasionally, a researcher may set suspicious or error-ridden responses to blanks (missing data) and use the good responses.

The chapter provides a formal introduction to the XL Data Analyst system that accompanies this textbook. Using a Microsoft Office Excel platform, with which most students are familiar, the XL Data Analyst provides two essential worksheets. The Data worksheet is composed of data labels in row 1 and raw data, normally numbers, in the other rows. The Define Variables worksheet is linked to the Data worksheet, and it holds the variable descriptions, value codes, and value labels that are used to define variables and to provide descriptive output for the XL Data Analyst's various tables and graphs. The chapter wraps up with descriptions of how to build your own XL Data Analyst data set, how to select subsets of your data set for analysis, and how to compute or add variables to your XL Data Analyst data set.

Key Terms

Data matrix (p. 226)
Data entry (p. 226)
Data coding (p. 226)
Date code book (p. 226)
Nonsampling errors (p. 226)
Fieldworkers (p. 227)
Intentional fieldworker errors (p. 227)
Unintentional fieldworker errors (p. 227)

Respondent errors (p. 227)
Intentional respondent errors (p. 227)
Unintentional respondent errors (p. 227)
Nonresponse (p. 227)
Refusal (p. 228)
Break-off (p. 229)
Item omission (p. 230)
Incomplete response (p. 230)
Yea-saying (p. 230)

Nay-saying (p. 231)
Middle-of-the-road pattern (p. 231)
Acceptable respondent (p. 232)
Data worksheet (p. 233)
Define Variables worksheet (p. 233)
Variable label (p. 233)
Variable description (p. 233)
Value code (p. 233)
Value label (p. 233)

Review Questions

1. What is a data matrix and how does data coding explain the numbers found in a data matrix?
2. Distinguish intentional from unintentional fieldworker errors.
3. Distinguish intentional from unintentional respondent errors.
4. Describe the three types of nonresponse possible in a survey.

5. How does a break-off differ from an item omission?
6. What, specifically, does a researcher look for during raw data inspection?
7. Distinguish a middle-of-the-road pattern from a yea-saying pattern.
8. List the three options open to a researcher with respect to how to handle data quality issues.
9. What are the two critical worksheets in the XL Data Analyst and how do they relate to each other?
10. Define each of the following:
    a. Variable label
    b. Variable description
    c. Value code
    d. Value label
11. What two options exist for a researcher who wishes to build his or her own data set for use with the XL Data Analyst?
12. What is the most important advice to remember when adding or computing a variable in an XL Data Analyst data set?

Application Questions

13. The following data matrix has ten respondents. There are seven questions on the survey (Q1–Q7). The possible answers for Q1–Q2 are "no" or "yes," coded 0 and 1, respectively. Questions Q3–Q4 are answered with "none," "somewhat," "a fair amount," and "very much," coded 1, 2, 3, and 4, respectively. Questions Q5–Q6 are satisfaction questions with possible answers of "very unsatisfied," "unsatisfied," "neither unsatisfied nor satisfied," "satisfied," and "very satisfied," coded 1, 2, 3, 4, and 5, respectively. Question Q7 is an open-ended question where the respondent provides his or her age. For each respondent, scrutinize the answers and indicate whether or not data quality error(s) is possibly apparent and, if so, identify the nature of the error. Also, indicate your judgment as to whether or not each is an "acceptable respondent."

Respondent	Q1	Q2	Q3	Q4	Q5	Q6	Q7
1	0	0			4	2	27
2	1	1	1	1	1	1	38
3	1	1	1	4	2	4	53
4	0	1	3	1			19
5							
6	0	1	3	4	3	3	
7	1	0	1	3	5	4	43
8	1	0	2	1	1	4	63
9	0	0	4	4	3	2	32
10	1	1	1	3	3	3	21

14. For all variables in the data matrix in question 13, indicate how each of the following aspects of the Define Variables worksheet should be set up in order for XL Data Analyst to perform analyses and create fully labeled tables.
    a. Variable labels
    b. Descriptions (of variables)
    c. Value codes
    d. Value labels
15. You work part time in a telemarketing company. Your compensation is based on the number of credit card applicants you sign up with the telemarketing approach. The company owner has noticed that the credit card solicitation business is slowing down, and so she decides to take on some marketing research telephone interview business. When you start work on Monday, she says that you are to do telephone interviews and gives you a large stack of questionnaires to have completed. What fieldworker errors are possible under the circumstances described here?

Case 10.1 **IHOP Improvement Survey**

Mary Yu graduated from college in June 2010. On graduation, she took a job as a marketing research assistant with the International House of Pancakes, known as "IHOP" and headquartered in Glendale, California. When Mary began working, the marketing research department was in the middle of a huge telephone survey of IHOP patrons across

North America. The objectives of the survey were to determine (1) how often and what time of day people eat at IHOP, (2) how satisfied they are with selected aspects of IHOP, (3) how satisfied they are overall with IHOP, (4) what IHOP advertising they recall, and (5) a demographic profile of the respondents.

Mary was assigned the responsibility of data analysis because she was fresh out of college. She was informed that

IHOP headquarters uses the XL Data Analyst program for its data analysis. All of the 5,000 respondents' answers are organized in a worksheet data set with variable labels in row 1. Of course, someone has to set up the XL Data Analyst so its output will be useful. This task is now Mary's responsibility. The questionnaire designers created a code sheet of the scales used in the survey. This code book is duplicated in the following table.

Variable	Response Scale Used (Data Code)
Age	Actual age in years
Family income	Ranges in $10,000 increments from below $10,000 (1) to over $100,000 (10)
Gender	Male (1), female (2)
Marital status	Single (1), married (2), other (3)
Family size	Number of adults; number of children under 18 living at home
How often they eat at IHOP	Estimated number of times per month
Time of day they are most likely to use IHOP	Early morning (1), midmorning (2), late morning (3), noontime (4), early afternoon (5), midafternoon (6), late afternoon (7), early evening (8), late evening (9), around midnight (10), in the wee small hours (11)
Satisfaction with each of five different aspects of IHOP	"Poor," "Fair," "Good," "Very good," or "Excellent" (coded 1, 2, 3, 4, 5, respectively)
Overall satisfaction with IHOP	"Extremely satisfied," "Somewhat satisfied," "Neither satisfied nor dissatisfied," "Somewhat dissatisfied," or "Extremely dissatisfied" (coded 5, 4, 3, 2, 1, respectively)
Recall of IHOP advertising	Yes or no for each of eight different advertising media: television, radio, Internet, billboards, coupons, store sign, flyer, and/or phone book ad (coded 0 = "No"; 1 = "Yes")

1. Indicate how Mary should set up the Define Variables worksheet in an XL Data Analyst data set file.

2. Describe how Mary should create a new variable that is equal to the total number of different advertising media where respondents recall seeing IHOP advertising.

Case 10.2 **Your Integrated Case**

The Advanced Automobile Concepts Survey Data Quality

It has been decided to use an online panel company as the specific data collection method for the Advanced Automobile Concepts survey. Among the reasons for this decision are (1) use of online questionnaire, (2) assurance of a random sample that represents U.S. households, (3) high response rate, (4) quick survey data collection, (5) low refusals to particular questions, (6) demographic, automobile ownership, and media preference responses in the online panel company's database so no need to ask these questions, and (7) reasonable total cost. Nick Thomas of Advanced Automobile Concepts has agreed that the selection of the online panel company is entirely up to CMG Research.

Cory Rogers's team at CMG Research has narrowed the choice to two different online panel companies that have made the "final cut," meaning that inspections of their

website descriptions, e-mail and telephone communications, and other factors have narrowed the set of possible providers. The costs of using either of these companies are highly comparable, so no single provider is favored at this time.

The CMG Research team is aware of a set of questions published by ESOMAR (European Society for Opinion and Marketing Research) entitled, "26 Questions to Help Research Buyers of Online Samples,"[23] and they decide to select six questions that are geared toward data quality. The competing online panel companies have prepared a short response to each of the six questions, as shown here.

Keeping the quality of the data as a foremost concern, compare the practices of these two competing panel companies, and recommend one that you think CMG Research should use for the Advanced Automobile Concepts survey. Why have you selected your choice over the competitor?

Question 1. *What experience does your company have with providing online samples for market research?*

Company A: We have conducted market research since 1999. We are the only panel company to take advantage of computer technology and provide a truly nationally representative U.S. sample online.

Company B: We have supplied online U.S. samples since 1990, Europe samples since 2000, and our Asian Panel went "live" in 2005. We have supplied approximately 5,000 online samples to our clients in the past ten years.

Question 2. *What are the people told when they are recruited?*

Company A: Individuals volunteer for our online panel via our website where they are informed that they will be compensated with redemption points based on the number of surveys in which they take part.

Company B: We recruit household members by asking them to join our panel, telling them they can have a say in the development of new products and services. They are rewarded with "credits" that they can use to claim products.

Question 3. *If the sample comes from a panel, what is your annual panel turnover/attrition/retention rate?*

Company A: Our voluntary drop-out rate is approximately 5% per month. If a panelist misses ten consecutive surveys, he/she loses his/her panel membership.

Company B: We do a 1-for-1 replacement for each panel member who drops out voluntarily (about 3% per year) or removed due to nonparticipation (about 2% per year).

Question 4. *What profile data are kept on panel members? For how many members is the data collected and how often is the data updated?*

Company A: We maintain extensive individual-level data, in the form of about 1,000 variables including demographics, household characteristics, financials, shopping and ownership, lifestyles, and more. All are updated every other year.

Company B: For each panelist, we have about 2,500 data points on demographics, assortment of goods and services owned, segmentation/lifestyle factors, health-related matters, political opinions, travel, financials, Internet usage, leisure activities, memberships, etc. Our updating is done annually.

Question 5. *Explain how people are invited to take part in a survey.*

Company A: Typically a survey invitation is sent via e-mail and posted on every selected panel member's personal member page. In either case, we have a link to the online survey location: "Click here to start your survey." The e-mail invitation is sent daily to selected panelists until the survey quota is filled.

Company B: Based on the client's sample requirements, we e-mail selected panelists with a link to the online survey. After 48 hours, if the panelist has not participated, we send a reminder, and again 48 hours after the reminder.

Question 6. *How does your company handle data quality issues?*

Company A: Our panel members sign a statement that they will be conscientious in responding to all questions in all surveys in which they participate.

Company B: In all surveys with most questions, we provide an option of "Refusal" or "Not applicable," where our panelists can indicate that they read the question but chose not to answer it for valid reasons. Furthermore, we advise our clients to not use "neutral" or "no opinion" response options unless they believe them to be absolutely necessary.

11

Summarizing Your Data

LEARNING OBJECTIVES

- To see an overview of the four types of data analysis performed by market researchers
- To understand summarization data analysis, including when to use percentage, average, mode, and standard deviation
- To become acquainted with the summarize function of your XL Data Analyst
- To learn how to create effective presentation tables for categorical and metric variable summarizations

Would You Say You Already Know How to Summarize Data?

When asked what is meant by data summarization, most students try to recall concepts they learned in their elementary statistics course. As a student, you may think, "Hmm, are they t tests, or standard deviations?" Surprisingly, you already know what they are; and furthermore, you use them frequently! Consider this: What is the first question you ask a college professor when test grades are given out? Of course, "What was the average score on the test?"

Suppose your professor answers, "The average is 75, which is a C letter grade." Your next thought is, "Wow! I hope I made a C, but I wonder how I did in comparison with the rest of the class." This thought gives rise to the second question, "What was the grade distribution? How many As, Bs, and Cs?"

By asking these two questions, you are using basic summarization analyses. Summarization analysis answers two fundamental questions: (1) How did the typical person respond? and (2) How different are the others from the typical person? When your professor says the average grade was 75, she is answering the first question. When she gives you the percentage of the class at various letter grades (A through F), she is answering the second question. Note that it was important to you to know answers to *both* questions. Knowing only the first tells you the average performance of the class. You know that a 75 is higher than a 55, but less than a 90 average. It certainly tells you something of value, doesn't it? But by only knowing the average, you still don't know how different the other scores are. It is unlikely, but entirely possible, that everyone scored a 75! It is also possible that no one scored a 75—in this case, some scored very high and some scored very low. Note how different this makes the interpretation of the 75 for the professor. In the first case, everyone is doing "average." In the second case, she has some outstanding

Would you want a hybrid automobile?

students and some who performed badly on this test. Again, we see why it is important to look at both these questions.

Let's think of a marketing research application of data summarization. In the integrated case regarding Advanced Automobile Concepts, we asked a sample of consumers questions about their lifestyles, demographics, magazine readership, automobile ownership, and type of new and efficient automobile they most preferred. Let's look at the question: "What is your preference for a standard size, four-seat hybrid automobile that gets 50 mpg in the city and 80 mpg on the highway?" The answers are measured on a 7-point scale, ranging from very undesirable (1) to very desirable (7).

In regard to our two fundamental questions about summarization analysis, first, What was the typical response to the question? Since we have a metric scale, "typical" means the arithmetic average. As you will learn in this chapter, when you want to calculate an average, you run the XL Data Analyst command "Averages," which gives you the following output.

Variable	Average	Standard Deviation	Minimum	Maximum	Sample
Preference: Standard four-seat hybrid	5.0	1.6	1	7	1,000

We see that our average is 5 on a 7-point scale. (This is the same as knowing our average test score was 75; and it alone gives us some information.) We know there is some preference for this auto; we don't have a really low score nor do we have an extremely high score. Our second question then is, How different are those who didn't have this "average" score? Statisticians use the term "variance" to describe the degree to which data vary.

One measure of variance is the "standard deviation," which in this example is 1.6 (see table). The higher this number, the more people differ from the average; the lower the number, the less they differ. Another measure of variance is the "range." We see in the table that some selected the minimum (1) and some selected the maximum (7). If we want to know how many scored in each of the seven different scale categories, then we would run another XL Data Analyst command, "Percents." The output is shown in the table here, and you should notice that the scale levels have labels because the value codes and value labels are set up in the XL Data Analyst file.

Preference: Standard Four-Seat Hybrid

Category	Frequency	Percent (%)
Very undesirable	31	3.1%
Undesirable	48	4.8%
Somewhat desirable	117	11.7%
Neutral	175	17.5%
Somewhat desirable	209	20.9%
Desirable	203	20.3%
Very desirable	217	21.7%
Total	1,000	100.0%

With these two tables alone, the marketing researcher has provided the client with all the summarization analysis necessary to understand the responses to this question. In this chapter you will learn when and how to run averages and percents in the XL Data Analyst. When you finish the chapter, you will be able to do more than simply articulate what is meant by summarization analyses. You will know how to use your powerful XL Data Analyst tool to generate them for you. You will also learn that summarization analysis is the "bread and butter" of most marketing research projects.

This chapter provides background on how a researcher describes the profile of a sample. That is, it describes the various ways a researcher summarizes the findings in a survey sample. It will introduce you to the analyses—such as percents and averages—to use, the proper or correct time to use them, and how to communicate them to clients who are anxiously awaiting the findings of the survey. The chapter begins our discussion of the various data analyses available to the marketing researcher. As you will soon learn, these are devices to convert formless data into meaningful information. These techniques summarize and communicate patterns found in the data sets that marketing researchers analyze.

As an overview to data analysis, we provide a brief introduction to each of the four types of data analysis: summarizing, generalizing, seeking differences, and identifying relationships. Because this chapter deals with summarizing data, we describe the data analyses that are appropriate to summarize, or describe, categorical and metric variables. We also show you how to use the XL Data Analyst to obtain these analyses with a data set. Next, we introduce the flow chart approach to deciding what data analysis to run. Finally, we provide tips on how to arrange and format these findings into effective tables.

Types of Data Analyses Used in Marketing Research

We will show you how to use the XL Data Analyst to perform summarization analyses, but first we provide a little background about data analyses. As you know from Chapter 10, the complementary processes of data coding and data entry result in a **data set,** defined as a matrix of numbers and other representations that includes all of the relevant answers of all the respondents in a survey. The researcher almost always uses computer tools to perform various types of **data analysis,** which is defined as the process of describing a data set by computing a small number of measures that characterize the data set in ways that are meaningful to the client.[1] Data analysis accomplishes one or more of the following functions: (1) It summarizes the data, (2) it generalizes sample findings to the population, (3) it compares for meaningful differences, and (4) it relates underlying patterns.[2] In other words, there are four types of analysis objectives: description, generalization, differences, and relationships that match our four data analysis functions.

Now, let's describe the appropriate type of data analysis a researcher uses in the case of each of the four research objective types. To facilitate your understanding of the various analyses, we have developed Table 11.1 as a handy reference and also as a way to preview the various data analyses described in your textbook.

> A data set is a matrix of numbers and other representations that includes all of the relevant answers of all the respondents in a survey.

> Data analysis is used to satisfy the objectives of description, generalization, differences, and relationships.

TABLE 11.1

Research Objectives and Appropriate Types of Data Analyses

Research Objective	Description of Analysis Appropriate to Objective	American Express College Student Survey Example*
Description	**Summarizing** the sample data with: ● Percentages and percentage distribution (categorical data) ● Averages, range, and standard deviation (metric data) (described in this chapter)	A total of 84% of the respondents owns at least one credit card, and the average total credit card debt is $3,173.
Generalization	**Generalizing** the sample findings to the population with: ● Hypothesis tests ● Confidence intervals (see Chapter 12)	American Express managers believe that 40% of college students own an American Express card, but this is not supported. Actually, between 18% and 28% own one.
Differences	**Comparing** averages or percents in the sample data to see if there are meaningful differences with: ● Percentage difference tests ● Averages difference tests (see Chapter 13)	A total of 88% of college seniors own a credit card, which was significantly different from 67% of college freshmen. College students in the Northeast own 4.3 credit cards, while those in the Midwest own 4.9 credit cards, on average, and significantly more.
Relationships	**Relating** variables to each other in a meaningful way with: ● Cross tabulations ● Correlations ● Regression analysis (see Chapter 14)	College students who own American Express cards were more likely to be attending professional schools and living off campus. They earn more income than nonowners. The target market for American Express is male and female students attending private rather than public schools.

*While some findings are fictitious, others are from the Sallie Mae publication, "How Undergraduate Students Use Credit Cards: Sallie Mae's National Study of Usage Rates and Trends 2009."

This section is an introduction to data analysis, so we will not delve into the specifics of each analysis type. It is important at this point, however, to provide you with a road map of what analyses are used by researchers, *and* when they are used. We use the following example throughout this section.

As you know from experience with unsolicited "junk" mail, credit card companies target college students, and they are quite successful for the most part.[3] However, one credit card company, American Express, as corporate policy does not target college students with such solicitations. Rather, it has opted to let college students apply online of their own choice. Consequently, American Express lags other cards with respect to college student market share. So, we will take a case of a survey that American Express has commissioned to better understand the college student credit card market. (Our example here is fictitious, but we know you can relate to this example of college students' use of credit cards.) The survey affects a representative sample of college students from public and private universities. In Table 11.1, we have included an example of each of the four data analyses in the American Express survey, and we will provide more examples in the following discussions.

Before we more fully describe the four research objectives and their respective proper data analyses, let's make an important distinction about the scales used by this researcher in the survey. In Chapter 8 we introduced you to categorical and metric scales. Recall that categorical scales have a level of measurement such that they place respondents into groups such as gender (male versus female), buyer type (buyer versus nonbuyer), marital status (single, married, separated, divorced), and the like. A metric scale is one where the respondent indicates an amount or quantity such as how many times, how much, how long, or how one feels on a synthetic metric scale such as a Likert scale (disagree–agree) or a 5-point anchored scale. Also in Chapter 8, we introduced you to the notion that the level of measurement dictates the *proper* data analysis. With this background revisited, we are ready to briefly describe the four types of data analysis.

Summarizing the Sample

With description research objectives, the researcher will perform **summarization analysis,** defined as describing the data in the sample with the use of percentages or averages.[4] In Chapter 8, we noted that if the variable under consideration is categorical, the proper summary analysis is a percentage distribution, whereas with a metric variable, the proper summary analysis is an average. Turning to our American Express example, two of its description objectives might be: (1) Do college students own credit cards; and (2) if so, how much is the total credit card debt that they are carrying? To summarize the data, the researcher would determine the following in the sample: (1) the percent of students who own a credit card and (2) the average dollars of credit card debt totals they report, as we have computed in Table 11.1. We will describe data summarization in much greater detail later in this chapter.

Generalizing the Findings

As you learned in Chapter 9, every probability sample has sample error, so there are procedures to use when the researcher desires to generalize his or her findings beyond the boundaries of the sample. **Generalization analysis** means that the researcher will conduct hypotheses tests and/or compute confidence intervals in order to make statements about the population that the sample represents. Returning to our American Express survey example, the researcher could test the actual percent of students who own an American Express credit card against what the American Express executives believe is the actual percent, which is a hypothesis test. That is, if the American Express executives believe that 40% of college students currently own an American Express credit card, the researcher could test his or her sample percent of respondents against 40% to see if the executives' belief is supported or refuted. If this hypothesis is refuted, the researcher can compute a 95% confidence interval as to the actual percentage of ownership of the American Express card. In Table 11.1, you will discover that the researcher found no support for the American Express executives' belief of 40% ownership, and in fact, the researcher estimated that between 18% and 28% of college students own an American Express credit card. We will describe these two generalization data analyses in Chapter 12.

Finding Meaningful Differences

Often clients, and consequently researchers, are interested in discovering meaningful differences between groups in the sample. Such differences, when found, can offer important marketing strategy insights. With **differences analysis,** the researcher identifies a categorical variable (such as gender) and compares the groups represented by that variable (males versus females) by analyzing their differences on a second variable. If the second variable is categorical (such as use or nonuse of our brand), then the researcher will perform a percentage differences analysis; but if the second variable is metric (how many purchases in the past month), the researcher will perform an averages differences test of some sort. In our American Express survey example, the American Express executives are interested in discovering differences between senior versus freshman students, so the researcher performed a percentage differences test for credit card ownership (categorical), finding that proportionately more seniors own a credit card than do freshman college students: 88% versus 67%. Similarly, regional differences are investigated with an averages difference test that finds Northeast college students own fewer credit cards than do Midwest college students: 4.3 versus 4.9 credit cards.

Although college students use credit cards, American Express is not owned by a large percentage.

Differences analysis is done by comparing percentages or averages.

Identifying Relationships

A client may wish to have a better understanding of the topics under study. In this case, the researcher can apply **relationship analysis,** which seeks to find useful connections or associations among two or more variables under study. If the researcher isolates two variables and both are categorical, he or she will perform cross-tabulation analysis, but if the two variables are metric, correlations will be used. Or the researcher may select several variables to see how they are related to a single critical variable, such as how demographics and lifestyle figure into the client's target market definition. In this case, the researcher will use regression analysis. Relationship analysis could be used to investigate student gender and American Express recognition (cross tabulation), credit card dollar expenditures, and number of credit cards owned (correlation), or perhaps to determine the college student demographic and/or lifestyle factors that relate to how appealing the American Express credit card is to college students (regression). Table 11.1 notes some relationships: Specifically, college student American Express cardholders tend to be majoring in professional school curricula, they live off campus, they have a higher income, and attend private schools. We devote Chapter 14 to relationship analyses.

Relationship analysis involves cross tabulations, correlations, or regression analysis.

In Figure 11.1, we identify two axes that underlie data analyses in general. The horizontal axis relates to the complexity of the analysis. Data analyses range from those that are very simple to those that are fairly complex. Figure 11.1 reveals that summarization using percentages, for example, is the most elementary, while relationship analysis such as regression is the most complicated type of analysis you will encounter in this textbook. The vertical axis we have labeled "Value of Findings," meaning that the findings of the analysis are more valuable with complicated data analyses, while simple analyses are less valuable. This is not to say

FIGURE 11.1

Types of Data Analysis
Used in Marketing
Research

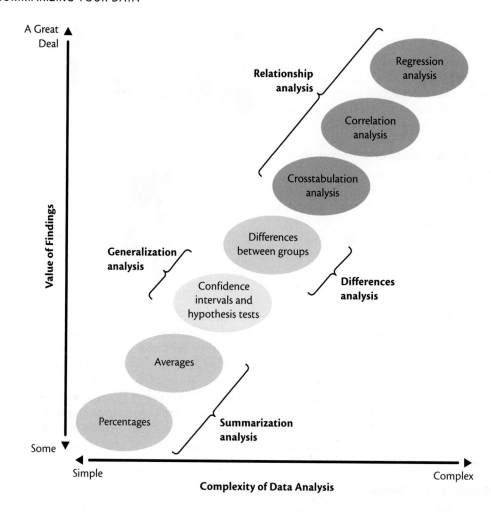

the simple analyses are not useful, for they are vital to researchers. However, as you move up the analysis balloons in Figure 11.1, the findings are typically more managerially valuable as they uncover patterns and relationships that often provide insight to marketing managers. You may want to refer back to this figure as you become more familiar with the various types of data analyses.

Summarizing Your Sample Findings

As promised, this chapter will now delve into summarization analysis, the simplest type of data analysis. The basic data analysis goal with all summarization is to report a few pieces of information that describe the most typical response to a question. At the same time, it is vital to summarize the degree to which all of the respondents share this typical response. The typical response is referred to as the **central tendency,**[5] while the expression of how similar respondents are to one another is referred to as **variability.**

The typical response is referred to as the central tendency.

Again, recall that there are two basic types of variables based on their level of measurement: categorical and metric. Because there are fundamental differences between these two, the summarization analysis is different. As a memory aid, Table 11.2 explains which analysis to perform for the central tendency, and the variability for categorical versus metric variables. The following sections detail the appropriate ways to summarize categorical and metric variables.

TABLE 11.2

Appropriate Summarization Analyses by Type of Scale

Type of Scale	Central Tendency (characterizes the most typical response)	Variability (indicates how similar the responses are)
Categorical scale (indicates groups)	Mode	Frequency or percentage distribution
Example: Gender	*Female*	*Female 56%* *Male 44%* *Total 100%*
Metric scale (indicates an amount or quantity)	Average	Range and/or standard deviation
Example: Age	*45.4 years*	*Range: 20 (minimum); 75 (maximum)* *Std. Dev. 6.3 years*

Summarizing Categorical Variables

When the researcher is working with a variable that is at the categorical level of measurement, the appropriate central tendency to use is the mode. The **mode** is a summarization measure defined as the value in a string of values that occurs most often. In other words, if you scanned a list of code numbers constituting a column for a categorical variable in a data matrix, the mode would be the number that appeared more than any other.

> The number that occurs most in a set of numbers is referred to as the mode.

You should note that the mode is a relative measure of central tendency, for it does not require that a majority of responses occurred for this value. Instead, it simply specifies the value that occurs most frequently, and there is no requirement that this occurrence is 50% or more. It can take on any value as long as it is the most frequently occurring number. If a tie for the mode occurs, the distribution is considered to be "bimodal," or "trimodal" if there is a three-way tie.

In truth, summarizing the mode (or modes) is not very informative with respect to relating how typical the mode is. It is better to summarize the variability of responses to a categorical question, using a **percentage distribution,** or a summary of the percent of times each and every category appears for the entire sample. Occasionally, a **frequency distribution** is used, which is a summary of the *number* of times each and every category appears for the entire sample, but a percentage distribution is much more intuitive as all of its categories will sum to 100%. Frequencies themselves are raw counts, and these frequencies are easily converted into percentages for ease of comparison. The conversion is arrived at very simply through a quick division of the frequency for each value by the total number of observations for all of the values, resulting in a percentage distribution. Glancing at a percentage distribution, a researcher or a client can easily assess the mode and the variability. Notice in Table 11.2 that the gender percentage distribution reveals that females are a slight majority which is more informative than the simple designation of "female" for the mode.

> With categorical data, one should use a frequency distribution or a percentage distribution to summarize the findings.

In other words, a frequency or percentage distribution is a tabulation of the responses to a categorical scale question in a survey. It quickly communicates how many respondents voted for each of the different answers for that question, and it reveals how much agreement or disagreement there is among the respondents. That is, it expresses the variability of their responses. The percentage distribution is preferred over frequencies because percentages are intuitive and easy to handle. Moreover, Figure 11.2 illustrates how quickly percentage distributions communicate variability when they are converted to bar charts. For instance, if our percentage distribution happened to have a great deal of agreement in it, then it would appear as a very steep, spike-shaped histogram such as the one for our "little variability" bar graph (drinking coffee); however, if the set happened to consist of many dissimilar numbers, then the bar graph would be much more spread out, with small peaks and valleys.

> Convert percentage distributions to bar charts to "see" the variability in the data.

FIGURE 11.2

Bar Chart Shows
Variability

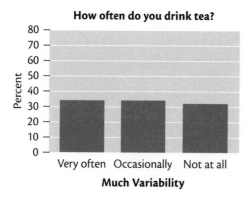

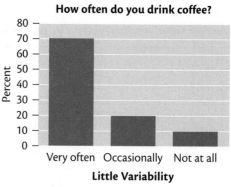

XLDA

To summarize a variable
using the XL Data
Analyst, use the
"Summarize" menu
command.

How to Summarize Categorical Variables with XL Data Analyst

To access the XL Data Analyst menu, simply click on the XL Data Analyst option on your Excel program menu and move your cursor over "Summarize." This will activate the drop-down menu under Summarize to reveal two options: "Percents" and "Averages." Since we are now dealing with categorical variables, the correct selection is "Percents." As you can see in Figure 11.3, a click on the Percent menu item will open up a selection window that you can use to select variables from your Advanced Automobile Concepts data set. Notice that you can use the check box to have pie graphs or cylinder graphs generated along with the tables for the variables you select. When you have completed your selection by highlighting or blocking the desired variables, a click on the "OK" button will cause XL Data Analyst to perform the percents summarization analysis.

Figure 11.4 shows the pie graph and percents table generated by XL Data Analyst. As you can see, we have the variable with the description "Size of home town or city." The pie chart clearly shows the breakdown of different sized cities represented in the sample. Under this graph is a table with this variable's description included in the table heading, the value labels such as "1 million and more," "500K to 1 million," and so forth noted, and the frequencies and percentages displayed. The table is formatted with a professional appearance, and you can copy and paste it into a research report or a presentation software program such as Microsoft PowerPoint. You can use Excel chart features or a chart template to create a stunning graphical presentation[6] of the findings with any XL Data Analyst percentage analysis. This work, as well, can be copied into a final report, PowerPoint, or any other compatible Windows program of your choice.

Summarizing Metric Variables

When dealing with metric variables, the researcher knows that the numbers are more than arbitrary codes. Instead, the numbers in metric variable columns in a data matrix represent real amounts reflecting quantities rather than categories. Even working with a synthetic metric variable where a labeled or number scale is used, the researcher knows that the numbers express amounts of feelings, evaluations, or opinions on the parts of the respondents. If you were given the task of identifying the central tendency number that typified all of the responses to a metric variable, you would soon realize that the best measure would be the **average**. As you can see in the formula, the average is computed by summing all of the numbers and dividing that sum by the number of respondents whose responses were included in that sum. The resulting number is the average or mean, a measure that indicates the central tendency of those values. It approximates the typical value in the set.

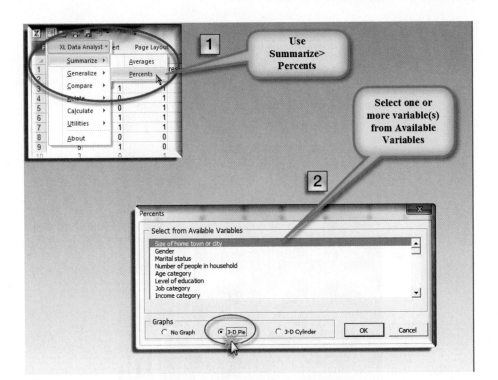

FIGURE 11.3

Using the XL Data Analyst to Select Variables for Percents Analysis

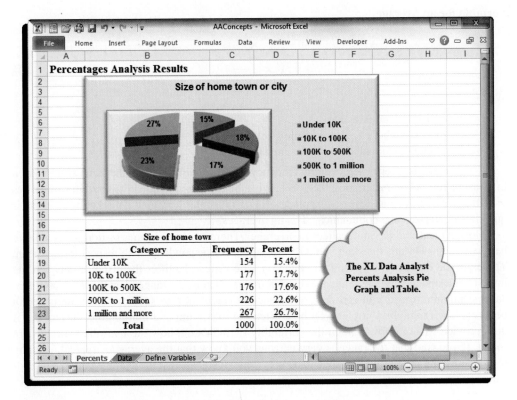

FIGURE 11.4

XL Data Analyst Percents Analysis Table

We can analyze the size of respondents' hometowns with a percentages table.

Formula for an Average

$$\bar{x} = \frac{\displaystyle\sum_{n}^{i=1} x_i}{n}$$

Where:

With a metric variable, use the average as the measure of central tendency.

x_i = each individual value
n = total number of cases (sample size)
Σ = signifies that all the x_i values are summed

The average is a very useful central tendency measure because when the same scale is used to measure various characteristics, the averages can be compared to quickly ascertain similarities or differences. Marketing Research Application 11.1 illustrates how global marketing research is quickly summarized and communicated using averages.[7]

How typical is this value called the average? There are two summarization analyses that help you to answer this question about the variability of respondents with respect to the mean. These are the range and the standard deviation. The **range** identifies the distance between the lowest value and the highest value in a set of numbers. That is, the range identifies the maximum and the minimum, and you can do a quick mental calculation to see how many units are in between. The range does not tell you how often the maximum and minimum occurred, but it does provide some information on the variability by indicating how far apart the extremes are found. If you find that the range is very narrow, you know that the average is typical of many respondents, but if you find the range to be very wide, it signals that the average may not be typical of most respondents.

The range identifies the smallest and the largest value in a set of numbers.

MARKETING RESEARCH APPLICATION 11.1

Global

Marketing Research Reveals Unique Australian Wine Lifestyle Segments

Marketing researchers investigating wine drinkers in Australia have created a metric scale that can be used to identify different wine consumer segments.[8] These researchers have developed a wine-drinking-specific lifestyle measure that captures how wine drinkers behave and think in situations such as (1) wine drinking occasions, (2) wine shopping, (3) wine qualities, (4) wine drinking rituals, and (5) consequences of wine drinking.

The most recent in a series of surveys have revealed distinct market segments. The graph illustrates the communication power of averages. The graph vividly depicts high, low, and "mixed" segments. Segment 1, the "high" segment, is consistently higher in wine-related lifestyle than is segment 2, the "low" segment. The graph reveals that segment 1 has integrated wine consumption deeply into their llifestyles, while segment 2 drinks wine, but to a markedly lower extent. The "mixed" wine-related lifestyle segment is clearly not like either the high or the low segment. Sometimes the mixed segment's average is above segment 1 average; sometimes it is below the segment 2's average, and on some of the wine-related lifestyle aspects, the mixed segment's average is between the low and high segments' averages. Thus, the average, when presented visually, such as in the accompanying figure, is a valuable data summarization concept.

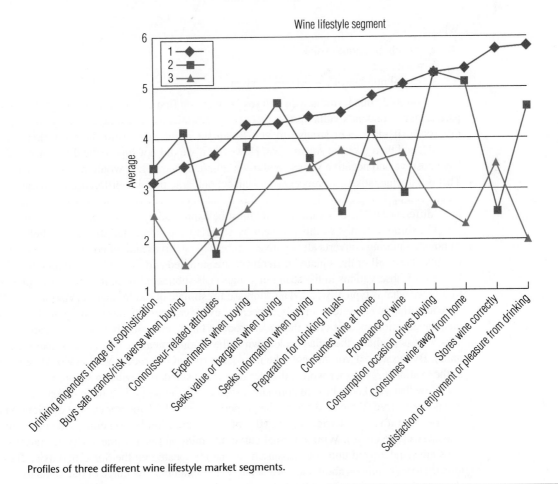

Profiles of three different wine lifestyle market segments.

While the range is somewhat informative about the variability of responses to a metric question, it does not tell anything about how respondents are spread across the range. For instance, are there a great many respondents whose answers are near the average and only a few at the limits of the range? Is it a situation with respondents spread evenly along the entire range, or are there many respondents bunched at one or both ends of the range with few near the average? The range offers no clues as to the answers to these questions that researchers and clients sometimes ask.

To answer these important questions about the summarization of metric data, researchers rely on another variability measure, called the standard deviation. The **standard deviation** indicates the degree of variability in the metric values in such a way as to be translatable into a normal or bell-shaped curve distribution. Although marketing researchers do not always rely on the normal curve interpretation of the standard deviation, they often encounter the standard deviation on computer printouts, and they usually report it in their tables. So, it is worthwhile to digress for a moment to discuss this statistical concept.

First, let's look at how a standard deviation is calculated. We have provided the formula below.

| The standard deviation is a measure of variability that uses a normal or bell-shaped curve interpretation. |

Formula for a Standard Deviation

$$standard\ deviation = \sqrt{\frac{\sum_{i=1}^{n}(x_i - \bar{x})^2}{n - 1}}$$

Where:

x_i = each individual value
$\bar{x}$ = average
n = total number of cases (sample size)

If you study this formula, you will realize that you first calculate the average, then you compare each respondent's value to the average by subtracting the average from it, and square that difference. It may seem strange to you to square differences, sum them up, divide them by $(n - 1)$, and then take the square root. However, if we did not square the differences, we would have positive and negative values; and if we summed them, there would be a cancellation effect. That is, large negative differences would cancel out large positive differences, and the numerator would end up being close to zero. But this result is contrary to what we know is the case with large differences: There is variation that must be expressed by the standard deviation.

The formula remedies this problem by squaring the subtracted differences before they are summed. Squaring converts all negative numbers to positives and, of course, leaves the positives positive. Next, all of the squared differences are summed and divided by one less than the number of total observations in the string of values (1 is subtracted from the number of observations to achieve what is typically called an "unbiased" estimate of the standard deviation). But we now have an inflation factor to worry about because every comparison has been squared. To adjust for this, the equation specifies that the square root be taken after all other operations are performed. This final step adjusts the value back down to the original measure (e.g., units rather than squared units). By the way, if you did not take the square root at the end, the value would be referred to as the "variance." In other words, the variance is the standard deviation squared.

Now that you know how to compute a standard deviation, it is time to review the properties of a normal curve. Table 11.3 shows the properties of a bell-shaped or normal distribution of values. Because it is symmetric, exactly 50% of the distribution lies on either side of the midpoint (the apex of the curve). With a normal curve, the midpoint is also the average. Standard deviations are standardized units of measurement that are located on the horizontal axis. They relate directly to assumptions about the normal curve. For example, the range of one standard deviation above and one standard deviation below the midpoint includes 68% of the total area underneath that curve. Because the bell-shaped distribution is a theoretical or ideal concept, this property never changes. Moreover, the proportion of area under the curve and within plus or minus any number of standard deviations from the mean is perfectly known.

TABLE 11.3

Normal Curve Interpretation of Standard Deviation

Number of Standard Deviations from the Mean	Percent of Area Under Curve[a]	Percent of Area to Right (or Left)[b]
± 1.00	68%	16.0%
± 1.96	95%	2.5%
± 2.58	99%	0.5%

[a]This is the area under the curve with the number of standard deviations as the lower (left-hand) and upper (right-hand) limits and the mean equidistant from the limits.

[b]This is the area left outside of the limits described by plus or minus the number of standard deviations. Because of the normal curve's symmetric properties, the area remaining below the lower limit (left-hand tail) is exactly equal to the area remaining above the upper limit (right-hand tail).

For the purposes of this presentation, normally only three standard deviation values are of interest to marketing researchers. Specifically, ± 2.58 standard deviations describes the range in which 99% of the area underneath the curve is found, ± 1.96 standard deviations is associated with 95% of the area underneath the curve, and ± 1.64 standard deviations corresponds to 90% of the bell-shaped curve's area. We have provided Figure 11.5 as a visual aid to the ± 1.96 standard deviations case that accounts for 95% of the area under the curve.

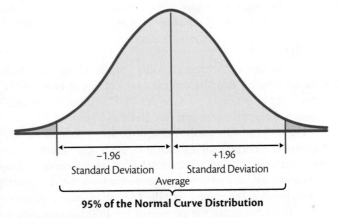

−1.96 Standard Deviation   +1.96 Standard Deviation
Average

95% of the Normal Curve Distribution

FIGURE 11.5

A Normal Curve with Its 95% Properties Identified

Whenever a standard deviation is reported along with an average, a specific picture should appear in your mind. Assuming that the distribution is bell shaped, the size of the standard deviation number helps you envision how similar or dissimilar the typical responses are to the average. If the standard deviation is small, the distribution curve is greatly compressed. On the other hand, with a large standard deviation value, the distribution curve is consequently stretched out at both ends.

As can be seen in Marketing Research Application 11.2, because managers are unfamiliar with statistical concepts and may misinterpret them, some marketing research companies provide explanations of various types.

A ±2.58 standard deviations pertains to 99%, while ±1.96 standard deviations pertains to 95% of the area under a bell-shaped curve.

How to Summarize Metric Variables with XL Data Analyst

The procedure for summarizing metric variables in XL Data Analyst is identical to the one for summarizing categorical variables, except you will select "Averages," as this is the proper analysis for a metric variable. That is, click on the XL Data Analyst option on your Excel program menu and move your cursor over "Summarize." This will activate the drop-down menu under Summarize to reveal "Percents" and "Averages." Because we are now dealing with metric variables, the

XLDA

MARKETING RESEARCH APPLICATION 11.2

Ethics

Ethical Marketing Research Companies Arm Clients with Statistical Understanding

As you might guess, marketing researchers are very comfortable with averages, percentages, standard deviations, and other statistical concepts. However, managers for whom marketing researchers work do not have the same comfort level, and it is entirely possible that a manager may misinterpret a marketing researcher's statements. For instance, if the researcher says, "The modal answer was 4," the manager might think that most or all of the respondents gave this answer. When the researcher says, "The standard deviation was 11.2," the manager may have no comprehension of what the researcher is saying. Ethical research companies may use any or a combination of the following to ensure that their client managers understand the analysis terminology used by its researchers: (1) prepared handbooks or glossaries defining marketing research terms, (2) appendices in reports that illustrate analysis concepts, (3) definitions of analysis terms embedded in reports when the manager first encounters them, or (4) footnotes or annotations with tables and figures that explain the analysis concepts used.

> To summarize a metric variable with the XL Data Analyst, use the Summarize-Averages command sequence.

correct selection is "Averages." A click on the Averages menu item will open up a standard Excel selection window that you can use to select one or more metric variables. When you have completed your selection, a click on the "OK" button will cause XL Data Analyst to perform the Averages Summarization analysis. Refer to Figure 11.3.

Figure 11.6 shows the Averages tables generated by XL Data Analyst for the Advanced Automobile Concepts survey metric variable "Gasoline emissions can contribute to global warming," measured on a 7-point scale, where 1 = very strongly disagree and 7 = very strongly agree. As you can see, this table is quite different from the Percents table, because metric data summarization involves the average, standard deviation, and range (minimum and maximum). The table in Figure 11.6 reveals that the average of the 1,000 respondents is 4.8, while the standard deviation is 2.3, and the minimum and maximum values are 1 and 7, respectively. Thus, the typical respondent's 4.8 corresponds to "agree" on the 7-point scale. (You can refer to the Define Variables worksheet to confirm this.) If you select more than one metric variable, the variables will be included in the same

FIGURE 11.6

XL Data Analyst Average Analysis Table

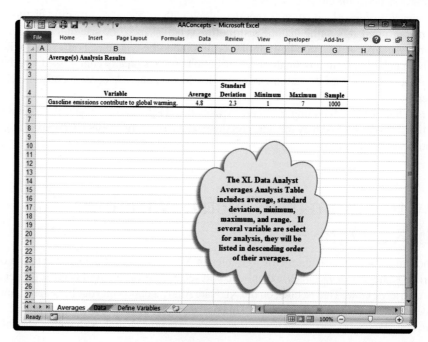

Variable	Average	Standard Deviation	Minimum	Maximum	Sample
Gasoline emissions contribute to global warming.	4.8	2.3	1	7	1000

The XL Data Analyst Averages Analysis Table includes average, standard deviation, minimum, maximum, and range. If several variable are select for analysis, they will be listed in descending order of their averages.

It is easy to determine the average age of respondents with the XL Data Analyst.

table, as it is most efficient to present them in this format; and the variables will be sorted in descending order, with the variable that has the highest average listed first and the variable with the lowest average listed last. If you want to make a graph, say comparing the means of selected metric variables, you can easily create one with the Excel chart feature and use the averages in the Averages table.

Flow Chart of Summarization Analysis

Because we have probably overloaded you with information about summarization analysis, we have created a flow chart of how to perform it with the XL Data Analyst. We recommend that you study it now, and earmark it for future reference. In Figure 11.7 you will see that when you want to summarize findings from your sample, select a variable and determine if it is categorical or metric. With a categorical variable, such as gender, use the XL Data Analysis menu sequence Summarize-Percents to obtain a percents table with an optional chart. With a metric, such as age in years, use the Summarize-Averages menu sequence to obtain a table that reports the average, standard deviation, minimum, and maximum. For guidelines on how to summarize data findings in a marketing research report, read Marketing Research Application 11.3.

Objective: Description of the sample (summarization)

Categorical variable → e.g. Hometownsize → XLDA: Summarize – Percents → Percents table and/or graph

Metric variable → e.g. Degree of agreement → XLDA: Summarize – Averages → Average, range, & standard deviation

FIGURE 11.7

Summarization Analysis Flow Chart

Our flow chart directs you on how to perform summarization analysis.

Understand the guidelines for preparing categorical data summarization tables.

Here are guidelines for preparing metric data summarization tables.

Practical Applications

MARKETING RESEARCH APPLICATION 11.3

How to Present Your Data Summarizations

In addition to being an analysis expert, a marketing researcher must be an excellent communicator of the findings of the survey. So, we have recommendations on how to organize and improve your XL Data Analyst summarization output for effective inclusion in a report or a PowerPoint presentation.[9] Although a table is the most common vehicle for presenting summarizations of data, a well-designed graph can dramatically illustrate findings as well.

Guidelines for Categorical Data Tables

The method of presenting a categorical data summarization finding includes the following:

- Use a descriptive title for the table.
- Do not report the frequencies alone, and not at all if a large sample is used.
- Report the percentages, either as whole numbers (e.g., 12%) or with a single decimal place (e.g., 11.9%); include a 100% total.
- Place percents in a vertically aligned column located close the categorical variable's labels (e.g., male, female) for ease of reading.
- If appropriate, arrange the labels in ascending or descending order of their percents.
- Highlight the modal percent with bold and/or enlarged font to aid the reader.
- Use a professional table format with a minimum of horizontal and vertical lines for the rows and columns.

Here is an example of an effective table.

Respondent's Gender

Category	Percent
Male	**50.5%**
Female	49.5%
Total	100.0%

Guidelines for Metric Data Tables

The method of presenting a metric data summarization finding includes the following:

- Use a descriptive title for the table.
- Use one decimal place unless convention demands otherwise (e.g., currency requires two decimal places for cents).
- Absolutely include the average(s).
- Typically include the standard deviation(s).
- Typically do not include the median or mode.
- Report the minimum and maximum unless the data are anchored by a scale such as a 5-point scale of agreement.
- When reporting the average(s) of a scale, include a table footnote to describe the scale (e.g., based on a scale where 1 = "poor" and 5 = "excellent").
- If more than one average is reported, arrange the table in ascending or descending order of the averages. (Note: The XL Data Analyst creates such tables in descending order.)
- Use a professional table format with a minimum of horizontal and vertical lines for the rows and columns.

Here is an example of an effective table reporting the findings for three metric variables.

Amount of Concern for Global Warming

Statement	Average[*]	Standard Deviation
I am worried about global warming.	6.1	1.5
Global warming is a real threat.	5.6	1.8
We need to do something to slow global warming.	5.3	1.9

[*]Based on a scale where 1 = "strongly disagree" and 7 = "strongly agree."

Summary

This chapter provides an overview of the different types of analysis typically conducted by marketing researchers on the data sets they obtain with their surveys. Data analysis is the process of describing a data set by computing a small number of measures that characterize the data set in ways that are insightful for the researcher and meaningful to the client.

Summarization analysis describes the data in the sample with the use of percentages or averages. Generalization analysis involves hypothesis tests and confidence intervals whereby the researcher infers his or her findings to the population represented by the sample. With differences analysis, the researcher seeks to discover meaningful disparities between groups of interest, and these differences may have important marketing strategy implications. Last, a researcher may seek to find useful connections or associations among two or more variables in the survey. If found, these may provide deeper understanding of the phenomenon under study.

The bulk of the chapter looks at summarization analyses. With a categorical variable, the proper analysis is to have XL Data Analyst create a percentage distribution where the mode can be quickly identified as the "typical" response. A pie or bar chart is a great visual aid for percentage distributions. In the case of a metric variable, the proper analysis is to have XL Data Analyst compute the average as the "typical" value, and standard deviation and range are provided as clues to the variability of the responses. Because categorical and metric variables require different summarization methods, a simple flow chart can direct you to the proper analysis. Finally, we show how easy it is to convert XL Data Analysis summarization analysis output into highly effective presentation tables for use in a research report or a PowerPoint presentation.

Key Terms

Data set (p. 243)
Data analysis (p. 243)
Summarization analysis (p. 244)
Generalization analysis (p. 244)
Differences analysis (p. 245)

Relationship analysis (p. 245)
Central tendency (p. 246)
Variability (p. 246)
Mode (p. 247)
Percentage distribution (p. 247)

Frequency distribution
 (p. 247)
Average (p. 248)
Range (p. 250)
Standard deviation (p. 252)

Review Questions

1. What is data analysis?
2. Describe summarization analysis and provide an example.
3. Describe generalization analysis and provide an example.
4. Describe differences analysis and provide an example.
5. Describe relationship analysis and provide an example.
6. With regard to complexity, how do the four types of data analysis compare?
7. With regard to value of the findings, how do the four types of data analysis compare?
8. What is meant by the term *central tendency*? Why is the central tendency an incomplete summarization of a variable?
9. When summarizing a categorical variable, what is the proper measure of central tendency, and why is it the proper measure? What is the proper measure of variability and why?
10. When summarizing a metric variable, what is the proper measure of central tendency, and why is it the proper measure?
11. Describe how a percentage distribution is computed.
12. When summarizing a metric variable, what is the most informative measure of variability, and why is it the most informative measure?
13. Describe how a standard deviation is computed.
14. With reference to the formula, show how the standard deviation takes into account the typicality of every respondent.
15. What is the relationship between a standard deviation and a normal curve?
16. What output is generated by the XL Data Analyst with the following types?
    a. Summarize-Average
    b. Summarize-Percent

Application Questions

17. In a survey on magazine subscriptions, respondents write in the names of magazines they subscribe to regularly. What measures of central tendency can be used? Which is the most appropriate and why?
18. A manager has commissioned research on a special marketing problem. He is scheduled to brief the board of directors on the problem's resolution in video conference tomorrow morning. The research director works late that night in the downtown San Francisco headquarters and completes the summarization data analysis, which will be sufficient for the presentation. However, less than an hour before the meeting, the manager calls him for an early-morning briefing on the survey's basic findings. The researcher looks around in his office and an idea flashes

in his head. He immediately grabs a blank questionnaire. What is he about to do to facilitate the quick communication of the study's basic findings to the manager?

19. A professor asks his students how many hours they studied for the last exam. He finds that the class average is 10.5 hours and the standard deviation is 1.5 hours. The minimum is 2 hours, and the maximum is 20 hours. How would you describe the typical student's study time for this professor's last exam?

20. In a survey, Valentine's Day rose buyers are asked to indicate what color of roses they purchased for their special friends. The following table summarizes the findings.

What color roses did you purchase last Valentine's Day?

Category	Frequency	Percent
Yellow roses	66	17.1%
White roses	78	20.3%
Red roses	159	41.3%
Mixed colors	82	21.3%
Total	385	100.0%

Describe the central tendency and variability apparent in this analysis.

21. An entrepreneur is thinking about opening an upscale restaurant. To help assess the market size, a researcher conducts a survey of individuals in the geographic target market who patronize upscale restaurants. The findings of the summarization analysis for two questions on the survey follow.

Variable	Average	Standard Deviation	Minimum	Maximum	Sample
Total amount spent in upscale restaurants per month	$150.11	$32.72	$5	$250	400
Average price expected to pay for an entree in an upscale restaurant	$28.87	$5.80	$16	$60	340

Describe the central tendency and variability apparent in this analysis.

Case 11.1 **The Prospective New Restaurant Survey**

Following is a questionnaire used in a survey to determine reactions to a proposed new restaurant.

Survey Questionnaire

1. Do you eat at an upscale restaurant at least once every two weeks?
   _____ Yes (Continue)   _____ No (Terminate)

2. How many total dollars do you spend per month in restaurants (for your meals only)?
   $_____

3. Now please read the following description of a restaurant and answer the following questions.
   A restaurant with a very elegant decor, offering very personal service in a spacious, semiprivate atmosphere, featuring menu items, traditional and unusual, prepared by chefs with international reputations. The atmosphere, food, and service at this restaurant meet a standard equal to that of the finest restaurants in the world. Menu items are priced separately, known as "a la carte," and the prices are what one would expect for a restaurant meeting or surpassing the highest restaurant standards in the world.

   How likely would it be for you to patronize this restaurant?
   _____ Very likely (1)
   _____ Somewhat likely (2)
   _____ Neither likely nor unlikely (3)
   _____ Somewhat unlikely (4)
   _____ Very unlikely (5)

4. Thinking again of the restaurant just described and remembering that drinks, appetizers, entrées, and desserts are priced separately (a la carte), what would you expect an average evening meal entrée item alone to be priced?
   $ _____

5. Would you describe yourself as one who listens to the radio?
   1. Yes (1)
   2. No (2) (Go to Question 7)

6. To which type of radio programming do you most often listen? Select only one.
   ____ Country & Western (1)
   ____ Easy Listening (2)
   ____ Rock (3)
   ____ Talk/News (4)
   ____ No Preference (5)

7. Would you describe yourself as a viewer of television local news?
   1. Yes (1)
   2. No (2) (Go to Question 9)

8. Which newscast do you watch most frequently? Select only one.
   ____ 7:00 am (1)
   ____ Noon (2)
   ____ 6:00 pm (3)
   ____ 10:00 pm (4)

9. Do you read the newspaper?
   1. Yes (1)
   2. No (2) (Go to Question 11)

10. Which section of the local newspaper would you say you read most frequently? Select only one.
    ____ Editorial (1)
    ____ Business (2)
    ____ Local (3)
    ____ Classifieds (4)
    ____ Life, Health & Entertainment (5)
    ____ No Preference (6)

11. Do you subscribe to *City Magazine*?
    1. Yes (1)
    2. No (2)

We are going to describe some characteristics of restaurants and we want you to tell us how strongly you would prefer each characteristic in a restaurant of your choice.

12. Waterfront view

13. Located less than a 30-minute drive from your home

14. A formal waitstaff wearing tuxedos

15. Unusual desserts such as "Baked Alaska" and "Flaming Bananas Foster"

16. A large variety of entrées

Response scale for Questions 12 through 21

____ Very strongly not prefer (1)
____ Somewhat not prefer (2)
____ Neither prefer nor not prefer (3)
____ Somewhat prefer (4)
____ Very strongly prefer (5)

17. Unusual entrées such as moose, bison, venison, and pheasant

18. Simple decor: tables, chairs, and a few wall decorations

19. Elegant decor: curtains, original paintings, fine furniture

20. A string quartet for background music

21. A jazz combo for background music

The following questions are asked for classification purposes only.

22. In which year were you born? _____

23. What is your highest level of education?
    ____ Less than high school (1)
    ____ Some high school (2)
    ____ High school graduate (3)
    ____ Some college (no degree) (4)
    ____ Associate degree (5)
    ____ Bachelor's degree (6)
    ____ Master's degree (7)
    ____ Doctorate degree (8)

24. What is your marital status?
    ____ Single (1)
    ____ Married (2)
    ____ Other (3)

25. Including children under 18 years of age living with you, what is your family size? _____

26. Please provide the zip code in which you live. _____

27. Which of the following categories best describes your before-tax household income?
    ____ < $15,000 (1)
    ____ $15,000–$24,999 (2)
    ____ $25,000–$49,999 (3)
    ____ $50,000–$74,999 (4)
    ____ $75,000–$99,999 (5)
    ____ $100,000–$149,999 (6)
    ____ $150,000+ (7)

28. What is your gender?
    _____ Male (1)
    _____ Female (2)

1. Assuming that the data set is comprised of only respondents who answered "Yes" to question 1, indicate those variables where missing data would be found even if every respondent answered every question he or she is supposed to answer.

2. Determine what variables are categorical and indicate the appropriate summarization analysis.

3. Determine what variables are metric scales and indicate appropriate summarization analysis.

Case 11.2 **Your Integrated Case**

Advanced Automobile Concepts Summarization Analysis

Cory Rogers was happy to call Nick Thomas to inform him that Advanced Automobile Concepts survey data were collected and ready for analysis. Of course, Rogers had other marketing research projects and meetings scheduled with present and prospective clients, so he called in his data analyst, Celeste Brown. Brown was a recently graduated marketing major who had worked as a marketing intern at CMG Research last year. She had worked on a few small CMG survey data sets, but she had not yet tackled any large projects. Rogers called Brown into his office and said, "Celeste, it is time to do some analysis on the survey we did for Nick Thomas of Advanced Automobile Concepts. I am going to assign you primary responsibility for all data analysis on this important project. For now, let's just get a feel for what the data look like. I'll leave it up to your judgment as to what analyses to run, but for now, do some summarizations in order to reveal the basic patterns and to gain an understanding of the nature of the variability in the data. Let's meet on Thursday at 2:30 pm to see what you have found."

Your task in Case 11.2 is to take the role of Celeste Brown, marketing analyst. The data set for the Advanced Automobile Concepts survey is now ready for summarization analysis. The file name is AAConcepts.xlsm, and it is in XL Data Analyst data file format. The instructor of your marketing research course will tell you how to access this data set. The data set sample represents American households, and it includes owners as well as nonowners of vehicles, because the hybrid vehicles being developed and marketed by the Advanced Automobile Concepts division of ZEN Motors will not "hit" the market for three to five more years.

The AAConcepts Define Variables worksheet defines the variables, but for easy reference, here is a list of the major variables in the survey. For any variables where the data coding is not clear in this case description, refer to the Define Variables worksheet.

All of the attitude variables are measured with a 7-point Likert scale, where 1 = "very strongly disagree" and 7 = "very strongly agree." The likelihoods of buying new automobile types are measured on a 100-point probability scale. The lifestyle types are measured on a 10-point scale, where 1 = "does not describe me at all" and 10 = "describes me almost perfectly." The preferences scale is a 7-point scale, with 1 = "very undesirable" and 7 = "very desirable."

Demographics
- Hometown size
- Gender
- Marital status
- Number of people in family
- Age category
- Education category
- Job type category
- Income category
- Dwelling type

Attitudes: Global Warming (Measure: 1–7)
- I am worried about global warming.
- Global warming is a real threat.
- We need to do something to slow global warming.

Attitudes: Gasoline Prices (Measure: 1–7)
- Gasoline prices will remain high in the future.
- Gasoline prices are too high now.
- High gasoline prices will impact what type of autos are purchased.

Automobile Ownership
- Primary vehicle price category
- Primary vehicle type
- Type of commuting

Attitudes: Gasoline Usage (Measure: 1–7)
- Gasoline emissions contribute to global warming.
- Americans use too much gasoline.
- We should be looking for gasoline substitutes.

Attitudes: Effects of New Automobile Types (Measure: 1–7)
- Very small autos with very high mpg will reduce fuel emissions.
- Very small autos with very high mpg will keep gas prices stable.
- Very small autos with very high mpg will slow global warming.
- Small autos with high mpg will reduce fuel emissions.
- Small autos with high mpg will keep gas prices stable.
- Small autos with high mpg will slow global warming.
- Hybrid autos that use alternative fuels will reduce fuel emissions.

Probabilities of Buying Hybrid Automobile Types (Measure: 0%–100%)

- Probability of buying a very small (one-seat) hybrid auto within three years?
- Probability of buying a small (two-seat) hybrid auto within three years?
- Probability of buying an economy-size hybrid auto within three years?
- Probability of buying a standard-size hybrid auto within three years?
- Probability of buying a large-size hybrid auto within three years?

Lifestyle Type (Measure: 1–10)

- *Novelist*—very early adopter, risk taker, "way out," "show off," want to be unique and special
- *Innovator*—Early adopter, less a risk taker than novelist, but into new technology; likes new products, but not a "show off"
- *Trendsetter*—Opinion leaders, well off financially and educationally, often the first adopters of new trends that are adopted by most of society

Favorite Television Show Type

- Comedy
- Drama
- Movies/Mini-series
- News/Documentary
- Reality, Science Fiction
- Sports

Favorite Magazine Type

- Business & Money
- Music & Entertainment
- Family & Parenting
- Sports & Outdoors
- Home & Garden
- Cooking–Food & Wine
- Trucks–Cars & Motorcycles
- News–Politics & Current Events

- Hybrid autos that use alternative fuels will keep gas prices down.
- Hybrid autos that use alternative fuels will slow global warming.

Preferences for Various Types of Hybrid Automobile Models (Measure: 1–7)

- Super cycle one-seat; 120+ mpg city
- Runabout sport two-seat; 90 mpg city, 120 mpg highway
- Runabout with luggage two-seat; 80 mpg city, 110 mpg highway
- Economy four-seat; 70 mpg city, 100 mpg highway
- Standard four-seat; 50 mpg city, 80 mpg highway

- *Forerunner*—Early majority of population, respected and fairly well off; not opinion leaders, but adopt new products before the "average" person
- *Mainstreamer*—Late majority of population, "average people" who are reserved and deliberate
- *Classic*—Laggards who cling to "old" ways

Favorite Radio Genre

- Classic Pop & Rock
- Country
- Easy Listening
- Jazz & Blues
- Pop & Chart
- Talk

Favorite Local Newspaper Section

- Editorial
- Business
- Local news
- National news
- Sports
- Entertainment

For each of the following questions, it is your task to determine the type of scale for each variable, so that you can conduct the proper summarization analysis with XL Data Analyst, and to interpret it.

1. What is the demographic composition of the sample?
2. What is the automobile ownership profile of respondents in the survey?
3. How do respondents feel about (1) global warming and (2) the use of gasoline?
4. What are the respondents' opinions about the effects of the use of various kinds of hybrid vehicles?
5. What size of "new" automobile (very small with very high mpg, small with high mpg, and hybrid using alternative fuels) do people in the sample believe are likely to have the most positive effects?
6. What type of hybrid automobile is the most attractive to people in the sample in terms of likelihood of purchase in the next three years? What type is the least attractive?

12

Generalizing Your Findings

Answering Clients' Questions About the Applicability of Research Findings

 Ipsos Forward Research

www.ipsos.com.

In their desire to have answers to their questions, clients often forget that a sample finding is at best an approximation of the truth. For example, let's suppose you've conducted some research and measured likelihood to purchase a client's proposed new product. This client has set an action standard that if the average on the 7-point scale is above 5.5, he will take the product to the next stage of product development. The results come in and the average is 6.0. This client immediately thinks, "That's great news! Now I start planning for the next stage in the development of my new product." But, a wise client might ask, "I wonder if we'd see 6.0 if we did the research over tomorrow?" This is indeed a wise question to ask because it recognizes that every finding is subject to sampling error. In fact, we will always have sampling error; it is inherent to the sampling process. This fact means the researcher's answer to the client's question is, "Yes, that number will likely vary if we conducted the research study over again tomorrow." In fact, because sampling error exists in every sample, that number is going to vary virtually every time we conduct a study.

However, we can generalize the 6.0 average by computing confidence intervals that will give the client a range within which we can expect our repeated surveys to fall. Granted, we will not take another survey, but we can use the average and standard deviation findings in our original survey and estimate what would be found if we had the luxury of repeating. In fact, a confidence interval allows us to make a statement such as, "If we conducted this study 100 times, 95 times out of the 100 studies, the mean to this question will fall between 5.7 and 6.3." Here we have answered the client's question in a meaningful way. The client now knows that even if we did multiple studies, it is highly unlikely that the mean will fall below 5.7. Since this is above our action standard of 5.5, the client can feel more assured in the decision to move forward in developing the new product.

Although they do not normally think about them, clients should be made aware of confidence intervals and how to interpret them. Similarly, clients sometimes have beliefs, or hypotheses, that are tested by the survey's findings, and again, it is the researcher's responsibility to use the appropriate generalization analyses that take into consideration sample size and variability. In this chapter, you will learn the basics of confidence intervals and hypothesis tests for averages and percentages.

Richard Homans, Senior Vice President and Managing Director, Ipsos Forward Research

Source: Richard Homans, Ipsos Forward Research.

As you learned in Chapter 11, measures of central tendency and measures of variability adequately summarize the findings of a survey. However, when a probability sample is drawn from a population, it is not enough to simply report the sample's summarization vehicles, for it is the population values that we want to know about. Every sample contains error meaning that the averages and percents will not fall on the population values. So, it is best to report a range that the client understands defines the true population value or what would be found if a census were feasible. In other words, every sample provides some information about its population, but there is always some sample error that must be taken into account.

Consequently, we begin the chapter by describing the concept of "generalization" and explaining the relationship between a sample finding and the population fact that it represents. We show you how your estimate of the population fact is more certain with larger samples and with more agreement in your respondents. From an intuitive approach, we shift to parameter estimation, where the population value is estimated with a confidence interval using specific formulas and knowledge of areas under a normal or bell-shaped curve. Specifically, we show you how to estimate both a percentage confidence interval and an average confidence interval. Our XL Data

Where We Are:

1. Establish the need for marketing research
2. Define the problem
3. Establish research objectives
4. Determine research design
5. Identify information types and sources
6. Determine methods of accessing data
7. Design data-collection forms
8. Determine the sample plan and size
9. Collect data
10. Analyze data
11. Prepare and present the final research report

Analyst performs these estimates, and we show examples. Next, we describe the procedure and computations for a hypothesis test for a percent or an average where the sample's finding is used to determine whether a hypothesis is supported or not supported. Again the XL Data Analyst does these analyses easily, and we show examples of hypotheses tests using the XL Data Analyst.

Generalizing a Sample's Findings

Using summarization analysis is perfectly acceptable when the researcher wishes to quickly communicate the basic nature of the central tendency and variability of the findings in a sample. However, when the researcher projects these findings to the population represented by the sample, there are procedures that must be used to reflect that samples always have some error. You learned in Chapter 9 that the error can be calculated for random samples and expressed as a $\pm$ value. Generalizing is using the known sample error, that is, the $\pm$ value, so as to determine an interval for the average or percentage. The researcher is then confident that this interval includes the true population average or percentage.

You will learn how to generalization analyses using XL Data Analyst.

We refer to a **sample finding** whenever a percentage or average or some other analysis value is computed with a sample's data. However, because of the sample error involved, the sample finding must be considered an approximation of the **population fact,** defined as the true value when a census of the population is taken and the value is determined using all members of the population. To be sure, when a researcher follows proper sampling procedures and ensures that the sample is a good representation of the target population, the sample findings are, indeed, *best* estimates of their respective population facts—but they will always be estimates that are hindered by the sample error.

Population facts are estimated using the sample's findings.

Generalization is the act of estimating a population fact from a sample finding.[1] It is important that you understand generalization, because this concept will help you understand estimation. Generalization is a form of logic in which you make an inference about an entire group based on some evidence about that group. When you generalize, you draw a conclusion from the available evidence. With generalization analysis, there are just two types of evidence: (1) the variability (less is more evidence) and (2) the sample size (more is more evidence).

Generalization is the act of estimating a population fact from a sample finding.

For example, if two of your friends each bought a new Chevrolet and they both complained about their cars' performances, you might generalize that all Chevrolets perform poorly, because both of your friends agree (less variability). On the other hand, if one of your friends complained about her new Chevy, whereas the other one liked his (less variability), then you might generalize that some, not all, Chevys have performance issues. So, your generalizations are greatly influenced by the preponderance of evidence that your friends agree. Now, let's add even more evidence. What if twenty of your friends (a larger sample) bought new Chevrolets, and they all complained about poor performance? Your inference that all Chevys are lemons would naturally be stronger or more certain than it would be in the case of only two friends' complaints.

For our purposes, you will soon find that generalization about any population's facts is a set of procedures where the sample size and sample findings are used to make estimates of these population values. For now, let us concentrate on the sample percentage, p, as the sample finding we are using to estimate the population percentage, π, and see how sample size enters into statistical generalization. Suppose that Chevrolet suspected that there were some dissatisfied Chevy buyers, and it commissioned two independent marketing research surveys to determine the amount of dissatisfaction that existed in its customer group. (Of course, our Chevrolet example is entirely fictitious. We don't mean to imply that Chevrolets perform in an unsatisfactory way.)

In the first survey, 100 ($n = 100$) customers who purchased a Chevy in the last six months are called on the telephone and asked, "In general, would you say that you are satisfied or dissatisfied with the performance of your Chevrolet since you bought it?" The survey finds that thirty-three respondents (33%) are dissatisfied. This finding could be generalized to the total population of Chevy owners who had bought one in the last six months, and we would say that there is 33% dissatisfaction. However, we know that our sample, which, by the way, was a probability sample, must contain some sample error, and in order to reflect this, you would have to say that there is *about* 33% dissatisfaction in the population. In other words, it might actually be more or less than 33% if we did a census, because the sample finding provided us with only an estimate.

In the second survey, 1,000 ($n = 1,000$) respondents—that's ten times more than in the first survey—are called on the telephone and asked the same question. This survey finds that 35% of the respondents are "dissatisfied." Again, we know that the 35% is an estimate containing sampling error, so now we would also say that the population dissatisfaction percentage is *about* 35%. This means that we have two estimates of the degree of dissatisfaction with Chevrolets. One is "about 33%" for the sample of 100, whereas the other is "about 35%" with the sample of 1,000.

How do we translate our answers (remember they include the word "about") into more accurate numerical representations? Let us say you could translate them into ballpark ranges. That is, you could translate them so we could say "33% $\pm$ x%" for the sample of $n = 100$ and "35% $\pm$ y%" for the sample of $n = 1,000$. How would x and y compare? To answer this question, think back on how your logical generalization was stronger with twenty friends than it was with two friends with Chevrolets. To state this in a different way, with a larger sample (more evidence), we have agreed that you would be more certain that the sample finding was accurate with respect to estimating the true population fact. In other words, with a larger sample size, you should expect the range used to estimate the true population value to be smaller. Intuitively, you should expect the range for y to be smaller than the range for x because you have a large sample and less sampling error. Table 12.1 illustrates how we would generalize our sample findings to the population of all Chevrolet buyers in the case of the 100 sample versus the 1,000 sample. (We will explain how to compute the ranges in Table 12.1 very shortly.)

As these examples reveal, when we make estimates of population values, such as the percentage (π) or average (μ), the sample finding percent (p) or average ($\bar{x}$) is used as the midpoint, and then a range is computed in which the population value is estimated, or generalized, to fall. The size of the sample, n, plays a crucial role in this computation, as you will see in all of the analysis formulas we present in this chapter.

Generalization is "stronger" with larger samples and less sampling error.

If your friend's new automobile had problems, you might think that particular automobile make was faulty.

TABLE 12.1

A Larger Sample Size Yields More Precision When Generalizing to Estimate Population Facts*

Sample	Sample Finding	Estimated Population Fact
100 randomly selected respondents	Sample finding: 33% of respondents report they are dissatisfied with their new Chevrolet.	Between 24% and 42% of all Chevrolet buyers are dissatisfied. 24%---------------|-----------------42% 33%
1,000 randomly selected respondents	Sample finding: 35% of respondents report they are dissatisfied with their new Chevrolet.	Between 32% and 38% of all Chevrolet 32%----------|----------38% 35%

*Fictitious example

Estimating the Population Value

Estimation of population values is a common type of generalization used in marketing research survey analysis. This generalization analysis is often referred to as **parameter estimation,** because the proper name for the population value is the **parameter,** or the actual population value being estimated. Typically, population parameters are designated by Greek letters such as π (percent) or μ (mean or average), while sample findings are relegated to lowercase Roman letters such as p (percent) or $\bar{x}$ (average or mean). As indicated earlier, generalization is mostly a reflection of the amount of sampling error believed to exist in the sample finding. When the *New York Times* conducts a survey and finds that readers spend an average of forty-five minutes daily reading the *Times*, or when McDonald's determines through a nationwide sample that 60% of all breakfast buyers buy an Egg McMuffin, both companies may want to determine more accurately how close these sample findings are to the actual population parameters. We will use these two examples to explain the estimation procedures for a percentage and for an average.

> Population facts or values are referred to as parameters.

How to Estimate a Population Percentage (Categorical Data)

CALCULATING A CONFIDENCE INTERVAL FOR A PERCENTAGE As noted, sometimes the researcher wants to estimate the population percentage (McDonald's example). A **confidence interval** is a range (lower and upper boundary) into which the researcher believes the population parameter falls with an associated degree of confidence (typically 95% or 99%). We will describe the way to estimate a percentage in this section. You should recall that percentages are proper when summarizing categorical variables.

The general formula for the estimation of a population percentage is written in notation form as follows:

Formula for a Population Percentage Estimation

$$p \pm z_\alpha \times \sqrt{\frac{p \times q}{n}}$$

Where:

p = sample percentage

z_α = z value for 95% or 99% level of confidence (α equals either 95% or 99% level of confidence)

$\sqrt{\dfrac{p \times q}{n}}$ = standard error of the percentage (sometimes designated as s_p)

> You estimate a population parameter using a confidence interval.

Typically, marketing researchers rely only on the 95% or 99% levels of confidence, which correspond to ± 1.96 (for $z_{.95}$) and ± 2.58 (for $z_{.99}$) standard errors, respectively. By far, the **most commonly used level of confidence** in marketing research is the 95% level corresponding to 1.96 standard errors. In fact, the 95% level of confidence is usually the default level found in statistical analysis programs. So, if you wanted to be 95% confident that your range included the true population percentage, for instance, you would multiply the standard error of the percentage, s_p, by 1.96 and add that value to the percentage, p, to obtain the upper limit, and you would subtract it from the percentage to find the lower limit. Notice that you have now taken into consideration the sample statistic p, the variability that is in the formula for s_p, the sample size n, which is also in the formula for s_p, and the degree of confidence in your estimate.[2] For a 99% confidence interval, substitute 2.58 for 1.96.

> Most marketing researchers use the 95% level of confidence.

Table 12.2 contains the formula and lists the steps used to estimate a population percentage. This table shows that estimation of the population percentage uses the sample finding to compute a confidence interval that describes the range for the population percentage. In order to estimate a population percentage, all you need is the sample percentage, p, and the sample size, n.

TABLE 12.2

How to Estimate the Population Value for a Percentage

Formula for 95% Confidence Interval Estimate of a Population Percentage

$$p \pm 1.96 \times \sqrt{\frac{p \times q}{n}}$$

Where:

p = percentage
$q = (100\% - p)$
n = sample size

Calculation of 95% confidence interval to estimate the population value range is as follows:

Step	Description	Chevrolet Example ($n = 100$)
Step 1	p is the percentage of times respondents chose one of the categories in a categorical variable.	The sample percent is found to be 33%, so $p = 33\%$
Step 2	q is always $100\% - p$.	$q = 100\% - 33\% = 67\%$
Step 3	*Standard error of the percentage (s_p):* divide p times q by the sample size, n, and take the square root of that quantity.	$s_p = \sqrt{\dfrac{p \times q}{n}} = \sqrt{\dfrac{33 \times 67}{100}} = 4.7\%$
Step 4	Multiply the standard error value by 1.96. Call it the *limit*.	Limit $= 1.96 \times 4.7\%$ $= 9.2\%$
Step 5	Subtract the limit from p to obtain the *lower boundary*. Then add the limit to p to obtain the *upper boundary*. These boundaries are the *95% confidence interval* for the population percentage.	Lower boundary: $33\% - 9.2\% = 23.8\%$ Upper boundary: $33\% + 9.2\% = 42.2\%$ The *95% confidence interval* is 23.8% to 42.2%

Following are sample calculations to help ensure that you understand how to apply the formula for the estimation of a population percentage. Let's take the McDonald's survey in which 60% of the 100 respondents were found to order an Egg McMuffin for breakfast at McDonald's. Here are the 95% and 99% confidence interval calculations.

Calculation of a 95% Confidence Interval for a Percentage

$$p \pm z_\alpha s_p$$

$$p \pm 1.96 \times \sqrt{\frac{p \times q}{n}}$$

$$60 \pm 1.96 \times \sqrt{\frac{60 \times 40}{100}}$$

$$60 \pm 1.96 \times 4.9$$

$$60 \pm 9.6$$

$$50.4\% - 69.6\%$$

Calculation of a 99% Confidence Interval for a Percentage

$$p \pm z_\alpha s_p$$

$$p \pm 2.58 \times \sqrt{\frac{p \times q}{n}}$$

$$60 \pm 2.58 \times \sqrt{\frac{60 \times 40}{100}}$$

$$60 \pm 2.58 \times 4.9$$

$$60 \pm 12.6$$

$$47.4\% - 72.6\%$$

Notice that the only thing that differs when you compare the 95% confidence interval computations to the 99% confidence interval computations in each case is z_α. As we noted earlier, z is 1.96 for 95% and 2.58 for 99% of confidence. The confidence interval is always wider for 99% than it is for 95% when the sample size is the same and variability is equal.

INTERPRETING A 95% CONFIDENCE INTERVAL FOR A PERCENTAGE The interpretation is based on the normal curve or bell-shaped distribution with which you are familiar. The **standard error** is a measure of the variability in a population based on the variability found in the sample. There usually is some degree of variability in the sample: Not everyone orders an Egg McMuffin, nor does everyone order coffee for breakfast. When you examine the formula for a **standard error of the percentage** (step 3 in Table 12.2), you will notice that the size of the standard error depends on two factors: (1) the variability, denoted as p times q, and (2) the sample size, n. The standard error of the percentage is larger with more variability and smaller with larger samples. What you have just discovered is exactly what you agreed to while working with the Chevrolet example: The more you found the Chevy owners to disagree (more variability), the less certain you were about your generalization, and the more Chevy owners you heard from, the more confident you were about your generalization.

> A confidence interval is computed with the use of the standard error measure.

If you theoretically took multiple samples and plotted the sample percentage, p, for all these samples as a frequency distribution, it would approximate a bell-shaped curve called the **sampling distribution.** The standard error is a measure of the variability in the sampling distribution based on what is theoretically believed to occur were we to take a multitude of independent samples from the same population. To help you understand how confidence intervals work, Figure 12.1 compares two cases. In the first case, the standard error of the percentage is 5%, while in the second case, the standard error is 2%. Notice that the two bell-shaped normal curves reflect the differences in variability, as the 5% curve with more variability is wider than the 2% curve that has less variability. The 95% confidence intervals are 50% to 70% and 56% to 64%, respectively. The larger standard error case has a larger interval, and the smaller standard error case has a smaller interval. The way to interpret a confidence interval is as follows: If you repeated your survey multiple times (literally, thousands of times), and plotted your *p*, or percentage, found for each on a frequency distribution, it would look like a bell-shaped curve, and 95% of your percentages would fall in the confidence interval defined by the population percentage ± 1.96 times the standard error of the percentage. In other words, you can be 95% confident that the population percentage falls in the range of 50% to 70% in the first case. Similarly, because the standard error is smaller (perhaps you have a larger sample in this case), you would be 95% confident that the population percentage falls in the range of 56% to 64% in the second case.

> The sampling distribution is a theoretical concept that underlies confidence intervals.

Obviously, a marketing researcher would take only one sample for a particular marketing research project, and this restriction explains why estimates must be used. Furthermore, it is the conscientious application of probability sampling techniques that allows us to make use of the sampling distribution concept. Thus, generalization procedures are direct linkages between probability sample design and data analysis. Do you remember that you had to grapple with accuracy levels when we determined sample size? Now we are on the other side of the table, so to speak, and we must use the sample size for our inference procedures. Confidence intervals must be used when estimating population values, and the size of the random sample used is always reflected in these confidence intervals.

> Confidence intervals depend on sample size and variability found in the sample.

As a final note in this section, but a note that pertains to all of the generalization analyses in this chapter, we want to remind you that the logic of statistical inference is identical to the reasoning process you go through when you weigh evidence to make a generalization or conclusion of some sort. The more evidence you have, the more precise you will be in your generalization. The only difference is that with statistical generalization we must follow rules that require the application of formulas so our estimates will be consistent with the assumptions of statistical theory. When you make a nonstatistical generalization, your judgment can be swayed

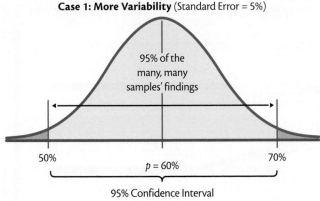

Case 1: More Variability (Standard Error = 5%)

95% of the many, many samples' findings

50%   *p* = 60%   70%

95% Confidence Interval

Because there is more variability, the 95% confidence interval is wider, meaning that 95% of the repeated samples' findings fall in a larger confidence interval of 50%–70%.

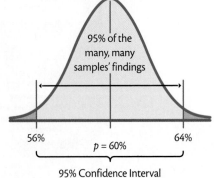

Case 2: Less Variability (Standard Error = 2%)

95% of the many, many samples' findings

56%   *p* = 60%   64%

95% Confidence Interval

Because there is less variability, the 95% confidence interval is narrower, meaning that 95% of the repeated samples' findings fall in a smaller confidence interval of 56%–64%.

FIGURE 12.1

The Variability Affects the Sampling Distribution Reflected in the 95% Confidence Interval for a Percentage by subjective factors, so you may not be consistent. In statistical estimates, however, the formulas are completely objective and perfectly consistent, and they are based on accepted statistical concepts.

Use the Generalize–Confidence Interval–Percentage menu sequence of the XL Data Analyst to direct it to produce confidence intervals.

HOW TO OBTAIN A 95% CONFIDENCE INTERVAL FOR A PERCENTAGE WITH XL DATA ANALYST As we have indicated from the beginning of this chapter, the analysis topic is generalization, and you will find that the XL Data Analyst has a major menu command called "Generalize." As you can see in Figure 12.2, the menu sequence to direct the XL Data Analyst to compute a confidence interval for a percentage is Generalize–Confidence Interval–Percentage. This sequence opens up the selection window where you can select the categorical variable in the top pane (Available Variables), and the various value labels for that variable will appear in the bottom (Available Categories). In our example, we will select "Primary vehicle type: SUV or van" as our chosen variable in the top pane, and then highlight the "Yes" category in the bottom pane. Clicking "OK" will prompt the XL Data Analyst to perform the confidence interval analysis.

The XL Data Analyst confidence interval analysis for the percentage of college students with high-speed cable modem access to the Internet is provided in Figure 12.3. When you study this figure, you will find that a total of 1,000 respondents answered this question, and 258 of them indicated that their primary vehicle is an SUV or van. This computes to a 25.8% value (258/1,000), and the table reports the lower boundary of 23.1% and the upper boundary of 28.5%, defining the 95% confidence interval for this percentage. Again, the proper interpretation of this boundary is that if we repeated our survey multiple times, 95% of the percentages found for high-speed cable connection would fall between 23.1% and 28.5%. The boundaries are so narrow for two reasons: (1) SUV or van accounts for only about one-quarter of the sample, so there is little variability, and (2) the sample size is fairly large.

FIGURE 12.2

Using the XL Data Analyst to Select a Variable Value for a Percentage Confidence Interval

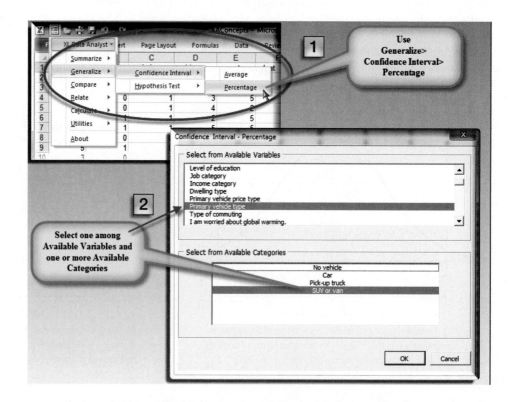

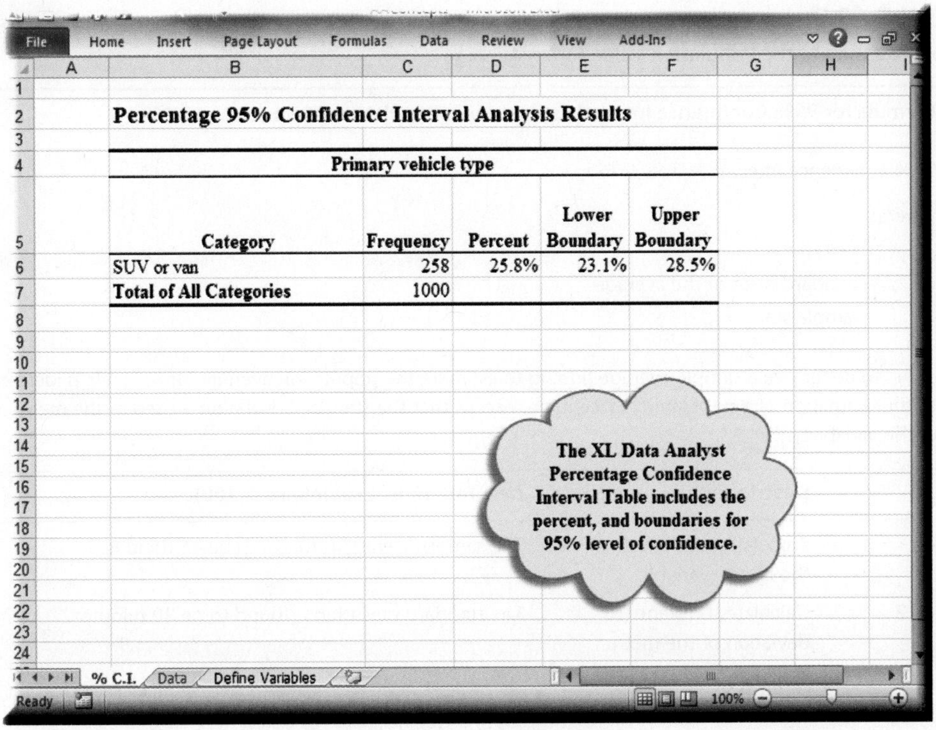

FIGURE 12.3

XL Data Analyst
Percentage Confidence
Interval Table

	Category	Frequency	Percent	Lower Boundary	Upper Boundary
Percentage 95% Confidence Interval Analysis Results					
Primary vehicle type					
SUV or van		258	25.8%	23.1%	28.5%
Total of All Categories		1000			

> The XL Data Analyst
> Percentage Confidence
> Interval Table includes the
> percent, and boundaries for
> 95% level of confidence.

How to Estimate a Population Average (Metric Data)

CALCULATING A CONFIDENCE INTERVAL FOR AN AVERAGE Here is the formula for the estimation of a population average in general notation.

Formula for a Population Average Estimation

$$\bar{x} \pm z_\alpha \times \frac{s}{\sqrt{n}}$$

Where:

$\bar{x}$ = sample average

z_α = z value for 95% or 99% level of confidence (1.96)

$\dfrac{s}{\sqrt{n}}$ = standard error of the percentage (sometimes designated as $s_{\bar{x}}$)

Table 12.3 describes how to calculate a 95% confidence interval for an average using our *New York Times* reading example, in which we found that our sample averaged forty-five minutes of reading time per day.

The procedure parallels the one for calculating a confidence interval for a percentage, except the standard deviation is used, as it is the correct measure of variability for a metric variable. With the formula for the **standard error of the average** (in Table 12.3), you should note the same logic that we pointed out to you with the percentage confidence interval: The standard error of the average is larger with more variability (standard deviation) and smaller with large samples (*n*).

Here is another example of the calculations of the confidence interval for an average using a sample of 100 *New York Times* readers where we have found a sample average of forty-five

> The confidence interval for an average uses the standard deviation as the measure of variability.

TABLE 12.3

How to Estimate the Population Value for an Average

Formula for 95% Confidence Interval Estimate of a Population Average

95% confidence interval $= \bar{x} \pm 1.96\, s_{\bar{x}}$

Where:

$\bar{x}$ = average

$s_{\bar{x}}$ = standard error of the average

n = sample size

To generalize a sample average finding to estimate the population average, the process is identical to the estimation of a population percentage, except that the standard deviation is used as the measure of the variability.

Step	Description	*New York Times* Example (n = 100)
Step 1	Calculate the average of the metric variable.	The sample average is found to be 45 minutes.
Step 2	Calculate the standard deviation of the metric variable.	The standard deviation is found to be 20 minutes.
Step 3	*Standard error of the average* = divide the standard deviation by the square root of the sample size.	$ss_{\bar{x}} = \dfrac{s}{\sqrt{n}}$ $= \dfrac{20}{\sqrt{n}} = \dfrac{20}{\sqrt{100}} = 2$
Step 4	*Limit* = multiply the standard error value by 1.96.	Limit $= 1.96 \times 2 = 3.9$
Step 5	*Lower boundary:* subtract the limit from average. *Upper boundary:* add the limit to the average. These boundaries are the *95% confidence interval* for the population percentage.	Lower boundary: $45 - 3.9 = 41.1$ minutes Upper boundary: $45 + 3.9 = 48.9$ minutes The *95% confidence interval* is 41.1 to 48.9 minutes

minutes and a standard deviation of twenty minutes. The 99% confidence interval estimate is calculated as follows:

Calculation of a 99% Confidence Interval for an Average

$$\bar{x} \pm z_\alpha s_{\bar{x}}$$

$$45 \pm 2.58 \times \frac{20}{\sqrt{100}}$$

$$45 \pm 2.58 \times 2$$

$$45 \pm 5.2$$

$$39.8 \text{ minutes} - 50.2 \text{ minutes}$$

As you learned with the percentage confidence intervals, the 99% confidence interval is wider because the standard error is multiplied by 2.58, while the 95% one is multiplied by the lower 1.96 value.

Confidence intervals can be used to estimate how much newspaper reading takes place in the population.

INTERPRETING A CONFIDENCE INTERVAL FOR AN AVERAGE The interpretation of a confidence interval estimate of a population average is identical to the interpretation of a confidence interval estimate for a population percentage: If you repeated your survey multiple times (again, literally thousands of times), and plotted your average number of minutes of reading the *New York Times* for each sample on a frequency distribution, it would look like a bell-shaped curve, and 95% of your sample averages would fall in the confidence interval defined by the population percentage $\pm$ 1.96 times the standard error of the average. In other words, you can be 95% confident that the population average falls in the range of 41.1 to 48.9 minutes. Of course, if the standard error is large (perhaps you have a smaller sample in this case), you would be 95% confident that the population average falls in the larger confidence interval that would result from your calculations.

> Interpretation of confidence intervals is identical regardless of whether you are working with a percentage or an average.

HOW TO OBTAIN A 95% CONFIDENCE INTERVAL FOR AN AVERAGE WITH XL DATA ANALYST If you examine Figure 12.4, you will notice that there are two options possible from "Generalize–Confidence Interval." One is for a percentage confidence interval, while the other is for an average confidence interval. The Average option opens up a Selection window

XLDA

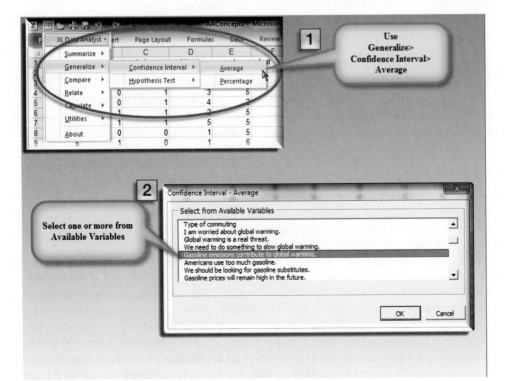

FIGURE 12.4

Using the XL Data Analyst to Select a Variable for an Average Confidence Interval

FIGURE 12.5

XL Data Analyst Average Confidence Interval Table

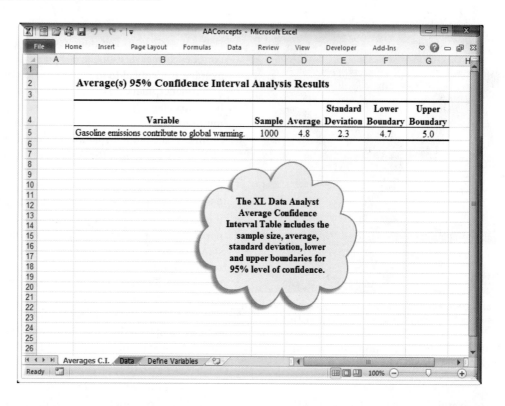

that can be seen in Figure 12.4. You select your metric variable(s) by highlighting it from among the Available Variables. When you click on "OK," the XL Data Analyst performs confidence interval analysis on the chosen metric variables.

In our Advanced Automobile Concepts data set example, we have selected the statement "Gasoline emissions contribute to global warming," which, you should recall, was responded to with a 7-point (very strongly disagree to very strongly agree) scale. You can see the results in Figure 12.5. The average response for the 1,000 respondents is 4.8, and the standard deviation is 2.3. (You may recall that we found these values when we did summarization analysis with this variable in Chapter 11.) The table here also reports the 95% confidence interval boundaries of 4.7 and 5.0. Thus, we have found that for the entire population of U.S. households, our estimate of the average response to the statement, "Gasoline emissions contribute to global warming" is this range, with translates to "agree" on the labeled scaled.

> The XL Data Analyst produces confidence intervals based on the 95% level of confidence.

Flow Chart of Generalization Analysis for Confidence Intervals

Figure 12.6 provides a flow chart of how to obtain confidence intervals with the XL Data Analyst. Here you will see that when you want to generalize findings from your sample to the population, first determine if that variable is categorical or metric. With a categorical variable, such as pick-up truck ownership, use the XL Data Analysis menu sequence Generalize–Confidence Interval–Percent to obtain the 95% level of confidence lower and upper boundaries for the sample percent. With a metric variable, such as number of persons in the household, use the Generalize–Confidence Intervals–Average menu sequence to obtain a table that reports the average and the 95% level of confidence lower and upper confidence interval values.

> Our flow chart directs you on how to obtain confidence intervals.

As a final comment on this topic, generalizations of survey sample findings to describe the population are useful in many ways. One important application of confidence intervals is in their use to generate market potential estimates. Marketing Research Application 12.1 shows

MARKETING RESEARCH APPLICATION 12.1

Practical Applications

How to Estimate Market Potential Using a Survey's Findings

A common way to estimate total market potential is to use buying intentions, which are assessments of buyers as to how likely they are to purchase some item in the future. Naturally, some consumers who say they will buy, do not, but then some who say they will not buy, do actually buy. Marketing researchers know from experience and common sense that an exact estimate of market potential is not possible, so they will use a range. The confidence interval range is highly acceptable and often used.

A question format used in the Advanced Automobile Concepts survey that can be related to sales potential is the probability measure. The survey asked respondents to indicate the probability (on a 0% to 100% scale) of buying certain types of hybrid automobiles in the next three years. For our illustration here, we will take the very small, three-wheel, one-seat commuter "cycle" hybrid model. Although the question was asked about each respondent's probability, we can combine them and apply the findings to the population. There is an estimated 114,825,428 American households (U.S. Census, 2010 estimate), and the survey is a probability sample of this population, so confidence intervals can be applied as follows:

Pessimistic Estimate	Best Estimate	Optimistic Estimate
	114,825,428 households	
12.3%	13.8%	15.2%
= 14,123,528	= 15,845,909	= 17,453,465
	÷ 3 years	
4,707,843	5,281,970	5,817,822

We use the lower confidence interval figure for the "pessimistic" estimate, the upper confidence interval value for the "optimistic" estimate, and the average probability value for the "best" estimate. Notice that the question was for a three-year time period, and since most business decisions are based on annual estimates, the estimated market potential per year is indicated in this table. The 95% confidence interval estimates are possible, but if multiple replications of the survey were to take place, most of the average probabilities of purchasing this hybrid model would fall between about 12% and about 15%.

how our Advanced Automobile Concepts survey findings can be used to estimate the market potential of one of the automobile concepts under consideration.

Testing Hypotheses About Percents or Averages

Sometimes someone, such as the marketing manager or marketing researcher, makes a prediction about the population value based on prior knowledge, assumptions, or intuition. This statement, called a **hypothesis,** commonly takes the form of an exact specification as to what is the population parameter. **Hypothesis testing** is a statistical procedure used to "support" (accept) or "not support" (reject) the hypothesis based on sample information.[3] With all hypothesis tests, you should keep in mind that the sample is the only source of current information

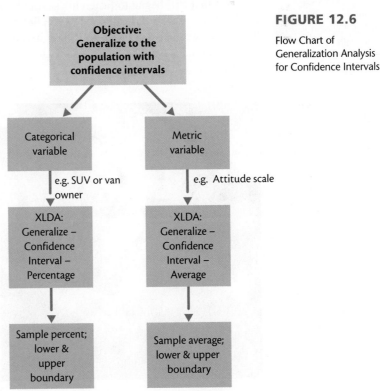

FIGURE 12.6

Flow Chart of Generalization Analysis for Confidence Intervals

When a manager or the researcher states what he or she believes will be the sample finding *before* it is determined, this belief is called a hypothesis.

about the population. Because our sample is a probability sample and therefore representative of the population, the sample results are used to determine whether or not the hypothesis about the population parameter has been supported.[4]

All of this might sound very technical, but it is actually a form of generalization that you do every day. You just do not use the words "hypothesis" or "parameter" when you do it. Here is an example to show how hypothesis testing occurs naturally. Your friend Bill does not wear his seat belt because he thinks only a few drivers actually wear them. But Bill's car breaks down, and he has to ride with his co-workers to and from work while it is being repaired. Over the course of a week, Bill rides with several different co-workers, and he notices that most of them buckle up. When Bill begins driving his car the next week, he begins fastening his seat belt.

This is intuitive hypothesis testing in action; Bill's initial belief that few people wear seat belts was his hypothesis. **Intuitive hypothesis testing** (as opposed to statistical hypothesis testing) is when someone uses something he or she has observed to see if it agrees with or refutes his or her belief about that topic. Everyone uses intuitive hypothesis testing; in fact, we rely on it constantly. We just do not call it hypothesis testing, but we are constantly gathering evidence that supports or refutes our beliefs, and we reaffirm or change our beliefs based on our findings. In other words, we generalize this new evidence into our beliefs so our beliefs will be consistent with the evidence. Marketing Research Application 12.2 illustrates that fact that you perform intuitive hypothesis testing quite often.

Obviously, if you had asked Bill before his car went into the repair shop, he might have said that only a small percentage of drivers, perhaps as low as 30%, wear seat belts. His week of car rides is equivalent to a sample of five observations, and he observes that a larger percent, perhaps 80%, of his co-workers buckle up. Because Bill's initial hypothesis is not supported by the evidence, he realizes that his hypothesis is in error, and it must be revised. If you asked Bill what percentage of drivers wear seat belts after his week of observations, he undoubtedly would have a much higher percentage in mind than his original estimate. The fact that Bill began to fasten his seat belt suggests he perceives his behavior to be out of the norm, so he has adjusted his belief and his behavior as well. In other words, his hypothesis was not supported, so Bill revised it to be consistent with what he now generalizes to be the actual case. The logic of statistical hypothesis testing is very similar to this process that Bill has just undergone.

Bill's seat belt example reveals that we do intuitive hypothesis testing all of the time.

After carpooling with his friends, Bill realized that he should buckle his seat belt in his own car.

Testing a Hypothesis About a Percentage

Here is the formula for a percentage hypothesis test.

Formula for a Hypothesis Test of a Population Percentage

$$z = \frac{p - \pi_H}{\sqrt{\dfrac{p \times q}{n}}}$$

Where:

p = sample percent
π_H = hypothesized population percentage

Table 12.4 provides formulas and lists the steps necessary to test a hypothesis about a percentage. Basically, hypothesis testing

MARKETING RESEARCH APPLICATION 12.2

Practical Applications

Intuitive Hypothesis Testing: We Do It All the Time!

People do intuitive hypothesis testing all the time to reaffirm their beliefs or to reform them to be consistent with reality. The following diagram illustrates how people perform intuitive hypothesis testing.

Here is an everyday example. As a student taking a marketing research class, you believe that you will ace the first exam if you study hard the night before the exam. You take the exam, and you score a 70%. Darn it! It sure looks like your score does not support your belief that one cram session will be enough to earn an A grade in this course. You now realize

that your belief (your hypothesis) was wrong, and you need to study more for the next exam. Because your hypothesis was not supported, you have to come up with a new one.

You ask a fellow student who did ace the exam, how much study time she put into studying, and she states "three solid nights." Notice that she has found evidence (her A grade) that supports her hypothesis, so she will not change her study habits belief. You, on the other hand, must change your hypothesis or suffer the consequences. Read the boxes and follow the arrows in the diagram below to see how your intuitive hypothesis testing comes out.

Your Hypothesis

| I believe that a one-night cram session is enough to ace the exam. This is my hypothesis. | I now believe that I need to study three solid nights to ace the next exam. This is my revised hypothesis. | I will hold this revised belief (hypothesis) as long as I continue to ace the exams. |

The Evidence

| Omigosh! I score a 70 on the exam. My belief (hypothesis) is not supported by the evidence, so I need to change it. | Woo Hoo! I score 95 on the next exam. My revised hypothesis is supported by the evidence. |

involves the use of four ingredients: the sample statistic (p in this case), the standard error (s_p), the hypothesized population parameter value (π_H in this case), and the decision to "support" or "not support" the hypothesized parameter based on a few calculations. The first two values were discussed in the section on percentage parameter estimation. The hypothesis is simply what the researcher hypothesizes the population parameter, π, to be before the research is undertaken. When these are taken into consideration by using the steps in Table 12.4, the result is a significance test for the hypothesis that determines its support (acceptance) or lack of support (rejection).

Tracking the logic of the equation for a percent hypothesis test, you can see that the sample percent, p, is compared to the hypothesized population percent, π_H. In this case, "compared" means "take the difference." They are compared because in a hypothesis test, one tests the **null hypothesis,** a formal statement that there is no (or null) difference between the hypothesized π value and the

> A hypothesis test gives you the amount of support for your hypothesis based on your sample finding and sample size.

TABLE 12.4

How to Test a Hypothesis for a Percentage

To test a hypothesis about a percentage, you must assess how close the sample percentage is to the hypothesized population percentage. The following example uses Bill's seat belt hypothesis and tests it with a random sample of 1,000 automobile drivers.

Step	Description	Seat Belt Example ($n = 1,000$)
Step 1	Identify π_H, the "hypothesized percent" that you (or your client) believe exists in the population.	Bill believes that 30% of drivers use seat belts.
Step 2	Conduct a survey and determine the sample percentage; call it p.	A sample of 1,000 drivers is taken, and the sample percent for those who use seat belts is found to be 80%, so $p = 80\%$.
Step 3	Determine the *standard error of the percentage*.	$$s_p = \sqrt{\frac{pq}{n}}$$ $$= \sqrt{\frac{(80 \times 20)}{1,000}}$$ $$= 1.26\%$$
Step 4	Calculate z: subtract Π_H from p and divide this amount by the standard error of the percent.	$$z = \frac{p - \pi_H}{s_p}$$ $$= \frac{(80 - 30)}{1.26}$$ $$= 39.7$$
Step 5	Compare the computed z to the critical z value of 1.96; determine whether the hypothesis is supported or not supported.	The computed z of 39.7 is greater than the critical z of 1.96, so the hypothesis is not supported.

p value found in our sample. This difference is divided by the standard error to determine how many standard errors away from the hypothesized parameter the sample percentage falls. All the relevant information about the population as found by our sample is included in these computations. Knowledge of areas under the normal curve then comes into play to translate this distance into a determination of whether the sample finding supports (accepts) or does not support (rejects) the hypothesis.

The example we have provided in Table 12.4 uses Bill's seat belt hypothesis that 30% of drivers buckle up their seat belts. To move our example from intuitive hypothesis testing and into statistical hypothesis testing, we have specified that Bill reads about a Harris Poll and finds that 80% of respondents in a national sample of 1,000 wear their seat belts. This is a 50% difference, but it must be translated into the number of standard errors, or the computed z value. In step 4 of Table 12.4, this calculated z turns out to be 39.7, but what does it mean?

As was the case with confidence intervals, the crux of hypothesis testing is the sampling distribution concept. Our actual sample is one of the multiple theoretical samples comprising the assumed bell-shaped curve of possible sample results using the hypothesized value as the center of the bell-shaped distribution. There is a greater probability of finding a sample result

FIGURE 12.7

95% Acceptance and
Rejection Regions for
Hypothesis Tests

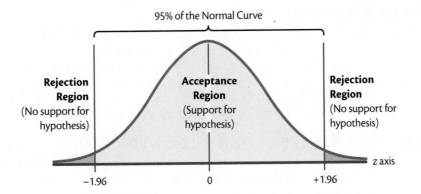

95% of the Normal Curve

Rejection Region (No support for hypothesis)

Acceptance Region (Support for hypothesis)

Rejection Region (No support for hypothesis)

z axis

−1.96   0   +1.96

close to the hypothesized mean, for example, than of finding one that is far away. But there is a critical assumption working here. We have conditionally accepted from the outset that the person who stated the hypothesis is correct. So, if our sample mean turns out to be within ± 1.96 standard errors of the hypothesized mean, it supports the hypothesis maker at the 95% level of confidence because it falls within 95% of the area under the curve. As Figure 12.7 illustrates, the sampling distribution defines two areas: the acceptance region that resides within ± 1.96 standard errors and the rejection region that is found at either end of the bell-shaped sampling distribution and outside the ± 1.96 standard errors boundaries. The hypothesis test rule is simple: If the z value falls in the acceptance region, there is support for the hypothesis, and if the z value falls in the rejection region, there is no support for the hypothesis. A computed z value of 39.7 is far greater than our 1.96 boundary, so as is indicated in step 5 of Table 12.4, the hypothesis is not supported.

Here is an example that will help crystallize your understanding of the test of a hypothesis about a percentage. What percent of U.S. college students own a major credit card? Let's say that you think three of every four college students (75%) own a MasterCard, Visa, or some other major credit card. A recent survey of 1,200 students on U.S. college campuses found that 84% have a major credit card.[5] The computations to test your hypotheses of 75% are as follows:

> The computed z value is used to assess whether the hypothesis is supported or not supported.

Example of a Percentage Hypothesis Test

$$z = \frac{p - \pi_H}{\sqrt{\dfrac{p \times q}{n}}}$$

$$= \frac{75 - 84}{\sqrt{\dfrac{84 \times 16}{1200}}}$$

$$= \frac{-9}{1.1}$$

$$= -8.2$$

Your hypothesis is not supported here, because the computed z value exceeds the critical value of 1.96. Yes, we realize that the result was *minus* 8.2, but the sign is irrelevant: You are comparing the absolute value of the computed z to the critical value of 1.96. The true percent of U.S. college students who own a credit card is estimated to be 81.8% to 86.2% at the 95% level of confidence. (We calculated the 95% confidence interval based on the sample finding.)

Why Use the 95% Significance Level?

By a very large majority researchers prefer to use the 95% significance level with its associated critical z value of ± 1.96. Granted, you may find a researcher who prefers to use the 99% significance level and its critical z value of ± 2.58; however, seasoned researchers are well aware of the ever-changing marketplace phenomena that they study, and they prefer to detect subtle changes early on. Consequently, they opt for the 95% one as it has a greater likelihood of not supporting clients' hypotheses and making them see these shifts and changes.

How Do We Know That We Have Made the Correct Decision?

What if Bill objects to your rejection? Which is correct—the hypothesis or the researcher's sample results? The answer to this question is always the same: Sample information is invariably more accurate than a hypothesis. Of course, the sampling procedure must adhere strictly to probability sampling requirements and assure representativeness. As you can see, Bill was greatly mistaken because his hypothesis of 30% of drivers wearing seat belts was 39.7 standard errors away from the 80% finding of the national poll. If Bill wants to dispute a national sample finding reported by the Harris Poll organization, he can, but he will surely come to realize that his limited observations are much less valid than the findings of this well-respected research industry giant.

Testing a Directional Hypothesis

A **directional hypothesis** is one that indicates the direction in which you believe the population parameter falls relative to some hypothesized average or percentage. If you are testing a directional ("greater than" or "less than") hypothesis, the critical z value is adjusted downward to 1.64 and 2.33 for the 95% and 99% levels of confidence, respectively. It is important that you understand that the hypothesis test formula does not change; it is only the critical value of z that is changed when you are testing a directional hypothesis. This adjustment is because only one side of the bell-shaped curve is involved in what is known as a "one-tailed" test. Of course, the sample percent or average must be in the right direction away from the hypothesized value, and the computed z value must meet or exceed the critical one-tailed z value in order for the hypothesis to be supported.

XLDA

HOW TO TEST A HYPOTHESIS ABOUT A PERCENTAGE WITH XL DATA ANALYST Again, we are interested in generalizing our findings to see if they support or fail to support our percentage hypothesis, so, as you can see in Figure 12.8, the menu sequence to direct the XL Data Analyst to accomplish this is Generalize–Hypothesis Test–Percentage. This sequence opens up the selection window where you can select the categorical variable in the top pane, and the various value labels for that variable will appear in the bottom pane. Notice at the bottom of the selection window, there is an entry box where we will enter our "Hypothesized Percent."

In our example, we will select "Dwelling type" as our chosen variable, and then highlight the "Single family" category. We have hypothesized that 50% of the population of U.S. households live in single-family dwellings. Clicking "OK" will prompt the XL Data Analyst to perform the hypothesis test.

Figure 12.9 is an annotated screenshot of an XL Data Analyst percentage hypothesis test analysis. You should immediately notice that this analysis produces a more detailed output than you have encountered thus far. First and foremost, there is a table that verifies that we have selected the Single family category answer for the Dwelling type variable, and it reveals that 45.2% of our 1,000 respondents answered "single family" to the dwelling type question. The table also shows our hypothesized percentage of 50% so we can verify that we have entered in our hypothesized percentage correctly. Immediately following the table are the results of three hypotheses tests. The main hypothesis test finding is presented first, and the XL Data Analyst finds insufficient support for our hypothesis of 50%, so it signals that our hypothesis is "not supported." Next, in case we had directional hypotheses in mind, the XL Data Analyst indicates that if we hypothesized that the percent was greater than 50%, this hypothesis lacks support and it is "not supported," but if we had hypothesized that the population percent is less than 50%, this hypothesis is "supported."

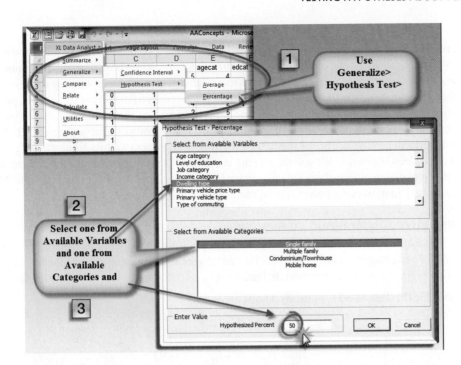

FIGURE 12.8

XL Data Analyst Selection Menu for a Percentage Hypothesis Test

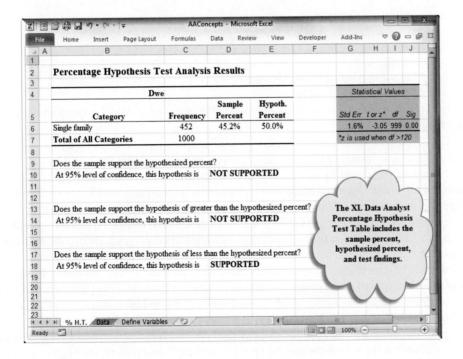

FIGURE 12.9

XL Data Analyst Output Table and Results for a Percentage Hypothesis Test

You should also notice that your XL Data Analyst provides the statistical values necessary to carry out the hypotheses tests. The standard error of the percentage, computed z (or t) value, associated degrees of freedom for using a t-distribution table, and the significance level are reported in case a user wishes to use them. However, since the XL Data Analyst assesses the hypothesized percentage and indicates whether or not the hypothesis is supported by the sample at the 95% level of confidence, there is scant need to be concerned with the statistical values. These are provided for the rare case where a researcher might feel the need to inspect them.

The XL Data Analyst tests both directional and nondirectional hypotheses in the same analysis.

Is It *t* or *z*? And Why You Do Not Need to Worry About It

The XL Data Analyst correctly decides whether to use a *t* value or a *z* value with hypothesis tests.

We have refrained from discussing the statistical values that appear on XL Data Analyst output, because you need to know only that it uses these values and tells you whether or not the hypothesis is supported. However, if you do inspect the statistical values, you may have noticed that there is reference to a *t* to *z* value. The *t* value is agreed by statisticians to be more proper than the *z* value,[6] but the *t* value does not have set critical values such as 1.96. It is not important for you to understand why, but it is worthwhile to inform you that whenever XL Data Analyst performs analysis, it uses the agreed-upon best approach, and its findings are correct based on the best approach. We use the *z* value in our explanations because it makes them simpler for you to understand as there are only a very few fixed critical values of *z* to deal with. Also, it is customary in marketing research books to use the *z* value formulas.

Testing a Hypothesis About an Average

Just as you learned that confidence intervals for averages follow the identical logic of confidence intervals for percentages, so is the procedure to test a hypothesis about an average identical to that for testing a hypothesis about a percent. In fact, a *z* value is calculated using the following formula.

Formula for the Test of a Hypothesis About an Average

$$z = \frac{\bar{x} - \mu_H}{\frac{s}{\sqrt{n}}}$$

The procedure for a hypothesis test for an average is identical to one for a percentage, except the equation uses values specific to an average.

Where:

$\bar{x}$ = sample average

μ_H = hypothesized population average

$\dfrac{s}{\sqrt{n}}$ = standard error of the average

You determine whether the hypothesis is supported or not supported using this formula applied to the steps in Table 12.4.

As is our custom, we will provide a numerical example of a hypothesis test for an average. Northwestern Mutual Life Insurance Company has a college student internship program which allows college students to participate in an intensive training program and to become field agents in one academic term. Via arrangements made with various universities in the United States, students receive college credit if they successfully complete this program. Rex Reigen, district agent for Idaho, believed, based on his knowledge of other programs in the country, that the typical college agent will earn about $3,750 in his or her first semester of participation in the program. He hypothesizes that the population parameter, that is, the average earning, will be $3,750. To check Rex's hypothesis, a survey was taken of current college agents, and 100 of these individuals were contacted through telephone calls. Each was asked to estimate the amount of money made in his or her first semester of work in the program. The sample average is determined to be $3,800, and the standard deviation is $350.

In essence, $3,750 is the hypothesized average of the sampling distribution of all possible samples of the same size that can be taken of the college agents in the country. The unknown factor, of course, is the size of the standard error in dollars. Consequently, although it is assumed that the sampling distribution will be a normal curve with the average of the entire distribution at $3,750, we need a way to determine how many dollars are within ± 1 standard error of the average, or any other number of standard errors of the average for that matter. The only information available that would help to determine the size of the standard error is the standard deviation obtained from the sample. This standard deviation can be used to determine a standard error with the application of the standard error formula you encountered in step 2 of Table 12.3.

The amount of $3,800 found by the sample differs from the hypothesized amount of $3,750 by $50. Is this amount a sufficient enough difference to cast doubt on Rex's estimate? Or, in other words, is it far enough from the hypothesized average to not support the hypothesis? To answer these questions, we compute as follows:

Calculation of a Test of Rex's Hypothesis That Northwestern Mutual Interns Make an Average of $3,750 in Their First Semester of Work

> The standard deviation and sample size are used to compute the standard error of an average.

$$z = \frac{\bar{x} - \mu_H}{\frac{s}{\sqrt{n}}}$$

$$= \frac{3,800 - 3,750}{\frac{350}{\sqrt{100}}}$$

$$= \frac{50}{35}$$

$$= 1.43 \quad \textit{Rex's hypothesis is accepted!}$$

The sample variability, s, and the sample size, n, have been used to determine the size of the standard error of the assumed sampling distribution. In this case, one standard error of the average is equal to $35. The difference of $50 is divided by $35 to determine the number of standard errors away from the hypothesized average the sample statistic lies, and the result is 1.43 standard errors. As is illustrated in Figure 12.10, 1.43 standard errors is within ± 1.96 standard errors of Rex's hypothesized average. It also reveals that the hypothesis is supported because it falls in the acceptance region.

How to Test a Hypothesis About an Average with XL Data Analyst

If the Advanced Automobile Concepts venture is to be successful, there must be attitudes in place that hybrid and/or alternative fuel vehicles will have some impact on carbon dioxide levels that may be contributing to global warming. Obviously, the principals believe this to be the case, so let's test this hypothesis. We will take the statement, "Hybrid autos that use alternative fuels will reduce fuel emissions" and test the principals belief that people "agree" with it. On the 7-point scale, "strongly agree" corresponds to a "5," so we will use the XL Data Analyst to see if the sample findings support this hypothesis.

To test the hypothesis that the average will be 5, you use the Generalize–Hypothesis Test–Average menu sequence to open up the selection window. Unlike the percentage hypothesis window, the average hypothesis test window has only one selection windowpane, as we must work with a metric variable. You will see in Figure 12.11 that we have selected the "Hybrid autos that

XLDA

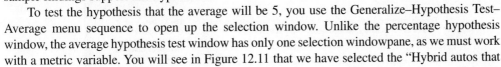

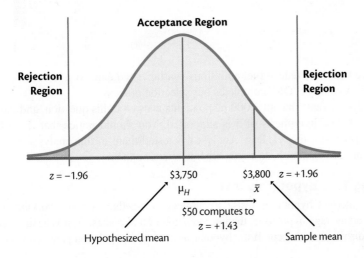

FIGURE 12.10

The Sample Findings Support the Hypothesis in This Example

FIGURE 12.11

XL Data Analyst Selection
Menu for an Average
Hypothesis Test

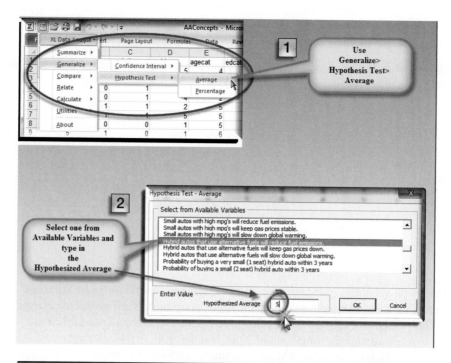

FIGURE 12.12

XL Data Analyst Output
Table and Results for an
Average Hypothesis Test

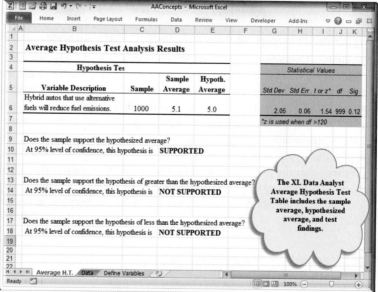

To have the XL Data
Analyst test a
hypothesis about an
average, select the
variable, input the
hypothesized average,
and click "OK."

use alternative fuels will reduce fuel emissions" variable and entered a "5" in the "Hypothesized Average" box. A click on "OK" completes our selection process.

Figure 12.12 reveals that all 1,000 respondents answered this question, and the average was found to be 5.1. Our hypothesis of 5 is supported. You should notice that if we had specified directional hypotheses, the XL Data Analyst has tested them in this analysis as well. Also, the statistical values are present in case you wish to examine them.

Interpreting Your Hypothesis Test

How do you interpret hypothesis tests? Regardless of whether you are working with a percent hypothesis or an average hypothesis, the interpretation of a hypothesis test is again directly linked to the sampling distribution concept. If the hypothesis about the population parameter is correct or true, then a high percentage of sample findings must fall close to this hypothesized value. In fact, if the hypothesis is true, then 95% of the sample results will fall between $\pm$ 1.96 standard errors of the hypothesized mean. On the other hand, if the hypothesis is incorrect, there is a strong likelihood that the sample findings will fall outside $\pm$ 1.96 standard errors.

In general, the further away the actual sample finding (percent or average) is from the hypothesized population value, the more likely the computed z value will fall outside the critical range, resulting in a failure to support the hypothesis. When this happens, the XL Data Analyst tells the hypothesizer that his or her assumption about the population is not supported. It must be revised in light of the evidence from the sample. This revision is achieved through estimates of the population parameter just discussed in a previous section. These estimates can be used to provide the manager or researcher with a new mental picture of the population through confidence interval estimates of the true population value.

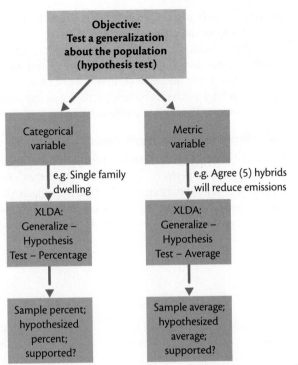

FIGURE 12.13

Hypothesis Test Flow Chart

> Interpretation of a hypothesis test is based on the sampling distribution concept.

Flow Chart of Generalization Analysis for Hypothesis Tests

As a means of summarizing our discussion of hypothesis tests and also to guide you when you are working with these tests, we have a flow chart (Figure 12.13) for hypothesis tests with the XL Data Analyst. With a categorical variable, such as a hypotheses that 25% of Americans own an economy car, use the XL Data Analysis menu sequence Generalize–Hypothesis Test–Percent to find whether or not it is supported at the 95% level of confidence. With a metric variable, such as a population average of neutral, or 4, on a 7-point scale, use the Generalize–Hypothesis Test–Average menu sequence to determine if it is supported by the sample.

How to Present Generalization Analyses

Our chapter concludes with recommendations on how to present generalization analyses findings in a final report.

Guidelines for Confidence Intervals

There are two options for confidence intervals: (1) the general case, and (2) findings-specific confidence intervals.

THE GENERAL CASE The marketing research industry standard, as well as an almost unanimous choice in opinion polling, is to simply state the sampling error associated with the survey sample size. For example, the report may say "findings are accurate to $\pm4\%$," or "the survey has an error of $\pm3.5\%$." This sample error, of course, is calculated using the sample error formula you learned in Chapter 9 and typically at the 95% level of confidence with $p = 50\%$, $q = 50\%$, and $z = 1.96$.

> Report confidence intervals either as a general $\pm x\%$ for the entire survey or with specific upper and lower boundaries for critical variables.

THE FINDINGS-SPECIFIC CASE You should realize that $p = 50\%$, $q = 50\%$ is the most conservative confidence interval estimate, for any combination of p and q other than $p = 50\%$, $q = 50\%$ will result in a smaller numerator in the standard error and, thus, a smaller confidence interval. Also, this formula only pertains to percentage findings, as the confidence intervals for findings about averages require the use of a different formula.

With the findings-specific approach, the researcher judges that there are findings that require more than the general case of reporting sample error. For instance, there may be findings that the client will use to answer critical questions or on which to base important decisions. Here, the researcher identifies all of the findings that he or she believes definitely require the reporting of findings-specific confidence intervals and provides them in a table that lists the 95% confidence interval lower and upper boundaries.

Guidelines for Hypothesis Tests

Report the confidence interval when a hypothesis is not supported.

The step-by-step approach to the presentation of hypothesis tests is as follows: (1) State the hypothesis; (2) by performing appropriate hypothesis test computations, state if the hypothesis is supported or not supported; and (3) if the hypothesis is not supported, compute confidence intervals to provide the client with the appropriate confidence intervals. If more than one hypothesis is tested, construct a table with items (1), (2), and (3) organized with descriptive headings.

Summary

This chapter begins by introducing you to the concept of generalization, in which you estimate a population fact with the use of a sample's finding. Note that with more evidence (large sample size) and less variability (standard error) generalization can be more precise. Estimation of a population percentage or average through the use of confidence intervals is sometimes called parameter estimation. With both parameters (average or percentage), we can use formulas for confidence intervals, which are provided in the chapter as well as examples of applications of these formulas and instructions on how to use XL Data Analyst to compute a percentage or an average confidence interval. A confidence interval is wider with more variation but smaller with larger sample sizes.

A researcher can test a hypothesis about a percentage or an average. That is, the researcher or manager may have a prior belief about what percent or average value exists in the population, and the sample findings can be used to assess the support or lack of support for this hypothesis. People often do intuitive hypothesis testing, either finding support for their beliefs or finding refuting evidence that causes them to modify their beliefs. The chapter provides formulas for hypothesis tests, examples of applications of these formulas, and instructions on how to use XL Data Analyst to test hypotheses for averages and percents. Finally, the chapter describes how to present confidence intervals and hypothesis tests in a marketing research report.

Key Terms

Sample finding (p. 264)
Population fact (p. 264)
Generalization (p. 264)
Parameter estimation (p. 266)
Parameter (p. 266)
Confidence interval (p. 266)

Most commonly used level
  of confidence (p. 267)
Standard error (p. 268)
Standard error of the percentage
  (p. 268)
Sampling distribution (p. 268)

Standard error of the average (p. 271)
Hypothesis (p. 275)
Hypothesis testing (p. 275)
Intuitive hypothesis testing (p. 276)
Null hypothesis (p. 277)
Directional hypothesis (p. 280)

Review Questions

1. Distinguish between sample findings and population facts. How are they similar, and how may they differ?
2. Define generalization, and provide an example of what you might generalize if you moved to a new city and noticed that you were driving faster than most other drivers.
3. What is a parameter, and what is parameter estimation?
4. Describe how a confidence interval can be used by a researcher to estimate a population percentage.
5. What two levels of confidence are used most often, and which one is most commonly used?

6. Using the formula for a confidence interval for a percentage, indicate the role of the following:
   a. Sample finding (percentage)
   b. Variability
   c. Level of confidence
7. Indicate how a researcher interprets a 95% confidence interval. Refer to the sampling distribution in your explanation.
8. In the case of a standard error of the average, indicate how it is affected by the following:
   a. Standard deviation
   b. Sample size
9. What is a hypothesis and what is the purpose of a hypothesis test? With a hypothesis test, what is the null hypothesis?

10. How does statistical hypothesis testing differ from intuitive hypothesis testing? How are they similar?
11. When performing a hypothesis test, what critical value of z is the most commonly used one, and to what level of significance does it pertain?
12. When the person who posited a hypothesis argues against the researcher who has performed the hypothesis test and not supported it, who should win the argument and why?
13. Using a bell-shaped curve, show the acceptance (supported) and rejection (not supported) regions for the following levels of confidence.
    a. 95% level of confidence
    b. 99% level of confidence
14. How does a directional hypothesis differ from a nondirectional one, and what are the two critical items to take into account when testing a directional hypothesis?

Application Questions

15. Here are several computation practice exercises in which you must identify which formula should be used and apply it. In each case, after you perform the necessary calculations, write your answers in the blank column.
    a. Determine confidence intervals for each of the following:

Sample Statistic	Sample Size	Confidence Level	Your Confidence Intervals?
Mean: 150 Std. Dev: 30	200	95%	
Percent: 67%	300	99%	
Mean: 5.4 Std. Dev: 0.5	250	99%	
Percent: 25.8%	500	99%	

    b. Test the following hypothesis and interpret your findings.

Hypothesis	Sample Findings	Confidence Level	Your Test Results
Mean = 7.5	Mean: 8.5 Std dev: 1.2 n = 670	95%	
Percent = 86%	p = 95% n = 1,000	99%	
Mean > 125	Mean: 135 Std dev: 15 n = 500	95%	
Percent < 33%	p = 31% n = 120	99%	

16. The manager of Washington State Environmental Services Division wants a survey that will tell her how many households in the city of Seattle will voluntarily identify environmentally hazardous household materials like old cans of paint, unused pesticides, and other such materials than cannot be recycled but should be disposed of, and then transport all of their environmental hazardous items to a central disposal center located in the downtown area and open only on Sunday mornings. A random survey of 500 households determines that 20% of households would do so, and that each participating household expects to dispose of about five items per year with a standard deviation of two items. What is the value of parameter estimation in this instance?

17. It is reported in the newspaper that a survey sponsored by *Forbes* magazine with 200 Fortune 500 company top executives has found that 75% believe that the United States trails Japan and Germany in automobile engineering. What percent of *all* Fortune 500 company top executives believe that the United States trails Japan and Germany?

18. Alamo Rent-A-Car executives believe that Alamo accounts for about 50% of all Cadillacs that are rented. To test this belief, a researcher randomly identifies twenty major airports with on-site rental car lots. Observers are sent to each location and instructed to record the number of rental company Cadillacs observed in a four-hour period. About 500 are observed, and 30% are observed being returned to Alamo Rent-A-Car. What are the implications of this finding for the Alamo executives' belief?

Case 12.1 **The Pets, Pets, & Pets Survey**

Pets, Pets, & Pets is a pet store located in a large regional mall. A research company conducted a survey using a random sample of 162 Pets, Pets, & Pets customers. The store has been provided with a summary of some analyses that were conducted using this sample.

	Times visited PPP in past year	Amount spent on last visit to PPP	How likely to buy at PPP next time (1-7 scale)	Number of pets owned
N	162	162	162	162
Average	4.4	$18.2	5.3	1.64
Mode	4	$15	4	1
Std. Deviation	4.98	$8.50	1.50	.77

Use Pets, Pets, & Pets how often?

	Frequency	Percent
Not Use Regularly	90	55.6%
Use Regularly	72	44.4%
Total	162	100.0%

Recommended Pets, Pets, & Pets to a friend?

	Frequency	Percent
No	29	17.9%
Yes	133	82.1%
Total	162	100.0%

Recall seeing a Pets, Pets, & Pets newspaper advertisement in the past month?

	Frequency	Percent
Yes	76	46.9%
No	86	53.1%
Total	162	100.0%

Use the information in this summary to determine answers to the following research questions.

1. How often did Pets, Pets, & Pets customers visit it last year?
2. How much did they typically spend on the last visit?
3. How likely are they to buy at Pets, Pets, & Pets on their next visit?
4. What percent are "regular" Pets, Pets, & Pets customers?
5. What percent has recommended Pets, Pets, & Pets to friends?
6. The manager at Pets, Pets, & Pets believes that, on average, store customers own two pets. Is this belief supported by the survey?
7. The manager also believes that Pets, Pets, & Pets monthly newspaper advertising is highly effective and reaches 80% of the store's customers. Is this belief supported by the survey?

Case 12.2 **Your Integrated Case**

The Advanced Automobile Concepts Survey Generalization Analysis

Cory Rogers was pleased with Celeste Brown's descriptive analysis. Brown had done all of the proper descriptive analyses, and she had copied the relevant tables and findings into a Word document with notations that Rogers could refer to quickly. Rogers says, "Celeste, this is great work. I am going to Nick Thomas in an hour to show him what we have found. In the meantime, I want you to look a bit deeper into the data. I have jotted down some items that I want you to analyze. This is the next step in understanding how the sample findings generalize to the population of the United States. I also have some hypotheses that I want you to test."

In the way of background, the data set for the Advanced Automobile Concepts survey has fifty variables that pertain to the following topics.

Demographics
Vehicle ownership
Probabilities of buying various types of hybrid vehicles in the next three years
Preferences for specific types of hybrid vehicles
Lifestyle
Favorite television show type
Favorite radio genre
Favorite magazine type
Favorite local newspaper section

The XL Data Analyst data set, called AAConcepts.xlsm, is comprised of 1,000 respondents who are a representative sample of American households. There is an estimated 14,825,428 American households (U.S. Census, 2010 estimate).

Your task here is to again take the role of Celeste Brown, marketing analyst. Using the Advanced Automobile Concepts data set, perform the proper analysis and interpret the findings for each of the following questions specified by Rogers.

1. What percent of the American public owns the following type of vehicle?
   a. Standard vehicle
   b. Luxury vehicle
   c. SUV or van
2. How does the American public feel about the following statements?
   a. Hybrid autos that use alternative fuels will reduce fuel emissions.
   b. Hybrid autos that use alternative fuels will keep gas prices down.
   c. Hybrid autos that use alternative fuels will slow global warming.
3. Principals at Advanced Automobile Concepts fully understand that there is resistance to change in Zen. There are some senior executives who grew up during America's "romance with the automobile" era of the 1950s and 1960s, and who believe that most Americans want a large and powerful automobile. These executives point out that SUVs are extremely popular despite global warming warnings that have been issued for the past decade and numerous gasoline price surges where filling up the gas tank of an SUV or a luxury automobile approached the $100 mark. These executives further believe that hybrid and alternative fuel automobiles are generally regarded by the American public as undesirable because they are perceived to be unattractive, boxy in appearance, and sluggish in acceleration. In fact, some of these senior executives believe that the probability of the American public buying the various hybrid vehicles in the next three years may resemble the following:

Hybrid Vehicle Type	Probability
Probability of buying a very small (one-seat) hybrid auto within three years?	5%
Probability of buying a small (two-seat) hybrid auto within three years?	5%
Probability of buying an economy size hybrid auto within three years?	15%
Probability of buying a standard size hybrid auto within three years?	15%
Probability of buying a large size hybrid auto within three years?	20%

Test these hypotheses with the findings from the survey.
4. Using the findings from the survey, estimate the number of vehicles of each of the following hybrid types that are expected to be purchased over the next three years.
   a. Very small (one-seat) hybrid auto
   b. Small (two-seat) hybrid auto
   c. Economy size hybrid auto
   d. Standard size hybrid auto
   e. Large size hybrid auto

13

Finding Differences

LEARNING OBJECTIVES

- To understand how market segmentation underlies differences analysis

- To learn how to assess the significance of the difference between two groups' percentages

- To learn how to assess the significance of the difference between two groups' averages

- To understand when "analysis of variance" (ANOVA) is used and how to interpret ANOVA findings

- To comprehend what analysis is used when the averages of two variables using the same metric scale are compared for differences

- To gain knowledge of the "Differences" analyses available with XL Data Analyst

A Marketing Research Professional Comments on the Importance of Differences Analysis

SOCRATIC
TECHNOLOGIES
Visit Socratic Technologies at www.sotech.com.

This quote about differences analysis is provided by William H. MacElroy, President, Socratic Technologies.

Over the years, I've seen many instances where true insights can be concealed by looking at just the simple average (mean). Consider the example where one group of people really likes a new product concept and another group of equal size dislikes it as passionately. If you just look at the mean purchase interest of both groups, you will be "averaging out" all the interesting findings and—even more importantly—will be looking at a level of interest that doesn't really represent anyone at all. Obviously, understanding the differences between groups and the "lay of the data" will highly influence who we recommend for the targeting of the new product.

To increase the usefulness of our analysis, we can examine differences between two proportions: differences between two means or differences between more than two means. In order to find valuable insights for our clients, it is important for marketing researchers to know the appropriate statistical tests to run and how the structure of the data distribution influences the correct choice of method. In this chapter you will learn all the tests that are appropriate for the three situations described herein. You will also learn how to run these tests using the XL Data Analyst and you will learn how to interpret the results.

As you learned in the previous chapter, it is possible to make inferences about measures of central tendency such as averages and percentages found in a random sample survey. These inferences take the form of confidence intervals or tests of hypotheses. A different type of inference concerns differences. That is, as MacElroy has described in his opening comments, the researcher can ask, "Are there statistically significant differences between two or more groups, and, if so, what are they?" In this chapter, we describe the logic of differences tests, and we show you how to use the XL Data Analyst to conduct various types of differences tests.[1]

William H. MacElroy,
President, Socratic
Technologies

We begin this chapter by discussing why differences are important to marketing managers. Next, we introduce you to differences (percentages or averages) between two independent groups, such as a comparison of AT&T versus Verison wireless telephone users on how satisfied they are with their wireless service. Then, we introduce you to ANOVA, a scary name but a simple way to compare the averages of several groups simultaneously and to quickly spot patterns of significant differences. Finally, we show you that it is possible to test whether a difference exists between the averages of two similarly scaled questions. For instance, do buyers rate a store higher in "merchandise selection" than they rate its "good values"? As in previous analysis chapters, we provide formulas and numerical examples, and also show you examples of XL Data Analyst procedures and output using the Advanced Automobile Concepts survey data set.

Why Are Differences Important?

Almost every marketer relies on market segmentation. In a nutshell, **market segmentation** holds that within a product market, there are different types of consumers who have dissimilar requirements, and these differences can be the bases of marketing strategies. For example, the Iams Company, which markets pet foods, has more than a dozen different varieties of dry dog food geared to the dog's age (puppy versus adult), weight situation (normal versus overweight), and activity (active versus inactive). Toyota Motors has nineteen models, including the economical Yaris, the four-door Avalon luxury sedan, the Highlander SUV, and the Tacoma truck. Even Boeing Airlines has eleven different types of commercial jets and a dozen configurations of freighter jets. The needs and requirements of each market segment differ greatly from others, and an astute marketer will customize his or her marketing mix to each target market's unique situation.[2]

Some differences, of course, are quite obvious, but as competition becomes more intense, with aggressive market segmentation and target marketing being the watchword of most companies in an industry, there is a need to investigate differences among consumer groups for consumer marketers and among business establishments for B2B marketers. In a nutshell, market segmentation relies on the discovery of significant differences through the application of the proper data analysis.[3] Of course, the differences must be meaningful and useful: Energetic, growing puppies need different nutritional supplements than do overweight, inactive, aging dogs with stiff joints, so Iams uses these different nutritional needs to formulate special types of dog food for these market segments.

In what might be considered an extreme example of market segmentation, Harrah's Entertainment, which operates twenty-six gambling casinos in thirteen U.S. states, has analyzed its slot machine players—estimated to be 25 million people—and claims to have identified ninety different market segmentation types based on age, gender, game preference, casino location, and other variables.[4] This segmentation analysis has revealed that one of these segments amounts to about one-third of its customers, yet it represents 80% of revenues. Also, Harrah's claims that by custom-tailoring its marketing strategies to various market segments, it has significantly increased its market share and become more profitable.

Analyzing for significant and meaningful differences is a discovery process. That is, the marketing researcher and manager formulate the research objectives with the goal of finding useful market segmentation differences in the total market, but there is no guarantee that significant and meaningful differences will be found. Data analysis is used to investigate for statistically significant differences, and there are rules and guidelines about how to decide when significant differences are indeed found. This chapter will inform you of the rules, and once you have learned them, you will be able to spot and interpret differences easily.[5]

Let's take the instance of a personal communication system company like Sprint and see how a researcher might look for market segment differences. There are three ways a researcher can analyze for differences in the service Sprint customers might want to (1) compare one group to another group, such as comparing men to women customers; (2) compare three or more groups, such as people who are single, those who are married without children, those who are married with teenagers living at home, and those who are married with one or more children in college; or (3) compare how important one service feature (such as rollover minutes) is compared to another service feature (such as sharing minutes with family members). You will learn how to perform differences tests for each of these three cases in this chapter.

Market segmentation is an important reason for analyzing differences.

Significant differences must be meaningful and useful.

There are three types of differences analysis performed by market researchers.

Testing for Significant Differences Between Two Groups

Often a researcher will want to compare two groups. That is, the researcher may have identified two independent groups such as walk-ins versus loyal customers, men versus women, or coupon users versus those who never use coupons, and he or she may want to compare their answers to the same question. This question of interest may use either a categorical scale or a metric scale. A categorical scale requires that the researcher compare the percentage for one group to the percentage for the other group, whereas he or she will compare averages group-to-group when a metric scale is involved. As you know by now, the formulas differ depending on whether percentages or averages are being tested. But, as you also can guess, the basic concepts involved in the formulas are identical.

Differences Between Percentages for Two Groups

When a marketing researcher compares two groups of respondents to determine whether or not there are statistically significant differences between them, the researcher is considering them to be two independent populations. That is, it is as though two independent surveys were administered, one for each group. The question to be answered then becomes, "Are the respective parameters of these two independent populations different?" But, as always, a researcher can work only with the sample results. Therefore, the researcher falls back on statistical concepts to determine whether the difference that is found between the two sample findings is a true difference between the two populations. You will shortly discover that the logic of differences tests is very similar to the logic of hypothesis testing that you learned in Chapter 12.

> When a researcher compares two groups in a survey, it is as though a separate survey were conducted with each group.

Gender is a demographic variable that is often used by marketers to segment their markets. Let's take the case of a DVD company that rents new-release DVDs online. The researcher uses the company database and pulls the orders from 100 randomly selected male customers and finds that 65% of them rented an "Action & Adventure" DVD last time. A different sample of 300 randomly selected female customers reveals that 40% rented an "Action and Adventure" DVD last time. In other words, we have a sample of males and a separate sample of females who rented DVDs from the company, and we have two percentages, 65% of the men and 40% of the women, who chose an "Action & Adventure" DVD last time they rented a DVD.

Are males and females different with respect to renting "Action & Adventure" DVDs? It sure seems so, as there is a 25% arithmetic (65% − 40%) difference, but you cannot be completely confident of your conclusion about two populations (men and women DVD renters) represented here because of sampling error. Sampling error is based on the sample sizes (100 men versus 300 women) and the variability of the percent of online DVD renters: 65% and 40%. Does this sound familiar to the logic we used when describing hypothesis tests?

> Differences analysis uses logic very similar to that in hypothesis tests.

A differences test can determine if men and women like action and adventure movies to the same degree.

To test whether a true difference exists between two group percentages, we test the null hypothesis that the difference in their population parameters is equal to zero. (We introduced you to the null hypothesis concept in Chapter 12.) The **alternative hypothesis** is that there is a true difference between the two group percentages (or averages) that we are comparing. The alternative hypothesis is, of course, the crux of market segmentation differences, so a marketing researcher is always hoping for the null hypothesis to *not* be supported. In other words, the researcher would very much like to report that significant differences were found because this is the first of the two conditions for market segmentation that we described earlier, namely, a significant difference.

To perform the test of significance of differences between two percentages, each representing a separate group (sample), the first step requires a comparison of the two percentages. By "comparison," we mean that you find the arithmetic difference between them. The second step requires that this difference be translated into a number of standard errors away from the hypothesized value of zero. Once the number of standard errors is known, knowledge of the area under the normal curve will yield an assessment of the support for the null hypothesis. Again, we hope this description sounds familiar to you, for it is almost exactly the procedure used to test a hypothesis, which we described in our previous chapter. The only departure is that in the present case, we are comparing two percents from two samples (p_1 to p_2), while in a hypothesis test for a percent, we compare the hypothesized percent to the percent in the sample (p to π_H).

Here is the formula for the test of the significance of the difference between two percentages.

Formula for Significance of the Difference Between Two Percentages

$$z = \frac{p_1 - p_2}{\sqrt{\dfrac{p_1 \times q_1}{n_1} + \dfrac{p_2 \times q_2}{n_2}}}$$

Where:

p_1 = percent for sample 1 and $q_1 = 100 - p_1$

p_2 = percent for sample 2 and $q_2 = 100 - p_2$

$\sqrt{\dfrac{p_1 \times q_1}{n_1} + \dfrac{p_2 \times q_2}{n_2}} = s_{p_1 - p_2} =$ standard error of the difference between two percents

Because we have two samples instead of the one that we worked with for a hypothesis test, the standard error term is calculated differently, called the **standard error of the difference between two percentages.**

Refer to Table 13.1 for step-by-step instructions on how to perform a test of the difference between two percents.

The sampling distribution under consideration now is the assumed sampling distribution of the differences between the percentages. That is, the assumption has been made that the differences have been computed for comparisons of the two sample percents for many repeated samplings. If the null hypothesis is true, this distribution of differences follows the normal curve, with an average equal to zero and a standard error equal to one. Stated somewhat differently, the procedure requires us, as before, to accept the (null) hypothesis as true until it lacks support from the statistical test. Consequently, the differences of (theoretically) hundreds of comparisons of the two sample percentages generated from multiple samplings would average zero. In other words, our sampling distribution is now the distribution of the difference between one sample and the other, taken multiple times.

Figure 13.1 shows the women's and the men's "Action & Adventure" DVD rental populations, represented by two bell-shaped sampling distribution curves. With the women renters' curve, the apex is at 40%, while the men's curve apex is at 65%. This shows that if we replicated our surveys multiple times, the central value for women renters would be 40%, and the central value for men renters would be 65% as to choice of "Action & Adventure" DVDs. In Figure 13.1 there is also the sampling distribution of the difference between two percents. Its apex is zero to

---

The null hypothesis holds that there is no difference between one group and the other.

A differences test is a comparison of one group's percent or average to the other's by way of simple subtraction. Then this value is divided by the standard error of the difference.

The standard error of the difference takes into account each group's percent and sample size.

TABLE 13.1

How to Determine If One Group's Percentage Is Different from Another Group's Percentage

Marketers are very interested in differences between groups because they offer potentially important market segmentation implications. As you might expect, the researcher assesses how close the percent for one group is to the percent for another group with a type of differences analysis. In this example, we are wondering if male DVD renters differ from female ones with respect to the "Action & Adventure" category. The steps are as follows:

Step	Description	Our Online DVD Rental Example
Step 1	Determine the percent and sample size for each of your two samples.	The rental company has found that 65% of the 100 males rented "Action & Adventure," while 40% of the 300 female customers rented this genre.
Step 2	Compare the two percentages by taking their arithmetic difference.	The difference is 65% − 40%, or 25%. (The sign does not matter.)
Step 3	Determine the *standard error of the difference between two percentages*.	$Standard\ error = \sqrt{\dfrac{65 \times 35}{100} + \dfrac{40 \times 60}{300}} = 5.55$
Step 4	Compute *z* by dividing the difference between the two sample percentages by the standard error of the difference between percents.	$z = 25/5.55$ $= 4.5$
Step 5	Using the critical *z* value, determine whether the null hypothesis is supported or not supported at your chosen level of confidence* (95% is customary, meaning a *z* of 1.96).	In our example, 4.5 is much larger than 1.96, so the null hypothesis is not supported. In other words, male and female renters are different in their choice of "Action & Adventure" DVDs.

*The significance level is provided automatically by practically any analysis program that you use.

represent the null hypothesis that there is no difference between the two populations. The standard error of the difference curve has a mean of zero, and its horizontal axis is measured with standard errors such that it embodies the assumptions of a normal, or bell-shaped, curve.

If we are computing our differences test manually, we compare the computed *z* value with our standard *z* of 1.96 for a 95% level of confidence, and the computed *z* in step 4 of Table 13.1 is 4.5. As you can see in Figure 13.1, 4.5 is certainly larger than 1.96. A computed *z* value that is larger than the critical *z* value amounts to no support for the null hypothesis because it falls outside the 95% area of our standard error of the difference curve. Thus, there is a statistically significant difference between the two percentages, and we are confident that if we repeated this comparison multiple times with a multitude of independent samples, we would conclude that there is a significant difference in at least 95% of these replications. Of course, we would never do multiple replications, but this is the statistician's basis for the assessment of significant differences between the two percents.

It is important that you study and understand Figure 13.1, as the sampling distributions concept and the standard error of the difference notion underlie every differences analysis we will describe in this chapter. In fact, we will refer back to Figure 13.1 in this chapter for this reason rather than build new figures that demonstrate the same concepts. It might be useful to also read Marketing Research Application 13.1 which illustrates the use of differences analysis.

The mean of the standard error of the differences is zero, and its distribution is a bell-shaped curve.

The notions in Figure 13.1 underlie all differences analyses described in this chapter.

FIGURE 13.1

Comparison of Women and Men Online Renters Sampling Distributions for "Action & Adventure" DVDs

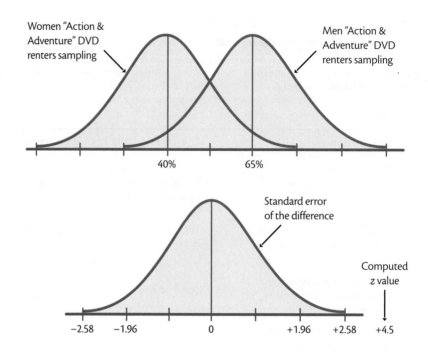

Directional hypotheses are also feasible in the case of tests of statistically significant differences. The procedure is identical to directional hypotheses that are stipulated in hypothesis tests. That is, you must first look at the sign of the computed z value to check that it is consistent with your hypothesized direction. Then you would use a cutoff z value such as 1.64 standard errors for the 95% level of confidence (2.33 standard errors for 99% level of confidence) because only one tail of the sampling distribution is being used.

> Differences analysis may be "directional" and the critical z value is adjusted accordingly.

USING THE XL DATA ANALYST TO DETERMINE THE SIGNIFICANCE OF THE DIFFERENCE BETWEEN TWO GROUP PERCENTS

XLDA

The XL Data Analyst can easily compare two mutually exclusive groups as to their respective percentage on a category of some variable. Let's assume that we are interested in seeing if there is a difference between people who live in dramatically differently sized hometowns and their commuting type, specifically the percent that commute in their vehicle alone. That is, we want to know if the percent of respondents living in huge cities (1 million and more residents) who commute alone is different from the percent of those who live in very small towns (under 10,000) who commute alone.

Figure 13.2 shows the selection menu sequence for the XL Data Analyst to accomplish this test. Notice that you use the command sequence of Compare–2 Group Percents. Next, select a Grouping Variable such as "Size of home town or city," and then you select 2 categories such as "1 million and more" and "Under 10K." . Next, you select "Type of commuting" as the Target Variable and highlight "Single occupancy" as the target group. We define a

MARKETING RESEARCH APPLICATION 13.1

Practical Applications

Do Spendthrifts Spend, and Are Tightwads Tight?

Here is an advanced example of two group differences analysis. Since the beginning of commerce, it has been observed that some consumers spend extravagantly while some are quite miserly in their expenditures. Researchers sought to identify and classify consumers with a scale that identifies spendthrifts versus tightwads.[6] In an attempt to study the spendthrift/tightwad trait, they compared the credit card usage and debt and the amount of savings of spendthrifts and tightwads. Through use of percentage differences tests using their published data, the following two graphs show where the significant differences were found.

The graphs illustrate that spendthrifts have greater credit card debt and less life savings, while tightwads have less credit card debt and greater life savings accounts. One striking difference is that almost three-quarters of tightwads pay off their credit card balances every month, while only about one-third of the spendthrifts are able to keep a zero credit card debt. The findings confirm that "tight" consumers actively manage their credit card debts and garner savings accounts benefits, while "spend" consumers experience credit management issues and endure the worries of meager savings to fall back on in the case of financial emergencies.

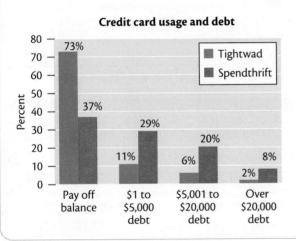

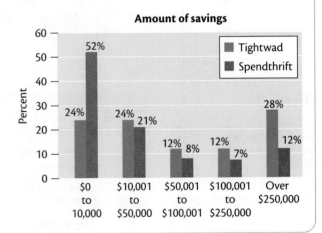

grouping variable as the variable that is used to identify the groups that are to be compared with respect to differences. The **target variable** is the variable on which the groups will be compared. Here, size of home town or city is the grouping variable, and the single occupancy category is the target variable's value.

The result of this difference analysis is found in Figure 13.3, and when you study this output, you will find that of the 267 large city respondents, 66.3% indicated "single occupancy," while of the 154 small town respondents, 50.6% responded identically as to type of commuting. The arithmetic difference is 15.6%, and at the bottom of the Difference Analysis Test table, the XL Data Analyst has reported that the hypothesis of equal percents (the null hypothesis) is "not supported." In other words, there is a true difference with respect to single occupancy commuting, and the Advanced Automobile Concepts principals should be informed that proportionately more very large city dwellers commute this way. Given that large city commutes normally require large amounts of gasoline, it is possible that these individuals are looking for more efficient vehicles such as hybrid and/or alternative fuel vehicles.

> With the XL Data Analyst, specify the grouping variable that defines the groups to compare, and then select the target variable's value that defines the nature of the comparison.

FIGURE 13.2

Using the XL Data Analyst to Set Up a Two-Group Percents Analysis

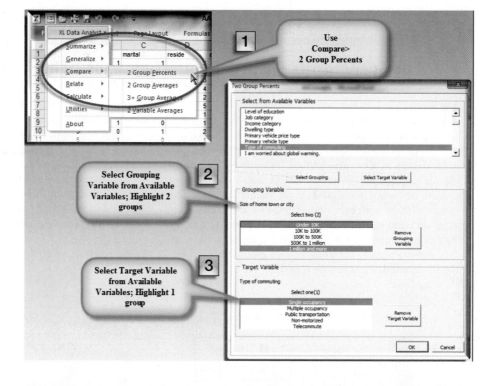

FIGURE 13.3

XL Data Analyst Two-Group Percents Differences Analysis Output

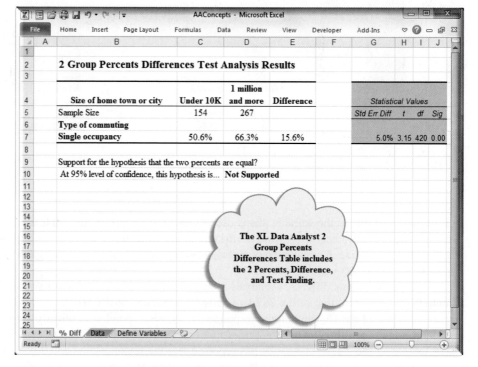

Differences Between Averages for Two Groups

The procedure for testing the significance of the difference between two averages from two different groups (samples) is identical to the procedure used in testing two percentages. As you can easily guess, however, the equations differ because a metric scale is involved. As with a

Some people may be looking for alternative fuel-efficient ways to commute to work.

percentages difference test, the average for one sample is "compared" to the average for the other sample. Recall that compared means "take the difference." This value is then divided by the standard error of the difference between averages, as shown in the following formula.

The procedure for comparing two group averages is identical to the one for comparing two group percents except for the substitution of appropriate formulas.

Formula for Significance of the Difference Between Two Averages

$$z = \frac{\bar{x}_1 - \bar{x}_2}{\sqrt{\dfrac{s_1^2}{n_1} + \dfrac{s_2^2}{n_2}}}$$

Where:

$\bar{x}_1 = $ average for sample 1
$\bar{x}_1 = $ average for sample 2
$s_1 = $ standard deviation for sample 1
$s_2 = $ standard deviation for sample 2
$n_1 = $ size of sample 1
$n_2 = $ size of sample 2
$\sqrt{\dfrac{s_1^2}{n_1} + \dfrac{s_2^2}{n_2}} = s_{\bar{x}_1 - \bar{x}_2} = $ standard error of the difference between two averages

The **standard error of the difference between two averages** is easy to calculate and again relies on the variability that has been found in the samples and their sizes. To illustrate how these significance of difference computations are made, we use the following example, which answers the question, "Do male teens and female teens drink different amounts of sports drinks?"

In a recent survey, teenagers were asked to indicate how many 20-ounce bottles of sports drinks they consume in a typical week. The descriptive statistics revealed that males consume 9 bottles on average and females consume 7.5 bottles of sports drinks on average. The respective standard deviations were found to be 2.0 and 1.2. Both samples were of size 100.

TABLE 13.2

How to Determine If One Group's Average Is Different from Another Group's Average

When metric data are being used, the researcher compares the averages. The procedure is identical to that used when comparing two percents; however, the formulas differ, as averages and standard deviations are appropriate for metric data. In our example, we are investigating the possible differences between males and females with respect to the number of bottles of sports drink they drink in a typical week. The steps are described below.

Step	Description	Our Sports Drink Example
Step 1	Determine the average, standard deviation, and sample size for each of your two samples.	We find that 100 males drink 9.0 bottles, while 100 females drink 7.5 bottles of sports drink per week, on the average. The standard deviations are 2.0 and 1.2, respectively.
Step 2	Compare the two averages by taking their arithmetic difference.	The difference is $(9.0 - 7.5)$ or 1.5. (The sign does not matter.)
Step 3	Determine the *standard error of the difference between two averages*.	$\text{Standard error} = \sqrt{\dfrac{2^2}{100} + \dfrac{1.2^2}{300}}$ $= \sqrt{.04 + .0144}$ $= .233$
Step 4	Calculate z by dividing the difference between the two sample averages by the standard error of the difference between averages.	$z = \dfrac{1.5}{0.233}$ $= 6.43$
Step 5	Using the appropriate statistical table, determine whether the null hypothesis is accepted or rejected at your chosen level of confidence.[*]	In our example, the significance level would be .000, so the null hypothesis is rejected. In other words, males and females are different with respect to the number of bottles of sports drink they consume in a typical week.

[*]The significance level is provided automatically by practically any analysis program that you use.

Table 13.2 presents a step-by-step explanation of the procedures used to test the null hypothesis that males and females are equal in number of bottles of sports drink consumed in a typical week.

Recall that Figure 13.1 illustrates how this analysis takes place. Since we are now working with averages, the two sampling distribution curves would be for the females' and males' averages, with the means of 7.5 and 9.0 under their respective apexes. The standard error of the difference curve would remain essentially as it appears in Figure 13.1, except the computed z value would now be 6.43.

A *statistical* significance level of, say, 95% merely implies that, if we were to do the study 100 times, then 95 times out of 100 the difference we observe now would repeat itself in the sample data. But statistical significance does not tell us anything about how important the difference is, regardless of the size of the difference we see in the observed data. *Practical* significance depends on whether or not there is a managerial application that uses the difference. That is, when the researcher reports a significant difference, it is up to the manager or the researcher working with the manager to assess the practical usefulness of the difference. When the difference is deemed to be important and useful to the marketing manager, then it has practical significance. Marketing Research Application 13.2 illustrates how significant findings can have practical significance for a marketing manager.

MARKETING RESEARCH APPLICATION 13.2

Global

How Differences of Means Analysis Helped a Scandinavian Bank with Its "Mature" Customers

Computer technology has significantly impacted the area of personal banking. In Europe, where wireless telephones are very prevalent, a bank in Finland worried about how its "elderly" customers would relate to banking using one's wireless phone. Researchers sought to compare younger bank customers who were using the mobile banking services to older customers who were less inclined to use it.[7] They administered several Likert statements to both groups of the bank's customers and compared the group averages. The statistically significant findings are listed in the accompanying table.

The differences tests reveal that older customers do have substantial worries about the security of their transactions, and specifically concerns about inputting incorrect information, connection breakdowns, wireless phone power loss, and security of their PINs. Accordingly, the Scandinavian bank was advised to launch a promotional campaign aimed at its "55+" customers to convince them of the security of mobile banking and safeguards against customer input errors and connection losses in midtransaction.

Opinion of Wireless Banking*	Young Customers	Old Customers
Usage barriers		
The use of changing PIN codes in mobile banking services is convenient. (reverse scored)	4.65	4.88
Risk barriers		
I fear that while I am paying a bill by mobile phone, I might make mistakes since the correctness of the inputted information is difficult to check from the screen.	4.64	5.04
I fear that while I am using mobile banking services, the battery of the mobile phone will run out or the connection will otherwise be lost.	4.22	4.67
I fear that while I am using a mobile banking service, I might tap out the information of the bill wrongly.	4.26	4.72
I fear that the list of PIN codes will be lost and end up in the wrong hands.	3.56	4.24
Image barriers		
In my opinion, new technology is often too complicated to be useful.	3.47	3.91

*Based on a scale where 1 = totally disagree and 7 = totally agree

USING THE XL DATA ANALYST TO DETERMINE THE SIGNIFICANCE OF THE DIFFERENCE BETWEEN TWO GROUP AVERAGES

XLDA

Since differences analysis is so vital to marketing research, the XL Data Analyst most definitely performs a difference analysis for the comparison of one group's average to the average of a separate group. To illustrate the operation of this analysis, we will tackle the question of whether or not differences exist between males' versus females' preference for the "super cycle" one-seat hybrid vehicle under consideration by the Advanced Automobile Concepts principals. Recall that the survey asked the question, "What is your preference for the super cycle one-seat hybrid?" and respondents indicated their likelihood on a 5-point balanced symmetric scale where 1 = very undesirable and 7 = very desirable. To illustrate the operation of the XL Data Analyst's two-group-averages comparison analysis, let's see if the

FIGURE 13.4

Using the XL Data
Analyst to Set Up a
Two-Group Averages
Analysis

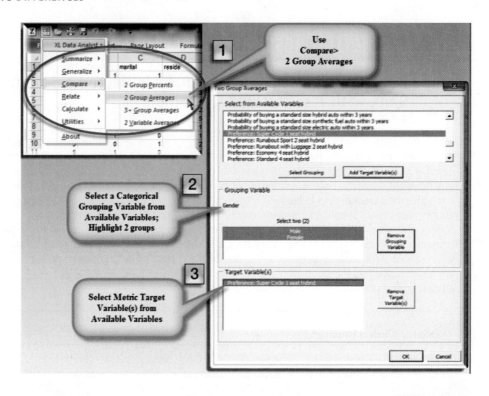

FIGURE 13.5

XL Data Analyst
Two-Group Averages
Differences Analysis
Output

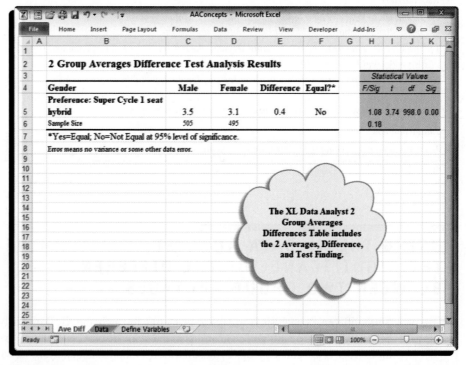

average for males is equal to the average for females. To direct the XL Data Analyst to perform
this analysis, use the Compare–2 Group Averages menu sequence that will open up the selection
window, as shown in Figure 13.4. Select the Grouping Variable of Gender and the two groups:
Male and Female will be automatically highlighted. Then add the preference variable into the
Target Variable window. (Note: You can select multiple Target Variables if you desire.)

Figure 13.5 contains the results of the XL Data Analyst's Two-Group Averages analysis. In the table, you can see that the Male and Female averages (3.5 and 3.1, respectively) are reported along with the number of students comprising each subsample (505 and 495, respectively). The arithmetic difference of 0.4 is indicated, and the hypothesis test outcome is also indicated. In this case, the "No" signifies that the null hypothesis that there is no difference between the two averages is not supported. That is, there is a significant difference between the two averages, with males students showing more interest in the Advanced Automobile Concepts than females in the U.S. population.

> To compare two group averages, specify the two groups with the grouping variable, then select the metric target variable with which the group averages will be computed.

Testing for Significant Differences for More Than Two Group Averages

When a researcher wants to compare the averages of several different groups, **analysis of variance,** sometimes called **ANOVA,** should be used to accomplish such multiple comparisons. The use of the word variance in the name "analysis of variance" is misleading—it is not an analysis of the standard deviations of the groups. To be sure, the standard deviations are taken into consideration, and so are the sample sizes, just as you saw in all of our other statistical inference formulas. Fundamentally, ANOVA (analysis of variance) is an investigation of the differences between the group averages to determine whether sampling errors or true population differences explain their failure to be equal.[8] That is, for our purposes, variance signifies differences between two or more groups' averages—do they vary from one another significantly? Although a term like ANOVA sounds frightfully technical, it is nothing more than a statistical procedure that compares the averages of several groups. The following sections explain to you the basic concepts involved with ANOVA and also how it can be applied to marketing research situations.

> The test of differences among more than two groups' averages is accomplished with ANOVA.

Why Use Analysis of Variance?

When you have two group averages to compare, you simply compare the average of one group to the other's average. When you have more than two groups, the comparisons become complicated, however. To illustrate, let's compare the averages of four different groups: A, B, C, and D. You will need to make the following six comparisons: A:B, A:C, A:D, B:C, B:D, and C:D. This process is tedious and makes it difficult to keep track of all the comparisons.

ANOVA is an efficient, convenient analysis that does all of these tests simultaneously. That's right—you only do one test, and the results tell you where the significant differences are found. ANOVA uses some complicated formulas, and we have found from experience that market researchers do not commit them to memory. Instead, a researcher understands the basic purpose of ANOVA, and becomes adept at interpreting ANOVA output. ANOVA's null hypothesis is that none of all possible group-to-group averages is significantly different: that is, there is not one single significant difference that exists between any possible pair of groups. The alternative hypothesis is that at least one pair is significantly different. When the null hypothesis is not supported in an ANOVA, follow-up analysis must be applied to identify where the significant differences are found.

> ANOVA is an efficient way to compare more than two groups' averages simultaneously.

Again, we will not provide details on ANOVA formulas other than to say that because multiple pairs of group averages are being tested, ANOVA uses the F test statistic, and the significance value that appears on standard statistical output is the degree of support for the null hypothesis. As you will soon find out, the XL Data Analyst does the statistical interpretation of ANOVA and, if it finds that the null hypothesis is not supported at the 95% level of confidence, it provides a table that shows you the various group averages and identifies which ones are significantly different.

Here is an example that will help you to understand how ANOVA works and when to use it. A major department store conducts a survey, and one of the questions on the survey is, "At what department did you last make a purchase for over \$250?" There are four departments where significant numbers of respondents made these purchases: (1) Electronics, (2) Home & Garden, (3) Sporting Goods, and (4) Automotive. Another question on the survey is, "How likely are you to return to this department to purchase another item for over \$250 the next time?" The respondents indicate how likely they are to do this on a 7-point scale where 1 = very unlikely and 7 = very likely. To summarize the findings, the researcher calculates the average of how likely each group is to return to the department store and purchase another major item from that same department.

How Likely Are Customers to Return?*

	Automotive	Electronics	Home & Garden	Sporting Goods
Group Average**	**2.2**	**5.1**	**5.3**	**5.6**
Automotive		2.2:5.1 Unequal	2.2:5.3 Unequal	2.2:5.6 Unequal
Electronics			5.1:5.3 Equal	5.1:5.6 Equal
Home & Garden				5.3:5.6 Equal

*Significant differences are noted by "unequal."
**Based on a scale where 1 = very unlikely and 7 = very likely to return to purchase another item in this department.

The researcher who is doing the analysis decides to compare these averages statistically with ANOVA, and the findings are provided in the table you see here. When you look at this table, you will find that the Automotive Department is definitely very different from the other three departments in the store. Its average is only 2.2, while the other departments' averages range from 5.1 to 5.6. To indicate where significant differences are found, the researcher places an "unequal" notation in the cell where the group row and the group column intersect. An "equal" notation indicates there is no significant difference between the two group means. For instance, in our illustrative table, the "unequal" in the Automotive row reveals that the Automotive Department average of 2.2 is different from the Electronics Department average of 5.1. In fact, the "unequal" notations denote that the Automotive Department's average is significantly different from each of the three other departments' averages. The "equal" entries denote that the averages for the other three departments are not significantly different from each other. In other words, there is a good indication that the patrons who bought an item for more than \$250 from the department store's Automotive Department are not as likely to buy again as are patrons who bought from any of the three other departments.

Again from Figure 13.1, the notions are relevant, except we now have four sampling distribution curves—one for each department. The Electronics, Home & Garden, and Sporting Goods sampling distribution curves would overlap a great deal, while the Automotive Department curve would stand separately on the lower end of the scale. Because ANOVA takes on all groups simultaneously, you would need to modify Figure 13.1 by adding a separate standard error of the difference curve for each of the six possible group-to-group comparisons, and you would see that the computed z value was large for every Automotive Department average comparison with each of the other three departments' averages.

The need to understand differences between multiple groups is fundamental not only to marketing researchers, but to other business researchers as well. Marketing Research Application 13.3 shows that differences analyses reveal why businesspersons encounter difficulties when dealing with individuals who originate from different cultural regions.[9]

> A researcher can see the differences (or lack thereof) among several groups' averages with a table based on ANOVA findings.

In a store, the service quality may differ from department to department.

Ethics

MARKETING RESEARCH APPLICATION 13.3

Multiple Groups Analysis Reveals Ethnical Philosophy Differences by Region of the Globe

Global business partnerships often encounter opposing beliefs as to what business practices or customs are acceptable. In order to understand cultural differences such as these, researchers sought to compare the ethnical orientations of university students who represented four different global regions: Anglo-American, Latin American, Far Eastern, and Arab. They measured and compared the ethnical orientation of these students. All four groups were found to have distinct and statistically significant differences. The ethnical orientations they found are presented in the following table.

These differences reveal that American businesspersons are pragmatic, and they attempt to grasp the opportunity of the moment. At the other extreme, Arab businesspersons value consistency, tradition, and formality. Asian businesspersons may appear to be confused or uncertain, but it is actually ethnical orientation that fosters this appearance, for they neither value the opportunity nor adhere to precedents; hence, they ponder business decisions for a considerable time. Finally, Latin American businesspersons may be opportunistic, depending on the nature of the decision at hand. Obviously, Anglo-American and Arab businesspersons have the greatest ethnical orientation distance between them, so one would predict more difficulties in the business relations between companies that reside in these two global regions.

Global Region	Ethnical Orientation	Description
Anglo-American	*Highly utilitarian*	*Considers every decision to be unique, so past precedents and consistency are unimportant.*
Latin American	*Moderately utilitarian*	*Considers some decisions to be unique, so past precedents may or may not be used.*
Far Eastern	*Deliberate*	*Does not have a strong decision-making orientation, so appears indecisive or a "fence sitter."*
Arab	*Traditional*	*Considers past precedents to be important, so the uniqueness of each decision is typically not considered.*

USING THE XL DATA ANALYST TO DETERMINE THE SIGNIFICANCE OF THE DIFFERENCE AMONG MORE THAN TWO GROUP AVERAGES

Previously, we illustrated the use of a two-group averages difference analysis by comparing the preferences of males versus females on their preferences for the super cycle one-seat hybrid vehicle under consideration. As you know, there are five age categories—18-24, 35-34, 35-49, 50-64, and 65 and older—and all five classes are represented in our random sample of U.S. households. So, this is precisely an instance where ANOVA applies. Figure 13.6 shows the menu commands and variable selection windows you use with the XL Data Analyst to set up three-plus–group averages analysis. Notice that the menu sequence is "Compare–3+ Group Averages," and the Grouping Variable is "Age category," while the Target Variable is "Preference: Super Cycle 1 seat hybrid."

Figure 13.7 reveals that the XL Data Analyst ANOVA output is in the same table format as our introductory example on the department store purchase intentions. That is, the ANOVA output table is arranged in ascending order based on the group averages, and an "equal" or "Not equal" is placed in the intersection cell for each possible pair of averages. An "Equal" notation means that there is a significant difference between the two averages, whereas a "Not equal" designation indicates that there is no support for the null hypothesis that the two group averages are equal. Granted, the table is a bit complicated when you first examine it; however, it is much more efficient than the ten different two-group average differences analyses that would be necessary if ANOVA was not available.

Examine the ANOVA table output in Figure 13.7 to ensure that it is apparent to you that those in the 18-24 group have the highest preference for the super cycle one-seat hybrid, and their average (4.9) is significantly different from all other groups. Those in the 50-64 group,

FIGURE 13.6

Using the XL Data Analyst to Set Up a Three-Plus–Group Averages Differences Analysis

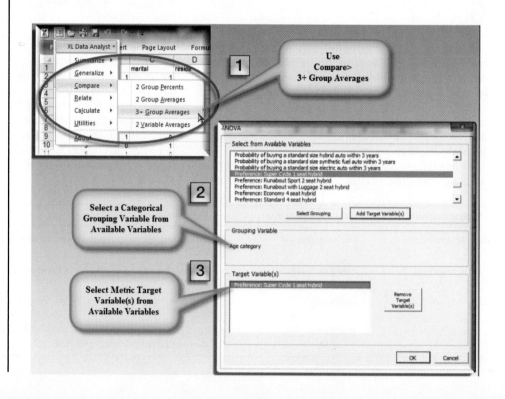

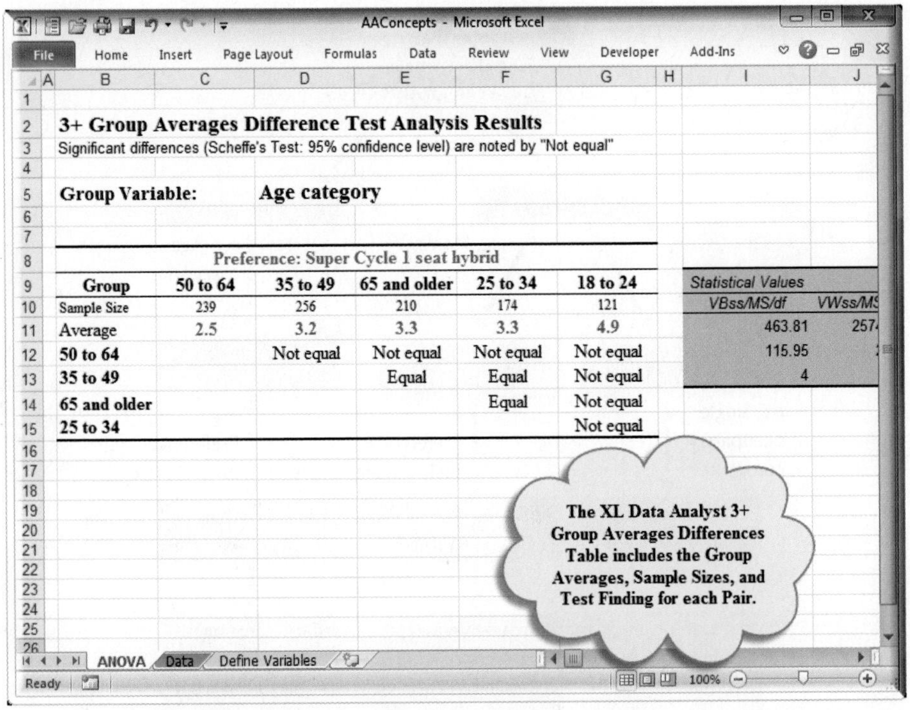

3+ Group Averages Difference Test Analysis Results

Significant differences (Scheffe's Test: 95% confidence level) are noted by "Not equal"

Group Variable: **Age category**

Preference: Super Cycle 1 seat hybrid

Group	50 to 64	35 to 49	65 and older	25 to 34	18 to 24
Sample Size	239	256	210	174	121
Average	2.5	3.2	3.3	3.3	4.9
50 to 64		Not equal	Not equal	Not equal	Not equal
35 to 49			Equal	Equal	Not equal
65 and older				Equal	Not equal
25 to 34					Not equal

Statistical Values	
VBss/MS/df	VWss/MS
463.81	257
115.95	
4	

FIGURE 13.7

XL Data Analyst Three-Plus–Group Averages Differences Analysis Output

in turn, have an average (2.5) that is significantly different from all other age categories. Finally, the averages of 35-49 (3.2), 65 and older (3.3), and 25-34 (3.3) are not significantly different. As with other XL Data Analyst results, the relevant statistical values are included for users with expertise and interest in examining them.

The three-plus–group average comparison of the XL Data Analyst is an ANOVA with an output table that indicates the pair(s) of averages that are significantly different.

Flow Chart of Differences Analyses for Groups

In Figure 13.8 you will find a flow chart of how to perform various differences tests when group percents or averages are involved. Note the first question, "How many groups are being compared?" With two groups, the next task is to ascertain if a categorical or a metric variable is under analysis. With a categorical variable, one does two group percents analysis, whereas with a metric variable, one does two group averages analysis. If the researcher is investigating among three or more groups and the variable under analysis is metric, then he or she uses three-plus group averages analysis, commonly known as ANOVA. (If the researcher is investigating a categorical variable with three-plus groups, a completely different analysis, called cross tabulation, is useful. This analysis is described in the next chapter.)

Testing for Significant Differences Between the Averages of Two Variables

The last differences analysis we will describe does not involve groups. Instead, it concerns comparing the average of one variable (question on the survey) to the average of another variable.[10] With this analysis, the entire sample is used, but two different variables are compared. For

FIGURE 13.8

Group Differences
Analysis Flow Chart

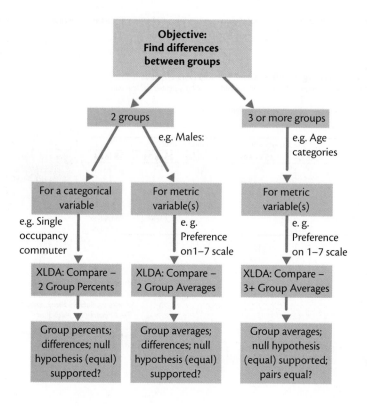

example, if a pharmaceuticals company was seeking to improve its cold remedy medication, a survey could be used to determine, "How important is it that your cold remedy relieves your _____?" using a 10-point scale of 1 = not important to 10 = very important for each of several cold symptoms such as "congestion," "cough," or "runny nose." The question then becomes, "Are any two average importance levels significantly different?" To determine the answer to this question, we must run an analysis to determine the significance of the difference between these averages; but the same respondents answered both questions, so you do not have two independent groups. In this case, you have two independent questions with one group. When you find significant differences between the averages of two variables such as ratings of importance or performance, you know that levels of the ratings are truly different in the population that the sample represents. Of course, the *two variables should be measured on the same metric scale*; otherwise, you are comparing apples to oranges.

> When comparing the averages of two variables, it is important that these variables be measured with the same scale.

A graph of the test for the difference in the averages of two variables would appear as you have seen in Figure 13.1. You now understand that the two bell-shaped curves would be the sampling distributions of the two variables being compared, and the apex of each one would be its average in the sample. When there is a small amount of overlap for the two curves, there is a true difference in the population averages. That is, if the survey were replicated multiple times, and the averages for all these replications were graphed, then they would appear similar to the bell-shaped curves in Figure 13.1, and the two averages would rarely, if ever, be equal (the null hypothesis). The formula for this statistical test is, in fact, similar to the one for the difference between two group averages. That is, the two averages are compared (take the difference), and this quantity is divided by the standard error of the difference to compute the z value. You can refer to the formula for the difference between two group averages for a conceptual understanding of the computations in this analysis. The logic we described still applies, but there must be an

> The difference analysis for the averages of two variables uses logic very similar to that used in the analysis of the difference between two group averages.

adjustment factor (that we will not discuss here) because there is only one sample involved. Directional hypothesis tests are possible as well.

USING THE XL DATA ANALYST TO DETERMINE THE SIGNIFICANCE OF THE DIFFERENCES BETWEEN THE AVERAGES OF TWO VARIABLES

As was indicated, the proper use of a differences test for two variables' averages requires that you select two metric variables that are measured with the same scale units. We might wonder if the overall preference of an economy hybrid vehicle differs from the preference for a standard model hybrid vehicle. Are these two averages significantly different, or is the arithmetic difference simply a reflection of sample size error and variability in the respondents' answers? To answer this question, we can use the XL Data Analyst to perform a Two-Variables Averages comparison. The menu sequence is Compare–2 Variable Averages, which opens up the selection menu for this procedure. In Figure 13.9, you can see that two selection window panes each list all of the available variables, so you must highlight a variable in the "Variable One" pane and another in the "Variable Two" pane to make a pair whose averages will be compared, and click this pair into the Selected Variable Pairs windowpane. You will see in Figure 13.9 that the "Preference: Economy 4 seat hybrid" and "Preference: Standard 4 seat hybrid" are selected, and they are identified as a "pair" in the selection windowpane. (Multiple pairs may be selected in a single analysis run, if desired.)

> Use the XL Data Analyst to select the pairs of metric variables whose averages are to be compared.

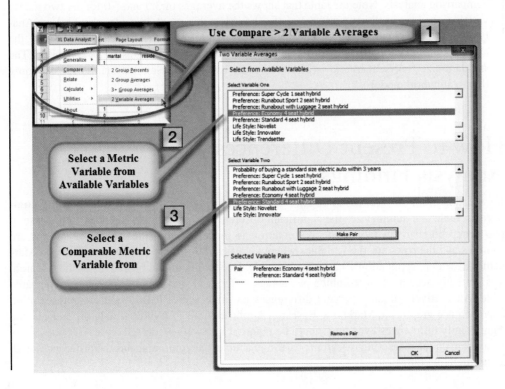

FIGURE 13.9

Using the XL Data Analyst to Set Up a Two-Variable Averages Differences Analysis

FIGURE 13.10

XL Data Analyst
Two-Variable Averages
Differences Analysis
Output

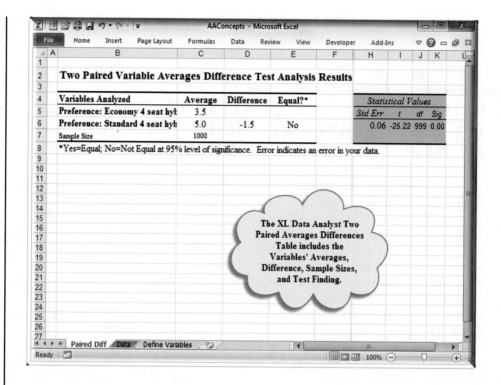

Figure 13.10 has the resulting XL Data Analyst output for our Two-Variable Averages comparison analysis. Note the table that shows the averages of 3.5 and 5.0 for the two metric variables, and the arithmetic difference of -1.5. Most important, however, the XL Data Analyst has indicated in this table that the difference is a significant difference. In other words, the null hypothesis that there is no difference between these two averages is not supported. The standard size four-seat hybrid is preferred more by U.S. households than is the economy four-seat hybrid model.

How to Present Differences Analysis Findings

In reporting group differences to clients, marketing researchers often construct a **group comparison table** that summarizes the significant differences in an efficient manner. In the case of two group comparison tables, the presentation is made side-by-side where the groups are columns and the rows are the variables where significant differences are found. Refer to Marketing Research Application 13.2 for such a table. Depending on the objectives of the research, it is perfectly acceptable to combine percentage differences and mean differences in the same table. Alternatively, if only percent differences are involved, a highly effective presentation approach is a graph (see Marketing Research Application 13.1). With variable differences, the significantly differences averages should be reported in a well-organized table. Of course, it is incumbent on the marketing researcher to design a table that communicates the differences with a minimum of confusion.

When the researcher is reporting differences found from ANOVA, the table presentation becomes more challenging as there can be overlaps of nonsignificant differences and significant differences. In this case, we recommend that the researcher use or modify the table generated in the XL Data Analyst 3+ groups analysis output (similar to the department store example table in the chapter).

Summary

The chapter discusses the reasons why differences are important to marketing managers. Basically, market segmentation implications underlie most differences analyses. It is important that differences are statistically significant, but it is also vital that they are meaningful as a basis of marketing strategy. Differences between two percentages in two independent samples can be tested for statistical significance. The chapter includes formulas and a step-by-step description of how the relevant statistical values are calculated and interpreted, and a description of the analysis test procedure using averages. In addition, the chapter introduces you to the differences analysis procedures in the XL Data Analyst, used to determine if two groups' percentages or two groups' averages are significantly different.

When a researcher has three or more groups and wishes to compare their various averages, the correct procedure involves analysis of variance, or ANOVA. ANOVA is a technique that tests all possible pairs of averages for all the groups involved and indicates which pairs are significantly different. We do not provide ANOVA formulas, as they are quite complicated, but we show how the XL Data Analyst is used to perform ANOVA and identify what pair(s) of group averages are significantly different. A flow chart helps to identify the proper group differences analysis to use. Finally, we briefly discuss the comparison of two variables' averages for significant differences. Here, the researcher is seeking to find real differences, for example, between the levels of ratings such as importance or performance that exist in the population represented by the sample being used in the analysis.

Key Terms

Market segmentation (p. 291)
Alternative hypothesis (p. 294)
Standard error of the difference
   between two percentages (p. 294)

Grouping variable (p. 297)
Target variable (p. 297)
Standard error of the difference
   between two averages (p. 299)

Analysis of variance
   (ANOVA) (p. 303)
Group comparison
   table (p. 310)

Review Questions

1. What are differences and why should marketing researchers be concerned with them?
2. What are the three ways a researcher can investigate for differences?
3. Why does the nature of the scale (categorical or metric) being used matter when performing a differences test?
4. What is the null hypothesis and what is the alternative hypothesis for a differences test?
5. When the percentages or the averages of two groups are compared, what is the nature of the comparison operation?
6. When a standard error of a difference (between percentages or averages) is computed, what two factors are taken into account, and how does each affect the size of the standard error?
7. Describe how a directional hypothesis about the difference between two percentages or two averages is tested.
8. What is ANOVA, and when is it used? Why is it termed efficient?
9. What is the null hypothesis in ANOVA?
10. How is a test of the difference between the averages of two variables different from a test of the difference between the averages of two groups with the same variable? How is it similar?

Application Questions

11. Are the following two sample results significantly different?

	Sample 1	Sample 2	Confidence Level	Your Finding?
a.	Mean: 10.6 Std. dev: 1.5 $n = 150$	Mean: 11.7 Std. dev: 2.5 $n = 300$	95%	
b.	Percent: 45% $n = 350$	Percent: 54% $n = 250$	99%	
c.	Mean: 1,500 Std. dev: 550 $n = 1,200$	Mean: 1,250 Std. dev: 500 $n = 500$	95%	

12. Demonstrate your understanding of your work in question 11 by drawing the sampling distributions of each case—a, b, and c—in the format presented in Figure 13.1 is on page 296.

13. A researcher is investigating different types of customers for a sporting goods store. In a survey, respondents have indicated how much they exercise in approximate minutes per week. These respondents have also rated the performance of the sporting goods store across twelve difference characteristics such as good value for the price, convenience of location, and helpfulness of the sales clerks. The researcher used a 7-point rating scale for these twelve characteristics, where 1 = poor performance and 7 = excellent performance. How can the researcher investigate differences in the ratings based on the amount of exercise reported by the respondents?

14. A shoe manufacturer suspects there are six market segments that it can use effectively in its target marketing: toddlers, middle-school children, high school students, young and active adults, professionals, and senior citizens. How many pairs of averages can be assessed for significant differences? Specify each separate pair.

15. A marketing manager of a Web-based catalog sales company uses a segmentation scheme based on the incomes of target customers. The segmentation system has four segments: (1) low income, (2) moderate income, (3) high income, and (4) wealthy. The company database holds information on every customer's purchases over the past several years, and the total dollars spent is one of the prominent variables. The marketing manager finds that the average total dollar purchases for the four groups are as follows:

Market Segment	Average Total Dollar Purchases
Low income	$101
Moderate income	$120
High income	$231
Wealthy	$595

Construct a table that is based on how the XL Data Analyst presents its findings for ANOVA that illustrates that the low- and moderate-income groups are not different from each other, but the other groups are significantly different from one another.

Case 13.1 **The *Daily Advocate* Lost Subscribers Survey**

The *Daily Advocate* is a newspaper serving the Capital City area, which accounts for about 350,000 households. The *Daily Advocate* has been the dominant daily newspaper in the area for the past fifty years. At one time, it was estimated that nine of ten Capital City–area households subscribed or otherwise bought the *Daily Advocate*. In the past decade, Capital City has undergone a growth spurt due primarily to three high-technology industrial "parks" where a great many Internet, computer equipment, and biotechnology companies have located. However, the circulation of the *Daily Advocate* did not experience a corresponding spurt; in fact, the circulation peaked in 1998, and it has been slowly declining ever since. It is now estimated that only seven of ten Capital City–area households subscribe to the *Daily Advocate*.

The circulation manager of the *Daily Advocate* commissions a market research study to determine what factors underlie the circulation attrition. Specifically, the survey is designed to compare current *Daily Advocate* subscribers with those who have dropped their subscriptions in the past year. A telephone survey is conducted with both sets of individuals. Following is a summary of the key findings—using a 95% level of confidence—from the study.

1. Why has the *Daily Advocate*'s circulation fallen in the face of a population boom in Capital City?
2. What marketing strategies should the *Daily Advocate* consider in order to sustain itself as the primary news vehicle in Capital City?

Variable Analyzed	Current Subscribers	Lost Subscribers	Difference	Finding
Length of residence in the city	*20.1 years*	*5.4 years*	*14.7 years*	*Not equal*
Length of time as a subscriber	*27.2 years*	*1.3 years*	*25.9 years*	*Not equal*
Watch local TV news program(s)	*87%*	*85%*	*2.0%*	*Equal*
Watch national TV news program(s)	*72%*	*79%*	*−7.0%*	*Equal*
Obtain news from the Internet	*13%*	*23%*	*−10.0%*	*Not equal*
Satisfaction* with:				
Delivery of newspaper	*5.5*	*4.9*	*0.6*	*Equal*
Coverage of local news	*6.1*	*5.8*	*0.3*	*Equal*
Coverage of national news	*5.5*	*2.3*	*3.2*	*Not equal*
Coverage of local sports	*6.3*	*5.9*	*0.4*	*Equal*
Coverage of national sports	*5.7*	*3.2*	*2.5*	*Not equal*
Coverage of local social news	*5.8*	*5.2*	*0.6*	*Equal*
Editorial stance of the newspaper	*6.1*	*4.0*	*2.1*	*Not equal*
Value for subscription price	*5.2*	*4.8*	*0.4*	*Equal*

*Average, based on a 7-point scale where 1 = very dissatisfied and 7 = very satisfied

Case 13.2 **Your Integrated Case**

The Advanced Automobile Concepts Survey Differences Analysis

Cory Rogers called a meeting with Nick Thomas, and Celeste Brown attended it. At the beginning of the meeting, Rogers's wife called with news that their five-year-old daughter was having a stomachache at school, and he was to pick her up and take her to the doctor. Rogers excused himself, saying, "I am sorry about this, but these things happen when you are a dual-career household. Celeste, sit with Nick for a bit and find out what questions he has about the survey findings. Then take a shot at the analysis, and we'll meet about it tomorrow afternoon. I am sure that Cory Junior will be over his stomach ailment by then."

After meeting for about twenty minutes, Brown understood that the Advanced Automobile Concepts division principals were encouraged by the findings of the survey which indicate that there is substantial demand for the various types of high-mileage hybrid automobiles under consideration. Depending on development costs, prices, and other financial considerations, it seems that any one or a combination of the hybrid automobiles could be viable. The next step in their planning is to identify the target market for each hybrid automobile type under consideration. This step is crucial to market strategy as it is known that the more precise the target market definition is, the more specific and pinpointed will be the marketing strategy. For a

first cut at the market segment descriptions, the survey included the following commonly used demographic factors.

- Gender
- Marital status
- Age category
- Education category
- Income category
- Home town size category

While the survey measured the likelihood of buying each hybrid type, Brown learned that Thomas considers preferences to be a better measure, because the hybrid model descriptions included seat size, mpg estimates, and styling notions.

Your task is to apply appropriate differences analysis to your AAConcepts XL Data Analyst data set to determine the target market descriptions for each of the five possible hybrid models.

1. Super cycle one-seat model; 120+ mpg city
2. Runabout sport two-seat model; 90 mpg city, 120 mpg highway
3. Runabout with luggage two-seat model; 80 mpg city, 110 mpg highway
4. Economy four-seat model; 70 mpg city, 100 mpg highway
5. Standard four-seat model; 60 mpg city, 80 mpg highway

14

Determining Relationships

LEARNING OBJECTIVES

- To learn what is meant by a "relationship" between two variables

- To understand when and how cross-tabulations with chi-square analysis are applied

- To become knowledgeable about the use and interpretation of correlations

- To learn about the application and interpretation of regression analysis

- To become proficient in the use of the XL Data Analyst to execute various types of relationship analyses

How Qualtrics Provides the "Total" Package

Visit Qualtrics at www.qualtrics.com.

We help many of our clients at Qualtrics with their marketing research projects. We do much more than help with the design of their questionnaires. In working closely with our clients, we often see that they are interested in knowing answers to such questions as: "Which package design is most effective in increasing awareness of our product on supermarket shelves?" "What type of pre-store opening promotion is most effective in producing sales during Grand Openings?" "Which customer demographic is most strongly related to product purchase/non-purchase?" "Which type of sales training method results in the least sales force turnover?" These are just a few of the questions our clients have in which they are really asking to understand the association between two variables. Which "type of pre-store promotion" is associated with "sales"? "Which package design is associated with the level of awareness?" In these examples, we have two variables and we wish to know if they are associated.

Marketing research projects can be conducted that will answer these questions. When marketing researchers collect the data needed

to answer the questions, they want to know if the pattern of association revealed in the data, if any, is statistically significant. That is, does the pattern revealed in the sample data exist in the population? Fortunately, statisticians have given us some tools to answer this question. You will learn about these tools in this chapter.

Scott Smith, Ph.D.
Founder, Qualtrics Inc.

Source: Scott Smith, Qualtrics.

This chapter illustrates the usefulness of statistical analyses beyond generalization and differences tests. Often marketers are interested in relationships among variables. For example, Frito-Lay wants to know what kinds of people, under what circumstances, choose to buy Doritos, Fritos, and any of the other items in the Frito-Lay line. A newspaper wants to understand the lifestyle characteristics of its prospective readers so that it is able to modify or change sections in the newspaper to better suit its audience. Furthermore, the newspaper desires information about various types of subscribers so as to communicate this information to its advertisers, helping them in copy design and advertisement placement within the various newspaper sections. For all of these cases, there are statistical procedures available, termed relationship analyses, that determine answers to these questions. Relationship analyses determine whether stable patterns exist between two (or more) variables; they are the central topic of this chapter.

We begin the chapter by describing what a relationship is and why relationships are useful concepts. Then we see how a cross-tabulation can be used to compute a chi-square value that, in turn, can be assessed to determine whether a statistically significant relationship exists between the two variables. We next move to a general discussion of correlation coefficients, and we illustrate the use and interpretation of correlations. The remainder of this chapter is devoted to regression analysis, which is a powerful predictive technique and one that fosters understanding of phenomena under study. As in our previous analysis chapters, we show you how to use the XL Data Analyst to perform these analyses and how to interpret the resulting output.

Where We Are:

1. Establish the need for marketing research
2. Define the problem
3. Establish research objectives
4. Determine research design
5. Identify information types and sources
6. Determine methods of accessing data
7. Design data-collection forms
8. Determine sample plan and size
9. Collect data
10. Analyze data
11. Prepare and present final report

What Is a Relationship Between Two Variables?

In order to describe a relationship between two variables, we first recall the scale characteristic called description, introduced in Chapter 7. Every scale has unique descriptors, sometimes called levels or labels, which identify the different positions on that scale. The term *levels* implies that the scale is metric, whereas the term *labels* implies that the scale is categorical. A simple categorical label is a "yes" or "no," for instance, if a respondent is a buyer (yes) or nonbuyer (no) of a particular product or service. Of course, if the researcher measured how many times a respondent bought a product, the level would be the number of times, and the scale would be metric because this scale would satisfy the assumptions of a real number scale.

A **relationship** is a consistent and systematic linkage between the levels or labels for two variables. Relationships are invaluable tools for the marketing researcher, because a relationship can be used for prediction and it fosters understanding of the phenomena under study. For example, if Canon finds that many of its mini HD camcorder buyers have children, it will predict that

> A relationship describes the linkage between the levels or labels for two variables.

315

If an airline finds a positive relationship between frequent flying and use of its website, it can design pop-up ads for "heavy" flyers.

those families with children who are thinking about purchasing a camcorder will be good prospects for its mini HD camcorder models. Furthermore, it seems logical that the parents are taking videos of their children, so Canon can use the promotional theme of "making memories" or "capturing special moments" because it understands that this is the primary purchasing motivation involved here.

Here is another example: If American Airlines discovers a relationship between the number of American Airlines frequent flyer miles and the amount of time that its customers spend on American's website, it can predict that heavy users of its website will also be its frequent flyers. Further, since frequent flyers take a lot of trips, they are undoubtedly checking out American's website for flight schedules for prospective trips or travel specials where they can use their frequent flyer miles benefits. So, if American can identify its frequent flyer website visitors by a registration process or cookies, it can direct pop-up advertisements or other information of interest to them.

Categorical Variables Relationships

In the instance of relationships between two categorical variables with labels, McDonald's knows from experience that breakfast customers typically purchase coffee, whereas lunch customers typically purchase soft drinks. For example purposes, our labels are "breakfast" and "lunch" for choice of meal, and "coffee" and "soft drink" for choice of drink. The relationship is in no way exclusive—there is no guarantee that a breakfast customer will always order coffee or that a lunch customer will always order a soft drink. In general, though, this relationship exists (see Figure 14.1). The relationship is simply that breakfast customers tend to purchase coffee and lunch customers tend to purchase soft drinks. So, you could make a prediction as to what type of drink would be ordered by the next McDonald's breakfast or lunch customer that you encounter, and you would feel fairly confident that your prediction would be correct most of the time. Often graphs such as the stacked cylinder graph in Figure 14.1 are excellent for communicating the nature of categorical variable relationships.

Stacked cylinder graphs can be used to show categorical variable relationships.

Cross-Tabulation Analysis

A graph such the one in Figure 14.1 provides visualization of a categorical variable relationship, but you should not develop one unless you are assured that the relationship is statistically significant, meaning that the pattern of the relationship will remain essentially as it is if you replicated your survey a great many times and averaged all of the findings. The analytical technique that assesses the statistical significance of categorical variable relationships is **cross-tabulation analysis.** With cross-tabulation, the two categorical variables are arranged in a **cross-tabulation table,** defined as a table in which data are compared using a row-and-column format. The intersection of a row and a column is called a **cross-tabulation cell.** As you will soon see, a cross-tabulation analysis accounts for all of the relevant label-to-label relationships and it is the basis for the assessment of statistical significance of the relationships.

Cross-tabulation analysis can be applied to categorical variables with more than two rows or columns. For example, let's ask a sample of college students, "Did you attend a movie in the past month?" The possible answers are "yes" and "no." We will also determine if the respondent is an "underclass student" or "upperclass student" or "graduate student," so we now have two rows and three columns in our cross-tabulation table (see Table 14.1). The columns are labeled Underclass Student or Upperclass Student or Graduate Student, whereas the rows are labeled either Yes or No for movie attendance in the past month. In addition, we have provided a column for the Row Totals, and a row for the Column Totals. The intersection cell for the Row Totals column and the Column Totals row is called the Grand Total.

TYPES OF FREQUENCIES AND PERCENTAGES IN A CROSS-TABULATION TABLE Table 14.1 is a **frequencies table** because it contains the raw counts for the cells based on the complete data set. From the grand total, we can see that there are 370 students in the sample, and from the row and column total cells, we can identify how many of each category of student classification (150, 170, and 50) and how many of "yes" versus "no" movie attendees (195 and 175) are in the sample. The cross-tabulation cell for "underclass student" and "yes" movie attendance reveals that there are 105 respondents, and the other intersection cells reveal their respective counts of respondents as well. So, a cross-tabulation table contains the raw counts and totals pertaining to all of the relevant cross-tabulation cells for the two categorical variables being analyzed.

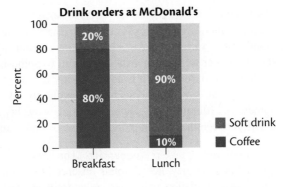

FIGURE 14.1

Example of a Relationship for Type of Drink Ordered for Breakfast and for Lunch at McDonald's

> Use a cross-tabulation table for the data defining possible relationships between two categorical variables.

> A frequencies table contains the raw counts of various relationships possible in a cross-tabulation.

TABLE 14.1

Cross-Tabulation Table for Movie Attendance and Student Classification

		Student Classification			
		Underclass Student	Upperclass Student	Graduate Student	Row Totals
Attended a Movie in the Past Month?	Yes	105	85	5	195
	No	45	85	45	175
Column Totals		150	170	50	370 **Grand Total**

CHI-SQUARE ANALYSIS OF A CROSS-TABULATION TABLE Chi-square (χ^2) analysis is the examination of frequencies for two categorical variables in a cross-tabulation table to determine whether the variables have a significant relationship.[1] The chi-square analysis begins when the researcher formulates a statistical null hypothesis that the two variables under investigation are not related. Actually, it is not necessary for the researcher to state this hypothesis in a formal sense, for chi-square analysis always explicitly takes this null hypothesis into account. Stated somewhat differently, chi-square analysis always begins with the assumption that no relationship exists between the two categorical variables under analysis.

Observed and Expected Frequencies. The raw counts in Table 14.1 are referred to as **observed frequencies,** as they are the totals observed by counting the number of respondents who are in each cross-tabulation cell, such as underclass students who did attend a movie.[2] Long ago, someone working with cross-tabulations discovered that if you multiplied the row total times the column total and divided that product by the grand total for every cross-tabulation cell, the resulting **expected frequencies** would perfectly embody these cell frequencies if there was no significant relationship present. Here is the formula for the expected cell frequencies.

Formula for an expected cell frequency

$$\text{Expected cell frequency} = \frac{\text{Cell column total} \times \text{Cell row total}}{\text{Grand total}}$$

The expected frequencies perfectly embody the null hypothesis (of no relationship), so the expected frequencies are a baseline, and if the observed frequencies are very different from the expected frequencies, there is reason to believe that a relationship does exist.

Computed Chi-Square Value We will describe this analytical procedure briefly in the hope that our description adds to your understanding of cross-tabulation analysis. The observed and expected cross-tabulation frequencies are compared by applying the following Chi-square formula, and the support or nonsupport of the null hypothesis is determined by inspecting the computed Chi-square value.

Chi-square formula

$$\chi^2 = \sum_{i=1}^{n} \frac{(\text{Observed}_i - \text{Expected}_i)^2}{\text{Expected}_i}$$

Where:

Observed$_i$ = observed frequency in cell i
Expected$_i$ = expected frequency in cell i
n = number of cells

The formula holds that each cross-tabulation cell expected frequency be subtracted from its associated observed frequency, and then that difference be squared to avoid a cancellation effect of minus and plus differences. Then the squared difference is divided by the expected frequency to adjust for differences in expected cell sizes. All of these are then summed to arrive at the computed chi-square value. We have provided a step-by-step description of this analysis[3] in Table 14.2.

By now, you should realize that when arriving at a computed value, a statistician will most certainly be comparing it to a table value to assess its statistical significance. In Table 14.2, we found a computed chi-square value of 55.1. We then have to consult with a chi-square value table to see if our computed chi-square value is greater than the critical table value. As with some statistical distributions, the chi-square distribution is not bell-shaped, and you must calculate the degrees of freedom with the formula in Table 14.2 in order to know where to look in the chi-square table for the critical value. Suffice it to say that with higher degrees of freedom,

TABLE 14.2

How to Determine If You Have a Significant Relationship Using Chi-Square Analysis

Step	Description	College Students Attending Movies Example ($n = 370$)				

Step 1 — Set up the cross-tabulation table and determine the cell counts known as the *observed frequencies*.

		Student Classification			
		Underclass Student	Upperclass Student	Graduate Student	Row Totals
Attended a Movie?	Yes	105	85	5	195
	No	45	85	45	175
Column Totals		150	170	50	370

Step 2 — Calculate the expected frequencies using the formula:

$$\text{Expected cell frequency} = \frac{\text{Cell Column total} \times \text{Cell row total}}{\text{Grand total}}$$

		Student Classification			
		Underclass Student	Upperclass Student	Graduate Student	Row Totals
Attended a Movie?	Yes	79.1	89.6	26.3	195
	No	70.9	80.4	23.6	175
Column Totals		150	170	50	370

Step 3 — Calculate the computed chi-square value using the chi-square formula.

$$\chi^2 = (105 - 79.1)^2/79.1 + (85 - 89.6)^2/89.6 + (5 - 26.3)^2/26.3 +$$
$$(45 - 70.9)^2/70.9 + (85 - 80.4)^2/80.4 + (45 - 23.6)^2/55.3$$
$$= 55.1.$$

Step 4 — Determine the critical chi-square value from a chi-square table, using the following formula: (Number of rows − 1) × (Number of columns − 1) = Degrees of freedom (*df*).

$$df = (2 - 1) \times (3 - 1)$$
$$= 2$$

You would need to use your computed *df* and a chi-square distribution table to find that the critical table value is 5.99.

Step 5 — Evaluate whether or not the null hypothesis of *no* relationship is supported.

The computed chi-square value of 55.1 is larger than the table value of 5.99, so the hypothesis is not supported. There *is* a relationship between student status and going to a movie in the past month.

the table chi-square value is larger, but there is no single value that can be memorized as in our 1.96 number for a normal distribution. A cross-tabulation can have any number of rows and columns, depending on the labels that identify the various groups in the two categorical variables being analyzed, and since the degrees of freedom are based on the number of rows and columns, there is no single critical chi-square value that we can identify for all cases.

Table 14.2 expresses that our computed value of 55.1 is, indeed, greater than the table value of 5.99, meaning that there is no support for our null hypothesis of no relationship. Yes, we do have a significant relationship, so now we can describe the relationship we have discovered.

How to Present a Significant Cross-Tabulation Finding

As illustrated when we introduced cross-tabulation analysis, the best communication vehicle in this case is a graph. Furthermore, we strongly recommend that you convert your raw counts (observed frequencies) to percentages for optimal communication. When you determine that a significant relationship does exist (that is, there is no support for the null hypothesis of no relationship), two additional cross-tabulation tables can be calculated that are valuable in revealing underlying relationships. The **column percentages table** divides the raw frequencies by their associated column total raw frequency, as shown in the following formula.

Formula for a column cell percentage

$$\text{Column cell percentage} = \frac{\text{Cell frequency}}{\text{Cell column total}}$$

The **row percentages table** presents the data with the row totals as the 100% base for each. That is, a row cell percentage is computed as follows:

Formula for a row cell percentage

$$\text{Row cell percentage} = \frac{\text{Cell frequency}}{\text{Cell row total}}$$

The advantage of row or column percentages is that they will sum to 100%, and a graph will show the composition of each row or column. Figure 14.2 presents the graphs for the column and row percents, respectively, for our college student/movie attendance example. Note that we have chosen orientations that communicate which percent formula was used: The column percents are in a vertical graph, and the row percents are in a horizontal graph.

It does not matter whether column percents or row percents are used, for the relationship that we have discovered to be significant is clear regardless of which graph we inspect: Underclass students tend to go to movies, upperclass students may or may not go, and graduate students rarely take in a movie.

How to Perform Cross-Tabulation Analysis with the XL Data Analyst

The XL Data Analyst performs cross-tabulation analysis and generates row and column percentage tables so that users can see the relationship patterns when they encounter a significant cross-tabulation relationship. As an exercise, consider the Advanced Automobile Concepts

FIGURE 14.2

Use of Column or Row Percents to Present a Significant Cross-Tabulation Relationship

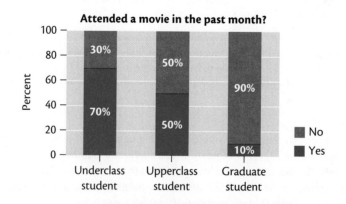

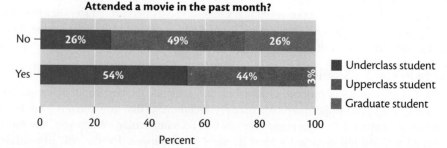

survey question asking respondents what is their favorite magazine type. Do you think that there is a relationship to gender? To ask this question differently, what gender would you expect to be associated with reading what types of magazines?

We'll use the XL Data Analyst to investigate this question. Figure 14.3 is the menu and selection window used to direct the XL Data Analyst to perform a cross-tabulation analysis. The menu sequence is Relate–Crosstabs, and this sequence opens up the selection window that you see in Figure 14.3. The Gender variable is selected as the Column Variable, and the Favorite Magazine Type variable is added into the Row Variable(s) window pane. Actually, it does not matter which categorical variable is placed in which selection windowpane, as the XL Data Analyst will generate a row percentages table as well as a column percentages table.

Figure 14.4 is the resulting output in the form of three tables. The first table is the Observed Frequencies table along with grand totals for rows and columns. The XL Data Analyst uses these to perform chi-square analysis, the result of which is provided immediately below the frequencies table. In this example, there is a significant relationship. The determination of a significant relationship signals that it is worthwhile to inspect the row percentages and/or the column percentages table(s) to spot the pattern of the relationship. The Column Percents table shows the male/female readership distribution of each magazine type. The Grand Total percent refers to both genders, so departures from this percentage are informative. Specifically, Business & Money, Home & Garden, and Trucks-Cars & Motorcycle magazines are read more by males, while Music & Entertainment magazines are read more by females.

In sum, the XL Data Analyst has flagged a significant cross-tabulation relationship, and its tables make the identification of the nature of the relationship an easy task. By the way, when the XL Data Analyst finds that there is no significant relationship in the cross-tabulation table, it does not provide the Column Percents table or the Row Percents table, as inspecting these tables with a nonsignificant relationship is not productive. For an example of the use of cross-tabulation analysis, see Marketing Research Application 14.1.

> Use the XL Data Analyst "Crosstabs" procedure to analyze a possible relationship between two categorical variables.

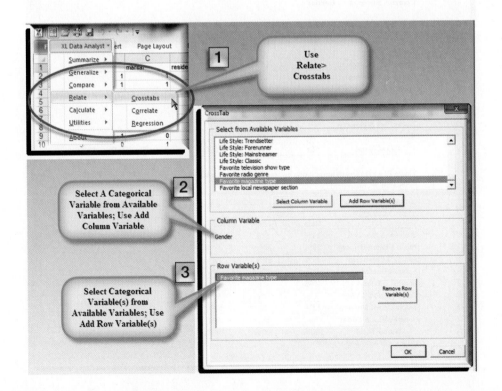

FIGURE 14.3

Using the XL Data Analyst to Set Up a Cross-Tabulation Analysis

Do men and women read the same types of magazines? Cross-tabulation analysis can investigate this question.

FIGURE 14.4

XL Data Analyst Cross-Tabulations Analysis Output

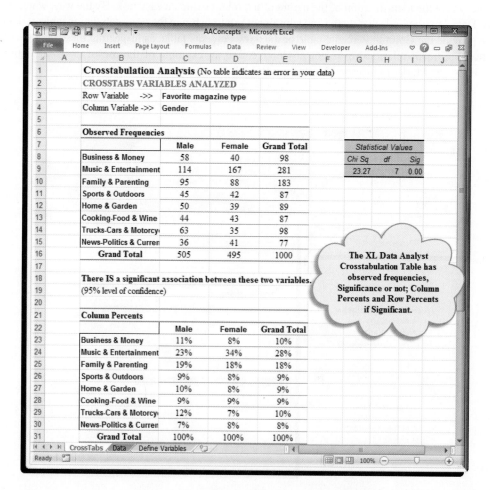

Crosstabulation Analysis (No table indicates an error in your data)

CROSSTABS VARIABLES ANALYZED

Row Variable   ->> Favorite magazine type

Column Variable ->> Gender

Observed Frequencies

	Male	Female	Grand Total
Business & Money	58	40	98
Music & Entertainment	114	167	281
Family & Parenting	95	88	183
Sports & Outdoors	45	42	87
Home & Garden	50	39	89
Cooking-Food & Wine	44	43	87
Trucks-Cars & Motorcy	63	35	98
News-Politics & Curren	36	41	77
Grand Total	505	495	1000

Statistical Values		
Chi Sq	df	Sig
23.27	7	0.00

There IS a significant association between these two variables.
(95% level of confidence)

Column Percents

	Male	Female	Grand Total
Business & Money	11%	8%	10%
Music & Entertainment	23%	34%	28%
Family & Parenting	19%	18%	18%
Sports & Outdoors	9%	8%	9%
Home & Garden	10%	8%	9%
Cooking-Food & Wine	9%	9%	9%
Trucks-Cars & Motorcy	12%	7%	10%
News-Politics & Curren	7%	8%	8%
Grand Total	100%	100%	100%

The XL Data Analyst Crosstabulation Table has observed frequencies, Significance or not; Column Percents and Row Percents if Significant.

MARKETING RESEARCH APPLICATION 14.1

Use of Exercise Equipment by Women in the United Arab Emirates

Home exercise equipment is experiencing a mini boom in at least one Arab country, the United Arab Emirates. In what might be the first survey on this topic, marketing researchers administered a questionnaire to 400 women living in Dubai, UAE.[4] They used cross-tabulations and Chi-square analysis to identify the following significant relationships. Their data have been reworked to create the following two cross-tabulation graphs.

The cross-tabulation graphs show the relationships between the primary reason for purchasing home exercise equipment (lose weight, look good, or get fit) with two demographic factors. Occupation is commonly used in Western research, and the finding is that UAE female students and housewives buy exercise equipment to lose weight, employees buy the equipment to look good, and business women buy the equipment to get fit. The pattern for religion is that Hindu and Muslim women purchase exercise equipment to lose weight, while Christian women in the UAE are purchasing this equipment to look good.

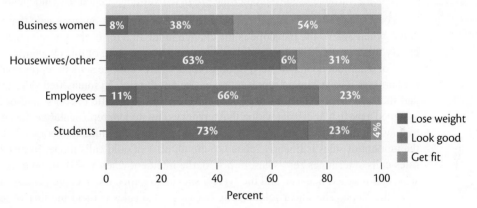

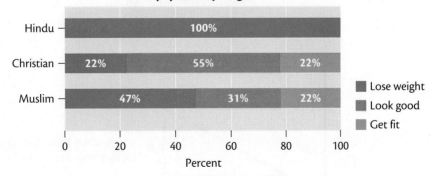

Correlation: Assessing Metric Variables Relationships

We now turn to the relationship between two or more metrically scaled variables. This is a more precise relationship, and one that you should find easy to visualize. Perhaps the most intuitive relationship between two metric variables is a **linear relationship,** sometimes called a straight-line relationship. Here, knowledge of the amount of one variable will automatically yield knowledge of the amount of the other variable as a consequence of applying the linear or straight-line formula that is known to exist between them. In its general form, a **straight-line formula** is as follows:

> The formula $y = a + bx$ describes a linear relationship between the variables y and x.

Formula for a straight line

$$y = a + bx$$

Where:

 y = the variable being predicted (called the "dependent" variable)
 a = the intercept
 b = the slope
 x = the variable used to predict the predicted variable (called the "independent" variable)

> A linear relationship is defined by its intercept, a, and its slope, b.

As you can see in Figure 14.5, the **intercept** is the point on the y-axis that the straight line "hits" when $x = 0$, and the **slope** is the change in the line for each one-unit change in x. We will clarify the terms independent and dependent in a later section of this chapter.

For example, South-Western Book Company hires college student representatives to work in the summer. These student representatives are put through an intensified sales training program and then are divided into teams. Each team is given a specific territory, and each individual is assigned a particular district within that territory. The student representative then goes from house to house in the district making cold calls, attempting to sell children's books. Let us assume that the amount of sales is linearly related to the number of cold calls made. In this special case, no sales calls determines zero sales, or $a = 0$, the intercept when $x = 0$. If, on average, every tenth sales call resulted in a sale and the typical sale is $62, then the average per call would be $6.20, or b, the slope. The linear relationship between total sales (y) and number of sales calls (x) is as follows:

Straight-line formula example

$$y = \$0 + \$6.20x$$

FIGURE 14.5

The Straight-Line Relationship Illustrating the Intercept and the Slope (General Case)

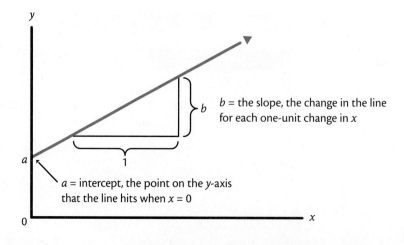

b = the slope, the change in the line for each one-unit change in x

a = intercept, the point on the y-axis that the line hits when $x = 0$

Thus, if the college salesperson makes 100 cold calls in any given day, the expected total revenues would be $620 ($6.20 times 100 calls). Certainly, our student sales rep would not derive exactly $620 for every 100 calls, but the linear relationship shows what is expected to happen on average.

Correlation Coefficients and Covariation

Of course, a perfectly linear relationship between two metric variables almost never occurs. The **correlation coefficient** is an index number, constrained to fall between the range of −1.0 and +1.0, that communicates both the strength and the direction of the linear relationship between two metric variables. The amount of linear relationship between two variables is communicated by the absolute size of the correlation coefficient, whereas its sign communicates the direction of the association. A plus sign means that the relationship is such that as one variable increases, the other variable increases. A negative sign means that as one variable increases, the other variable decreases.

> A correlation coefficient expresses the amount of covariation between two metric variables.

Stated in a slightly different manner, a correlation coefficient indicates the degree of covariation between two variables. **Covariation** is defined as the amount of change in one variable systematically associated with a change in another variable. The greater the absolute size of the correlation coefficient, the greater is the covariation between the two variables, or the stronger is their relationship regardless of the sign.

We can illustrate covariation with a **scatter diagram,** which plots data pairs in an x- and y-axis graph. Here is an example: A marketing researcher is investigating the possible relationship between total company sales for Novartis, a leading pharmaceuticals sales company, in a particular territory and the number of salespeople assigned to that territory. At the researcher's fingertips are the sales figures and number of salespeople assigned for each of twenty different Novartis territories in the United States. It is possible to depict the raw data for these two variables on a scatter diagram, as shown in Figure 14.6. A scatter diagram plots the points corresponding to each matched pair of x and y variables. In this figure, the vertical axis (y) is Novartis sales for the territory, and the horizontal axis (x) contains the number of salespeople in that territory.

> A scatter diagram will portray the amount of covariation between two metric variables.

The arrangement or scatter of points falls in a long ellipse. Any two variables that exhibit systematic covariation will form an elliptical pattern on a scatter diagram. Of course, this particular scatter diagram portrays the information gathered by the marketing researcher on sales and the number of salespeople in each territory and only that information. In actuality, the scatter diagram could have taken any shape, depending on the relationship between the points plotted for the two variables concerned.[5]

Three different scatter diagrams are portrayed in Figure 14.7. Each scatter diagram result indicates a different degree of covariation. For instance, you can see that the scatter diagram depicted in Figure 14.7a is one in which there is no apparent association or relationship between the two variables, because the points fail to create any identifiable pattern. They are clumped into a large, formless shape. Those points in Figure 14.7b indicate a negative relationship between variables x and y; higher values of x tend to be associated with lower values of y. Those points in Figure 14.7c

> There is a relationship between the number of pharmaceutical salespersons in a territory and the sales level for that territory.

FIGURE 14.6

A Scatter Diagram
Showing Covariation

FIGURE 14.7

Scatter Diagrams
Illustrating Various
Relationships

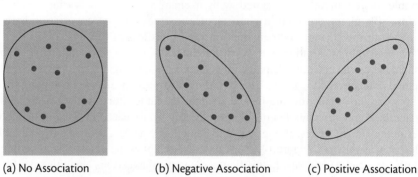

(a) No Association   (b) Negative Association   (c) Positive Association

> The elliptical shape of a scatter diagram for two metric variables translates to the direction and size of their correlation coefficient.

are fairly similar to those in Figure 14.7b, but the angle or the slope of the ellipse is different. This slope indicates a positive relationship between *x* and *y*, because larger values of *x* tend to be associated with larger values of *y*.

What is the connection between scatter diagrams and correlation coefficients? The answer lies in the linear relationship described earlier in this chapter. Look at Figure 14.7, and Figures 14.8b and 14.8c and you will see that all of them form ellipses. Imagine taking an ellipse and pulling on both ends. It would stretch out and become thinner until all of its points fell on a straight line. If you happened to find some data with all of its points falling on the axis line and you computed a correlation, you would find it to be exactly 1.0 (+1.0 if the ellipse went up to the right and −1.0 if it went down to the right).

Now imagine pushing the ends of the ellipse until it became the pattern in Figure 14.7a. There would be no identifiable straight line. Similarly, there would be no systematic covariation. The correlation for a ball-shaped scatter diagram is zero because there is no discernible linear relationship. In other words, a correlation coefficient indicates the degree of covariation between two variables, and you can envision this linear relationship as a scatter diagram. The form and angle of the scatter pattern are revealed by the size and sign, respectively, of the correlation coefficient.

Correlation analysis has the great, handy ability of relating two variables that are of very different measurements. For instance, you can correlate a buyer's age with the number of times he or she purchased the item in the past year, you can correlate how many miles a commuter drives in a week to how many minutes of talk radio he or she listens to, and you can correlate how satisfied customers are with how long they have been loyal customers. You can use correlation with disparate metric scales because there is a standardization procedure in the computation of a correlation that eliminates the differences between the two measures involved.

STATISTICAL SIGNIFICANCE OF A CORRELATION Working with correlations is a two-step process. First, you must assess the statistical significance of the correlation. If it is significant, you can take the second step, which is to interpret it. With respect to the first step, a correlation coefficient that is not statistically significant is taken to be a correlation of zero. Let us emphasize this point: You must always first determine the statistical significance of a correlation coefficient, and if it is not significant, you must consider it to be a zero correlation regardless of its computed value. To repeat, a correlation that is not statistically significant has no meaning at all because of the **null hypothesis for a correlation,** which states that the population correlation coefficient is equal to zero. If this null hypothesis is rejected (that is, there is a statistically significant correlation), then you can be assured that a correlation other than zero will be found in the population. But if the sample correlation is found to not be significant, the population correlation will be zero.

> With correlation analysis, the null hypothesis is that the population correlation is equal to zero.

How do you determine the statistical significance of a correlation coefficient? Tables exist that give the lowest value of the significant correlation coefficients for given sample sizes. However, most computer statistical programs will indicate the statistical significance level of the computed correlation coefficient. Your XL Data Analyst evaluates the significance and reports whether the correlation is significant at the 95% level of confidence.

RULES OF THUMB FOR CORRELATION STRENGTH After you have established that a correlation coefficient is statistically significant, we can talk about some general rules of thumb concerning the strength of the relationship. Correlation coefficients that fall between +1.00 and +.81 or between −1.00 and −.81 are generally considered to be "strong." Those correlations that fall between +.80 and +.61 or −.80 and −.61 generally indicate a "moderate" relationship. Those that fall between +.60 and +.41 or −.60 and −.41 denote a "weak" association. Any correlation that falls between the range of ±.21 and ±.40 is usually considered indicative of a "very weak" association between the variables. Finally, any correlation that is equal to or less than ±.20 is typically uninteresting to marketing researchers because it rarely identifies a meaningful association between two variables. We have provided Table 14.3 as a reference on these rules of thumb. As you use these guidelines, remember two things: First, we are assuming that the statistical significance of the correlation has been established. Second, researchers make up their own rules of thumb, so you may encounter someone whose guidelines differ slightly from those in this table.[6]

> Use guidelines in Table 14.3 to judge the strength of a statistically significant correlation coefficient.

THE PEARSON PRODUCT MOMENT CORRELATION COEFFICIENT The **Pearson product moment correlation** measures the linear relationship between two metric-scaled variables. The formula for calculating a Pearson product moment correlation is complicated, and researchers never compute it by hand, as they invariably find these on computer output. However, some instructors believe that students should understand the workings of the correlation coefficient formula, plus it is possible to describe the formula and point out how covariation is included and how the correlation coefficient's value comes to be restricted to −1.0 to +1.0. We have described this formula and pointed out these items in Marketing Research Application 14.2.

TABLE 14.3

Rules of Thumb About Correlation Coefficient Size

Coefficient Range	Strength of Relationship*
±.81 to ±1.00	Strong
±.61 to ±.80	Moderate
±.41 to ±.60	Weak
±.21 to ±.40	Very weak
±.00 to ±.20	None

*Assuming the correlation coefficient is statistically significant.

MARKETING RESEARCH APPLICATION 14.2

Practical Applications

How to Compute a Pearson Product Moment Correlation

Marketing researchers almost never compute a correlation, but it is insightful to learn about this process. The computational formula for a Pearson product moment correlation is provided here, and a brief description of its components will help you see how the concepts we have discussed in this chapter fit together.

Formula for Pearson product moment correlation

$$r_{xy} = \frac{\sum_{i=1}^{n}(x_i - \bar{x})(y_i - \bar{y})}{ns_x s_y}$$

Where:

x_i = each x value
$\bar{x}$ = average of the x values
y_i = average y values
$\bar{y}$ = average of the y values
n = number of paired cases
s_x, s_y = standard deviations of x and y, respectively

The numerator requires that the x_i and the y_i of each pair of x, y data points be compared (via subtraction) to its average, and that these values be multiplied. The sum of all these products is referred to as the cross-products sum, and this value represents the covariation between x and y. Recall that we represented covariation on a scatter diagram in our introduction to correlation earlier in this section of the chapter.

The covariation is divided by the number of xy pairs, n, to scale it down to an average per pair of x and y values. This average covariation is then divided by both the standard deviation of the x values and the standard deviation of the y values. This adjustment procedure eliminates the measurement differences in the x units and the y units (x might be measured in years, and y might be measured on a 1 to 10 satisfaction scale). The result constrains the correlation, r_{xy}, to fall within a specific range of values, and this range is between -1.0 and $+1.0$, as indicated earlier as well.

XLDA

The XL Data Analyst computes the correlation coefficient, assesses its significance, and relates its strength.

HOW TO PERFORM CORRELATION ANALYSIS WITH THE XL DATA ANALYST A common application of correlation analysis with surveys such as the Advanced Automobile Concepts survey is its use in the investigation of relationships between hybrid vehicle preferences and lifestyle variables. In our survey, respondents were administered a 10-point scale anchored with "Does not describe me at all" and "Describes me perfectly," measuring their lifestyle as to the degree to which they are novelist, innovator, trendsetter, forerunner, mainstreamer, or classic. Is there a relationship between lifestyle orientation and preference for a certain model of the prospective hybrid vehicles? Figure 14.8 shows the XL Data Analyst menu sequence for correlation analysis. The menu sequence is Relate–Correlate, which opens up the selection window. As you can see in the figure, Preference: Super Cycle One-seat Hybrid is chosen as the Primary Variable, while all six lifestyle types are clicked into the Other Variable(s) window pane.

Figure 14.9 shows the resulting XL Data Analyst output for correlation. The table reveals computed correlations and sample sizes (1,000 in all cases), and all correlations are statistically significant from zero (the null hypothesis). However, only one is stronger than weak according to our rules of thumb about correlation sizes. The $+.79$ correlation for preference for the one-seat super cycle hybrid and the novelist lifestyle reveals that there is moderate positive association between these two variables. These two variables covary, suggesting that if the Advanced Automobile Concepts principals developed a one-seat hybrid super cycle, it would be useful to target the novelist lifestyle market segment, as this vehicle concept is definitely attractive to these individuals.

How to Present Correlation Findings

Marketing researchers usually have a "target" or a "focal" variable in mind, and they look at correlations of other variables of interest with this target variable. The XL Data Analyst output for correlation handles this concept well, as it specifically asks for the "primary variable."

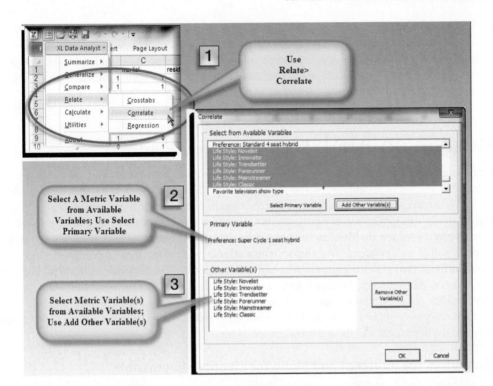

FIGURE 14.8

Using the XL Data
Analyst to Set Up a
Correlation Analysis

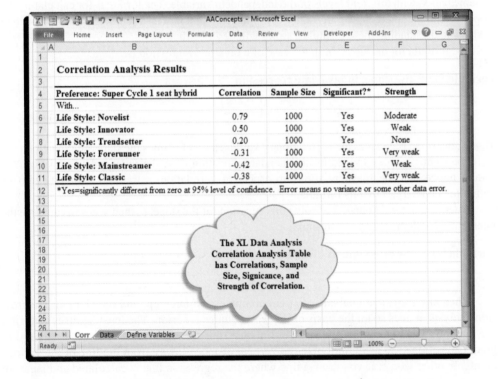

FIGURE 14.9

XL Data Analyst
Correlation Analysis
Output

We recommend a table where the target variable is clearly indicated, probably in the table title, and the statistically significant positive and negative correlations are identified and separated. For each, the correlations should be reported in descending order based on the absolute size. In this way, the reader's attention is drawn first to the positively related variables, and he or she can see the pattern from strong to weak positive correlations. Next, attention is drawn to the negatively associated variables, and again, one can see the pattern from strong to weak negative correlations. If the researcher thinks it appropriate, a third column can be added to the table, and the designations of Strong, Moderate, Weak, and so on, can be placed beside each correlation according to the rules of thumb strength levels identified in this chapter.

Regression Analysis

Regression analysis assesses the straight-line relationship between a metric dependent variable, y, and a metric independent variable, x.

Regression analysis is a predictive analysis technique in which two or more variables are used to predict the level of another by use of the straight-line formula, $y = a + bx$, that we described earlier. When a researcher wants to make an exact prediction based on a correlation analysis finding, he or she can turn to regression analysis.[7] **Bivariate regression analysis** is a case in which only two variables are involved in the predictive model, and one is called dependent while the other is called independent. The **dependent variable** is the one that is predicted, and it is customarily termed y in the regression straight-line equation. The **independent variable** is the one that is used to predict the dependent variable, and it is the x in the regression formula. We must quickly point out that the terms *dependent* and *independent* are arbitrary designations and are customary to regression analysis. There is no cause-and-effect relationship or true dependence between the dependent and the independent variables.

Computing the Intercept and Slope for Bivariate Regression

To compute a and b, one needs a number of observations of the various levels of the dependent variable paired with different levels of the independent variable. The formulas for calculating the slope (b) and the intercept (a) are rather complicated, but some instructors are in favor of their students understanding these formulas, so we will describe them here.

The formula for the slope, b, in the case of a bivariate regression is:

Formula for b, the slope, in bivariate regression

$$b = r_{xy} \frac{s_y}{s_x}$$

That is, the slope is equal to the correlation of variables x and y times the standard deviation of y, the dependent variable, divided by the standard deviation of x, the independent variable. You should notice that the linear relationship aspect of correlation is translated directly into its regression counterpart by this formula.

When you use your data set to solve this equation for the slope, b, then you can calculate the intercept, a, with the following formula.

Formula for a, the intercept, in bivariate regression

$$a = \bar{y} - b\bar{x}$$

Regression analysis computes the intercept, a, and the slope, b, of a straight-line relationship between x and y using the least squares criterion.

When any statistical analysis program computes the intercept and the slope in a regression analysis, it does so on the basis of the least squares criterion. The **least squares criterion** is a way of guaranteeing that the straight line that runs through the points on the scatter diagram is positioned so as to minimize the vertical distances away from the line of the various points. In other words, if you draw a line where the regression line is calculated and measure the vertical distances of all the points away from that line, it would be impossible to draw any other line that would result in a lower total of all of those vertical distances. So, regression analysis determines the best slope and the best intercept possible for the straight-line relationship between the independent and dependent variables for the data set that is being used in the analysis.

Testing for Statistical Significance of the Intercept and the Slope

The values for *a* and *b* must be tested for statistical significance. The intercept and slope that are computed are sample estimates of population parameters of the true intercept, α (alpha), and the true slope, β (beta). The tests for statistical significance are tests as to whether the computed intercept and computed slope are significantly different from zero (the null hypothesis). To determine statistical significance, regression analysis requires that a *t* test be used for each parameter estimate. The interpretation of these *t* tests is identical to other significance tests you have seen; that is, if the computed *t* is greater than the table t value, the null hypothesis is not supported, meaning that the computed intercept or slope is not zero, it is the value determined by the regression analysis.

> Statistical tests determine whether the calculated intercept, *a*, and slope, *b*, are significantly different from zero (the null hypothesis).

Making a Prediction with Bivariate Regression Analysis

How do you make a prediction? The fact that the line is a best-approximation representation of all the points means we must account for a certain amount of error when we use the line for our predictions. Figure 14.10 shows how the prediction works. The regression prediction uses a confidence interval that is based on a standard error value. To elaborate, we know that the scatter of points does not describe a perfectly straight line, because a perfect correlation of $+1.0$ or -1.0 almost never is found. So our regression prediction can only be an estimate.

Generating a regression prediction is conceptually identical to estimating a population average using a confidence interval range rather than stipulating an exact estimate for your prediction. Regression analysis provides for a **standard error of the estimate,** which is a measure of the accuracy of the predictions of the regression equation. This standard error value is analogous to the standard error of the mean you used in estimating a population average from a sample, but it is based on **residuals,** which are the differences between each predicted *y* value for each *x* value in the data set compared to the actual *x* value.[8] That is, regression analysis takes the regression equation and applies it to every *x* value and determines what you might envision as the average difference away from the associated actual *x* value in the data set. The differences, or residuals, are translated into a standard error of the estimate value, and you use the standard error of the estimate to compute confidence intervals around the predictions that you make using the regression equation. The prediction process is accomplished by applying the following equation.

> When making a prediction with a regression equation, use a confidence interval that expresses the sample error and variability inherent in the sample used to compute the regression equation.

95% confidence interval for a predicted *y* value using a regression equation

Predicted $y = a + bx$

Confidence interval = Predicted $y \pm (1.96 \times$ standard error of the estimate$)$

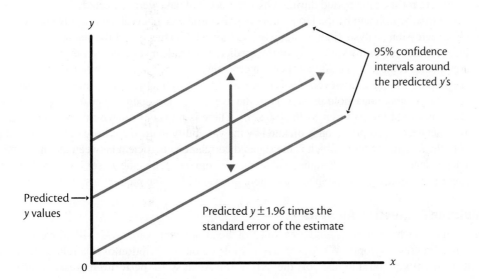

Predicted → *y* values

Predicted $y \pm 1.96$ times the standard error of the estimate

95% confidence intervals around the predicted *y*'s

FIGURE 14.10

To Predict with Regression, Apply a Confidence Interval Around the Predicted *Y* Value(s)

One of the assumptions of regression analysis is that the points in the scatter diagram will be spread uniformly and in accord with the normal curve assumptions over the regression line. The points are congregated close to the line and become more diffuse as they move away from the line. In other words, a greater percentage of the points are found on or close to the line than are found further away. The great advantage of this assumption is that it allows the marketing researcher to use his or her knowledge of the normal curve to specify the range in which the dependent variable is predicted to fall. The interpretation of these confidence intervals is identical to interpretations for previous confidence intervals: Were the same prediction made many times and an actual result determined each time, the actual results would fall within the range of the predicted value 95% of these times.

Let us use the regression equation to make a prediction about the dollar amount of grocery purchases that would be associated with a certain family size. In this example, we have asked respondents to provide us with their approximate weekly grocery expenditures and the number of family members living in their households. A bivariate regression analysis is performed, and the regression equation is found to have an intercept of $75 and a slope of +$125. So to predict the weekly grocery expenditures for a family of four, the computations would be as follows:

Calculation of average weekly grocery expenditures for a household of four individuals

$$y = a + bx$$
$$\text{Expenditures} = \$75 + (\$25 \times 4 \text{ members})$$
$$= \$75 + \$100$$
$$= \$175$$

The analysis finds a standard error of the estimate of $20, and this value is used to calculate the 95% confidence interval for the prediction.

Calculation of 95% confidence interval for the prediction of average weekly grocery expenditures for a household of four individuals

$$\$175 \pm 1.96 \times \$20$$
$$\$175 \pm \$39.20$$
$$\$135.8 - \$214.2$$

The interpretation of these three numbers is as follows: For a typical family represented by the sample, the expected average weekly grocery purchases amount to $175, but because we are using a sample's estimates, the weekly expenditures would not be exactly that amount. Consequently, the 95% confidence interval reveals that the purchases figure should fall between $136 and $214 (rounded values). Of course, the prediction is valid only if conditions remain the same as they were for the time period during which the original data were collected.

You may be troubled by the large range of our confidence interval, and rightly so. How precisely a regression analysis finding predicts is determined by the size of the standard error of the estimate, a measure of the variability of the predicted dependent variable. In our grocery expenditures example, the average dollars spent on groceries per week may be predicted by our bivariate regression findings; however, if we repeated the survey many, many times, and made our $175, four-member household prediction of the average dollars spent every time, 95% of these predictions would fall between $136 and $214. There is no way to make this prediction range more exact because its precision is dictated by the variability in the data. Researchers sometimes refer to the **R-square value,** which is the squared correlation coefficient between the independent and dependent variable. The R-square value ranges from 0 to 1, and the closer it is found to 1, the stronger is the linear relationship and the more precise will be the predictions.

Researchers use the *R*-square value (the squared correlation) to judge how precise a regression analysis finding will be when used in a prediction.

Multiple Regression Analysis

Now that you have a basic understanding of bivariate regression, we will move on to an advanced regression topic. When we have completed our description of this related topic, we will instruct you on the use of the XL Data Analyst to perform regression analysis.

Multiple regression analysis is an expansion of bivariate regression analysis such that more than one independent variable is used in the regression equation. The addition of independent variables makes the regression model more realistic because predictions normally depend on multiple factors, not just one. The regression equation in multiple regression has the following form.

Multiple regression equation

$$y = a + b_1x_1 + b_2x_2 + b_3x_3 + \cdots + b_mx_m$$

Where:

  y = the dependent, or predicted, variable
  x_i = independent variable i
  a = the intercept
  b_i = the slope for independent variable i
  m = the number of independent variables in the equation

As you can see, the inclusion of other independent variables is displayed by inserting b_ix_i variables to the equation. We still have retained the basic $y = a + bx$ straight-line formula, except now we have multiple x variables, and each one is added to the equation, changing y by its individual slope. The treatment of each independent variable in this manner conforms to the straight-line assumptions of multiple regression analysis. This is sometimes known as **additivity,** because each new independent variable is added on to the regression equation. Of course, it might have a negative coefficient, but it is added on to the equation as another independent variable.

> Multiple regression "adds" more independent variables to the regression equation.

WORKING WITH MULTIPLE REGRESSION Everything about multiple regression is essentially equivalent to bivariate regression except you are dealing with more than one independent variable. The terminology is slightly different in places, and some statistics are modified to take into account the multiple aspect, but for the most part, concepts in multiple regression are analogous to those in the simple bivariate case.

Let's look at a multiple regression analysis result so you can better understand the multiple regression equation. Let's assume that we are working for Lexus, and we are trying to predict prospective customers' intentions to purchase a Lexus. We have performed a survey that included an attitude-toward-Lexus variable, an attitude-toward-current-automobile variable, and an income variable. We then applied multiple regression analysis and found that these three independent variables and the intercept were statistically significant. Here is the result.

Lexus purchase intention multiple regression equation example

  Intention to purchase a Lexus = 2
         + 1.0 × Attitude toward Lexus (1–5 scale)
         − 0.5 × Attitude toward current auto (1–5 scale)
         + .25 × Income level (1–10 scale)

This multiple regression equation says that you can predict a consumer's intention to buy a Lexus level if you know three variables: (1) attitude toward Lexus, (2) attitude toward present automobile, and (3) income level using a scale with ten income grades. Furthermore, we can see the impact of each of these variables on Lexus purchase intentions. Here is how to interpret the equation. First, the average person has a "2" intention level, or some small propensity to want to buy a Lexus. Attitude toward Lexus is measured on a 1–5 scale, and with each attitude scale point, intention to purchase a Lexus goes up 1 point. That is, an individual with a strong positive attitude of 5 will have a greater intention than one with a weak attitude of 1. With increasing positive feelings about one's current automobile, the intention decreases by 0.5 for each level on the 5-point scale. Finally, the intention increases by 0.25 with each increasing income level.

Here is a numerical example for a potential Lexus buyer whose attitude is 4, attitude toward present auto is 3, and income is 8. (We will not use a confidence interval as we just want to illustrate how a multiple regression equation operates.)

Multiple regression can be used to predict how likely someone is to purchase a luxury automobile.

Calculation of Lexus purchase intention using the multiple regression equation

$$
\begin{aligned}
\text{Intention to purchase a Lexus} ={} & 2 \\
& + 1.0 \times 4 \\
& - .5 \times 3 \\
& + .25 \times 8 \\
={} & 6.5
\end{aligned}
$$

Multiple regression is a very powerful tool, because it tells us which factors predict the dependent variable, which way (the sign) each factor influences the dependent variable, and even how much (the size of b_i) each factor influences it. Just as was the case in bivariate regression analysis, it is possible to compute the strength of the linear relationship between the independent variables and the dependent variable with multiple regression. **Multiple R,** also called the **coefficient of determination,** is a handy measure of the strength of the overall linear relationship. As was the case in bivariate regression analysis, the multiple regression analysis model assumes that a straight-line (plane) relationship exists among the variables. Multiple R ranges from 0 to $+1.0$ and represents the amount of the dependent variable "explained," or accounted for, by the combined independent variables. High multiple R values indicate that the regression plane applies well to the scatter of points, whereas low values signal that the straight-line model does not apply well.

Researchers use multiple R to assess how much of the dependent variable, y, is accounted for by the multiple regression result they have found.

Multiple R is like a lead indicator of the multiple regression analysis findings. It is often one of the first pieces of information provided in a multiple regression output. Many researchers mentally convert the multiple R into a percentage. For example, a multiple R of .75 means that the regression findings will explain 75% of the dependent variable. The greater the explanatory power of the multiple regression finding, the better and more useful it is for the researcher. However, multiple R is useful only when the multiple regression finding has only significant independent variables. There is a process called "trimming" in which researchers make iterative multiple regression analyses, systematically removing nonsignificant independent variables until only statistically significant ones remain in the analysis findings.[9]

USING "DUMMY" INDEPENDENT VARIABLES A **dummy independent variable** is defined as one that is scaled with a categorical 0-versus-1 coding scheme. The 0-versus-1 code is traditional, but any two adjacent numbers could be used, such as 1-versus-2. A requirement of multiple regression analysis is that all variables are metric. However, in certain instances, a marketing researcher may want to use an independent variable that is categorical and identifies only two groups. It is not unusual, for instance, for the marketing researcher to wish to use a two-label variable, such as gender, as an independent variable, in a multiple regression problem. For instance, a researcher may want to use gender coded as 0 for male and 1 for female as an independent variable; or a buyer–nonbuyer dummy variable as an independent variable. In these instances, it is usually permissible to slightly violate the assumption of metric scaling for the independent variable to come up with a result that is in some degree interpretable.

> It is permissible to cautiously use a few categorical variables with a multiple regression analysis.

THREE USES OF MULTIPLE REGRESSION Bivariate regression is used only for prediction, whereas multiple regression can be used for (1) prediction, (2) understanding, or (3) as a screening device.[10] You already know how to use regression analysis for prediction, as we illustrated it in our bivariate regression analysis example: Use the statistically significant intercept and beta coefficient values with the levels of the independent variables you wish to use in the prediction, and then apply 95% confidence intervals using the standard error of the estimate.

As a tool for understanding, multiple regression is complicated because independent variables are often measured with different units, so it is wrong to make direct comparisons between the calculated betas. For example, it is improper to directly compare the beta coefficient for family size to another for money spent per month on personal grooming, because the units of measurement are so different (people versus dollars). The solution to this problem is to standardize the independent variables through a quick operation that involves dividing the difference between each independent variable value and its mean by the standard deviation of that independent variable. This results in what is called the **standardized beta coefficient.** When they are standardized, direct comparisons may be made between the resulting betas. The larger the absolute value of a standardized beta coefficient, the more relative importance it assumes in predicting the dependent variable. With standardized betas, the researcher can directly compare the importance of each independent variable with others. Most statistical programs provide the standardized betas automatically. Marketing Research Application 14.3 illustrates the use of standardized beta coefficients.

> Researchers study standardized beta coefficients in order to understand the relative importance of the independent variables as they impact the dependent variable.

A third application of multiple regression analysis is as a **screening device,** meaning that multiple regression analysis can be applied by a researcher to "narrow down" many considerations to a smaller, more manageable set. That is, the marketing researcher may be faced with a large number and variety of prospective independent variables, and he or she may use multiple regression as a screening device or a way of spotting the salient (statistically significant) independent variables for the dependent variable at hand. In this instance, the intent is not to determine a prediction of the dependent variable; rather, it may be to search for clues as to what factors help the researcher understand the behavior of this particular variable. For instance, the researcher might be seeking market segmentation bases and could use regression to spot which demographic and lifestyle variables are related to the consumer behavior variable under study.

HOW TO USE THE XL DATA ANALYST TO PERFORM REGRESSION ANALYSIS The first step in multiple regression analysis is to identify the dependent and independent variables. For our example, we will use the "probability of buying a standard size hybrid auto within three years" as our dependent variable. Logically, we would expect this probability to be related to demographics, beliefs, and attitudes. A requirement of regression is that the dependent variable be metric, meaning interval or ratio scaled. Our probability of buying satisfies this requirement

XLDA

MARKETING RESEARCH APPLICATION 14.3

Ethics

What Factors Predict the Success of Business Ethics Taught in MBA Programs?

Researchers sampled students from 75 different MBA programs across the United States to identify aspects of these

Factor	Standardized Beta
Number of incorporation methods used	0.26
Required core course(s)	0.15
Quality of program management	0.15
Integrated case studies within most courses	0.15
Referred to in most courses	0.12
Willingness to recommend school	0.08
Quality of curriculum	0.08
Quality of faculty	0.06

programs related to the perceived effective incorporation of ethics into these MBA programs.[11] Using regression analysis, they found eight factors that were related to this perceived effectiveness. The factors and their standardized beta coefficients are listed here.

The findings reveal that the most important factor is the teaching of business ethics using a variety of methods, including speakers, required core course(s), integrated case studies within some courses, referred to in most courses, elective course(s), and workshops. The next three factors, in terms of importance, are teaching business ethics as a required core course, overall quality of the MBA program, and incorporation of business ethics case studies with most of the course in the MBA program. Of the eight statistically significant factors, the quality of the MBA faculty is the least important aspect.

for the dependent variable. However, if you review the questionnaire and coding system used for the income as well as for hometown size, age, and education, you will come to realize that the codes define ordinal scales. For instance, a 5 pertains to hometowns of 1 million and more, a 4 corresponds to 500K to 1 million, and a 3 designates a hometown of between 100K and 500K people. Because the size ranges are not equal, the code numbers are not metric.

In any regression, it is best to use realistic values, because they are easiest to interpret. Consequently, we will recode the hometown size, age, education, and income values to represent the midpoints of the various ranges designated on the questionnaire. Naturally, not every respondent's value falls on the midpoint, but we can make the assumption that while some have actual values above the midpoint and some have actual values below the midpoint, these will average to be the midpoint or very close to it for all respondents who fall into that particular range. Here are the recode values that we use to convert our four demographic variables into values that are metric. For hometown size, we will use thousands: $1 = 5, 2 = 55, 3 = 300, 4 = 750$, and $5 = 1,500$. For years of age, $1 = 17, 2 = 21, 3 = 30, 4 = 42, 5 = 57$, and $6 = 70$. For years of education, $1 = 9, 2 = 12, 3 = 14, 4 = 16$, and $5 = 18$; and for \$10,000 of income, $1 = 20, 2 = 37.5, 3 = 62.5, 4 = 100$, and $5 = 150$. If you are tracking this recoding carefully, you no doubt have noted cases where the lower or upper limit of the range is not specified, such as "\$125,000 and higher" for income. In these cases, we chose a value that is reasonable. If you wish to work with our recoded variables, you may recode your AAConcepts data set, or you can chose to use the XL Data Analyst data set, named AAConcepts.Recoded.xlsm.

The XL Data Analyst has been developed to allow you to perform regression analysis. To illustrate multiple regression analysis in action, and to simultaneously familiarize you with how to direct the XL Data Analyst to perform regression analysis, we will take as our dependent variable the question, "Probability of buying a standard size hybrid vehicle." This is a metric variable because the response scale was a 1–100 probability scale. Figure 14.11 shows the menu sequence and selection window for setting up regression analysis with the XL Data Analyst. Notice that the menu sequence is Relate–Regression, which opens up the Regression selection window. We have selected our probability variable into the Dependent Variable windowpane, and we have

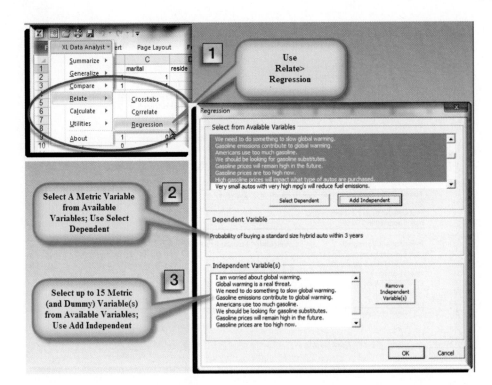

selected some demographic factors (e.g., size of hometown or city, gender, GPA, number of people in household) and nine global warming and gasoline-related attitude items as the independent variables.

Figure 14.12 contains the results of this multiple regression analysis. There are two tables in Figure 14.12. First, the XL Data Analyst computes the full multiple regression analysis using all of the independent variables. It presents the beta coefficients, the standardized beta coefficients, and the result of the significance test for each independent variable's beta. Since one or more independent variables resulted in a nonsignificant beta coefficient—meaning that even though a coefficient value is reported in the first table, its true population value is 0—the XL Data Analyst reruns the analysis with the nonsignificant independent variables omitted from the analysis. The final result is in the second table, where all independent variables now left in the regression analysis results have significant beta coefficients. Thus, the trimmed findings table is the one to use in the interpretation of the regression findings.

> The XL Data Analyst removes nonsignificant independent variables in its multiple regression analysis procedure.

We can now interpret our multiple regression finding. We will first use the signs of the beta coefficients in our interpretation. All four statistically significant independent variables have positive signs (no sign means positive), so as, for example, income and education increase, so does the probability of buying a standard size hybrid auto. Next, we can use the standard beta coefficients to better our understanding of the demand for standard sized hybrid automobiles. The belief that high gasoline prices will impact the type of autos purchased in the future has a much larger value (.49) than any other variable, and it is five times more important than income, education, or age, which are approximately equal in importance.

HOW TO PRESENT REGRESSION ANALYSIS FINDINGS To properly apply the regression result as a predictive equation, the following aspects are recommended: (1) dependent variable, (2) statistically significant independent variables, (3) intercept, (4) beta coefficients, including signs, (5) adjusted R^2, and (6) standard error of the estimate. A preferred format for reporting the statistically significant findings of the use of multiple regression as a predictive tool is a multiple regression equation where the beta coefficients and independent variables are listed. It is useful

FIGURE 14.12

XL Data Analyst Multiple
Regression Analysis
Output

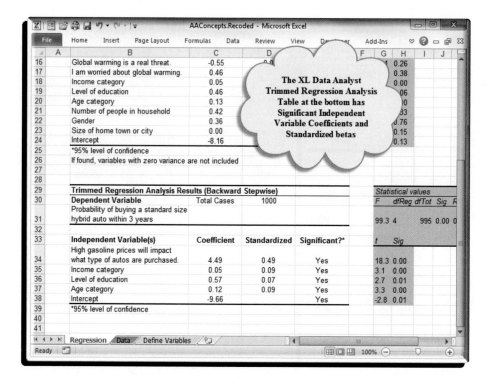

to identify the measurement scales used for the independent variables so the reader can apply the findings to any combination of the levels of the independent variables.

When regression is used as a screening device or for understanding, the items to report are (1) dependent variable, (2) statistically significant independent variables, (3) signs of beta coefficients, and (4) standardized beta coefficients for the significant variables. A handy format is the one used in the XL Data Analysis Trimmed Regression table. It is advisable to arrange the statistically significant independent variables by the absolute values of their standardized beta coefficients so the reader can easily see the relative importance from most to least.

FINAL COMMENTS ON MULTIPLE REGRESSION ANALYSIS There is a great deal more to multiple regression analysis, but it is beyond the scope of this textbook to delve deeper into this topic.[12] The coverage in this chapter introduces you to regression analysis, and it provides you with enough information about it to run uncomplicated regression analyses with your XL Data Analyst, identify the relevant aspects of the output, and interpret the findings.[13] However, we have barely scratched the surface of this complex data analysis technique. There are many more assumptions, options, statistics, and considerations involved. In fact, there is so much material that whole textbooks exist on regression. Our descriptions are merely an introduction to multiple regression analysis to help you comprehend the basic notions, common uses, and interpretations involved with this predictive technique.[14]

> Multiple regression is a complicated topic that requires a great deal more study to master.

Flow Chart on Relationship Analyses

In Figure 14.13 you will find a flow chart of how to decide what form of relationships analysis to perform. As shown, the first consideration is whether or not a dependent variable is involved. If not, then it is a matter of determining if the variables are categorical or metric. With categorical variables, one does cross-tabulation analysis. With metric variables and no dependent variable, the proper analysis is to use correlations. Finally, with a dependent metric variable and (mostly) metric independent variables, the correct choice is to perform regression analysis.

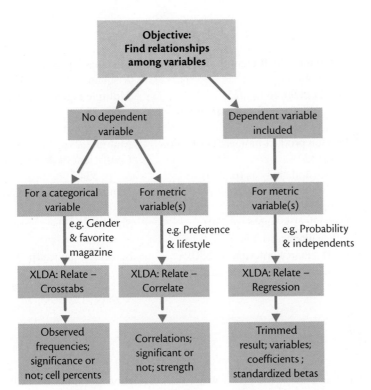

FIGURE 14.13

Flow Chart for
Relationships Analyses

Summary

This is the last data analysis chapter in the textbook, and it deals with relationships between two or more variables and how these relationships can be useful for prediction and understanding. The first type of relationship involves two categorical variables where the researcher deals with the co-occurrence of the labels that describe the variables. That is, raw counts of the number of instances are computed to construct a cross-tabulation table. This table is then used in the application of chi-square analysis to evaluate whether a statistically significant relationship exists between the two variables being analyzed. If so, then the research turns to graphs or percentage tables to envision the nature of the relationship.

Correlation analysis can be applied to two metric variables, and the linear relationship between them can be portrayed in a scatter diagram. The correlation coefficient indicates the direction (by its sign) and the strength (by its magnitude) of the linear relationship. However, only statistically significant correlations can be interpreted, and by rules of thumb provided in the chapter, a correlation must be larger than $\pm.81$ to be "strong."

Correlation leads to bivariate regression, in which the intercept and slope of the straight line are estimated and assessed for statistical significance. When statistically significant findings occur, the researcher can use the findings to compute a prediction, but the prediction must be cast in a confidence interval because there is invariably some error in how well the regression analysis result performs. Multiple regression analysis is appropriate when the researcher has more than one independent variable that may predict the dependent variable under study. With multiple regression, the basics of a linear relationship are retained, but there is a different slope (b) for each independent variable, and the signs of the slopes can be mixed. Generally, independent variables should be metric, although a few dummy-coded (e.g., 0,1) independent variables may be used in the independent variables set. A multiple regression result can be used to make predictions; moreover, with standardized beta coefficients, you can gain understanding of the phenomenon as it is permissible to compare these to each other and to interpret the relative importance of the various independent variables with respect to the behavior of the dependent variable.

Key Terms

Relationship (p. 315)
Cross-tabulation analysis (p. 317)
Cross-tabulation table (p. 317)
Cross-tabulation cell (p. 317)
Frequencies table (p. 317)
Chi-square (χ^2) analysis (p. 318)
Observed frequencies (p. 318)
Expected frequencies (p. 318)
Column percentages table (p. 320)
Row percentages table (p. 320)
Linear relationship (p. 324)
Straight-line formula (p. 324)
Intercept (p. 324)
Slope (p. 324)

Correlation coefficient (p. 325)
Covariation (p. 325)
Scatter diagram (p. 325)
Null hypothesis for a correlation
    (p. 327)
Pearson product moment correlation
    (p. 327)
Regression analysis (p. 330)
Bivariate regression analysis
    (p. 330)
Dependent variable (p. 330)
Independent variable (p. 330)
Least squares criterion (p. 330)
Standard error of the estimate (p. 331)

Residuals (p. 331)
R-square value (p. 332)
Multiple regression analysis
    (p. 333)
Additivity (p. 333)
Multiple R (p. 334)
Coefficient of determination
    (p. 334)
Dummy independent variable
    (p. 335)
Standardized beta coefficient
    (p. 335)
Screening device (p. 335)

Review Questions

1. What is a relationship between two variables, and how does a relationship help a marketing manager? Give an example using a demographic variable and a consumer behavior variable, such as satisfaction with a brand.
2. What is the basis for a cross-tabulation table? What types of variables are best analyzed with a cross-tabulation table relationship and why?
3. Illustrate how a cross-tabulation cell occurs in a cross-tabulation table. Provide an example using the variables of gender (categories: male and female) and vehicle type driven (SUV, sedan, sports car).
4. Describe chi-square analysis by explaining the following:
   a. Observed frequencies
   b. Expected frequencies
   c. Chi-square formula
5. When a researcher finds a statistically significant chi-square result for a cross-tabulation analysis, what should the researcher do next?
6. Use a scatter diagram and illustrate the covariation for the following correlations:
   a. −.99
   b. +.21
   c. +.76
7. Explain why the statistical significance of a correlation is important. That is, what must be assumed when the correlation is found to not be statistically significant?
8. Describe the connection between a correlation and a bivariate regression analysis. In your discussion, specifically note (1) statistical significance, (2) sign, and (3) use or application.
9. Relate how a bivariate regression analysis can be used to predict the dependent variable. In your answer, identify the independent and dependent variables, intercept, and slope. Also, give an example of how the prediction should be accomplished.
10. When a regression analysis is performed, what assures the researcher that the resulting regression equation is the best or optimal regression equation? Explain this concept.
11. How does multiple regression differ from bivariate regression? How is it similar?
12. Define and note how each of the following is used in multiple regression:
   a. Dummy independent variable
   b. Standardized beta coefficients
   c. Multiple R
13. How should you regard your knowledge and command of multiple regression analysis that is based on its description in this chapter? Why?

Application Questions

14. A researcher has conducted a survey for Michelob Light beer. There are two questions in the survey being investigated in the following cross-tabulation table.

	Michelob Light		
	Buyer	Nonbuyer	Totals
White collar	152	8	160
Blue collar	14	26	40
Totals	166	34	200

The computed chi-square value of 81.6 is greater than the chi-square table critical value of 3.8. Interpret the researcher's findings.

15. Following is some information about ten respondents to a mail survey concerning candy purchasing. Construct the various types of cross-tabulation tables that are possible. Label each table, and indicate what you find to be the general relationship apparent in the data.

Respondent	Buy Plain M&Ms	Buy Peanut M&Ms
1	Yes	No
2	Yes	No
3	No	Yes
4	Yes	No
5	No	No
6	No	Yes
7	No	No
8	Yes	No
9	Yes	No
10	No	Yes

16. Morton O'Dell is the owner of Mort's Diner, which is located in downtown Atlanta, Georgia. Mort's opened up about twelve months ago, and it has experienced success, but Mort is always worried about what food items to order as inventory on a weekly basis. Mort's daughter, Mary, is an engineering student at Georgia Tech, and she offers to help her father. She asks him to provide sales data for the past ten weeks in terms of pounds of food bought. With some difficulty, Mort comes up with the following list.

Week	Meat	Fish	Fowl	Vegetables	Desserts
1	100	50	150	195	50
2	91	55	182	200	64
3	82	60	194	209	70
4	75	68	211	215	82
5	66	53	235	225	73
6	53	61	253	234	53
7	64	57	237	230	68
8	76	64	208	221	58
9	94	68	193	229	62
10	105	58	181	214	62

Mary uses these sales figures to construct scatter diagrams that illustrate the basic relationships among the various types of food items purchased at Mort's Diner over the past ten weeks. She tells her father that the diagrams provide some help in his weekly inventory ordering problem. Construct Mary's scatter diagrams with Excel to indicate what assistance they are to Mort. Perform the appropriate correlation analyses with the XL Data Analyst and interpret your findings.

17. A pizza delivery company like Domino's Pizza wants to predict how many of its pizzas customers order per month. A multiple regression analysis finds the following statistically significant results.

Variable	Coefficient or Value
Intercept	+2.6
Pizza is a large part of my diet.*	+.5
I worry about calories in pizzas.*	−.2
Gender (1 = female; 2 = male)	+1.1
Standard error of the estimate	+.2

*Based on a scale where 1 = "strongly disagree," 2 = "somewhat agree," 3 = "neither agree nor disagree," 4 = "somewhat agree," and 5 = "strongly agree."

Compute the predicted number of pizzas ordered per month by each of the following three pizza customers.

a. A man who strongly agrees that pizza is a large part of his diet but strongly disagrees that he worries about pizza calories

b. A woman who is neutral about pizza being a large part of her diet and who somewhat agrees that she worries about calories in pizzas

Segmentation Variable	Compact Automobile Buyer	Sports Car Buyer	Luxury Automobile Buyer
Demographics			
Age	−.28	−.15	+.59
Education	−.12	+.38	
Family Size	+.39	−.35	
Income	−.15	+.25	+.68
Lifestyle/Values			
Active		+.59	−.39
American Pride	+.30		+.24
Bargain Hunter	+.45	−.33	
Conservative		−.38	+.54
Cosmopolitan	−.40	+.68	
Embraces Change	−.30	+.65	
Family Values	+.69		+.21
Financially Secure	−.28	+.21	+.52
Optimistic		+.71	+.37

c. A man who somewhat disagrees that he worries about pizza calories and is neutral about pizza being a large part of his diet

18. Segmentation Associates, a company that specializes in using multiple regression as a means of describing market segments, conducts a survey of various types of automobile purchasers. The table on the previous page summarizes a recent study's findings. The values are the standardized beta coefficients of those segmentation variables found to be statistically significant. Where no value appears, that regression coefficient was not statistically significant.

Interpret these findings for an automobile manufacturer that has a compact automobile, a sports car, and a luxury automobile in its product line.

Case 14.1 **Friendly Market Versus Circle K**

Friendly Market is a convenience store located directly across the street from a Circle K convenience store. Circle K is a national chain, and its stores enjoy the benefits of national advertising campaigns, particularly the high visibility these campaigns bring. All Circle K stores have large red-and-white store signs, identical merchandise assortments, standardized floor plans, and they are open 24-7. Friendly Market, in contrast, is a one-of-a-kind "mom-and-pop" variety convenience store owned and managed by Billy Wong. Billy's parents came to the United States from Taiwan when Billy was ten years old. After graduating from high school, Billy worked in a variety of jobs, both full and part time, and for most of the past ten years, Billy has been a Circle K store employee.

In 2002, Billy made a bold move to open his own convenience store. Don's Market, a mom-and-pop convenience store across the street from the Circle K, went out of business, so Billy gathered up his life savings and borrowed as much money as he could from friends, relatives, and his bank. He bought the old Don's Market building and equipment, renamed it Friendly Market, and opened its doors for business in November 2008. Billy's core business philosophy is to greet everyone who comes in and to get to know all his customers on a first-name basis. He also watches Circle K's prices closely and seeks to have lower prices on at least 50% of the merchandise sold by both stores.

To the surprise of the manager of the Circle K across the street, Friendly Market has prospered. In 2009, Billy's younger sister, who held a master's degree from Indiana University, conducted a survey of Billy's target market to gain a better understanding of why Friendly Market was successful. She drafted a simple questionnaire and did the telephone interviewing herself. She used the local telephone book and called a random sample of over 150 respondents whose residences were listed within three miles of Friendly Market. She then created an XL Data Analyst data set with the following variable descriptions and values.

Question	Value Labels
Do you use Friendly Market regularly?	*0 = No; 1 = Yes*
Do you use Circle K regularly?	*0 = No; 1 = Yes*
Where do you live?	*1 = Own home; 2 = Rent*
What is your gender?	*1 = Male; 2 = Female*
What is your work status?	*1 = Work full time;* *2 = Work part time* *3 = Retired/Do Not Work*
Do you pass by Friendly Market/Circle K corner to/from work?	*0 = No; 1 = Yes*

In addition to these demographic questions, respondents were asked if they agreed (coded with a 3), disagreed (coded with a 1), or neither agreed nor disagreed (coded with a 2) with each of the following five different lifestyle statements.

I often shop for bargains.
I always pay cash.
I like quick, easy shopping.
I shop where they know my name.
I am always in a hurry.

The data set for this case accompanies this textbook. It is named "FriendlyMarket.xlsm." Use the XL Data Analyst to perform the relationship analyses necessary to answer the following questions.

1. Do customers patronize both Friendly Market and Circle K?
2. What demographic characteristics profile Friendly Market's customers? That is, what characteristics are related to patronage of Friendly Market?
3. What demographic characteristics profile Circle K's customers? That is, what characteristics are related to patronage of Circle K?
4. What is the lifestyle profile related to Friendly Market's customers?

Case 14.2 **Your Integrated Case**

The Advanced Automobile Concepts Survey Relationships Analysis

Cory Rogers was very pleased with the way the Advanced Automobile Concepts was shaping up. Celeste Brown, the CMG data analyst, had applied differences analysis using the preferences for the various hybrid models that might be developed, and she had found a unique demographic target market profile for each model. Brown had summarized her findings into a professional PowerPoint presentation that she and Rogers presented to Nick Thomas and his assembled managers just yesterday. The presentation was one of the smoothest possible, and Thomas's development team members became very excited and animated when they realized that Advanced Automobile Concepts had a possibility of five "winner" hybrid model vehicles to work with. In fact, at the end of the meeting, Thomas had decided to go ahead with a preliminary marketing plan for each model.

Thomas informed Rogers and Brown that Zen Motors places a huge amount of emphasis on its communications, investing millions of dollars every year in many different types of advertising to convince prospective customers that the Zen Motors models are the best possible choices. Thomas explained, "Zen does not shotgun its advertising. Everything is based on solid marketing research that reveals the media usage characteristics of each target market. That is why I insisted on including the media usage information in our AAC survey. Zen corporate will most certainly shoot us down if we come to it with any preliminary marketing plan for any hybrid model that does not have advertising recommendations based on media usage research. I did not realize at the time that we would be working on all five hybrid models, but each of my development teams will need whatever media usage findings you can come up with for its particular model."

Rogers and Brown are in a meeting the following day to discuss further analysis for the Advanced Automobile Concepts project. Rogers says, "I recall that we have a lot of detail on the media habits of the AAC survey respondents. Let's see, it includes favorite television show type, radio genre, magazine type, and local newspaper section. Nick Thomas called this morning and asked if we could have our findings to him inside of a week, so I guess he and his team are moving very fast. Nick also told me that he spoke to the Zen Motors advertising group, and they have strong preferences as to what demographic factors should be used for what media. Nick says that for television, they prefer to use age; for newspaper and television, they prefer to use education; and for magazines, they prefer to use income."

Brown says, "Needs it yesterday, so what is new? Seriously, I can get to it by the end of this week and have it ready to present early next week, assuming no glitches." Rogers concludes the meeting with, "Great, just let me know on Friday morning how it is coming, as I told Nick I will call him on that day to set up the presentation."

Your task in Case 14.2 is to revisit Case 13.2 where Celeste Brown (that is, you) used differences analyses to find the unique demographic profiles for each of the five possible new hybrid models.

- Super cycle one-seat model; 120+ mpg city
- Runabout sport two-seat model; 90 mpg city, 80 mpg highway
- Runabout with luggage two-seat model; 80 mpg city, 70 mpg highway
- Economy four-seat model; 70 mpg city, 60 mpg highway
- Standard four-seat model; 60 mpg city, 50 mpg highway

1. Use each unique hybrid model demographic profile to determine whether or not statistically significant associations exist, and if they do, recommend the specific media vehicles for radio, newspaper, television, and magazines. Do not forget to use the Zen Motors advertising division's preferred demographic.
2. What is the lifestyle of each of the possible target markets, and what are the implications of this finding for the advertising message that would "speak" to this market segment when the hybrid model is introduced?
3. Perform the proper analyses to identify the salient demographic, belief, and/or attitude factors that are related to preferences for each of the five different hybrid models under consideration. With each hybrid automobile model, prepare a summary that:
   a. Lists the statistically significant independent variables (use 95% level of confidence).
   b. Interprets the direction of the relationship of each statistically significant independent variable with respect to the preference for the hybrid model concerned.
   c. Assesses the strength of the statistically significant independent variables as they join to predict the preferences for the hybrid model concerned.

15

Preparing and Presenting Your Research Report

LEARNING OBJECTIVES

- To appreciate the importance of the marketing research report

- To learn about an online report writing tool, the iReportWriter Assistant, that will help you write better reports

- To know what material should be included in each part of the marketing research report

- To learn the basic guidelines for writing effective marketing research reports

- To learn how to organize the written report by making effective use of headings and subheadings

- To know how to use visuals such as figures, tables, charts, and graphs

- To learn how to make pie and bar charts using XL Data Analyst and Excel

- To understand there are ethical considerations in preparting visuals

- To learn the basic principles for presenting your report orally

Introducing the iReportWriter Assistant

Interpersonal communication? Why should I study that? I talk to people all the time; I've done it all my life. I communicate with people all day. I write papers and emails all the time. I don't need to be taught something that just comes naturally. Do you feel that way about communication? If so, let's explore a couple of other questions. Have you ever listened to an entire presentation only to wonder what the point of the speech was? Do you find yourself carrying on a conversation with someone only to realize you don't know what the person has been talking about for the last five minutes? Have you ever read a report to find you have learned nothing from it? If you answered yes to any of these questions, you see the importance of learning effective communication. Communication is an essential tool for your success in business. But don't be fooled into thinking it will be any easier to attain than any other business fundamental. As John Powell said, "Communication works for those who work at it."[1] William B. Chiasson, CFO of Leapfrog Enterprises and former senior vice president and CFO of Levi Strauss and Company, gave the following statement as advice for MBA graduates: "Anyone pursuing an MBA should emphasize communication and interpersonal skills, the ability to work in small and large teams, and the ability to work with people in a multi-disciplinary capacity."[2] The business world is without a doubt calling out for good communicators. If you want to be prepared for your career, you must ensure that you have the needed communication skills.

A career in marketing requires a variety of communication skills including the ability to present research results in a spoken and written manner. But writing a marketing research report for the first time can be a bit daunting and confusing. The authors of your textbook recognize the sometimes overwhelming job of the research report and have provided an online tool to help you understand this job.

In this chapter you will be introduced to a new online report writing tool, called iReportWriter Assistant. This tool takes you through the entire report writing process. You begin with the prewriting steps of analyzing your purpose, anticipating your audience, and adapting the message to the audience. Next, you research your topic (a process discussed in great detail in this textbook), organize your information into a workable outline, and compose your first draft. Much of the work is done after these six steps while you revise, proofread, and evaluate whether your report will accomplish your purpose.[3]

Heather Howard
Donofrio, Ph.D.,
Business
Communications

Other aspects of the report to consider are the citations (the style to be used), grammar, and professional graphics. All parts of the report should be as flawless as possible for the report to be effective. (Your product is a reflection of you and your company.) The online writing tool will ensure that you have the information needed to create a masterful marketing research report that can contribute to a successful business career.

Source: Heather Donofrio.

We asked Dr. Heather Donofrio to introduce you to this chapter in our opening vignette. One of the points she makes clear is the importance of being an effective communicator, both written and oral. If you have been following our integrated case, Advanced Automobile Concepts, you know that the data analysis for Nick Thomas's project is finished. Cory Rogers and his CMG Research team have worked diligently to investigate the market potential of hybrid cars for Advanced Automobile Concepts, and they are ready to prepare their findings and recommendations for presentation. You might think the bulk of their work is finished, but that is not the case. Now begins the task of sifting through the hundreds of pages of computer output and other information to determine what to present and then how to present it clearly and effectively. When the members of the team have prepared the written report, they will also need to decide which elements are critical to include in the oral presentation to the client.

Compiling a market research report is a challenging (and sometimes daunting) task. You must decide what parts need to be in the report, what content needs to be in each part, what kinds of visuals to include, and what format to follow for headings and subheadings. Though report writing is our final chapter this does not indicate that it is less important than our other topics have been.[4] On the contrary, it means that communicating the results of your research is the culmination of the entire process. Being able to do so effectively and efficiently is critical to your success. In fact, all of your outstanding data and significant findings and recommendations are meaningless if you cannot communicate them in such a way that the client knows what you have said, understands your meaning, and responds appropriately.

The Importance of the Marketing Research Report

The **marketing research report** is a factual message that transmits research results, vital recommendations, conclusions, and other important information to the client, who in turn bases his or her decision making on the contents of the report. This chapter deals with the essentials of writing and presenting the marketing research report. Researchers must provide client value in the research report. The marketing research report is the product that represents the efforts of the marketing research team, and it may be the only part of the project that the client will see. If the report is poorly written, riddled with grammatical errors, sloppy, or inferior in any way, the quality of the research (including its analysis and information) becomes suspect and its credibility is reduced. If organization and presentation are faulty, the reader may never reach the intended conclusions.

> The marketing research report is a factual message that transmits research results, vital recommendations, conclusions, and other important information to the client, who in turn bases his or her decision making on the contents of the report.

If, on the other hand, all aspects of the report are done well, the report will not only communicate properly, but it will also serve to build credibility. Marketing research users,[5] as well as marketing research suppliers,[6] agree that reporting the research results is one of the most important aspects of the marketing research process. Many managers will not be involved in any aspect of the research process but will use the report to make business decisions. Effective reporting is essential, and all of the principles of organization, formatting, good writing, and good grammar must be employed.

> The time and effort expended in the research process are wasted if the report does not communicate effectively.

Improving the Efficiency of Report Writing

You are probably thinking, based on the report writing that you have done thus far in your college career, that writing a marketing research report is a formidable task. You are right. It is complex, involved, and can be very time consuming. However, in recent years several technological advances have greatly improved report writing. There are several software tools now available to help researchers gain efficiency in report writing. For example, Burke Inc. provides its clients with access to its online reporting tool, Digital Dashboard, which allows clients to watch data come in as they are being collected and organizes data into presentation-quality tables. Readers can examine total results or subgroup analysis of any type. Thus, **online reporting software** electronically distributes marketing research reports to selected managers in an interactive format that allows each user to conduct his or her own analyses. We've tried to make your report writing more efficient as well. We have prepared the iReportWriter Assistant, which you can access on the website for this textbook. The iReportWriter Assistant is explained in more detail in Marketing Research Application 15.1.

> Report writing can be complex, involved, and time consuming. However, if you read this chapter closely you will take a great step toward being a more effective and efficient report writer!

The report represents the effort of the entire research team, but it may be the only part of the project seen by the client.

Organizing Your Written Report

Marketing research reports are tailored to specific audiences and purposes, and you must consider both in all phases of the research process, including planning the report. Before you begin writing, then, you must answer some basic questions: What message do you want to communicate? What is your purpose? Who is the audience? Are there multiple audiences? What does your audience know? What does your audience need to know? What are your audience's interests, values, concerns? These and other questions must be addressed before you decide how to structure your report. Doing so will help you see things through the eyes of your audience and increase the success of your communication. This is your opportunity to ask that basic (and very critical) question from the reader's point of view: "What's in it for me?"

Once you have answered these basic questions, you need to determine the format of your document. If the organization for which you are conducting the research has specific guidelines for preparing the document, you should follow them. However, if no specific guidelines are provided, there are certain elements that must be considered when you are preparing the report. These elements can be grouped in three sections: front matter, body, and end matter. See Table 15.1 for details.

Have you been given a required format to follow? If not, there are guidelines on the elements a report should contain.

Front Matter

The **front matter** consists of all pages that precede the first page of the report—the title page, letter of authorization (optional), letter/memo of transmittal, table of contents, list of illustrations, and abstract/executive summary.

Front matter consists of all pages that precede the first page of the report.

TITLE PAGE   The **title page** (Figure 15.1) contains four major items of information: (1) the title of the document, (2) the organization/person(s) for whom the report was prepared, (3) the

MARKETING RESEARCH APPLICATION 15.1

Practical Applications

Your iReportWriter Assistant

Because report preparation is so critical to the marketing researcher, you have been provided with a tool to guide you through the marketing research report writing process. This tool, the iReportWriter Assistant, provides an overall discussion of the research report from the prewriting step (analyzing your purpose, anticipating your audience, and adapting the message to the audience) through the research step (including research that you have learned about in this text, organization of your information into a workable outline, and composition of your *first* draft), and finally to the revision step (revision, proofreading, and evaluation of whether or not your report will accomplish your purpose).

Writing Process PowerPoints

There is a file that describes the basics of writing a research report.

Templates to Help You Get Started

The iReportWriter Assistant helps provides templates for the title page and list of illustrations along with letters of authorization and transmittal, table of contents, research objectives, and method. Headings and subheadings are also explained so that the information you provide in a report is clear and flows well.

Help with Grammar and Citations

Despite the statistical accuracy and thorough coverage you may provide in your report, if your grammar is lacking, readers may question your ability, dedication, and effectiveness. An online grammar help is also provided with the iReportWriter Assistant. Last, it is likely that that you have used information from other sources. Proper citation is not only polite, it is a requirement in order to avoid plagiarism (also discussed on the iReportWriter Assistant). You will probably be using one of two citation styles: APA (from the American Psychological Association) or MLA (from the Modern Language Association). Either is an acceptable citation form, but they differ in format. Some report writers find this part of the report a bit confusing, but never fear. The iReportWriter Assistant will provide the information needed for citing sources, including online sources.

An Example Report

As a final help to budding research report writers, an example of a proper marketing research report is supplied. Check it out before writing or compare your own report to it during the revision step.

To access the iReportWriter Assistant, go to www.pearsonhighered .com/burns on the Companion Website link for this text.

---

organization/person(s) who prepared the report, and (4) the date of submission. If names of individuals appear on the title page, they may be in either alphabetical order or some other agreed-upon order; each individual should also be given a designation or descriptive title, if appropriate.

Without being overly long, formal research reports should have titles that are as descriptive as possible. Note that the title of the Advanced Automobile Concepts report provides the reader with a good idea of what is contained in the report. Research report titles should be informative to the point that the potential reader knows the key purposes or goals of the research. It should not be "catchy" or "cute." Rather, it should be professional and to the point. The title should be centered and printed in all uppercase (capital) letters. Other items of information on the title page should be centered and printed in upper- and lowercase letters. The title page is counted as page i of the front matter; however, no page number is printed on it (see Figure 15.1). On the next page, the printed page number will be ii.

> The letter of authorization is the marketing research firm's certification to do the project.

LETTER OF AUTHORIZATION The **letter of authorization** is the marketing research firm's certification to do the project and is optional. It is particularly helpful in large organizations because it provides other users of the report with the name, title, and department of the individual(s) who authorized the project. It may also include a general description of the nature of the research project, completion date, terms of payment, and any special conditions of the research project requested by the client or research user. If you allude to the conditions of your

TABLE 15.1

Elements of a Marketing Research Report

A. Front Matter

1. Title Page
2. Letter of Authorization
3. Letter/Memo of Transmittal
4. Table of Contents
5. List of Illustrations
6. Abstract/Executive Summary

B. Body

1. Introduction
2. Research Objectives
3. Method
4. Findings
5. Limitations
6. Conclusions, or Conclusions and Recommendations

C. End Matter

1. Appendices
2. Endnotes

authorization in the letter/memo of transmittal, the letter of authorization is not necessary in the report. However, if your reader may not know the conditions of authorization, inclusion of this document is helpful.

LETTER/MEMO OF TRANSMITTAL Use a **letter of transmittal** to release or deliver the document to an organization for which you are not a regular employee. Use a **memo of transmittal** to deliver the document within your own organization. The letter/memo of transmittal describes the general nature of the research in a sentence or two and identifies the individual who is releasing the report. The primary purpose of the letter/memo of transmittal is to orient the reader to the report and to build a positive image of the report. It should establish rapport between the writer and receiver. It gives the receiver a person to contact if questions arise.

> Use a letter for transmittal outside your organization and a memo within your own organization.

The writing style in the letter/memo of transmittal should be personal and slightly informal. Some general elements that may appear in the letter/memo of transmittal are a brief identification of the nature of the research, a review of the conditions of the authorization to do the research (if no letter of authorization is included), comments on findings, suggestions for further research, and an expression of interest in the project and further research. It should end with an expression of appreciation for the assignment, acknowledgment of assistance from others, and suggestions for follow-up. Personal observations, unsupported by the data, are appropriate.

TABLE OF CONTENTS The **table of contents** helps the reader locate information in the research report. The table of contents (Figure 15.2) should list all sections of the report that follow; each heading should read exactly as it appears in the text and should identify the number of the page on which it appears. If a section is longer than one page, list the page on which it begins. Indent subheadings under headings. All items except the title page and the table of contents are listed with page numbers in the table of contents. Front-matter pages are numbered with lowercase Roman numerals: i, ii, iii, iv, and so on. Arabic numerals (1, 2, 3) begin with the introduction section of the body of the report.

> The table of contents helps the reader locate information in the research report.

FIGURE 15.1

Example of a Title Page
for a Marketing Research
Report

ADVANCED AUTOMOTIVE CONCEPTS:
A MARKETING RESEARCH STUDY
TO DETERMINE CAR MODEL PREFERENCES
AND PROFILE MARKET SEGMENTS

Prepared for
Mr. NickThomas

Prepared by
Cory Rogers
CMG Research, Inc.

July, 2010

> If the report contains
> tables and/or figures,
> include in the table of
> contents a list of
> illustrations along with
> the page numbers on
> which they appear.

LIST OF ILLUSTRATIONS If the report contains tables and/or figures, include in the table of contents a **list of illustrations** along with the page numbers on which they appear. All tables and figures should be included in this list by their respective titles, to help the reader find specific illustrations that graphically portray the information. **Tables** are words or numbers that are arranged in rows and columns; **figures** are graphs, charts, maps, pictures, and the like. Because tables and figures are numbered independently, you may have both a Figure 1 and a Table 1 in your list of illustrations. Give each a name, and list each in the order in which it appears in the report.

ABSTRACT/EXECUTIVE SUMMARY Your report may have many readers. Some of them will need to know the details of your report, such as the supporting data on which you base your

FIGURE 15.2

Example of a Table of
Contents for a Marketing
Research Report

Table of Contents

conclusions and recommendations. Others will not need as many details but will want to read the conclusions and recommendations. Still others with a general need to know may read only the executive summary. Therefore, the **abstract** or **executive summary** is a "skeleton" of your report. It serves as a summary for the busy executive or a preview for the in-depth reader. It provides an overview of the most useful information, including the conclusions and recommendations. The abstract or executive summary should be written carefully and concisely. It should be single spaced and should briefly cover the general subject of the research, the scope of the research (what the research covers/does not cover), identification of the type of methodology used (e.g., a mail survey of 1,000 homeowners), conclusions, and recommendations.

> The abstract or executive summary is a "skeleton" of your report.

Report Body

The **body** is the bulk of the report. It contains an introduction to the report, a description of how your research was performed, a presentation of your findings, a statement of limitations, and a list of conclusions and recommendations. It is best to think of the report as a resource document that will be used by various people in the future. Only a few people will read it in its entirety. Most will read the executive summary, conclusions, and recommendations. Therefore, formal reports are repetitious. For example, you may specify the research objectives in the executive summary and refer to them again in the findings section as well as in the conclusions section. Also, do not be concerned that you use the same terminology to introduce the tables and/or figures. In lengthy reports, repetition actually enhances reader comprehension.

> The body of the report contains the introduction, methodology, discussion of results, limitations, and conclusions and recommendations.

INTRODUCTION The **introduction** to the marketing research report begins the body of the report and orients the reader to its contents. With respect to format, we recommend that the first page of the body contain the title "Introduction," centered at the top of the page. This page is counted as page 1, but no page number is printed on it. All other pages throughout the document are numbered consecutively. The introduction should contain a statement of the background situation leading to the problem, the statement of the problem, and a summary description of how the research process was initiated. It should contain a statement of the general purpose of the report and also the specific objectives for the research.

RESEARCH OBJECTIVES We recommend that the **research objectives** follow the introduction as a separate section (see Table 15.1). The listing of research objectives follows the statement of the problem, since the two concepts are closely related. The list of specific research objectives often serves as a good framework for organizing the results section of the report.

METHOD The **method** follows the research objectives and describes, in as much detail as necessary, how the research was conducted, including a description of the data collection method, questionnaire design, sample plan, sample size, and analysis overview. It is customary to organize these as subheadings in the method section. Supplementary information should be placed in the appendix.

> The method describes in detail how the research was conducted.

The method section does not need to be long, but it should provide sufficient information for the reader to understand how the research was performed and how the results were achieved. It should be clear enough that other researchers could conduct a comparable study in the future.

FINDINGS The **findings** section is the most important and most detailed portion of the report. This section should be organized around the research objectives for the study. Normally, the findings are presented in tables, charts, figures, and other appropriate visuals that are accompanied by short narrative descriptions. As a general rule, it is wise to outline your findings section before you write the report. The survey questionnaire itself can serve as a useful aid in organizing your results because the questions are often grouped in a logical order or in purposeful sections. Another useful method for organizing your results is to individually print all tables and figures and arrange them in a logical sequence. Once you have the results

> The findings section is the major portion of your report and should logically present the findings of the research.

outlined properly, you are ready to write the introductory sentences, definitions (if necessary), review of the findings (often referring to tables and figures), and transition sentences to lead into the next topic.

LIMITATIONS The **limitations** section is an honest accounting of major aspects of the research that constrain or temper the findings and conclusions. No research is fautless, but all research projects strive to be as accurate as possible. So, the limitations section should note major issues, indicate why each one exists, and either mention how they affect the findings or how the research was carried out to minimize the effects of the limitation. For example, the sample size might be smaller than desired due to financial considerations, but the sample will be accurate to some ±%. Typical limitations in research reports often focus on but are not limited to factors such as time, money, size of sample, and personnel. Here is an example of how a limiation might be couched: "The reader should note that this study was based on a survey of students at State University. Care should be exercised in generalizing these findings to other university populations."

CONCLUSIONS AND RECOMMENDATIONS Conclusions and recommendations may be listed together or in separate sections, depending on the amount of material you have to report. In any case, you should note that conclusions are not the same as recommendations. **Conclusions** are the deductions and inferences that have come about based on the research findings. **Recommendations** are suggestions for how to proceed based on the conclusions. Unlike conclusions, recommendations may require knowledge beyond the scope of the research findings themselves, that is, information on conditions within the company, the industry, and so on. Therefore, researchers should exercise caution when making recommendations. The researcher and the client should determine prior to the study whether the report is to contain recommendations and build a working relationship that fosters useful recommendations.[7] A clear understanding of the researcher's role will result in a smoother process and will help avoid conflict. Although a research user may desire the researcher to provide specific recommendations, both parties must realize that the researcher's recommendations are based solely on the knowledge gained from the research report, not familiarity with the client. Other information, if made known to the researcher, could totally change the researcher's recommendations. If recommendations are required and if a report is intended to initiate further action, however, recommendations are the important map to the next step. Writing recommendations in a bulleted list and beginning each with an action verb help to direct the reader to the logical next step.

> Conclusions are outcomes or decisions based on results. Recommendations are suggestions for how to proceed based on conclusions.

End Matter

The **end matter** comprises the **appendices,** which contain additional information the reader may refer to for further reading that is not essential to reporting the data. Appendices contain the "nice to know" information, not the "need to know." Therefore, that information should not clutter the body of the report but should instead be inserted at the end for the reader who desires or requires additional information. Tables, figures, additional reading, technical descriptions, data collection forms, and appropriate computer printouts are some elements that may appear in the appendix. Each appendix should be labeled with both a letter and a title, and each should appear in the table of contents. A reference page or endnotes (if appropriate) should precede the appendix.

> End matter contains additional information that the reader may refer to for further reading but that is not essential to reporting the data.

Following Guidelines and Principles for the Written Report

The parts of the research report have been described. However, you should also consider their form and format and their style.

Form and Format

The form and format of a report includes headings, subheadings, and visuals.

> Headings and subheadings act as signals and signposts to serve as a road map for a long report.

HEADINGS AND SUBHEADINGS In a long report, readers need signals and signposts that help them find their way. Headings and subheadings perform this function. **Headings** indicate the topic of each section. All information under a specific heading should relate to that heading, and **subheadings** should divide that information into segments. A new heading should introduce a change of topic. Choose the kind of heading that fits your purpose—single word, phrase, sentence, question—and consistently use that form throughout the report. If you use subheadings within the divisions, the subheadings must be parallel to one another but not to the main headings.

Visuals

> Visuals can dramatically and concisely present information that might otherwise be difficult to comprehend.

Visuals are tables, figures, charts, diagrams, graphs, and other graphic aids. Used properly, they can dramatically and concisely present information that might otherwise be difficult to comprehend. A **table** systematically presents numerical data or words in columns and rows. A figure translates numbers into graphical displays so that findings can be comprehended visually. Examples of figures are graphs, pie charts, and bar charts.

Visuals should tell a story; they should be uncluttered and self-explanatory. Even though they are self-explanatory, the key points of all visuals should be explained in the text. Each visual should be titled and numbered. A visual should be placed on the same page either immediately before or immediately after it is referenced in the text. Of course, if sufficient space is not available, insert a page break at the end of the text and locate the visual on the following page. Additional information on preparing visuals is presented later in this chapter.

Style

> Stylistic devices can make the difference in whether or not your reader gets the message as you intended it.

Style is the way one writes a report. It includes aspects such as word choice, sentence structure, and voice. Here are ten guidelines for the style of your marketing research report.

1. Avoid long paragraphs (usually those with more than nine printed lines). Using long paragraphs is a strategy for burying a message, not for communicating, because most readers do not read the middle contents of long paragraphs. Use short paragraphs with an identifiable topic sentence to state the main idea. See Marketing Research Application 15.2 to help you become a better paragraph writer.
2. Capitalize on white space. The lines immediately before and immediately after white space (the beginning and the end of a paragraph) are points of emphasis. So are the beginning and the end of a page. Therefore, place more important information at these strategic points.
3. Use jargon sparingly. Some of your audience may understand technical terms; others may not. When in doubt, properly define the terms for your readers. If many technical terms are required in the report, consider including a glossary of terms in an appendix to assist the less-informed members of your audience.
4. Use strong verbs to carry the meaning of your sentences. Instead of "making a recommendation," "recommend." Instead of "performing an investigation," "investigate."
5. Use active voice. Voice indicates whether the subject of the verb is doing the action (active voice) or receiving the action (passive voice). For example, "The marketing research was conducted by Judith" uses passive voice. "Judith conducted the marketing research" uses active voice. Active voice is direct and forceful, and active voice uses fewer words.

MARKETING RESEARCH APPLICATION 15.2

Practical Applications

Developing Logical Paragraphs

"**A** paragraph is a group of related sentences that focus on one main idea."[a] The first sentence should include a topic sentence, which identifies the main idea of the paragraph. For example: "The research identified four major competitive strengths," is a good topic sentence because it notifies the reader that the paragraph will describe competitive strengths. Next, the body of the paragraph provides the main idea of the topic sentence by giving more information, analysis, or examples. For example, continuing from the topic sentence example given above: "Sustained brand loyalty was found to be the most significant strength." So, the paragraph has moved from the topic to one of the specifics, and the reader naturally expects the other specifics to follow in the paragraph.

Paragraphs should close with a sentence that signals the end of the topic and indicates where the reader is headed. For example: "Apart from these four competitive strengths, the research also revealed two important competitive weaknesses, which will be discussed next." Note this last sentence contains a transitional expression. A transitional expression is a word, or group of words, that tells readers where they are heading. Some examples include *following, next, second, third, at last, finally, in conclusion, to summarize, for example, to illustrate, in addition, so,* and *therefore*.[b]

Limiting the length of paragraphs should encourage good communication. As a rule, paragraphs should be short. Business communication experts believe most paragraphs should be under or around the 100-word range.[c] This is long enough for the topic sentence and three or four sentences in the body of the paragraph. The paragraph should never cover more than one main topic. For complex topics, break them into several paragraphs.

[a]Ober, S. (1998). *Contemporary Business Communication* (3rd ed.). Boston: Houghton Mifflin, 121.
[b]Ober, 123.
[c]Bovee, C., and Thill, J. (2000). *Business Communication Today* (6th ed.). Upper Saddle River, NJ: Prentice Hall, 153.

6. Eliminate extra words. Write your message clearly and concisely. Combine and reword sentences to eliminate unnecessary words. Remove opening fillers and eliminate unnecessary redundancies. For example, instead of writing, "There are 22 marketing research firms in Newark," write, "Twenty-two marketing research firms are located in Newark." Instead of saying, "the end results," say, "the results."

7. Avoid unnecessary changes in tense. Tense tells if the action of the verb occurred in the past (past tense—*were*), is happening right now (present tense—*are*), or will happen in the future (future tense—*will be*). Changing tenses within a document is an error writers frequently make.

8. In sentences, keep the subject and verb close together. The farther apart they become, the more difficulty the reader has understanding the message and the greater the chance for errors in subject-verb agreement.

9. Use faultless grammar. If your grammar is in any way below par, you need to take responsibility for finding ways to improve. Poor grammar can result in costly errors and loss of your job. It can jeopardize your credibility and the credibility of your research. There is no acceptable excuse for poor grammar.

10. Edit carefully. Your first draft is not a finished product; neither is your second. Edit your work carefully, rearranging and rewriting until you communicate the intent of your research as efficiently and effectively as possible. Some authors suggest that as much as 50% of your production time should be devoted to improving, editing, correcting, and evaluating an already written document.[8]

Of course, no report is complete until it is carefully and thoroughly proofread for grammar, spelling, and all the other little slip-ups that can occur when one writes a long and detailed document.

Using Visuals: Tables and Figures

Visuals assist in the effective presentation of numerical data. The key to a successful visual is a clear and concise presentation that conveys the message of the report. The selection of the visual should match the presentation purpose for the data. Common visuals and their purpose are listed here.[9]

Tables identify exact values.
Graphs and *charts* illustrate relationships among items.
Pie charts compare a specific part of the whole to the whole.
Bar charts and *line graphs* compare items over time or show correlations among items.
Flow diagrams introduce a set of topics and illustrate their relationships.
Maps define locations.
Photographs present an aura of legitimacy because they are not "created" in the sense that other visuals are created. Photos depict factual content.
Drawings focus on visual details.

A discussion of some of these visuals follows in the next section.

Tables

> Tables allow the reader to compare numerical data.

Tables allow the reader to compare numerical data. Effective table guidelines are as follows:

1. Use no or only one decimal place (12% or 12.2%) unless more are called for by convention ($12.23).
2. Place items you want the reader to compare in the same column, not the same row.
3. If you have many rows, darken alternate entries or double-space after every five entries to assist the reader to accurately line up items.
4. Total columns and rows when appropriate (100%).

Pie Charts

> Pie charts are particularly useful for illustrating relative size or static comparisons.

Pie charts are useful when you want to illustrate the *relative* sizes or *proportions* of one component versus others. For example, if you wanted to illustrate to your reader the proportions of consumers that preferred different types of radio programming, a pie chart would be an excellent tool for showing the relative sizes of each type of programming preference. Basically, a pie chart is a circle divided into sections. Each section represents a percentage of the total area of the circle associated with one component. Today's data analysis programs easily and quickly make pie charts. Some guidelines for pie charts are as follows:

1. Have a limited number of segments (eight, at most).
2. Place labels outside the pie slices to enhance readability for small slices.
3. Include an understandable legend.[10]

Marketing Research Application 15.3 describes how to create a professionally appearing pie chart with Excel.

Bar Charts

Bar charts are used often in reporting survey data because they are easy to interpret. They are useful to report the magnitude of response or to show magnitude or response comparisons between groups. They are also useful for illustrating change over time. Several types of bar charts can be used. Some guidelines for bar charts are as follows:

1. Put bars in logical order or arrangement.
2. Label both axes.
3. Ensure that bars are visually distinct.

Using more than eight slices in a pie chart often leads to confused interpretation.

4. Use major and minor gridlines sparingly.
5. Place labels near or in bars subject to readability.

Marketing Research Application 15.4 describes how to create a professionally appearing bar chart with Excel.

Ensuring Ethical Visuals

An **ethical visual** is totally objective in terms of how information is presented in the research report. Sometimes misrepresenting information is intentional (as when a client asks a researcher to misrepresent the data in order to promote his or her "pet project") or it may be unintentional. In the latter case, those preparing a visual are sometimes so familiar with the material being presented that they falsely assume that the graphic message is apparent to all who view it.

To ensure that you have objectively and ethically prepared your visuals, be sure to do the following:

1. Double- and triple-check all labels, numbers, and visual shapes. A faulty or misleading visual discredits your report and work.
2. Exercise caution if you use three-dimensional figures. They may distort the data by multiplying the value by the width and the height.
3. Make sure all parts of the scales are presented. Truncated graphs (having breaks in the scaled values on either axis) are acceptable only if the audience is familiar with the data.

Ethics

An ethical visual is one that is totally objective in terms of how information is presented in the research report.

MARKETING RESEARCH APPLICATION 15.3

Practical Applications

Steps in Making an Enhanced Pie Chart

If you are like other marketing researchers, you may want to enhance your written report or presentation by using some of the improved graph features on Excel 2010. This Marketing Research Application will take you step-by-step to accomplish this goal.

Step in Excel	Illustration

Step 1: Use Excel to make an Exploded Pie chart. *Select an XL Data Analyst Summarize-Percents table and insert the pie chart. Be sure that you have correctly set up the value codes and the value labels. Here is the pie chart that is generated using the Advanced Automobile Concepts data set percent summarization analysis with the variable, "Primary vehicle price type."*

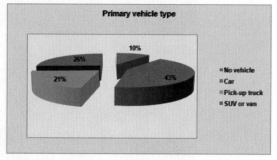

Step 2: Change the pie chart, if you want. *If you want to change the pie chart type or use some other type of graph for this chart, click on the graph to activate it, and then use the Chart tools menu to open up the chart options. With the Design menu on, click on Change Chart Type to open up a menu of options. You can select any one of these displayed on the scrolling window menu for your chart. Of course some chart types, such as line charts, are not appropriate for a percentage summarization table.*

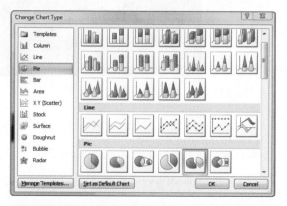

Step 3: Make the pie slices look much better. *Assuming that the exploded pie chart is your choice, you can change the appearance of the slices. Just click on any one slice. Then left-click and choose "Format Data Series" to open up the Format Data Series options window. The 3-D format option will assist you in choosing a bevel (the edge of each pie slice) and the material (texture or smooth surface) for the slices. Here, we have chosen the circle bevel for the top and bottom of the slices, and the metal material display.*

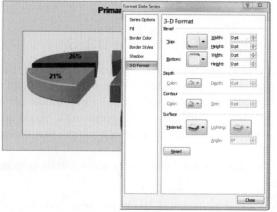

Step in Excel	Illustration

Step 4: Format the plot area. *The plot area is the area that surrounds the pie chart slices. It is quite simple to make this part of your graph look very impressive by clicking on the plot area and then right-clicking to bring up the Excel– Format Plot Area options. Here you can use Fill Gradient fill, and then use the preset colors to select the background. Notice the wide array of preset colors available to you. You can also change the angle of the gradient. If you do not wish to use a preset plot area color, you can experiment with your own color and gradient stops.*

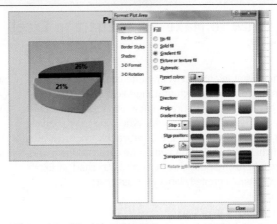

Step 5: Consider using a picture file to personalize your graph. *Click on the outer chart area and then right-click and select Format Chart Area. The options are identical to those in step 4, and we chose to use "Picture or texture fill." By clicking the "File" button, you can browse to find a picture file on your personal computer. The picture used in our example is just a stock one that comes with Microsoft Office, but you could use your own photos, graphics from a website, or any other photo file that is appropriate.*

Step 6: Enhance the chart title, legend, and plot area. *If you used a picture or changed the chart area background, it is possible that the chart title and legend are now difficult to read. Both can be enhanced (separately) by selecting them via point-and-click and then using Format Chart Title or Format Legend Menus. The options are similar to those in other chart format menu windows. Of course, you can also use any of Excel's many format options (3-D, shadow, glow, etc.) to make aspects of your graph, title, and legend stand out.*

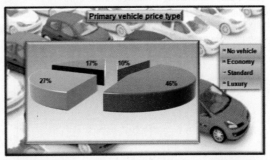

Step 7: Save your chart as a template for future charts. *If you have a chart appearance that you want to use consistently in your report or presentation, you can save this format as a template, and use Excel's chart template feature to apply it to each of the XL Data Analyst's basic pie charts.*

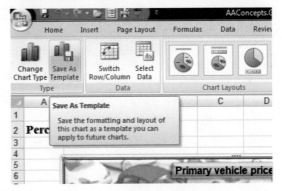

MARKETING RESEARCH APPLICATION 15.4

Practical Applications

How to Make a Bar Chart in Excel

You may want to enhance your written or oral report with a figure in the form of a bar chart using Micro Excel 2010 Chart Tools. Bar charts are often used in marketing research reports because they are easily interpreted. When you have a limited number of bars (six or less), use a vertical bar chart (called a *Column* chart in Excel). When you have seven or more bars, consider a horizontal bar chart (called a *Bar* chart in Excel). Finally, you should properly label your bar chart.

For our example we want to compare the averages of beliefs about hybrid vehicles' effects on gasoline prices, fuel emissions, and global warming. Recall that these statements were measured with a 7-point Likert scale where 1 = very strongly disagree and 7 = very strongly agree. So, do a Summarize—Averages analysis using all three statements used in the survey.

Steps in Making a Bar Chart

Step in Excel	Illustration
Step 1: Make a basic bar chart. *With your cursor, select the statements and averages in the XL Data Analyst table that results. Then use Excel's Insert menu to select the type of column chart you want to use. We used the 2-D column option. This will generate a basic bar chart.*	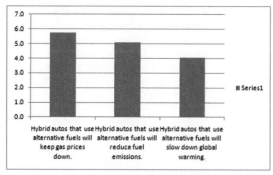
Step 2: Use "Chart Tools Design-Change Chart Type" to select a better bar chart appearance. *There are several options for bar-, cylinder-, or pyramid-shaped charts. We have selected the "clustered cylinder" one.*	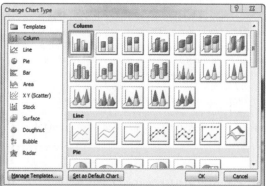 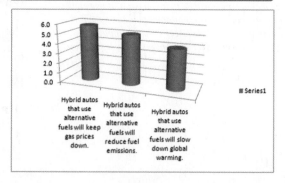

Steps in Making a Bar Chart

Step in Excel	Illustration

Step 3: Use chart appearance features to greatly improve the appearance of your bars. *The "Design" tab opens with a great many Chart Styles options as to the appearance of the bars in your graph. Some options provide for a dark or grayed plot background. Note that we have selected and applied the 3-D beveled metallic green appearance for the cylinders.*

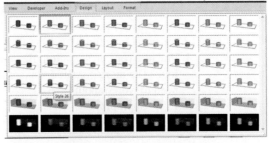

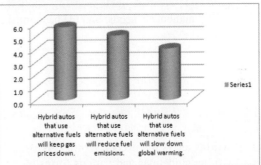

Step 4: Use Excel's Chart features to create a professional final bar chart. *There are many enhancements available for backgrounds, fonts, labels, and other aspects of Excel charts. These enhancements are available on practically all Excel charts, and you can use them to create a professional-quality final bar chart such as the one shown here.*

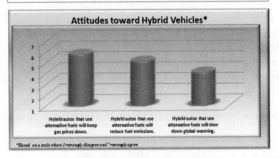

Presenting Your Research Orally

It is common to perform an oral summary of the research work. The purpose of the **oral presentation** is to succinctly present the information and to provide an opportunity for questions and discussion. The presentation may be accomplished through a simple briefing with the client, or it may be a formal presentation to several people. Telephone, compressed video, Internet, or other conferencing technology may be employed. In any case, says Jerry W. Thomas, CEO of Decision Analyst, research reports should "be presented orally to all key people in the same room at the same time." He believes this is important because many people don't read the research report and others may not understand all the details of the report. "An oral presentation ensures that everyone can ask questions to allow the researchers to clear up any confusion."[11] It also ensures that everyone hears the same thing.

To be adequately prepared when you present your research orally, follow these steps:

1. Identify and analyze your audience. Consider the same questions you addressed at the beginning of the research process and at the beginning of this chapter.
2. Find out the expectations your audience has for your presentation. Is the presentation formal or informal? Does your audience expect an electronic slide show?
3. Present your points succinctly and clearly.[12] The written report will serve as a reference for further reading.
4. Practice your presentation. Be comfortable with what you are going to say and how you look. The more prepared you are and the better you feel about yourself, the less you will need to worry about jitters.
5. Dress appropriately.

One communication consultant offers the following succinct guidelines for a presentation: (1) Keep it tight, meaning short; (2) keep it simple; (3) keep it relevant or focused on the audience's needs; and (4) be enthusiastic in your presentation.[13]

Summary

Our online report writing aid is the iReportWriting Assistant. It has report writing guidelines and various forms of assistance such as how to set up headings and subheadings, grammar, and citation guides. It even has a complete sample marketing research report.

The final stage of the marketing research process is the preparation and presentation of the marketing research report. The marketing research report is a factual message that transmits research results, vital recommendations, conclusions, and other important information to the client, who in turn bases decision on the contents of the report. The report writing and presentation stage is a vital stage of the marketing research process. This importance is attributed to the fact that, regardless of the care taken in the design and execution of the research project itself, if the report does not adequately communicate the project to the client, all is lost. In most cases, the report is the only part of the research process actually seen by the client.

Marketing research reports should be tailored to their audiences. Reports are typically organized into the categories of front matter, body, and end matter. Each of these categories has subparts, with each subpart having a different purpose. Conclusions are based on the results of the research, and recommendations are suggestions based on conclusions.

Guidelines for writing the marketing research report include proper use of headings and subheadings, which serve as signposts and signals to the reader, and proper use of visuals such as tables and figures. Style considerations include understanding the structure of paragraphs, spare use of jargon, strong verbs, active voice, consistent tense, conciseness, and varied sentence structure and length. Editing and proofreading, preferably by reading the report aloud, are important steps in writing the research report. Care should be taken to ensure that all presentations are clear and objective to the reader.

Report writers should understand the effective use of visuals such as tables and figures. Pie charts and bar charts can be effectively used to aid in communicating research results in a report. This chapter contains specific keystroke instructions on building pie charts and bar charts using XL Data Analyst and Excel. Many visual aids may be distorted so that they have a different meaning to the reader. This means that ethical considerations must be made in the preparation of the research report.

In some cases, marketing researchers are required to orally present the findings of their research project to the client. Guidelines for making an oral presentation include knowing the audience, its expectations, and the key points you wish to make; correctly preparing visuals; practicing; checking out presentation facilities and equipment prior to the presentation; having backup systems; and being positive.

Key Terms

Review Questions

1. Briefly explain the features of the iReportWriting Assistant.
2. Discuss the relative importance of the marketing research report to the other stages in the marketing research process.
3. What are the components of the marketing research report?
4. When should you include or omit a letter of authorization?
5. When should a letter of transmittal versus a memo of transmittal be used?
6. What is the difference between a table and a figure?
7. Why is the abstract or executive summary important?
8. What should be covered in the body of the report?
9. What are your options regarding placement of the research objectives in the report?
10. Discuss what information should be included in the method section of the report.
11. What is found in the findings section and how is this information logically organized?
12. Distinguish conclusions from recommendations.
13. Why are headings and subheadings important to use?
14. Illustrate the differences between levels of headings.
15. What are guidelines to preparing tables, pie charts, and bar charts?
16. What are guidelines to preparing ethical visuals?

Application Questions

17. Assume you have conducted a marketing research project for your university and that the project basically consists of providing them with a descriptive study of the student population. You've collected demographic information and information on students' attitudes toward various campus services and student life activities. Write a title page for the report. Would you use a memo or letter of transmittal? Write it.
18. Using your XL Data Analyst and Excel, prepare a pie chart and a bar chart using any data you have.
19. Why do you think we included a discussion of ethics in preparing visuals? If you wanted to make your pie chart or bar chart you prepared in the question above unethical, describe what you could do.
20. Now look at some of the answers you have written above. Evaluate your answers in light of the information contained in this chapter in Marketing Research Application 15.2 on developing logical paragraphs.
21. Visit your library and ask your reference librarian if he or she is aware of any marketing research reports (you can also ask for "reports written by faculty of the university") that have been placed in the library. Chances are good that you will be able to find several reports of various kinds. Examine the reports. What commonalities do they have in terms of the sections that the authors have created? Look at the sections carefully. What types of issues were addressed in the introduction section? The method section? How did the authors organize all of the information reported in the findings section? Are recommendations different from conclusions?

Case 15.1 **Your Integrated Case**

Advanced Automobile Concepts: Using iReportWriter Assistant

Cory Rogers was about to write up the first draft of the final report for Advanced Automobile Concepts (AAC). He decided to go to the online report writing module he learned when he took his first marketing research course in college. Because the iReportWriter Assistant is constantly updated, Rogers knew he would have access to the latest links and information that would assist him in writing his report. Nick Thomas of AAC had told Rogers that ZEN Motors had its own marketing research department and that the department heads were eager to read his report. Rogers knew that they would be particularly interested in technical issues such as how the sample size was determined and the margin of error. He had also had a frank discussion with Thomas about conclusions and recommendations. Thomas had told him, "Cory I want to know what the numbers say. What are the conclusions based on those numbers? In terms of how to proceed, I will meet with my top staff members and we will make those decisions. We have to factor in many constraints that, frankly, I am not even aware of at this point."

As a trained marketing researcher, Rogers was very familiar with the steps in the marketing research process. Knowledge of these steps was useful in writing the "method" section of his marketing research reports. For example, Rogers knew that he should address the types and sources of information used in the report; he should also address the research design and why it was chosen over other designs; he knew the sampling plan and sample size should also be included in the "method" section. Rogers made a list of topics he should cover and he started organizing these topics in terms of headings and subheadings that would eventually be used in the final report.

Rogers thought, "Ah, yes! I have to properly cite every source I have used in this report." He dreaded this part. As many times as he had written a report, remembering every detail that goes in a reference was just something that would not stay in his memory bank. Yet, he knew it was important to use the proper form for his reference list.

Before you start on the questions that follow, access the iReportWriter Assistant by going to www.pearsonhighered.com/burns and click on the Companion Website link for this text. Now read over the major topics covered in the iReportWriter Assistant before you read the following questions. Once you are finished reviewing the contents of the iReportWriter Assistant you should be ready to answer the following questions.

1. What is it about the information in the case above that Rogers should consider doing before he actually begins to write the report? Name some specific issues Rogers should address.
2. Should Rogers include the standard "Conclusions and Recommendations" section of the report? Why or why not?
3. We are told that Rogers has made a list of issues to include in the "Method" section of the report. What, if anything, is included in the iReportWriter Assistant that could help him ensure that he has included everything?
4. What section of the iReportWriter Assistant should Rogers seek out to help him with properly citing the secondary sources used in the marketing research report?

Case 15.2 **Your Integrated Case**

Advanced Automobile Concepts: Making a PowerPoint Presentation

Cory Rogers completed the report for Advanced Automobile Concepts. He decided he wanted to make some PowerPoint slides to use in his presentation of the findings. Working in Word, he wrote a title to his presentation: Advanced Automobile Concepts: A Marketing Research Study to Determine Car Model Preferences and Profile Market Segments. Then he wrote out several other comments that he wanted to include in the beginning of his presentation, such as the research objectives, and several issues dealing with the method used, such as the sample plan and the sample size. When Rogers wrote out a number of the statements that he thought would help him communicate the purpose and method of the study, he turned his attention to presenting the findings.

Rogers thought he would begin his presentation of the study with a description of the sample, often referred to as a "profile of the sample." He noticed that for Gender and Marital Status there were only two categories (male, female; and married, unmarried) for each question. He decided to just orally report the percentages of the categories. However, for some of the other variables, there were several categories of response and he felt he would communicate the results better by showing the frequency distribution table. He prepared a frequency distribution of the responses to these questions using XL Data Analyst. He continued by making several key analyses of the data using XL Data Analyst.

1. Using a word processing program, write out several of the statements that you think would be appropriate to present to the client, Nick Thomas, for an oral presentation.

2. Import the statements you prepared in question 1 into PowerPoint using copy and paste. Experiment with different color text and font sizes and styles.

3. Using the XL Data Analyst, run several frequency distributions. Using Excel or Microsoft Word, select a table style that embodies the guidelines for good tables provided in this chapter. Make any modifications to the table style that result in an effective table format.

4. Using Excel, make a bar chart of the answers to the question regarding the variable, "Americans Use Too Much Gasoline." Experiment with the different options of bar charts available to you in Excel. Select a bar chart and import that chart into PowerPoint using copy and paste. Experiment with making edits on your slide.

Endnotes

Chapter 1

1. Keefe, L. M. (2004, September 15). What is the meaning of "marketing"? *Marketing News*, pp. 17–18. Chicago: American Marketing Association.
2. Vargo, S. L., and Lusch, R. F. (2004). Evolving to a new dominant logic for marketing. *Journal of Marketing*, vol. 68, no. 1, pp. 1–17.
3. Shostack, G. L. (1977). Breaking free from product marketing. *Journal of Marketing*, vol. 41, no. 2, p. 74. Shostack's original example used General Motors.
4. Hodock, C. L. (2007). *Why Smart Companies Do Dumb Things*. Amherst, NY: Prometheus Books, 181.
5. Drucker, P. (1973). *Management: Tasks, Responsibilities, Practices*. New York: Harper & Row, 64–65.
6. Glancey, J. (1999, October). The private world of the Walkman. *The Guardian*.
7. Kotler, P., and Keller, K. (2009). *Marketing Management*. Upper Saddle River, NJ: Prentice Hall, 19.
8. Ibid.
9. Bennett, P. D. (Ed.). (1995). *Dictionary of Marketing Terms* (2nd ed.). Chicago: American Marketing Association/NTC Books, 169.
10. Ibid., 165.
11. Glossary of Terms, Retrieved February 21, 2010, from the Marketing Research Association, www.mra-net.org/resources.
12. Ibid.
13. Merritt, N. J., and Redmond, W. H. (1990). Defining marketing research: Perceptions vs. practice. *Proceedings: American Marketing Association*, pp. 146–50.
14. Market research: Pre-testing helps ad effectiveness. (2003, May 8). *Marketing*, p. 27.
15. Tracy, K. (1998). *Jerry Seinfeld: The entire domain*. Secaucus, NJ: Carol Publishing Group, 64–65.
16. Marconi, J. (1998, June 8). What marketing aces do when marketing research tells them, "don't do it!" *Marketing News*. Also see Zangwill, W. (1993, March 8). When customer research is a lousy idea. *Wall Street Journal*, p. A12.
17. Heilbrunn, J. (1989, August). Legal lessons from the Delicare affair—1. United States. *Marketing and Research Today*, vol. 17, no. 3, pp. 156–60. Also see Frederickson, P., and Totten, J. W. (1990). Marketing research projects in the academic setting: Legal liability after *Beecham vs. Yankelovich*, in L. M. Capello et al., eds., *Progress in Marketing Thought: Proceedings of the Southern Marketing Association*, 250–53.
18. Hodock, *Why Smart Companies Do Dumb Things*, 157.
19. Market research: Pre-testing helps ad effectiveness.
20. Chocolate good for the heart. . . . (2001, September). *Candy Industry*, vol. 166, no. 9, p. 11. Retrieved May 6, 2010, from ABI/INFORM Global (Document ID: 84497286).
21. Business Ignorance. (2004, August). *Industrial Engineer*, vol. 36, no. 8, p. 12.
22. The description of the MIS is adapted from Kotler and Keller, *Marketing Management*.
23. Bakker, Gerben. (2003, January). Building knowledge about the consumer: The emergence of market research in the motion picture industry. Industry overview. *Business History*, vol. 45, no. 1, p. 101 (29).

Chapter 2

1. Bartels, R. (1976). *The History of Marketing Thought* (2nd ed). Columbus, OH: Grid, 124–25.
2. You can see a list of past Parlin Award winners since 1945, at http://themarketingfoundation.org/parlin_recipients.html.
3. Hardy, H. (1990). *The Politz Papers: Science and Truth in Marketing Research*. Chicago: American Marketing Association.
4. Bartels, *The History of Marketing Thought*, 125.
5. Jack J. Honomichl received a bachelor of science degree from Northwestern University and a master's degree from the University of Chicago; Mr. Honomichl has spent a good part of his life in the research industry. He has held executive positions with the Marketing Information Center, a subsidiary of Dun & Bradstreet; Audits & Surveys Inc.; MRCA; and the *Chicago Tribune*. He frequently contributes to *Advertising Age* and the American Marketing Association's *Marketing News*. His book on the industry,

entitled *Honomichl on Marketing Research*, is published by National Textbook Company, Lincolnwood, IL. He has published nearly 400 articles in the trade and the academic press. He was inducted into the Market Research Council's Hall of Fame at the Yale Club in New York in 2002. Other members of the Hall of Fame include such notables as Arthur C. Nielsen Sr., George Gallup Sr., David Ogilvy, Marion Harper, Daniel Yankelovich, Daniel Starch, Ernest Dicter, Alfred Politz, and Elmo Roper.

6. Much of the following was excerpted from Honomichl, J. (2006). Jack J. Honomichl on the marketing research industry, in A. C. Burns and R. F. Bush, eds., *Marketing Research* (5th ed.). Upper Saddle River, NJ: Pearson/Prentice Hall, 40–41.

7. *Global Market Research 2009.* (2009). Amsterdam, The Netherlands.

8. Honomichl, J. (2010, June 30). Honomichl Top 50. *Marketing News.* Also see Honomichl, J. (2009, June 30). Honomichl Top 50. *Marketing News*; and Honomichl, J. (2008, June 15). Economy stunts industry growth. *Marketing News*, pp. H2–H3, ff.

9. Honomichl, J. (2010, June 30). Honomichl Top 50. *Marketing News.*

10. Honomichl, J. (2009, June 30). Honomichl Top 50. *Marketing News*, p. 53.

11. Ibid., p. 22.

12. Ibid., pp. 23–24.

13. Ibid., p. 33.

14. Ibid., p. 24.

15. Malhotra, N. K. (2007). *Marketing Research* (5th ed.). Upper Saddle River, NJ: Prentice Hall, 17.

16. Kinnear, T. C., and Root, A. R. (1994). *Survey of Marketing Research: Organization Function, Budget, and Compensation.* Chicago: American Marketing Association, 38.

17. Ibid., 12.

18. Personal communication with the authors from Creative & Response Research Service Inc., August 12, 2003.

19. Krum, J. R. (1978, October). B for marketing research departments. *Journal of Marketing*, vol. 42, pp. 8–12; Krum, J. R., Rau, P. A., and Keiser, S. K. (1987–1988, December–January). The marketing research process: Role perceptions of researchers and users. *Journal of Advertising Research*, vol. 27, pp. 9–21; Dawson, S., Bush, R. F., and Stern, B. (1994, October). An evaluation of services provided by the marketing research industry. *Service Industries Journal*, vol. 14, no. 4, pp. 515–26; Austin, J. R. (1991). An exploratory examination of the development of marketing research

service relationships: An assessment of exchange evaluation dimensions, in M. C. Gilly et al., eds., *Enhancing Knowledge Development in Marketing*, 1991 AMA Educators' Conference Proceedings, Chicago: American Marketing Association, 133–41; Swan, J. E., Trawick, I. F., and Carroll, M. G. (1981, August). Effect of participation in marketing research on consumer attitudes toward research and satisfaction with a service. *Journal of Marketing Research*, pp. 356–63; also see Malholtra, N. K., Peterson, M., and Kleiser, S. B. (1999, Spring). Marketing research: A state-of-the-art review and directions for the 21st century. *Journal of the Academy of Marketing Science*, vol. 27, no. 2, pp. 160–83.

20. See Neal, W. D. (2002, September 16). Shortcomings plague the industry. *Marketing Research*, vol. 36, no. 19, p. 37ff.

21. See, for example: McManus, J. (2004, April 1). Stumbling into intelligence: Market research organizations are trying to grab a bigger piece of the pie. *American Demographics*, vol. 26, p. 3.

22. Wilson, S., and Macer, T. (2007). *The 2007 Confirmit Annual Market research Software Survey.* London, UK: meaning, 19.

23. How can we increase our email marketing response rates? (2002). *CRM Magazine.* Retrieved from DestinationCRM.com.

24. See a review of this in: Braunsberger, K., Wybenga, H., and Gates, R. (2007). A comparison of reliability between telephone and web-based surveys. *Journal of Business Research*, vol. 60, pp. 758–64.

25. Fienberg, H. (2008, January). Do not call registry update. *Alert!* vol. 46, no. 1, pp. 14–15.

26. Berkowitz, D. (2003, October 24). Harsh realities for marketing research. Retrieved October 27, 2003, from eMarketer.com.

27. Fienberg, H. (2008, May). New FCC ruling on auto-dialer calls to cell phones: Are you in compliance? *Alert!* vol. 46, no. 5, pp. 38–39.

28. Schultz, D. E. (2005, February 15). MR deserves blame for marketing's decline. *Marketing News*, p. 7; and Schultz, D. E., Schultz, H. F., and Haigh, D. (2004, September). A roadmap for developing an integrated, audience-focused, market research-driven organization. *ESOMAR World Congress.* Readers seeking more information on Schultz's suggested remedy are encouraged to read the ESOMAR paper.

29. The following paragraphs are based on: Mahajan, V., and Wind, J. (1999, Fall). Rx for marketing research: A diagnosis of and prescriptions for recovery of an ailing discipline in the business world. *Marketing Research*, pp. 7–13.

30. Honomichl, J. (2003). *The Marketing Research Industry: As Old Order Crumbles a New Vision Takes Shape.* Barrington, IL: Marketing Aid Center.

31. Young, R. A., Weiss, A. M., and Stewart, D. W. (2006). *Marketing Champions: Practical Strategies for Improving Marketing's Power, Influence, and Business Impact.* Hoboken, NJ: Wiley.

32. Mahajan and Wind, pp. 7–13.

33. Schultz, MR deserves blame for marketing's decline; Schultz et al., A roadmap for developing an integrated, audience-focused, market research-driven organization.

34. Blackwell, R. D. (1998). Why the new market research? An interview. *Inc.*, vol. 20, no. 10, p. 86.

35. Clancy, K., and Krieg, P. C. (2000). *Counterintuitive Marketing: Achieve Great Results Using Uncommon Sense.* New York: The Free Press.

36. Witt, L. (2004). Inside intent. *American Demographics*, vol. 26, p. 2.

37. Honomichl, *The Marketing Research Industry*; Krum, B for marketing research departments; Krum et al., The marketing research process; Dawson et al., An evaluation of services provided by the marketing research industry; Austin, An exploratory examination of the development of marketing research service relationships; Swan et al., Effect of participation in marketing research on consumer attitudes; Malholtra et al., Marketing research.

38. Quoted in Chakrapani, C. (2001, Winter). From the editor. *Marketing Research*, vol. 13, no. 4, p. 2.

39. What's wrong with marketing research? (2001, Winter). *Marketing Research*, vol. 13, no. 4, p. 4.

40. Dawson, S., Bush, R. F., and Stern, B. (1994, October). An evaluation of services provided by the market research industry. *Service Industries Journal*, vol. 111, pp. 515–26.

41. McDaniel, S., Verille, P., and Madden, C. S. (1985, February). The threats to marketing research: An empirical reappraisal. *Journal of Marketing Research*, pp. 74–80; Akaah, I. P., and Riordan, E. A. (1989, February). Judgements of marketing professionals about ethical issues in marketing research. *Journal of Marketing Research*, pp. 112–20; Laczniak, G. R., and Murphy, P. E. *Marketing Ethics.* Lexington, MA: Lexington Books; Ferrell, O. C., and Gresham, L. G. (1985, Summer). A contingency framework for understanding ethical decision making in marketing. *Journal of Marketing Research*, pp. 87–96; Reidenbach, R. E., and Robin, D. P. (1990). A partial testing of the contingency framework for ethical decision making: A path analytical approach, in L. M. Capella, H. W. Nash, J. M. Starling, and R. D. Taylor, eds., *Progress in Marketing Thought.* Proceedings of the Southern Marketing Association, 121–28; LaFleur, E. K., and Reidenbach, R. E. (1993). A taxonomic construction of ethics decision rules: An agenda for research, in T. K. Massey Jr., ed., *Marketing: Satisfying a Diverse Customerplace.* Proceedings of the Southern Marketing Association, 158–61; Reidenbach, R. E., LaFleur, E. K., Robin, D. P., and Forest, P. J. (1993). Exploring the dimensionality of ethical judgements made by advertising professionals concerning selected child-oriented television advertising practices, in T. K. Massey Jr., ed., *Marketing: Satisfying a Diverse Customerplace*, 166–70; Klein, J. G., and Smith, N. C. (1994). Teaching marketing research ethics in business school classroom, in R. Achrol and A. Mitchell, eds., *Enhancing Knowledge Development in Marketing.* A.M.A. Educators' Conference Proceedings, 92–99.

42. See Kelley, S., Ferrell, O. C., and Skinner, S. J. (1990). Ethical behavior among marketing researchers: An assessment. *Journal of Business Ethics*, vol. 9, no. 8, p. 681ff.

43. See Whetstone, J. T. (2001, September). How virtue fits within business ethics. *Journal of Business Ethics*, vol. 33, no. 2, pp. 101–14; and Pallister, J., Nancarrow, C., and Brace, I. (1999, July). Navigating the righteous course: A quality issue. *Journal of the Market Research Society*, vol. 41, no. 3, pp. 327–42.

44. Hunt, S. D., Chonko, L. B., and Wilcox, J. B. (1984, August). Ethical problems of marketing researcher. *Journal of Marketing Research*, vol. 21, pp. 309–24.

45. For an excellent article on ethics see: Hunt, S. D., and Vitell, S. (1986). A general theory of marketing ethics. *Journal of Macromarketing*, pp. 5–16.

46. Hunt et al., Ethical problems of marketing researcher.

47. For an excellent discussion of these two philosophies relative to marketing research see: Kimmel, A. J., and Smith, N. C. (2001, July). Deception in marketing research: Ethical, methodological, and disciplinary implications. *Psychology & Marketing*, vol. 18, no. 7, pp. 672–80.

48. Bowers, D. K. (1995, Summer). Confidentiality challenges. *Marketing Research*, vol. 7, no. 3, pp. 34–35.

49. Hunt et al., Ethical problems of marketing researcher.

50. Hoffman, T. (2003). Market research providers confront credibility concerns; IT chiefs say they want ethics policies and disclosures stated more clearly. *Computerworld*, vol. 37, no. 41, p. 4ff.

51. Hodock, C. L. (2007). *Why Smart Companies Do Dumb Things.* Amherst, NY: Prometheus Books, 318–19.

52. Ensing, D. (2008, October). Let me help you with that. *Quirk's Marketing Research Review*, pp. 30–36.

53. Kiecker, P. L., and Nelson, J. E. (1989). Cheating behavior by telephone interviewers: A view from the trenches, in P. Bloom et al., eds., *Enhancing Knowledge Development in Marketing*. Chicago: A.M.A. Educators' Conference Proceedings, 182–88.

54. Hunt et al., Ethical problems of marketing researcher.

55. Ibid.

56. Jarvis, S. (2002, February 4). CMOR finds survey refusal rate still rising. *Marketing News*, vol. 36, no. 3, p. 4. Also see: D. K. Bowers. (1997). CMOR's first four years. *Marketing Research*, vol. 9, pp. 44–45; Shea, C. Z., and LeBourveau, C. (2000, Fall). Jumping the "hurdles" of marketing research. *Marketing Research*, vol. 12, no. 3, pp. 22–30.

57. Oliver, J., and Eales, K. (2008). Re-evaluating the consequentialist perspective of using covert participant observation in management research. *Qualitative Market Research: An International Journal*, vol. 11, no. 3, pp. 344–57.

58. Kimmel, A. J., and Smith, N. C. (2001, July). Deception in marketing research: Ethical, methodological, and disciplinary implications. *Psychology & Marketing*, vol. 18, no. 7, pp. 663–89.

59. Shing, M., and Spence, L. (2002). Investigating the limits of competitive intelligence gathering: Is mystery shopping ethical? *Business Ethics: A European Review*, vol. 11, no. 3, p. 343ff.

60. Mail abuse prevention system definition of spam. Retrieved March 1, 2002, from www.mail-abuse.org/standard.html.

61. New law: Is spam on the lam? *Managing Technology*. Retrieved December 6, 2003, from www.knowledge.wharton.upenn.edu.

62. The author makes no pretense that this is an original case. Rather, this case has been adapted from Sparks, J. R., and Hunt, S. D. (1998). Marketing researcher ethical sensitivity; conceptualization, measurement, and exploratory investigation. *Journal of Marketing*, vol. 62, no. 2, pp. 92–109.

Chapter 3

1. Others have broken the marketing research process down into different numbers of steps. Regardless, there is widespread agreement that using a step-process approach is a useful tool for learning marketing research.

2. Neal, William D. (2002). Linking marketing strategy and marketing research, in C. Chakrapani, ed., *Decisions That Click*. Toronto: Professional Marketing Research Society.

3. Goodman, J., and Beinhacker, D. (2003, October). By the numbers: Stop wasting money! *Quirk's Marketing Research Review*. Retrieved December 12, 2008, from Quirks.com.

4. For some insights on marketing research during hard economic times see: Anonymous. (2010, February). What is the best way to conduct research during a difficult economy? *PRweek* (U.S. Ed., New York), vol. 13, no. 2, pp. 51–52.

5. Adapted from Adler, L. (1979, September 17). Secrets of when, and when not to embark on a marketing research project. *Sales & Marketing Management Magazine*, vol. 123, p. 108.

6. Hagins, B. (2010, May). The ROI on calculating research's ROI (J. Rydholm, ed.). *Quirk's Marketing Research Review*, vol. 14, pp. 52–58.

7. Adapted from Adler, Secrets of when, and when not to embark on a marketing research project.

8. Wilson, S., and Macer, T. *The 2007 Confirmit Annual Market Research Software Survey*. London, 6.

9. This example was provided by Doss Struse to one of the authors. At the time, Mr. Struse was Director of Marketing Research for Betty Crocker®.

10. Personal communication with Lawrence D. Gibson. Also see: Gibson, L. D. (1998, Spring). Defining marketing problems: Don't spin your wheels solving the wrong puzzle. *Marketing Research*, vol. 10, no. 4, pp. 5–12.

11. Getzels, J. W., and Csikszentmihalyi, M. (1975). *Perspectives in Creativity*. Chicago: Aldine Publishing Co.

12. Raiffa, H. (1968). *Decision Analysis*. Reading, MA: Addison-Wesley Publishing Co.

13. The operative product word: Ambitiousness. (1996, December 21). *Advertising Age*, p. 14; Murtaugh, P. (1998, May). Consumer research: The big lie. *Food & Beverage Marketing*, p. 16; and Parasuraman, A., Grewal, D., and Krishnan, R. (2004). *Marketing Research*. Boston: Houghton Mifflin, 41–42.

14. Koten, J., and Kilman, S. (1985, July 15). Marketing classic: How Coke's decision to offer 2 colas undid 4½ years of planning. *Wall Street Journal*, p. 1.

15. Gibson, Defining marketing problems.

16. Ibid., p. 7.

17. Retrieved November 13, 2003, from www.dictionary.com.

18. Kotler, P. (2003). *Marketing Management: Analysis, Planning, Implementing, and Control* (11th ed.). Upper Saddle River, NJ: Prentice Hall, 102.

19. For example, see: Gordon, G. L., Schoenbachler, D. D., Kaminski, P. F., and Brouchous, K. A. (1997). New product development: Using the salesforce to identify opportunities. *Business and Industrial*

Marketing, vol. 12, no. 1, p. 33; and Ardjchvilj, A., Cardozo, R., and Ray, S. (2003, January). A theory of entrepreneurial opportunity identification and development. *Journal of Business Venturing*, vol. 18, no. 1, p. 105.

20. Kotler, *Marketing Management*, 103.

21. Webster, C. M., Seymour, R., and Daellenbach, K. (2010). "Behind closed doors": Opportunity identification through observational research. *Qualitative Market Research*, vol. 13, no. 1, pp. 24–35. Retrieved March 30, 2010, from ABI/INFORM Global (Document ID: 1945882771).

22. Nachay, K. (2010, January). Mintel predicts 2010 flavor trends. *Food Technology*, vol. 64, no. 1, p. 10. Retrieved March 30, 2010, from Research Library (Document ID: 1966978711).

23. Personal communication with Lawrence D. Gibson. Also see: Gibson, Defining marketing problems.

24. Semon, T. (1999, June 7). Make sure the research will answer the right question. *Marketing News*, vol. 33, no. 12, p. H30.

25. "Students may be surprised to learn that there is little agreement in the advertising industry as to what constitutes a 'better' advertising claim at the testing stage. The researcher is often saddled with the task of measuring the quality of the claims and with defining what a better claim should be. It would be helpful if the firm has a history of testing claims and has reached agreement on what constitutes a 'better' claim. In the end the definition of 'better' must be based on consensus or the decision cannot be made." Quote provided to the authors by Ron Tatham, Ph.D.

26. Adapted from Dictionary.com. Retrieved November 15, 2003. Also see Bagozzi, R. P., and Phillips, L. W. (1982, September). Representing and testing organizational theories: A holistic construal. *Administrative Science Quarterly*, vol. 27, no. 3, p. 459.

27. Ibid.

28. Smith, S. M., and Albaum, G. S. (2005). *Fundamentals of Marketing Research*. Thousand Oaks, CA: Sage Publications, Inc., 349.

29. Dictionary. American Marketing Association. Retrieved December 10, 2003, from www.marketingpower.com.

30. Bearden, W. O., Netemeyer, R. G., and Mobley, M. F. (1993). *Handbook of Marketing Scales*. Newberry Park, CA: Sage Publications, Inc.; Bearden, W. O., and Netemeyer, R. G. (1999). *Handbook of Marketing Scales: Multi-item Measures for Marketing and Consumer Behavior Research*. Thousand Oaks, CA: Sage Publications, Inc.; and Bruner, G. C., Hensel, P. J., and James, K. E. (2005). *Marketing Scales Handbook: A Compilation of Multi-Item Measures for Consumer Behavior and Advertising*. Chicago: American Marketing Association.

31. Moser, A. (2005). Take steps to avoid misused research pitfall. *Marketing News*, vol. 39, no. 15, p. 27.

32. See: Insights based on 30 years of defining the problem and research objectives, in A. C. Burns and R. F. Bush, *Marketing Research* (5th ed.). Upper Saddle River, NJ: Pearson Prentice Hall, 92–93.

33. See: Evgeniou, T., and Cartwright, P. (2005). Barriers to information management. *European Management Journal*, vol. 23, no. 3, pp. 293–99.

34. See Jones, S. (2006). Problem-definition in marketing research: Facilitating dialog between clients and researcher. *Psychology and Marketing*, vol. 2, no. 2, pp. 83–92.

35. Jones, p. 83.

36. Kane, C. (1994, November 28). New product killer: The research gap. *Brandweek*, vol. 35, no. 46, p. 12.

37. Rogers, K. (1970). The identity crisis of the marketing researcher, in J. Siebert and G. Wills (eds.), *Marketing Research*, Middlesex: Penguin; Small, R. J., and Rosenberg, L. J. (1975). The marketing researcher as a decision-maker: Myth or reality? *Journal of Marketing*, vol. 39, no. 1, pp. 2–7; Crawford, C. M. (1977). Marketing research and the new product failure rate. *Journal of Marketing*, vol. 41, no. 2, pp. 51–61; and Channon, C. (1982). What do we know about how research works. *Journal of the Market Research Society*, vol. 24, no. 4, pp. 241–315.

Chapter 4

1. For an interesting look at experimentation in the hospitality industry see: Lynn, A., and Lynn, M. (2003). Experiments and quasi-experiments: Methods for evaluating marketing options. *Cornell Hotel and Restaurant Administration Quarterly*, vol. 44, no. 2, pp. 75–84. Retrieved May 6, 2010, from ABI/INFORM Global (Document ID: 341111711).

2. Singleton, D. (2003, November 24). Basics of good research involve understanding six simple rules. *Marketing News*, pp. 22–23.

3. For an excellent in-depth treatment of research design issues, see Creswell, J. (2003). *Research Design: Qualitative, Quantitative, and Mixed Methods Approaches*. Thousand Oaks, CA: Sage Publications.

4. Personal communication with Holly McLennan, Marketing Director, 1-800-GOT-JUNK? on April 27, 2005; and Martin, J. (2003, October 27). Cash from trash: 1-800-Got Junk? *Fortune*, vol. 148, p. 196.

5. For one example, see Parasuraman, A., Berry, L. L., and Zeithaml, V. A. (1991, Winter). Refinement and reassessment of the SERVQUAL scale. *Journal of*

Retailing, vol. 67, no. 4, p. 420ff. A small effort of exploratory research on this topic will find many references on measuring service quality.

6. Stewart, D. W. (1984). *Secondary Research: Information Sources and Methods.* Newbury Park, CA: Sage; Davidson, J. P. (1985, April). Low cost research sources. *Journal of Small Business Management*, vol. 23, pp. 73–77.

7. Knox, N. (2003, December 16). Volvo teams up to build what women want. *USA Today*, p. 1B.

8. Bonoma, T. V. (1984). Case research in marketing: Opportunities, problems, and a process. *Journal of Marketing Research*, vol. 21, pp. 199–208.

9. Kinnear, T. C., and Taylor, J. R. (1991). *Marketing Research: An Applied Approach.* New York: McGraw-Hill, 142.

10. Sudman, S., and Wansink, B. (2002). *Consumer Panels* (2nd ed.). Chicago: American Marketing Association. This book is recognized as an authoritative source on panels.

11. Lohse, G. L., and Rosen, D. L. (2002, Summer). Signaling quality and credibility in Yellow Pages advertising: The influence of color and graphics on choice. *Journal of Advertising*, vol. 30, no. 2, pp. 73–85.

12. Wyner, G. (2000, Fall). Learn and earn through testing on the Internet: The Web provides new opportunities for experimentation. *Marketing Research*, vol. 12, no. 3, pp. 37–38.

13. In fact the Healthcare Reform bill signed into law in March 2010 by President Obama will require the FDA to develop standards requiring restaurant chains with twenty or more outlets to provide food labeling.

14. See, for example: Montgomery, D. (2001). *Design and Analysis of Experiments.* New York: John Wiley & Sons; and Kerlinger, F. N. (1986). *Foundations of Behavioral Research* (3rd ed.). New York: Holt, Rinehart, and Winston.

15. Campbell, D. T., and Stanley, J. C. (1963). *Experimental and Quasi-experimental Designs for Research.* Chicago: Rand McNally.

16. Calder, B. J., Phillips, L. W., and Tybout, A. M. (1992, December). The concept of external validity. *Journal of Consumer Research*, vol. 9, pp. 240–44.

17. Gray, L. R., and Diehl, P. L. (1992). *Research Methods for Business and Management.* New York: Macmillan, 387–90.

18. Brennan, L. (1988, March). Test marketing. *Sales Marketing Management Magazine*, vol. 140, pp. 50–62.

19. Miles, S. (2001, January 17). MyTurn is cutting back in unusual way. *Wall Street Journal*, Eastern edition.

20. Churchill, G. A., Jr. (2001). *Basic Marketing Research* (4th ed.). Fort Worth, TX: Dryden Press, 144–45.

21. Spethmann, B. (1985, May 8). Test market USA. *Brandweek*, vol. 36, pp. 40–43.

22. Melvin, P. (1992, September). Choosing simulated test marketing systems. *Marketing Research*, vol. 4, no. 3, pp. 14–16.

23. Ibid. Also see Turner, J., and Brandt, J. (1978, Winter). Development and validation of a simulated market to test children for selected consumer skills. *Journal of Consumer Affairs*, pp. 266–76.

24. Greene, S. (1996, May 4). Chattanooga chosen as test market for smokeless cigarette. *Knight-Ridder/Tribune Business News*. Retrieved on March 7, 2004, from Lexis-Nexis.

25. Power, C. (1992, August 10). Will it sell in Podunk? Hard to say. *Business Week*, pp. 46–47.

26. Murphy, P., and Laczniak, G. (1992, June). Emerging ethical issues facing marketing researchers. *Marketing Research*, p. 6.

27. Ezzy, D. (2001, August). Are qualitative methods misunderstood? *Australian and New Zealand Journal of Public Health*, vol. 25, no. 4, pp. 294–97.

28. Clark, A. (2001, September 13). Research takes an inventive approach, *Marketing*, pp. 25–26.

29. Rydholm, J. (2010, May). Steering in the right direction. (J. Rydholm, ed.). *Quirk's Marketing Research Review*, vol. 14, pp. 26–32.

30. Smith, S. M., and Whitlark, D. B. (2001, Summer). Men and women online: What makes them click? *Marketing Research*, vol. 13, no. 2, pp. 20–25.

31. Piirto, R. (1991, September). Socks, ties and videotape. *American Demographics*, p. 6.

32. Modified from Tull, D. S., and Hawkins, D. I. (1987). *Marketing Research* (4th ed.). New York: Macmillan, 331.

33. Greenbaum, T. I. (1988). *The Practical Handbook and Guide in Focus Group Research.* Lexington, MA: D.C. Heath.

34. Stoltman, J. J., and Gentry, J. W. (1992). Using focus groups to study household decision processes and choices, in R. P. Leone and V. Kumar, eds., *Educator's Conference Proceedings: Vol. 3: Enhancing Knowledge Development in Marketing.* Chicago: American Marketing Association, 257–63.

35. Last, J., and Langer, J. (2003, December). Still a valuable tool. *Quirk's Marketing Research Review*, vol. 17, no. 11, p. 30.

36. Kleber, D. (2010, March 22). Focus groups want to pay for your opinion. *The Atlanta (GA) Journal–Constitution*, p. D.4; also see: Wellner, A. (2003, March). The new science of focus groups. *American Demographics*, vol. 25, no. 2, p. 29ff.

37. Seidler, S. (2010, May). Qualitative research panels: A new spin on traditional focus groups (J. Rydholm, ed.). *Quirk's Marketing Research Review*, vol. 14, pp. 18–20.

38. Perez has shown how seating arrangements may affect focus groups. See: Perez, R. (2010, May). Shaping the discussion (J. Rydholm, ed.). *Quirk's Marketing Research Review*, vol. 14, pp. 34–40.

39. Thomas, J. (1981). Focus groups and the American dream. *White Papers, Decision Analyst, Inc.* Retrieved December 16, 2003, from www.decisionanalyst.com.

40. Langer, J. (2001). *The Mirrored Window: Focus Groups from a Moderator's Viewpoint*. New York: Paramount Market Publishing, 4.

41. Ibid., 11.

42. Flores Letelier, M., Spinosa, C., and Calder, B. (2000, Winter). Taking an expanded view of customers' needs: Qualitative research for aiding innovation. *Marketing Research*, vol. 12, no. 4, pp. 4–11.

43. Kahan, H. (1990, September 3). One-on-ones should sparkle like the gems they are. *Marketing News*, vol. 24, no. 18, pp. 8–9.

44. Roller, M. R. (1987, August 28). A real in-depth interview wades into the stream of consciousness. *Marketing News*, vol. 21, no. 18, p. 14.

45. Kahan, One-on-ones should sparkle like the gems they are.

46. An interesting article on recent developments in depth interviewing is Wansink, B. (2000, Summer). New techniques to generate key marketing insights. *Marketing Research*, vol. 12, no. 2, pp. 28–36.

47. Kates, B. (2000, April). Go in-depth with depth interviews. *Quirk's Marketing Research Review*, vol. 14, no. 4, pp. 36–40.

48. Mitchell, V. (1993). Getting the most from in-depth interviews. *Business Marketing Digest*, vol. 18, no. 1, pp. 63–70.

49. Reynolds, T. J., and Gutman, J. (1988). Laddering, method, analysis, and interpretation. *Journal of Advertising Research*, vol. 28, no. 1, pp. 11–21.

50. An example is Piirto, R. (1990, December). Measuring minds in the 1990s. *American Demographics*, vol. 12, no. 12, pp. 30–35.

51. Dictionary. American Marketing Association. Retrieved December 16, 2003, from www.marketing power.com.

52. Ibid.

53. Taylor, C. (2003, December). What's all the fuss about? *Quirk's Marketing Research Review*, vol. 17, no. 11, pp. 40–45.

54. Miles, L. (2003, December 11). Market research: Living their lives. *Marketing. Market Research Bulletin.*

Retrieved May 20, 2005, from www.brandrepublic.com.

55. For an example of ethnographic research in kitchens see: Elwood, M. (2010, May). Of stovetops and laptops (J. Rydholm, ed.). *Quirk's Marketing Research Review*, vol. 14, pp. 42–45.

56. Much of the content of this case was taken from a discussion with marketing researcher, Doss Struse.

Chapter 5

1. For an example of using secondary data for a marketing research project, see Castleberry, S. B. (2001, December). Using secondary data in marketing research: A project that melds Web and off-Web sources. *Journal of Marketing Education*, vol. 23, no. 3, pp. 195–203.

2. Quirk's Marketing Research Review. (2010, May). Survey monitor: Boomers and Gen X the most spend-happy; millennials buy more per trip (J. Rydholm, ed.). *Quirk's Marketing Research Review*, vol. 14, pp. 10, 59.

3. Weiss, M. J. (2003, September 1). To be or not to be. *American Demographics*. Retrieved October 30, 2003, from Lexis-Nexis.

4. Tootelian, D. H., and Varshney, S. B. (2010). The grandparent consumer: A financial "goldmine" with gray hair? *The Journal of Consumer Marketing*, vol. 27, no. 1, pp. 57–63. Retrieved May 5, 2010, from ABI/INFORM Global (Document ID: 1945854611).

5. Kotler, P., and Keller, K. L. (2009). *Marketing Management* (13th ed.). Upper Saddle River, NJ: Pearson Prentice Hall, 143.

6. Senn, J. A. (1988). *Information Technology in Business: Principles, Practice, and Opportunities.* Upper Saddle River, NJ: Prentice Hall, 66.

7. Grisaffe, D. (2002, January 21). See about linking CRM and MR systems. *Marketing News*, vol. 36, no. 2, p. 13.

8. Drozdenko, R. G., and Drake, P. D. (2002). *Optimal Database Marketing.* Thousand Oaks, CA: Sage Publications.

9. Kotler and Keller, 143–45.

10. McKim, R. (2001, September). Privacy notices: What they mean and how marketers can prepare for them. *Journal of Database Marketing*, vol. 9, no. 1, pp. 79–84.

11. America's experience with Census 2000. (2000, August). *Direct Marketing*, vol. 63, no. 4, pp. 46–51.

12. Actually, virtually all these firms offer some customization of data analysis, and many offer varying methods of collecting data. Still, while customization

is possible, these same companies provide standardized processes and data.

13. *Tapestry Segmentation, Segment Summaries.* (2009). Redlands, CA: ESRI. Also taken from *Tapestry Segmentation Reference Guide.* (no date). Redlands, CA: ESRI.

14. See: www.smrb.com/web/guest/core-solutions/tipping-point-segments.

15. Arbitron offers data for national, network, and local radio programming. See: http://arbitron.com.

Chapter 6

1. Malhotra, N. (1999). *Marketing Research: An Applied Orientation* (3rd ed.). Upper Saddle River, NJ: Prentice Hall, 125.

2. See Oishi, S. M. (2003). *How to Conduct In-person Interviews for Surveys.* Thousand Oaks, CA: Sage Publications, 6.

3. Cleland, K. (1996, May). Online research costs about one-half that of traditional methods. *Business Marketing*, vol. 81, no. 4, pp. B8–B9.

4. Maronick, T. (2009, Spring). The role of Internet survey research: Guidelines for researchers and experts. *Journal of Global Business and Technology*, vol. 5, no. 1, pp. 18–31.

5. Heerwegh, D. (2009). Mode differences between face-to-face and Web surveys: An experimental investigation of data quality and social desirability effects. *International Journal of Public Opinion Research*, vol. 21, no. 1, pp. 111–21.

6. See Macer, T. (2002, December). CAVI from OpinionOne. *Quirk's Marketing Research Review.* Retrieved March 15, 2004, from www.quirks.com.

7. Bourque, L., and Fielder, E. (2003). *How to Conduct Self-administered and Mail Surveys* (2nd ed.). Thousand Oaks, CA: Sage Publications.

8. Jang, H., Lee, B., Park, M., and Stokowski, P. A. (2000, February). Measuring underlying meanings of gambling from the perspective of enduring involvement. *Journal of Travel Research*, vol. 38, no. 3, pp. 230–38.

9. Ericson, P. I., and Kaplan, C. P. (2000, November). Maximizing qualitative responses about smoking in structured interviews. *Qualitative Health Research*, vol. 10, no. 6, pp. 829–40.

10. Gillian, E., and Jowell, R. (2009). Prospects for mixed-mode data collection in cross-national surveys. *International Journal of Marketing Research*, vol. 51, no. 2, pp. 267–69.

11. Roller, M., and Linelle, B. (2009, February). A volunteered response. *Quirk's Marketing Research Review*, vol. 23, no. 2, pp. 24–32.

12. See Jacobs, H. (1989, Second Quarter). Entering the 1990s: The state of data collection—From a mall perspective. *Applied Marketing Research*, vol. 30, no. 2, pp. 24–26; Lysaker, R. L. (1989, October). Data collection methods in the *U.S. Journal of the Market Research Society*, vol. 31, no. 4, pp. 477–88; Gates, R., and Solomon, P. J. (1982, August/September). Research using the mall intercept: State of the art. *Journal of Advertising Research*, pp. 43–50; and Bush, A. J., Bush, R. F., and Chen, H. C. (1991). Method of administration effects in mall intercept interviews. *Journal of the Market Research Society*, vol. 33, no. 4, pp. 309–19.

13. See Ghazali, E., Mutum, A. D., and Mahbob, N. A. (2006). Attitude towards online purchase of fish in urban Malaysia: An ethnic comparison. *Journal of Food Products Marketing*, vol. 12, no. 4, pp. 109–28; or Wang, Y., and Heitmeyer, J. (January 2006). Consumer attitude toward US versus domestic apparel in Taiwan. *International Journal of Consumer Studies*, vol. 30, no. 1, pp. 64–74.

14. Frost-Norton, T. (June 2005). The future of mall research: Current trends affecting the future of marketing research in malls. *Journal of Consumer Behaviour*, vol. 4, no. 4, 293–301.

15. Hornik, J., and Eilis, S. (1989, Winter). Strategies to secure compliance for a mall intercept interview. *Public Opinion Quarterly*, vol. 52, no. 4, pp. 539–51.

16. At least one study refutes the concern about shopping frequency. See DuPont, T. D. (1987, August/September). Do frequent mall shoppers distort mall-intercept results? *Journal of Advertising Research*, vol. 27, no. 4, pp. 45–51.

17. Bush, A. J., and Grant, E. S. (1995, Fall). The potential impact of recreational shoppers on mall intercept interviewing: An exploratory study. *The Journal of Marketing Theory and Practice*, vol. 3, no. 4, pp. 73–83.

18. Frost-Norton, The future of mall research.

19. Bourque and Fielder, *How to Conduct Telephone Interviews*.

20. Sheppard. J. (2000, April). Half-empty or half-full? *Quirk's Marketing Research Review*, vol. XIV, no. 4, pp. 42–45.

21. See, for example, Xu, M., Bates, B. J., and Schweitzer, J. C. (1993). The impact of messages on survey participation in answering machine households. *Public Opinion Quarterly*, vol. 57, pp. 232–37; Meinert, D. B., Festervand, T. A., and Lumpkin, J. R. (1992). Computerized questionnaires: Pros and cons, in Robert L. King, ed., "Marketing: Perspectives for the 1990s." *Proceedings of the Southern Marketing Association*, pp. 201–06.

22. Remington, T. D. (1993). Telemarketing and declining survey response rates. *Journal of Advertising Research*, vol. 32, no. 3, pp. RC-6–RC-7.

23. Brennan, M., Benson, S., and Kearns, Z. (2005, Quarter 1). The effect of introductions on telephone survey participation rates. *International Journal of Market Research*, vol. 47, no. 1, p. 65.

24. Snaith, T. (2009, August). Mobile research—The fifth methodology? *Quirk's Marketing Research Review*, vol. 23, no. 8, pp. 26–30.

25. At the extreme, it is reported that Chinese research companies monitor at least 50% of all telephone interviews. See: Harrison, M. (2006, Winter). Learning the language. *Marketing Research*, vol. 18, no. 4, pp. 10–16.

26. Gates, R. H., and Jarboe, G. R. (1987, Spring). Changing trends in data acquisition for marketing research. *Journal of Data Collection*, vol. 27, no. 1, pp. 25–29; also see Synodinos, N. E., and Brennan, J. M. (1998, Summer). Computer interactive interviewing in survey research. *Psychology and Marketing*, pp. 117–38.

27. DePaulo, P. J., and Weitzer, R. (1994, January 3). Interactive phone technology delivers survey data quickly. *Marketing News*, vol. 28, no. 1, p. 15.

28. Jones, P., and Palk, J. (1993). Computer-based personal interviewing: State-of-the-art and future prospects. *Journal of the Market Research Society*, vol. 35, no. 3, pp. 221–33.

29. For a "speed" comparison, see Cobanoglu, C., Warde, B., and Moeo, P. J. (2001, Fourth Quarter). A comparison of mail, fax and Web-based survey methods. *International Journal of Market Research*, vol. 43, no. 3, pp. 441–52.

30. Bruzzone, D., and Shellenberg, P. (2000, July/August). Track the effect of advertising better, faster, and cheaper online. *Quirk's Marketing Research Review*, vol. XIV, no. 7, pp. 22–35.

31. Miller, P. (2008). Web survey methods. *Public Opinion Quarterly*, vol. 72, no. 5, pp. 831–35.

32. Miles, L. (2004, June 16). Online market research panels offer clients high response rates at low prices. *Marketing*, p. 39.

33. Grecco, C. (2000, July/August). Research non-stop. *Quirk's Marketing Research Review*, vol. XIV, no. 7, pp. 70–73.

34. Greenberg, D. (2000, July/August). Internet economy gives rise to real-time research. *Quirk's Marketing Research Review*, vol. XIV, no. 7, pp. 88–90.

35. Frazier, D., and Rohmund, I. (2007, July/August). The real-time benefits of online surveys. *Electric Perspectives*, vol. 32, no. 4, pp. 88–91.

36. See, for example, Deutskens, E., Jong, A., Ruyter, K., and Wetzels, M. (2006, April). Comparing the generalizability of online and mail surveys in cross-national service quality research. *Marketing Letters*, vol. 17, no. 2, pp. 119–36; Coderre, F., St-Laurent, N., and Mathieu, A. (2004, Quarter 3). Comparison of the quality of qualitative data obtained through telephone, postal and email surveys. *International Journal of Market Research*, vol. 46, no. 3, pp. 347–57; or Kaplowitz, M. D., Hadlock, T. D., and Levine, X. (2004, Spring). A comparison of Web and mail survey response rates. *Public Opinion Quarterly*, vol. 68, no. 1, pp. 94–111; Sparrow, N., and Curtice, J. (2004). Measuring the attitudes of the general public versus Internet polls: An evaluation. *International Journal of Market Research*, vol. 46, no. 1, pp. 23–44.

37. See: Bourque and Fielder, *How to Conduct Self-administered and Mail Surveys*.

38. Nonresponse is a concern with any survey, and our understanding of refusals is minimal. See, for example, Groves, R. M., Cialdini, R. B., and Couper, M. P. (1992). Understanding the decision to participate in a survey. *Public Opinion Quarterly*, vol. 56, pp. 475–95.

39. Anderson, R. C., Fell, D., Smith, R. L., Hansen, E. N., and Gomon, S. (2005, January). Current consumer behavior research in forest products. *Forest Products Journal*, vol. 55, no. 1, pp. 21–27.

40. Grandcolas, U., Rettie, R., and Marusenko, K. (2003). Web survey bias: Sample or mode effect? *Journal of Marketing Management*, vol. 19, pp. 541–61.

41. See, for example, McDaniel, S. W., and Verille, P. (1987, January). Do topic differences affect survey nonresponse? *Journal of the Market Research Society*, vol. 29, no. 1, pp. 55–66; Whitehead, J. C. (1991, Winter). Environmental interest group behavior and self-selection bias in contingent valuation mail surveys. *Growth & Change*, vol. 22, no. 1, pp. 10–21; or Brennan, M., and Charbonneau, J. (2009, Summer). Improving mail survey response rates using chocolate and replacement questionnaires. *Public Opinion Quarterly*, vol. 73, no. 2, pp. 368–78.

42. A large number of studies have sought to determine response rates for a wide variety of inducement strategies. See, for example, Fox, R. J., Crask, M., and Kim, J. (1988, Winter). Mail questionnaires in survey research: A review of response inducement techniques. *Public Opinion Quarterly*, vol. 52, no. 4, pp. 467–91. Also see Yammarino, F., Skinner, S., and Childers, T. (1991). Understanding mail survey response behavior. *Public Opinion Quarterly*, vol. 55, pp. 613–39.

43. Conant, J., Smart, D., and Walker, B. (1990). Mail survey facilitation techniques: An assessment and

proposal regarding reporting practices. *Journal of the Market Research Society*, vol. 32, no. 4, pp. 369–80.

44. Jassaume Jr., R. A., and Yamada, Y. (1990, Summer). A comparison of the viability of mail surveys in Japan and the United States. *Public Opinion Quarterly*, vol. 54, no. 2, pp. 219–28.

45. Brown, S. (1987). Drop and collect surveys: A neglected research technique? *Journal of the Market Research Society*, vol. 5, no. 1, pp. 19–23.

46. See: Ibeh, K. I. N., and Brock, J. K-U. (2004, Quarter 3). Conducting survey research among organisational populations in developing countries. *International Journal of Market Research*, vol. 46, no. 3, pp. 375–83; Ibeh, K., Brock, J. K-U., and Zhou, Y. J. (2004, February). The drop and collect survey among industrial populations: Theory and empirical evidence. *Industrial Marketing Management*, vol. 33, no. 2, pp. 155–65.

47. A recent industry study identified effectiveness, demand for a specific modality, cost, speed of data collection, and available resources as the top five selection criteria when selecting a data collection modality. See Research Industry Trends Report. (2004, April). Prepared by Pioneer Marketing Research for Dialtek L.P. (available at www.dialtek.com).

48. For an example of a new data collection method, see Wentz, L. (2004, April 12). Mindshare to read 20,000 media minds. *Advertising Age*, vol. 75, no. 15, p. 1.

49. Philpott, G. (2005, February). Get the most from Net-based panel research. *Marketing News*, vol. 39, no. 2, p. 58.

50. Gerlotto, C. (2003, November). Learning on the go: Tips on getting international research right. *Quirk's Marketing Research Review*, p. 44.

51. Weiss, L. (2002, November). Research in Canada. *Quirk's Marketing Research Review*, p. 40.

52. Ilieva, J., Baron, S., and Healey, N. M. (2002, Quarter 3). Online surveys in marketing research: Pros and cons. *International Journal of Market Research*, vol. 44, no. 3, pp. 361–76.

53. Ho, D. Y. H. (2009, November). The rules are changing. *Quirk's Marketing Research Review*, vol. 23, no. 11, pp. 32–36.

Chapter 7

1. Sometimes open-ended questions are used to develop closed-ended questions that are used later. See, for example, Erffmeyer, R. C., and Johnson, D. A. (2001, Spring). An exploratory study of sales force automation practices: Expectations and realities. *Journal of Personal Selling and Sales Management*, vol. 21, no. 2, pp. 167–75.

2. Fox, S. (2001, May). Market research 101. *Pharmaceutical Executive*, Supplement: *Successful Product Management: A Primer*, p. 34.

3. Ideally, respondents should respond to the scale as having equal intervals. See, for example, Crask, M. R., and Fox, R. J. (1987). An exploration of the interval properties of three commonly used marketing research studies: A magnitude estimation approach. *Journal of the Market Research Society*, vol. 29, no. 3, pp. 317–39.

4. Scale development requires rigorous research. See, for example, Churchill, G. A. (1979, February). A paradigm for developing better measures of marketing constructs. *Journal of Marketing Research*, vol. 16, pp. 64–73, for method; or Ram, S., and Jung, H. S. (1990). The conceptualization and measurement of product usage. *Journal of the Academy of Marketing Science*, vol. 18, no. 1, pp. 67–76, for an example.

5. As an example, see McMullan, R., and Gilmore, A. (2003, March). The conceptual development of customer loyalty measurement: A proposed scale. *Journal of Targeting, Measurement, and Analysis for Marketing*, vol. 11, no. 3, pp. 230–43.

6. See, for example, Wellner, A. S. (2002, February). The female persuasion. *American Demographics*, vol. 24, no. 2, pp. 24–29; Wasserman, T. (2002, January 7). Color me bad. *Brandweek*, vol. 43, no. 1, p. 2; or Wilke, M., and Applebaum, M. (2001, November 5). Peering out of the closet. *Brandweek*, vol. 42, no. 41, pp. 26–32.

7. The order of the response scale does not seem to affect responses. See, for example, Weng, L., and Cheng, C. (2000, December). Effects of response order on Likert-type scales. *Educational and Psychological Measurement*, vol. 60, no. 6, pp. 908–24.

8. The Likert response format, borrowed from a formal scale development approach developed by Rensis Likert, has been extensively modified and adapted by marketing researchers so much, in fact, that its definition varies from researcher to researcher. Some assume that any intensity scale using descriptors such as "strongly," "somewhat," "slightly," or the like is a Likert variation. Others use the term only for questions with agree–disagree response options.

9. For an example of this research see: Harcar, T., and Kaynak, E. (2008). Life-style orientation of rural US and Canadian consumers: Are regio-centric standardized marketing strategies feasible? *Asia Pacific Journal of Marketing and Logistics*, vol. 20, no. 4, pp. 433–54. Retrieved May 27, 2010, from ABI/INFORM Global (Document ID: 1572046571).

10. Another way to avoid the halo effect is to have subjects rate each stimulus on the same attribute and then move

to the next attribute. See Wu, B.T.W., and Petroshius, S. (1987). The halo effect in store image management. *Journal of the Academy of Marketing Science*, vol. 15, no. 1, pp. 44–51.

11. The halo effect is real and used by companies to good advantage. See, for example, Moukheiber, Z., and Langreth, R. (2001, December 10). The halo effect. *Forbes*, vol. 168, no. 15, p. 66; or Anonymous. (2002, March 11). Sites seeking advertising (the paid kind). *Advertising Age*, vol. 73, no. 10, p. 38.

12. Some authors recommend using negatively worded statements with Likert scales to avoid the halo effect; however, evidence argues convincingly against this recommendation: Swain, S. D., Weathers, D., and Niedrich, R. W. (February, 2007). Assessing three sources of misresponse to reversed Likert items. *Journal of Marketing Research*, vol. 45, no. 1, pp. 116–31.

13. Garg, R. K. (1996, July). The influence of positive and negative wording and issue involvement on responses to Likert scales in marketing research. *Journal of the Marketing Research Society*, vol. 38, no. 3, pp. 235–46.

14. See, for example, Leigh, J. H., and Martin Jr., C. R. (1987). "Don't know" item nonresponse in a telephone survey: Effects of question form and respondent characteristics. *Journal of Marketing Research*, vol. 29, no. 3, pp. 317–39.

15. See also Duncan, O. D., and Stenbeck, M. (1988, Winter). No opinion or not sure? *Public Opinion Quarterly*, vol. 52, pp. 513–25; and Durand, R. M., and Lambert, Z. V. (1988, March). Don't know responses in survey: Analyses and interpretational consequences. *Journal of Business Research*, vol. 16, pp. 533–43.

16. Semon, T. T. (2001, October 8). Symmetry shouldn't be goal for scales. *Marketing News*, vol. 35, no. 21, p. 9.

17. See, for example, Crask, M. R., and Fox, R. J. (1987). An exploration of the interval properties of three commonly used marketing research studies: A magnitude estimation approach. *Journal of the Market Research Society*, vol. 29, no. 3, pp. 317–39.

18. Some researchers claim the use of a 0–10 scale over the telephone is actually better than a 3-, 4-, or 5-point scale. See Loken, B., et al. (1987, July). The use of 0–10 scales in telephone surveys. *Journal of the Market Research Society*, vol. 29, no. 3, pp. 353–62.

19. Elms, P. (2000, April). Using decision criteria anchors to measure importance among Hispanics. *Quirk's Marketing Research Review*, vol. 15, no. 4, pp. 44–51.

20. The authors are well aware of the need for multi-item scales in order to assess reliability and validity. However, practitioners rely greatly on single-item scales that have face validity. These are recommended single-item scales with face validity.

Chapter 8

1. A review of research on questionnaire design is reported in: McColl, E. et al. (2001). Design and use of questionnaires: A review of best practice applicable to surveys of health service staff and patients. *High Technology Assessment*, vol. 5, p. 31.

2. For examples on questionnaire development in a variety of settings go to *Google Scholar* and search "questionnaire development."

3. Malhotra, N. (2007). *Marketing Research: An Applied Orientation* (5th ed.). Upper Saddle River, NJ: Pearson Prentice Hall, 143.

4. Many marketing research studies have used observation. See, for example: Kimes, S. E., and Mutkoski, S. A. (1991). Assessing customer contact: Work sampling in restaurants. *Cornell Hotel and Restaurant Administration Quarterly*, vol. 32, no. 1, p. 82. Retrieved May 13, 2010, from ABI/INFORM Global (Document ID: 274132); Solomon, P. J., Bush, R. F., and Hair, J. F. (1976). White and black consumer sales response to black models. *Journal of Marketing Research*, vol. 13, no. 4, p. 431; and Bush, R. F., Gwinner, R. F., and Solomon, P. (1974). White consumer sales response to black models. *Journal of Marketing*, vol. 38, no. 2, p. 25.

5. Malhotra, 322–23.

6. Susan, C. (1994). Questionnaire design affects response rate. *Marketing News*, vol. 28, p. H25; and Sancher, M. E. (1992). Effects of questionnaire design on the quality of survey data. *Public Opinion Quarterly*, vol. 56, pp. 206–17.

7. For a more comprehensive coverage of this topic, see Baker, M. J. (2003, Summer). Data collection—Questionnaire design. *Marketing Review*, vol. 3, no. 3, pp. 343–70.

8. Babble, E. (1990). *Survey Research Methods* (2nd ed.). Belmont, CA: Wadsworth Publishing Co., 131–32.

9. In custom-designed projects, the researcher must develop a questionnaire for the project at hand. If the research calls for standardized information, as for example, a tracking study, the "questions" have already been determined.

10. Hunt, S. D., Sparkman, R. D., and Wilcox, J. (1982, May). The pretest in survey research: Issues and preliminary findings. *Journal of Marketing Research*, vol. 26, no. 4, pp. 269–73.

11. Dillman, D. A. (1978). *Mail Telephone Surveys: The Total Design Method.* New York: John Wiley & Sons, Inc.

12. Interested readers may wish to read: Wood, R. T., and Williams, R. J. (2007, February). "How much money do you spend on gambling?" The comparative validity of question wordings used to assess gambling expenditure. *International Journal of Social Research Methodology*, vol. 10, no. 1, pp. 63–77.

13. Loftus, E., and Zanni, G. (1975). Eyewitness testimony: The influence of the wording of a question. *Bulletin of the Psychonomic Society*, vol. 5, pp. 86–88.

14. Adapted and modified from Payne, S. L. (1951). *The Art of Asking Questions* (1st ed.). Princeton, NJ: Princeton University Press. Current source is the 1980 edition, chap. 10.

15. Several other marketing research textbooks advocate question focus. See: Baker, Data Collection. Practitioners also recommend sharp focus. See: Anonymous. (2008, February). Do's and don'ts. *CRM Magazine*, vol. 12, no. 2, p. 13-13 (special issue).

16. Webb, J. (2000, Winter). Questionnaires and their design. *Marketing Review*, vol. 1, no. 2, pp. 197–218.

17. Ibid.

18. Question clarity must be achieved for respondents of different education levels, ages, socioeconomic strata, and even intelligence: Noelle-Neumann, E. (1970, Summer). Wanted: Rules for wording structured questionnaires. *Public Opinion Quarterly*, vol. 34, no. 2, pp. 191–201.

19. Webb, Questionnaires.

20. For memory questions, it is advisable to have respondents reconstruct specific events. See, for example, Cook, W. A. (1987, February-March). Telescoping and memory's other tricks. *Journal of Advertising Research*, vol. 27, no. 1, pp. RC1–RC8.

21. Baker, Data collection.

22. Connell, S. (2002, Winter). Travel broadens the mind: The case for international research. *International Journal of Marketing Research*, vol. 44, no. 1, pp. 97–108.

23. Lerman, D., Maxwell, S., Jallat, F., and Reed, G. (2006). Single language surveys: An efficient method for researching cross-cultural differences. *Advances in Consumer Research–Latin American Conference Proceedings*, vol. 1, pp. 63–64.

24. Sinickas, A. (2005, December/January). Cultural differences and research. *Strategic Communication Management*, vol. 9, no. 1, p. 12.

25. For tips on using a translation service, see: Podrovitz, B., and Stejskal, J. (2005, November). Success in any language. *Quirk's Marketing Research Review*, vol. 19, no. 10, pp. 38–42.

26. Baker, Data collection.

27. Webb, Questionnaires.

28. Baker, Data collection.

29. Webb, Questionnaires.

30. Patten, M. (2001). *Questionnaire Research*. Los Angeles: Pyrczak Publishing, 9.

31. See, for example, Anonymous. (2008, May). More ways to build a better survey. *HR Focus*, vol. 85, no. 5, pp. 13–14.

32. Brennan, M., Benson, S., and Kearns, Z. (2005, Quarter 1). The effect of introductions on telephone survey participation rates. *International Journal of Market Research*, vol. 47, no.1, pp. 65–74.

33. There is some evidence that mention of confidentiality has a negative effect on response rates, so the researcher should consider not mentioning it in the introduction even if confidentiality is in place. See Brennan et al., The effect of introductions on telephone survey participation rates.

34. Screens can be used to quickly identify respondents who will not answer honestly. See Waters, K. M. (1991, Spring-Summer). Designing screening questionnaires to minimize dishonest answers. *Applied Marketing Research*, vol. 31, no. 1, pp. 51–53.

35. For recommended guidelines for introductions in "b-to-b" surveys, see Durkee, A. (2005, March). First impressions are everything in b-to-b telephone surveys. *Quirk's Marketing Research Review*, vol. XIX, no. 3, pp. 30–32.

36. While we advocate common sense, researchers are mindful of question order effects. See, for instance, Latflin, L., and Hansen, M. (2006, October). *Quirk's Marketing Research Review*, vol. 20, no. 9, pp. 40–44.

37. Smith, R., Olah, D., Hansen, B., and Cumbo, D. (2003, November/December). The effect of questionnaire length on participant response rate: A case study in the U.S. cabinet industry. *Forest Products Journal*, vol. 53, no. 11/12, pp. 33–36.

38. Webb, Questionnaires.

39. Bethlehem, J. (1999/2000, Winter). The routing structure of questionnaires. *International Journal of Market Research*, vol. 42, no. 1, pp. 95–110.

40. Baker, Data collection.

41. At least one group-administered survey found that question sequence had no effect on cooperation rate. See: Roose, H., De Lange, D., Agneessens, F., and Waege, H. (2002, May). Theatre audience on stage: Three experiments analyzing the effects of survey design features on survey response in *Audience Research. Marketing Bulletin*, vol. 13, pp. 1–10.

42. They also represent new presentation and format considerations that need to be researched. See, for example, Healey, B., Macpherson, T., and Kuijten, B. (2005, May). An empirical evaluation of three web

survey design principles. *Marketing Bulletin*, vol. 16, pp. 1–9; or Christian, L. M., Dillman, D. A., and Smyth, J. D. (2007, Spring). Helping respondents get it right the first time: The influence of words, symbols, and graphics in web surveys. *Public Opinion Quarterly*, vol. 71, no. 1, pp. 113–25.

43. Highly sophisticated questionnaire design systems have a great many question formats and types in their libraries, and they sometimes have algorithms built into them to arrange the questions into a logical format. See Jenkins, S., and Solomonides, T. (1999/2000, Winter). Automating questionnaire design and construction. *International Journal of Market Research*, vol. 42, no. 1, pp. 79–95.

44. While very efficient, "check all that apply" questions have recently been found to be slightly less effective than "forced choice" or "yes/no" question formats. See, Smyth, J. D., Christian, L. M., and Dillman, D. A. (Spring, 2008). Does "yes or no" on the telephone mean the same as "check-all-that-apply" on the web? *Public Opinion Quarterly*, vol. 72, no. 1, pp. 103–13.

45. At least one author says to not pretest is foolhardy: Webb, Questionnaires.

46. Some authors refer to "pretesting" as "piloting" the questionnaire, meaning "pilot testing" the questionnaire. See: Baker, Data collection.

47. Normally pretests are done individually, but a focus group could be used. See Long, S. A. (1991, May 27). Pretesting questionnaires minimizes measurement error. *Marketing News*, vol. 25, no. 11, p. 12.

48. For a detailed description of the goals and procedures used in pretesting, see Czaja, R. (1998, May). Questionnaire pretesting comes of age. *Marketing Bulletin*, vol. 9, pp. 52–64.

49. For a comprehensive article on pretesting, see Presser, S., Couper, M. P., Lessler, J. T., Martin, E., Martin, J., Rothgeb, J. M., and Singer, E. (2004, Spring). Methods for testing and evaluating survey questions. *Public Opinion Quarterly*, vol. 68, no. 1, pp. 109–30.

Chapter 9

1. See, for example, Lenth, R. (2001, August). Some practical guidelines for effective sample size determination. *American Statistician*, vol. 55, no. 3, pp. 187–93; Williams, G. (1999, April). What size sample do I need? *Australian and New Zealand Journal of Public Health*, vol. 23, no. 2, pp. 215–17; or Cesana, B. M, Reina, G., and Marubini, E. (2001, November). Sample size for testing a proportion in clinical trials: A "two-step" procedure combining power and confidence interval expected width. *American Statistician*, vol. 55, no. 4, pp. 288–92.

2. By "real" we mean that there is some value that truly represents the average height of everyone in your class. We could approximate this by carefully measuring everyone in the class, alternating persons taking the measurements, and taking several measurements of each person and then averaging all the measurements. The point is, there is some "real" value in the population though we rarely ever know what that value is. These values are called parameters by statisticians.

3. See, for example, Stephen, E. H., and Soldo, B. J. (1990, April). How to judge the quality of a survey. *American Demographics*, vol. 12, no. 4, pp. 42–43.

4. See Bradburn, N. M., and Sudman, S. (1988). Polls and surveys: Understanding what they tell us; Cantril, A. H. (1991). The opinion connection: Polling, politics, and the press; Cantril, A. H. Public opinion polling, retrieved from Answers.com on April 29, 2007; Landon in a landslide: The poll that changed polling. Retrieved from www.historymatter.gmu.edu on April 29, 2007.

5. We use percents throughout this chapter because they are more intuitive than averages.

6. There are myriad other considerations that can factor into sample size calculation and are beyond the scope of this book. See, for example, Parker, R. A., and Berman, N. G. (2003, August). Sample size: More than calculations. *American Statistician*, vol. 57, no. 3, pp. 166–71.

7. See Shiffler, R. E., and Adams, A. J. (1987, August). A correction for biasing effects of pilot sample size on sample size determination. *Journal of Marketing Research*, vol. 24, no. 3, pp. 319–21.

8. For a caution on this approach, see Browne, R. H. (2001, November). Using the sample range as a basis for calculating sample size in power calculations. *The American Statistician*, vol. 55, no. 4, pp. 293–98.

9. Foreman, J., and Collins, M. (1991, July). The viability of random digit dialing in the UK. *Journal of the Market Research Society*, vol. 33, no. 3, pp. 219–27; and Hekmat, F., and Segal, M. (1984). Random digit dialing: Some additional empirical observations, in D. M. Klein and A. E. Smith, eds., *Marketing Comes of Age: Proceedings of the Southern Marketing Association*, 176–80.

10. Of course there are other methods such as taking all the listings and putting them in a hat and blindly drawing each until the sample size is reached. This method, the blind-draw, is used frequently for small populations. Nevertheless, this would require considerable effort assuming a large population.

11. For a somewhat more technical description of cluster sampling, see Carlin, J. B., and Hocking, J. (1999,

October). Design of cross-sectional surveys using cluster sampling: An overview with Australian case studies. *Australian and New Zealand Journal of Public Health*, vol. 23, no. 5, pp. 546–51.

12. In fact, systematic sampling is a form of cluster sampling.

13. See also Sudman, S. (1985, February). Efficient screening methods for the sampling of geographically clustered special populations. *Journal of Marketing Research*, vol. 22, pp. 20–29.

14. Bradley, N. (1999, October). Sampling for Internet surveys: An examination of respondent selection for Internet research. *Journal of the Market Research Society*, vol. 41, no. 4, p. 387.

15. Academic marketing researchers often use convenience samples of college students. See Peterson, R. A. (2001, December). On the use of college students in social science research: Insights from a second-order meta-analysis. *Journal of Consumer Research*, vol. 28, no. 3, pp. 450–61.

16. Wyner, G. A. (2001, Fall). Representation, randomization, and realism. *Marketing Research*, vol. 13, no. 3, pp. 4–5.

17. For an application of referral sampling, see Moriarity Jr., R. T., and Spekman, R. E. (1984, May). An empirical investigation of the information sources used during the industrial buying process. *Journal of Marketing Research*, vol. 21, pp. 137–47.

18. For a detailed description of how to select a quota sample, see Baker, M. (2002, Autumn). *Marketing Review*, vol. 3, no. 1, pp. 103–20.

19. Paramar, A. (2003, February). Tailor techniques to each audience in Latin market. *Marketing News*, vol. 37, no. 3, pp. 4–6.

20. The nature of sample bias for online surveys is just becoming known. See, for example, Grandcolas, U., Rettie, R., and Marusenko, K. (2003, July). Web survey bias: Sample or mode effect? *Journal of Marketing Management*, vol. 19, no. 5/6, pp. 541–61.

21. For an historical perspective and prediction about online sampling, see Sudman, S., and Blair, E. (1999, Spring). Sampling in the twenty-first century. *Academy of Marketing Science*, vol. 27, no. 2, pp. 269–77.

22. Internet surveys can access hard-to-reach groups. See Pro and con: Internet interviewing. (1999, Summer). *Marketing Research*, vol. 11, no. 2, pp. 33–36.

23. See, as an example, Dahlen, M. (2001, July/August). Banner advertisements through a new lens. *Journal of Advertising Research*, vol. 41, no. 4, pp. 23–30.

24. For a comparison of online sampling to telephone sampling, see Cooper, M. P. (2000, Winter). Web surveys: A review of issues and approaches. *Public Opinion Quarterly*, vol. 64, no. 4, pp. 464–94.

25. Grossnickle, J., and Raskin, O. (2001, Summer). What's ahead on the Internet. *Marketing Research*, vol. 13, no. 2, pp. 8–13.

26. Miller, T. W. (2001, Summer). Can we trust the data of online research? *Marketing Research*, vol. 13, no. 2, pp. 26–32.

27. Bradley, N. (1999, October). Sampling for Internet surveys: An examination of respondent selection for Internet research. *Journal of the Market Research Society*, vol. 41, no. 4, p. 387.

Chapter 10

1. Personal communication, quoted by permission.

2. Interviewer errors have been around for a very long time. See Snead, R. (1942). Problems of field interviewers. *Journal of Marketing*, vol. 7, no. 2, pp. 139–45.

3. These problems are international in scope. See Kreitzman, L. (1990, February 22). Market research: Virgins and groupies. *Marketing*, pp. 35–38, for the United Kingdom.

4. There is a move in the United Kingdom for interviewer certification. See Hemsley, S. (2000, August 17). Acting the part. *Marketing Week*, vol. 23, no. 28, pp. 37–40.

5. For a set of recommendations, see Harrison, D. E., and Krauss, S. I. (2002, October). Interviewer cheating: Implications for research on entrepreneurship in Africa. *Journal of Developmental Entrepreneurship*, vol. 3, no. 7, pp. 319–30.

6. Epstein, W. M. (2006, January). Response bias in opinion polls and American social welfare. *Social Science Journal*, vol. 43, no. 1, pp. 99–110.

7. Intentional errors are especially likely when data is supplied by competitors. See Croft, R. (1992, Third Quarter). How to minimize the problem of untruthful response. *Business Marketing Digest*, vol. 17, no. 3, pp. 17–23.

8. See also, Conrad, F., and Schober, M. (2000, Spring). Clarifying question meaning in a household survey. *Public Opinion Quarterly*, vol. 64, no. 1, pp. 1–28.

9. Based on: Bronner, F., and Kuijlen, T. (2007). The live or digital interviewer. *International Journal of Market Research*, vol. 49, no. 2, pp. 167–90.

10. Coleman, L. G. (1991, January 7). Researchers say nonresponse is single biggest problem. *Marketing News*, vol. 1, no. 25, pp. 32–33; Landler, M. (1991, February 11). The "bloodbath" in market research. *Business Week*, pp. 72, 74; and Jarvis, S. (2002, February 4).

CMOR finds survey refusal rate still rising. *Marketing News*, vol. 3, no. 4, p. 36.

11. Anonymous. (2003, Spring). The case for caution: This system is dangerously flawed. *Public Opinion Quarterly*, vol. 67, no. 1, pp. 5–17.

12. Baim, J. (1991, June). Response rates: A multinational perspective. *Marketing & Research Today*, vol. 2, no. 19, pp. 114–19.

13. Jarvis, S. (2002, February 4). CMOR finds survey refusal rate still rising. *Marketing News*, vol. 36, no. 3, p. 4.

14. Mitchel, J. O. (2002, Fall). Telephone surveys: The next buggy whip? *LIMRA's MarketFacts Quarterly*, vol. 4, no. 21, p. 39.

15. Groves, R. M., Couper, M. P., Presser, S., Singer, E., Tourangeau, R., Acosta, G. P., and Nelson, L. (2001, First Quarter). Experiments in producing nonresponse bias. *Public Opinion Quarterly*, 2006 Special Issue, vol. 70, no. 5, pp. 720–36.

16. Tourangeau, R., and Yan, T. (2007, September). Sensitive questions in surveys. *Psychological Bulletin*, vol. 133, no. 5, pp. 859–83.

17. Jarvis, S. (2002, February). CMOR finds survey refusal rate still rising. *Marketing News*, vol. 36, no. 3.

18. Groves, R. M., Presser, S., and Dipko, S. (2004, Spring). The role of topic interest in survey participation decisions. *Public Opinion Quarterly*, vol. 68, no. 1, pp. 2–31.

19. Some authors use the term "unit nonresponse" to refer to item omissions. See, for example, Hudson, D., Seah, L-H., Hite, D., and Haab, T. (2004). Telephone presurveys, self-selection, and non-response bias to mail and Internet surveys in economic research. *Applied Economics Letters*, vol. 11, no. 4, pp. 237–40.

20. Shoemaker, P. J., Eichholz, M., and Skewes, E. A. (2002, Summer). Item nonresponse: Distinguishing between don't know and refuse. *International Journal of Public Opinion Research*, vol. 14, no. 2, pp. 193–201.

21. For yea-saying and nay-saying, see Bachman, J. G., and O'Malley, P. M. (1985, Summer). Yea-saying, nay-saying, and going to extremes: Black–white differences in response styles. *Public Opinion Quarterly*, vol. 48, pp. 491–509; and Greenleaf, E. A. (1992, May). Improving rating scale measures by detecting and correcting bias components in some response styles. *Journal of Marketing Research*, vol. 29, no. 2, pp. 176–88.

22. Fisher, S. (2007). How to spot a fake. *Quirk's Marketing Research Review*, vol. 21, no. 1, p. 44.

23. *www.esomar.org/index.php/26-questions.html*.

Chapter 11

1. It is important for the researcher and client to have a partnership during data analysis. See, for example, Fitzpatrick, M. (2001, August). Statistical analysis for direct marketers—in plain English. *Direct Marketing*, vol. 64, no. 4, pp. 54–56.

2. For an alternative presentation, see Ehrnberg, A. (2001, Winter). Data, but no information. *Marketing Research*, vol. 13, no. 4, pp. 36–39.

3. Fitzgerald, K. (2003, June). They're baaaaack: Card marketers on campus. *Credit Card Management*, vol. 3, no. 16, p. 18.

4. The use of descriptive statistics is sometimes called "data reduction," although some authors term any appropriate analysis that makes sense of data, "data reduction." See: Vondruska, R. (1995, April). The fine art of data reduction. *Quirk's Marketing Research Review*, online archive.

5. Some authors argue that central tendency measures are too sterile. See, for example, Pruden, D. R., and Vavra, T. G. (2000, Summer). Customer research, not marketing research. *Marketing Research*, vol. 12, no. 2, pp. 14–19.

6. Gutsche, A. (2001, September 24). Visuals make the case. *Marketing News*, vol. 35, no. 20, pp. 21–23.

7. Ghose, S., and Lowengart, O. (2001, September). Perceptual positioning of international, national and private brands in a growing international market: An empirical study. *Journal of Brand Management*, vol. 9, no. 1, pp. 45–62.

8. Based on Bruwer, J., and Li, E. (2007). Wine-related lifestyle (WRL) market segmentation: Demographic and behavioural factors. *Journal of Wine Research*, vol. 18, no. 1, pp. 19–34.

9. Some guidelines are drawn from: Ehrenberg, A. (2001, Winter). Data, but no information. *Marketing Research*, vol. 13, no. 2, pp. 36–39.

Chapter 12

1. In statistical jargon, one uses statistical inference (generalization) to estimate a population parameter (population fact) from the sample statistic (sampling finding).

2. Instructors may find this article useful when teaching confidence intervals: Blume, J. D., and Royall, R. M. (2003, February). Illustrating the law of large numbers (and confidence intervals). *American Statistician*, vol. 57, no. 1, pp. 51–57.

3. We are aware of the disconnect between applied statistical testing and classical statistical testing; however, we opt for the applied approach here. Refer to Hubbard, R., Bayarri, M. J., Berk, K. N., and

Carlton, M. A. (2003, August). Confusion over measures of evidence (*p*'s) versus errors (α's) in classical statistical testing. *American Statistician*, vol. 57, no. 3, p. 171.

4. Some disciplines, such as psychology and medicine, encourage their researchers to refrain from performing hypothesis and to report confidence intervals instead. See: Fidler, F., Cumming, G., Burgman, M., and Thomason, N. (2004, November). Statistical reform in medicine, psychology and ecology. *Journal of Socio-Economics*, vol. 33, no. 5, pp. 615–30; Fidler, F., Thomason, N., Cumming, G., Finch, S., and Leeman, J. (2004, February). Research article editors can lead researchers to confidence intervals, but can't make them think statistical reform lessons from medicine. *Psychological Science*, vol. 15, no. 2, pp. 119–26.

5. Anonymous. (2009, April 17). College credit card use breaks records, research finds. *CardLine*, vol. 9, no. 16, p. 14.

6. Traditionally, statistics textbooks have advised the use of *t* over *z* when the sample size is 30 or less; however, since the variance is typically unknown in marketing research data, the *t* is preferable up to 120.

Chapter 13

1. One author considers *t*-tests (differences tests) to be one of the most important statistical procedures used by marketing researchers. See: Migliore, V. T. (1996). If you hate statistics. . . . *Quirk's Marketing Research Review*, electronic archive.

2. For a contrary view, see Mazur, L. (2000, June 8). The only truism in marketing is they don't exist. *Marketing*, p. 20.

3. Unfortunately, the nature of statistical significance is not agreed to; see: Hubbard, R., and Armstrong, J. S. (2006). Why we don't really know what statistical significance means: Implications for educators. *Journal of Marketing Education*, vol. 28, no. 2, pp. 114–20.

4. Brandt, J. R. (2003, January/February). Meet your new market. *Chief Executive*, no. 185, p. 8.

5. Meaningful difference is sometimes called "practical significance." See: Thompson, B. (2002, Winter). "Statistical," "practical," and "clinical": How many kinds of significance do counselors need to consider? *Journal of Counseling and Development*, vol. 30, no. 1, pp. 64–71.

6. Rick, S., Cryder, C., and Loewenstein, G. (2008). Tightwads and spendthrifts. *Journal of Consumer Research*, vol. 34, no. 6, pp. 767–82.

7. Laukkanen, T., Sinkkonen, S., Kivijarvi, M., and Laukkanen, P. (2007). Innovation resistance among mature consumers. *Journal of Consumer Marketing*, vol. 24, no. 7, pp. 419–27.

8. For illumination, see Burdick, R. K. (1983, August). Statement of hypotheses in the analysis of variance. *Journal of Marketing Research*, vol. 20, pp. 320–24.

9. This example is based on Kumar, K., and Strandholm, K. (2002, July/August). American business education: Effect on the ethical orientation of foreign students. *Journal of Education for Business*, vol. 77, no. 6, pp. 345–50.

10. This procedure is sometimes called a "paired samples" test. For an example of the use of paired samples *t*-tests, see Ryan, C., and Mo, X. (2001, December). Chinese visitors to New Zealand: Demographics and perceptions. *Journal of Vacation Marketing*, vol. 8, no. 1, pp. 13–27.

Chapter 14

1. For advice on when to use chi-square analysis, see Hellebush, S. J. (2001, June 4). One chi square beats two *z* tests. *Marketing News*, vol. 35, no. 11, pp. 12–13.

2. It is not advisable to use cross-tabulations analysis with Chi-square when there are cases of cell frequencies of less than five cases. See: Migliore, V. (1998). *Quirk's Marketing Research Review*, electronic archive.

3. Here are some articles that use cross-tabulation analysis: Burton, S., and Zinkhan, G. M. (1987, Fall). Changes in consumer choice: Further investigation of similarity and attraction effects. *Psychology in Marketing*, vol. 4, pp. 255–66; Bush, A. J., and Leigh, J. H. (1984, April/May). Advertising on cable versus traditional television networks. *Journal of Advertising Research*, vol. 24, pp. 33–38; and Langrehr, F. W. (1985, Summer). Consumer images of two types of competing financial institutions. *Journal of the Academy of Marketing Science*, vol. 13, pp. 248–64.

4. McKechnie, D., Grant, J., Korepina, V., and Sadykova, N. (2007). Women: Segmenting the home fitness equipment market. *Journal of Consumer Marketing*, vol. 24, no. 1, pp. 18–26.

5. For a more advanced treatment of scatter diagrams, see Goddard, B. L. (2000, April). The power of computer graphics for comparative analysis. *Appraisal Journal*, vol. 68, no. 2, pp. 134–41.

6. See, for example, Branch, W. (1990, February). On interpreting correlation coefficients. *American Psychologist*, vol. 45, no. 2, p. 296.

7. See also, Gibson, L. (2007). Irreverent thoughts: Just what are correlation and regression? *Marketing Research*, vol. 19, no. 2, pp. 30–33.

8. Residual analysis can take many forms. See, for example, Dempster, A. P., and Gasko-Green, M. (1981). New tools for residual analysis. *Annals of Statistics*, vol. 9, pp. 945–59.

9. Our description pertains to "backward" stepwise regression. We admit that this is a simplification of stepwise multiple regression.

10. For readable treatments of problems encountered in multiple regression applied to marketing research, see Mullet, G. (1994, October). Regression, regression. *Quirk's Marketing Research Review*, electronic archive; Mullet, G. (1998, June). Have you ever wondered . . .? *Quirk's Marketing Research Review*, electronic archive; Mullet, G. (2003, February). Data abuse. *Quirk's Marketing Research Review*, electronic archive.

11. Grady, B., and Edgington, R. (2008). Ethics education in MBA programs: Effectiveness and effects. *International Journal of Management and Marketing Research*, Graduate Management Admission Council, vol. 1, no. 1, pp. 49–69.

12. We admit that our description of regression is introductory. Two books that expand our description are Lewis-Beck, M. S. (1980). *Applied Regression: An Introduction*. Newbury Park, CA: Sage Publications; and Schroeder, L. D., Sjoffquist, D. L., and Stephan, P. E. (1986). *Understanding Regression Analysis: An Introductory Guide*. Newbury Park, CA: Sage Publications.

13. At least one marketing researcher thinks that regression analysis is so complex that it actually clouds reality. See: Semon, T. T. (2006). Complex analysis masks real meaning. *Marketing News*, vol. 40, no. 12, p. 7.

14. Regression analysis is commonly used in academic marketing research. Here are some examples: Callahan, F. X. (1982, April/May). Advertising and profits 1969–1978. *Journal of Advertising Research*, vol. 22, pp. 17–22; Dubinsky, A. J., and Levy, M. (1989, Summer). Influence of organizational fairness on work outcomes of retail salespeople. *Journal of Retailing*, vol. 65, pp. 221–52; Frieden, J. B., and Downs, P. E. (1986, Fall). Testing the social involvement model in an energy conservation context. *Journal of the Academy of Marketing Science*, vol. 14, pp. 13–20; and Tellis, G. J., and Fornell, C. (1988, February). The relationship between advertising and product quality over the product life cycle: A contingency theory. *Journal of Marketing Research*, vol. 25, pp. 64–71. For an alternative to regression analysis, see Quaintance, B. S., and Franke, G. R. (1991). Neural networks for marketing research. In King, R. L. (ed.), *Marketing: Toward the Twenty-First Century. Proceedings of the Southern Marketing Association*, 230–35.

Chapter 15

1. Powell, J. (1995). *Will the Real Me Please Stand Up?: 25 Guidelines for Good Communication*. Notre Dame, IN: Ave Maria Press.

2. Owens, J. (2003). The moral high ground. *Marshall News*, pp. 50–51.

3. The source of this writing process is: Guffey, M. E. (2006). *Essentials of Business Communication* (7th ed.). Florence, KY: South-Western College.

4. We wish to acknowledge that this chapter was originally written by M. Howard, Ph.D., and H. Donofrio, Ph.D., assisted us in updating the chapter. Both Dr. Howard and Dr. Donofrio are experts in business communications.

5. We wish to acknowledge that this chapter was originally written by M. Howard, Ph.D.; and H. Donofrio, Ph.D., assisted us in updating the chapter. Both Dr. Howard and Dr. Donofrio are experts in business communications.

6. Deshpande, R., and Zaltman, G. (1982, February). Factors affecting the use of market research information: A path analysis. *Journal of Marketing Research*, vol. 19, pp. 14 – 31.

7. Deshpande, R., and Zaltman, G. (1984, February). A comparison of factors affecting researcher and manager perceptions of market research use. *Journal of Marketing Research*, vol. 21, pp. 32–38.

8. Antilla, R., and Blake, B. F. (2009, May). Translating "researcher-speak" into "executive-ese." *Quirk's Marketing Research Review*, vol. 23, no. 5, pp. 24–28.

9. Guffey, M. E. (2000). *Business Communication: Process and Product* (3rd ed.). Cincinnati: South-Western College Publishing, 103.

10. Tutee, E. R. (1983). *The Visual Display of Quantitative Information*. Cheshire, CT: Graphics Press.

11. For an excellent in-depth discussion on the use of pie charts, see: Fink, A. (2003). *How to Report on Surveys*. Thousand Oaks, CA: Sage Publications, 5–9.

12. Thomas, J. (2001, November). Executive excellence. *Marketing Research*, pp. 11–12.

13. For some guidelines on PowerPoint presentations, see: Murray, M. (2006, October). Make the results come alive. *Quirk's Marketing Research Review*, vol. 20, no. 9, pp. 58–66.

Credits

Chapter 1

Pages 2, 3: Courtesy of Jon Last. Page 6 (top left, bottom left, top right, bottom right): Courtesy of NewProductWorks®, The Innovation Resource Center of GfK Strategic Innovation (formerly Arbor Strategy Group). Page 10: Photodisc/Siri Stafford/Thinkstock.

Chapter 2

Pages 20, 21: Courtesy of Kristen Darby, Marketing Research Association. Page 23: Courtesy of Jack Homomichl. Page 28: Courtesy of Ted Donnelly. Page 33: Courtesy of Jennifer Cattel, Certification Manager, Marketing Research Association. Page 36: Courtesy of Ted Donnelly, Ph.D., PRC, Vice President, Baltimore Research. Page 38: Comstock/Thinkstock.

Chapter 3

Pages 46, 47: Courtesy of Colleen Moore-Mezler. Page 51: Comstock Images/Thinkstock. Page 52: AbleStock.com/Hemera Technologies/Getty Images/Thinkstock. Page 55 (top): Courtesy of Qualtrics (logo); (bottom): Courtesy of Survey Sampling International (logo). Page 66: Stockbyte/Thinkstock.

Chapter 4

Pages 78–79: Courtesy of Herb Sorenson. Page 82: AbleStock.com/Hemera Technologies/Getty Images/Thinkstock. Page 86: Courtesy of Alison Babcock, Ipsos Public Affairs. Page 94: BannaStock/Thinkstock. Page 98: Courtesy of Philip Trocchia. Pages 99, 100: Courtesy of Holly O'Neill.

Chapter 5

Pages 106, 107: Courtesy of Cristi Allen, Decision Analyst. Page 108 (top): Courtesy of Cristi Allen, Decision Analyst; (bottom): Courtesy of Dr. Dennis Tootelian. Pages 117, 118: Courtesy of U.S. Census Bureau, www.census.gov. Page 121: Courtesy of Brent Roderick, ESRI. Page 122: Digital Vision/Maria Teijeiro/Thinkstock. Page 123: Courtesy of Brent Roderick, ESRI.

Chapter 6

Pages 128–129: Courtesy of Luis Pamblanco, Intercampo. Pages 131, 132: Stockbyte/Thinkstock. Page 139: BannaStock/Thinkstock. Page 143: Brand X Pictures/Thinkstock.

Chapter 7

Pages 152, 153: Courtesy of Bill Neal, SDR Consulting. Page 157: Courtesy of Brand X Pictures Collection. Page 161: Courtesy of Ron Bush. Page 163: Courtesy of Photos.com Collection.

Chapter 8

Page 175: Courtesy of Lifesize Collection. Page 182: Courtesy of Pixland Collection. Page 187: Courtesy of Photodisc Collection. Page 194: Courtesy of Tulay Girard.

Chapter 9

Pages 196, 205: Courtesy of Ilene Siegalovsky, Survey Sampling International.

Chapter 10

Pages 224, 225: Courtesy of Raina Hawley. Page 227: Comstock/Jupiterimages/GettyImages/Thinkstock. Page 229: Photos.com/Jupiterimages/GettyImages/Thinkstock. Page 231: Photodisc/Thinkstock. Page 235: Goodshoot/Thinkstock.

Chapter 11

Page 241: Courtesy of Jupiterimages. Page 245: Courtesy of PhotoObjects.net. Page 250: Courtesy of Brand X Pictures. Page 255: Courtesy of John Howard.

Chapter 12

Pages 262, 263: Courtesy of Richard Homans, Ipsos Forward Research. Page 265: Courtesy of Jupiterimages. Page 273: Courtesy of George Doyle. Page 276: Courtesy of Digital Vision.

Chapter 13

Pages 290, 291: Courtesy of William MacElroy. Page 293: Courtesy of PhotoObjects.net. Pages 299, 305: Courtesy of Digital Vision.

Chapter 14

Page 314 (logo, photo): Courtesy of Scott Smith, Qualtrics. Page 316: Courtesy of Creatas. Page 322: Courtesy of David De Lossy. Page 325: Courtesy of Comstock. Page 334: Courtesy of Jupiterimages.

Chapter 15

Page 345: Courtesy of Heather Donofrio. Page 347: Courtesy of Polka Dot Images. Page 357: Courtesy of Creatas.

Index

Name Index

Subject Index